D0860900

# EXPOSITORY PREACHING AND TEACHING
## Revelation

# EXPOSITORY PREACHING AND TEACHING
## Revelation



By

Owen L. Crouch

College Press Publishing Company, Joplin, Missouri

Printed and bound in the
United States of America


Library of Congress Catalog Card Number: 85-071665
International Standard Book Number: 0-89900-207-2

TO

my father and mother

who

left a pattern of faith and an ideal of learning!

# PREFACE

Regardless of one's personal point of view something of value for the student of Revelation appears in this volume. Differences of interpretation need not deter from the very practical use of the diagrams of the text. If the reader holds to a particular point of view with such vigor and feeling then he quite probably should ignore the sections Some Expository Thoughts. The rest of this work should prove very practical for the student no matter what his method of approach.

The basic contribution is the analysis of each sentence of the Greek text. This appears in the form of a diagram visible to the eye. For the student unfamiliar with Greek the English appears above the Greek. So in effect, besides the Greek diagrams, it offers diagrams of a quite literal English translation.

As each paragraph or unit of thought develops it appears in the form of an English translation. Accompanying the translation is an outline of that particular section of the book.

With each of the diagrams, usually on the facing page, are notes in explanation of the diagram. These notes do not constitute a commentary in the accepted sense of the term. They are an attempt to help the student follow the diagrams as they picture the various grammatical relationships in the sentences. As space is available an occasional observation appears about the history or meaning of a word.

Finally there are Some Expository Thoughts on each section of Revelation as divided by the outline of the book. Hopefully these may prove of value in stimulating ideas for expository work. Revelation is a book of hope for the oppressed believer. It needs exposing in its natural setting. Revelation was written to stir faith and encourage loyalty to Christ in a time of severe stress. The kind of faith and hope which it engendered when first written it will fan into flame again in similar situations.

In approaching any book for serious study one's presuppositions are determinative. The viewpoint with which one starts signals rather clearly the conclusions at which one will arrive. This is particularly true in the approach to Revelation. For this reason it is doubly important that we place the book as nearly as possible in the original setting that prompted its writing. Having done that, it is imperative that we trace the author's thought by analyzing each sentence. That is the chief contribution of the present volume. It is my hope and prayer that each thoughtful student of the New Testament may find herein some measure of help in his effort to follow the Revelator's unfolding thought.

Nashville, Tennessee
January 12, 1984

Owen L. Crouch

## CONTENTS

## Diagrams and Notes

## THE IMPORTANCE OF CONTEXT

Truth is universal. It may not be accepted everywhere but it is true any time, everywhere, in time and eternity. Truth is true when spoken by a pervert, liar or Satan himself. He may misdirect it, distort it, alter its context, bury it under an avalanche of falsehoods but he cannot change the truthfulness of truth. Truth is universal. If it's true it's true in Paris, Moscow, Wasington, on the moon, Mars or distant Neptune. Truth is absolute, not relative.

But when written or spoken truth comes in a context. And the context is local, temporal, relative; not absolute. That charges an author with the task of avoiding obscurities about historical and social backgrounds. The reader must perceive clearly. And the reader must consider closely every aspect of the background until the author's point is clear. Communication demands comprehension of context. In both author and reader such honesty is imperative.

"Values caught are more pervasive than values taught." Some might question the truth of that quotation. It's conceivable that certain values taught become just as pervasive as those caught. Yet, once taught the value must become a part of the experiential life of him who is taught. In other words, for it to become his very own he must "catch" that which he's taught. Thus even when taught, to be permanently valuable teaching must be caught.

Assuming the quotation above to be true, it stands as all truth stands, universal. It's true in all places and times. But in quoting the above the entire sentence is not cited. Nor is there a hint as to the book, article, or paragraph from which it is extracted. Seen in its total context that truth refers to a specific point that a certain author wants to make. And his point supports a thesis he's developing. Moreover, the author directs his essay to a particlar audience.

The full sentence says, "With an uncommitted audience, values caught are more pervasive than values taught." In light of this opening phrase the sentence is more forceful not to say clearer. The author includes all "uncommitted." He's not concerned as to what they're uncommitted, only that an uncommitted audience is more liable to "catch" something. The very lack of commitment makes one vulnerable. He who is "caught" by some person, cause, ideology, or enthusiasm is open to being "taught." So, by adding a qualifying phrase the truth quoted is modified by a bit of context.

Now to cite a larger portion of the paragraph of which the above quote is the final sentence. "Whoever heard of 'The Satan Hour' as a TV show? Such a program would have to buy its way into the market as religious time or be given away as sustaining programming on religiously oriented stations....Yet, Satan's shows are more 'religious' than religious shows are. He sows his seeds --literally infuses his seeds--into them so that his values are caught. With an uncommitted audience, values caught are more pervasive than values taught." In this larger context the author introduces a hypothetical unlikely TV program called "The Satan's Hour.' He seeks to illustrate how a TV program whose aim would "sell" Satan's sadistic sensualism would fail in its goal if aired in a direct hard sell. On the other hand the diabolic aim is attained by not making an overt approach. It is achieved by planting evil's own subtle seeds of sin in a regular commercially sponsored program. The lure of the "pleasure of sin for a season" can be communicated better in a program with a background of golden, purple, firery sunset and an idyllic tropical beach to distract attention from a display of drunken, sexual violence of a baudy party in the scene. The approach of evil is subtle and to the subconscious, not direct. The evil is blanketed under the color of God's beautiful creation. The human heart is "caught." Once caught it may then be taught.

What is the larger context in which this paragraph and this sentence is found? It is a four-page article in the religious journal CHRISTIANITY TODAY of April 8, 1983. The article, "Selling" the Gospel in Secular Markets (pgs.20-23) develops the idea that the Christian world is beginning to learn that the secular society can be reached better through the "secular mass communication media" than by direct religious media programs.

The essay cites numerous examples of magizines, radio, TV and motion picture productions that are sold to regular commercial sponsors. They aren't "religious" programs. They are "secular" in the sense that they deal with themes geared to the commercial "secular" markets. But planted in these programs lie buried principles which are definitely spiritually oriented. They deposit in the "secular" mind basic Christian spiritual values of faith, integrity, morality,responsibility, family purity and such like. The thesis of the essay rises clearly in the next to last paragraph in the words of our quotation, "values caught are more pervasive than values taught." After reading the article and noting his examples the words of the quotation clinch the argument in a form calculated to "catch" the reader. We may forget details but will recall the theme. The quote is like a text to a sermon, a topic sentence in a paragraph, a sign on a marquee at a theatre. It presents a universal truth. But placed in a context it heralds an updated technique of spreading the truth of God's gospel.

Nothing is more important than context in deciphering meaning. This is no less true of biblical literature than of the so-called secular media. The 32nd and 51st Psalms come to vibrant life when read as the outpouring of the soul of king Davis suffering under the conviction of his adulterous affair with Bathsheba and the subsequent murder of her husband. The prophecies of Jeremiah must be read in the context of the historical events of the decline and fall of Judah and Jerusalem. He spoke to specific situations which shaped his messages of doom or promise. And his words had to mean something to his generation before they could have meaning for later generations. For Jeremiah to be understood in 20th century America he must be seen in 7th-6th century B.C. Jerusalem. The prophet's word is timeless and universal. But it was spoken in a time-place context in a particular crisis.

Context not only involves word, sentence, paragraph, chapter or article but it includes the magazine or book in which these occur. Moreover, any book is written in a historical-social context and in a geographical locale. Personality, linguistic, literary methods and style of the author must be included in the concept of total context. That Matthew was a Jew, a publican, and one of the twelve helps in arriving at a clearer understanding of some passages in the Gospel of Matthew. And that Luke was a Greek, a physician, and a companion of Paul throws a flood of light on a number of passages in his Gospel.

In approaching Revelation context may be ignored only at the price of distortion. I may have pure motives and sincere commitment but they won't lessen the defacement of meaning if I disregard the context from which and for which the book initially emerged.

The book of Revelation is classed as prophecy and rightly so. But it is written in the form of an epistle. 1:4-5 includes normal characteristics of first-century salutations. It's similar in wording and tone to the salutations of Paul. Certainly it has more of a salutation than I John. As an epistle it was written to specific readers alluded to in 1:3.

It must also be observed that as prophecy it's message is designed to be "kept" more than a formula for unveiling a hidden future. Like all prophecy it's basic purpose is to influence conduct rather than to predict future events. In fact, when the future is predicted it's in order that it inspire to present obedience. John writes "Blessed the one keeping and those hearing the words of the prophecy and keeping the things written in it."(1:3) The bottom line of prophecy is preaching. Without doubt Amos predicted as Acts 15:15-18 confirms. But the greater part of Amos is addressed to the practical problems of 8th century Israel. The major predictive elements relate to threats of judgment on <u>that</u> generation. In the same manner the book of Revelation is a message for its first readers living under the dark threat of Roman persecution. It was designed to give hope, appeal to repentance, fortify resistence to the enemies of Christ. At its best prophecy is practical preaching. And Revelation was written prophecy more than preached prophecy!

Introductory problems are left to standard commentaries. We conclude the apostle John to be the responsible author, at least the human agent to whom the visions came. He wrote during the reign of Domitian (81-96 A.D.). Other Emperors had accepted divine worship but Domitian demanded that he be worshipped as God under threat of severe persecution. Provincial officials, especially in the province of Asia, served as efficient executioners of the Domitian policy. At the point of Emperor worship Christians confronted head on the power of Imperial Rome. Shall the believer pay divine honors to the emperor and thereby disown supreme allegiance to Christ? The issue was clear cut. Can the sovereignty of Caesar and that of God in Christ be accepted at the same time? Will the power of Christ prevail over the power of Caesar? Is God or Caesar sovereign? The book of Revelation answers such questions. It offers faith, hope, and victory against what seems to be tremendous odds.

The aged John, a political exile, was on the isle of Patmos "on account of the word of God and his testimony to Jesus."(1:9) For years he gave pastoral service to the churches of the province of Asia. Now, as their leader, he had been struck down. The power of Empire had turned against the churches. It threatened the existence of Christianity. It insisted that Caesar be acknowledged as God. But believing in the sovereignty of the living God John refused to yield. And the influence of his leadership in faith dominated the Christian movement in Asia. How can he continue his witness of Christ to the imperiled churches? How can he inspire hope, energize faith, nourish conviction in the ultimate victory of righteousness? Can he communicate his vision of victory in spite of government censorship? Apocalypse was a method that could reveal his message to the Christian communities while concealing it from investigating authorities. Jewish apocalyptic writings provided a perfect code language for such an undertaking.

John alerts his readers that the work is written in symbolic language. "And he <u>signified</u> (ἐσήμανεν) it,..." (1:1) While this verb does not of necessity imply symbolic writing it includes such an idea. And in view of the nature and content of the book of Revelation, in this context, it clearly means "symbolized." The normal principles involved in exegesis apply to Revelation as to any of the biblical books. But in addition the reader must be aware that this book uses the symbols current in apocalyptic literature. He who ignores the meaning of the symbols is inviting a distorted message.

The book of Revelation has a practical purpose. It's design is to bolster faltering faith, to strengthen weakening courage, to stir fires of loyalty to Christ enough to overcome torture and death. It's not history written before it happened, but ammunition to fight present battles. It's not a prediction of an Armageddon of tanks, planes, and bullets. Rather it is to supply moral and spiritual ammunition for the life and death struggle of the spiritual forces of Christ against the vicious forces of Satan as embodied in Roman Imperial government. Any prediction about the future is embedded within the mortal combat between Christianity and Rome, especially Rome as incorporated in the cult of Emperor worship. The authorities in the province of Asia were saddled with the responsibility of enforcing the cult. The Roman beast authorized its provincial beast to enforce the sovereignty of Rome against the sovereignty of God and His Christ. Revelation was written to unveil the certain triumph of God's people in the terrible conflict.

Because the book of Revelation describes the principles of triumph of God's cause over the Roman government's assault it stands as a pattern of victory for all history. Any government that abuses its God-given task of maintaining an orderly society and turns its power against the eternal Christ is doomed to the same defeat. God in Christ is sovereign in this world. He moves through history with the inexorable progress of "feet of burnished brass." The entire book must be read in the light of its original context. Every word relates to a larger context, its sentence, paragraph, and the life situation which inspired the pen of John.

## PROPHETS AND PROPHECY!

Prophecy has been so long associated with fortelling and predicting that the primary meaning of the term seems novel. Yet to predict, while a legitimate meaning, is secondary. Acquired from years of special application of the primary sense prophecy has become "predicting." The word comes from two Greek terms. Preposition πρό means "fore" or "before" but not exclusively or even primarily time. It meant "before" in terms of place or idea. When used of time it isn't always foretell but also to "go forward." It may give the sense of superiority ("above all") as in Jas.5:12. When used with the verb φημί (to speak) the basic meaning is "to speak forth." Prophecy was to bring forth a message from God in a crisis. It was a warning of impending danger coupled with promises of hope and encouragement. A prophet was a man with a message in a moral crisis which augured doom. Imbedded in the message were promises of the fulfillment of God's ultimate purpose. When such a message was applied to specific crises it inevitably drew forth predictions of what would happen. Gradually prediction became closely associated with the term.

But the primary idea in prophecy is still speaking forth the word of God in a crisis. This is the basic function of preaching. To preach is to bring God's message relative to a moral, ethical or spiritual crisis. The fact that the twentieth century preacher relies on the written revelation in the Bible to supply the content of his prophetic message in no way lessens his function as prophet. From the crises of the past he brings to bear the messages of the biblical prophets to the crises of the present. He is still a man with God's message in a crisis.

But to be prophetic the modern prophet must place the biblical message in its original setting in order to know how to bring it to bear in his contemporary setting. One does not teach the word of God by merely opening the Bible and saying, "this is what this message means to me." What it meant to the prophet who first spoke it is the essential element. What the life situation was that first prompted the prophet to speak is basic to biblical preaching.

No book in the Bible, not even Proverbs, is a collection of lofty moral maxims collected willy-nilly and jumbled together for inspirational devotions. The books are "prophetic" compositions. They are messages written or assembled by men of God who were responding to moral needs of individuals, communities, or nations. Each book has a thesis. Every paragraph develops, supports, and clarifies the idea of the prophetic writer. It intends to influence moral action. This is true whether the book be Revelation or the Gospel of Mark. The point and purpose of prophecy is not in the foretelling of events yet to happen. Rather it is the revelation of the truth of God as it relates to a vital problem of human life. The central significance of the prophetic word is God's truth about sin, redemption, repentance, hope. The revelation of the truth is the main thing, not what's going to happen tomorrow, next year or in the coming centuries.

## REVELATION: AN OUTLINE

The Prologue. 1:1-8
(1)Superscription. 1:1-3
(2)Salutation. 1:4-8

PART ONE

1. The Reigning Christ among the Churches. 1:9-3:22
(1)Vision of the Sovereign Christ. 1:9-20
(2)Letters to seven churches. 2:1-3:22
2. The Court of Heaven. 4:1-5:14
(1)The Reigning God. 4:1-11
(2)The Redeeming Lamb. 5:1-14
3. Breaking Six of the Seven Seals. 6:1-17
4. Interlude: Sealing of God's Servants. 7:1-17
5. Breaking of the Seventh Seal: Seven Trumpets. 8:1-9:21
6. Two Interludes: Visions of Consolation. 10:1-11:13
(1)The Prophet Eats a Little Book. 10:1-11
(2)The Temple Measured; The Two Prophets. 11:1-13
7. Sounding the Seventh Trumpet; God's Sovereignty. 11:14

PART TWO

8. The Christ and the Conflict. 12:1-17
(1)Birth of Messiah.
(2)Fall of Satan,
(3)Persecution of the Woman.
9. The Forces of Evil. 13:1-18
(1)The Dragon, Satan;
(2)First Beast, Rome;
(3)Second Beast; Emperor Worship.
10. The Forces of Righteous Judgment. 14:1-15:8
(1)God's Christ, the Lamb. 14:1-6
(2)God's Judgment. 14:7-20
(3)God's Wrath. 15:1-8
11. The Seven Bowls of Wrath. 16:1-21
12. Judgment on the Great Harlot. 17:1-18:24
(1)The Scarlet Woman. 17:1-18
(2)Rome's Allies. 18:1-20
(3)Doom for the city of Rome.18:21-24
13. Victory of the Christ. 19:1-20:10
(1)Rejoicing of the saints. 19:1-10
(2)Defeat of the Beast and Allies. 19:11-21
(3)Binding of Satan. 20:1-3
(4)The Reign of Martyrs and Saints. 20:4-6
(5)Final Defeat of Satan. 20:7-10
(6)Resurrection,Judgment, Defeat of Death. 20:11-15
14. Destiny of the Redeemed. 21:1-22:5
(1)Coming of the New Age. 21:1-8
(2)The New Jerusalem. 21:9-22:5

Conclusion. 22:6-21

## APOCALYPTIC LITERATURE

The book of Revelation is apocalyptic literature. This kind of writing blossomed for four centuries from 200 B.C. to 200 A.D. After the Babylonian Captivity Israel as God's people struggled to maintain itself in an alien world. It fell under the iron heel of powerful political overlords. When suffering touched the depths prophetic voices arose to herald the victory of God's people and the establishment of God's kingdom. The seedbed of adversity sprouted apocalypses. Present suffering was strongly contrasted to future glory. God's personal invasion into the world's affairs became the scarlet thread of hope in these apocalyptic visions. The unrighteous were to meet their just judgmental fate while the people of God would be vindicated in their righteousness. The purpose of apocalypses was to neutralize doubt and apostasy. The sure overthrow of Satan and his beastial instruments coupled with the final victory of God's righteous kingdom was the theme threading its way through all such literature. Apocalypses bred faith and hope amidst doubt and despair.

If one doesn't recognize apocalypse as a literary method he'll not read Revelation with proper appreciation. Failure to familiarize oneself with this kind of literature is like placing the pyramid of Cheops in New York's Times Square. It's out of its natural setting; it is an anomaly which loses a lot of its meaning.

One feature of this kind of literature is its cryptic, veiled manner of speech. But the very danger which birthed it dictated the cabalistic method. If persecuting authorities perceived the meaning the lives of both author and reader would be threatened. So by its nature apocalypse was written to conceal and reveal; conceal from the non-initiated and reveal to the initiated. The modes of thought that formed the very fabric of all such literature saturate the book of Revelation. At least one must be familiar with the fact of the presence of such kind of literature if he would at all follow the thread of thought in our Revelation. In a despairing situation God's man used this type of writing to keep faith and hope at white heat.

The following are non-canonical apocalyptic books. The book of Enoch, The Assumption of Moses, The Secrets of Enoch, The book of Baruch, and Fourth Ezra. It would not be time wasted to read one or two of these works. That will contribute two things to the reader of our New Testament Revelation. First, it will reveal that our book is not an isolated island in an unchartered literary sea. It was a form of communication familiar to first century audiences. Second, the words, phrases, symbols and style of writing will give the reader a thought vocabulary with which to read with greater insight the Revelation of the New Testament.

There are a few characteristics of apocalypses with which it is wise to be familiar. An apocalypse arose out of a specific historical situation. Knowledge of that predicament is essential to a sound understanding of the book. A fruit tree is not to be viewed suspended in the air between the heavens and the earth.

It belongs rooted firmly in its earth-bound soil of a fruit orchard. As literature Revelation is not a freak oddity uprooted from the soil of human history. On the contrary, the history of late first-century Rome in conflict with the sovereignty of God in Christ germinated this message of victory and hope. If we are to get God's word from the book it must be read in the light of that historical situation.

Apocalypses were generally pseudonymous. In the inter-testament period the "law" came to be viewed as "adequate, infallible," and "valid dogma." Hence if any author would get a reading he resorted to attaching his writing to some ancient revered name. In this respect Revelation was different. It was not limited to such a restraint. It makes its own claim to authorship. In the late first century the author felt compelled to identify himself in order to get a reading from the audience at which he aimed. Knowledge of its human source, one as well known as John, was essential to its being accepted by the churches of the province of Asia.

Apocalypses are characterized by visions peopled with grotesque animals, weird dragons, flying fowl and ornately garmented people. As with other features these are symbolic of people, principles, and situations.

Apocalyptic writings, though rooted in present persecutions, are geared to future victories. God is pictured as present in current events that God's people may be sure of a part in future events.

Symbols are conspicuous in all apocalyptics. Dragons and beasts symbolize authorities and governments. Birds, heavenly bodies, swords, colors, all have their symbolic significance in the code language of apocalypses. Of interest is the following list of the symbolism of numbers:

"2" = strength, courage, energy.
"3" = father, mother, child, the "divinest life can offer."
So "3" became symbol of the divine; the Trinity!
"4" = Four directions of compass, hence symbol of
natural creation; the human number.
"7" = the number of perfection. 3 + 4 = 7, ultimate perfection.
"10" = A complete full-rounded human being has ten fingers.
10 became symbol of completeness.
10x10x10 = 1000 ultimate completeness.
"3½" = one half of 7 = incompleteness; falling short,
unrealized aspirations, an indefinite length.
"6" = One short of completion; defeat, stroke of doom;
somewhat like the modern "13"!!!

## METHODS OF INTERPRETING REVELATION

Throughout history numerous methods of approach to the study of Revelation have surfaced. This has resulted in a conflicting babel of voices. But shall we abandon reading Revelation because of impious partisans with opposing views? Hardly! Such would be a Satanic device to get us to ignore God's message of hope. Revelation was given by God to reveal something important. Shall we not listen when God speaks? He expects us to make the effort to hear that which he has spoken. Abuse is no reason for non-use. We need the hope which the book brings to our needs in time of despair.

One fact for sure stands out. The method of approach determines the outcome. The point of departure predicts the point of arrival. Thus it behooves the student to canvass with care the methods of approach before he launches on his own journey.

Included here are several methods of approach to the study of Revelation.

Futurist. In this approach the book is treated as entirely eschatological, a document of unfulfilled prophecy. Events of chapters 4 through 19 are to take place within a space of seven years, the period of "tribulation" of Daniel 9:24-27. They will come at the close of the "church age." Christ will come at Armaggedon to rescue his own and will reign with them on earth 1000 years.

Continuous-Historical. This views Revelation as a history of the church before it happened. It foresees various periods of history, particularly church history, in symbolic forms. It details the Roman apostasy and other aberations.

Philosophy of history. A book dealing with God's governing of all men in all ages. It's not a description of actual events but is a revealing of those powers inherent in all events. It reveals principles which embody themselves whenever conditions demanding them appear in history. It describes ageless, timeless processes not tied to any particular historical situation.

Preterist. This approach assumes that everything was fulfilled in the past at the time of Roman persecution in the first century. Except for Christ's "second coming," the final judgment and the perfected state of the redeemed all is a matter of the past.

Historical background. In this view the author addressed the Christians of his own time for their benefit. His was a practical aim of encouraging hope in times of despair. It was written in code language. Furthermore, he used many Old Testament terms but with New Testament meanings. It was addressed to the imagination in order to create an impression, the certainty of the Christians' victory in the face of impossible odds.

## A TRANSLATION OF REVELATION 1:1-3

The revelation of Jesus Christ which God gave to him to show to his bondservants. (It consists of) the things which it's necessary to come to pass shortly. And he, having sent through his angel, symbolized to his bondservant John, who testified the word of God and the testimony of Jesus Christ however many (things) which he saw. Blessed is the one reading and the ones hearing the words of the prophecy, and the ones keeping the things which have been written in it; for the time is near.

## AN OUTLINE OF REVELATION 1:1-3

<u>God's Prophet and Prophecy!</u>

Revelation is an unveiling of something veiled; an uncovering of that which is concealed; a drawing back of a curtain!

This particular revelation is "symbolized" (ἐσήμανεν) in the form of the generally accepted form of apocalyptic literature. It is given in "signs" whose meanings were known to the recipients and the revealer but to none others. To those who knew the signs of the code it revealed; to others it concealed.

I. THE SOURCE OF THE REVELATION. vs.1

1. God is the ultimate source, the divine. vs.1a

2. Angels the intermediate agents. vs.1c

3. John the human prophet. vs.1d

II. PROPHET AND THE PROPHECY. vss.1d-2

1. The prophet is a "slave." "My servants the prophets..." They are a special breed whose life and message are wholly determined by the call and message of God.

2. This prophet's testimony was twofold:
   (a) The "word" of God.
   (b) The "testimony of Jesus Christ."

3. God's prophet is a man with a message in a crisis. The crisis determines the message and often the method.

III. THE PRACTICAL PURPOSE OF PROPHECY. vs.3

1. To be read - preached!

2. To be heard - "take heed that you hear!"

3. To be obeyed - its goal is not prediction but obedience.

Blessing comes, not in solving the puzzle of the prophet but in hearing and heeding the divine message channeled through the prophet.

## Revelation 1:1–2

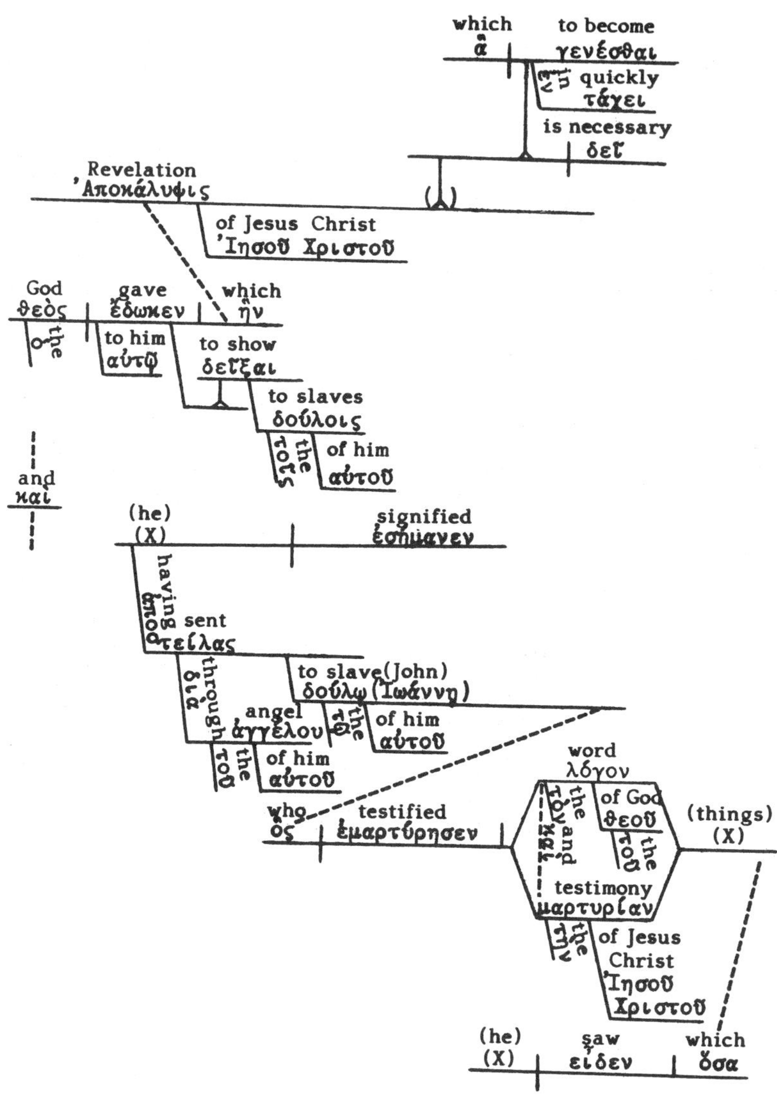

## THE DIAGRAM OF REVELATION 1:1-2

The period at the close of verse two in Nestle's text would indicate the end of a sentence. However, the first part of verse one up through τάχει is a self-contained idea. Since it has no finite verb it probably should not be classed as a sentence. It's almost of the nature of a title and may have been considered such by the author. The word Ἀποκάλυψις appears in the nominative and stands as the sole prominent idea. It is limited by three modifying ideas though no verb asserts anything about this "Revelation." The genitive "of Jesus Christ" specifies whose unveiling it is. It is the "uncovering of Jesus Christ." Most commentators think that "Jesus Christ" is a subjective genitive. That is, in view of the relative clause (ἣν) "...which God gave to him..." they see the unveiling as something God gave to Jesus Christ." But there is nothing in the words, their relationship to each other, or the context that won't allow this to be a normal objective genitive after an action noun. In other words this indeed is a revealing given by God to Jesus Christ but it is of Jesus Christ as the content of what is revealed. No other part of the New Testament surpasses this book in its unveiling of the glorified Christ, his place in guiding human history to its destined end.

The other descriptive elements are in the form of two relative clauses. The one introduced by ἃ is in apposition to ἀποκάλυψις. The relative is accusative of general reference with aorist infinitive γενέσθαι which serves as subject to the verb δεῖ; "...which things to become shortly is necessary..." The phrase ἐν τάχει is adverbial in function and tells when these things are to come to pass, that is, "shortly" or "soon."

The other relative has ἣν introducing it. It defines the source and ultimate authority of the revealing as being God. The purpose of the revelation is presented in aorist infinitive δεῖξαι. It was "to show to his slaves."

The remainder of the verses constitutes a complex sentence. The independent clause states, "he signified..." Aorist ἐσήμανεν is a verb built off the noun σῆμα = sign. Here it indicates that "he" (probably Jesus) gave the revelation in signs. He symbolized the truth. Obviously this book is a communication given in symbols. This clause plainly says so. ἀποστείλας is a circumstantial aorist participle suggesting the manner by which the action was executed; "...sent through his angel..." διὰ with genitive displays an agent through whom he sent the symbolic revelation.

Dative δούλῳ is indirect object registering the person to whom the revelation was sent. To that is appended a relative clause ushered in by ὃς. It is adjectival describing "his slave John" as one "who testified the word of God etc..." λόγον and μαρτυρίαν form a compound direct object. In apposition to this compound object is an understood "things" that serves as antecedent to the relative ὅσα. This relative introduces another adjective dependent clause describing the "things" as "things which he saw." ὅσα is quantitative relative = "howevermany things."

## Revelation 1:3

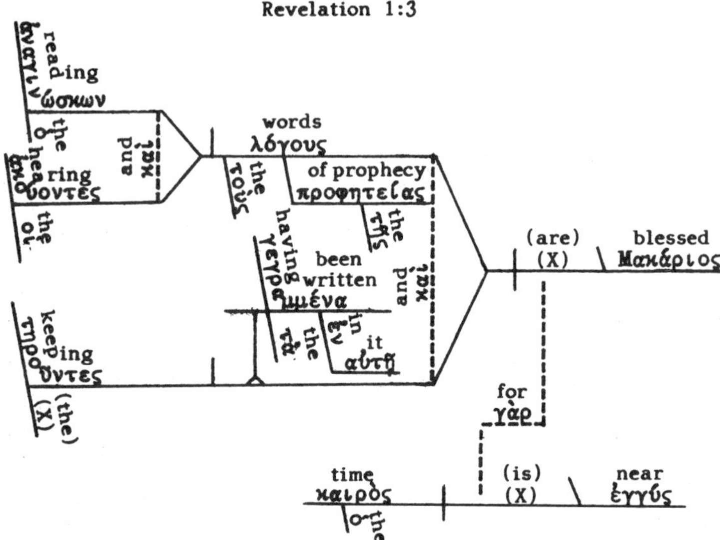


Two independent clauses make of this a compound sentence. The initial clause has a two-pronged compound subject. The first prong of that subject is itself a compound of two elements. The complete subject reads, ""The one reading and the ones hearing the words of the prophecy and (the) ones keeping the things having been written in it..." Having thus identified the subject the author goes on to affirm that such ones "are blessed..." The second clause states, "the time is near." It gives not only the reason why such ones are blessed but also why he, the author, believes they are "blessed." Time for fulfillment is near.

"The one reading" does not refer to the student reading in a suquestered library. In the days before printing scrolls were not plentiful and those available were expensive. So "the one reading" refers to the specially equipped public reader who led in worship. Accordingly "the ones hearing" consisted of the audience who was listening in the public worship.

The third attributive participle τηροῦντες (ones keeping) shows quite clearly that "prophecy" was not something merely to satisfy impertinent human curiosity. It was something to be "kept" when heard. Prophecy is a message from a man of God with a message for a crisis in life, personal, national, or community! It's a practical message to be "obeyed" rather than a puzzle to be solved. The "blessing" comes in the "keeping" of the "messages (λόγους) of the prophecy," once having heard them read. All three of the participles in the subject are attributive presents. The linear action of the present tense in all three may be classed as iterative; repeated action.

## EXPOSITORY THOUGHTS ON 1:1-3

Revelation is the drawing back of a curtain. The props and actors on the stage of history become visible. God is the producer, Jesus Christ the "star," the Holy Spirit the director. Those who see make up the audience. The tragedy played out in history is the story of Redemption.

The ultimate origin of any or all real revelation is the living God. No matter what form or method revelation takes its source is God. He who is "truth" alone can reveal truth. Energy may take the shape of gas, liquid or solid but regardless of its form its physical source is the sun. Thus it is with revealed truth. Miracle, parable, historical event, law, poetry, prose, prophecy, literal, symbol, fire or flood—these are but the clothes. The body is the essence revealed.

But God uses agents through which his revelations are given. On the divine side are his angelic messengers. He "makes his angels (messengers) winds, And his ministers a flame of fire." (Heb.1:7) It is but natural that God use "natural" means as his "ministering servants." Hidden within the visible, sensual forms of life are the innumerable agents hastening to do God's bidding. Part of their task is that of revealing!

On the human side are his "servants the prophets." In the present instance God's "bondservant John" was his human agent. Of that holy band of twelve the aged John alone was left to speak a final word in God's age-long unveiling of himself and his redemptive purpose for man. The story is about to be completed. And that last word which "God gave to show to his servants" is "that which is about to come to pass shortly," namely, eternal victory in the face of apparent defeat.

A prophet of God is not his own man. He belongs mind, body, and soul to his God, the "possessor of heaven and earth." Hence his message is determined by God. The historical situation in which the prophet lives shapes the vocabulary, style and form of his message. Since Jesus ministry in the flesh John had "testified the word of God and the testimony of Jesus Christ." And for that same testimony he was now exiled on the isle of Patmos. But now there is added to his testimony the "revealing of Jesus Christ which God gave to him to show..."

It is popular to say that the "to him" in 1:1 indicates that God gave this revelation to Jesus Christ. Thus the genitive "...of Jesus Christ..." is said to be subjective. It's the revelation which Jesus Christ received. This might be true. But even if it is (which is doubtful) the content of the book itself presents Jesus Christ as being the content of what is revealed. HE is the central figure, the key to victory, the lamb who gains the sovereignty for God. Furthermore, the fact that genitive "Jesus Christ" follows an action noun "revealing"(ἀποκάλυψις)strongly favors "Jesus Christ" as being objective genitive. If God gave the revelation to Jesus Christ, it was also about Jesus Christ. He is the sum and substance, center and circumference, core and content of that which the book contains.

Before the printing press, radio, TV, and all the devices for rapid communication, prophetic voices were entirely dependent on public or private assemblies to announce their news. Three elements were present wherever communication took place--the reader, the listener, and the heeder! To serve any practical use news had to be heralded, heard, and heeded! Even now, with all our technological advances, the same three ingredients must be involved if news, good or bad, is to have any practical effect in life. Thus it was that John pronounced his readers "blessed" if and when they gave attention to "reading," "hearing," and "keeping" the "words of the prophecy" which he was now writing.

When originally written the book of Revelation was designed to sway conduct. It's immediate aim was to affect faith, encourage hearts, stimulate hope, and lead persecuted Christians to continued loyal obedience. It dealt with immediate, current threats, not false deviations a thousand years hence. Thus the Revelation fell into the pattern of all biblical literature, that is, "that the man of God may be thoroughly furnished unto every good work..."

"Blessed (is) the one reading..." says John. He's not thinking of reading for relaxation; nor of the scholar laboring in the library. He has in mind the public readers who preside over the public worship of those struggling threatened churches of Asia. He who read and preached the "good news" of Christ's redemptive love was "blessed." He kept fanning into flame the embers of the gospel smouldering in the hearts of God's persecuted people. In order to hear someone must "read" and proclaim! "How beautiful are the feet of them who preach the gospel of peace, and bring glad tidings of good things."

"Blessed (are) the ones hearing..." says John. The reading of the news is not for the sake of the reader but of him who hears. In its nature news is to be spread abroad that others may know the news. "Take heed that you hear" is as essential as "blessed is the one reading." News in a deserted house, an empty auditorium, or an abandoned city is of no practcial value. News is to be read and proclaimed where it is news; and to whom it is news.

Furthermore, "take heed <u>how</u> you hear" is as essential <u>"that"</u> you hear. One's attitude as <u>he</u> hears determines what he hears. He who listens to learn will learn. He who listens to condemn will learn little or nothing. He's self-condemned.

"Blessed (are) the ones keeping..." adds John. The end of all prohetic preaching is obedience. "Be you doers of the word and not hearers only, deceiving your own selves." He who hears the words of prophecy and does not do cheats no one but himself. Faith, hope and love are generated more by obedience to divine revelation than all the charisma of God. There's no substitute for heeding the prophetic word of God. The book of Revelation is full of moral demands for the soul! Prophecy is to be <u>kept</u>!. "Blessed are the ones keeping the things having been written in the prophecy."

## A TRANSLATION
### Revelation 1:4-8

John to the seven churches, the ones in Asia: Grace to you and peace from the being one, and the 'was' one, and the coming one, and from the seven spirits which (are) before his throne, and from Jesus Christ, the faithful witness, the first-born from the dead and the one ruling the kings of the earth. To the one loving us and who loosed us out from our sins in his blood. And he made us (to be) kingdom, priests to his God and father, to him the glory and the strength unto the ages of the ages. Amen.

Behold, he is coming with the clouds and every eye shall see him, and those who pierced him and all the tribes of the earth shall mourn over him. Yea, amen!

I am the alpha and the omega, says the Lord God, the being one and the 'was' one and the coming one, the almighty!

## AN OUTLINE OF REVELATION 1:4-8

### A Salutation from the Eternal God!

When a letter arrives the return on the envelope often measures the eager anticipation with which we open. This salutation identifies the sender's dignity, nature and authority. It's content ought excite us to eager reading and prompt obedience. This letter is from the Eternal, worthy of reading and heeding.

I. THE WRITER AND THE DESTINATION. vs.4a
   1. John, trusted pastor.
   2. "The seven churches." The whole of God's people.

II. THE SENDER, THE ETERNAL, LIVING, REIGNING GOD. vss.4b-5a
   1. The eternal God.
      (a)"the being one..." I AM THAT I AM.
      (b)"the 'was' one..." "Before the mountains were brought forth, thou art God."
      (c)"the one coming..." He's in all the future!
   2. "From the seven spirits..." The Holy Spirit. The "breath" of life" to all that has life.
   3. From Jesus Christ
      (a)"Faithful witness"
      (b)"First-born from the dead."
      (c)"Ruler of the kings of the earth."

III. THE RECIPIENTS, "US" THE REDEEMED. vss.5b-6
   1. He "loosed us from our sins."
   2. He "made us into a kingdom."
   3. We function as priests in behalf of God to the world.
   4. For all this we extend "glory, strength," honor to Him!

IV. HIS FUTURE "COMING." vss.7-8
   1. He is coming again "with the clouds."
   2. It's to be universal. "Every eye shall see..."
   3. Including "the ones who pierced him."
   4. Universal reaction. "All tribes shall mourn over him..."

Conclusion: The Eternal is the "Almighty" one. It is well to "hear and heed."

John
Ἰωάννης
(sends)
(X)
(greetings)
(X)
vs. 4a
to churches
ἐκκλησίαις
the
ταῖς
seven
ἑπτὰ
the
ταῖς
in
ἐν
Asia
Ἀσίᾳ
the
τῇ

grace
χάρις
and
καὶ
peace
εἰρήνη
(be)
(X)
to you
ὑμῖν
and
καὶ
and
καὶ
from
ἀπὸ
being
ὤν
the
ὁ
was
ἦν
the
ὁ
com
ἐρχό
ing
μενος
the
ὁ
and
καὶ
and
καὶ
from
ἀπὸ
witness
μάρτυς
the
ὁ
faithful
πιστός
the
ὁ
vss. 4b–5a
Jesus Christ
Ἰησοῦ Χριστοῦ
firstborn
πρωτότοκος
the
ὁ
of dead
νεκρῶν
the
τῶν
and
καὶ
rul
ἄρ
ing
χων
the
ὁ
kings
βασιλέων
the
τῶν
earth
γῆς
the
τῆς
from
ἀπὸ
spirits
πνευμάτων
the
τῶν
seven
ἑπτὰ
which
ἃ
(are)
(X)
before
ἐνώπιον
throne
θρόνου
the
τοῦ
of him
αὐτοῦ

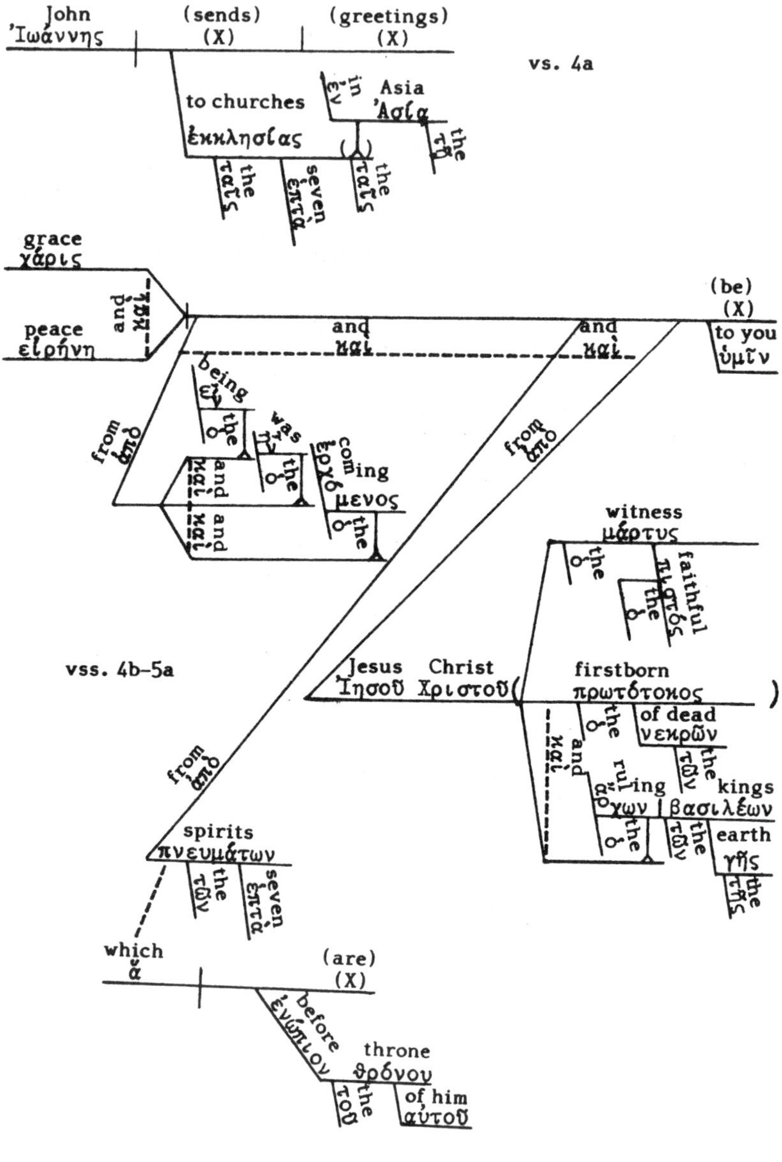

## THE DIAGRAM OF 1:4-5a

Verse 4a appears as a single simple sentence. Subject is Ἰωάννης. No identification as to which John is added because he was a familiar figure to the first readers of this epistle. The verb and its object are "understood."

The diagram is a good device for visualizing relationships of thought as linked in a sentence. But sometimes the emotional impact is weakened by diagramming. In order to be a sentence both subject and predicate are necessary. But to gain dramatic effect subject or predicate may be left unstated. They are "understood" as here in 1:4a. In reading, dramatic effect is heightened by leaving out "sends greetings." But to give the full sentence the diagram fills in the implied verb and its object.

Verses 4b-5a constitute a complex sentence. It has one basic clause, "Grace and peace (be) to you..." A brief dependent clause is attached to describe πνευμάτων, "which are before his throne." The compound subject of the main clause is the normal first century words used in most Christian salutations, "Grace and peace." "Grace" reflects the merciful gift of God; "peace" indicates the result in the heart of him who knows God's grace. The two words combine the greetings of two cultural segments of antiquity, the Greek "grace" and the Hebrew "peace" (shalom). They appear in a number of New Testament epistles.

Three adverbial phrases sprout from the main clause; "from the being one," "from the seven spirits," and "from Jesus Christ." They identify the source from which grace and peace are to come.

These three incorporate a remarkable construction. The author struggles to convey ideas too exalted for human language. He must disregard normal grammatical useage to get his idea on paper. The definite article ὁ with the present active participal ὢν isn't at all abnormal. Nor is it with present middle (defective) participle ἐρχόμενος. These are normal attributive participles, "the one being" and "the one coming." But to place the article with a finite verb ἦν is unusual. About the best English can do is to render it "the 'was' one." In our translation we have treated this verb ἦν as if it were an adjective; "the being one, and the 'was' one, and the coming one." It is a supreme effort to transpose into human language the idea of the exalted eternity of the living God. This "grace and peace" was to derive from Him who "always is, always was, and always will be." He has no limitation of time. He's the great I AM!

Not only do grace and peace derive from the eternal God but also "from the seven spirits," that is, from the Holy Spirit, the life breath of the living God. And these "spirits" are further described by a relative adjectival clause, "which (are) before his throne."

The third source is "from Jesus Christ." In apposition to "Jesus Christ" is a three-pronged combination: (1)"the faithful witness," (2)"the first-born of the dead" and (3)the attributive participial expression, "the one ruling the kings of the earth."

Revelation 1:5b-6

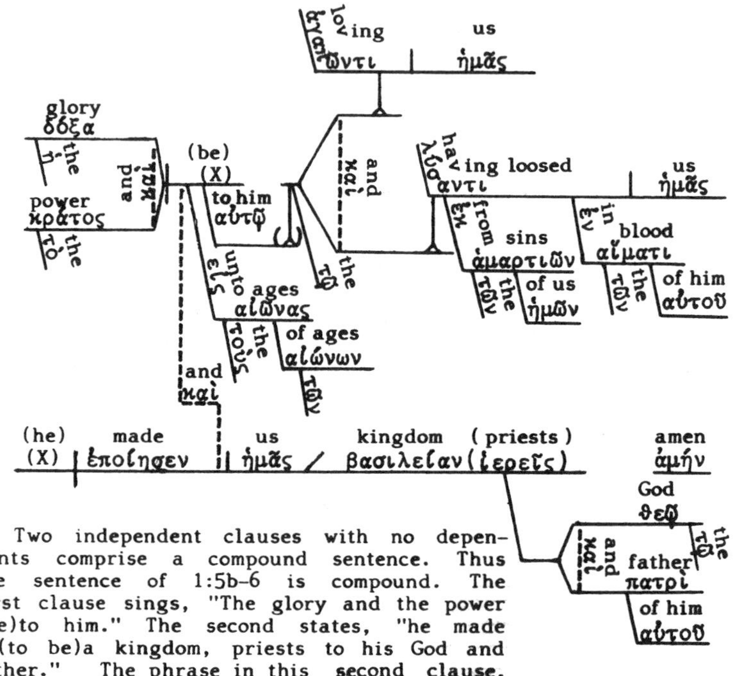


Two independent clauses with no dependents comprise a compound sentence. Thus the sentence of 1:5b-6 is compound. The first clause sings, "The glory and the power (be)to him." The second states, "he made us(to be)a kingdom, priests to his God and father." The phrase in this second clause, "to his God and father " might rightly modify the verb ἐποίησεν (made) as adverbial. We have elected to place it under ἱερεῖς as if it were adjectival = "his God-and-father priests." The word which is translated "priests" is in apposition to βασιλείαν(kingdom) which in turn is objective complement of ἡμᾶς. That which he made us to be is a "kingdom." And each separate citizen is to be functioning as a priest in behalf of God.

In the first clause the subject is the compound "the glory and the power." Such is to be ascribed "to him." This "to him" is more explicitly defined by a brace of attributive participles in apposition to αὐτῷ (to him). Present tense, continued action of ἀγαπῶντι is contrasted with punctiliar of aorist λύσαντι. His loving us is continuous and unbroken; his "having loosed us from our sins" looks to a specific point in history when the "loosing" took place. The ἐκ and ἐν phrases are adverbial. "From our sins" answers the question from where. He removed our sins "from us." The ἐν phrase answers how. He removed our sins "in his blood." His life's blood was the means he used in the removal of sins.

## EXPOSITORY THOUGHTS ON 1:4-8

Without communication there is no unity, no fellowship, no sense of "belonging." The letters of John, Paul, and others bound the scattered first-century churches together. The congregations were not lonely chips tossed to and fro on stormy waters. They were a flotilla of God's warships attacking the strongholds of sin. "John to the seven churches, the ones in Asia" is the semaphore that helped the many churches to move as one fleet.

Furthermore, John's choice of "seven" is symbolic. There were certainly more than seven churches in the Roman province of Asia. Besides the seven of verse 11 we know for sure of one, that at Colossae. Without doubt there were many others. John's "seven" is his signal that he's writing to the _whole_ church. Not only the seven named but all those unnamed. _And_ not just in Asia but in all the world. And we might add, through all time. The Revelation is a message for the entire church of God.

Though the apostle is the human author he bears a word of "grace and peace" from exalted sources. The letter's ultimate source is three-fold. It's from the living God, the Spirit of God and the Son of God. This trinity of sources is really the deity behind, in and through all creation including man. Deity expresses himself in three methods of disclosure.

As supreme He is "the being One, and the 'was' One, and the coming One." He is the great "I AM" who, without being locked into time, eternally _is_. John thus presents Deity as the "living God."

The letter also comes from "the seven spirits..." Seven signifies "perfection." Thus this is John's way of saying that the Holy Spirit is a prime source of his writing. Lest any doubt this he adds, "...which (are) before his throne..." These "seven spirits" are always in the presence of God. They are the "breath of God" ever breathing his energy into his word, his will, his purposes of redemption. Declaring that his letter was "from the seven spirits" John lays claim to the Holy Spirit as his guide in writing. The Revelation is _inspired_!

This Revelation comes also from Jesus Christ. And this Jesus is identified by three explications. He is "the faithful witness." In "the days of his flesh" he bore true testimony to God's plan for man. Both in deed and doctrine he revealed. He faithfully revealed the sinful condition of man, he revealed God's moral standard for man, he revealed Himself as the priestly Saviour for man, he revealed the eternal destiny of man. He's "the faithful witness."

Moreover, Jesus Christ is "the firstborn of the dead." The term "firstborn" is not declaring that Jesus as the Christ isn't coexistent with God. It is declaring that he is the "first" of a long line of human beings whom the grave disgorges as a baby comes from the womb. The fact is, it's because he _is_ eternally coexistent with God that such a birth from the cemetery is possible. Death and the grave could not hold _him_. If Christ be not the "firstborn from the dead" there'll be noone so "born." He's the "resurrection and the life!"

Besides this, Jesus Christ is "the one ruling the kings of the earth." It was not Caesar who was sovereign but Jesus. At the outset after describing Jesus as one of his sources John sets forth the Christ as sovereign. This is the basic conflict that drew forth the Revelation. Who is ruler? Christ or Caesar? When first Gabriel disclosed to the virgin that she would birth a son he said, "...God will give to him the throne of his father David, and he will reign over the house of Jacob forever."(Luke 1:32-33) He was a "born king." At the trial of Jesus Pilate asked, "Are you then a king? Jesus answered, You say that I am a king. For this have I come into the world..." He lived as king, he died as king, he reigns as king, "the one ruling the kings of the earth." In this very book (11:15) at the blast of the seventh trumpet the announcement of the sovereignty of God in Christ forms a climax of the conflict. Voices in heaven shouted, "The kingdom of the world became the kingdom of our Lord and his Christ, and he shall reign forever and ever." History confirms the sovereignty of Christ. From Caesar who challenged the sovereignty of Christ in the first century to modern Caesars, governments that oppose the Christ's ruling authority have waned and fallen. The Domitians, Napoleons, Hitlers and Stalins have flashed their rebellious swastikas through the years. Each has finally fallen under the sovereign power of righteousness. God's moral sway has been built into the moral universe. He who challenges it breaks himself upon it be he individual or government. Christ is <u>now</u> reigning; not only king over his kingdom but he rules "the kings of the earth."[4]

Reference to Christ as source of the Revelation leads John to ascribe "glory and honor" to him for what he has done in our behalf. "To the one loving us and who loosed us from our sins in his blood..." He loves us; he looses us! When it faced our lostness the unbroken love of Christ dissolved our sin and its consequences. He did what love had to do. He "loosed us from our sin." And he did it "in his blood," that is, in the sacrifice of his life's blood at calvary. It's not lack of clothing, food, knowledge or skills. It's sin, an inner weakness of spirit, that is our undoing. So it is this point at which Christ attacks. He "loosed us from our sins!"

But he didn't stop there. He didn't cleanse the house and then leave it empty, unattended. "He made us into a kingdom, priests to his God and father..." A king must have a kingdom. He "made <u>us</u>" into his kingdom. He transformed us from rebellious truants <u>into</u> a redeemed citizenry.

Moreover, we are a kingdom of "priests." Man must have a priest. Human nature recoils from familiar association with the Holy God. What can filth have in common with purity, darkness with light, ignorance with knowledge? Indeed, man will have a priest. And though it is true that he who "loosed us from our sins" is our great High Priest, interceding at the Father's right hand, he has made "us" to function in this world as a priestly kingdom. The church is God's psychotherapist institution. Christians mediate the sin-dissolving, burden-lifting gospel in God's behalf. "As the father sent me so send I you."

The Christ is not only a figure in the past he's a figure in the future! "Behold! He comes with the clouds..." The certainty of his "second" coming is as certain as his first. In his coming again he gathers unto himself all lines of ancient prophetic words (Dan.7:13, Zech.12:10-14)

Furthermore, his future coming shall be visible and universal. "Every eye shall see him..." As the angels said at his ascension, "This Jesus who was received up from you into heaven shall thus come in like manner as you beheld him going."(Acts 1:11) Jesus himself assured the Sanhedrin (Mark 14:62) "You shall see the son of man sitting at the right hand of power and coming with the clouds of heaven." As sure as is the word of Christ so sure is his coming again. This is the hope of the church. The Christian lives with this expectation.

And why shall he come again? For what purpose is he coming? "...and they who pierced him...shall see him and all the tribes of the earth shall mourn over him." It is for the consummation of redemption and the finale of judgment that he comes again. The sight of him whom they pierced shall justify judgment on those who pierced him. That same sight shall be the joy of those who received him. The cross of Christ both saves and condemns. It's God's means of man's redemption. It's the proof of just judgment on those who perpetrated it. It's the expression of man's most heinous guilt; the means of his most certain salvation. "All the tribes of the earth shall mourn over him..." Both saved and lost shall stand in awesome mourning. The one at the amazing grace; the other at the astounding sin!

Once again John underlines the authenticity of his message by calling attention to the timelessness of the God who inspires him. "I, even I, let no doubt exist that it is I" who declares all this Revelation and who makes these things come to pass. "I am the Alpha and the Omega, says the God, the being One and the 'was' One, and the coming One, the Almighty." Who can doubt either the substance or certainty of this Revelation! It is well to hear and heed what the "Almighty" has to say!

Revelation 1:7–8

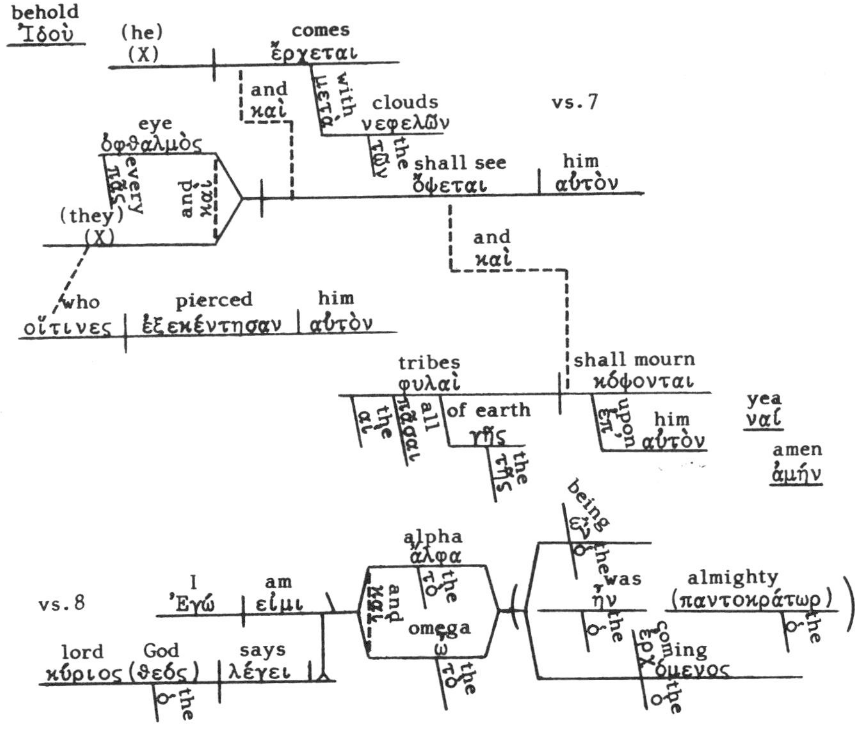

## THE DIAGRAM OF 1:7-8

Verse seven frames a compound-complex sentence. It entertains three independent ideas. One dependent clause hangs from a second prong of the compound subject of the second independent clause.

The first independent clause states positively, "He comes..." How he's going to come is introduced by the prepositional phrase "with the clouds." The phrase is adverbial in function.

The second of the independent expressions has a compound subject, "every eye and they..." Just who the "they" are is noted by the adjectival dependent clause, "who pierced him." When he comes "every eye shall see him" and that includes with particular emphasis "they who pierced him." When he comes again they who pierced the Lord shall not avoid facing him whom they abused and killed. The relative clause makes prominent that fact.

The final of the three independents reaffirms the universality of the "second" coming. The subject involves "all the tribes of the earth." The predicate adds to "every eye shall see" the fact that "all the tribes shall mourn." The idea of "mourning" may suggest that "all the tribes" did less than receive him as Lord and Saviour. Yet even those who received him and rejoiced in his first coming shall enter into the somber reality of judgment that comes upon those who rejected. The undertone seems to be on judgment associated with his future coming. Prepositional phrase ἐπ' αὐτὸν is adverbial; it deals with the question as to why the tribes shall mourn. They shall mourn "upon the basis of him." That is to say, His coming, his ministry, his death, his resurrection, and all that's associated with his first coming forms the basis upon which "all the tribes shall mourn" at his second.

The sentence of verse seven begins and ends with exclamations. "Behold" and "Yea, amen!" This instills dramatic power to the whole somber thought in the sentence.

Verse eight contains a complex sentence of two clauses. The independent element, with rising emotion, posits, "Lord, the God says,..." The absence of the definite article with κύριος, while awkward in English, is suggestive in Greek. It subtly implies that this one who speaks is of the nature of one who is Lord(Master). Who this "Lord" is appears in the appositional ὁ θεός. And that which he "says" is set forth in the dependent noun clause, object of the verb "says." This object clause declares, "I am the alpha and the omega." The "alpha and omega" are both parts of a compound predicate nominative. They point back to and are identified with the "I" as subject. The simple symbolism of the "alpha" and the "omega" is plain. They, being the first and last letters in the Greek alphabet, symbolize in another way the eternity of the living, ever-present God. This can hardly be doubted when we note that in apposition is repeated the earlier expression, "the being one," "the 'was" one," and "the coming one." Then there is added another appositional expression, "the almighty." He's not only eternal and living, he is all-powerful! When we look at παντοκράτωρ in its constituent parts it suggests, "the ruler of all things." In its New Testament usage reference isn't so much to God's involvement at creation as to his presence in creation.

Revelation 1:9–11

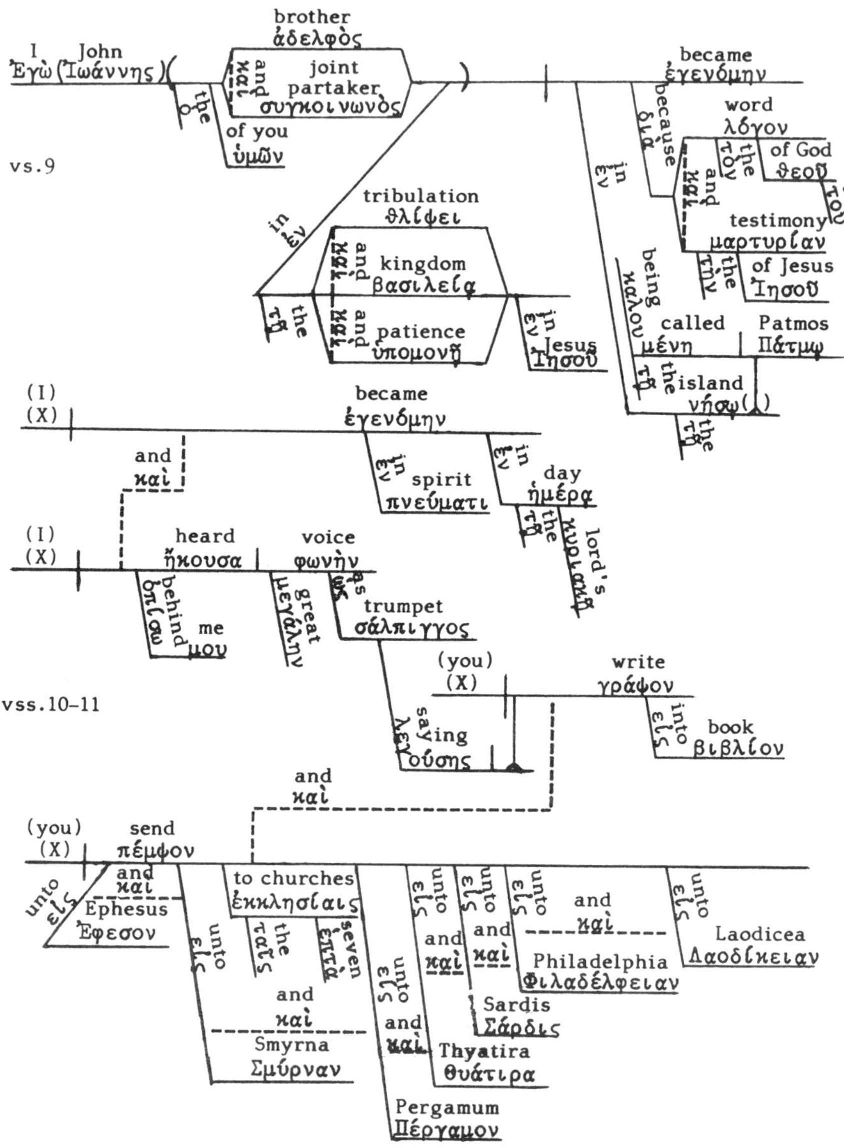

## THE DIAGRAM OF 1:9–11

The one clause of verse nine, when stripped of all modifying expansions, states "I became." So, as to its classification, the sentence is simple.

The subject "I" is quite boldly emphatic because the writer uses the personal pronoun ἐγὼ. Then he identifies the "I" by adding his personal name "John" in apposition. Another appositional expression is attached to identify further John as "brother and joint partner." An additional description of John is inserted by means of prepositional phrase introduced by ἐν. The phrase is adjectival in force. John is the "in tribulation-kingdom-patience partner." Further, this triad is more than just general "tribulation etc." that all men endure. It is tribulation that comes because he, John, is "in Jesus."

The verb in this sentence is not "was" but "became." ἐγενόμην represents more than constant existence. It pictures a "becoming," an entering into a state not previously present, an outflowering of an implanted potential. John "became" a prisoner on Patmos rather than "was" a prisoner. The reason why this state of affairs became is set forth in the διὰ phrase; "because of the word of God and testimony to Jesus." The genitive Ἰησοῦ is objective. It was the "testimony" which John gave about Jesus. The things which Jesus said and did formed the content of that to which John testified. On the other hand, the genitive θεοῦ seems more of a possessive idea, a subjective genitive. The word was "God's word."

Verses 10–11 contain four clauses, two independents and two dependents. It is compound-complex. The two independents declare, "I became...and...I heard voice..."

Under the verb "became" of the first main clause are two ἐν phrases serving as adverb ideas. The first "in spirit" answers the question <u>where</u>, while "in the Lord's day" indicates <u>when</u>.

In the second clause φωνὴν is direct object of ἤκουσα. One might expect a simple normal genitive "of trumpet" (σάλπιγγος) to modify "voice." But ὡς barges in = "as trumpet." The diagram treats the ὡς as a preposition. Describing "trumpet" is the present circumstantial participle λεγούσης, "saying." As direct object of this "saying" and giving the content of what was said are two dependent noun clauses. First: "(You) write in a book." And second: "(you) send..." Indirect object indicating <u>to whom</u> he is to send his writing is, "to the seven churches."

Then the author proceeds to name the specific churches as symbolically representing all the congregations in the province of Asia. The choice of these particular churches is not only symbolic of the entire church in Asia but was quite practical in purpose. These cities were major centers in a well-defined postal system. Government runners, corporate carriers, and other such institutions used these as primary points to which vital correspondence was sent; and from which the same messages were relayed to other cities of which these seven served as hubs. John found these established communication centers important to him not only as symbolic but as a ready-made customary way of rapid communication.

## Revelation 1:12-13

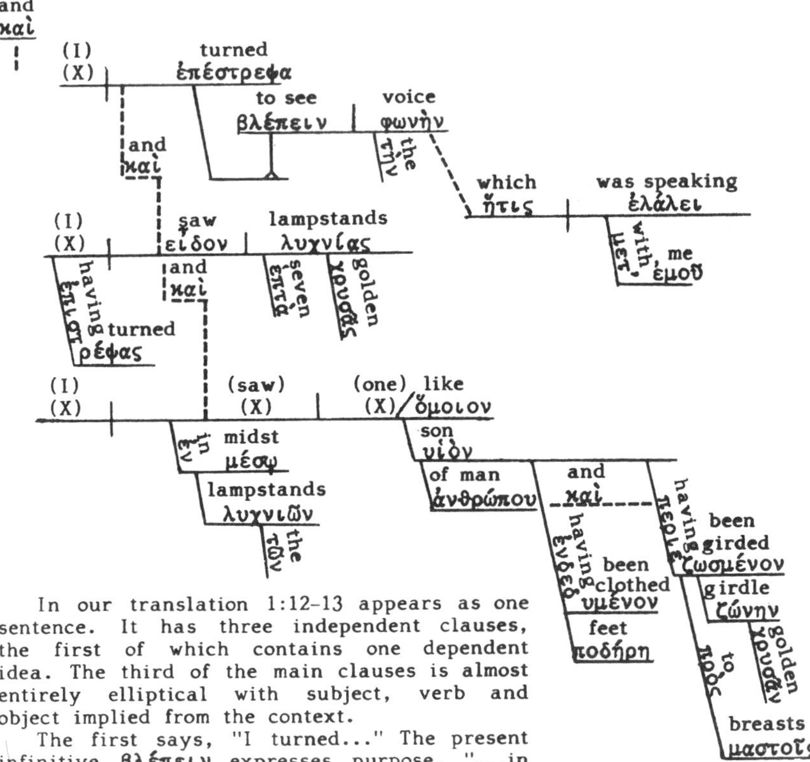


In our translation 1:12-13 appears as one sentence. It has three independent clauses, the first of which contains one dependent idea. The third of the main clauses is almost entirely elliptical with subject, verb and object implied from the context.

The first says, "I turned..." The present infinitive βλέπειν expresses purpose, "...in order to see the voice..." The relative clause ushered in by ἥτις is adjectival describing "voice." Imperfect tense ἐλάλει gives a dramatic vividness that would be lacking in a matter-of-fact aorist. It sketches a moving picture of an animated flow of speech.

Modifying the subject "I" of the second main clause is aorist active circumstantial participle ἐπιστρέψας = "having turned." It is temporal and may be rendered as relative, "when I turned." The point action of the aorist focuses on a point antecedent to the action in the main verb. "When I turned I saw..."

ὅμοιον of the third main clause is objective complement. ὅμοιον would be expected to have instrumental υἱῷ after it but here the accusative υἱὸν appears. In fact some ancient manuscripts have the instrumental. Two circumstantial participles add descriptions to υἱὸν, "having been clothed and having been girdled." Both are perfect tense calling attention to the permanancy of the action. Whatever clothing and girdling symbolize it's permanent.

TRANSLATION

Revelation 1:9-20

I John, your brother and partner in the affliction, and kingdom and patience in Jesus, came (to be) in the isle, the one called Patmos, because of the word of God and the testimony to Jesus. I got in the spirit on the Lord's day and I heard behind me a great voice as a trumpet saying, "What you see write in a book and send to the seven churches: unto Ephesus and unto Smyrna and unto Pergamum and unto Thyatira and unto Sardis and unto Philadelphia and unto Laodicea." And I turned to see the voice which was speaking with me and, having turned, I saw seven golden lampstands and amid the lampstands (I saw one) like a son of man having been clothed to the feet and having been girdled about the breast with a golden girdle. And his head and his hair were white as wool, white like snow (is white); and his eyes were as a flame of fire, and his feet like burnished bronze as having been refined in a furnace and his voice as (the) voice of many waters. And (he was) having in his right hand seven stars and out of his mouth (was) going a sharp two-edged sword and his face (was) as the sun shines in its power. And when I saw him I fell to his feet as dead and he placed his hand upon me saying, "Quit fearing! I am the first and the last and the living one. And I became dead and look, I am living unto the ages of the ages and I hold the keys of the death and of the hades. Write therefore which things you saw and which things are and which things are about to come to pass after these things. The mystery of the seven stars which you saw upon my right hand and the seven golden lampstands (is this): the seven stars are the messengers of the seven churches and the lampstands are the seven churches."

AN OUTLINE OF REVELATION 1:9-20

The Exalted Christ Commissions the Prophet!

This is a message of hope to God's people, "the seven churches."

I. THE EXILE. 1:9-10
   1. "I John, your brother and partner."
   2. Exiled because of the Word and Witness to Jesus.
   3. At worship: (a)"in the Spirit" (b)"heard a voice."

II. THE COMMISSION. 1:11
   1. "Write what you see."
   2. Destination: "the seven churches." God's people.

III. VISION OF THE VICTORIOUS CHRIST. 1:12-20
   1. Controls the destiny of the churches. vss. 12-13
      And of the ministry. vs.16a & 20a
   2. His Person: royalty, purity, insight, relentless progress, revelation, offensive weapon, light.
   3. As "first and last" he's eternal, encompassing history.
   4. Victor over death hence eternally alive.
   5. Holds the "keys" of life and death.

Conclusion: This message springs from the victorious Christ through a suffering brother. It's a down-to-earth word that meets man at the level where he must live. It's to be read with hope in troublous times.

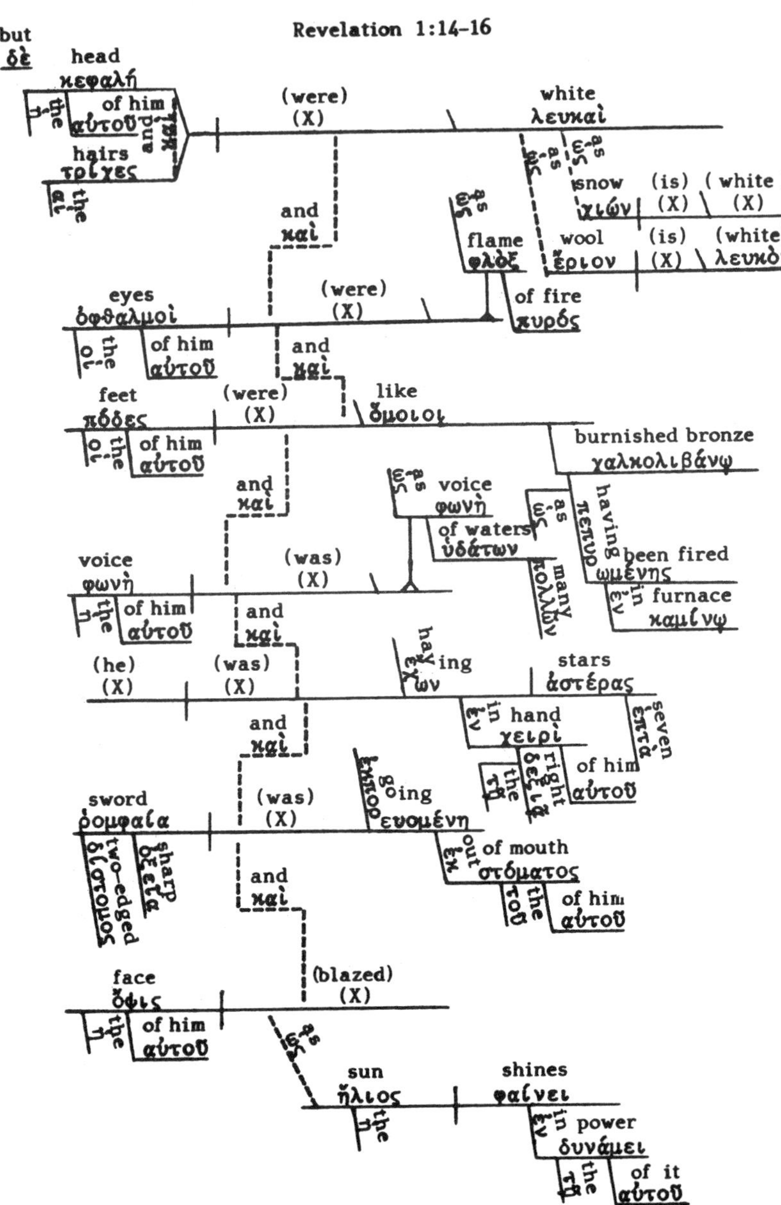
but
δὲ
head
κεφαλὴ
the
ἡ
of him
αὐτοῦ
and
καὶ
hairs
τρίχες
the
αἱ
(were)
(X)
white
λευκαὶ
as
ὡς
snow
χιὼν
(is)
(X)
( white )
(X)
wool
ἔριον
(white)
λευκὸν
and
καὶ
eyes
ὀφθαλμοὶ
the
οἱ
of him
αὐτοῦ
flame
φλὸξ
of fire
πυρὸς
feet
πόδες
of him
αὐτοῦ
like
ὅμοιοι
burnished bronze
χαλκολιβάνῳ
having been fired
πεπυρωμένης
in
ἐν
furnace
καμίνῳ
voice
φωνὴ
of waters
ὑδάτων
many
πολλῶν
(was)
(X)
(he)
having
ἔχων
stars
ἀστέρας
seven
ἑπτὰ
hand
χειρὶ
right
δεξιᾷ
τῇ
sword
ῥομφαία
two-edged
δίστομος
sharp
ὀξεῖα
going
ἐκπορευομένη
out
ἐκ
of mouth
στόματος
τοῦ
face
ὄψις
(blazed)
sun
ἥλιος
shines
φαίνει
power
δυνάμει
of it

## THE DIAGRAM OF 1:14-16

The sentence of 1:14-16 continues describing the apocalyptic "son of man" who becomes the chief figure in Revelation. The sentence consists of ten clauses. Seven of them are independent. The first has two dependent adverb clauses of comparison modifying the predicate adjective "white." Tacked onto the final of these independents is another ὡς adverbial dependent of comparison. Thus the sentence is to be categorized as compound-complex.

The seven independent clauses follow a rather uniform pattern each one joined to the next by the coordinating conjunction καὶ.

The first has a compound subject, "His head and hairs..." The predicate adjective λευκαὶ looks back to the subject. The plural is normal with a double subject but it seems influenced by the plural "hairs" as being the most prominent feature about the head. It is the white hair that furnishes the symbol of purity for which the writer is striving. To heighten the whiteness of the white he throws in two ὡς clauses of comparison. "Wool" was a familiar product. Sheep herders were a daily sight in any pastoral land, certainly in John's home land of Palestine. "Snow" and its glistening whiteness was not unkown even in the warm Mediterranean lands. Snowclad mountains were relatively frequent sights.

The next independent clause depicts, "his eyes (were) as flame of fire." The presence of ὡς doesn't keep "flame" from performing as a predicate nominative. The whole phrase is predicate.

The third independent characterizes "his feet" to be "like burnished bronze." ὅμοιοι is predicate adjective followed by a normal instrumental case χαλκολιβάνῳ. Describing this "burnished bronze" is the perfect passive participle πεπυρωμένης = having been fired. It's a circumstantial. The tense is in keeping with the permanent hardness of the metal gained by being fired in a furnace.

The fourth of the independents declares, "his voice (was) as voice of many waters." Once again the whole ὡς phrase is treated as predicate nominative.

In the fifth independent the present participle ἔχων supplements an understood "was." Together they make a periphrastic imperfect tense; "he was having." Such periphrastic expressions usually give more prominence to the linear aspect of the tense. This "son of man" continuously kept control of the "stars" (the ministers) of the churches. The prepositional phrase "in his right hand" indicates <u>where</u> he held the stars. This apocalyptic person guided with his right hand the progress and destiny of the ministry of the church.

Another periphrastic imperfect enlivens the sixth independent clause. "A sharp two-edged sword <u>was going out</u> of his mouth." Here again the sword feature was a continuing ongoing thing. The sword symbolized the word of God uninterruptedly "going out" of the mouth of the "son of man."

The final of the independents, with the aid of its ὡς dependent, produces a vivid impression of brilliance. "...his face (blazed) as the sun shines in its power." The verb "blazed" or some such word is needed to match the brilliance of the shining noonday sun as presented in the dependent clause. If his "face" is to accord with the brilliance of the shining sun the author must find a strong matching word. We are suggesting "blaze."

Revelation 1:17–18

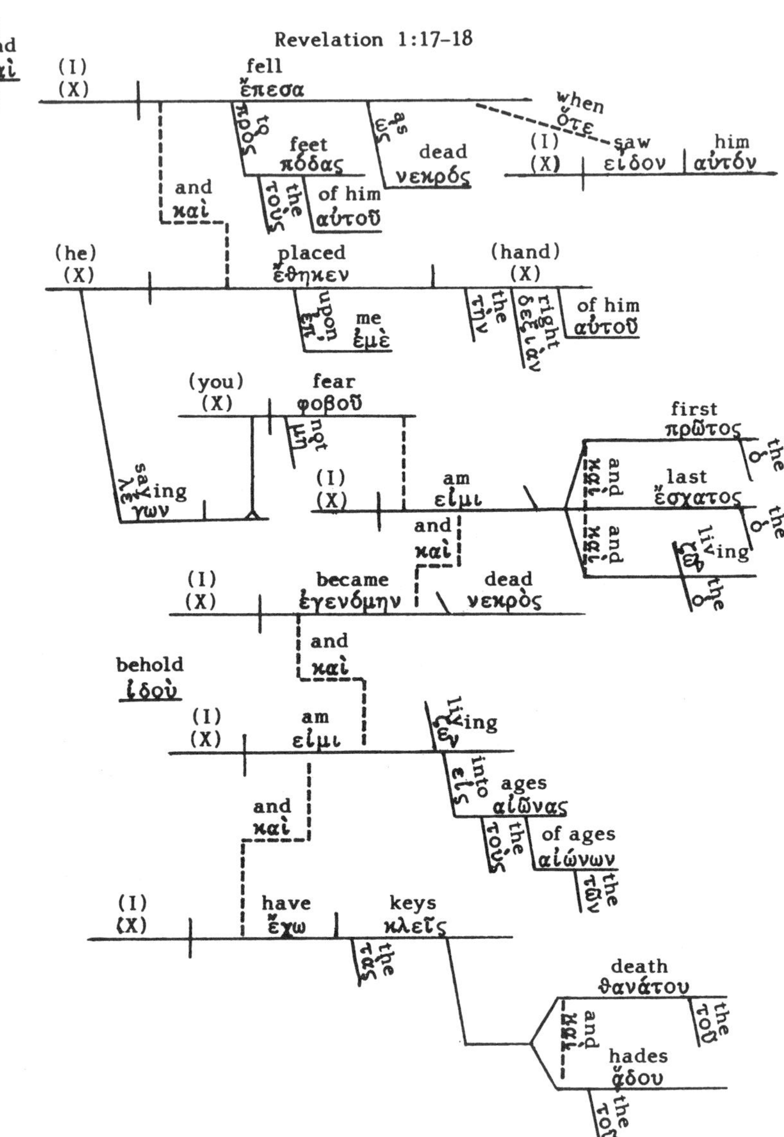

## THE DIAGRAM OF 1:17-18

Verses 17-18 formulate one sentence of eight clauses. Two are independent and six are dependent. The main action of the two independents state what John did and how the "son of man" responded. "I fell...and...he placed his right hand..." A temporal subordinate clause informs when John fell, that is, "when I saw him..." The phrase introduced by ὡς might be treated as another dependent clause, "...as (though I were) dead..." But the diagram has it as an adverbial phrase modifying the verb "fell." "I fell like one dead." Another adverbial phrase modifies "fell" by telling where John fell; "to his feet."

The second independent clause unveils how this awesome figure reassured the frightened apostle. "..and he placed his right hand upon me..." The "upon me" is a prepositional phrase used as an adverb answering the question where.

The remainder of the sentence is made up of a present active circumstantial participle λέγων = "saying" followed by five noun clauses each of which serves as a direct object of the participle.

First comes the exhortation, "Quit fearing..." The verb φοβοῦ is present imperative middle. Linear action in a present imperative shows itself by one of two meanings. Either "Quit what you're doing" or "Don't have the habit of doing what you're doing." The context must be the determining factor. Here it seems that the Lord is exhorting John to "Quit being afraid!"

The next four dependent clauses furnish solid reasons why John should "quit fearing." One is: "I am the first and the last and the living one." The idea of "first and last" nerves the apostle by reminding him that he, the Lord, encompasses all time from birth to death. And that's true whether it be the birth and death of the indivdual or that of the universe. To all and to any he is the "first and the last." The attributive present participle ζῶν, "the living one" inspires with the knowledge that he encompasses all time and eternity.

The next two dependent ideas are a couple that need each other to make the essential point of either. First, "I became dead" points to an event in history, the crucifixion of the Christ. But it also prepares for the startling fact of the next clause which informs that death had no effect on him; "I went right on living," and moreover, "I am living forever and forever..." The present tense of the participle makes prominent the fact that the Lord "went right on living..." He didn't die and then "become alive." He did not cease living even though he experienced death. And the fact that this is a supplementary participle, part of a periphrastic expression, adds even more emphasis to the force of this linear action.

In the final of the dependent clauses the speaker presents a figure familiar to all people, that of "keys." "I have the keys of the death and of the hades." The present tense of the verb ἔχω suggests that he possesses and keeps possession of that which unlocks both the fact and the meaning of "death and hades." There need be no fear, no mystery about such threatening things since the "son of man" has the keys that unlock their ability to imprison men through fear.

Revelation 1:19-20

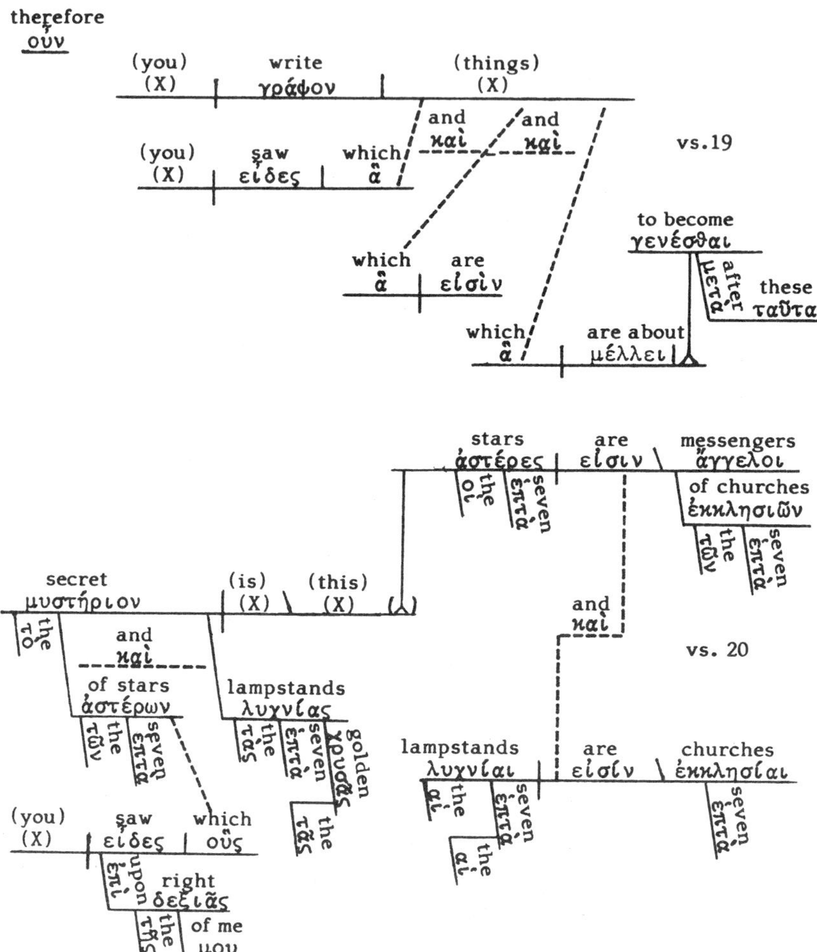

## THE DIAGRAM OF REVELATION 1:19-20

The introductory particle οὖν expresses consequence, "therefore." This renews his command of verse 11, "Write." Now, however, he is to write the "things which you saw." That is, now that you have seen the exalted, living, victorious Christ, "therefore write.."

The sentence is complex since it has but one independent clause with the other three being dependents. All three dependents are adjectival; all three describe an understood "things," object of the verb "write" of the main clause.

In the first of the dependent clauses the relative pronoun ἃ is neuter accusative. It is direct object of εἶδες. But in the next two dependents the relative is neuter nominative because it serves as subject in each clause.

It seems to trouble some observers that a neuter plural is subject of the plural εἰσὶν while it is subject of the singular μέλλει. It is normal Greek for a neuter plural to be used with a singular verb. So that should create no problem. If there is a problem it would be why use a neuter plural with a plural verb? Especially since the normal rule appears in the third dependent? The irregularities of the grammar in the Revelation is one question that offers food for speculation for many scholars and for which none have come up with a sure answer. It's possible that the author deliberately violated rules in order to stimualte attention in what he was writing. That's as good a surmise as any!

Verse 20 embodies a complex arrangement. It has three dependent clauses amplifying the basic idea of the independent, "The secret (is this)." Describing "secret" are two genitives, "of stars" and "of lamp stands." The genitive case in some way or other specifies the kind of thing that is described. It is similar to an adjective in function but describes more sharply. It's the "stars" kind of secret and the "lampstands" kind of mystery.

The relative οὓς clause is adjectival describing "stars." And by virtue of the conjunction καὶ it also describes the "lampstands."

An understood "this" serves as predicate nominative after understood verb "is." Defining the "this" is an appositional noun clause stating, "the seven stars are the seven messengers..." The word ἄγγελος in its primary sense means "messenger." "Angel" as a meaning comes later as a specialized use of the term. It seems best to use "messenger" here. Possibly referring to the "ministers" of the seven churches. And note once again the genitive ἐκκλησιῶν specifying the "kind" of messengers.

The final of the three dependent clauses states, "the lampstands are seven churches." It also is a noun clause in apposition to the predicate nominative "this" of the main clause.

If one has any doubts that the book of Revelation offers its message by means of symbols the words of the exalted "son of man" should remove them. He here states plainly that "stars" are "messengers" and that "lampstands" are "churches." This not only makes clear these immediate symbols but this example furnishes a plain hint to the reader to look for meanings lying behind and beyond the symbols.

## EXPOSITORY THOUGHTS ON 1:9-20

The electrifying rapture of victory! Who has not felt it? The wretched pang of defeat! Who has not wallowed in it? Defeat is no fun at any level! A grade school ball game, a business reverse, a disrupted marriage, or a world wide armed conflict!

Has there ever been a more humiliating defeat than that of Jesus Christ? Betrayed by a friend, denied by a comrade, mobbed by his people, executed as a public menace! Is that not the prototype of defeat? Now, two generations later his church is being subjected to the same agony of defeat. The Roman empire with its military force, economic controls, social regimentation has set itself against the church. Jesus is being crucified again. The issue was clear: life with Caesar! or death with Christ!

Satan did not exhaust his efforts against Christ 2000 years ago. He's alive in today's world. He operates through control over the forces of institutions, notably government and its bureaucratic powers. Every move of a materialistic age over the mind, heart, and thought through social organizations helps reproduce such terrifying conditions that led John on Patmos to write Revelation.

### The vision of victory

"The revelation of Jesus Christ" is something which God gave "to show."(1:1) In verses 10-11 John describes how he "...was in the spirit..." and "heard a great voice...saying, 'Write...the things which you see.'" When the startled apostle turned he says, "I saw..." So his message is not fantasy nor illusion. John saw and himself experienced what he writes.

And what did John see that Sunday morning when the loud voice sounded behind him? He saw "seven golden lampstands." And he saw in the midst of the lampstands "one like unto the son of man." And what indeed suggests victory in a bunch of flickering lights with a weirdly dressed man walking among them?

That which the apostle saw signified something other than what he saw. Stars on the flag symbolize states but they aren't states. Lampstands symbolize something other than lamps. And this weirdly dressed man signifies someone other than just a grotesque old man. In verse 20 John indicates that "...the lampstands are the seven churches." The number seven signifies the whole, complete, entire church. The author thus says that this oddly dressed man moves with freedom, authority, and concern among the churches; that they are under his supervision and control. He is Lord over the whole church. The very term "son of man" identifies this man as the Christ moving with firm confidence among his beleaguered churches as he guides them to their destiny.

Examine the details of the man's appearance! The white hair, the flaming eyes, the protruding sword, the feet of burnished brass, the voice of many waters, the seven stars, his "appearance as the sun shining in its power." These are symbolic signs which spoke to lives threatened under the harsh heel of imperial Rome. And they still speak hope for any who live in fear of the power of government threatening to invade personal lives of faith.

The snow-white head says that this "son of man" is pure and therefore eternal. For the only thing that abides is purity. Sin is "for a season" but the whiteness of virtue is forever.

And those flames of fire blazing from his eyes? He sees with uncompromising severity into the buried depths of every soul. He "discerns the thought and intent of the heart. Before him no man is hidden, but all are open and naked before him with whom we have to do."(Heb.4:13) "Even before a word is on my tongue, lo, O Lord, thou knowest it altogether."(Psalm 139:4)

And his feet! They gleam "like burnished brass refined in a furnace." Feet are for walking. How can mortal flesh halt the progress of him who steadily moves with the indestructible strength of refined metal? Can any calamity in history, any tower of Babel, any invention or technology of man stay the sure progress of the "son of man" and his redemptive love? Nothing! He survives wars, famines, depressions, national and international upheavals. No crisis of man's making or the devil's devising traps him off-guard. Christ moves through century after century with firmness of metal against flesh.

In the sound of his voice flows the message of "many waters." Like the mighty Mississippi gathers into its bosom the waters from mountains and miles of tributary streams so Christ collects the revelations of the patriarchs and prophets of antiquity. He sums up all that God has spoken "to the fathers in the prophets." His word is final; his message the ultimate manifesto from God to man. The "Word became flesh." In his person he gathers up "the way, the truth, and the life."

From his mouth projects a "sharp two-edged sword." A sword symbolizes the power of government. "All authority in heaven and on earth has been given unto me" says Jesus. He has the authority to command and the power to judge. So the day is at hand when the petty power and arrogant presumption of the kings of the earth shall be humbled by the sword of the "son of man"." And what shall become of the presumptuous pride of men who invade his church, usurp his royal prerogative and disrupt his kingdom by their overbearing assumed authority? The church isn't a democracy; it's a kingdom and the "son of man" is its king. He has the right of the sword; the power to determine God's program of redemption. What man dare usurp that responsibility?

A final feature of this "son of man" is his face. It is "like the sun shining in full strength." As the sun is the source of light, heat and life on this planet so the son of God is the source of the light of truth, the warmth of love, and the life that overcomes death. The courts and councils of men, local, national or international, are as blind men fumbling in the dark. The "son of man" is the full-orbed noon day sun "shining in its strength."

### The thrill of victory

What is the practical significance of this bewildering cryptic vision of John on the isle of Patmos? What is its abiding message?

When the aged apostle saw this unearthly vision his initial reaction was one of fear. He "fell as though dead." Then came the reassuring voice, "Quit being afraid! I am the first and the last and the living one. I became dead and behold, I am living forever and ever. And I have the keys of death and hades." What a word of hope to an imprisoned man! What inspiration to churches facing aggressive governmental persecution!

It is heartening to observe how Christ treats death. He almost ignores it. Mentions it only to reveal that he holds the key that unlocks whatever binding force death has. Jesus did not say, "I died and I arose in order to live again." No! He said, "I am the living one. I became dead but went right on living." Jesus went through that death men fear so much like a man walking through an open door. It was as though death didn't exist. He declares, "I walked right through it. Yes, I died, but I went right on living. It wasn't even a contest. I held all the trump cards." While in the flesh Jesus said, "As the father has life in himself, so he gave the son to have life in himself."(Jn.5:26) There's just no way to bury "life." We bury corpses, but not life! If men try to hide, chain, imprison, bury, seal, the "living one" he just goes right on living. There's no prison, no bars, no dungeon, no grave that can keep life from living. It simply breaks through all restraints and goes right on.

Christ is victor! He's victor because he's pure and therefore eternal. He's victor because his flaming eyes see into the soul of all humanity. He's victor because nothing can stop his relentless tread through history (or my personal life). He's victor because in him are gathered all the voices of the past. He's victor because from him proceeds the only genuine universal power to govern. He has "all authority." He's like the "sun in its strength." Nothing dark can endure in the light of his person. "The Lord is the stronghold of my life; of whom shall I be afraid?...I believe that I shall see the goodness of the Lord in the land of the living! Wait for the Lord; be strong, and let your heart take courage; yea, wait for the Lord."(Psalm 27:1, 12-13)

Jesus said, "He that lives and believes on me shall never die." In other words, We shall walk through death even as he - as if it doesn't even exist. Then we shall "see him as he is."

A thirty-two year old daughter of a devoted father suddenly, without warning died. Though it was a devastating shock his faith never faltered. When he later had reason to counsel with his daughter's friend, who herself was within a few days of death, he said, "When you see Ruth, tell her 'Hi!'" The living Christ interprets death as a door to life not a dungeon to darkness. Death is the door through which we walk to say "Hi!" to Christ and all who are victors because of Him.

## THE SEVEN CITIES

1. Ephesus: The City of Change. 2:1-7
   (1)Changes in character of the city as determined by population.
      (a)First, villages surrounded by local sanctuary.
      (b)In 1100 B.C. Greek colonists established a city.
      (c)In 560 Croesus conquered and moved the city back from higher ground to be next to temple of Artemis.
      (d)After 287 Lysimachus turned it back into a Hellenistic and moved it back to higher ground.
   (2)Changes in location.
   (3)Changes in natural environment from seaport to inland.
   (4)Changes in outward forms of religious expression.

2. Smyrna: The City of Life. 2:8-11
   (1)Greeks found it as colony before 1000 B.C. Destroyed by king Alyattes in 600 B.C.
   (2)Refounded by Lysimachus about 290 B.C. But throughout the interval a loose group of settlements called "Smyrna" was in existence but not as a free, sovereign Greek city.
   (3)Its beauty a sign of its creative life, regular block streets, groves of trees, harbor, hills. The "crown of Smyrna.
   (4)Live activity in every branch of literature.
   (5)Zephyrus, a refreshing westerly breeze up the gulf to allay the summer heat from early afternoon to sunset. A "pleasant coolness through the city."

3. Pergamum: The City of Authority. 2:12-17
   (1)The natural physical situation of the city impresses with the sense of power and authority. Its vast rock-hill plants its foot upon a broad plain. The rock rules the valley with an impression of size, permanence, strength, authority.
   (2)Its coinage and history reveals its political headship from 282 B.C. onward. In 133 Attalus III bequeathed the city to the Romans It was the capital of the province 2½ centuries.
   (3)The official capital became the center of the Imperial cult.

4. Thyatira: The City from Weakness Made Strong. 2:18-29
   (1)Originated as a garrison city its importance lay in its military strength. Yet as a military base it was weak for it lay in a open valley gentle hills, no acropolis. So from a natural weakness it had to be made strong.
   (2)The function in history of the city was to guard against an ever-threatening danger between rival powers.
   (3)Its native Anatolian religion characterized its situation. Its god, Tyrimnos, on war horse and battle axe going out to conquer his enemies.
   (4)When this letter was written it was after a century of Roman peace. Industry commerce, trade guilds dominated life and furnished the issue: Is Christianity to be absorbed into Graeco Roman society, morbid, unhealthy, fast, highly developed?

## THE SEVEN CITIES
(continued)

5. Sardis: The City of Death. 3:1-6
   (1)Natural environment and history furnish the frame for the letter. History of the city became pattern of the church.
      (a)Natural surrounding. 1500 foot high rock plateau joined only on south by narrow neck. Impregnable!
      (b)History: Capitol from "time there were princes in Lydia." Great, wealthy, invincible - "against which none could strive and prevail."
      (c)Twice it fell; "as a thief in the night." In 546 under Croesus. Again 320 years later Antiochus II conquered it. Both times because only one side guarded.
   (2)The famous Sardis: its history "past and done." Though it appeared to be living it was already dead. "Pretensions unjustified, promise unfulfilled, appearance without reality, confidence that heralded ruin." "Appearance of strength, the mask of weakness."
   (3)History of the city furnished pattern for the history of the church. A name for life after it was already dead!

6. Philadelphia: The Missionary Church. 3:7-13
   (1)The district possessed by Eumenes 189 B.C. Founded for purpose of spreading Greek language and letters in East Lydia and Phrygia. By 19 A.D. Greek the only tongue spoken in Lydia. Successful mission from the start.
   (2)In 17 A.D. earthquake destroyed the city. Frequent quakes for years made people live under daily threat of disaster. Some went out to open country dreading "day of trial."
   (3)From appreciation for Imperial help took a new name from the Imperial god. Neokaisareia (New Caesar).
   (4)Philadelphia (and Smyrna) became the most long-lived of the seven cities. More influential; as mission church would

7. Laodicea: The City of Compromise. 3:14-22
   (1)Built by Antiochus II in 261-246 B.C. at a critical juncture of the East-West road system through Lycus valley. A commercial, financial, manufacturing center.
   (2)Famous for black wool; also medical school.
   (3)It knew no extremes; in this lay its main characteristic. As successful trading center it adapted to others' needs, pliable, accomodating, full of spirit of compromise.
   (4)The church was neither this nor that; irresolute, undecided, lacking in initiative, self-satisfied.
   (5)The church could not evaluate its spiritual condition. Thought itself rich when poor; having sight when blind.

## A TRANSLATION
Revelation 2:1-7

To the church in Ephesus write: These things says the one holding the seven stars in his right hand, the one walking in the midst of the seven golden lampstands, "I know your works and your labor and your patience and that you are not able to bear evil and that you tried the ones calling themselves apostles though they're not and you found them false. And you are continuing to have patience; and you endured on account of my name, and you have not grown weary.

But I have against you that you have left your love, that which you had at the first. Therefore, be remembering from where you have fallen and repent and produce your first works. But if not, I'm going to come to you and I will remove your lampstand out of its place, except you repent.

But this you do have, that you are hating the work of the Nicolaitans, which (works) I also hate.

The one having ears is to hear what the spirit is saying to the churches. To the one overcoming, I will give to him to eat out of the tree of life which is in the paradise of God."

## AN OUTLINE OF REVELATION 2:1-7
Loveless Loyalty

Loyalty in doctrine and deed to the living Christ is laudible. But loyalty without love lacks life.

I. HISTORY MARKS EPHESUS AS A CITY OF CHANGE.
   1. Changes in character of the population.
      (a)First, villages surrounding a religous shrine.
      (b)In 1100 B.C. Greek colonists established a city. It was at the foot of Mt. Koressos.
   2. Changes in location.
      (a)In 560 Croesus conquered and moved the city back from higher ground to be near temple of Artemis.
      (b)After 287 Lysimachus restored it into a Hellenistic city and moved it back to higher ground.
   3. Changed from seaport to an inland city.
   4. Changes in forms of religious expression.

II. THE CHURCH AT EPHESUS WAS A CHURCH THAT CHANGED.
   1. Said Jesus, "I know your works...your first works."
      (a)"Toil," "Patience," "tested" false apostles, endured, didn't grow weary." You "hated" properly.
      (b)A negative mark: "You left your love" that which you had at "the first." You changed!

III. AN EXHORTATION, A WARNING, AND A PROMISE.
   1. "Remember whence you've fallen." Be aware of a change.
   2. "Repent." Change your mind!
   3. "Do the first works." Change your motive back to love.
   4. Warning: Removal of the church as light!
   5. Promise: To eat from "the tree of life."

The Ephesians hated the works of the Nicolaitans ("which I also hate.") without hating the Nicolaitans. But they needed to do those works and have that hate from a heart of love. A deed is not good until it is properly motivated.

## A TRANSLATION
### Revelation 2:8-11

And to the messenger of the church in Smyrna write: These things says the first and the last, who became dead and lived, "I know your affliction and your poverty (but you are rich) and the blasphemy of the ones calling themselves Jews and are not but are a synagogue of Satan. Quit fearing (the things) which you are about to suffer. Behold, the devil is about to throw (some) of you into prison in order that you might be tried, and you will have affliction ten days. Go on being faithful unto death and I will give to you the crown of life.

The one having ears is to hear what the spirit is saying to the churches. The one overcoming shall not be harmed out of the second death."

## AN OUTLINE OF REVELATION 2:8-11
### Living Though Dead!

"Even if he should die, the one believing on me shall live." Jesus does not say "he shall live again. No! He shall go right on living! He who wears the crown which is life cannot be hurt by death at any time in any form.

I. HISTORY MARKS SMYRNA AS A CITY OF LIFE.
   1. Founded as a free Greek city before 1000 B.C. Destroyed in 600 B.C. Went on living as an Anatolian community.
   2. Refounded about 290 B.C. Beauty of its streets, groves, harbor, hills, literary life, and Zephyrus breeze brought fame for its energetic life as "The crown of Smyrna."
   3. No conquest, no disaster ever permanently broke Smyrna as a living city.
   4. Had the record of being the earliest, most faithful ally of Rome since before Rome's greatness.

II. LIFE OF THE CHURCH IMAGES THE LIFE OF THE CITY
   1. The experience of Christ forms the message to the church.
      (a)"The first and the last." "The living one."(cf.1:17b)
      (b)Who "became dead and right on living." He didn't die and after some time live again. His life persisted through death. So would the church!
   2. "I know your affliction" past and future. But it's limited. "Ten days" will be its limits.
   3. "Go on being faithful" as you always have been. Such faithfulness will result in the "crown" which is life.
   4. You are a poor church but are really rich.
      (a)For you intelligently defend against false Jews.
      (b)You're faithful when imprisoned by Satan.

The Smyrnians had an unblemished record. They seemed to be poor but had real wealth; experienced apparent death but had real life. They lived not only in but through death and decay. The "one overcoming shall not be hurt out of the second death." What, after all, can death do to life?

## A TRANSLATION
### Revelation 2:12-17

And to the messenger of the church in Pergamum, write: These things says the one having the sharp two-edged sword, "I know where you are dwelling, where the throne of Satan is. And you are holding tight my name and did not deny your faith in me, and in the days of Antipas my faithful martyr, who was put to death in your presence where Satan dwells.

But I have against you a few things, that you have there ones holding the teaching of Balaam, who was teaching Balak to throw a stumbling block before the sons of Israel, to eat idol sacrifices and to fornicate. Thus you have also ones holding the doctrine of the Nicolaitans after the same manner. Repent therefore! But if not, I am coming to you quickly and will do battle with them with the sword of my mouth.

The one having ears is to hear what the spirit is saying to the churches. To the one overcoming, I will give to him of the manna, that having been hidden, and I will give to him a white stone and upon the stone a new name having been written, (a name) which no one knows except the one receiving (it)."

## AN OUTLINE OF REVELATION 2:12-17
### The Right of the Sword!

In Rome the sword symbolized the highest authority, the "right of the sword"(jus gladii) with which the proconsul was invested. Pergamum as provincial capital held this "right of the sword." But the real jus gladii proceeded out of the mouth of the risen Christ, "the one having the sharp two-edged sword."

I. PERGAMUM, CITY OF OFFICIAL AUTHORITY.
   1. Its natural situation gave Pergamum its position of power.
      (a)Massive rock mound in the broad Caicus plain.
      (b)Though not on a trade route its dominating location forced on it the authority of kingship.
      (c)Its leadership in Asia culminated in 133 B.C. when Attalus III bequeathed the kingdom to Rome. For 2½ centuries ruled as Rome's provincial capital.

II. THE SAINTS WHERE SATAN DWELLS
   1. The government the "throne of Satan." The official power which opposes the church with the "right of the sword."
   2. Faithfulness of the church.
      (a)Did not deny faith in Christ as Lord.
      (b)The example of Antipas the martyr.
   3. Warning as to some saints holding false teachings.
      (a)Teaching of Balaam; idols and fornication.
      (b)Teaching of the Nicolaitans.
   4. Exhortation with a warning. "Repent." Or expect "the right of the sword" to be exercised.
   5. Promises to the faithful.
      (a)To eat of the hidden manna.
      (b)White stone with its secret name.

The real "right of the sword" is possessed by the saints. The Christian has a superior "white stone," and "secret name."

## A TRANSLATION
### Revelation 2:18-29

And to the messenger of the church in Thyatira write: These things says the son of God, the one having his eyes as a flame of fire, and his feet like burnished brass. "I know your works and your love and your faith and your service and your patience; and your last works are greater than your first.

But I have against you that you are permitting the woman Jezebel, the one calling herself 'the prophetess.' And she's teaching and deceiving my servants to fornicate and to eat idol sacrifices. And I gave her time that she might repent, and she doesn't will to repent from her fornication. Behold, I'm throwing her onto a great couch and those adulterating with her into great afflicton if they don't repent from her works. And her children I will kill in death; and all the churches shall know that I am the one searching (the) inward parts and (the) heart, and I will give to each of you according to your works.

But to you, the rest of you in Thyatira who do not hold this teaching, who didn't get to know the 'deep things of Satan,' as they say, I am not casting upon you (any) other burden. But that which you have keep until whenever I shall come.

And the one overcoming and the one keeping my works unto the end, to him I will give power over the nations and he will shepherd them with an iron rod as earthen vessels are shattered, as I also have received from my father, I will also give to him the morning star.

The one having ears is to hear what the spirit says to the churches.

## AN OUTLINE OF REVELATION 2:18-29
### From Weakness Made Strong

Strength is the harvest when weakness is mixed with faith.

I. THYATIRA, A CITY, THOUGH WEAK, MADE STRONG.
   1. Founded as a garrison city between rival powers. Though naturally weak its position demanded strength.
   2. In peace time manufacturing and trade; bronze, brass and royal fabrics etc. Many workers' guilds.

II. DESTINY OF THE CITY THE HERITAGE OF THE CHURCH.
   1. He who speaks has "feet of burnished bronze." He moves with irresistable strenth of hardest metal.
   2. His commendation: past works; present growth "more than the first."
   3. Complaint: Jezebel teaches "Christianized idolatry."
   4. Warning: her followers killed "according to their works."
   5. His promises:
      (a)"...until I come..." He is coming again.
      (b)"...power over the nations...shepherd with a rod of iron..." The Christian really rules, not Rome.
      (c)...the morning star..." The herald of day.

The weakest is promised to be the strongest. The Christian, true victor, triumphs by the death which the persecutor pronounces.

## A TRANSLATION
Revelation 3:1-6

And to the messenger of the church in Sardis, write: "These things says the one having the seven spirits of God and the seven stars, "I know your works, that a name you have that you live, and yet you are dead. Be ever watching, and get the remaining things which are about to die, established. For I have not found your works fulfilled before my God. Therefore, be remembering how you have received and heard, and be keeping them and repent. If, then, you don't watch, I will come as a thief, and you won't recognize what sort of hour I will come upon you.

But you do have a few names in Sardis who did not defile their garments and they will walk with me in white, because they are worthy. The one thus being victorious will be clothed in white garments, and I will not leave his name out of the book of life, and I will confess his name before my father and before his angels.

The one having ears is to hear what the spirit says to the churches.

## AN OUTLINE OF REVELATION 3:1-6
A Mask for Weakness!

The threat of death so often unmasks the bold front with which we face the world. An arrogant display of strength is a mask behind which we hide to forget our failures.

I. APPEARANCE OF LIFE VERSUS THE REALITY OF DEATH.

1. The church at Sardis had the look of life but possessed the doom of death. vs.1b
   (a)The city: An impregnable acropolis. Defended only on narrow neck on one side.
   (b)History: had fallen twice; failed to guard one of the precipitous sides. Had a "name" of living but "was dead."
   (c)History of the church patterned after the city. "I have not found your works fulfilled before my God." Had the trappings but no life.

II. TWO EXHORTATIONS AND A PROMISE.

1. Be alert!
   (a)"Be watching." Especially at the unguarded points.
   (b)"Establish the things that are remaining." Finish those unfinished projects; complete what you started.
2. Remember and return to the fundamentals of the gospel.
   (a)"Remember" what you got in Christ.
   (b)"Remember" the message entrusted to you.
3. A Promise to a "few who have not defiled their garments."
   (a)In a dead church are a few choice souls.
   (b)To be given white (pure) garments.
   (c)To walk in white in fellowship with the Christ.
   (d)Names recorded in the citizens' roll in the city of God.
   (e)They will be honored at the great assize.

He who holds the "seven spirits of God" holds power to accomplish these things. Recognize and receive him.

## A TRANSLATION
### Revelation 3:7-13

And to the messenger of the church in Philadelphia write: These things says the holy, the true, the one having the key of David, the one opening and no one shall shut, and shutting and no one opens. "I know your works. Behold, I present before you a door having been opened which no one is able to shut, because you have little power and you kept my word and did not deny my name. Behold, I give of the synagogue of Satan, of the ones calling themselves Jews, and they are not but are lying--behold, I will make them that they shall come and worship before your feet, and they shall know that I loved you. Because you kept the word of my patience, I also will keep you from the hour of trial, the one being about to come upon the whole inhabited earth to try the ones dwelling on the earth. I come quickly! Hold fast that which you have that no one take your crown.

The one overcoming, I will make him (to be) a pillar in the temple of my God and he will not go out any more and I will write upon him the name of my God and the name of the city of my God, the new Jerusalem, the one coming down out of heaven from my God. (And I will write upon him) my new name.

The one having ears is to hear what the spirit is saying to the churches."

## AN OUTLINE OF REVELATION 3:7-13
### The Church of the Open Door!

Missions is the mission of the church. He who "holds the key of David" locks and unlocks the doors of opportunity. They who enter find a new name.

I. PHILADELPHIA MARKED BY THREE NOTABLE FEATURES.
   1. Founded and functioned as a missionary city. To spread Greek culture in a Lydian environment.
   2. Its people lived in constant dread of a "day of trial." Hence many people lived outside the city in shacks.
   3. It adopted a new name from its Imperial benefactor.

II. THE CHURCH FULFILLING ITS MISSION.
   1. He who providentially guides the church is:
      (a)Holy and true. He imparts what he is.
      (b)"Opens and shuts." Controls providential opportunities.
   2. The faithful church.
      (a)Though "little in power" you "kept my word."
      (b)"Did not deny my name."
   3. Promises to the church.
      (a)Victorious before false Jews.
      (b)Security. "I will keep you from the hour of trial."
      (c)Stability. You shall be "pillar in the temple of God."
      (d)Permanence. "You shall not go out any more."
      (e)A new name. Redeemed character; for the citizens of the city of God.

Success of the church comes, not from "talent" or skill or self-made "doors." It comes from opening oneself to him who holds the key that locks and unlocks life's providences.

## A TRANSLATION
### Revelation 3:14-22

And to the messenger of the church in Laodicea write: These things says the true One, the faithful and true witness, the beginning of the creation of God, "I know your works that you are neither cold nor hot; would that you were cold or hot. Thus because you are lukewarm and neither hot nor cold, I am about to spew you out of my mouth. And because you are saying, 'I am rich and have gotten wealthy and I have no need,' and (because) you don't know that you are wretched and miserable and poor and blind and naked, I counsel you to purchase from me gold having been refined of fire in order that you might get rich, and white garments that you may clothe yourself and the shame of your nakedness not be manifested. And (I counsel you) to anoint your eyes with eye-salve that you might see.

If I love, I reprove and discipline whom (I love). Therefore, ever be zealous and repent. Behold, I am standing at the door and knocking. If anyone shall hear my voice and open the door, I'll enter to him and will dine with him and he with me. The one overcoming, I will give to him to sit with me on my throne as I overcame and sat with my father on his throne.

The one having ears is to hear what the spirit says to the churches.

## AN OUTLINE OF REVELATION 3:14-22
### The Wretched Rich

There's no healing for him who is ill and refuses to recognize that he's sick.

I. THE DISTINCTION OF LAODICEA.
1. The distinction of Laodicea was that it wasn't distinct.
2. It knew no extremes. As a trading center it adapted to others; pliable, accomodating, compromising.
3. Church patterned itself after the city.

II. THE CHURCH RECEIVED NO PRAISE.
1. This the one church for which Jesus had no praise. He sees more in an honest opponent than a tepid friend.
2. Neither hot or cold but nauseating in lack of commitment.
3. Self-deceived in spiritual evaluation.
   (a)Claimed "I am rich" though really poor.
   (b)Self-sufficient due to wealth, health, and culture. But really naked, sick, barren in spirit.

III. THE REMEDEY.
1. The fact of this letter implies there's a remedy available.
2. The remedy:
   (a)Recognize reality; poor, naked, blind, misery.
   (b)Purchase pure gold, good medicine, white garments from the honest salesman, the good physician.
   (c)"Be zealous! Repent!"

Motives: Fellowship at mealtime: "Behold I stand at the door and knock..." Sovereignty with Christ in his Messianic rule. "If anyone open..." But I must open the door!

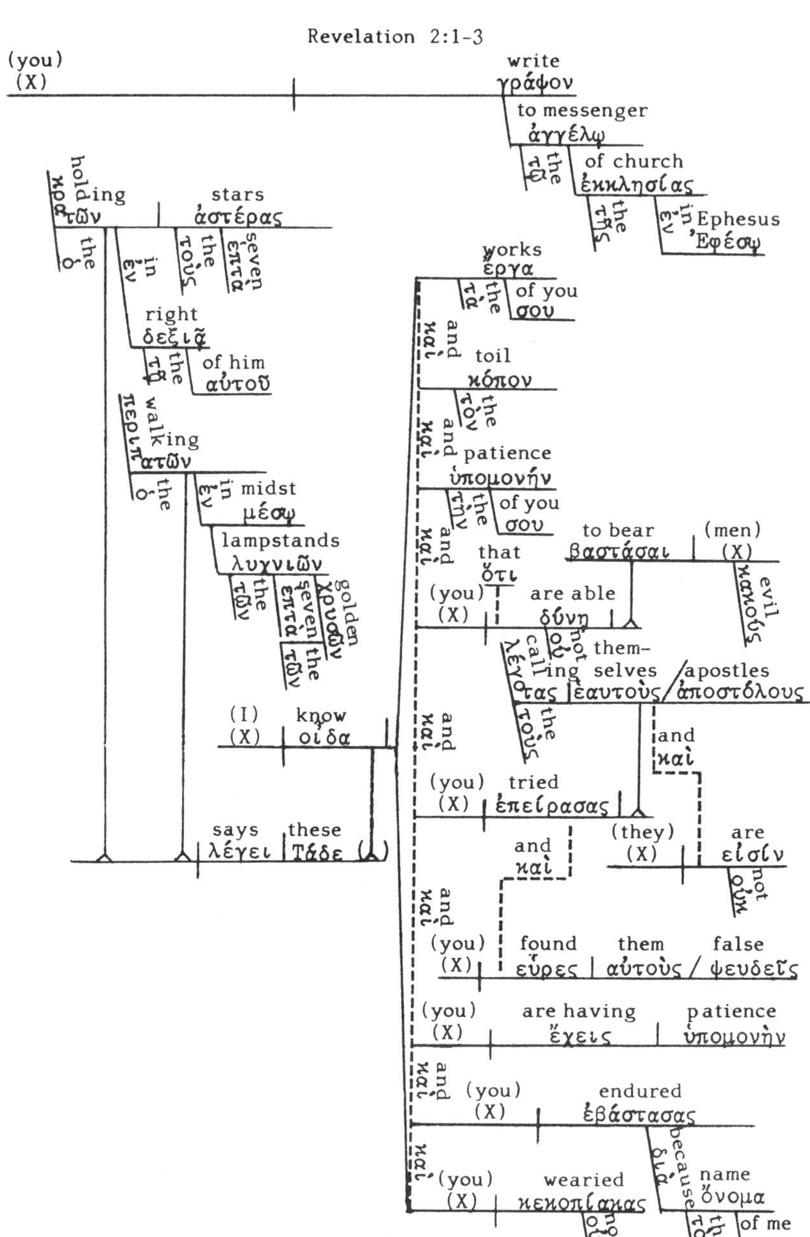
(you) (X)
write γράψον
to messenger ἀγγέλῳ
the τῷ
of church ἐκκλησίας
the τῆς
in ἐν
Ephesus Ἐφέσῳ
holding κρατῶν
the ὁ
stars ἀστέρας
the τοὺς
seven ἑπτὰ
in ἐν
right δεξιᾷ
the τῇ
of him αὐτοῦ
walking περιπατῶν
the ὁ
in ἐν
midst μέσῳ
lampstands λυχνιῶν
the τῶν
seven ἑπτὰ
golden χρυσῶν
the τῶν
(I) (X)
know οἶδα
says λέγει
these Τάδε
works ἔργα
the τὰ
of you σου
and καὶ
toil κόπον
the τὸν
and καὶ
patience ὑπομονήν
the τὴν
of you σου
and καὶ
that ὅτι
(you) (X)
are able δύνῃ
not οὐ
to bear βαστάσαι
(men) (X)
evil κακούς
calling λέγοντας
the τοὺς
themselves ἑαυτοὺς
apostles ἀποστόλους
and καὶ
(you) (X)
tried ἐπείρασας
(they) (X)
are εἰσὶν
not οὐκ
and καὶ
(you) (X)
found εὗρες
them αὐτοὺς
false ψευδεῖς
(you) (X)
are having ἔχεις
patience ὑπομονὴν
and καὶ
(you) (X)
endured ἐβάστασας
because διὰ
name ὄνομα
the τὸ
of me μου
καὶ
(you) (X)
wearied κεκοπίακας
not οὐ

## THE DIAGRAM OF 2:1-3

Chapter two includes letters to "the seven churches" of the Roman province of Asia. The first is to Ephesus and encompasses the first seven verses. At the head of each letter in the form of instruction to the writer is the aorist imperative, "Write." The diagram treats this opening exhortation as a single simple sentence. Each time it appears, other than the bare clause "You write," there is appended only the adverbial phrase giving the name of the church to whom the particular letter is addressed. "To the messenger of the church in _________."

2:2b-3 consists of one complex sentence. The independent clause really has a double subject, a compound without any conjunction joining them. The subject consists of two attributive participles. "The one holding the stars...the one walking in the midst..." Both participles are present tense expressing continuing action. The "one like to a son of man" is ever-present, continually controlling the ministry. He is also constantly guiding the destiny of the churches.

The predicate of this main clause declares, "...says these things..." The content of what he says is more fully expressed in a long noun clause direct object in apposition to the **Τάδε,** object of **λέγει.** "I know your works...etc..."

This noun clause makes the claim, "I know..." What he knows blossoms out in an eight-branched object. The first three of these objects that branch out are nouns: "your works." "the toil," and "your patience."

The other five of these direct objects consists of brief dependent clauses. The first of these noun-direct object dependent clauses asserts "that you are not able to bear evil men." The second of these clauses advances a step in showing just how serious the church at Ephesus was in its unwillingness to tolerate evil men. "You tried the ones calling thmselves apostles..." Note that this dependent clause has within it its own dependent, "and they are not." And yet another noun-object clause (not one of the five) that parallels "you tried" is "and you found them false."

The last three of these five noun-object clauses give a full picture of the patient endurance under extreme stress of this loyal Ephesian congregation. They say, "you are having patience," "you endured," and "you have not wearied." It should be noted that each of these final three clauses uses a different tense in its verb. ἔχεις is present, linear action; it calls attention to an ongoing patience, a continuing willingness to stay true to their commitment to pure doctrinal standards. The point action aorist ἐβάστασας focuses attention on the fact of their endurance more than a description of it. The prepositional phrase, "because of my name" may even suggest that ἐβάστασας looks to that crucial point in time when they refused to bow down to Caesar as Lord. Or to some such specific testimony to the person of the Lord Christ. The final clause has the perfect κεκοπίακας = "you have not wearied." And you still don't weary of bearing the load of faithful testimony.

Revelation 2:4-7

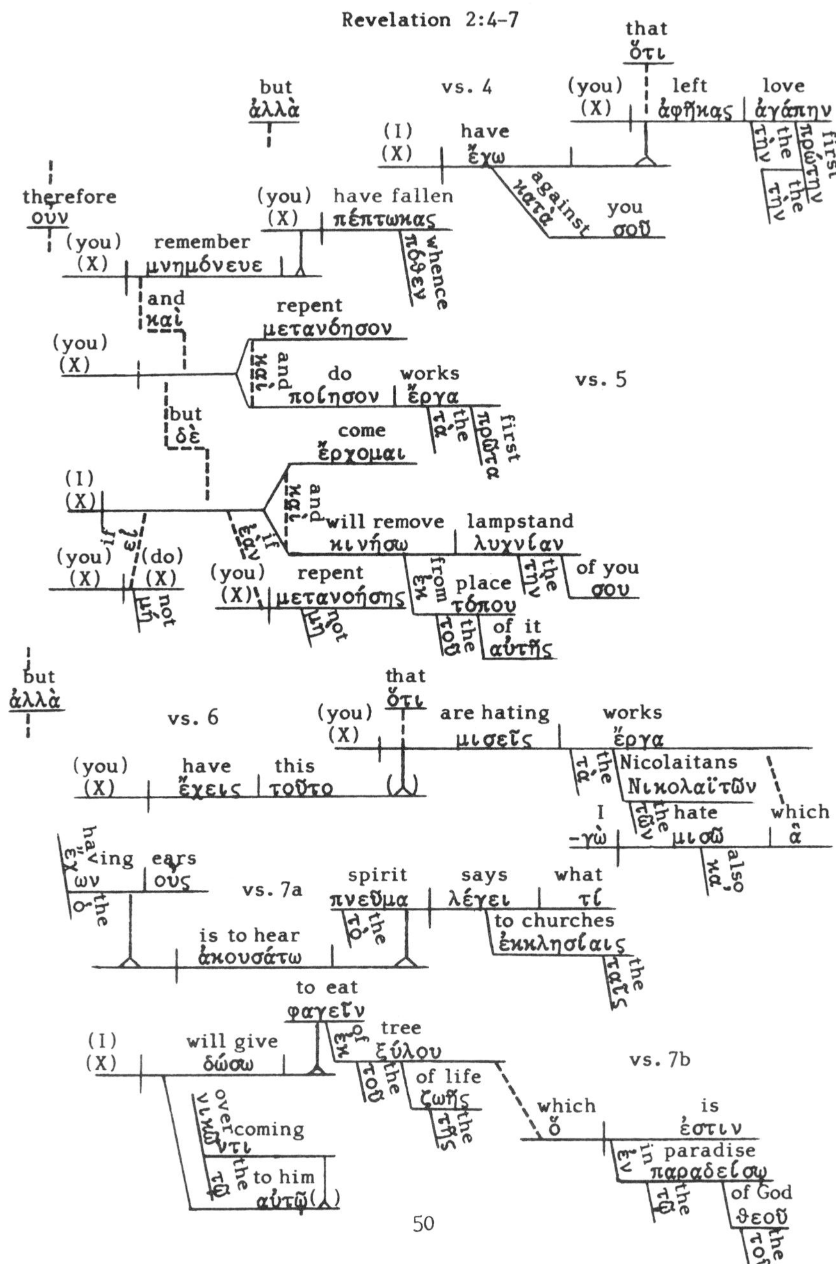

## THE DIAGRAM OF 2:4-7

The sentence of 2:4 is complex. The main clause asserts, "I have this against you..." Then a noun clause introduced by ὅτι inserts the object of ἔχω declaring, "that you left the first love." Present tense "I have" contrasts with aorist of the dependent "you left." The Lord goes on holding as he looks to the specific point at which they departed from love.

Verse five enfolds six clauses, three independent and three dependent. μνημόνευε of the first independent clause is present tense imperative. The Lord urges them to "go on remembering." In other words, "do not ever be forgetting..." Then as object he includes a noun clause with perfect tense πέπτωκας = "you have fallen." The perfect tense takes into view a point in the past at which they fell away and it admits of the dangerous fact that they are still in that "fallen away" condition.

Therefore, the second of the independents urges an immediate change by the use of two aorist imperatives, "repent and do the first works." The choice of aorists is appropriate because they suggest both urgency and immediacy. "First works" as direct object of ποίησαν refers to works that spring from love.

The third of the independents has a compound predicate which incorporates present indicative "come"(ἔρχομαι) and future "will remove"(κινήσω). The present is probably futuristic, "I am going to come" while the future is normal point action indicating an actual point at which the Lord would "remove the lampstand." That is, he would eliminate that church. This clause presents an unusual incidence. It has two supporting "if" clauses. The writer starts out with a first class condition, "if (you do) not, and you won't..." It assumes they won't repent. By the time he gets to the end of his clause he repeats the "if" but changes to the third class ἐὰν "if you don't repent but you might."

Two subordinate clauses following one independent makes verse six a complex sentence. "You have this" forms the independent idea. ὅτι announces a noun clause in apposition to τοῦτο object in the main clause. ἔργα is direct object and it is described by the genitive Νικολαΐτων. This genitive specifies the kind of works which they hate. An added description of these works is presented by the relative ἃ clause, "which I also hate."

Verse 7a constitutes another complex idea with only two clauses. Subject is the present attributive participle, "the one having ears." The present imperative ἀκουσάτω has an instant insistent ring that won't entertain any suggestion of "not hearing." "The one having ears is obligated to hear, no excuses acceptable." Precisely what he is to hear is set forth in the dependent noun clause, "what the spirit says to the churches."

The final sentence on this page (vs.7b) is also complex. Its chief clause proposes a promise, "I will give." The aorist infinitive φαγεῖν is object of the main verb "will give." The source from which the eating is to be derived is expressed by ἐκ with ablative ξύλου. That "tree" is described by the adjectival ὅ clause, "which is in the paradise of God."

Revelation 2:8–11

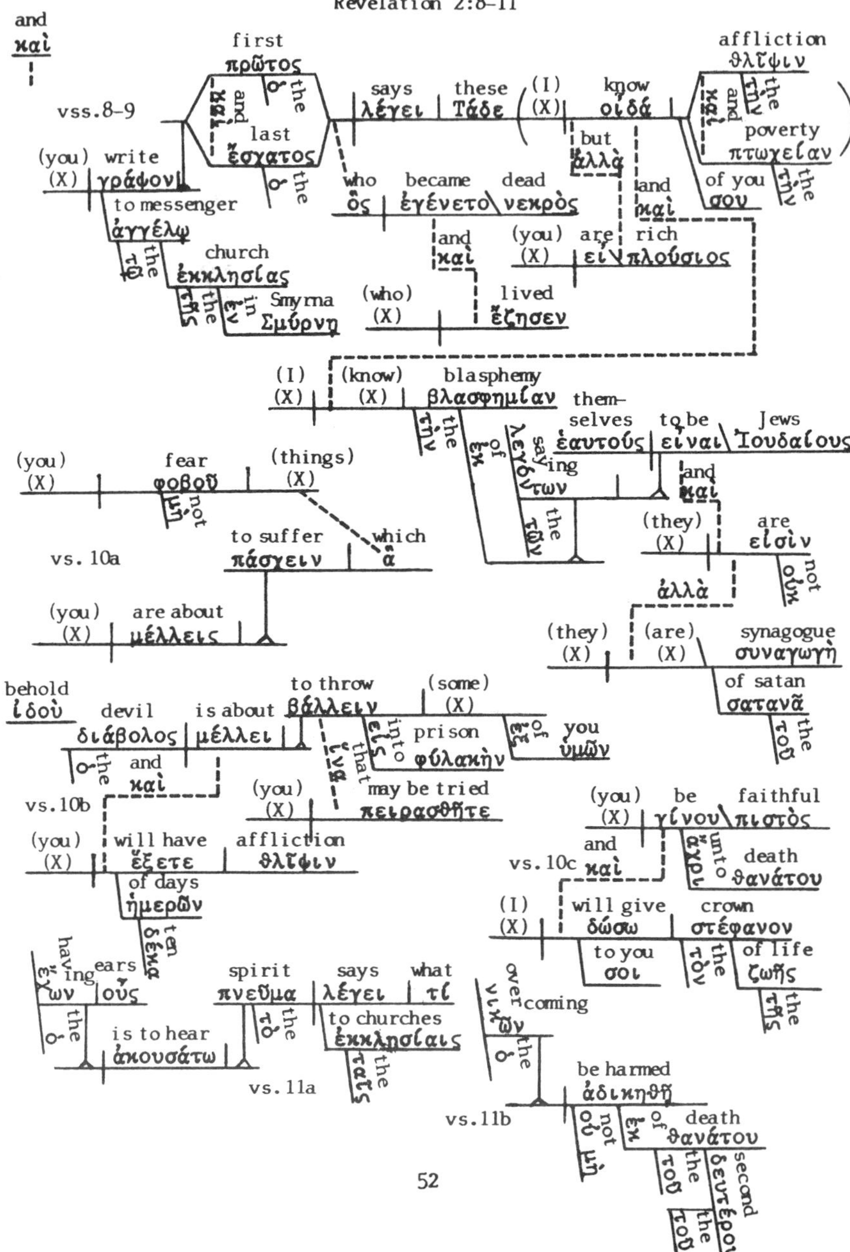

## THE DIAGRAM OF 2:8-11

The diagram alters how it presents the introductory instruction "write." Instead of a separate simple sentence the clause "You write" is treated as an independent clause of a complex. The full sentence extends through verse 9. It's just a judgment whether to include what to write as object of imperative "write."

As diagrammed eight dependent clauses appear. Besides, there is an attributive participle with infinitive phrase that is equivalent to a clause, "the one calling themselves Jews..."

The initial dependent says, "The first and the last says..." The object of "says" is "these"(τάδε). In apposition to τάδε is another subordinate clause, "I know your affliction and poverty." In order to conserve space on the page this appositional isn't put on the usual pedestal but on the same line as τάδε. Hanging from this clause are four more dependents. Each of the four are themselves coordinate with "I know your affliction etc..." and hence are themselves also appostional. Within this group of four hangs also the above mentioned participial, "the ones calling themselves Jews." One of these four, "but you are rich," is practically parenthetical. It is set off by the adversative "but."

In the participial expression, the participle "saying" has for its direct object the infinitive εἶναι with ἑαυτούς as accusative of general reference and Ἰουδαίους as predicate accusative.

Two other relative clauses must be noted. They are adjective in function, introduced by relative ὅς and are descriptive of the subjects; "who became dead and lived." The aorists of these clauses are suggestive. "Became" recognizes the point of death. But the aorist ἔζησεν doesn't look to a point at which he "became alive," but rather "he went right on living." The Aktionsart is basically linear. So even in the aorist the tense merely looks at the entire process of living as a point. When Jesus died he "went right on living." Death never phased him; it was but one more incident in his ongoing living. The aorist is not a description of his living but an announcement of the fact.

Verse 7a is a brief complex which is an exhortation to "Quit fearing..." The relative ἃ clause is adjectival describing understood "things," "...which you are about to suffer."

The sentence of 10b involves a compound-complex scheme. Two independent clauses say, "The devil is about to throw" and "you will have affliction..." One adverbial purpose clause explains <u>why</u> the devil will throw: "that you may be tried."

The two clauses of 10c signify a compound. First, an exhortation, "be faithful" followed by a promise, "I will give..." Present γίνου urges, "go on being faithful..." The future δώσω centers on the point at which the promise is fulfilled.

Verse 11a reproduces the complex sentence of verse 7a.

Verse 11b ranks as a simple sentence. Its subject is present articular attributive participle, "the one overcoming." Negative οὐ μὴ is most emphatic, "...shall <u>not</u> be harmed." ἐκ with ablative expresses the source from which harm may have been expected, that is, "out of the second death."

Revelation 2:12-13

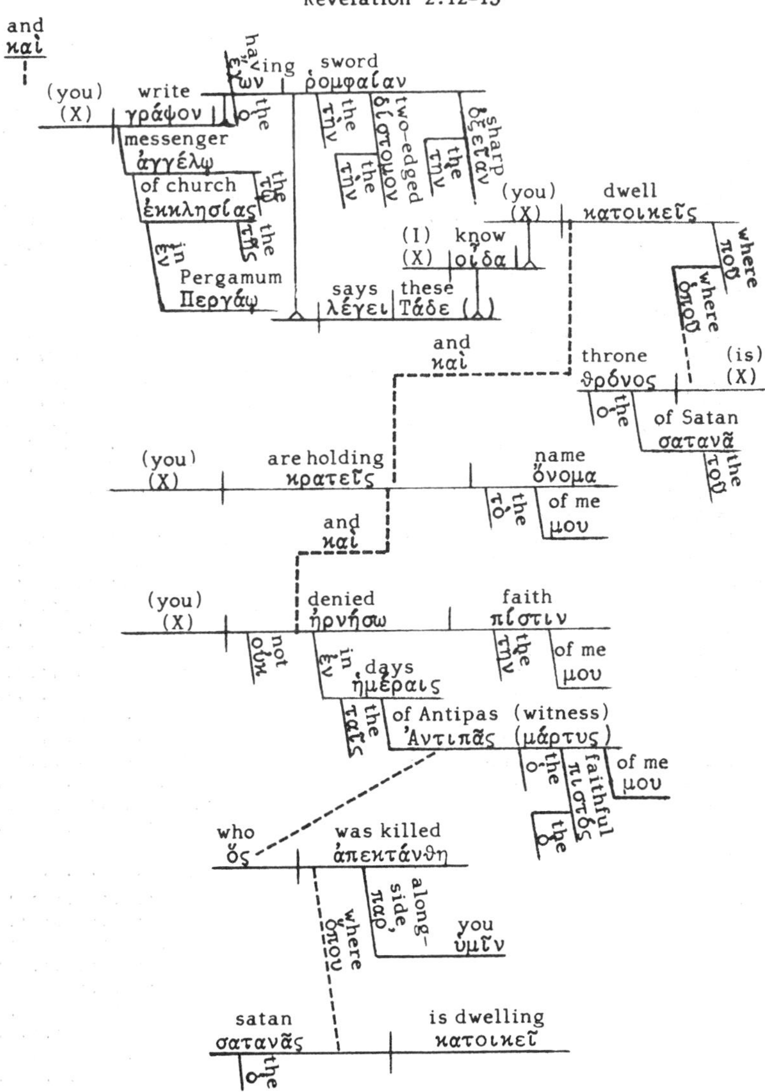

## THE DIAGRAM OF 2:12-13

Once again the diagram is placing the introductory exhortation as the independent clause of what then becomes a complex sentence. Jesus charges John: "You write to the messenger of the church in Pergamum." As direct object of this main clause is the dependent noun clause which declares: "The one having the sharp two-edged sword says these..." Present articular participle ἔχων with its object ῥομφαίαν serves as subject.

Next comes another subordinate noun clause, "I know." It is in apposition to τάδε. The οἶδα of this clause has for its direct object a third noun clause, "you dwell." Tacked on to this clause is yet another dependent, this time adverbial, "where the throne of Satan (is)."

Paralleling the object clause "you dwell"(object of οἶδα) are two more noun clauses. Each of these would also be added objects of οἶδα. They read: "you are holding my name" and "you denied not my faith." Both ὄνομα and πίστιν are limited by the genitive pronoun μου. But the genitive with "name" is possessive or subjective genitive whereas the genitive with "faith" is objective. It's not the faith which Jesus possessed that they "denied not." It is the faith which they had in Jesus. It was their faith of which Jesus was the object that they "did not deny." He was the center and substance of what they believed.

Another feature of these three object clauses worthy of notice is the use of tenses. κατοικεῖς = "you are dwelling" is linear present. κρατεῖς = "you are holding' is also linear present. But οὐκ ἠρνήσω = "denied not" is aorist. Pergamum was the politcal capitol of the province, that is, "where Satan dwells." And because to "live where Satan lives" was a continuous, ever-present pressure so their "holding fast" his name was a continuous experience. In fact, that they "did not deny" was also an ongoing repeated experience. However, the aorist tense gathers all their separate opportunities to deny and lumps them into one great act of loyalty. This probably is because one well-known martyrdom took place on one occasion during a period of many days of a particularly special persecution. This particular period is set forth in the adverbial ἐν phrase, "In the days of Antipas, my faithful martyr."

This Antipas is described further by an adjective dependent clause inaugurated by the relative ὅς, "who was killed at your side." The prepositional παρ' phrase is used adverbially to tell where he was martyred. παρά literally means alongside. This expression seems to suggest that Antipas met his martyrdom in their presence as eye-witnesses; a prominent, public execution.

One final dependent clause again identifies the city of this famous martyr as being "where Satan dwells." It is an adverb clause answering the question where. Once more the present tense κατοικεῖ insists on the idea of Satan's constantly continuing activity in the capitol city of Pergamum.

Revelation 2:14-16

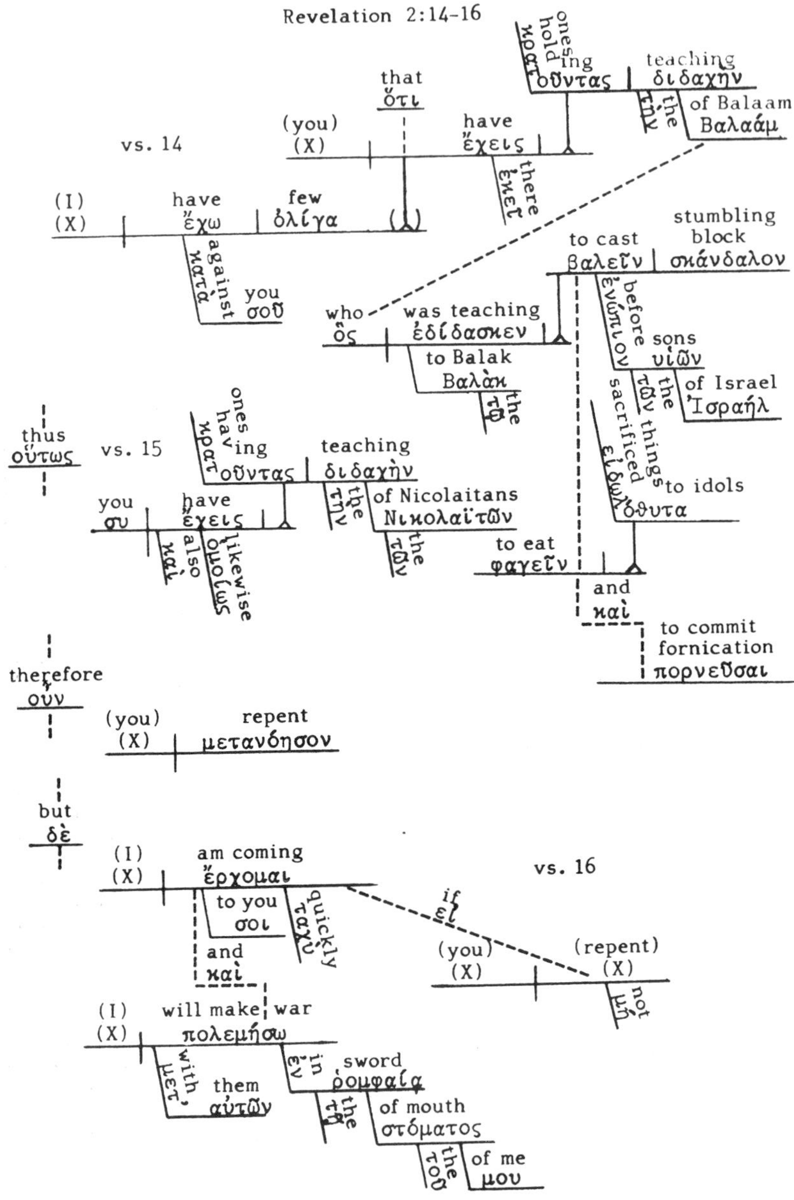

## THE DIAGRAM OF 2:14-16

Verse 14 presents a combination of clauses to be classed as complex. Besides its one independent two dependent clauses fill out the framework.

The independent affirms, "I have against you a few (things)." As far as the diagram is concerned the adjective ὀλίγα appears as a substantive, direct object of ἔχω. "Few" implies "things." ὅτι instigates a noun clause in apposition to the "few." It reads, "that you have there ones holding the teaching of Balaam." Present participle κρατοῦντας appears as direct object of ἔχεις. The relative pronoun ὅς brings in an adjective clause descriptive of Balaam, "who was teaching Balak..." ἐδίδασκεν is imperfect that calls attention to the unremitting efforts to keep on teaching. As direct objects of this "teaching" three aorist infinitives appear. They give the detailed content of that which Balaam was teaching; "to cast...to eat...to commit fornication." All three infinitives are aorists whereas the verb "was teaching" of which they are objects is linear imperfact. The imperfect calls attention to the historic reality of the persistent, repeated times that Balaam did the teaching. The writer could have used linear presents in the infinitives to describe the process of throwing, eating and fornicating. But he chose aorists which turn more attention on the skills involved than the processes. An experienced farmer might teach a young beginner the necessity of plowing as over against the process or "how to" plow. So Balaam "was teaching" the prerequisite for these evils if destruction of Israel was to be accomplished.

The sentence of verse 15 has only one complete clause, hence is classed as simple. The sentence is introduced by adverb οὕτως which serves also as somewhat of a conjunction idea to relate what follows to the preceeding sentence. Coupled with καὶ it reads, "thus also..." The clause states, "you are having..." Present tense ἔχεις does not indicate that they "got" but that they "possess." The participial phrase appears as direct object, "ones having the teaching of the Nicolaitans." Again, the present tense κρατοῦντας centers on the continuous "holding" of this false teaching than the "getting" of it. It was an ongoing disease not a twenty-four hour rash.

Verse 16 might be treated as one sentence or two. The diagram has the brief command, "Therefore, you repent" as one simple sentence. The aorist tense of the verb "repent" gives an urgency to the command. It has an abrupt curtness designed to shake into action him who hears.

Then follows closely the alternative, "But if you do not repent I am coming..." The "if" clause is dependent adverbial and adds the complex idea. It is a first class condition determined as fulfilled. "If you don't repent and you won't then the following will happen..." There are two independent clauses so it is to be classed as compound complex. "I am coming" and "I will make war" are the bare essentials of the independents. Together they form the apodosis (the conclusion) of the condition.

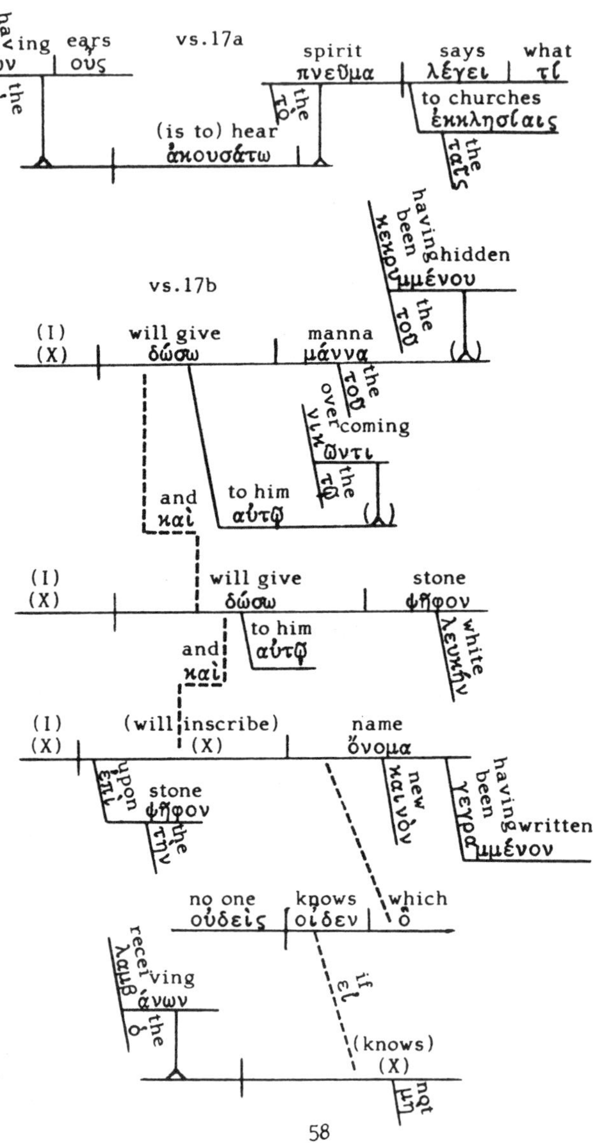
vs.17a
having
ἔχων
ears
οὖς
the
ὁ
(is to) hear
ἀκουσάτω
spirit
πνεῦμα
the
τό
says
λέγει
what
τί
to churches
ἐκκλησίαις
the
ταῖς
vs.17b
(I)
(X)
will give
δώσω
manna
μάννα
the
τοῦ
having been hidden
κεκρυμμένου
the
τοῦ
overcoming
νικῶντι
the
τῷ
and
καὶ
to him
αὐτῷ
(I)
(X)
will give
δώσω
stone
ψῆφον
white
λευκὴν
to him
αὐτῷ
and
καὶ
(I)
(X)
(will inscribe)
(X)
name
ὄνομα
upon
ἐπὶ
stone
ψῆφον
the
τὴν
new
καινὸν
having been written
γεγραμμένον
no one
οὐδεὶς
knows
οἶδεν
which
ὃ
if
εἰ
receiving
λαμβάνων
the
ὁ
(knows)
(X)
not
μὴ

## THE DIAGRAM OF 2:17

The sentence of 17a is the third time this complex arrangement has been presented in Revelation. (see 2:7, 11) So far as the structure of this sentence is concerned no added comment need be made. Because it has one main and one dependent clause it is complex. The subject of the main clause is by now the familiar "the one having ears..." Article ὁ guarantees that the participle is attributive. Its present tense gives assurance of continued action; "the one possessing..." Continuous privilege brings with it continuous obligation. "What the spirit says to the churches" is a noun-object clause in the form of an indirect question after verb of hearing. Interrogative pronoun τί is direct object of the present λέγει.

The very fact that this sentence is exactly reproduced with each of the letters to "the seven churches" vouches for the urgency of the exhortation. And it underscores how very important the truth is: the privilege of having ears brings with it the responsibility of hearing.

Verse 17b involves three independent plus two dependent ideas. Thus it is to be classed as compound-complex sentence. The three main clauses pledge, "I will give manna...I will give stone...I (will inscribe) name..." In the first clause the direct object μάννα is expanded by an articular perfect participle "having been hidden." The perfect tense announces the fact that the manna not only was hidden but still is.

Another attributive participle νικῶντι has the present tense. That reminds the reader that the victory involved in "overcoming" Satan's sword had been an unrelenting continuous struggle. This participle is in apposition to the indirect object αὐτῷ.

In the third of these independents ὄνομα is direct object of the implied verb "will inscribe." The prepositional phrase, "upon the name" is used adverbially to indicate where the name will be inscribed. To the direct object, "name," is attached the perfect passive participle "having been written." It is probably best taken as circumstantial predicate. The perfect tense intimates that this "new name" has been permanently written.

A dependent adjectival clause describing "name" is announced by the relative ὃ "which no one knows." And this relative clause itself is the conclusion (apodosis) of a first class negative condition determined as fact. "If the one receiving does not (know) and we assume he doesn't, no one is knowing..."

It is worth a brief note here to call attention to the fact that the term ὄνομα "name" in human history has a great deal more significance than just the means of distinguishing one person or thing from another. ὄνομα carries with it the personality and character of the person so named. So when the promise is stated. "I will inscribe a new name..." it is promising a radically new personality and character. This idea gains support from the fact that καινὸν means a "new kind" as to quality rather than "new" in reference to time. The redeemed person is given a new quality of character, not merely new in terms of time sequence

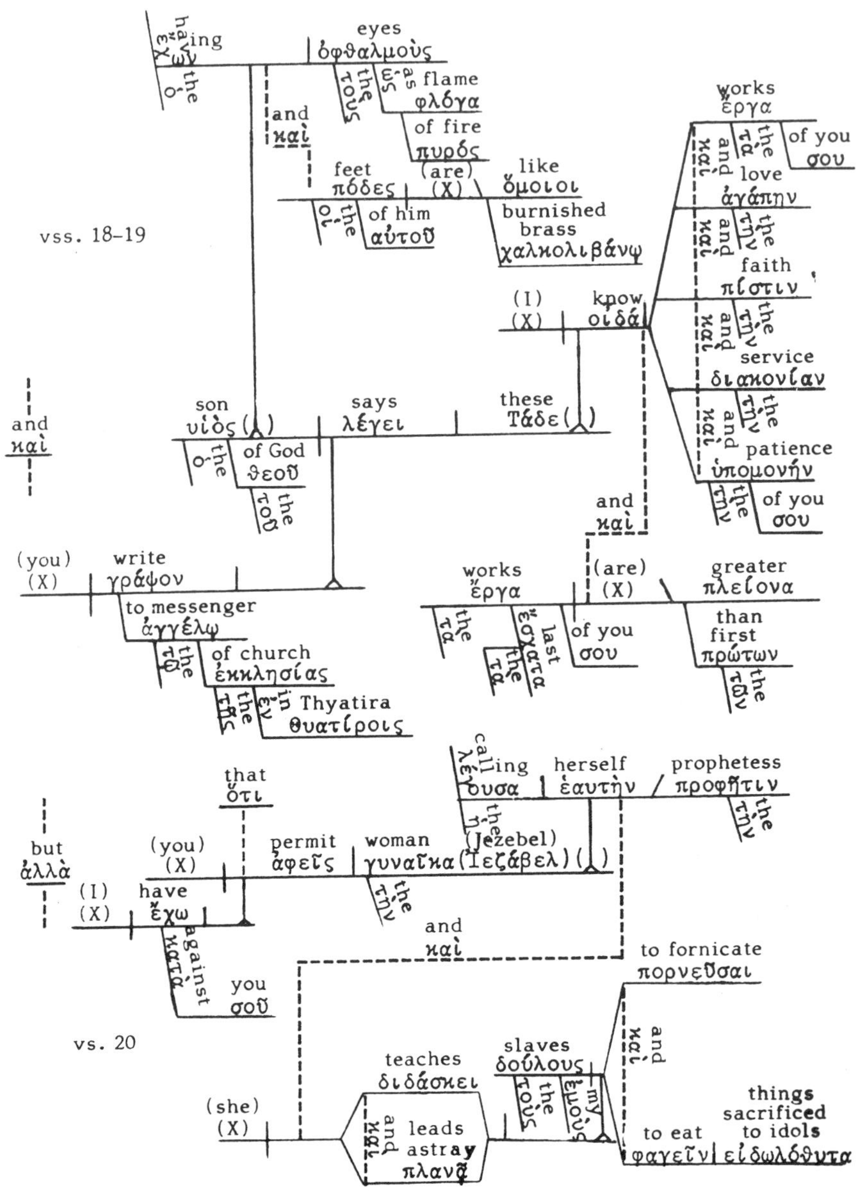
vss. 18-19
having
ἔχων
the
ὁ
eyes
ὀφθαλμοὺς
the
τοὺς
as
ὡς
flame
φλόγα
of fire
πυρός
and
καὶ
feet
πόδες
the
οἱ
of him
αὐτοῦ
(are)
(X)
like
ὅμοιοι
burnished brass
χαλκολιβάνῳ
(I)
(X)
know
οἶδά
works
ἔργα
the
τὰ
of you
σου
and
καὶ
love
ἀγάπην
the
τὴν
faith
πίστιν
service
διακονίαν
patience
ὑπομονήν
and
καὶ
son
υἱὸς
the
ὁ
of God
θεοῦ
the
τοῦ
says
λέγει
these
Τάδε
(you)
(X)
write
γράψον
to messenger
ἀγγέλῳ
the
τῷ
of church
ἐκκλησίας
the
τῆς
in
ἐν
Thyatira
Θυατίροις
works
ἔργα
the
τὰ
last
ἔσχατα
(are)
(X)
of you
σου
greater
πλείονα
than first
πρώτων
the
τῶν
vs. 20
but
ἀλλὰ
(I)
(X)
have
ἔχω
against
κατὰ
you
σοῦ
that
ὅτι
(you)
(X)
permit
ἀφεῖς
woman
γυναῖκα
the
τὴν
(Jezebel)
(Ἰεζάβελ)
calling
λέγουσα
the
ἡ
herself
ἑαυτὴν
prophetess
προφῆτιν
the
τὴν
(she)
(X)
teaches
διδάσκει
and
καὶ
leads astray
πλανᾷ
slaves
δούλους
the
τοὺς
my
ἐμοὺς
to fornicate
πορνεῦσαι
to eat
φαγεῖν
things sacrificed to idols
εἰδωλόθυτα

## THE DIAGRAM OF 2:18-20

If we take, as in the previous letter, the opening command to "write" as part of the sentence of 2:18-19 then it classifies as complex. "Write to the messenger of the church in Thyatira" is the independent clause. The phrase translated "in Thyatira" stands between definite article "the" and "church." In other words, it is a phrase that serves as attributive in force. Though somewhat awkward it might be rendered, "the in-Thyatira church."

A dependent noun clause stands as object of γράφον that reads, "...the son of God says these..." A compound appositional expression is inserted to expand further the subject. This compound appositional has a somewhat irregular construction. First the writer uses attributive present participial phrase, "the one having the eyes as flame of fire." Then instead of having another accusative object of the participle the writer changes to a noun clause with nominative πόδες as subject; "his feet (are) like burnished brass." At any rate this compound construction certifies this "son of God" as the one who appeared in chapter one.

In apposition to τάδε ("these") is another noun clause, "I know your works...etc..." The verb οἶδα has a series of direct objects each of which is set forth with marked distinction by a definite article; "the works of you, and the love, and the faith, and the service, and the patience of you." The presence of the article with each of these attributes serves to make each one quite distinctive.

Another noun clause in apposition to τάδε parallels "I know." It says, "...your last works (are) greater than your first." The ablative πρώτων expresses the standard of comparison following comparative πλείονα.

After reciting so many admirable qualities the Lord uses a strong adversitive conjunction ἀλλὰ ("but") to set in sharp contrast an unpleasant feature of the Thyatirian church. The sentence is complex. The independent element reproves, "I have against you..." The substance of what he has against them is introduced in the ὅτι noun clause, direct object of ἔχω; "that you permit the woman, Jezebel..." Besides the appositional "Jezebel," the present participial expression "the one calling herself prophetess..." appears. This too is an appositional idea. The apposition extends to another clause. But the construction changes from participle to a full clause connected by coordinating conjunction καὶ; "and she teaches and leads astray..." Both these verbs in this compound predicate are linear action presents. They emphasize the fact that this Jezebel "goes on teaching" and "keeps on leading astray..." Direct objects of the verbs are the two aorist infinitives "to fornicate" and "to eat." Those who do the "fornicating" and the "eating" are presented by the accusative of general reference δούλους. Another accusative εἰδωλόθυτα serves as direct object of the infinitive φαγεῖν. When we recall that, though in fixed forms, all infinitives function in a case we realize that there are four accusatives in the object of this predicate, "teaches and leads astray." Six if we include the article and pronoun modifying the noun "slaves."

# Revelation 2:21-23

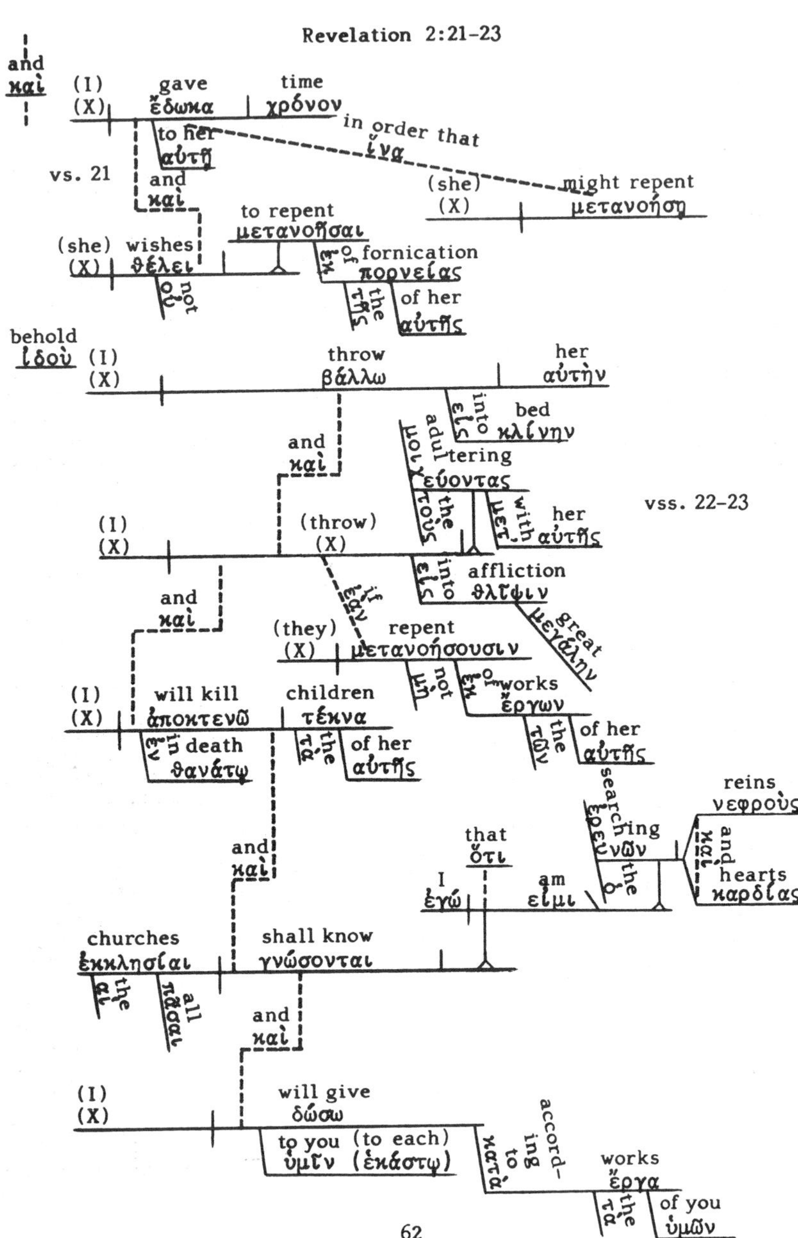

## THE DIAGRAM OF 2:21-23

Verse 21 frames a compound-complex sentence. It has two clauses that are independent joined together by conjunction καί. From the first clause hangs a dependent purpose clause.

The first clause states, "I gave her time." αὐτῇ is dative case expressing indirect object. The dependent clause is introduced by subordinating conjunction ἵνα. It states the reason why the Lord "gave her time," - "in order that she might repent."

The second of the independents in a parallel clause gives the response of Jezebel to the opportunity to repent; "she does not will to repent of her fornication." Aorist ἔδωκα of the first main clause presents the offer of the Lord as fact without calling attention to what no doubt were repeated opportunities. An aorist does not deny action as repeated; it just doesn't affirm it. But the present θέλει is a negative linear which does focus attention on her repeated refusals. Aorist infinitive "to repent" is direct object of the verb. The point action of aorist suits well the basic idea of "repent" which represents a decisive, single resolution to "change the mind." The preposition ἐκ with ablative πορνείας reveals well the ablative idea of "separation." To "repent" means that one separates himself from something or someone.

The sentence of verses 22-23 involves five independent clauses plus two dependent expressions. Hence it is compound-complex. "I throw her into bed" is the initial independent. The verb βάλλω is probably a futuristic present for the "if" clause attached to the second independent applies to this clause also. Since she is left the option of repenting it is possible that she choose to repent. In that case he would not throw her into bed.

The direct object αὐτὴν of the first clause is matched in the second by the articular present participle μοιχεύοντας. Also the prepositional phrases "into bed" and "into great affliction" balance. They each are used adverbially answering the questions where. The "bed" is used figuratively for her "Christianized idolatry" though that may include literal fornication. The ἐὰν clause ushers in a third class conditional undetermined but with prospect of determination. She might repent but probably she won't!

The third independent threatens, "I will kill her children in death." Again, the prepositional phrase "in death" functions here as an adverb. ἐν is used only with locative case but here this is the so-called "instrumental" use of ἐν. The killing is conceived of by the writer as taking place "in death." The English reads more smoothly by translating, "by means of."

The most outstanding feature of the fourth independent clause is its direct object. It's the noun clause introduced by declarative ὅτι; "...that I am the one searching reins and hearts." By use of personal pronoun ἐγώ the subject is very emphatic, "I on my part." Then the attributive participle with its objects forms a predicate nominative referring back to the subject.

The final independent promises, "I will give to each of you according to your works." The pronoun ἑκάστῳ is in apposition to ὑμῖν. It distinguishes each separate person of the "you."

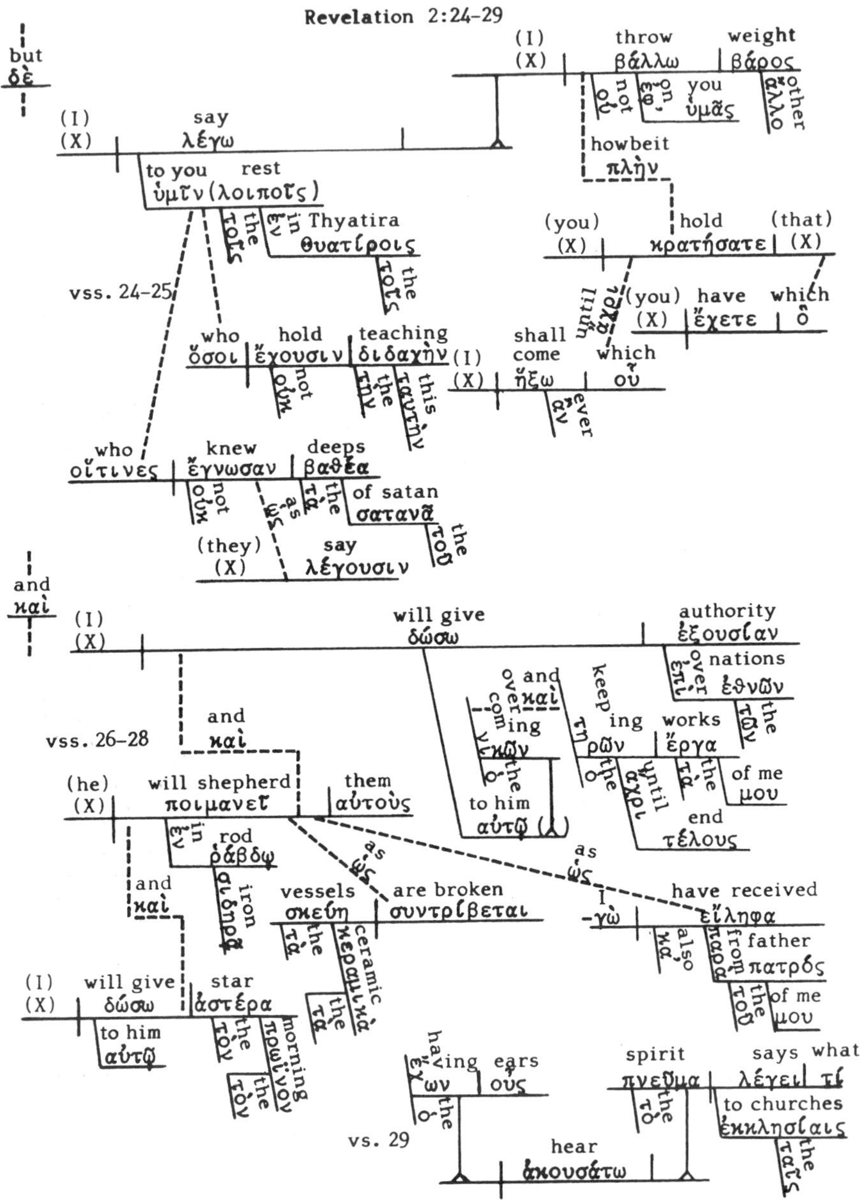

Revelation 2:24-29
but
δὲ
(I)
(X)
say
λέγω
to you
rest
ὑμῖν (λοιποῖς)
the
τοῖς
in
ἐν
Thyatira
Θυατίροις
the
τοῖς
vss. 24-25
who
ὅσοι
hold
ἔχουσιν
not
οὐκ
teaching
διδαχὴν
the
τὴν
this
ταύτην
who
οἵτινες
knew
ἔγνωσαν
not
οὐκ
deeps
βαθέα
the
τὰ
of satan
σατανᾶ
the
τοῦ
as
ὡς
(they)
(X)
say
λέγουσιν
(I)
(X)
throw
βάλλω
weight
βάρος
not
οὐ
on
ἐφ'
you
ὑμᾶς
other
ἄλλο
howbeit
πλὴν
(you)
(X)
hold
κρατήσατε
(that)
(X)
until
ἄχρι
(you)
(X)
have
ἔχετε
which
ὃ
(I)
(X)
shall come
ἥξω
ever
ἂν
which
οὗ
and
καὶ
(I)
(X)
will give
δώσω
authority
ἐξουσίαν
over
ἐπὶ
nations
ἐθνῶν
the
τῶν
and
καὶ
over coming
νικῶν
the
ὁ
keeping
τηρῶν
the
ὁ
works
ἔργα
the
τὰ
of me
μου
until
ἄχρι
end
τέλους
to him
αὐτῷ
vss. 26-28
and
καὶ
(he)
(X)
will shepherd
ποιμανεῖ
them
αὐτοὺς
in
ἐν
rod
ῥάβδῳ
iron
σιδηρᾷ
as
ὡς
vessels
σκεύη
the
τὰ
ceramic
κεραμικὰ
the
τὰ
are broken
συντρίβεται
as
ὡς
I
ἐγὼ
also
κἀ
have received
εἴληφα
from
παρὰ
father
πατρός
the
τοῦ
of me
μου
and
καὶ
(I)
(X)
will give
δώσω
star
ἀστέρα
to him
αὐτῷ
the
τὸν
morning
πρωϊνόν
the
τὸν
having
ἔχων
the
ὁ
ears
οὖς
vs. 29
hear
ἀκουσάτω
spirit
πνεῦμα
the
τὸ
says
λέγει
what
τί
to churches
ἐκκλησίαις
the
ταῖς

## THE DIAGRAM OF 2:24-29

Beginning with the independent clause, "I say to you..." the sentence of 2:24-25 blossoms out with seven subordinate clauses. One trunk sprouting seven branches produces a complex scheme.

As direct object of the main verb, "I say" is a brace of noun clauses, "I do not throw weight" and "you hold (that)..." Where he proposes not to throw "other weight" is told in the adverb prepositional "on you." The tenses in these two clauses contrasts linear present "am throwing" with aorist, "hold fast." Present represents a continuous, ongoing repeated refusal; aorist fits the decisive finality of that which the Lord exhorts. An understoood demonstrative "that" is object of κρατήσατε. An adjective clause amplifies the demonstrative, "...which you have..." Another dependent clause hangs from "hold fast," this time adverbial introduced by ἄχρι = "until which (time) I come." Relative οὗ appears in the diagram as object of ἥξω. It could be placed as an adjective modifying an implied "things."

Under λέγω of the main clause is indirect object ὑμῖν, "to you." Two adjective clauses describe this indirect object. (1)"Who are not holding this teaching..." Linear action of present ἔχουσιν is worth noting. There was an ongoing consistency in their "not holding" this compromising teaching. Subject ὅσοι is quantitative relative, "howevermany of you..." (2)Subject of the next dependent adjectival is the qualitative relative οἵτινες, "who by your nature..." ἔγνωσαν is ingressive aorist, "didn't get to know..."

The final clause of the sentence inserted by ὡς is of the nature of a parenthesis; "as they say..." It picks up a current saying going the rounds and refers it to the claims of the Jezebel party. It may have a subtle touch of sarcasm.

Verses 26-28 house a compound-complex grouping. Three independent clauses make three promises: "I will give authority," "he will shepherd them," and "I will give the morning star." The kind of authority promised finds expression in the ἐπὶ prepositional phrase modifying ἐθνῶν. It's "over the nations authority." The indirect object αὐτῷ designates to whom he will give that authority. In apposition to αὐτῷ are two attributive present participles, "the one overcoming" and "the one keeping my works..." The nominative case in conjunction with the dative of αὐτῷ reflects the habit of the writer to ignore grammatical agreement. In this instance he begins the sentence with these nominatives as though they were to be subjects. In mid stream he changes the construction and leaves these hanging without case agreement. They could be classed as nominative absolutes. The diagram prefers to put them in apposition to the dative. They're that in sense if not in form.

The two ὡς clauses stemming from "will shepherd" are adverbial in function. They set up standards of comparison: (1)"as vessels are broken..."and (2)"as I have received..." Perfect "have received" spotlights the permanence of the authority he had received from his father. Present passive "are broken" reflects an often repeated incident when handling ceramics.

Verse 26 repeats the complex of 7, 11, and 17.

Revelation 3:1-3a

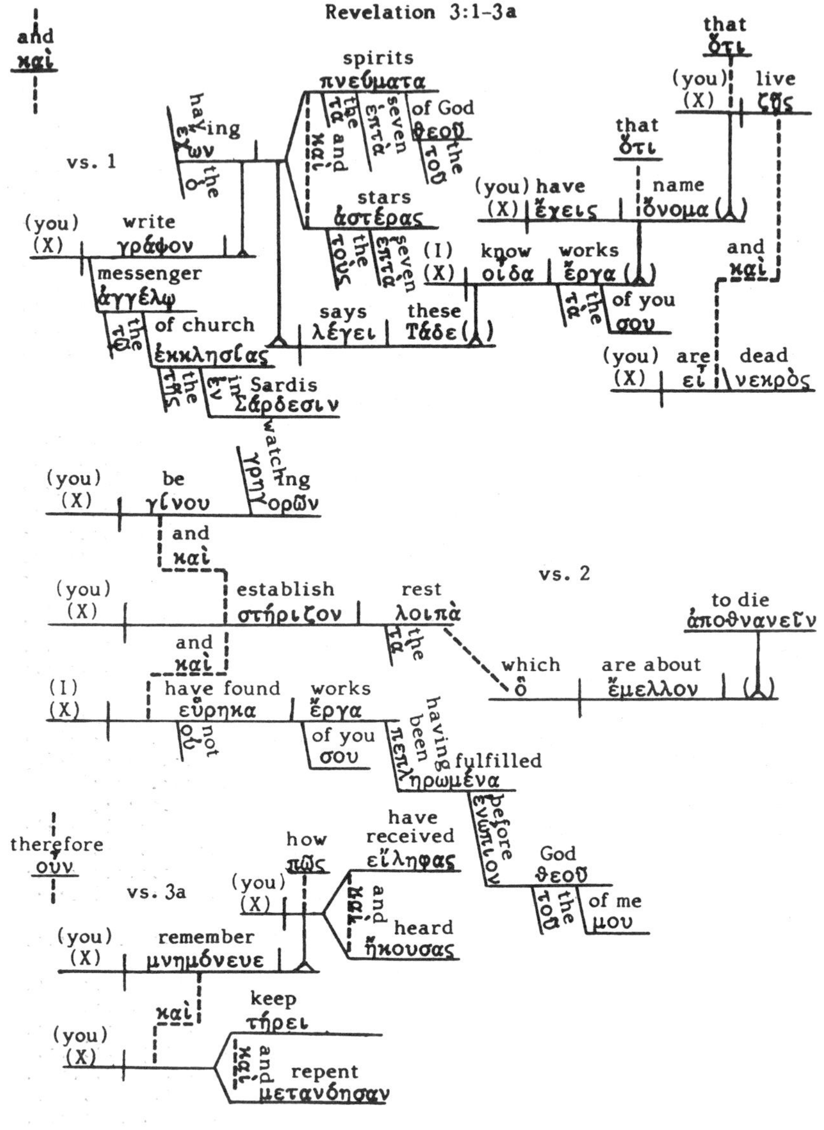

## THE DIAGRAM OF 3:1-3a

In the complex sentence of verse one the exhortation, "You write" is the independent element. The remainder of the sentence consists of five dependent concepts all of which are noun clauses.

The first of the five is direct object of "write." Its subject is attributive participle ἔχων with its objects "spirits" and "stars." "The one having says these..." is the full clause. Τάδε is treated in the diagram as though it were a noun, object of λέγει. It might have been placed as adjective modifying an understood "things." In apposition to τάδε is a second noun clause, "I know your works." ἔργα is direct object of λέγει. "Works" itself has a noun clause in apposition, "that you have a name. Yet another appositional clause appears, this time expanding more specifically the "name," that is, "that you are living..." A companion clause says, "and you are dead." The conjunction καὶ which joins these two has almost the force of an adversative "but."

Verse two contains three independent clauses: "you be watching," "you establish the rest..." and "I have not found..." The verbs employ three different tenses. The "be watching" of the first is a periphrastic present γίνου γρηγορῶν. Such a construction intensifies the force of linear action. "You go on watching; don't a moment from watching..." The aorist of the second independent (στήριζον) by its punctiliar action concentrates on the need for resolute decision. There were many things that needed to be established. And these might call for a repetition of iterative linear action. But the speaker used the aorist to enforce his notion that a once-for-all decision is demanded. Tense is not necessarily the kind of action that takes place. It is rather the kind of action which the speaker-writer wants the listener-reader to envision.

The third independent clause changes from exhorting "you" to stating something about "I". Perfect εὕρηκά indicates that what he "has not found" remains that way. He still hasn't found. Describing object "works" is perfect passive participle "having been fulfilled." The predicate force of this descriptive of "works" is striking. It's not that the Lord hadn't found works. But he hadn't found "works having been completed." The participle carries the main idea. So it is at least a circumstantial idea. It could even be supplementary to the verb "have found." But if viewed that way the diagram should have it on the line carrying εὕρηκά.

The one dependent idea in the sentence is adjective describing λοιπὰ, "which (things) are about to die."

The sentence of 3a encloses a compound-complex. The two independent elements are exhortations. "You be remembering..." and "you be keeping and repent." That which you are to be remembering is expressed in a noun clause, object of μνημόνευε, "how you have received and heard." πῶς here is not an adverb so much as declarative, "how that." Remember the fact not the manner. Perfect εἴληφας points out that what they "received" they still possess. But aorist ἤκουσας, while not denying that they still retain the effects, calls special attention to the point at which they heard.

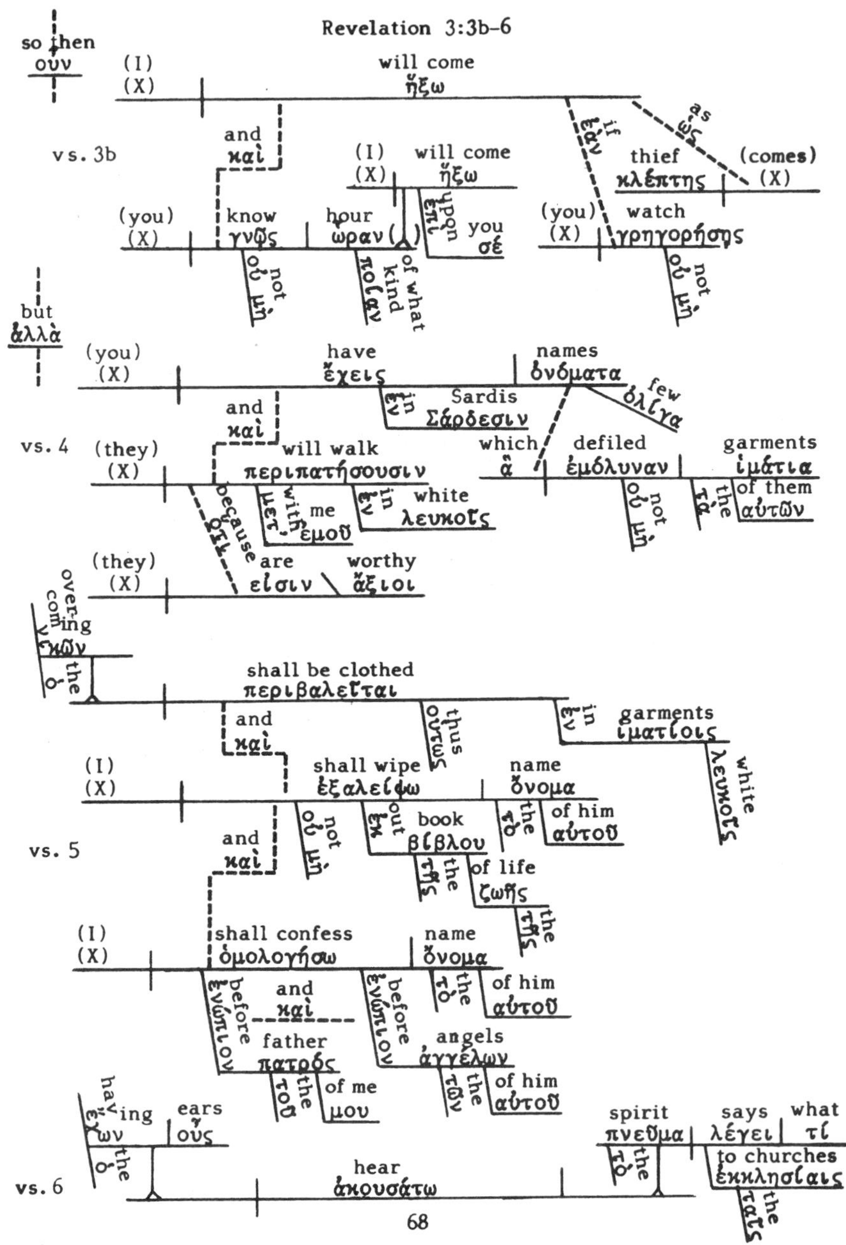
Revelation 3:3b-6
so then
οὖν
vs. 3b
(I)
(X)
will come
ἥξω
and
καὶ
if
ἐὰν
as
ὡς
thief
κλέπτης
(comes)
(X)
(I)
(X)
will come
ἥξω
upon
ἐπι
you
σέ
(you)
(X)
know
γνῷς
not
οὐ μὴ
hour
ὥραν
of what kind
ποίαν
(you)
(X)
watch
γρηγορήσῃς
not
οὐ μὴ
but
ἀλλὰ
(you)
(X)
have
ἔχεις
names
ὀνόματα
few
ὀλίγα
in
ἐν
Sardis
Σάρδεσιν
vs. 4
and
καὶ
(they)
(X)
will walk
περιπατήσουσιν
with
μετ'
me
ἐμοῦ
in
ἐν
white
λευκοῖς
because
ὅτι
which
ἃ
defiled
ἐμόλυναν
not
οὐ μὴ
garments
ἱμάτια
the
τὰ
of them
αὐτῶν
(they)
(X)
are
εἰσιν
worthy
ἄξιοι
over-coming
νικῶν
the
ὁ
shall be clothed
περιβαλεῖται
thus
οὕτως
in
ἐν
garments
ἱματίοις
white
λευκοῖς
and
καὶ
(I)
(X)
shall wipe
ἐξαλείψω
name
ὄνομα
the
τὸ
of him
αὐτοῦ
not
οὐ μὴ
out
ἐκ
book
βίβλου
the
τῆς
of life
ζωῆς
the
τῆς
vs. 5
and
καὶ
(I)
(X)
shall confess
ὁμολογήσω
name
ὄνομα
the
τὸ
of him
αὐτοῦ
before
ἐνώπιον
and
καὶ
father
πατρός
the
τοῦ
of me
μου
before
ἐνώπιον
angels
ἀγγέλων
the
τῶν
of him
αὐτοῦ
having
ἔχων
the
ὁ
ears
οὖς
vs. 6
hear
ἀκουσάτω
spirit
πνεῦμα
the
τὸ
says
λέγει
what
τί
to churches
ἐκκλησίαις
the
ταῖς
68

## THE DIAGRAM OF 3b-6

Verse 3b displays a compound-complex sentence of five clauses. Two are independent and three are dependent. The first independent declares, "I will come..." Two dependents are attached to this declaration. ἐὰν introduces a third class condition undetermined but with prospect of determination. It relates a condition which will occasion his coming: "...if you do not repent..." The double negative οὐ μὴ is the very strongest. The other dependent, also adverbial, uses ὡς as its introductory conjunction. It's a comparative idea stating how he will come, "...as a thief.."

The second independent in 3a makes a statement, "you do not know what kind of hour..." ποίαν is an interrogative adjectival pronoun which contains the flavor of quality, that is, what kind..." In apposition to "hour" is a noun clause, "I will come upon you."

Verse four opens with strong adversative conjunction ἀλλὰ, "but." The church at Sardis had the appearance of life but was really dead. The Lord hadn't said any good about it. So now when he is about to call attention to some choice souls he introduces the fact with a very strong "But!" Two independent clauses give a compound flavor. But two subordinate ideas make it a compound-complex sentence. The first of the main clauses announces, "You are having a few names..." In the ancient biblical world "name" (ὄνομα) had a great deal more significance than a handle by which one person is distinguished from another. It indicated the total person, his character, personality, position, influence, etc. So the word "names" here means "persons." Describing this word ὀνόματα is an adjective clause proposed by the relative ἃ, "which defiled not their garments."

The second of the independent clauses promises, "they will walk with me in white..." A supporting reason underlying that promise is an adverbial ὅτι clause, "because they are worthy."

Verse five structures a three-pronged compound sentence. All three clauses are independent and each carries a promise designed to encourage "the one overcoming," subject of the first clause. This subject is linear action present attributive participle νικῶν. The linear action doesn't look to a point of victory; it is looking at victory as a process going on.

The second independent pledges, "I will not wipe out..." Here again ὄνομα is more than wiping something written down in a book; its eliminating a person from citizenship. The genitive ζωῆς modifying βίβλου specifies the kind of book involved. It's the book which is life.

The last of the three clauses is another encouraging promise, "I will confess his name(person)..." Two prepositional phrases, "before my father" and "before his angels" are adverb in function. They reveal where the confession is to be made. The "few souls" in the Sardian church got little recognition in that dead church. But this promise held out before them a wider recognition than they could ever have dreamed.

The sentence of verse six is complex. It is the same as in 2:7, 11, 17, and 29.

Revelation 3:7-8

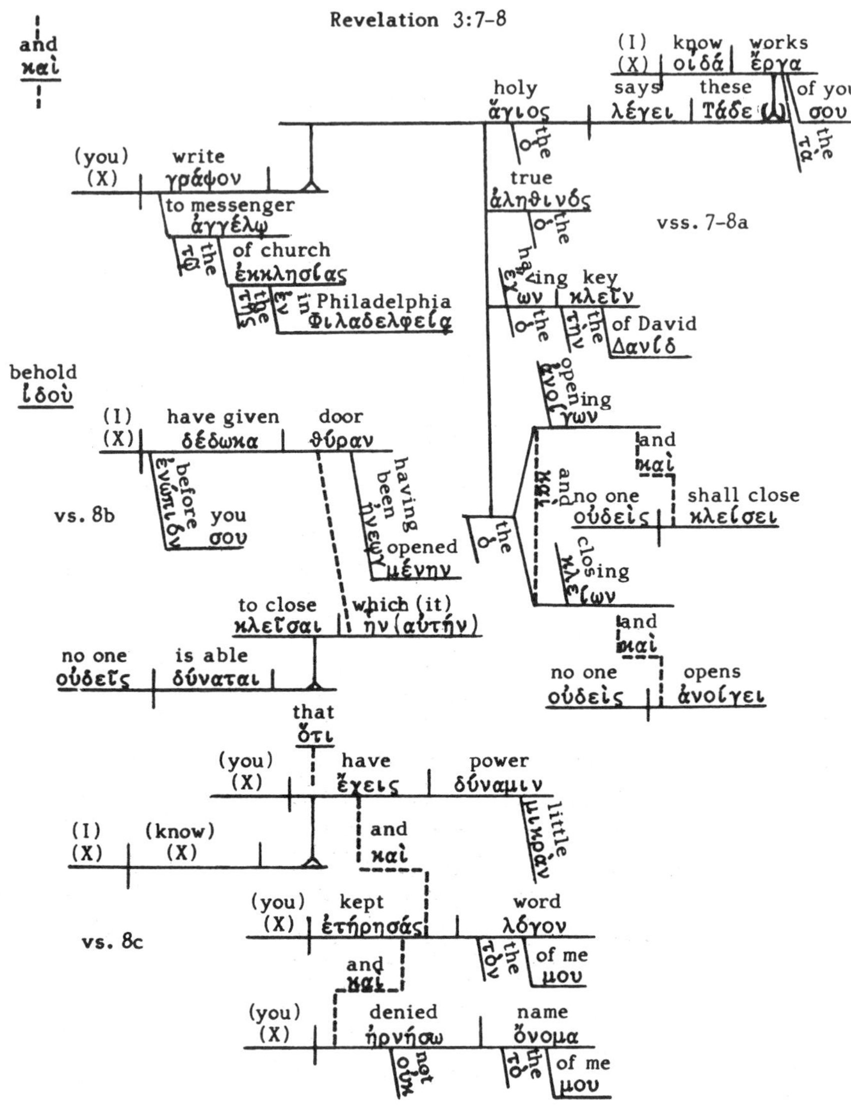

## THE DIAGRAM OF 3:7-8

Again the "son of man" who appeared in the first chapter of the Revelation urgently insists, "You write..." That exhortation forms the independent portion of the complex sentence of verses 7-8a. The direct object of "write" is a dependent noun clause which itself contains three noun clauses.

That noun clause, object of "write," has a seven-point subject. It consists of two articular adjectives which perform the role of substantives. Then follows three articular attributive participles. To each of the last two of these participles there is joined a dependent clause. Each of these clauses expands the idea of the participle to which it is joined by καὶ. The entire subject says, "The holy(one), the true(one), the one having the key of David, the one opening and no one shall close, and closing and no one opens,..." By the time a reader wades through this lengthy subject he's forgotten that it is a subject and the mind struggles to announce the verb and its adjuncts. To resolve that problem of style it is best to use the object first, "these things"(τάδε), then the verb followed by this lengthy subject. Thus it reads, "These things says the holy, the true, the one having the key...etc..." The noun clause, "I know your works" is in apposition to Τάδε.

The sentence embraced by 8b is complex with two clauses. The independent announces a providential fact, "I have given a door." Just where that door is is depicted in an adverbial phrase "before you." ἐνώπιόν is an adjective but used here with the force of a preposition with genitive. It literally means "right in the presence of your face." θύραν("door") is object of perfect δδέδωκα the action of which signifies that the gift is still in effect. To paint further the permanence of this gift the circumstantial perfect participle "having been opened"(ἠνεῳγμένην)is tacked onto "door" as added emphasis that the door of opportunity still stands open. The rest of the sentence consists of a dependent adjective clause describing this "door" as one "which no one is able to close." That entire clause gives emphasis that the providential gift of a door of opportunity remains open. αὐτήν is redundant though its very presence adds a note of finality. κλεῖσαι is aorist infinitive. The punctiliar action turns attention to the point (not attained) at which a door might be forced shut with an explosive snap. Forces of evil put pressure on the door but they can never "slam it shut."

Verses 7 through 8 form one unbroken sentence in Nestle's text. But the diagram breaks it into three sentences. The sentence of 8c must borrow its whole main clause from the "I know" of the earlier noun clause in apposition to τάδε. Then after this implied independent "I know" there follow three noun clauses. Each serves as an object of "know." The first declares, "...that you have little power..." ἔχεις as present pictures the perpetual lack of power so characteristic of the Philadelphian church. But the next two of these noun clauses have aorist tenses: "you kept my word" and "you did not deny my name." The keeping of his word in itself extended over the entire stretch of their lack of power. But by the aorist the writer looks at their entire effort as one successful point. Furthermore, at no point did they deny.

Revelation 3:9–10

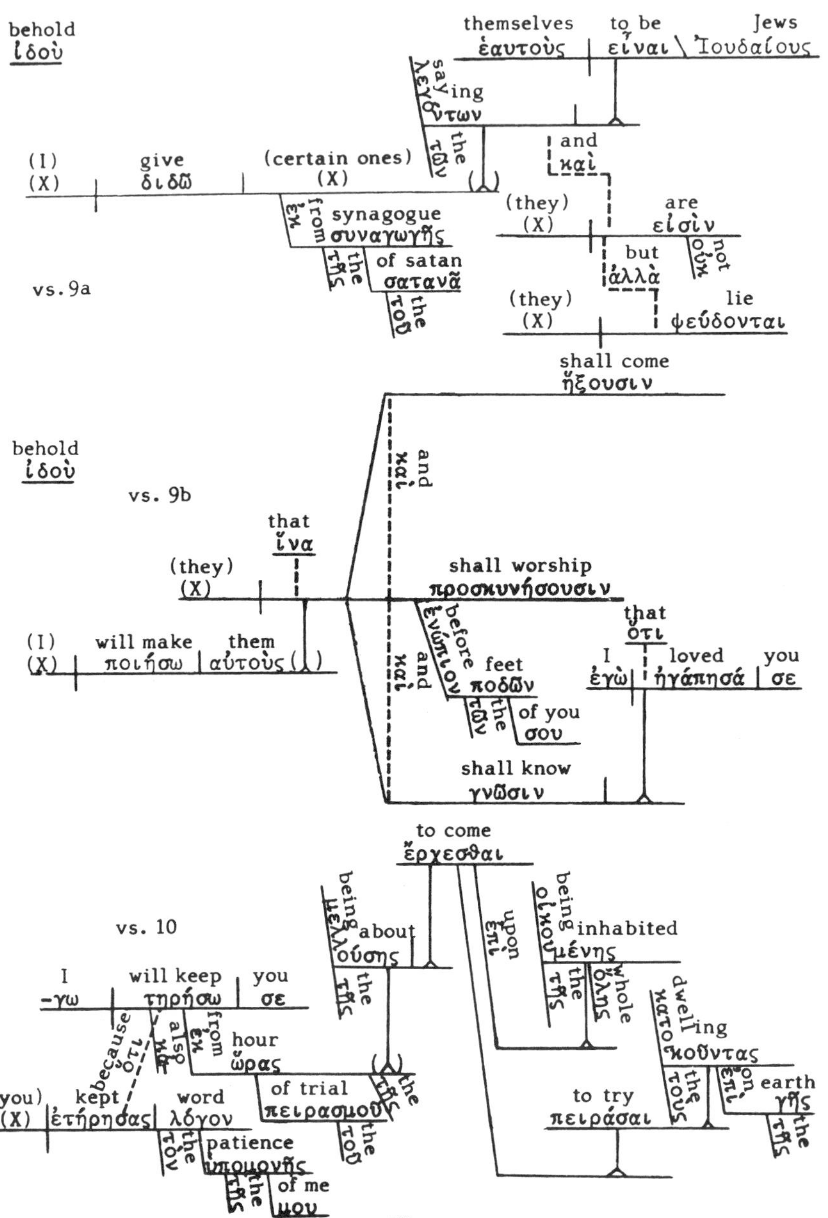

## THE DIAGRAM OF 3:9-10

Verse 9a encases a complex sentence. The independent clause announces, "I give (certain ones)..." Obviously the "certain ones," as object, is implied from the context. But the ἐκ phrase identifies the source from whence these "certain ones" came; hence it's adverbial in function. In apposition to the understood object "certain ones" is the articular attributive present participle "the ones saying"(λεγόντων). As object of this participle is infinitive εἶναι with accusative of general reference ἑαυτοὺς as so-called "subject" and Ἰουδαίους as predicate accusative. Two dependent noun clauses are added to complete the sentence: "they are not" and "they lie." These clauses are also in apposition to implied object "certain ones" of the main clause.

Verse 9b also frames a complex sentence. The main clause states, "I will make them..." Precisely what he will make them to do is presented in the noun clause proposed by conjunction ἵνα. It is a purport (object) clause. The diagram shows this purport noun clause as in apposition to the object αὐτοὺς. However, it might be thought of as an objective complement. In any case it fills out the idea of the object "them" by revealing what the "them" should do. Three things he "will make them" do: (1)"that they shall come, (2)that they shall worship," (3)"that they shall know..." This third of the predicates "shall know" has itself a noun clause as its direct object. It is introduced by ὅτι; "that I loved you."

It might be well for the student of Greek to take note that there is very little practical difference in function between the ἵνα and the ὅτι clauses. Both are noun dependent clauses. Both of them express the content of the action in the verb of which each is object or as with ἵνα apposition to the object.

Yet a third complex sentence on this page is that contained in verse 10. "I will keep you..." is the independent idea. The presence of personal pronoun ἐγώ is noticeably emphatic (as it was in verse 9b). It centers pronounced attention on the personal involvement of the Lord in watching over his people. One reason why the Lord was so concerned about keeping them is expressed in the ὅτι adverb clause, "because you kept the word of my patience." Another adverbial idea is that of the ἐκ phrase "from the hour of trial..." It tells when the Lord "will keep." Further amplifying "the hour" is an attributive present participle "the one being about to come..." Modifying the present infinitive ἔρχεσθαι is the aorist infinitive expressing purpose πειράσαι. As direct object of this aorist infinitive is an attributive present participle translated "the ones dwelling..." Where they dwell is set forth in the ἐπὶ phrase, "upon the earth."

Another adverbial idea modifying infinitive ἔρχεσθαι is introduced by preposition ἐπὶ with present attributive participle οἰκουμένης = "the whole inhabited earth." The phrase indicates where the threatened "hour" is "being about to come."

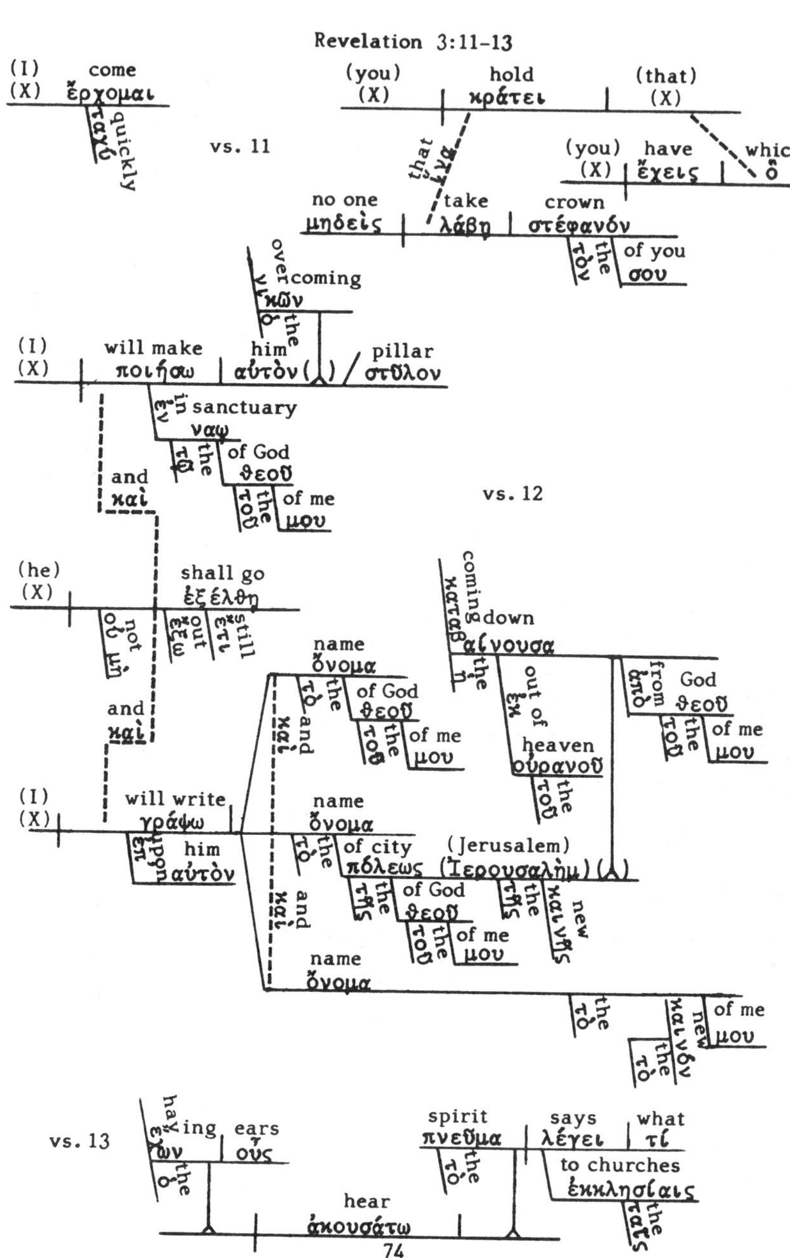

Revelation 3:11-13
(I)
(X) ἔρχομαι
come
ταχύ
quickly
vs. 11
(you)
(X)
κράτει
hold
(that)
(X)
(you)
(X)
ἔχεις
have
ὃ
which
ἵνα
that
μηδεὶς
no one
λάβῃ
take
στέφανόν
crown
τὸν
the
σου
of you
ὁ
the
νικῶν
overcoming
(I)
(X)
ποιήσω
will make
αὐτὸν
him
στῦλον
pillar
ἐν
in
ναῷ
sanctuary
τῷ
the
θεοῦ
of God
τοῦ
the
μου
of me
καὶ
and
vs. 12
(he)
(X)
ἐξέλθῃ
shall go
οὐ μὴ
not
ἔξω
out
ἔτι
still
καὶ
and
(I)
(X)
γράψω
will write
ἐπ'
upon
αὐτὸν
him
ὄνομα
name
τὸ
the
θεοῦ
of God
τοῦ
the
μου
of me
καὶ
and
ὄνομα
name
τὸ
the
πόλεως
of city
(Ἰερουσαλὴμ)
(Jerusalem)
τῆς
the
θεοῦ
of God
τοῦ
the
μου
of me
τῆς
the
καινῆς
new
ἡ
the
καταβαίνουσα
coming down
ἐκ
out of
οὐρανοῦ
heaven
τοῦ
the
ἀπὸ
from
θεοῦ
God
τοῦ
the
μου
of me
καὶ
and
ὄνομα
name
τὸ
the
καινόν
new
τὸ
the
μου
of me
vs. 13
ὁ
the
ἔχων
having
οὖς
ears
ἀκουσάτω
hear
τὸ
the
πνεῦμα
spirit
λέγει
says
τί
what
ἐκκλησίαις
to churches
ταῖς
the
74

## THE DIAGRAM OF 3:11-13

As the diagram presents verse 11 two sentences are involved. The first is simple: "I come quickly." Whether the adverb ταχύ should be translated "quickly" or "shortly" is a matter to be determined by the context. It is safe to render it "quickly" for whenever he comes it will be "quickly" as a "thief in the night."

The second sentence of verse 11 is complex in structure. It holds two dependent clauses aside from the independent clause. The main idea is an exhortation, "You be holding (that)..." The linear action of the present κράτει insists on a continuing alertness to ever "be holding..." The purpose for which they should "go on holding" is inserted by the ἵνα adverb clause, "that no one take the crown from you..." Aorist λάβῃ graphically contrasts with the present of the main clause. If one should grow lax in "holding" at any given moment an adversary might grab ("take") one's crown. The sudden stealing of the crown is appropriate to the point action of aorist; the linear present suits the idea of alertly "holding" onto that which one has.

A second dependent clause is included by neuter relative ὃ. It is adjectival and describes the understood object of the main clause, a demonstrative "that."

Three independent clauses verify the sentence of verse 12 to be compound in form. The first of the three declares, "I will make him..." "Pillar"(στῦλον) is objective complement; it reveals that into which the Lord promises to "make him." But in order to state more clearly precisely who this "him" is the speaker inserts an attributive participle νικῶν. It is in apposition to the pronoun object αὐτὸν. The present tense of this participle enforces the idea of "overcoming" as being a process going on. It's a descriptive present.

The second of the independent clauses says, "he shall not go out any more..." The negative is doubled (οὐ μὴ) and therefore quite prominent in the clause. In fact the adverb ἔτι helps to underscore the negative aspect; "he shall <u>not</u> go out <u>any more</u>."

The third independent idea adds another promise; "I will write..." Where he will write is set forth in the adverb phrase "upon him." Precisely <u>what</u> the Lord will write is contained in a three-fold compound object "name." The "name of my God..," the "name of the city of my God..." and "my new name." The word ὄνομα means more than just a distinguishing mark. It denotes some trait that characterizes the essence of the one so named. So this three-fold naming of the redeemed saint entails the giving of the character of God(deity), the security of the city, the quality of the Saviour to the saint. The second time ὄνομα appears it is amplified by two appositionals: "Jerusalem" and attributive participle "the one coming down..." Two prepositional adverb phrases modify this participle. One tells from whence the city is "coming down," that is, "...from heaven..." The other tells from whom the city is "coming down," That is, "...from my God..."

Verse 13 repeats what has by now become a refrain in this part of the book. "The one having ears is to hear what the spirit says..."

Revelation 3:14-16

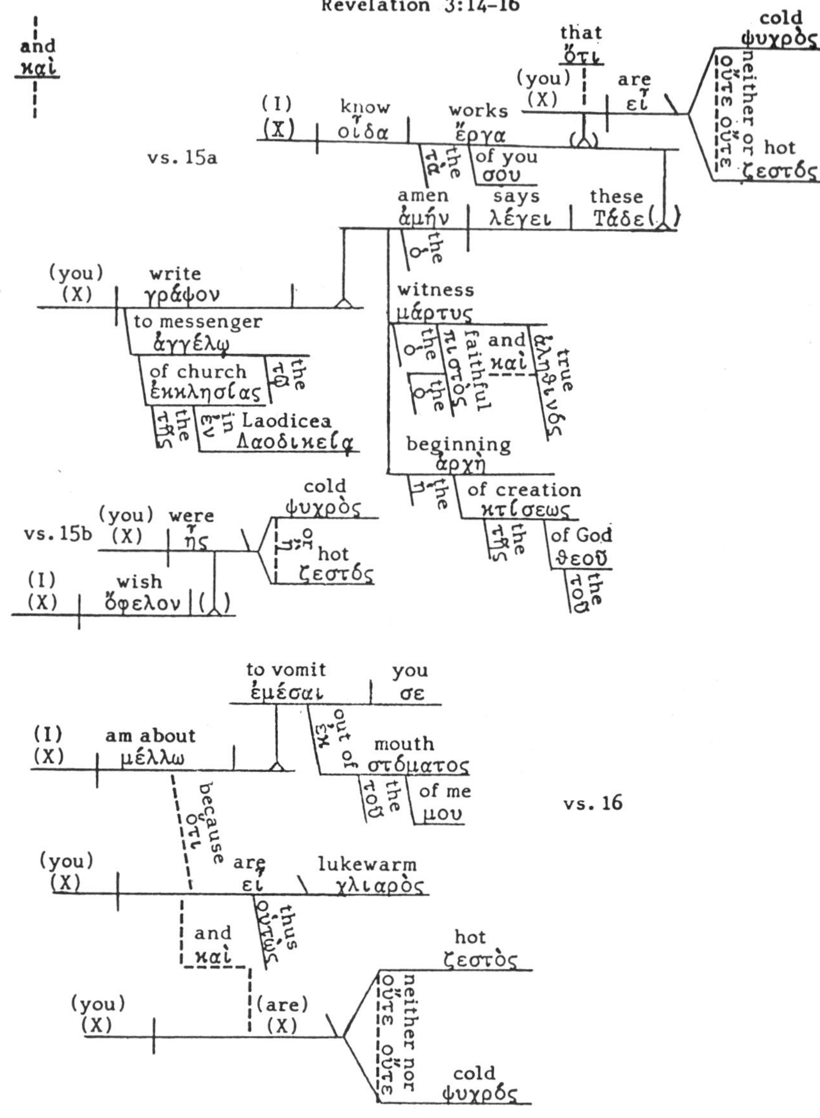

## THE DIAGRAM OF 3:14-16

Three sentences adorn this page. All three are complex. As in his address to the earlier six churches so in this seventh the independent clause enjoins the apostle: "You write." Again he is to write "to the messenger." ἀγγέλῳ is dative of indirect object. Genitive ἐκκλησίας specifies the kind of "messenger." He is the "messenger of the church." The prepositional phrase "in Laodicea" locates the place in which the church exists.

Direct object of the verb "write" of the main clause, is a dependent noun clause, "the amen says these..." The subject ἀμήν is more fully identified by two added epithets. They are probably best classified as ideas in apposition to the "amen." The diagram has not placed them on the normal pedestal. But in order to conserve space on the page has hung them below the horizontal line on which the "amen" rests. First the "amen" is defined as "the faithful and true witness." Then as "the beginning of God's creation." This expression is not meant to indicate that the Lord Jesus was a "created" being. But that he is the ABC, the basic essence on which creation came into being. He is not the "beginning" in terms of time. But rather the "beginning" in terms of essence, purpose, rudimentary elements!

A second dependent noun clause is in apposition to τάδε. It reads, "I know your works..." Once again another dependent noun clause expands that clause; it is in apposition to the direct object noun ἔργα. It accuses, "that you are neither cold or hot." Their works were sufficient to identify them with the Christian movement but not boiling (ζεστός) with enthusiasm.

The independent clause of verse 15b uses ὄφελον "I wish..." This form is really the 2nd aorist indicative active of ὀφείλω without any augment. Here it is expressing a wish about the present. The precise content of that which he wished is contained in a noun clause direct object of this main verb: "(that) you were cold or hot."

The sentence of verse 16 has three clauses two of which are dependent. The independent element has present indicative active μέλλω with its object infinitive ἐμέσαι in the aorist. His anticipation and preparation "to spit" was an ongoing transaction. But when it came to the act of spitting that was a decisive deed expressed best by a point action aorist.

The two dependent ideas of verse 16 are adverbial causal clauses governed by ὅτι. They state the positive and negative reasons why the Lord felt nauseated by the tepid type of faith of these Laodicean Christians. It was "...because you are lukewarm and neither hot nor cold."

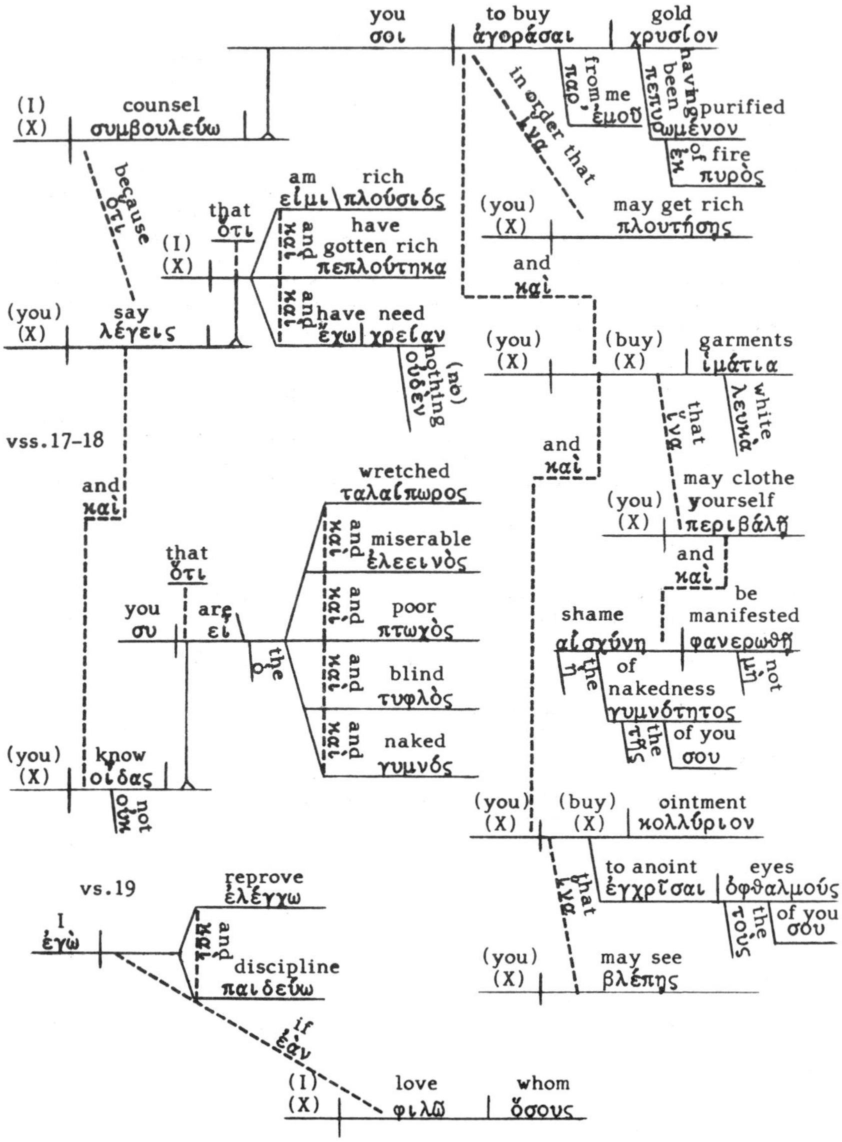

you σοι
to buy ἀγοράσαι
gold χρυσίον
(I) (X) counsel συμβουλεύω
from παρ'
me ἐμοῦ
in order that ἵνα
having been purified πεπυρωμένον
of fire ἐκ πυρὸς
because ὅτι
that ὅτι
am εἰμι
rich πλούσιός
(I) (X)
and καὶ
have gotten rich πεπλούτηκα
(you) (X) may get rich πλουτήσῃς
and καὶ
(you) (X) say λέγεις
and καὶ
have ἔχω
need χρείαν
(no) nothing οὐδὲν
(you) (X) (buy) (X) garments ἱμάτια
white λευκὰ
that ἵνα
vss.17-18
and καὶ
and καὶ
wretched ταλαίπωρος
(you) (X) may clothe yourself περιβάλῃ
and καὶ miserable ἐλεεινὸς
that ὅτι
and καὶ
be manifested φανερωθῇ
you σὺ
are εἶ
the ὁ
and καὶ poor πτωχὸς
shame αἰσχύνη
the ἡ
of nakedness γυμνότητος
not μὴ
and καὶ blind τυφλὸς
the τῆς
of you σου
and καὶ naked γυμνός
(you) (X) know οἶδας
not οὐκ
(you) (X) (buy) (X) ointment κολλύριον
to anoint ἐγχρῖσαι
eyes ὀφθαλμούς
the τοὺς
of you σου
that ἵνα
(you) (X) may see βλέπῃς
vs.19
reprove ἐλέγχω
I ἐγὼ
and καὶ
discipline παιδεύω
if ἐὰν
(I) (X) love φιλῶ
whom ὅσους

## THE DIAGRAM OF REVELATION 3:17-19

Chapter 3:17-18 encloses a sentence of 59 words filling eleven clauses (if we classify the infinitive construction as a clause) and is to be classed as complex. The only independent element says, "I counsel..." Linear action of the present tense of the verb rendered "counsel" suggests that the Lord continues to exhort and counsel them.

Two ὅτι clauses of cause display reasons why he offers such counsel; "because you are saying" and "because you know..." A noun clause, object of λέγεις, launched by declarative ὅτι gives the content of what the Laodiceans were "saying." That is, "that I am rich and have gotten rich and have no need." A second ὅτι ushers in another noun clause direct object of οἶδας This object clause gives the content of what the Laodiceans do not know; "...that you are wretched and miserable and poor and blind and naked." These are two good reasons why the Lord offers his counsel.

Aorist infinitive ἀγοράσαι is direct object of συμβουλεύω with dative pronoun σοι as its so-called "subject" rather than the more normal accusative of general reference. Strictly speaking this is not a clause. But for practical purposes it functions as a noun clause, object of "counsel," "that you buy gold..." The adverb ἵνα clause stemming off of the infinitive is purpose; "that you may get rich."

Another noun clause, object of the main verb "counsel," states a second item in the list of what the Lord counsels them; "(that you buy) white garments..." Two ἵνα purpose clauses support the counsel as to why they ought buy white garments; "that you may clothe yourself" and that "the shame of your nakedness be not manifested."

Yet a third noun clause, object of the main verb "counsel," appears: "(that you buy) ointment to anoint your eyes..." Hanging from that clause is another ἵνα adverbial purpose clause stating the reason why they should buy ointment; "in order that you might go on seeing."

An interesting observation is that the earlier three ἵνα clauses used point action aorists but this fourth one has present tense to emphasize that they "go on seeing" rather than to "get sight." In the earlier purpose clauses the Laodiceans hadn't yet gotten rich. They just thought they had. Material riches gave them the illusion of wealth. Nor did they have clothing; they just supposed they had; they were really naked. But, though their vision was blurred, they were not yet entirely blind. If they bought ointment from the Lord they "might go on seeing" and not lose their sight.

The sentence of verse 19 has but two clauses; one independent and one dependent, hence is complex in structure. The "if" clause is the protasis of a third class condition, undetermined but with some prospect of determination. "If I love whom...and I most likely will..." The conclusion is stated in the independent clause which declares, "I reprove and discipline." Love guarantees reproof and discipline" wherever and whenever it is needed for growth or protection.

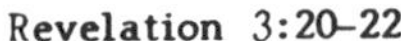

behold
ἰδοὺ

vs. 20a

(I) (X) | stand ἕστηκα | before ἐπὶ | door θύραν | the τὴν

and καὶ

(I) (X) | knock κρούω

vs. 20b

(I) (X) | shall enter εἰσελεύσομαι | to πρὸς | him αὐτὸν

if ἐάν

anyone τις | shall hear ἀκούσῃ | voice φωνῆς | the τῆς | of me μου

and καὶ

shall open ἀνοίξῃ | door θύραν | the τὴν

and καὶ

(I) (X) | shall dine δειπνήσω | with μετ' | him αὐτοῦ

and καὶ

he αὐτὸς | shall dine (X) | with μετ' | me ἐμοῦ

vs. 21

(I) (X) | will give δώσω | to him αὐτῷ

to sit καθίσαι | with μετ' | me ἐμοῦ | on ἐν | throne θρόνῳ | the τῷ | of me μου

overcoming νικῶν | the ὁ | ( )

as ὡς

I -γὼ | also καὶ

overcame ἐνίκησα

and καὶ

sat ἐκάθισα | with μετὰ | father πατρὸς | the τοῦ | of me μου | on ἐν | throne θρόνῳ | the τῷ | of him αὐτοῦ

vs. 22

having ἔχων | the ὁ | ears οὖς

hear ἀκουσάτω

spirit πνεῦμα | the τὸ | says λέγει | what τί | to churches ἐκκλησίαις | the ταῖς

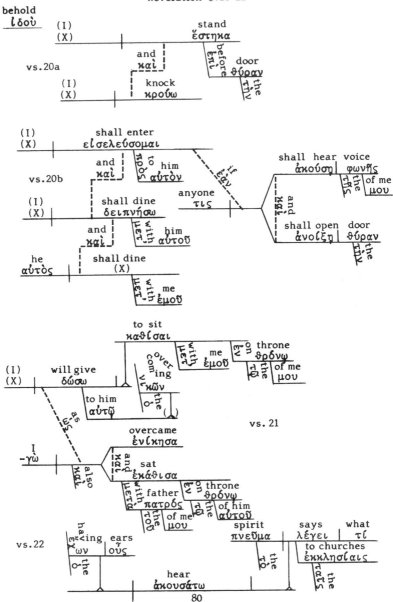

## THE DIAGRAM OF REVELATION 3:20-22

The two clauses of the sentence of 3:20a are equal in rank and hence form the frame for a compound combination. They state, "I stand and I am knocking." The prepositional phrase, "before the door" is adverbial in function for it tells where he stands. Perfect tense ἕστηκα suggests that the Lord "has taken a stand and still stands." κρούω is iterative present depicting the Lord's persistent repetition of knocking. Both tenses enhance the idea that the Lord doesn't intend to give up his effort to enter. If he doesn't get in it will be the refusal of the Laodiceans to open the door.

The sentence of 20b employs four clauses three of which are independent. So it classifies as compound-complex. All three of the independent ideas are based on the one dependent idea which is a 3rd class conditional "if" clause. It's undetermined but with some prospect of determination. "If anyone shall hear my voice and shall open the door...and it's quite likely someone will..." The verbs "hear" and "open" are both aorist subjunctives. Both tense and mode suit the speculative uncertainty of the "if." But if the "if" does became a reality then there follows a three-fold effect as expressed in the three independent ideas: "I shall enter," "I shall dine" and ("he shall dine.")

The ὡς of verse 21 advances a dependent adverb clause of comparison. It sets up a standard by which the idea in the main clause may be measured. "As I overcame and sat..." is the scale on which I shall gauge how much "I will give to him, the one overcoming, to sit with me on my throne." The sentence frames a complex arrangement. Personal pronoun αὐτῷ appears as indirect object of δώσω. The articular attributive present participle νικῶν is in apposition to the dative pronoun even though it is in the nominative case. This reflects the grammatical inconsistency appearing numbers of times throughout Revelation. It agrees in sense though not in grammar. The linear action of the present tense of νικῶν calls attention to the fact that the victory of him who "overcomes" is not accomplished by a single effort but is an ongoing operation. "Overcoming" is a series of successful efforts rather than one supreme isolated impulse.

Verse 22 presents once again the refrain "The one having ears is to hear what the spirit says to the churches." In form it is complex. The fact that the plural ἐκκλησίαις is used in each instance when in fact only a single church is involved in each appearance of this sentence suggests that the message to each single church is really intended for all the churches. In other words, each message is for the entire Christian church throughout the Roman province of Asia. Indeed, for the whole church, world wide and age long!

Furthermore, it is the "spirit" that is sending the message, not just the apostle John. The author lays claim to be the vehicle of the Spirit of God in bringing his message.

ἀκουσάτω is aorist imperative. It represents a command; at least a strong exhortation. "The one having (present) ears..." has a responsibility that he who doesn't have ears does not have. Blessing brings privilege; privilege brings accountability!

## A TRANSLATION
### Revelation 4:1-11

After these things I saw, and Behold! A door having been opened in the heaven, and the first voice which I heard as a trumpet speaking with me, saying, "Come up here and I will show to you which things are necessary to come after these things." At once, I got in the spirit. And behold a throne was set in heaven and upon the throne one sitting; and the one sitting (was) like in appearance to jasper and sard stone, and a rainbow encircled the throne in appearance like emerald. And twenty four thrones (were) encircling the throne and upon the thrones twenty four elders seated, having been clothed in white garments, and upon their heads golden crowns. And out of the throne goes lightnings and noises and thunders. And seven lamps of fire (were) burning before the throne which are the seven spirits of God. And before the throne, as it were, a glassy sea like crystal; and in the midst of the throne and encircling the throne(were)four living creatures full of eyes before and behind. And the first living creature (was) like a lion, and the second living creature (was) like an ox, and the third living creature (was) having his face as of man, and the fourth living creature (was) like a flying eagle. And the four living creatures, one by one of them, (were) each having six wings, (and) they are full of eyes without and within; and they are not having rest day and night saying, "Holy, holy, holy, Lord, the God, the Almighty, the was one and the being one, and the coming one."

And whenever the living creatures shall give glory and honor and praise to the one sitting upon the throne, the one living unto the ages of the ages, the twenty four elders shall fall down before the one sitting upon the throne and they shall worship the living one unto the ages of the ages. And they shall throw their crowns before the throne, saying, "You, the Lord and our God, are worthy to receive the glory and the honor and the power, because you created all things and because of your will they were and are created."

## AN OUTLINE OF REVELATION 4:1-11

### The Sovereign God!

"I got in the spirit." A vision of God seen through "an opened door."

I. THE SOURCE OF GOD'S SOVEREIGNTY. vss. 3-7
   1. Seven characteristics of the "one sitting on the throne."
      (a)He is "spirit." (b)Timeless. (c)King over kings.
      (d)Source of "natural" powers. (e)Of spiritual powers.
      (f)Image of holiness. (g)Origin of creature life.

II. SUCH A ONE IS WORTHY OF WORSHIP. vss. 8-11
   1. All "living creatures" worship him.
   2. All religion honors him.

"Worthy art thou" by right of creation! Let all worship!

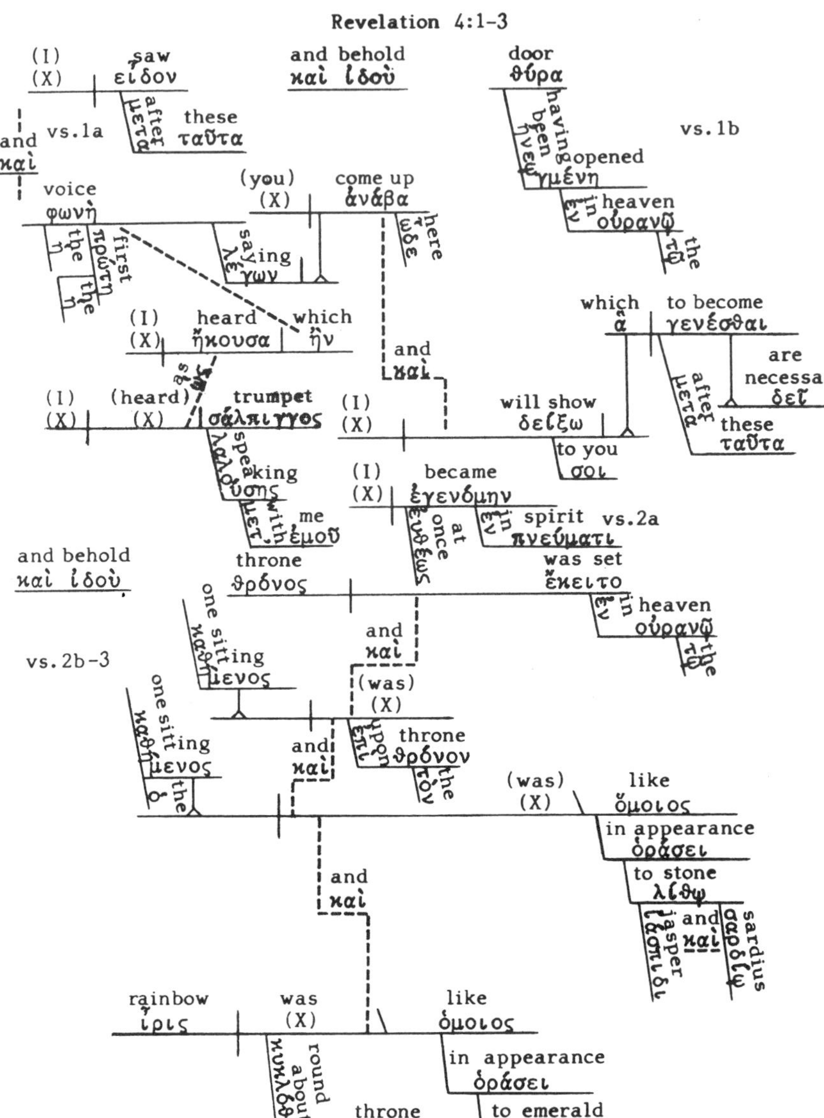

vs.1a
(I) (X) saw εἶδον
after μετὰ these ταῦτα
and καὶ
and behold καὶ ἰδοὺ
door θύρα
having been opened ἠνεῳγμένη
in ἐν heaven οὐρανῷ the τῷ
vs.1b
voice φωνὴ
the ἡ
first πρώτη
saying λέγων
(you) (X) come up ἀνάβα
here ὧδε
(I) (X) heard ἤκουσα
which ἣν
as ὡς
(I) (X) (heard) (X) trumpet σάλπιγγος
speaking λαλούσης
with μετ᾽ me ἐμοῦ
and καὶ
(I) (X) will show δείξω
to you σοι
which ἃ
to become γενέσθαι
are necessary δεῖ
after μετὰ these ταῦτα
(I) (X) became ἐγενόμην
at once εὐθέως
in ἐν spirit πνεύματι
vs.2a
and behold καὶ ἰδοὺ
throne θρόνος
was set ἔκειτο
in ἐν heaven οὐρανῷ the τῷ
vs.2b-3
one sitting καθήμενος
and καὶ
(was) (X)
upon ἐπὶ throne θρόνον the τὸν
one sitting καθήμενος the ὁ
(was) (X) like ὅμοιος
in appearance ὁράσει
to stone λίθῳ
jasper ἰάσπιδι and καὶ sardius σαρδίῳ
rainbow ἶρις
was (X)
like ὅμοιος
round about κυκλόθεν
throne θρόνου the τοῦ
in appearance ὁράσει
to emerald σμαραγδίνῳ

## THE DIAGRAM OF 4:1-3

Grammatically verse 1a, "After these things I saw," is a complete sentence. But before the writer gives an object indicating what he saw he starts again with an exclamatory "and behold!" Then when he does relate what he saw he uses a nominative "door" with an added circumstantial perfect participle. That which John "saw" was a "door having been opened in heaven." But in structure we treat verse 1a as a distinct simple sentence, "I saw after these." "A door having been opened..." is either a nominative absolute or a simple sentence if one wants to look on the participle as taking the place of a finite verb. If so it would read, "And behold! A door (has been) opened in heaven." Perfect tense of participle ἀνεῳγμένη intimates that the door was propped open so as to stay open.

The diagram begins a new sentence with nominative φωνὴ. It is the subject of the only independent clause. That clause hasn't any expressed verb unless λέγων be thought of as supplementary to an unexpressed copula "was." In that case it would read "The first voice (was) saying..." The diagram has opted to treat λέγων as circumstantial modifying subject φωνὴ, "the first voice (spoke) saying..." Also modifying subject "voice" is dependent adjective clause, "which I heard." Inserted to enlarge on that clause is the adverbial dependent "as though(I heard)a trumpet speaking with me..." Circumstantial participle λαλούσης agrees in case with σάλπιγγος although refers back to "voice" in idea.

Direct objects of λέγων are two noun clauses, "come up here." and "I will show you..." Object of δείξω revealing what he will show is another noun clause. Subject of this clause is aorist infinitive γενέσθαι with its accusative of general reference ἃ. The verb of the clause is δεῖ. Literally it would read, "...which to become after these things is necessary."

Verse 2a is handled as a separate sentence. It is simple in structure. "Immediately I became (was) in spirit."

The sentence which encompasses verses 2b-3 has four independent clauses, hence is compound. The initial independent idea sets the scene, "And behold, a throne was set in heaven..." ἔκειτο is imperfect middle of κεῖμαι to be set or stood. Used frequently as passive of τίθημι.

The second clause says, "...one sitting (sat) upon the throne.." The verb must be suggested by the context. "Upon the throne" is adverbial denoting <u>where</u> he sat.

Subject of the <u>third</u> clause is a repeat of that of the second, the attributive present participle καθήμενος. Here however it is used with the definite article. It's the article of previous reference. As the context makes clear both participles refer to God. But the picture of "one sitting" depicts more vividly than the abstract "God." A sovereign "sits" to rule. God is the ruling sovereign, hence he is the "one sitting." ὅμοιος normally takes associative-instrumental case as it does here.

The last of the four clauses describes the environment of the throne. "A rainbow, encircling the throne, (was) like in appearance to emerald."

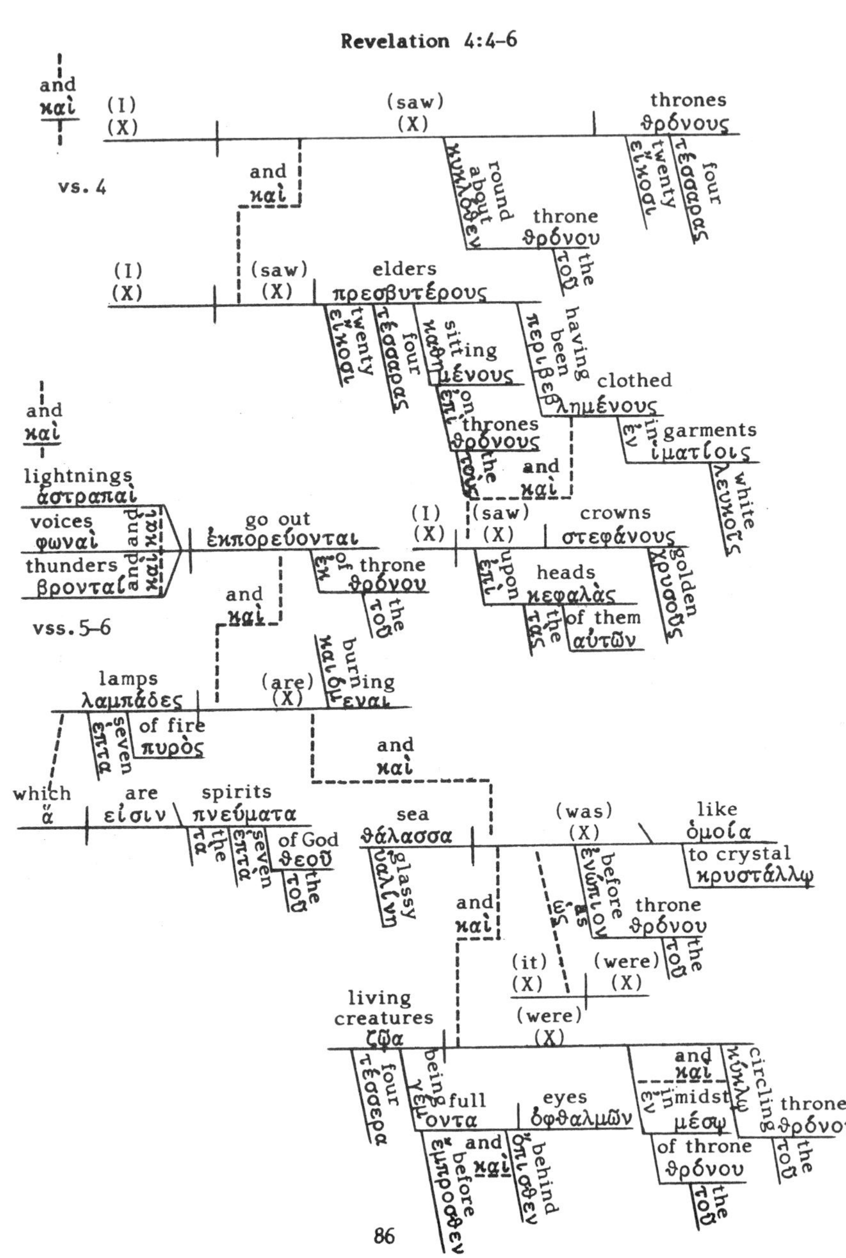
and
καὶ
(I)
(X)
(saw)
(X)
thrones
θρόνους
twenty
εἴκοσι
four
τέσσαρας
round about
κυκλόθεν
throne
θρόνου
the
τοῦ
vs. 4
and
καὶ
(I)
(X)
(saw)
(X)
elders
πρεσβυτέρους
twenty
εἴκοσι
four
τέσσαρας
sitting
καθημένους
on
ἐπὶ
thrones
θρόνους
the
τοὺς
having been clothed
περιβεβλημένους
in
ἐν
garments
ἱματίοις
white
λευκοῖς
and
καὶ
(I)
(X)
(saw)
(X)
crowns
στεφάνους
golden
χρυσοῦς
upon
ἐπὶ
heads
κεφαλὰς
the
τὰς
of them
αὐτῶν
and
καὶ
lightnings
ἀστραπαὶ
voices
φωναὶ
thunders
βρονταί
and
καὶ
go out
ἐκπορεύονται
of
ἐκ
throne
θρόνου
the
τοῦ
vss. 5-6
and
καὶ
lamps
λαμπάδες
seven
ἑπτὰ
of fire
πυρὸς
(are)
(X)
burning
καιόμεναι
which
ἅ
are
εἰσιν
spirits
πνεύματα
the
τὰ
seven
ἑπτὰ
of God
θεοῦ
the
τοῦ
and
καὶ
sea
θάλασσα
glassy
ὑαλίνη
(was)
(X)
like
ὁμοία
to crystal
κρυστάλλῳ
before
ἐνώπιον
throne
θρόνου
the
τοῦ
as
ὡς
(it)
(X)
(were)
(X)
and
καὶ
living creatures
ζῷα
four
τέσσερα
(were)
(X)
being full
γέμοντα
eyes
ὀφθαλμῶν
before
ἔμπροσθεν
and
καὶ
behind
ὄπισθεν
in
ἐν
midst
μέσῳ
of throne
θρόνου
the
τοῦ
and
καὶ
circling
κύκλῳ
throne
θρόνου
the
τοῦ

## THE DIAGRAM OF 4:4-6

Though the sentence of verse four has at least two (possibly three) independent clauses all of them need verbs to be supplied from the context. So the diagram fills in with "I saw..."

The first clause announces, "(I saw) encircling the throne twenty four thrones..." κυκλόθεν is an adverb formed from an adjective meaning ring or circle. Here it serves as a preposition in an adverbial phrase; it locates where the 24 thrones were.

The second of the independents declares, "(I saw) twenty four elders." The elders are described by two circumstantial participles. Present καθημένους reveals them as "sitting." Where they're sitting is pictured by the phrase "upon the thrones." A perfect participle follows περιβεβλημένους "having been clothed in white..." The tense says that they not only had been clothed but still were.

It is at this point at which one must decide whether the clause stating "(I saw) golden crowns..." is independent or dependent. It may justifiably be viewed as either. But the diagram has attached it to the participle and thus treats it as dependent. In idea it seems more closely related to a description of the elders than a parallel thought to "I saw elders." The author is certainly free to change the structure in ideas that are parallel. And he often does. If it is correct to classify this as a dependent clause then the sentence is compound-complex. Otherwise it would be compound.

No such question need be raised in the sentence encased in verses 5-6. Four independent and two dependent clauses make it compound-complex. The first independent has a compound subject, "Lightnings and voices(noises)and thunderings..." The fact that all three are without a definite article suggests that these booming roars of creation are symbolic of something beyond themselves. Do they not suggest the manifold power of him who is "sitting" on the throne?

The second of the independents insists that "seven lamps of fire (are) burning." Present participle καιόμεναι in conjunction with understood copula "was" forms a periphrastic. It's a vivid descriptive present. No doubt can be entertained but that this picture of "lamps of fire" is symbolic. The dependent adjective clause puts forward precisely what the lamps symbolize, "which are the seven spirits of God."

Symbolism continues in the third main clause: "...glassy sea like crystal (was) before the throne..." Crystal is sparkling pure and to the ancients the sea was that which separated friends and loved ones. God is the one who is completely "other," totally beyond human kind! The ὡς seems to suggest an adverbial idea thrust in to place limits on pushing the symbolism too far: "as it were!" and thus it appears as an additional dependent idea.

The final of the four independent clauses depicts more fully the appearance and location of the "four living creatures." Present participle γέμοντα with its adjuncts describes them as "being full of eyes before and behind." Do the numerous eyes signify unlimited intelligent capacity? Two more phrases play the role of adverb; "in midst of the throne" and "in a circle about the throne." They tell where.

## Revelation 4:7–8

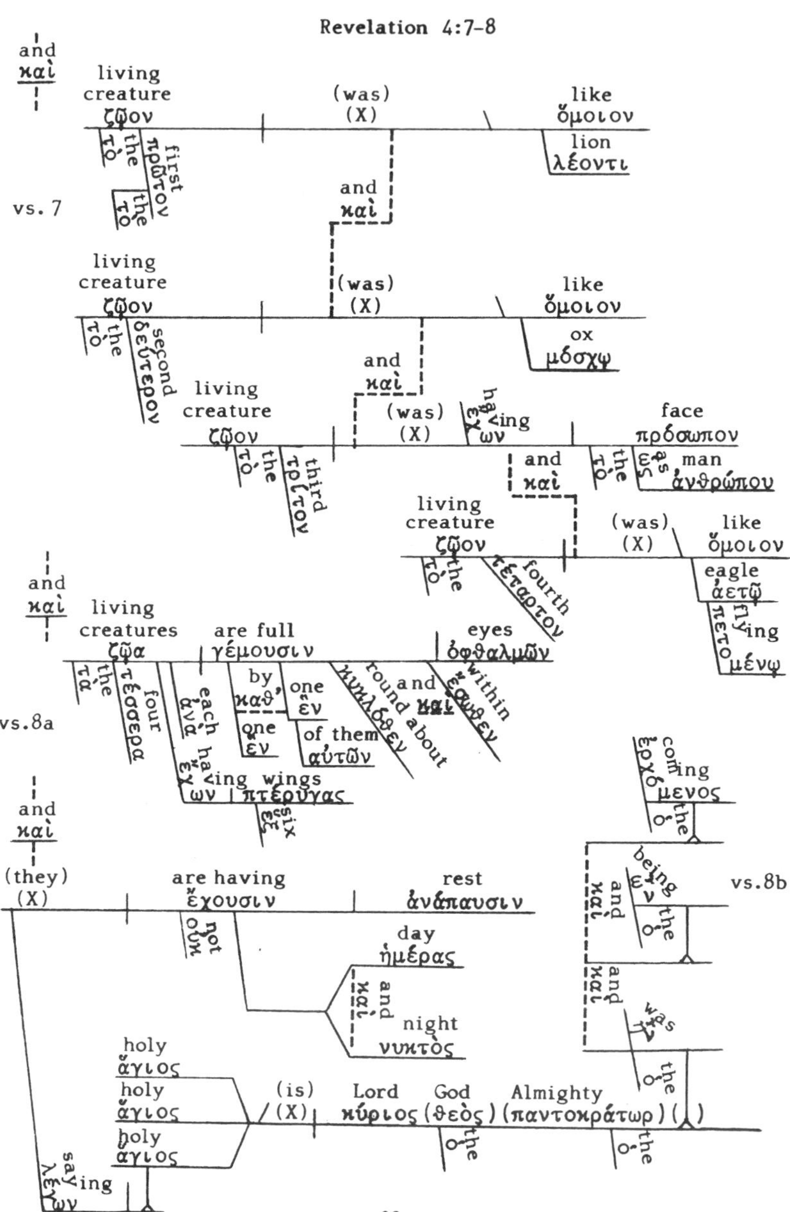

## THE DIAGRAM OF 4:7-8

Four clauses of equal rank form the framework of verse seven, hence it contains a compound sentence. Each of the four describes one of the "living creatures." Except for a variation in the third they adopt a pattern of subject, an implied connecting verb "was," then predicate adjective ὅμοιον and its modifier. (1)"The first living creature (was) like a lion," (2)"the second living creature (was) like an ox," (4)"the fourth living creature (was) like a flying eagle." (3)The third of the clauses varies its verb by using a supplementary predicate participle with the understood copula "was" to form a periphrastic imperfect, "was having." Furthermore, the descriptive element with direct object "face" uses ὡς ἀνθρώπου instead of the instrumental case as in the other three. ὡς appears as a practical preposition with genitive.

In form verse 8a is simple. Stripped of modifiers it declares, "...living creatures are full of eyes." The subject is neuter plural but it has nominative masculine present participle ἔχων modifying it: "each having six wings..." ἀνὰ is used here in a distributive sense, "one by one by one," that is to say, "each one."

Verse 8b exhibits but two clauses, one independent and the other dependent. That classes it as a complex sentence. The main clause proposes a negative declarative statement, "they are not having rest day and night." To be noticed is the genitives in the expression of time "day and night" modifying the main verb. One might expect accusative extent of time but we note the genitive instead. Is this an example of the author's laxity in grammatical usage? Or is he calling attention to the "kind of time" rather than the extent of time? There is <u>no kind of time</u> at which God's creation ceases in its energetic activity or its praise of his holiness!

The word translated "rest" here does not in this context hint of any weariness on the part of God's creation. The word derives from preposition ἀνά = "up" plus παύω = "to cause to cease." The noun indicates a ceasing from activity.

λέγων is present circumstantial participle modifying the subject "they." The present tense underscores their unceasing praise. The direct object of the participle is the noun clause: "the Lord God Almighty, the was one and the being one and the coming one (is) holy, holy, holy!"

The poetic beauty of the song of praise is enhanced by placing the adjectices "holy, holy, holy" first where the subject is normally placed. The diagram shows them in this position though as a matter of fact they are predicate adjectives. The subject is κύριος "Lord" expanded considerably by three appositional expressions: "God," "Almighty," and the triology, "the was one and the being one and the coming one." Though it is decidedly unusual in a diagram we have placed the adjectives first in an effort to preserve the poetic emotional effect.

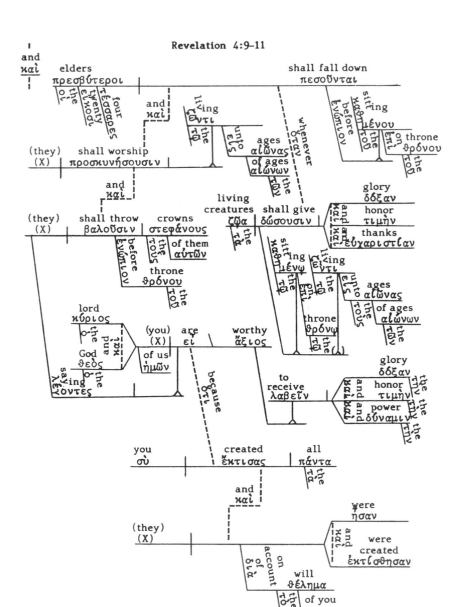

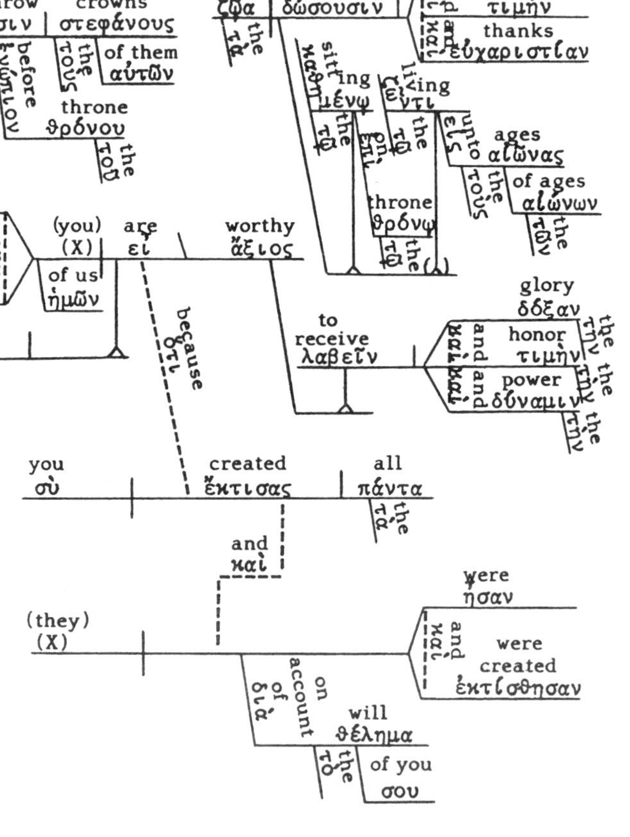
and καὶ
elders πρεσβύτεροι
οἱ the
εἴκοσι twenty
τέσσαρες four
shall fall down πεσοῦνται
and καὶ
living ζῶντι
τῷ the
unto εἰς
ages αἰῶνας
of ages αἰώνων
τῶν the
whenever ὅταν
sitting καθημένου
before ἐνώπιον
τοῦ the
on ἐπὶ
throne θρόνου
τοῦ the
(they) (X)
shall worship προσκυνήσουσιν
and καὶ
living creatures ζῷα
τὰ the
shall give δώσουσιν
glory δόξαν
and καὶ
honor τιμὴν
and καὶ
thanks εὐχαριστίαν
(they) (X)
shall throw βαλοῦσιν
crowns στεφάνους
τοὺς the
of them αὐτῶν
before ἐνώπιον
throne θρόνου
τοῦ the
sitting καθημένῳ
τῷ the
on ἐπὶ
throne θρόνῳ
τῷ the
living ζῶντι
τῷ the
unto εἰς
ages αἰῶνας
τοὺς the
of ages αἰώνων
τῶν the
lord κύριος
ὁ the
and καὶ
God θεὸς
ὁ the
saying λέγοντες
(you) (X)
are εἶ
worthy ἄξιος
of us ἡμῶν
because ὅτι
to receive λαβεῖν
glory δόξαν
τὴν the
and καὶ
honor τιμὴν
τὴν the
and καὶ
power δύναμιν
τὴν the
you σὺ
created ἔκτισας
all πάντα
τὰ the
and καὶ
(they) (X)
were ἦσαν
and καὶ
were created ἐκτίσθησαν
on account of διά
will θέλημα
τὸ the
of you σου

## THE DIAGRAM OF 4:9-11

A combination of seven clauses in verses 9-11 forges a compound-complex sentence. Three are independent; four are dependent.

The independent members make three assertions about the elders. First, "the twenty four elders shall fall down." Then, "they shall worship." Last, "they shall throw their crowns..."

The verb in the first clause has two modifying ingredients, both adverbial. "Before the one sitting on the throne" denotes where they "shall fall down." The articuler present attributive participle "the one sitting" appears twice in this sentence. By this construction, rather than the abstract "God," the author makes clearer the scope of God's work as sovereign. A reigning monarch sits to rule; "on the throne" is where he sits. The present tense "is sitting" stresses the continuing aspect of God's sovereignty.

The clause introduced by ὅταν also plays the role of adverb. It answers the question as to when. "Whenever the living creatures shall give..." then "the twenty four elders shall fall..." ὅταν is an indefinite conjunction = "whenever." It doesn't look to one definite, specific point of "when." "Whenever" suggests that there's more than once when the living creatures "shall give glory...etc ..." The present participle "to the one sitting" reappears as indirect object. But this time note that in apposition is another present attributive, "to the one living unto the ages..." This "One" is not only sitting continuously but he is one who "goes on living" perpetually. He is not only reigning God but he is also the "living God."

The second of the independent units has this same present attributive participle τῷ ζῶντι as direct object of the verb "shall worship." The dative case in the direct object after προσκυνέω is appropriate. It reflects the intense personal element involved in worship of living people to living God.

The last of the three main clauses unveils the sincerety and completeness of their worship; "...they shall throw their crowns..." Nothing is held back! A "crown" is symbolic of one's personal right to choose and live his own life. Thus no secret reserve is kept back for oneself. To reinforce this ultimate giving of self these twenty four elders sing a song of praise. Their song is introduced by the present circumstantial participle λέγοντες = "saying." What they are saying is expressed in the noun clause, object of the participle. "You are worthy, the Lord and the God of us." The subject is "you." In apposition so as to make stand out clear and prominently are the two nouns "the Lord" and "the God." Definite article "the" is with both "Lord" and "God." It indicates that "Lord"(Master) is "the" God.

ὅτι thrusts in a final brace of dependent adverb clauses of cause. They give the underlying ground on which is based the worthiness of the Lord to receive absolute worship. His worth ultimately rests on his creative will as God. "Because you created the all (things)" and because "they were (existed) and were created on account of your will." God had within himself the innate power to create. Besides, he brought creation into existence, not on someone else's advice but "because of his own will."

## EXPOSITORY THOUGHTS ON 4:1-11

"In the beginning God created..." With these lofty words the Bible begins its steadfast unfurling of God's sovereignty. As first and last cause God rules all creation.

"The Lord sat as king at the flood; yea, the Lord sits as king forever."(Ps.29:10) At the flood God exercised his royal rule in judgment. Nor has he abdicated that sovereign throne. At a critical rescue of Israel some sons of Korah sang, "God reigns over the nations; God sits upon his holy throne."(Ps.47:8) In a vast variety of ideas, topics and revelations the Bible develops the ever-present theme of God's sovereignty. God "sits on his holy throne." But not in holy isolation. He is intimately and immanently ruling within his creation.

### The throne of God

Revelation 4:1-11 reports the first vision John saw through the "opened door" when the "first voice" said "Come up here and I will show you..." It's the primary impression when he "got in the Spirit..."(Rev.4:1,2) He saw a "throne set in heaven, and one sitting upon the throne..."

And who sat on heaven's throne? The question is answered in 4:11; "...worthy are you, our Lord and God, to receive the glory..." "God reigns!" This forms the substratum of the entire book of Revelation, not to say of the Bible. Any time one looks through heaven's opened door the feeling which eclipses all else is the supreme sovereignty of God. No vision of heaven or earth is true that displaces the living God from his throne.

### The twenty four thrones

But God's throne was not the only throne that John saw in this initial vision of heaven. "And twenty four thrones (were) encircling the throne and upon the thrones twenty four elders seated, having been clothed in white garments, and upon their heads golden crowns." Both the number 24 plus the fact that "elders" occupied these "twenty four thrones" symbolize some relative simple truths. Twelve is the divine three and the human four multiplied. There were 12 tribes of Israel, the Old Testament "people of God." And the 12 apostles of Christ were the spearhead of the New Testament "people of God." Which is to say that the 12 elders symbolize the "people of God," that is, religion as reflected in both O.T. and N.T. religious expressions. Furthermore, the fact they sat on thrones says that they were reigning kings on whose heads rested "crowns," symbol of their royal power. Whatever rule, authority, or power these religions held, they cast their crowns in submissive praise and adoration before the sovereign God.

Besides these "crowns" the "twenty four elders" were clothed in "white robes." The dirt of sin, the corruption of rebellion, the mortality of knavish, immoral human nature had been whitened. Redeemed humanity, cleansed and ruling over sin and self, gave all praise to him who created them; and then, when they became lost, redeemed them. All religion looks to God as sovereign king. "God sits upon his holy throne." This is revealed in Revelation!

## The praise of Creation

Not only "elders" but all creation lifts its voice in adoring praise to "the one sitting on the throne." John saw "in the midst of the throne and encircling it four living creatures..." One "like a lion," king of wild beasts. Another "like an ox," steady and strongest of domestic animals. A third "like the face of a man," the wisest divinest of creatures. A fourth "like a flying eagle," the swiftest of birds. These encompass all creation. And they each have "six wings full of eyes within and without" symbolizing the sleepless, ceaseless activity of the whole created order. As the invention of a genius, or the masterpiece of a skilled artist gives undying praise to its maker so the "natural" creation in its daily functioning gives its perpetual praise to "the one sitting on the throne" of the universe.

Besides, there's a vital link between creation's unending praise and the breath(spirit)of God. John tells of "seven lamps of fire burning before the throne" which he identifies as "the seven spirits of God," that is, the Holy Spirit of God. It's not without significance that the word "spirit" (πνεῦμα) and "breath" are the same. The Spirit of God is the life breath of all living. God not only "breathed into man the breath of life" but he incessantly breathes into all his creation his spirit, his "breath of life." In return, in its perfect function, it offers lasting praises to him its Creator. These symbols say the same as the Psalmist "Let everything that has breath praise the Lord."(Ps.150:6) "...the four living creatures...never cease saying, 'holy, holy, holy, Lord God Almighty, the was one, and the being one, and the coming one.'"

## What God is like!

"No one has ever seen God at any time."(Jn.1:18) Who can sketch a drawing, sculpture a statue, or paint a portrait of God? No word in man's language can embody an adequate concept of God. John makes no effort to "describe" God. That lies beyond his literary skill. So he tackles the task by creating an impression of what God is like. He selects the symbols of two precious stones and the emerald green from the rainbow. God "in appearance" is "like" the crystal, transparant brilliance of a "jasper stone." He is "like" the "blood red" sardius. And the bow circling the throne is "like in appearance" to the "emerald green" of the rainbow, symbol of God's mercy in the midst of judgment. The precious stones suggest the transparent purity, the eternal brilliance, the life, particularly life redeemed, flowing from him who sits on the throne. Life, pure, eternal, redeemed is the glory, the nature, of God who rules from heaven's throne. As far as words can impress this best sets forth the "likeness" of God. But the Revelator is aware that Jesus said, "He that has seen me has seen the Father."(Jn.14:9) That aspect of God he will symbolize later. How he rules is not the idea here but the fact that he reigns eternally.

What's the basis of God's sovereignty? First, by right of creation: "...because you created all things." Second, "...through your will they were and were created." No man, no angel, no celestial council urged God to rule. It was HIS idea!!

## A TRANSLATION
### Revelation 5:1-14

And I saw on the right of the one sitting upon the throne a book having been written on (the) inside and (the) back, having been sealed with seven seals. And I saw a mighty angel proclaiming in a loud voice,

"Who is worthy to open the book and to loosen its seals?"

And no one was being able in the heaven, neither upon the earth, nor under the earth to open the book nor to look (into) it.

And I began to weep profusely because no one worthy was found to open the book nor to see (into) it.

And one of the elders says to me: "Quit weeping! Behold! The Lion, the one of the tribe of Judah, the root of David, conquered to open the book and (to loosen) its seven seals."

And in the midst of the throne and of the four living creatures and in the midst of the elders I saw, as though he had been slaughtered, a lamb, standing, having seven horns and seven eyes, which are the seven spirits of God having been sent into all the earth. And he came and ("Look!) he has taken (the book) out of the right (hand) of the one sitting upon the throne."

And when he took the book, the four living creatures and the twenty four elders fell before the lamb, each having a zither and golden bowls full of incenses, which are the prayers of the saints. And they are singing a new song saying,

> "Worthy are you to take the book and to open its seals,
> because you were slaughtered and you purchased for God
> in your blood out of every tribe and tongue and people
> and nation, and you made them for your God a kingdom
> and priests, and they shall rule upon the earth."

And I saw, and I heard (the) voice of many angels encircling the throne and of the living creatures and of the elders. And their number (was) myriads of myriads and thousands of thousands; In a loud voice they (were) saying

> "Worthy is the lamb, the one having been slaughtered
> to take the power and wealth and wisdom and might
> and honor and glory and blessing."

And every creature which (is) in the heaven and upon the earth and under the earth and on the sea, and all the (things) in them, I heard saying,

> "To the one sitting upon the throne and to the lamb (be)
> the blessing and the honor and the glory and the strength
> unto the ages of the ages."

And the four living creatures were saying, "Amen!"

And the elders fell down and worshipped!

## AN OUTLINE OF REVELATION 5:1-14
### The Slaughtered Lamb!

Who does not want to know the mysteries of God? What thinker, philosopher, theologian, poet or prince would not welcome knowledge of God's governing grace?---assuming it is grace! Why the suffering of the innocent? Why such brutality? Why fire, earthquake, storm, and flood? Why war, famine, pestilence, disease? Why do men have the instincts of heaven but are mortal in destiny? Why so divine in potential yet so weak in fact?

I. THE SEALED SECRET.
  1. The book containing the secret.
    (a)It belongs to God. It's "on God's right (hand)."
    (b)Written "front and back." Full and overflowing.
    (c)Sealed with seven seals. Securely closed from any who would pry it open. There IS an explanation.
  2. The search.
    (a)"Who is worthy?" It takes "worth" not strength. Truth not attained by force but by moral value.
    (b)Universal challenge offered, in heaven, earth, hell.
    (c)The weeping prophet! He, the representative of God before man, had no message if no one found to explain and interpret God to man.

II. THE REVEALED SECRET, THE SLAUGHTERED LAMB!
  1. The secret is known, the victory won.
    (a)Victory was promised: Lion of Judah; root of David.
    (b)He "conquered" in order to reveal God's secret book.
  2. The lamb the agent of God's sovereignty and victory.
    (a)He was slaughtered in a humilating death.
    (b)He's not dead but "standing" up and active.
    (c)Seven horns - perfect power.
    (d)Seven eyes - perfect insight(omniscience).
    (e)His rule "in all the earth." Universal!
  3. He is making it known. "He has taken" the book!

III. THE WORSHIPPERS.
  1. The four living creatures. All creation.
  2. Twenty four elders. All religion
     They worship with zither and prayer.
  3. Myriads of angels encircling the throne
     sing a "new" song of redemption.
  4. The lamb universally recognized as "worthy."

Those who want a winner will turn to the lamb of God who "takes away the sin of the world." The war is over; the victory won! It's up to me to accept <u>my</u> share in the victory!

## Revelation 5:1-4

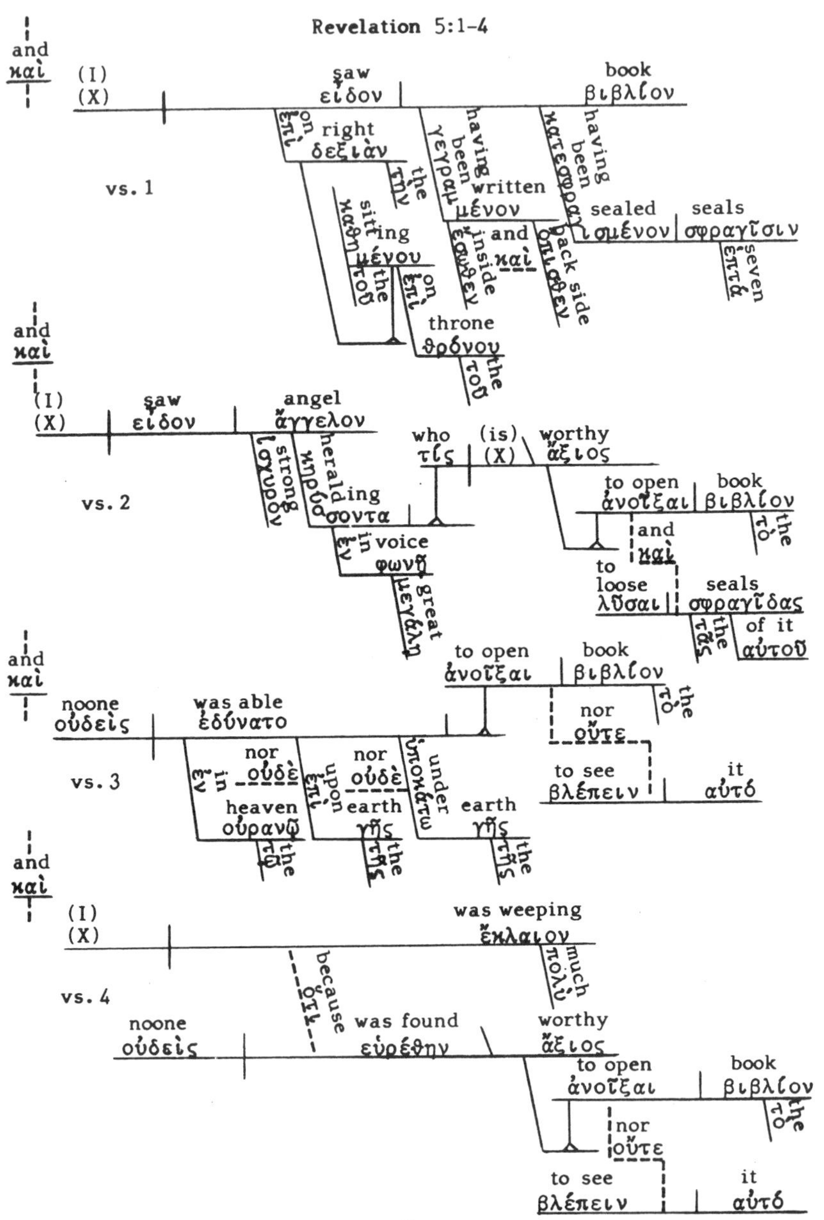

## THE DIAGRAM OF 5:1-4

Of the four verses on this page each envelops one sentence. In structure the first frames a simple sentence; the second a complex; the third a simple; and the fourth a complex.

Reduced to its minimum the first says, "I saw book." Disclosing where the book was is the prepositional adverb expression "on the right..." Further specifying the kind of "right" is the attributive genitive participle "the one sitting on the throne." Two perfect participles describe the condition of the book. As diagrammed they appear as circumstantial, "having been written"(γεγραμμένον) and "having been sealed"(κατεσφραγισμένον). Their perfect tenses say that the writing and sealing were permanently fixed. The words translated "inside" and "outside"("front and back")not only indicate where the writing was but also suggest that the book was bursting with the fulness of its contents.

The second sentence of the page declares that he saw something else besides a book. "I saw an angel..." A present active participle describes that which the angel was doing when John saw him. He was "heralding..." The manner in which he was heralding appears in an adverbial phrase "in a great voice." The content of what he was heralding comes to the fore in a noun clause, direct object of the participle. It's in the form of a question, "Who (is) worthy?" Two infinitive phrases suggesting result hang from the adjective "worthy." -- "worthy to open the book" and "worthy to loose the seals."

In view of the fact that we do not classify infinitive phrases as clauses the sentence of verse three is simple. "No one was able" is the affirmation of the bare clause. But the verb finds completion in the two epexegetic infinitives, "able to open" and "able to see..." The tense of ἀνοῖξαι is aorist while that of βλέπειν is present, punctiliar contrasted with linear. Apparently many tried "to open" the book. This implies numerous efforts. But all attempts are lumped together as a single point-action failure. That's what the aorist says. The change to the linear action vividly dramatizes that the failure "to look" was a frustrating ongoing matter. To show the inability "to look into the book" as an experience common to every place three prepositional phrases are employed: "in," "on," and "under" the earth. Each of these phrases is, of course, adverbial in function.

The last sentence on this page is a complex of two clauses. The dependent is an adverb clause of cause prefaced by ὅτι. It gives the reason which underlies the action presented in the independent clause. "Because no one was found worthy to open the book nor to look into it, I began to weep."

The verb of the main clause is the imperfect, indicative, active ἔκλαιον "I was weeping." Adverbial adjective "much" adds a note of vexation to the intensity of his feelings over no one's being able to uncover the secrets sealed within the scroll. Even more revealing of his feelings is the imperfect tense. It is probably best taken to be an inchoative imperfect. That is, "I began to weep..." Facing the hopelessness of finding the secret of God's providential sovereignty he "burst into tears..."

Revelation 5:5–7

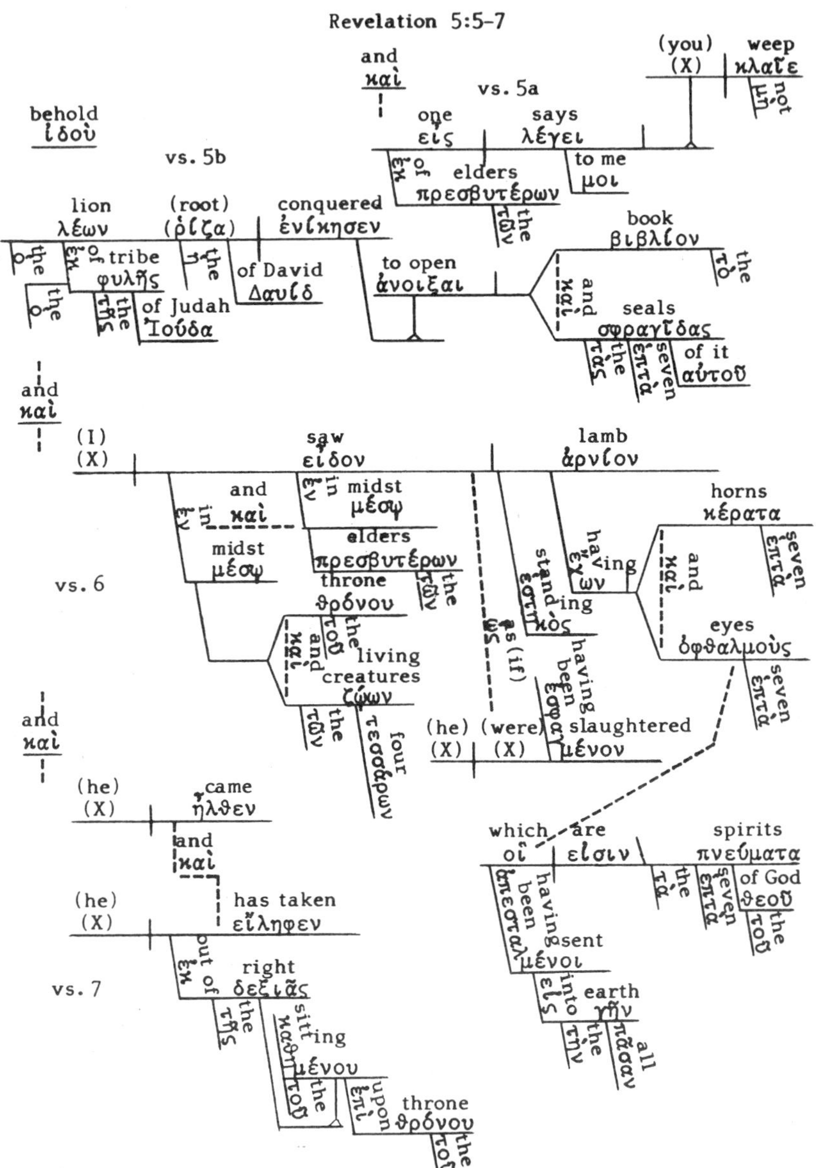

## THE DIAGRAM OF 5:5-7

Only nine words make up the sentence of 5a yet it is a complex of two clauses. Subject of the independent element is the numeral "one." Which "one" is indicated by ἐκ with ablative: "one of the elders." The verb of the main clause is present λέγει the direct object of which is the noun dependent clause, "Quit weeping!" The present tense κλαῖε in the imperative with negative means, in this context, "Quit" what you're doing.

Verse 5b could be dealt with as another object of λέγει of 5a. It is merely the continuation of that which "one of the elders says..." However, the diagram presents it as a separate simple sentence. It basically states, "...lion conquered..." The result of his having conquered is expressed in the infinitive phrase, "...so as to open the book etc..." Who this "lion" was is signified first by ἐκ with ablative, "of the tribe of Judah..." It is further distinguished by the noun ῥίζα in apposition: "the root of David.."

Verse six charts a complex sentence of three full clauses. The chief clause says, "I saw a lamb..." Answering the question as to where he saw the lamb are two ἐν phrases used as adverbs, "in midst of throne..." and "in midst of elders..." Also modifying the verb is an adverbial clause of concession announced by ὡς "as if (he were) having been slaughtered." ἐσφαγμένον in connection with the understood "were" forms a periphrastic pluperfect. It could be translated "...as though he had been slaughtered..." The tense impressively makes prominent the permanency of the slaughter of the lamb. It's a fact accomplished and its effects continue indefinitely. Two participial verbal expressions add their descriptions to the object "lamb." Perfect ἑστηκὸς "standing" has the force of a present tense. This slaughtered lamb is no longer pictured as lifeless for he's now "standing," living, expectant, powerful and all-knowing. These last two attributes come out in the second of these present participles ἔχων "having seven horns and seven eyes..." Horn is the symbol of power; seven of perfect power. Eye is symbol of omniscient insight; seven of perfect penetrating discernment. To insure the import of "the seven eyes" there is added a descriptive adjective clause announced by relative οἵ, "which are the seven spirits of God." These seven spirits, as elsewhere, are symbolic of the Holy Spirit. There is also appended a perfect circumstantial participle further describing the "seven spirits" as "having been sent into all the world." Perfect tense suggests that they are sent permanently. ἀπεσταλμένοι takes its case and gender from the relative οἵ rather than the πνεύματα.

Verse seven embodies a compound sentence of two clauses. It reads, "He came and he has taken out of the right..." The verb of the first clause ἦλθεν is a simple historical aorist. It's the normal tense in narrative unless something unusually compelling leads an author to a more moving descriptive device. This author became so excited at that which he was witnessing that he turned from the more prosaic aorist to the dramatic perfect. The second clause has εἴληφεν, "he has taken." John is more than just a reporter; he's emotionally involved. This perfect dramatizes his personal interest in what's going on.

## Revelation 5:8–10

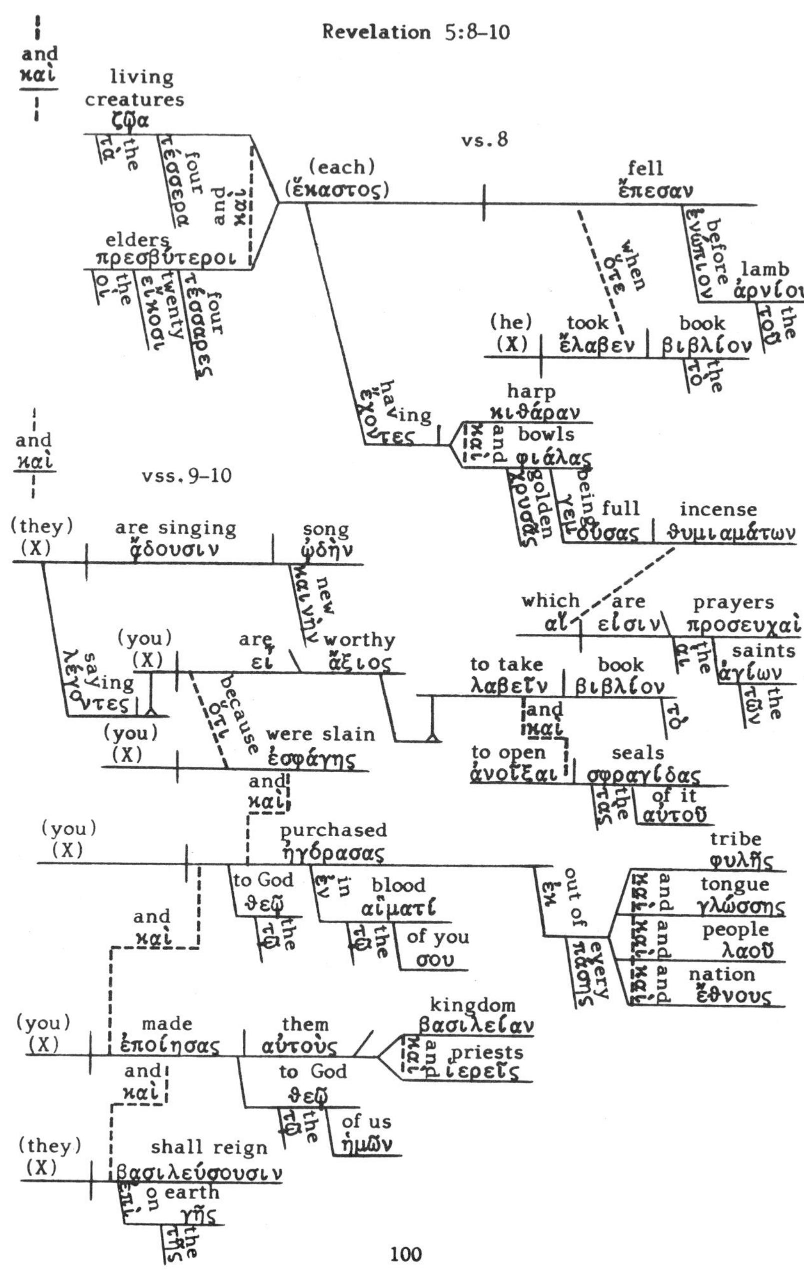

THE DIAGRAM OF 5:8-10

."The four living creatures and the twenty four elders fell before the lamb" is the one independent clause of verse eight. Prefaced to this main idea a temporal adverb clause indicates when they fell in worship, that is, "when he took the book." The inserting of the adjective ἕκαστος "each" in apposition serves to individualize the "living creatures" and the "elders." Describing the "each" is present circumstantial participle ἔχοντες "having." Though "each" is singular the modifying participle is plural. It agrees in sense with the plural "creatures" and "elders." In "harps and bowls" the participle has a compound object. A present circumstantial participle γεμούσας "being full" describes "bowls." Verbs of filling take genitives hence θυμιαμάτων is object of the verbal "being full." This object is described by the adjective clause introduced by relative αἵ, "which are the prayers of the saints."

The clause "they are singing a new song" constitutes the only independent clause in verses 9-10. The verb "are singing" is an example of a descriptive present. It portrays a moving picture of a concert in process. Adjective καινὴν "new" means a new kind of song in distinction from new in terms of time.

Present circumstantial participle λέγοντες modifies the subject "they" and serves to introduce a noun clause telling what the content of the song is. The noun clause is direct object of the participle "saying." The substance of the song is "You are worthy."

Subordinating conjunction ὅτι leads into four adverb dependent clauses. They each advance a cause on which the lamb's worthiness of worship rests. First, "because you were slain..." The death wounds of the lamb revealed the worth of the lamb.

Second, "and (because) you purchased to God in your blood..." Apart from his intrinsic worth he paid the price which made him worthy. Three adverbial ideas modify this verb "purchased." "To God"(θεῷ) is dative, the case of personal interest. Dative shows advantage or disadvantage. In this instance the dative means that he made the purchase "for the advantage of God." The expression "in the blood..." indicates the means of the purchase. The ἐκ phrase speaks of multiple sources out of which the purchase was made.

The third dependent declares another reason why he was worthy; because "you made them a kingdom and priests to our God." The accusative nouns βασιλεῖαν "kings" and ἱερεῖς "priests" are both objective complements filling out the meaning of the direct object "them"(αὐτοὺς). "Kingdom" is singular while "priests" is plural. The lamb made "them" into a unified corporate body, the "people of God." But they retain their individual personalities, each separate one serving in a redemptive role as a priest to God.

The fourth of the clauses, besides giving another cause for his worth, also sums up the consequence of the lamb's slaughter, his purchase, and his making them into a kingdom of priests. The clause proclaims: "...they shall reign..." Very significant is the prepositional adverb phrase "on the earth." The reign of the saints of God is to be "on the earth" in the here and now.

Revelation 5:11-13

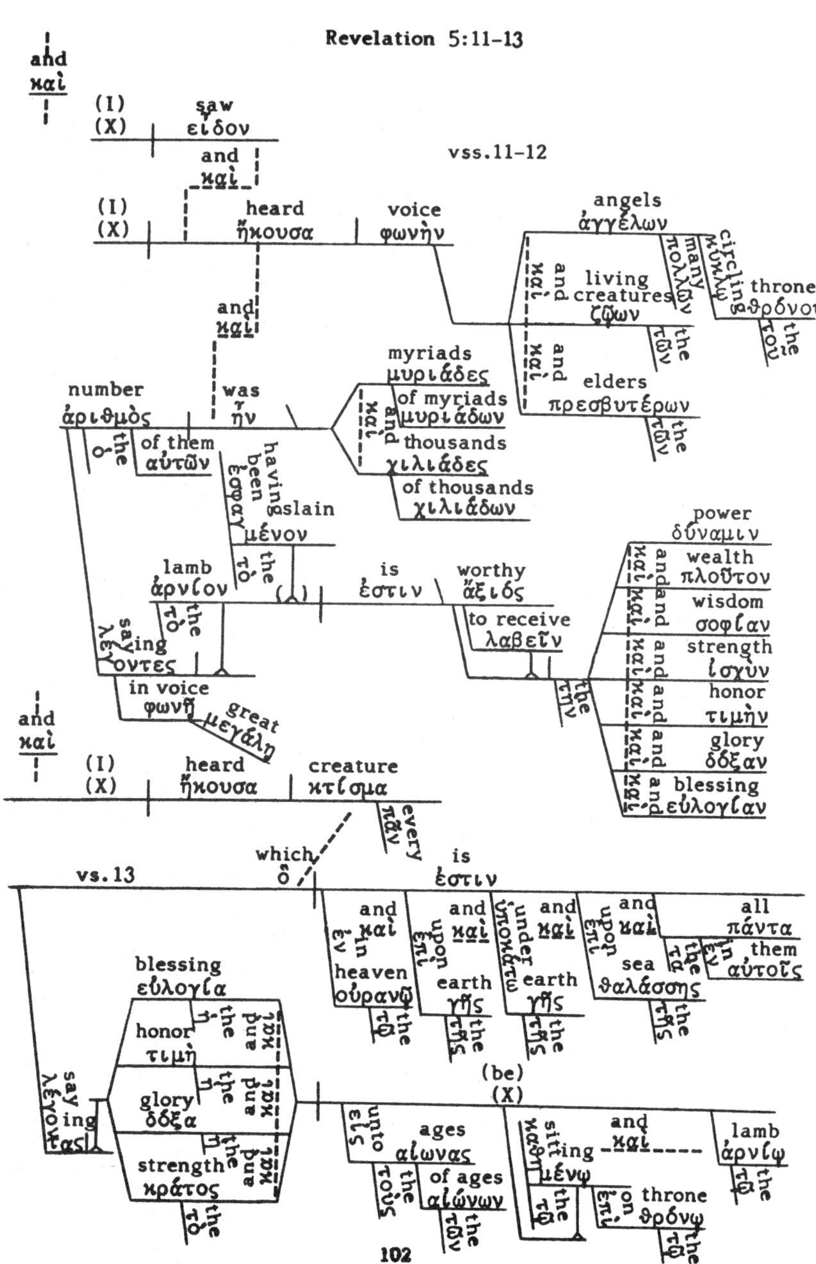

## THE DIAGRAM OF 5:11-13

Verses 11-12 constitute a compound-complex sentence of three independent clauses and one subordinate. Deprived of all modifying elements the three main members state, "I saw...I heard...the number was..." The first of the three has no modifiers; it simply says, "I saw."

The second of these three incorporates a direct object (φωνὴν) which indicates what was heard, a "voice." The kind of voice that was heard appears in three genitives, "angels," living creatures," and "elders." The first of the three genitives(ἀγγέλων)is described by two adjectival modifers. "Many" is just a simple genitive adjective agreeing in case and number. But the expression κύκλῳ is an instrumental literally meaning "in circle." Added to the term "circle" is genitive θρόνου to specify the kind of circle; it's a circle around "the throne." This entire expression seems to describe "angels" rather than as adverb telling where "I heard."

The third of the main clauses declares, "...the number of them was myriads of myriads and thousands of thousands..." The words translated "myriads" and "thousands" are plural predicate nominatives referring back to singular subject ἀριθμὸς. Circumstantial participle λέγοντες modifying "number" is also plural. These agree according to sense, not grammar.

The one dependent idea is a noun clause, object of participle "saying." It gives the content of what was being said: "...the lamb, the one having been slain, is worthy..." Subject of this dependent clause, "the lamb," is further identified by the articular attributive perfect participle ἐσφαγμένον "the one having been slain." Aorist infinitive λαβεῖν is an adverbial accusative expressing result after predicate nominative "worthy." As a verbal the infinitive has a compound object of seven elements all tied together under one article τὴν; "the power and wealth and wisdom and strength and honor and glory and blessing."

The one independent clause of verse 13 declares, "I heard every creature." While that clause, being independent, is self-sufficient it would be much impoverished without the two dependent clauses which fill out this complex sentence. The first of the dependents is adjectival describing κτίσμα = creature. It is introduced by the neuter nominative relative pronoun ὃ. Five adverbial phrases answer the question where; "in the heaven and upon the earth and under the earth and upon the sea, and all the things in them..." Present circumstantial participle "saying" introduces another dependent feature. It is a noun clause direct object of the verbal aspect in the participle. Subject of the clause is the compound idea, "the blessing and the honor and the glory and the strength." The verb "be" or "be given" is implied. An adverbial phrase answering the question how long modifies the understood verb; "unto the ages of the ages." Dative, the case of personal interest, is appropriate for indirect objects καθημένῳ and ἀρνίῳ, "the one sitting" and "the lamb." "The one sitting" represents an attributive present participle.

## EXPOSITORY THOUGHTS ON 5:1-14

Human life which promises such wonderful beauty turns out to be so wickedly baneful. Why? Men are born with instincts for eternity but end up with the decay of death! Why are we created with divine potential but inherit mortal weakness? Instead of peace, power, and purity we experience war, weakness, and wickedness. The brutality of human life with its war, famine, pestilence, and disease leads to doubt as to the power and goodness of God. Is this the best that God could make? What is the secret of human existence? What is the meaning of such a sordid existence as this world offers to human beings? Can the secret of God's governing grace (assuming it is grace) be discovered? Who can explain it?

### The sealed secret

God holds the book containing the secret of his providence. It is full and overflowing with adequate information for it's written "front and back," within and without. Nothing is omitted to satisfy the most demanding conscience. There IS an explanation satisfactory to the most sensitive moral soul. But alas! it is "sealed with seven seals." It is totally and tightly shut to human discovery. No one in heaven, earth or hell can unlock the of God's governing in history. Who can explain the riddle of God's dealings with humanity? Philosophers have ineptly fumbled in the darkness of their ignorance. Poets have lit some flickering lights, soon blown out under the gusts of human misery. Religious thinkers have offered their theological guesses as they grope in their dark moral decay. Man's pain in his moral illiteracy is enough to make a strong man weep. In fact, John confesses that when he saw that no one in "heaven, earth, or under the earth was able to open the book, or to look therein" that he "began to weep much." It's part of humanity's burden that no one can come up with an answer as to the why of human existence? And why God allows such enormous brutal suffering!

But there is an answer! There's one who emerged in history who broke the tightly sealed book of God. "Weep not; behold, the Lion of the tribe of Judah, the root of David, overcame to open the book and the seven seals." What man couldn't and can't discover, God intended to reveal. In the dawn of revelation God promised that Judah, "a lion's whelp," would pass on his ruling scepter to "him to whom it belongs."(Gen.49:9f) And "upon the throne of David" would sit "a shoot from the stump of Jesse...the government will be upon his shoulder."(Is.9:6,11:1) This promised one is he who is "worthy" to open God's book. He can explain the mysteries of God's governing grace and thus relieve the anguished cry of man.

Moreover, man doesn't have to wait for some unknown distant day. The victory of God's grace is already past, a happening in history. Said the elder, "...the root of David overcame to open the book..." God's conquering of evil is an event that has already occurred; it's a matter of record. God's mystery of grace can now be opened, explained, enjoyed!

## The revealed secret

John's attention was captured by a "lamb, standing as if he'd been slaughtered." Lambs don't normally have "horns" but this one had "seven," symbol of perfect power, complete authority. He also had "seven eyes" which, says John, "are the seven spirits of God sent into all the earth." The power of the lamb's horns extends, by God's Spirit, through all creation. In his excitement John can scarcely contain himself. He bursts out, "He's taken the book! He's taken it right out of God's hand." Then followed in rapid succession three doxologies from "the prayers of the saints," and from "thousands of thousands" of angels. Added to these, praise came from "every created thing in heaven, earth, under the earth, the sea and all things in them..." The four living creatures confirmed the praise with their "Amen" while the elders bowed in worship! It would appear that the entire universe was relieved and pleased with the fact that the slain lamb took God's book; and with the fact that he revealed what was in it!

Chapter four revealed the absolute ultimate authority of God as the reigning ruler of the universe. But here's the marvel, the secret of God's rule. He rules by a slaughtered lamb. "Behold, the lamb of God that takes away the sin of the world."(Jn.1:29) It's through pain that God relieves man's pain; it's by suffering that God cures suffering; it's by "reverses" that God makes "advances" in the task of "making man in our image." His perfect power(seven horns)is exercised from a throne in the shape of a cross. And this power of redemption is universally available in "all the earth" for the spirit of God(seven spirits)operates universally.

The "new song" of the prayers of the saints proclaimed, "Worthy art thou...to open the seals...for you were slain..." The thousands upon thousands of angels cried in their loudest voice, "Worthy is the lamb that has been slaughtered..." So it's the slain lamb who redeems man. He also offers his own death as the pattern of God's method of reigning in a sin-stained world.

Fire, earthquake, storm, flood, war, famine, pestilence, are not periods at the end of the sentence. They aren't the final chapter. They're part of the plot, creating the tension that makes life a tragedy of pain. Yet not a final defeat. "If any man would be my disciple he is to deny himself, take up his cross and follow me." This is the paradox of God's rule. No cross! No crown! Every "suffering for righteousness sake" is a cross that brings me closer to the "image of God" into which God is shaping me. Each failure is a step up as measured by God's moral yardstick. "Chastening does not seem for the present joyful but greivous; afterward it yields peaceable fruit to ones being exercised by it."(Heb.12:11) The cross, pain because of righteousness, is a chisel in the divine sculptor's skilled hand by which he is carving a man into his "likeness."

In view of God's grace how can it be but that "every created thing" should say, "Unto him that sits on the throne, and unto the lamb, the blessing, and the honor, and the glory, and the strength unto the ages of the ages." The lamb slain is God's secret!

## A TRANSLATION
## Revelation 6:1-17

And when the lamb opened one of the seven seals, I saw and I heard one of the four living creatures saying, "Come!" And I saw, and Behold!! A white horse! And the one sitting on it (was) having a bow. And a crown was given to him and he, conquering, went out that he might conquer.

And when he opened the second seal I heard the second living creature saying, "Come!" And another horse, firey red, came out. And to take peace from the earth was given to him. to the one sitting on the horse; and that they shall kill one another. And a huge sword was given to him.

And when he opened the third seal, I heard the third living creature saying, "Come!" And I saw, and Behold! A black horse! And the one sitting upon it (was) having scales in his hand. And I heard (that which seemed) like a voice in the midst of the four living creatures saying, "A measure of wheat for a denarius and three measures of barley, a denarius. But don't hurt the oil and the wine.

And when he opened the fourth seal, I heard the voice of the fourth living creature saying, "Come!" And I saw, and Behold! A greenish yellow horse. And the one sitting upon it. his name (was) Death. And Hades was following with him and power was given to them over a fourth of the earth to kill in sword and in famine and in death and by the wild beasts of the earth.

And when he opened the fifth seal, I saw under the altar the souls of the ones having been slaughtered on account of the word of God and on account of the witness which they were having. And they cried with a loud voice saying, "O Master, the holy and true, how long (is it) that you don't judge and avenge our blood from the ones dwelling upon the earth?" And a white robe was given to each of them; and it was told them that they shall rest until their fellow servants and their brethren and the ones about to be killed, as they (were), should be fulfilled.

And when he opened the sixth seal, I looked and a great earthquake became; and the sun became darkened like sackcloth of hair; and the entire moon became like blood and the stars of heaven fell unto the earth as a fig tree, being shaken by the wind, drops its unripe figs; and the heaven was withdrawn like a scroll having been rolled up. And from their places were removed every mountain and island. And the kings of the earth and the great ones and the generals and the rich and the strong and every slave and freedman hid themselves in the caves and in the rocks of the moutains and they say to the mountains and to the rocks, "Fall upon us and hide us from the face of the one sitting on the throne and from the wrath of the lamb, because the great day of their wrath is come and who is able to stand?"

## AN OUTLINE OF REVELATION 6:1-17

Breaking the Seven Seals of History

Do the facts of history sustain the idea that God is just? Is God really sovereign in control of men and events? If so, why conquest? war? famine? death? If God is supreme why have his people suffered from evil governments? Egypt, Babylon, Greece, Rome? And on into the present? Hitler, Stalin, and our own government with ever increasing force invading personal religious conscience of its citizens?

Furthermore, why are we living under constant fear of the world's end by a firey atomic cataclysm?

I. THE LAMB OF GOD "OPENS" THE SECRETS OF THE SEALS. 6:1

1. The lamb identified. The lamb is "worthy" because he was "killed and purchased" the right.(5:9,12)
2. The sovereignty of God is exercised in the slain lamb. Rev.11:15 declares, "the sovereignty of the world became (that) of our Lord and his Christ and he shall reign unto the ages of the ages." All between the first seal and the proclamation of 11:15 to be understood in terms of God's rule in the slain lamb, that is, the gospel.
3. The facts of recent history furnish the frame for the visions of the seven seals.
   (a)The Old Testament.
   (b)Maccabean revolt.
   (c)Rome under Nero.

II. THE OPENING OF THE SEALS. 6:2-17

1. The Four Horsemen. vss.2-8
   (a)The white horse-the Conquerer. A universal ordeal. Yet conquerer conquered by conquerer! He who "takes the sword shall die by the sword."
   (b)Second horseman; "fiery red." War! If he's to master he must make war. He's then destroyed by war.
   (c)The black horseman of Famine. War brings scarcity of food; starvation wages and prices. So the cycle moves relentlessly on to its own destruction.
   (d)The "pale green" horse of Death. Followed by Hades who gathers up the corpses of the earlier three. All these four must be read in view of gospel facts.
2. The Fifth Seal. 6:9-11
   (a)God's people do suffer and die in this world as it is.
   (b)Just recompense on evil rulers does come.
   (c)Saints who have suffered are safe "under the altar."
   (d)They wear "white robes" of victory and purity.
   (e)They are one with living brethren yet to suffer.
3. The sixth Seal. 6:12-17
   The end of history not an accident with no purpose but a goal reached with moral, ethical meaning for present trials.

The consummation contains the validation of God's truth revealed in history. The meaning of the cross in view of the end.

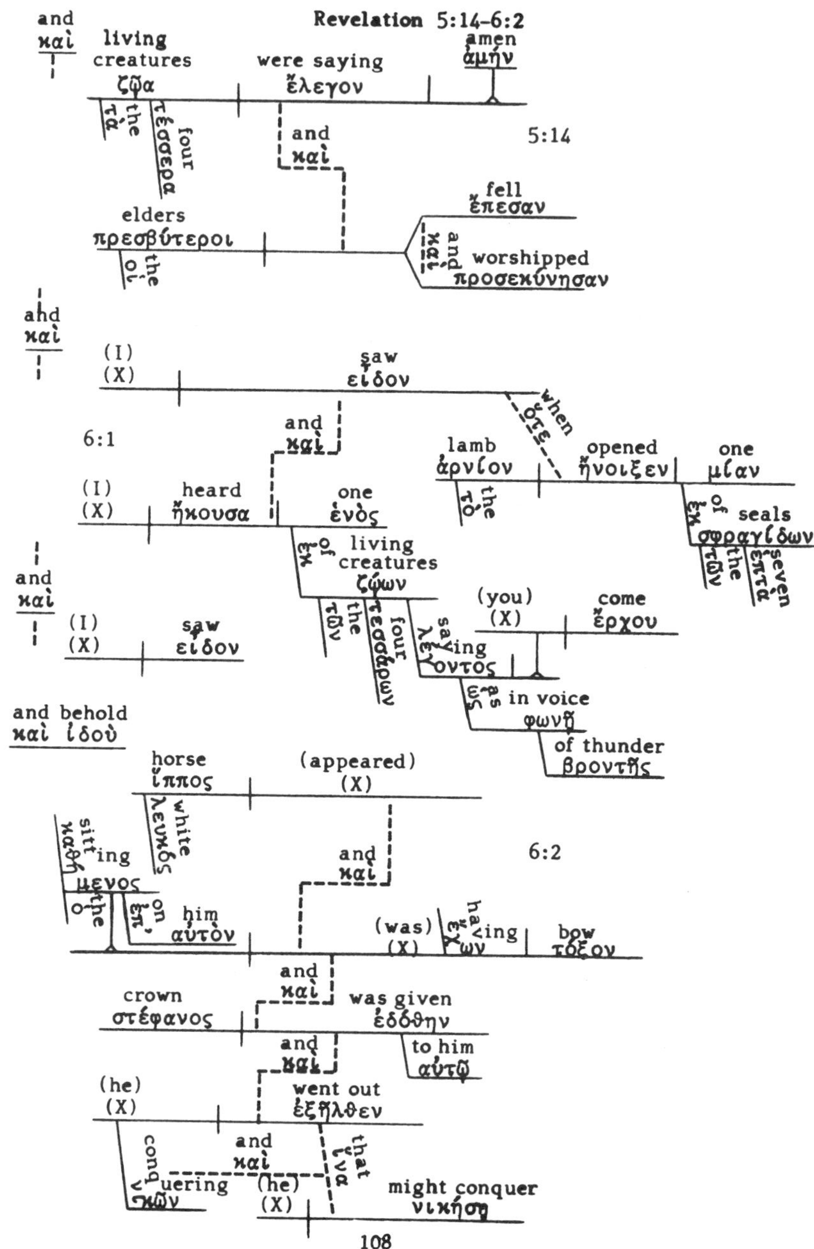
Revelation 5:14–6:2
and
καὶ
living creatures
ζῷα
τὰ the
τέσσερα four
were saying
ἔλεγον
amen
ἀμήν
5:14
and
καὶ
elders
πρεσβύτεροι
οἱ the
fell
ἔπεσαν
καὶ and
worshipped
προσεκύνησαν
and
καὶ
(I)
(X)
saw
εἶδον
when
ὅτε
6:1
lamb
ἀρνίον
τὸ the
opened
ἤνοιξεν
one
μίαν
ἐκ of
seals
σφραγίδων
τῶν the
ἑπτὰ seven
and
καὶ
(I)
(X)
heard
ἤκουσα
one
ἑνὸς
ἐκ of
living creatures
ζῴων
τῶν the
τεσσάρων four
λέγοντος saying
(you)
(X)
come
ἔρχου
ὡς as
in voice
φωνῇ
of thunder
βροντῆς
and
καὶ
(I)
(X)
saw
εἶδον
and behold
καὶ ἰδοὺ
horse
ἵππος
λευκός white
(appeared)
(X)
6:2
καθήμενος sitting
ὁ the
ἐπ' on
him
αὐτὸν
and
καὶ
(was)
(X)
ἔχων having
bow
τόξον
and
καὶ
crown
στέφανος
was given
ἐδόθη
to him
αὐτῷ
and
καὶ
(he)
(X)
went out
ἐξῆλθεν
νικῶν conquering
and
καὶ
that
ἵνα
(he)
(X)
might conquer
νικήσῃ
108

## THE DIAGRAM OF REVELATION 5:14-6:2

Revelation 5:14 contains a sentence of two equal clauses. It is compound in its pattern. The first clause echoes the approval of "the four living creatures" to the song of universal praise of the preceding sentence. "The four living creatures were saying, 'Amen.'" ἔλεγον is imperfect indicative active. It is probably a distributive imperfect; each separate "living creature" personally said the "Amen." ἀμήν is an indeclinable verbal particle here used as a noun, direct object of "were saying." It expresses solemn approval of a prayer, praise, song, exhortation etc.

The second clause of this compound sentence has a compound predicate; "the elders fell and worshipped." The verbs are both aorists, "they fell and worshipped." The physical act of falling was point action. The spiritual act of "worship" was linear in its Aktionsart but focused to a point in the way the author chose to present the attitude and act of worship.

The first verse of chapter six accommodates a compound-complex sentence. It possesses two independent clauses and two dependent. The adverbial conjunction ὅτι is the harbinger of the first of the dependent clauses. It announces <u>when</u> the action of the main verbs took place; "...when the lamb opened one of the seven seals..." It was then that "I saw...and...I heard..." Precisely <u>what he</u> heard is seen in direct object ἑνὸς. It is genitive after <u>verb of</u> hearing. ἐκ with ablative ζῴων is an example of the ablative in the partitive sense as indeed ἐκ with partitive ablative appeared in the temporal ὅτε clause. As an added predicate description to ζῴων is present circumstantial participle λέγοντες. It is genitive in case but singular in number; its number is probably influenced by ἑνὸς. Adverb ὡς practically functions as a preposition introducing the phrase, "as in a great voice." The participle "saying" has for its direct object the noun clause of exhortation, "You come!"

Strictly speaking, the "I saw" with which 6:2 opens is a simple sentence. But it serves as an exclamatory interjection coupled with the "and behold!" Leaving this double barrelled interjection aside the remainder of the sentence is compound-complex. It employs four independent clauses. It also has one dependent clause joined by conjunction καὶ to a circumstantial participle.

The first clause simply states, "white horse (appeared)..." The second is a bit more entangled with an attributive participle as subject of a paraphrastic verb; "...the one sitting on him (was) having a bow..." ἔχων is present active participle supplementing an implied "was" forming the paraphrastic. The third clause returns to a simple idea; "...crown was given to him..."

The final of the four independents states "he went out." But to it is joined the adverbial ἵνα clause of purpose, "in order that he might conquer." The circumstantial participle νικῶν is to be classed as purpose. As adjective the participle describes subject "he" but as verb it is present tense, linear action. It also suggests the adverbial purpose idea paralleling the full ἵνα clause.

Revelation 6:3-4

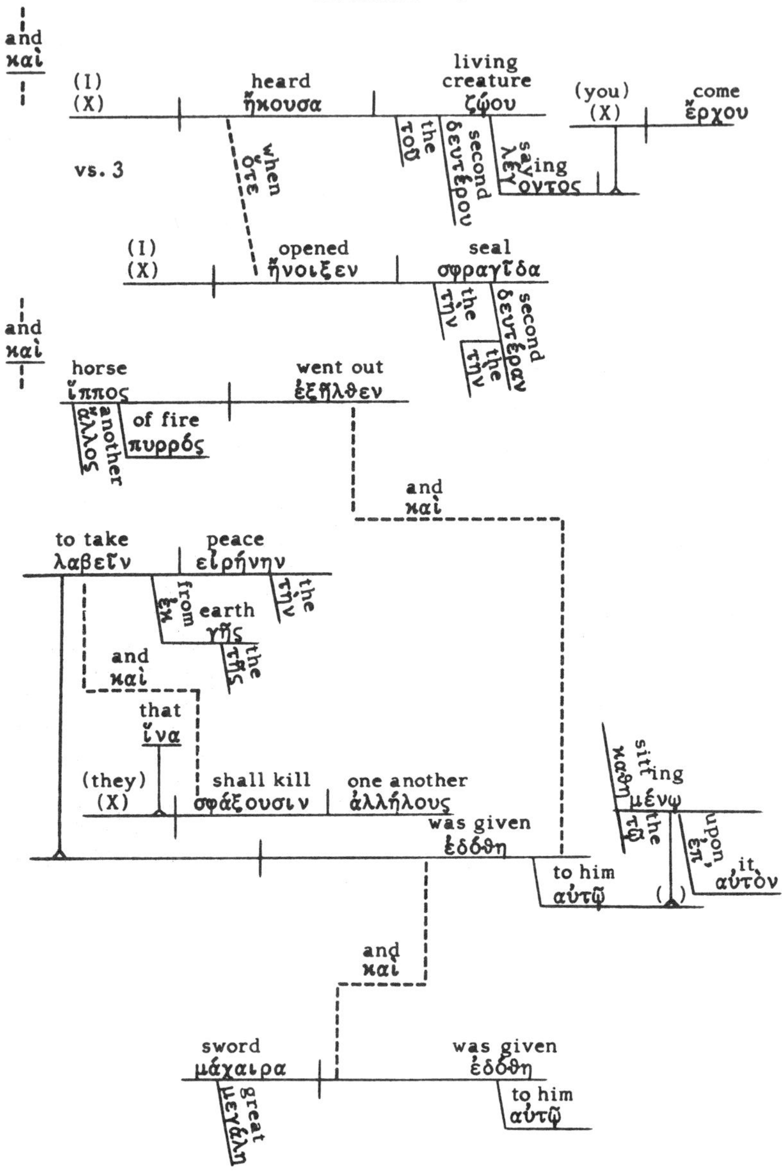

# THE DIAGRAM OF REVELATION 6:3-4

The invitation of the second "living creature" to "Come" is incorporated in a three-clause complex sentence. The main clause of verse five states, "I heard the second living creature..." Direct object ζῴου is genitive case after ἤκουσα. Describing this object is the present circumstantial participle λέγοντος = "saying." As direct object of that participle is the dependent noun clause, "You come!" The point of time at which John heard this invitation of the second living creature is put forward in the dependent adverbial clause introduced by ὅτε, "when he opended the second seal."

What John envisioned when he responded to the invitation to "come" is set forth in three clauses of verse four. It is a compound-complex sentence with three independent units. The first declares, "Another horse went out..." The kind of horse is specified by genitive πυρρός = firey red.

The next two of the independents have as their verb the first aorist indicative passive ἐδόθη = was given. To whom it "was given" appears in both clauses in an indirect object αὐτῷ, to him! To identify more clearly who this "him" is the present attributive participle καθημένῳ is added in apposition; "the one sitting upon him."

**Subject** of "was given" of the second independent is a compound combination consisting of an infinitive phrase and a noun clause prefixed by ἵνα. That an infinitive is subject is quite normal since it by definition is a verbal-noun. And as verb it's nothing unusual to take a direct object as here in "peace." This infinitive also has the prepositional phrase "from the earth" serving as adverb indicating "from whence."

Normally an infinitive with object and modifiers such as this is called a phrase rather than a clause because it has no subject. Yet here it performs a similar function as the full ἵνα clause certainly does. Without question "that they shall kill one another" is a clause. So sometimes it may seem quite arbitrary to force grammatical classifications on the way we write and speak. Yet we do need to organize our human speech so as to be able to ferret out the tangled involvement of human thought. In the present instance the ἵνα clause seems to spell out in more explicit details just what is occasioned in "taking peace from the earth."

The final independent clause is really a repeat summary of the idea in the second clause. But this time the author uses the symbol of "sword" as a sign embodying the "taking peace from the earth." It reads "...a great sword was given to him."

## Revelation 6:5–6

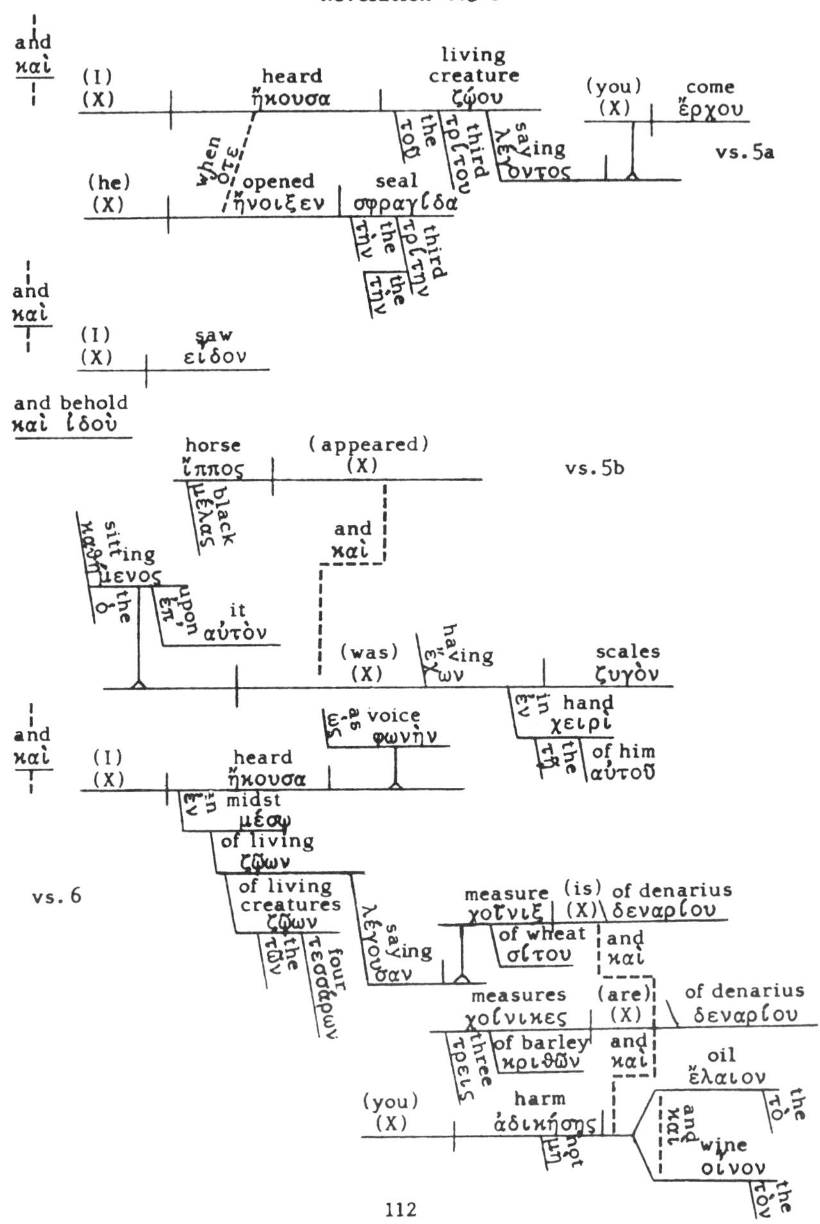

## THE DIAGRAM OF REVELATION 6:5-6

In structure the sentence of 6:5a is exactly the same as that of 6:3. It is a complex with a temporal ὅτε clause indicating when the action of the main clause took place. And it also has the noun clause, direct object of participle λέγοντος. The only difference of any kind is the numeral "three" in place of "two."

As in 6:2 so here in 6:5b the full clause "I saw" appears with interjection "behold" as a kind of double-barrelled exclamation. It serves to express the excited enthusiasm of the author having the vision and thereby more effectively grabs the attention of the reader.

The sentence of 6:5b itself is a compound of two clauses. The first clause attests, "A black horse (appeared)..." Among the ancients the adjective translated "black" held the idea of something sinister or dreadfully sad, horrible or unlucky. Its presence here suggests Famine, the rueful results of the two previous horses of Conquest and War!

The second clause of this compound sentence has for its subject an attributive participial phrase, "the one sitting upon it." The prepositional expression "upon it" is adverbial in function telling where the rider was sitting. The verb consists of an understood "was"(ἦν) plus present active participal ἔχων. Together they form a peraphrastic imperfect. Such a construction paints a more vivid picture of the linear action involved. A point action would merely have reported the fact that the rider "had scales." By use of the imperfect, particularly the paraphrastic form, the author throws on the screen of imagination a colorful moving picture.

Once again we note the use of a prepositional phrase "in his hand" to tell <u>where</u> he was having the scales. Any phrase will function in one of three ways. Either as noun, adjective, or adverb.

Verse six comprises a complex sentence. Its one independent clause asserts "I heard." The direct object of the verb "heard" would normally be the simple noun φωνὴν. But here the adverbial particle ὡς is thrust in. The full idea might be expressed: "I heard as though I were hearing a voice..." That would entail a full additional dependent clause. However, the diagram treats the ὡς phrase as direct object of the main verb. The phrase "in the midst" is adverbial. It tells <u>where</u> the voice was or <u>from whence</u> the voice came.

By joining the present circumstantial participle λέγουσαν to φωνὴν the writer says he heard something "like" a voice. Possibly that of one of those "creatures." The participal has three dependent noun clauses as direct objects. They are: "A measure of wheat (is) for a denarius," "three measures of barley (are) for a denarius," and "don't harm the oil and the wine." The genitive δεναρίου, appearing twice here, is genitive of price.

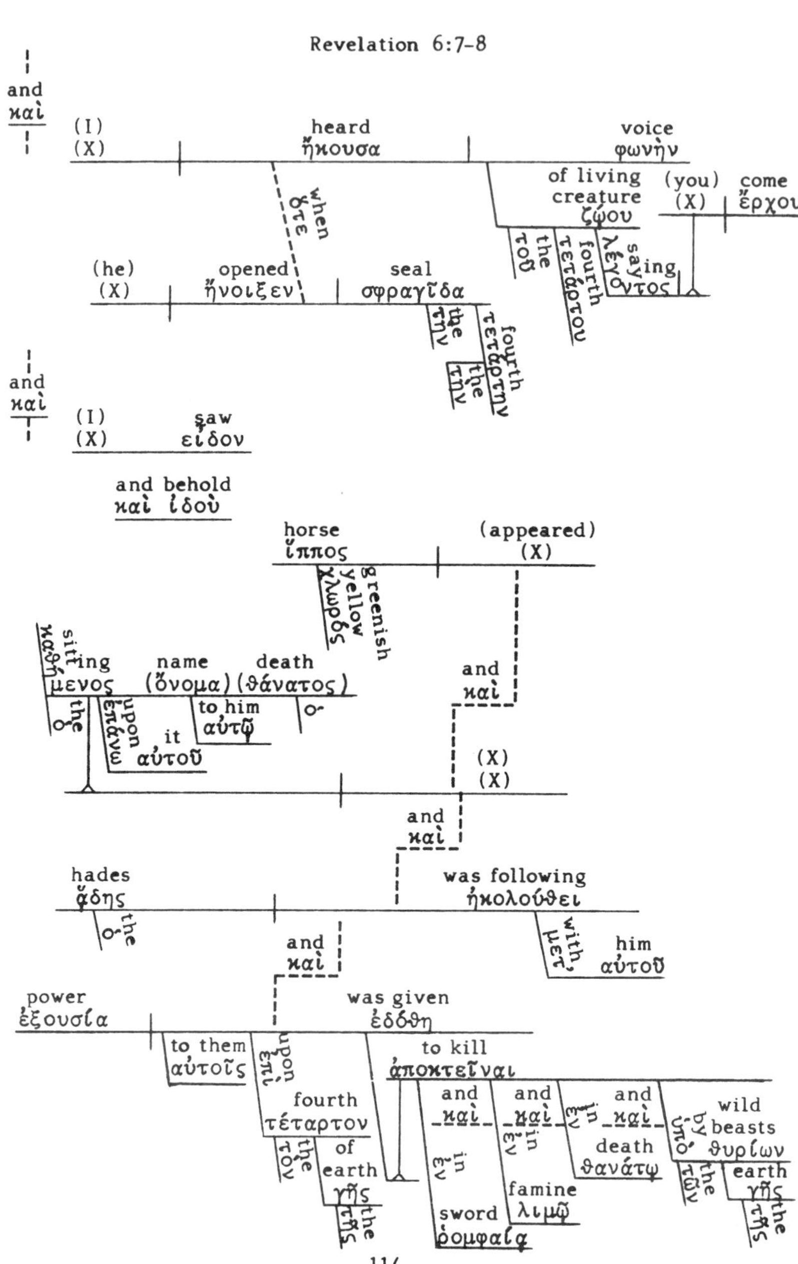
and
καὶ
(I)
(X)
heard
ἤκουσα
voice
φωνὴν
when
ὅτε
of living
creature
ζῴου
the
τοῦ
fourth
τετάρτου
saying
λέγοντος
(you)
(X)
come
ἔρχου
(he)
(X)
opened
ἤνοιξεν
seal
σφραγῖδα
the
τὴν
fourth
τετάρτην
the
τὴν
and
καὶ
(I)
(X)
saw
εἶδον
and behold
καὶ ἰδοὺ
horse
ἵππος
(appeared)
(X)
greenish
yellow
χλωρός
sitting
καθήμενος
the
ὁ
upon
ἐπάνω
it
αὐτοῦ
name
(ὄνομα)
to him
αὐτῷ
death
(θάνατος)
ὁ
and
καὶ
(X)
(X)
and
καὶ
hades
ᾅδης
the
ὁ
was following
ἠκολούθει
with
μετ'
him
αὐτοῦ
and
καὶ
power
ἐξουσία
was given
ἐδόθη
to them
αὐτοῖς
upon
ἐπὶ
fourth
τέταρτον
the
τὸ
of
earth
γῆς
the
τῆς
to kill
ἀποκτεῖναι
and
καὶ
in
ἐν
sword
ῥομφαίᾳ
and
καὶ
in
ἐν
famine
λιμῷ
in
ἐν
and
καὶ
death
θανάτῳ
by
ὑπὸ
wild
beasts
θηρίων
the
τῶν
earth
γῆς
the
τῆς

## THE DIAGRAM OF REVELATION 6:7-8

The sentence which tells of the opening of the fourth seal is exactly the same category as that of 6:3 and 6:5a. Note comments at those points. The sentence, of course, is complex.

Verse eight develops a compound sentence of four independent clauses. After a repetition of the double injerjection, "I saw and behold!" the first clause introduces the fourth horse; "A pale greenish-yellow horse (appeared)..."

The second clause of this sentence is similar in structure to the second clause of the compound sentence of 6:5b. But there is a noticeable difference. In 6:5b the subject-participle καθήμενος is followed by a paraphrastic verb "(was) having" and a direct object. But here in 6:8, though we have the same participial subject, there is no expressed verb with an object. In thought (though not formally) the clause might have read, "the one sitting upon it (was having) a name of death..." However, the author placed "name" as direct object of the subject participle. Then he put "death" in apposition to "name." He inserted also the αὐτῷ as dative of possession to indicate <u>whose</u> name was "death." What verb is to be supplied in this clause must be determined from the context. It might be, "...the one sitting... (also appeared...)"

The third clause says, "and the Hades was following with him..." The imperfect ἠκολούθει represents durative action in past time. As usual it presents a moving picture of the action rather than an aoristic snapshot. It's much more descriptive! The concern of prepositional phrase μεθ' is adverbial. It's worth while to note the μετά with Genitive suggests the idea of "fellowship." "Hades was following in fellowship with Death!" Both Death and Hades are personified; as Death executes, Hades swallows up the spirits of those killed in death.

The last of the four clauses relates that "...power was given to them..." The extent of this power is still not the ultimate for it extends only "upon the fourth part of the earth..." Thus the ἐπὶ phrase is adverbial telling how far. The purpose of the power's being given finds expression in the aorist infinitive "to kill." The means by which the killing takes place appears in three phrases using ἐν with locative plus one using ὑπὸ and ablative.

A word about ἐξουσία is in order. It derives from present participle of εἰμί = I am (οὖσα) and preposition ἐκ = out of. It is the kind of power that springs from "being." It's not arbitrary power imposed from without but that which is inherent, springing from within because of the nature of things. It's not the power of a fast-falling pile-driving hydraulic hammer but rather the power of the growing herb that cracks the concrete because of the upward surge of life within the green plant. In the present use of the term here it suggests that death has within it the inherent power to kill. Death is not arbitrarily "sent" by God. But death has been placed in the seed of sin in such a way that death is the inevitable fruit. "In the day that you eat you will surely die." That's not arbitrary; its in the nature of things.

Revelation 6:9-11

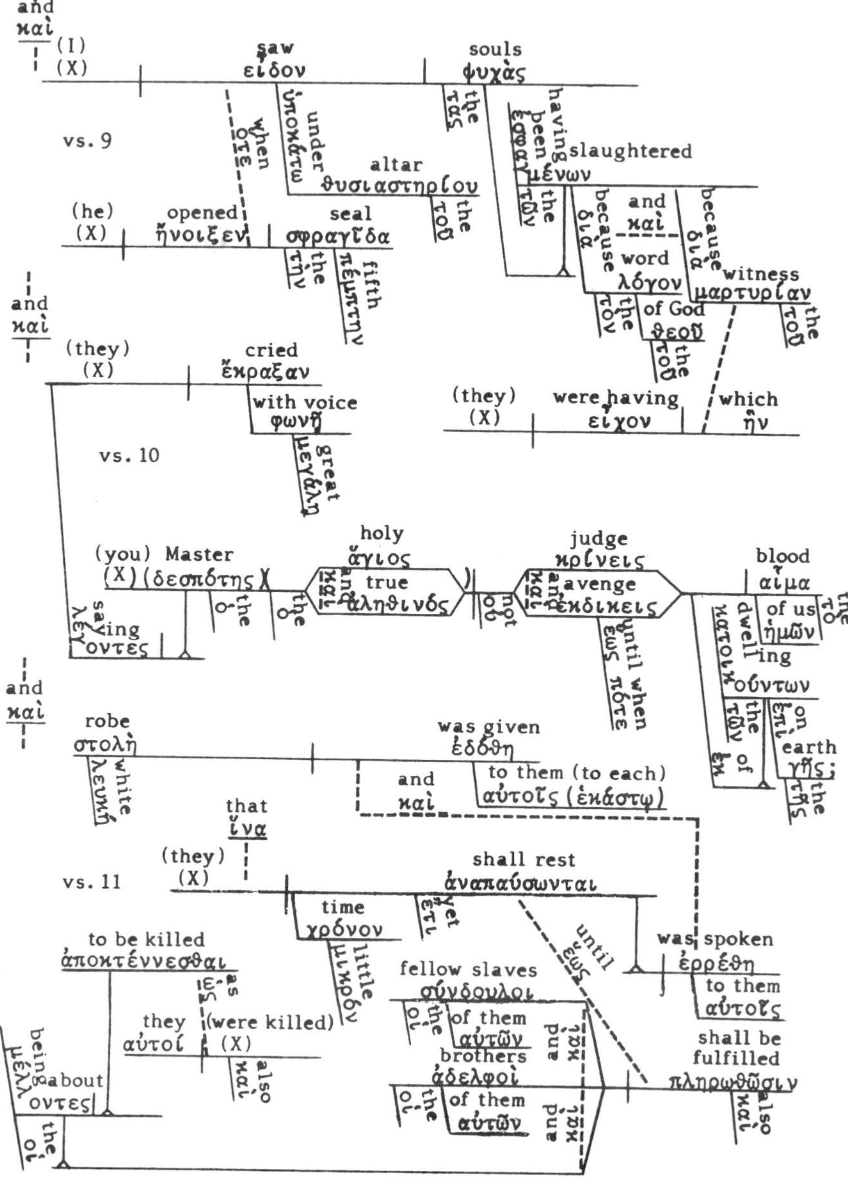

## THE DIAGRAM OF REVELATION 6:9–11

Verse nine embraces a complex sentence of three clauses. The independent member affirms, "I saw the souls..." When he saw the souls is testified to in the ὅτε adverb clause, "when he opened the fifth seal." Where the souls were that he saw is designated by the prepositional phrase, "under the altar." ὑποκάτω, an improper preposition, is used with the ablative case. Suffix -τηρ indicates place. Hence θυσιαστηρίου indicates the place where a sacrifice takes place, that is, an altar. Thus here "under the altar" seems to suggest that these "souls" which John saw are secure under the "place of the sacrifice." To point out more definitely which souls he saw the apostle introduces the attributive perfect passive participle ἐσφαγμένων = "the ones having been slaughtered." Why they were slaughtered appears in two adverb phrases using διά with accusative, "because of the word of God" and "because of the testimony..." This "testimony" is described by an adjective dependent clause, "which they were having."

Verse ten embodies another complex composition. "They cried" is the independent statement. The instrumental φωνῇ with adjective is an adverbial phrase indicating how much they cried.

The dependent portion of verse ten appears as a noun clause direct object of circumstantial participle λέγοντες. The subject "you" is sharply emphatic by virtue of δεσπότης in apposition. This word translated "Master" suggests unrestricted power of total ownership. The subject is further sharpened by the addition of two adjectives under the influence of one article, "the holy and true..." Finishing out the clause in the form of a rhetorical question the cry of the altar-secured saints implores, "...are you not judging and avenging our blood from the ones dwelling on the earth?" ἐκ with present active attributive participle "the ones dwelling" intimates that vengeance finds its origins in something within "the ones dwelling on the earth." In their having wronged the saints lies the source of the need for vengeance on the part of him who is essentially "holy and true."

The sentence of verse 11 is compound-complex in its structure. The two independent clauses inform us that "...a white robe was given" and "that they shall rest was spoken to them..." The rest of the sentence consists of a dependent segment introduced by the subordinating temporal conjunction ἕως = until. Subject of this dependent unit is a three-part compound combination, "their fellow-slaves and their brothers and the ones being about to be killed.." Both participle μέλλοντες and its object infinitive ἀποκτέννεσθαι are present. The linear idea in the usage here would seem to be distributive. The infinitive is not so much describing the deaths as indicating the successive death of each separate one of "their fellow-slaves and their brothers." Modifying the infinitive is dependent adverb clause of comparison, "as they also (were killed)." The entire subordinate ἕως clause reads, "...until their fellow-slaves and their brothers and the ones being about to be killed, as they also (were killed) shall be fulfilled."

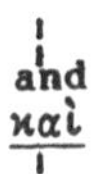
and
καὶ
(I)
(X)
saw
εἶδον
when
ὅτε
(he)
(X)
opened
ἤνοιξεν
seal
σφραγῖδα
the
τὴν
sixth
ἕκτην
the
τὴν
and
καὶ
earthquake
σεισμὸς
great
μέγας
became
ἐγένετο
and
καὶ
sun
ἥλιος
the
ὁ
became
ἐγένετο
black
μέλας
like
ὡς
sackcloth
σάκκος
of hair
τρίχινος
and
καὶ
moon
σελήνη
the
ἡ
whole
ὅλη
became
ἐγένετο
like
ὡς
blood
αἷμα
and
καὶ
stars
ἀστέρες
the
οἱ
of heaven
οὐρανοῦ
the
τοῦ
fell
ἔπεσαν
unto
εἰς
earth
γῆν
the
τὴν
as
ὡς
fig tree
συκῆ
being shaken
σειομένη
by
ὑπὸ
wind
ἀνέμου
great
μεγάλου
casts
βάλλει
unripe
ὀλύνθους
the
τοὺς
of her
αὐτῆς
and
καὶ
heaven
οὐρανὸς
the
ὁ
was separated
ἀπεχωρίσθη
like
ὡς
book
βιβλίον
having been rolled up
ἑλισσόμενον
and
καὶ
mountain
ὄρος
and
καὶ
island
νῆσος
every
πᾶν
were moved
ἐκινήθησαν
out of
ἐκ
places
τόπων
the
τῶν
of them
αὐτῶν

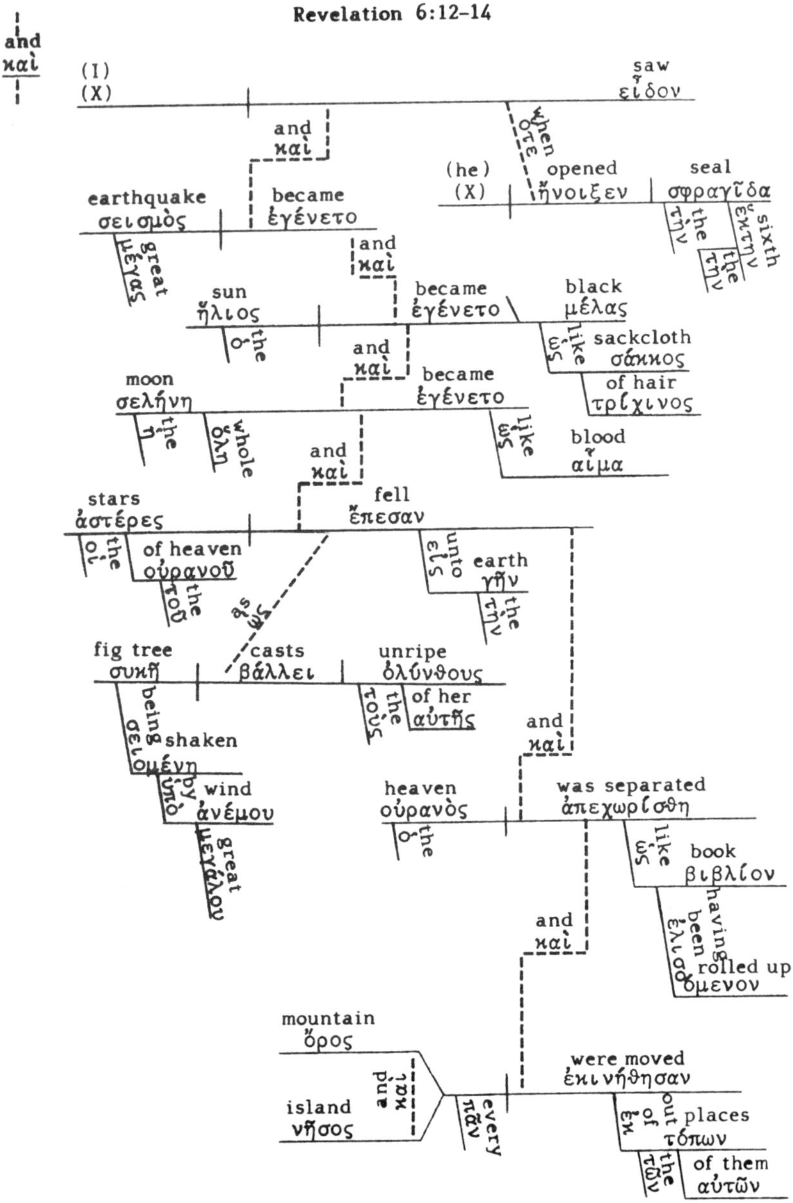

## THE DIAGRAM OF REVELATION 6:12-14

The text treats 6:12-14 as one sentence. It entertains seven independent clauses. To the first and fourth of these is attached adverbial subordinate clauses. Thus the sentence is classified as compound-complex.

The initial declaration is, "I saw..." Exactly when he saw is set forth in the adverbial ὅτε clause: "...when he opened the sixth seal..."

The second of the independent units tells what the author saw "when he opened..." That is, "a great earthquake became..." In this and the next two clauses the verb is 2nd aorist ἐγένετο. "Became" is more than "was" as "become" is more than "is" or "be" as indeed γίνομαι is different than εἰμί. It signifies something vital, potential, latent within that pushes its way out from within until it is outwardly manifest. Something interior becomes exterior!

A third independent clause states, "the sun became black..." The diagram presents an expression introduced by ὡς = "as" to describe predicate adjective μέλας. As the diagram has it ὡς is treated as prepositional adverb like any normal preposition with a noun. This is certainly acceptable. However, it might be conceived of as an eliptical dependent clause: "...as a sackcloth of hair (is black)..." ὡς appears twice more in this sentence and is treated in similar fashion.

The fourth independent member moves to describe what happened to the moon: "the entire moon became like blood." Here is the second use of the adverbial preposition ὡς; "like blood."

In the fifth independent component the author tells what he saw happen to the stars. "The stars of heaven fell to the earth." At this point instead of the prepositional use of ὡς he inserts a full adverbial clause of comparison introduced by ὡς; "as a fig tree, being shaken by a great wind, casts her unripe (figs.)" σειομένη is present passive participle of σείω = shake, agitate. The context suggests a temporal idea, "when shaken..." Present tense of this participle combines with present tense βάλλει to give a vivid picture of what always happens to unripe figs during a heavy windstorm; it's customary, repeated action. These presents contrast with aorist ἔπεσαν of the independent clause. The stars in a once-for-all decisive event "fell" just as unripe figs customarily fall during storms.

The verb in the sixth main clause ἀπεχωρίσθη in the diagram is translated "was separated." In Acts 15:39 it means "to separate yourselves from." Here the separation is "like a scroll (book) "having been rolled up" and stored away. The idea is that the heaven was rolled up and taken away. The aorist tense presents the fact as fact without any attempt to describe the action.

The final of the seven independent clauses brings that which John "saw" in this vision to a conclusion. Starting with a "great earthquake" he saw disturbing effects on sun, moon, stars, heaven and now "every mountain and island." They "were removed out of their places." All seven of the main clauses use the narrative aorist to present the action. The aorist reports; linear action tenses describe.

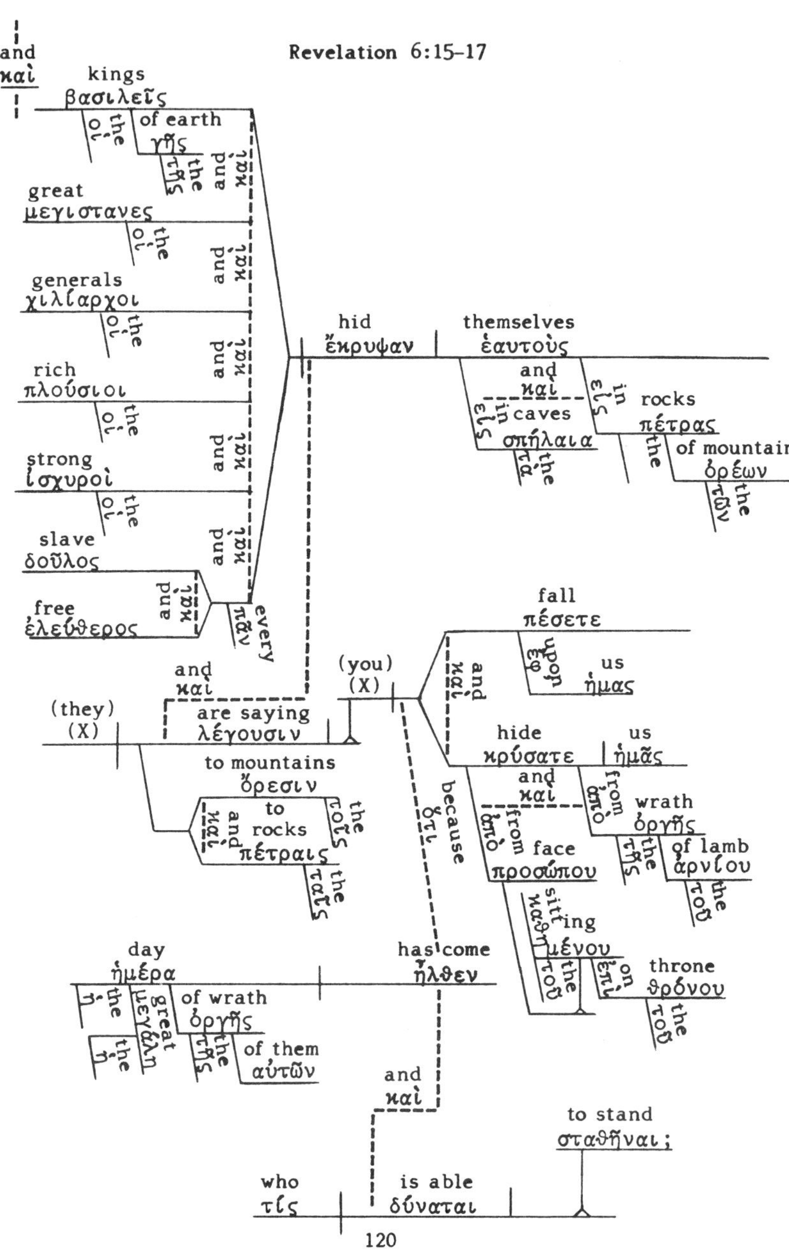
and
καὶ
kings
βασιλεῖς
the
οἱ
of earth
γῆς
the
τῆς
and
καὶ
great
μεγιστανες
the
οἱ
generals
χιλίαρχοι
the
οἱ
rich
πλούσιοι
the
οἱ
strong
ἰσχυροὶ
the
οἱ
slave
δοῦλος
and
καὶ
free
ἐλεύθερος
every
πᾶν
hid
ἔκρυψαν
themselves
ἑαυτοὺς
in
εἰς
caves
σπήλαια
the
τὰ
in
εἰς
rocks
πέτρας
the
of mountains
ὀρέων
the
τῶν
(they)
(X)
are saying
λέγουσιν
to mountains
ὄρεσιν
the
τοῖς
to
rocks
πέτραις
the
ταῖς
(you)
(X)
fall
πέσετε
upon
ἐφ
us
ἡμας
hide
κρύσατε
us
ἡμᾶς
from
ἀπὸ
face
προσώπου
sitting
καθημένου
the
τοῦ
on
ἐπὶ
throne
θρόνου
wrath
ὀργῆς
of lamb
ἀρνίου
because
ὅτι
day
ἡμέρα
the
ἡ
great
μεγάλη
of wrath
ὀργῆς
of them
αὐτῶν
has come
ἦλθεν
who
τίς
is able
δύναται
to stand
σταθῆναι;

## THE DIAGRAM OF REVELATION 6:15-17

As the diagram appears 6:15-17 comprises a compound-complex sentence of five clauses. The first of its two independent clauses has a somewhat extensive subject. It's made up of six separate components. Of these six each of the first five displays its own definite article. For this reason each of the five stands out distinctly: "the kings of the earth, and the great, and the generals, and the rich, and the strong..." The last of the six subjects is itself a compound, "every slave and free..." The second member of these two, the word "free," in the extent of its idea encompasses the first five elements of the compound subject. All these five classes of people constitute the "free." They plus the "slaves" make up all humanity as embodied in the Graeco-Roman civilization of the first century A.D.

The first independent clause declares, "And the kings etc...hid themselves..." The second records, "they are saying..."

The first of the three dependent clauses is a noun clause, direct object of the verb λέγουσιν. "...you fall upon us and hide us..." The aorist imperatives πέσετε and κρύσατε are quite appropriate to the action requested. When a man tries to escape from the "face" of God and the "wrath of the lamb" he invokes immediate decisive results. He doesn't want prolonged disintegration. He prefers quick annihilation. Aorists are appropriate to such feelings.

Modifying aorist κρύσατε are two adverb phrases both of which are introduced by preposition ἀπὸ = from: "...from the face of the one sitting on the throne" and "from the wrath of the lamb..." The preposition ἀπό is only used with the ablative case, the case of separation. These two ἀπό phrases dramatize the ultimate fear of sin-filled man in the presence of absolute holiness of the reigning holy one "sitting on the throne," not to mention abused and rejected love of the slain lamb. "Hide us" is the anguished cry of the lost! The sinful want to be removed "from" the presence of Him who is sinless; and from the lamb whose sacrificial love bridged the gap between sin and salvation.

One clear reason for such terrified cries is set forth by the ὅτι adverbial clause of cause: "because the day of their wrath came..." The wrath of God which has been inexorably working throughout life comes to a climax. Wrong thinking, wrong feeling, wrong doing is now to come face to face with its own results. "The day of his wrath came!"

A second adverb causal clause raises an inevitable question: "...and who is able to stand?" To ask is to answer such a question. No one is able to stand. Aorist active infinitive σταθῆναι as direct object of δύναται fills out the meaning of the verb, "..is able to stand?"

## EXPOSITORY THOUGHTS ON 6:1-17

The "lamb opened one of the seals..." The lamb's opening the seals signifies that Jesus Christ explains certain facts as they relate to the sovereignty of God. Certain questions find answers in the light of God's supreme kingship. These questions the lamb deals with in the symbol of breaking the seven seals. The problems are problems because God does rule in human events.

From the dawn of history Conquest, followed by War, Famine and Death has been the baneful curse of humanity. The first four seals represent the recurring appearance of these four afflictions of the race. First came the white horse and "the one sitting upon him (was) having a bow..." The Parthians, not the Romans, used the bow with their cavalry, a scourge from the East! This horseman designates the curse of conquest; he "went out conquering that he might conquer." "You covet and cannot obtain; so you fight and make war.(Jas.4:2) There's ever a Hitler, a Napoleon, a Domitian to conquer. In an immoral society there will always be one who lusts to conquer.

Conquest arouses resistance. That prompts the second horseman, the red horse of War, to ride. "And to take peace from the earth was given to him...and that they should kill one another. And a huge sword was given to him." The Conquerer must invade; the invaded declares war. Because God is king this is a law of life. "All who take the sword shall perish by the sword." He who commits evil shall be destroyed by that evil. This is God ruling in Christ.

The third horseman rides a black horse. He holds aloft a "balance in his hand." And a voice cried, "A measure of wheat for a day's wage, a denarius. Three measures of barley for a denarius." An inevitable result of war is famine, a shortage of food, a skyrocketing of prices until a day's wage scarcely buys enough to keep body and soul together. If God is king why allow the pains of famine? The real question is, "If God be sovereign in a moral, spiritual universe, how can he not allow famine?" It's the conquerer and war-monger, the greedy profiteer, who disregards moral right. If a moral king rules, suffering of famine follows immorality as night follows day. It's because God in Christ does rule that evil inflicts pain on the innocent and the good.

The fourth seal unveils a rider on a "pale green" horse. He represents "Death." And "Hades followed after." These twin evils swallow up a "fourth part of the earth" with "sword, famine, death, and wild beasts." Like a gleaner he garners in his net the gory results of the three previous horsemen. Yet it's not total for his gorging is limited to a "fourth part of the earth."

If God is good, supremely and solely moral, honoring right as right and wrong as wrong then it's certain that immoral behaviour is the seed the harvest of which is Conquest, War, Famine, and Death. If Christ identified with sinners his death reveals the fact and method of God's sovereign rule.

Opening the fifth seal reveals the injustices committed against those who were "slain for the word of God..." How can God be "good" and be so blind to the inequities perpetrated against the righteous? "Vengeance belongs to me" says the Lord but he seldom seems to vent his promised vengeance! The lamb offers two answers to this "problem" of faith. First, "...a white robe was given to each of them." He who is genuinely good but suffers for "his testimony" does not decline in the quality of his goodness. He who is truly righteous and becomes a martyr to his righteousness does not suffer any loss of righteousness. In fact, just the contrary. He is given the "white robe" of God's purity. His very martyrdom sealed his righteousness. His death demonstrates his redemption. Moreover, "Be patient! Rest yet a little while until your fellow-servants meet their unjust death." "Blessed are you when men shall persecute you for so did they persecute the prophets." Crimes committed against the righteous in a sin-afflicted world is an identifying badge. Injustice is the mark of "belonging" to the select group of the people of God. In addition, "yet a little while" wrongs will be righted!

Human history is not a cycle with no end. It is a journey with a definite goal. It's a line, not a circle! It has a consummation. It's not a stream dissipated in the sands of a desert. It is a river contributing to the vast open sea of ongoing life in eternity. The opening of the sixth seal ties the traumatic events of history's end to man's present moral struggle. The end is a goal to be acheived therefore it relates to present moral conflict. A school commencement is not an isolated event unrelated to the years that went before, classes, study halls, home work, tests, social activity and sports. In fact, the graduation projected its effects into these earlier years of effort. The commencement and what lay beyond it motivated the years of toil. So it is with the sixth seal. It unveiled the fact of the "end event" as a generating motivating power in present struggles. In view of history's goal one must be faithful to today's witness. If not, then one will find himself among those "kings, captains, rich, strong, bond, and free" who "hid themselves in the caves and the rocks of the mountains" saying, "Fall on us, and hide us from the wrath of the lamb; for the great day of their wrath is come; who is able to stand?"

If one looks on the "end" of personal life (or the "end" of human history) merely as a dead "end" then present life has no meaning. Man's potential is that of deity but he has the life of an insect. No moral or spiritual purpose in present life is visible if the final issue is a zero. Why have a gun if it has no target or shoots only blanks? So the end of the present cosmic order has no meaning unless God be present and His purposes be taken into account. The breaking of the sixth seal makes clear that the consummation of history involves God's judgment. God at the "end" projects ethical and moral values into present human struggle. The "end" explains all God's deeds in history; it verifies faith. The end of history interprets the meaning of history. Man lives a life of moral and spiritual worth in view of the God at the "end."

## A TRANSLATION
Revelation 7:1-17

After this I saw four angels standing upon the four corners of the earth, holding (back) the four winds of the earth in order that no wind should blow upon the earth neither upon the sea neither against any tree. And I saw another angel coming up from the rising of (the) sun holding (the) seal of the living God. And in a loud voice he shouted to the four angels to whom it was given to harm the earth and the sea, saying, "Don't harm the earth nor the sea nor the trees until we seal the servants of our God upon their foreheads."

And I heard the number of those having been sealed, 144,000 having been sealed out of every tribe of Israel:

of the tribe of Judah 12,000 having been sealed,
of the tribe of Reuben 12,000,
of the tribe of Gad 12,000,
of the tribe of Asher 12,000,
of the tribe of Naphtali 12,000,
of the tribe of Manasseh 12,000,
of the tribe of Simeon 12,000,
of the tribe of Levi 12,000,
of the tribe of Issachar 12,000,
of the tribe of Zebulun 12,000,
of the tribe of Joseph 12,000,
of the tribe of Benjamin 12,000 having been sealed.

After these things I saw, and behold, a great crowd whom no one was able to number out of every nation and tribes and peoples and tongues, standing before the throne and before the lamb, having been clothed with white robes and palm branches in their hands. And they are shouting in a loud voice saying, "The salvation to our God, to the one sitting upon the throne, and to the lamb."

And all the angels stood encircling the throne and the elders and the four living creatures. And they fell before the throne on their faces and worshipped God, saying, "Amen! The blessing and the glory and the wisdom and the thanksgiving and the honor and the power and the might to our God unto the ages of the ages! Amen."

And one of the elders answered saying to me, "These, the ones having been clothed in white robes--Who are they and from whence did they come?" And I said to him; "My Lord! <u>You</u> know!" And he said to me; "These are the ones coming out of the great tribulation and they washed their robes and whitened them in the blood of the lamb. Because of this they are before the throne of God and are serving him day and night in his sanctuary and the one sitting upon the throne will tabernacle over them. They shall not hunger any more, neither shall they thirst any more, nor shall the sun fall upon them nor any scorching, because the lamb, the one in the midst of the throne, will shepherd them and will guide them unto the springs of the waters of life; and God will wipe away every tear from their eyes."

## AN OUTLINE OF REVELATION 7:1-17

### The Sealing of the Saints

Where do the righteous stand in a world of unrighteousness? What security can God's people expect in a world of insecurity? When one is "in" the world but not "of" the world what certainty can he count on amid the devestation of destruction? When the "wrath of God" prevails through the four horsemen of the apocalypse what is the Christian's hope?

I. SEALING OF THE SAINTS ON THE EARTH. 7:1-8
   1. Destruction delayed. vs.1
   2. The angel with God's seal. vs.2-3
   3. All God's people on earth provided with protection. vss.4-8
      (a) The 144,000 are God's people.
      (b) The 144,000 are all of God's people on earth.
      (c) Their sealing comes from "the rising of the sun."

II. THE SAINTS "BEFORE THE THRONE." 7:9-12
   1. The "great crowd" standing "before the throne." vs.9-10
      (a) Beyond measurement.
      (b) Universal in origin.
      (c) Purified and victorious.
      (d) Filled with peace and joy.
      (e) Praising God for salvation realized.
   2. The worship of the heavenly inhabitants.
      (a) The angels, elders, and four living creatures.
      (b) The substance of their worship.
         "The blessing" "the glory" "the wisdom" "the thanks giving" "the honor" "the power" and "the might."

III. THE SECURITY OF GOD'S PEOPLE IN HEAVEN. 7:13-17
   1. The identity of the innumerable multitude.
      (a) Those in possession of their eternal redemption.
      (b) They have come out of "the great tribulation."
      (c) Have been whitened by the "blood of the lamb."
         Their salvation was of God's doing; not their's.
   2. The promises they inherit.
      (a) Service in the presence of God.
      (b) No hardship anymore from natural creation.
      (c) Unrestrained access to the sources of life.
      (e) God the personal, ever-present strength and comfort.

Christians are not to expect removal from the human earthly experience. The "great tribulation" is the common lot of all humanity, saved or unsaved. God doesn't save his own "from" it. But he does redeem, guide and save through it. And even by means of it! The "great tribulation" must be lived and evaluated in the light of the security which endures "unto the ages of the ages." Present suffering not to be compared with future glory!

## Revelation 7:1

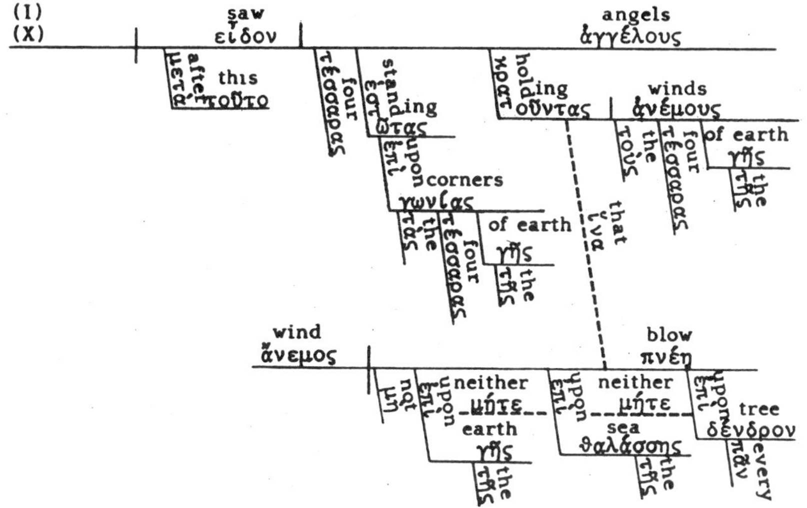


THE DIAGRAM OF REVELATION 7:1

This verse contains a complex sentence of two clauses. Deprived of all modifiers the independent element states, "I saw angels." The prepositional phrase "after this" tells when. Two participles inform as to some circumstances that surround the seeing of the angels. "Upon the four corners of the earth" is a prepositional phrase used adverbially to indicate where the angels were standing. The noun translated "winds" is direct object of participle "holding" and so designates what the angels were holding.

ἵνα is a subordinating conjunction introducing an adverbial clause of purpose, "...in order that wind might not blow..." μὴ is the normal negative with subjunctive. Note the negative goes with verb rather than the subject ἄνεμος. The three ἐπὶ phrases denote where a "wind might not blow." Note also that γῆς and θαλάσσης are genitive case whereas δένδρον is accusative. A subtle difference in idea but still a difference to be noted. The wind didn't blow "on" either earth or sea. It didn't blow "against" any tree.

ἑστῶτας and κρατοῦντας are participles, the first one perfect, the second present. Participles are not verbs used as adjectives; nor are they adjectives used as verbs. They are verbal adjectives. They function as verbs and adjectives at the same time. These are probably best classified as predicate circumstantial.

Revelation 7:2–3

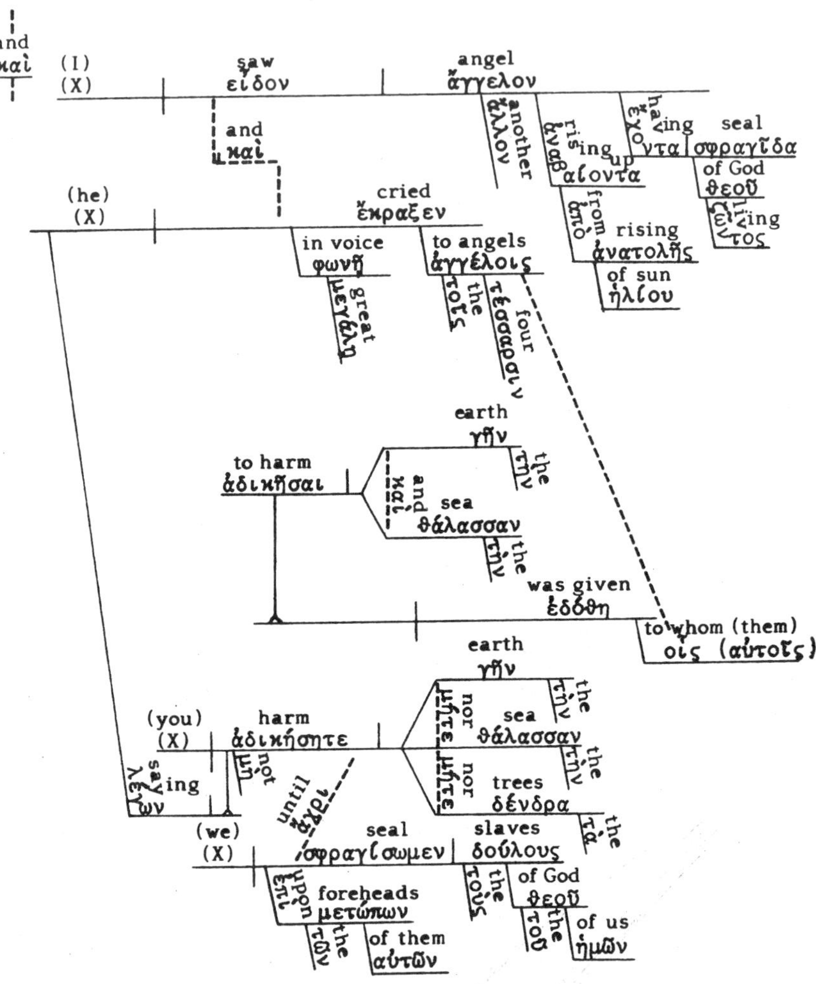

## THE DIAGRAM OF REVELATION 7:2-3

Verses 2-3 contain one sentence of five clauses, two independent and three dependent. The independent segments sav. "I saw angel" and "he cried."

As in the preceding sentence two participles modify the direct object "angel." ἀναβαινοντα is present tense, descriptive temporal linear action, "as (he) was rising up..." ἔχοντα presents parallel action, "having God's seal..." Another present participle ζῶντος describes God as "living." In its verbal aspect a participle may take an object as here ἔχοντα has for its object σφραγῖδα.

The verb ἔκραξεν has two noun combinations modifying it. First comes locative φωνῇ = "in a loud voice." Then follows an indirect object in dative ἀγγέλοις = "to the four angels." Dropping off of the dative noun translated "angels" is an adjective clause ushered in by the relative pronoun οἷς. The 3rd personal pronoun "to them" (αὐτοῖς) is redundant; the diagram places it in apposition to the relative. The expression may be translated: "...to whom it was given to them..."

The author was under pressures of both political and religious persecution. Moreover, the excitement generated by the visions being given him was enough to disturb any normal style of writing he possessed. A number of redundancies and grammatical lapses may be accounted for in such ways.

This adjective clause (οἷς) has for its subject an infinitve phrase, "to harm the earth and the sea..." ἀδικῆσαι is aorist active infinitive. As noun it is subject of the clause; as verb it takes a compound direct object, "the earth and the sea."

That which the angel "cried" is set forth in the two remaining subordinate clauses. The present circumstantial participle λέγων modifies "he" the subject of "cried." Object of participle "saying" is the noun clause "Don't harm the earth nor the sea nor the trees." Negative μὴ with aorist subjunctive ἀδικήσητε means "don't even begin to harm."

The final dependent clause is a temporal adverbial prefaced by ἄχρι = until we seal the slaves of our God on their foreheads." The conjunction ἄχρι with aorist subjunctive introduces "indefinite action for the future" whereas the future inidicative is used in 17:7. The aorist σφραγίσωμεν is effective = "until we get them sealed..."

The ἐπὶ prepositional phrase indicates where the seal is placed, "upon their foreheads." θεοῦ is a possessive genitive telling whose slaves get the sealing. They are "the slaves of God," not someone else's.

## Revelation 7:4-8

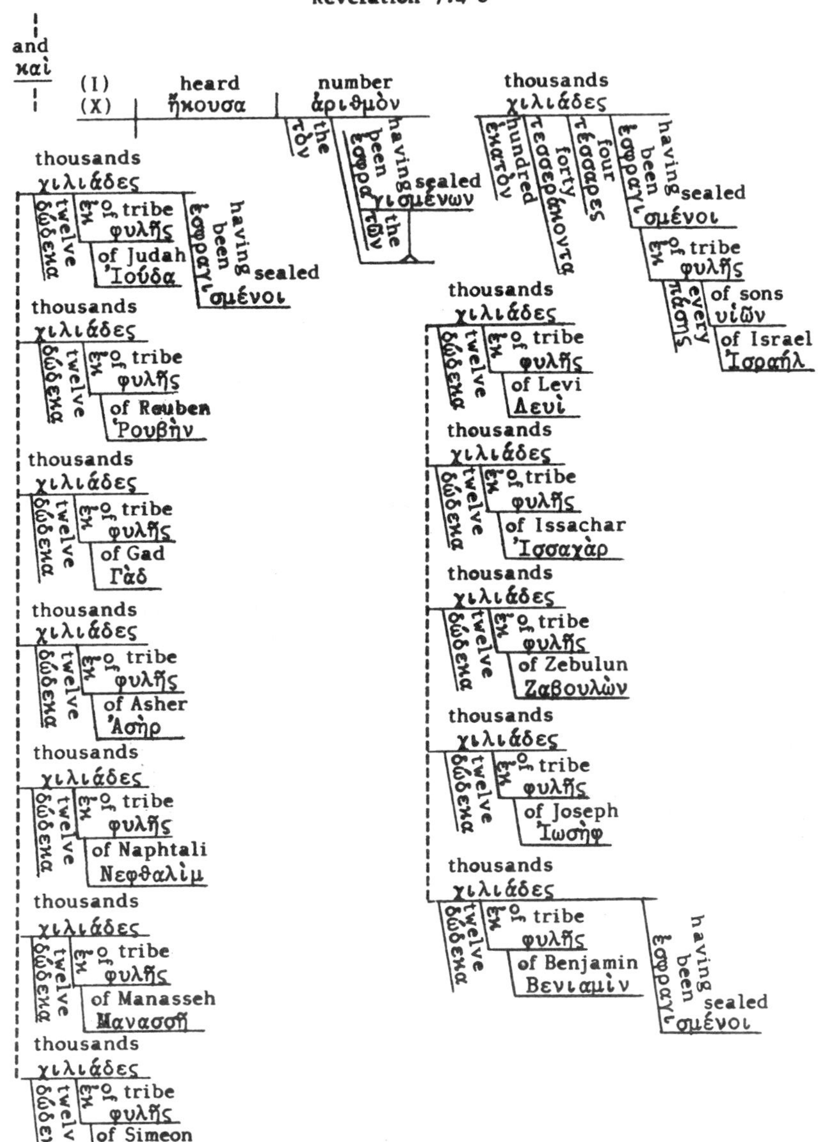

## THE DIAGRAM OF 7:4-8

The four verses of 7:4-8 enfolds only one full sentence. And that is a simple sentence of six words: "And I heard the number of the ones having been sealed." χιλιάδες is quite naturally accusative as direct object of the verb. Accusative case limits an idea in "content, scope or direction." Here it states the content of what he "heard." Besides the definite article, it is described by the genitive perfect passive articular participle ἐσφραγισμένων. The participle is attributive. Its perfect tense suggests the durability of the "sealing." This 144,000 had been ensured with the divine seal and still was.

So far as the basic thought is concerned the author might have concluded the sentence without any expansion. In fact, grammatically the sentence is concluded. But he goes on to expand without use of clause or sentence. He first adds a nominative absolute, "hundred forty four thousands having been sealed of every tribe of Israel's sons." By placing the appositional idea χιλιάδες as nominative absolute the author certainly makes it stand out with a great deal more prominence. Furthermore, after thus spotlighting the total 144,000 he proceeds to break the full number down into 12,000 to each tribe. He begins with the tribe of Judah from whom the Christ came and ends with the tribe of Benjamin. Each of these also appears as a nominative plural probably to be thought of as in agreement with the χιλιάδες of the initial nominative absolute.

Of the twelve tribes named in this passage two of them were never considered tribes in the original division. Neither Joseph nor Levi ever obtained a heritage in the parceling out of tribal territories. Levi gained the privilege of serving in the priestly function. Joseph inherited only through his sons Ephraim and Manasseh. The author was too knowledgable of Old Testament facts and traditions for these abberations to have been accidental. The entire passage is symbolical. The meaning lies beyond the mere numbers and names involved. But whatever were the author's intent it doesn't affect the grammatical structure. The sentence is simple in form with added nominative absolutes.

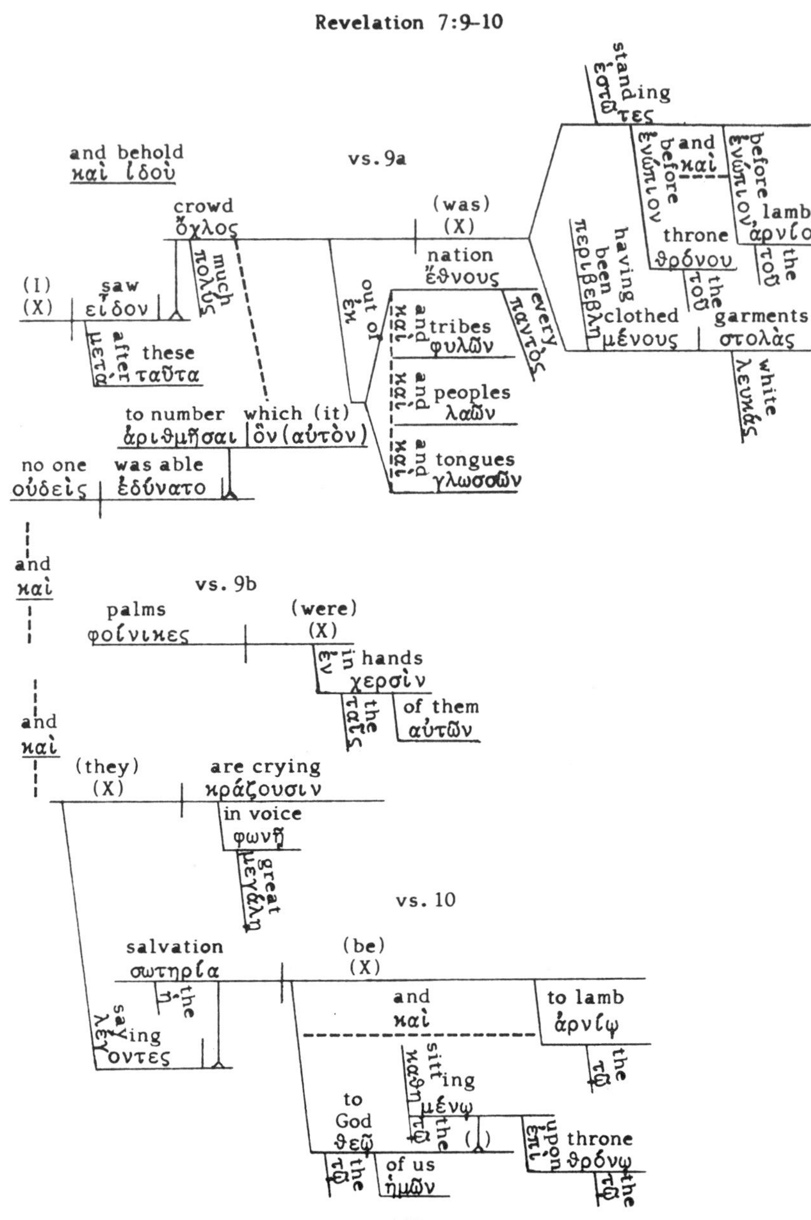
vs. 9a
and behold
καὶ ἰδοὺ
(I)
(X)
saw
εἶδον
after these
μετὰ ταῦτα
crowd
ὄχλος
much
πολύς
(was)
(X)
out of
ἐκ
nation
ἔθνους
every
παντὸς
and
καὶ
tribes
φυλῶν
peoples
λαῶν
tongues
γλωσσῶν
to number
ἀριθμῆσαι
which (it)
ὃν (αὐτὸν)
no one
οὐδεὶς
was able
ἐδύνατο
standing
ἑστῶτες
before
ἐνώπιον
throne
θρόνου
the
τοῦ
lamb
ἀρνίου
having been clothed
περιβεβλημένους
garments
στολὰς
white
λευκάς
vs. 9b
palms
φοίνικες
(were)
(X)
in
ἐν
hands
χερσὶν
the
ταῖς
of them
αὐτῶν
(they)
(X)
are crying
κράζουσιν
in voice
φωνῇ
great
μεγάλῃ
vs. 10
salvation
σωτηρία
the
ἡ
saying
λέγοντες
(be)
(X)
to lamb
ἀρνίῳ
to God
θεῷ
of us
ἡμῶν
sitting
καθημένῳ
upon
ἐπὶ
throne
θρόνῳ

## THE DIAGRAM OF 7:9-10

Verse 9a sprouts a complex sentence of three clauses. The basic independent idea states: "...I saw..." That which he saw is put in a noun clause, "a great crowd (was) standing." This clause functions as object of the verb "saw." Perfect participle ἑστῶτες is predicate, supplementing an understood "was" thus making a periphrastic "was standing." The same construction applies also to perfect participle περιβεβλημένους = having been clothed. Direct object στολὰς is accusative after verb of clothing. Where they "were standing" finds expression in the adverbial phrases, "before the throne" and "before the lamb." This crowd which John "saw" is identified as to its make-up by the four-pronged phrase introduced by ἐκ, "out of every nation and tribes and peoples and tongues." In addition to that an adjective clause also describes the "crowd." It reads, "...which no one was able to number it..." The pronoun αὐτὸν (it) is redundant since the relative ὃν already expressed the direct object of the infinitive ἀριθμῆσαι.

According to Nestle's text verse 9b is included as part of the sentence in 9a. If so, that would mean that the entire verse is compound-complex. But the diagram treats verse 9b as a separate sentence. It is simple in form stating, "And palms (were) in their hands."

Another complex sentence arises in verse ten. The independent clause uses a dramatic present in its verb, "they are shouting in a loud voice..." Instead of reporting the fact of the crowd's loud shout in tenses reflecting past action he changes to the more vivid dramatic present. Such a use of this linear present after "I saw" and "were standing etc." reflects the overflowing emotional flush in John as he experienced this vision. It is as if John were impelled into the crowd's feelings. He feels their cry and himself enters more completely into what they shout.

The content of the crowd's cry is expressed in a noun clause, object of circumstantial present participle λέγοντες = saying. "The salvation (be) to our God, the one sitting upon the throne and to the lamb." The presence of the definite article "the" with "salvation" indicates that the "salvation" is not just a salvation from immediate crises. It's "the" salvation from sin, death and all sin's consequences including the present crisis. The shout of praise goes for the totality of "the" salvation!

The ones to whom the shout is lifted is expressed in datives, the case of personal interest. It's praise "to" God and "to" the lamb. "God" is further defined by the present attributive participle καθημένῳ = the one sitting upon the throne." The participle is in apposition to θεῷ.

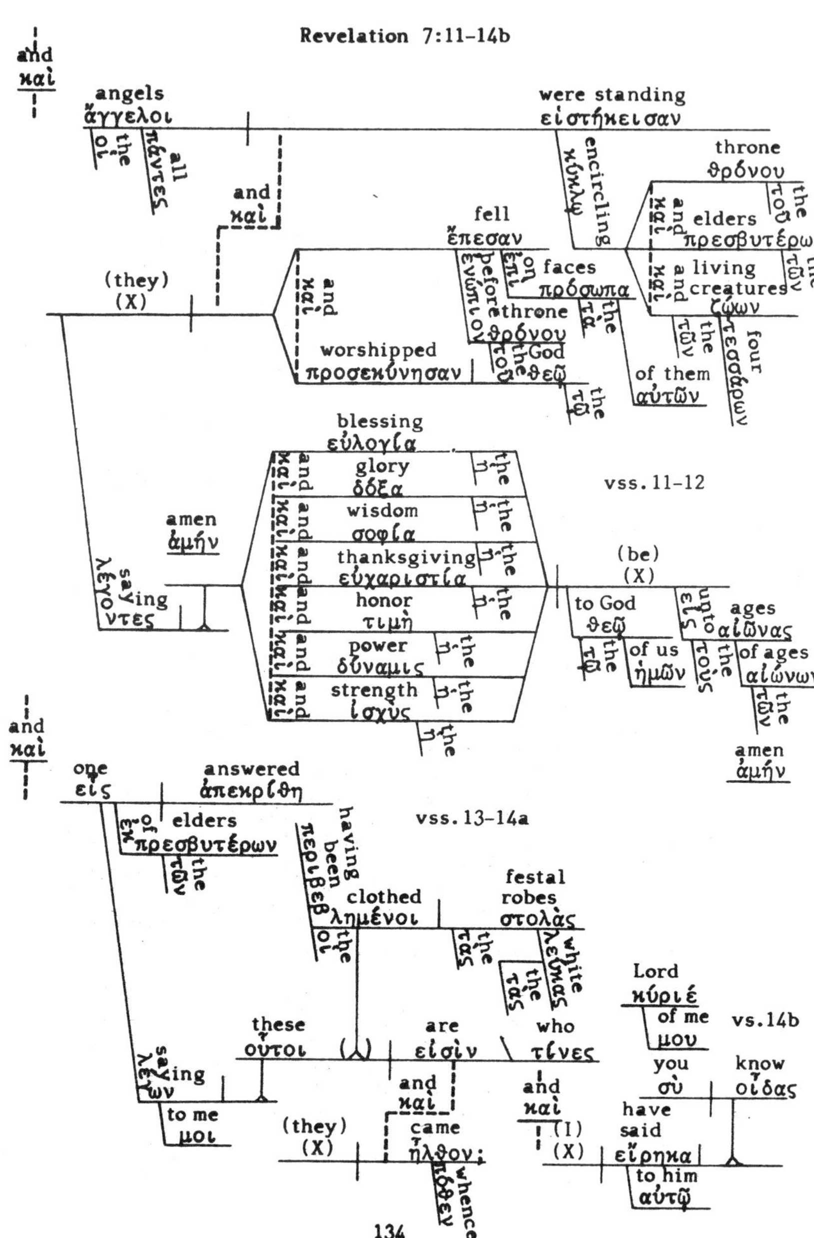
and
καὶ
angels
ἄγγελοι
the
οἱ
all
πάντες
were standing
εἱστήκεισαν
encircling
κύκλῳ
throne
θρόνου
the
τοῦ
and
καὶ
elders
πρεσβυτέρων
the
τῶν
and
καὶ
living creatures
ζῴων
the
τῶν
four
τεσσάρων
fell
ἔπεσαν
on
ἐπὶ
faces
πρόσωπα
the
τὰ
of them
αὐτῶν
before
ἐνώπιον
throne
θρόνου
the
τοῦ
worshipped
προσεκύνησαν
God
θεῷ
the
τῷ
(they)
(X)
saying
λέγοντες
amen
ἀμήν
blessing
εὐλογία
glory
δόξα
wisdom
σοφία
thanksgiving
εὐχαριστία
honor
τιμὴ
power
δύναμις
strength
ἰσχὺς
the
ἡ
vss. 11-12
(be)
(X)
to God
θεῷ
the
τῷ
of us
ἡμῶν
unto
εἰς
ages
αἰῶνας
the
τοὺς
of ages
αἰώνων
the
τῶν
amen
ἀμήν
one
εἷς
answered
ἀπεκρίθη
of
ἐκ
elders
πρεσβυτέρων
the
τῶν
vss. 13-14a
having been clothed
περιβεβλημένοι
the
οἱ
festal robes
στολὰς
the
τὰς
white
λευκὰς
the
τὰς
saying
λέγων
to me
μοι
these
οὗτοι
are
εἰσὶν
who
τίνες
and
καὶ
(they)
(X)
came
ἦλθον;
whence
πόθεν
and
καὶ
(I)
(X)
Lord
κύριέ
of me
μου
vs. 14b
you
σὺ
know
οἶδας
have said
εἴρηκα
to him
αὐτῷ

## THE DIAGRAM OF 7:11-14b

Verses 11-12 encase a compound-complex sentence. There are two independent clauses and one dependent. The second independent has a compound predicate of two verbs. Stripped of their modifying elements the independents state: "...angels were standing" and "...they fell...and...worshipped." εἱστήκεισαν is pluperfect but with the force of an imperfect = "was standing." This contrasts sharply with the aorists translated "fell" and "worshipped" of the second independent element. Standing is an ever continuous action; to fall and worship is looked on as a single act. At least attention is focused on the act more than its continuance.

κύκλῳ is a preposition used with genitive; here with three genitives, "throne, elders, living creatures." Taking the text as is without emendation the angels formed a large circle about the throne and the "elders and living creatures" which themselves were in a circle around the throne. It's understandable that the angels would encircle the entire company all of whom were praising "the one sitting on the throne."

The verb "fell" has two modifying details. "Before the throne" is adverbial telling where; "on their faces" is adverbial expressing manner. ἐνώπιον is used with genitive; ἐπί the accusative. The verb translated "worshipped" has dative θεῷ for direct object. The personal interest of the dative is appropriate for the idea involved in "worship" of the living God.

The dependent clause appears as a noun clause object of present circumstantial participle λέγοντες = "saying." It has a seven part compound subject. And each of the seven has its own definite article which makes each characteristic stand out with distinct eminence: "the blessing and the glory and the wisdom and the thanks and the honor and the power and the strength..." The clause is a doxology enclosed by "amen" before and after.

The sentence of 13-14a is complex. "One of the elders answered" is the independent clause. ἀπεκρίθη is aorist passive of defective verb ἀποκρίνομαι so it is active in meaning though passive in form. Though no question had been asked "one of the elders" stepped in to "answer" the situation, the thought implied in the situation. That which he answered is contained in the noun clause object of circumstantial participle λέγων. The "answer" contains two clauses: "These are who?" and "Whence did they come?" Perfect participle περιβεβλημένοι = "having been clothed" is attributive and is in apposition to subject οὗτοι. Its tense emphasizes the enduring quality of the "white robes" with which "these" had been clothed.

Verse 14b contains John's puzzlement in response to the pointed inquiry of the elder. The sentence is complex in form. The independent clause uses dramatic perfect εἴρηκα = "I have said." The tense calls attention to the vividness of John's confusion as he answered the elder. Vocative κύριέ is an address of respect, not worship. The use of personal pronoun σύ as subject in the noun clause "you know" is quite emphatic.

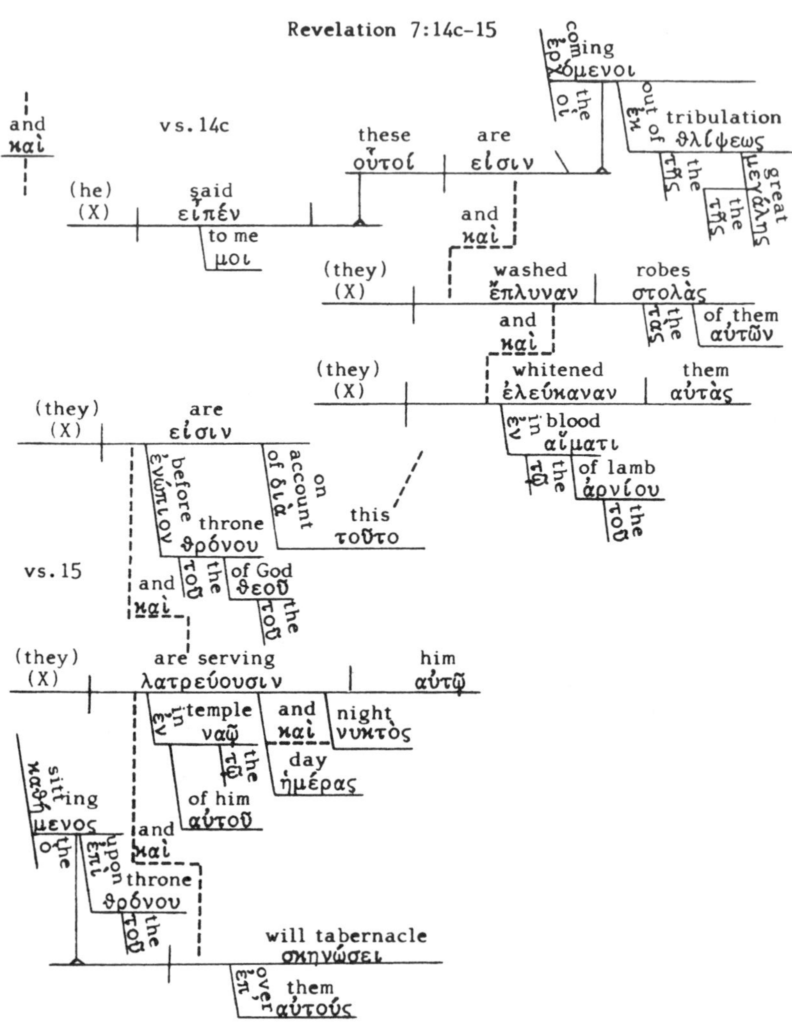
Revelation 7:14c-15
vs. 14c
and
καί
(he)
(X)
said
εἰπέν
to me
μοι
these
οὗτοί
are
εἰσιν
coming
ἐρχόμενοι
the
οἱ
out of
ἐκ
tribulation
θλίψεως
the
τῆς
great
μεγάλης
the
τῆς
and
καί
(they)
(X)
washed
ἔπλυναν
robes
στολὰς
the
τὰς
of them
αὐτῶν
and
καί
(they)
(X)
whitened
ἐλεύκαναν
them
αὐτὰς
in
ἐν
blood
αἵματι
the
τῷ
of lamb
ἀρνίου
the
τοῦ
(they)
(X)
are
εἰσιν
before
ἐνώπιον
throne
θρόνου
the
τοῦ
of God
θεοῦ
the
τοῦ
on account of
διὰ
this
τοῦτο
vs. 15
and
καί
(they)
(X)
are serving
λατρεύουσιν
him
αὐτῷ
in
ἐν
temple
ναῷ
the
τῷ
of him
αὐτοῦ
and
καί
night
νυκτὸς
day
ἡμέρας
sitting
καθήμενος
the
ὁ
upon
ἐπὶ
throne
θρόνου
the
τοῦ
and
καί
will tabernacle
σκηνώσει
over
ἐπ'
them
αὐτούς

## THE DIAGRAM OF 7:14c-15

The last half of verse 14 develops a complex arrangement. The main clause reports the fact and content of the elder's response. "He said to me" is the independent clause. The content of what he said is contained in three noun clauses objects of aorist εἰπέν.

The first of the dependents identifies who this "great crowd" of innumerable white-robed people was. "These are the ones coming out of the great tribulation..." The articular present attributive participle ἐρχόμενοι = "coming" serves as predicate adjective referring back to subject οὗτοί (these). In further describing "the ones coming" the speaker uses the ablative. The case suits well the idea of separation involved in these saints coming through and separating from the suffering of the tribulation. Tribulation grows out of being saintly in a sinful society.

The next two of these object-noun clauses relate what was done to and for this multitude from "every nation..." "They washed their robes" and "they whitened them in the blood of the lamb." The present tense of the participle ἐρχόμενοι suggests the regular and continuing flow of "ones coming" in an ever unbroken stream. In contrast the verbs of the last two of the dependent clauses are both aorists reflecting point action. Their robes "got washed" and "became white" at a specific point in history.

The διὰ τοῦτο of verse 15 ties the sentence of verse 15 to that of verse 14c. "On account of this..." On account of what? That which he had just stated in verse 14c, that is, because their robes had been "washed and whitened..." The diagram shows the phrase as adverbial under εἰσιν; it is almost a conjunction in force. Another adverbial phrase appears under εἰσιν. "Before the throne of God"(ἐνώπιον) indicates where!

This sentence of verse 15 is a three-clause compound one. The three clauses affirm: "they are...they serve...the one sitting will tabernacle..."

λατρεύουσιν is present active indicative of λατρεύω = "to serve." The verb derives from λάτρις = "hired servant." Originally it meant "to work for hire." It developed into the idea of general service. Finally it took on the particular meaning of "religious service to God," especially the ritual service of priests to God. This "great crowd" of white-robed palm-waving people from "every nation" obviously refers to the redeemed who inhabit heaven. The priesthood of believers is here dramatically presented as they "serve" God "day and night" in spiritual religious worship. The genitives "day and night" indicate the kind of time, that is unceasingly, around the clock, so to speak. Extent of time would have used accusative.

In the third of the clauses the subject shifts from "they" to "the one sitting." This refers to God as sovereign. God "will tabernacle over them." That is to say, God will protect them. He will be as a tent to them shielding from sand, wind, rain, heat, cold and storm. The whole chapter presents a pause to reassure the saints of their security through the threatening storm.

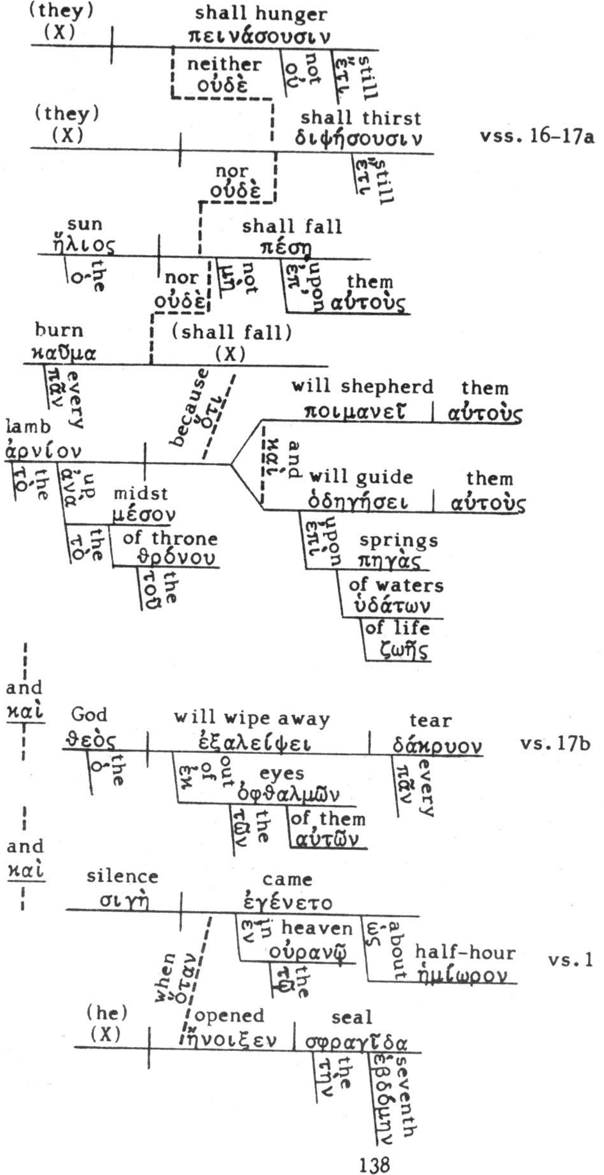
(they) (X)
shall hunger πεινάσουσιν
neither οὐδὲ
not οὐ
still ἔτι
(they) (X)
shall thirst διψήσουσιν
still ἔτι
nor οὐδὲ
sun ἥλιος
the ὁ
shall fall πέσῃ
not μὴ
upon ἐπ'
them αὐτοὺς
nor οὐδὲ
burn καῦμα
every πᾶν
(shall fall) (X)
because ὅτι
lamb ἀρνίον
the τὸ
up ἀνὰ
midst μέσον
the τὸ
of throne θρόνου
the τοῦ
will shepherd ποιμανεῖ
them αὐτοὺς
and καὶ
will guide ὁδηγήσει
them αὐτοὺς
upon ἐπὶ
springs πηγὰς
of waters ὑδάτων
of life ζωῆς
vss. 16-17a
and καὶ
God θεὸς
the ὁ
will wipe away ἐξαλείψει
tear δάκρυον
every πᾶν
out of ἐκ
eyes ὀφθαλμῶν
the τῶν
of them αὐτῶν
vs. 17b
and καὶ
silence σιγὴ
came ἐγένετο
in ἐν
heaven οὐρανῷ
the τῷ
about ὡς
half-hour ἡμίωρον
vs. 1
when ὅταν
(he) (X)
opened ἤνοιξεν
seal σφραγῖδα
the τὴν
seventh ἑβδόμην

## THE DIAGRAM OF 7:16-8:1

The way in which the "one sitting on the throne" will cast his tabernacling canopy of protection over the saints is set forth in the sentence of verse 16-17a. In four independent clauses it states four explicit needs which God supplies. Then follows a dependent clause which gives the logical reason why such needs can be supplied. The sentence is obviously compound-complex.

The first independent says, "They shall not hunger any more..." The second refers to another physical human need; "...neither shall they thirst any more..." To those who must live in and through this kind of world of time, taste, space and weight there's no way to portray the infinite joy of heaven's experience except in negative terms. They "shall not hunger...not thirst..." How else could one tell what it will be?

The third and fourth independent clauses continue the negative sketch of heavenly experience. The two items reflect Israel's desert experience under the heat of the sun and its burning rays. "The sun shall not fall upon them neither shall any scorching burn (fall on them)..." By implication the verb of the fourth clause comes from aorist subjunctive πέσῃ of the third clause. The verbs of the first two clauses are future indicatives. So far as the kind of action is concerned there's not much difference, if any, between future indicative and aorist subjective. Both are future as to time; both are point action.

The one dependent clause of the sentence is an adverbial causal introduced by ὅτι. The clause gives the underlying reason why the protection described in the four earlier clauses is assured. It's "because the lamb will shepherd them and will guide them..." ποιμανεῖ and ὁδηγήσει are future indicatives. Here the symbolism of the book is quite striking. A "lamb" is performing the function of a "shepherd" and "guide" instead of the one needing shepherding and guiding, wholly incongruous were it not symbolic language.

The expression τὸ ἀνὰ μέσον is equivalent to ἐν μέσῳ = "in midst." The diagram places it as though an adjective describing ἀρνίον. And it does perform an adjectival function. For practical purposes it takes the place of a dependent adjective clause, "who was mid-point before the throne."

Verse 17b embodies a simple sentence. It continues the negative portrait of the heavenly security of the saints. "God shall wipe away every tear..." ἐκ with ablative ὀφθαλμῶν is normal expression for separation.

The sentence of 8:1 belongs to the next vision. It's a complex sentence of two clauses. The independent idea reports, "silence became..." Where is an adverbial idea of ἐν with locative: "in the heaven." How long the "silence" obtained is in ὡς with accusative: "about half-hour." Another adverbial idea of when appears in the subordinate clause ushered in by ὅταν = "whenever he opened the seventh seal." The verbs in both clauses are aorists reporting facts as facts rather description of the facts.

## EXPOSITORY THOUGHTS ON 7:1-17

"Who is able to stand?" Those on earth who have the "seal of our God on their foreheads." Also that innumerable multitude in heaven of "every nation...clothed with white robes...shouting, 'Salvation to our God.'" 7:1-8 depicts the security of God's people on earth. 7:9-17 that of all God's people in heaven.

The angels "at the four corners of the earth" restrain the destructive judgments until God's people are secured. Believers fall heir to the judgmental disturbances hurled against a sinful earth. But God hasn't abandoned them. They get God's "seal" to mark them as safe. Not safe from hurt but from being destroyed by the hurts. Living or dying, they're secure!

144,000 divided equally between the tribes of Israel symbolizes the complete totality of God's people here on earth. The names of Old Testament clans plus the deviation of two of the tribes from the normal twelve supports the symbolic use of the number. The 12 tribes were God's people. This multiple of 12 is the author's way of saying that God's people, Jew and Gentile, enjoy God's protecting care through all their earth-life's suffering. Conquest, war, famine etc. will not destroy their soul's safety. "Who's able to stand?" Spiritual Israel; God marks them as his!

Moreover, all God's people shall stand. John was given a glimpse of a "great crowd whom no one was able to number of every nation..." This unnumbered crowd standing "before the throne" was not only universal in origin but also wore "white robes" of cleansing. They waved "palm branches" of victory. And their shout was one of praise for salvation wrought in their behalf: "Salvation to our God..."

Joining the chorus in their victory song heaven's "angels," the "elders and four living creatures(all creation)" added their worship "The blessing and the glory and the wisdom and the thanks and the honor and the power and the might to our God forever."

And who is this crowd "whom no one could number?" John challenged the "elder" to tell him. They are identified as being (1)"the ones coming out of the great tribulation." That is, those who have been God's people on earth, passed through their suffering for right in a sinful order and now, having passed through, are safe "before the throne." (2)Ones who "washed their robes white in the blood of the lamb." That is, redeemed by Christ's death, purified from sin by God's grace and are now safely serving him in heaven's security.

And there's something else about this innumerable host. They are heirs of certain promises. (1)They "are serving him day and night." That is, endlessly. Their priestly, religious devotion and godly service is not counted by time. It's an eternal serving in the presence of the living God. (2)They want for neither food or drink. Nor do they suffer the heat of desert sun, affliction from "natural" causes. They have unrestrained access to the "waters of life." (3)God is their comforter for he "shall wipe every tear from their eyes." Such is the security of the saints! They alone can stand!

## A TRANSLATION
### Revelation 8:1-9:21

And when he opened the seventh seal, silence settled in heaven, about half an hour. And I saw the seven angels, the ones who stand before God. And seven trumpets were given to them.

And another angel, having a golden censure, came and stood by the altar. And much incense was given to him that he might give (it) with the prayers of all the saints upon the golden altar, the one before the throne. And the smoke of the incense went up with the prayers of the saints out of the angel's hand before God.

And the angel has taken the censure and filled it from the fire of the altar and hurled it unto the earth. And thunderings and noises and lightning flashes (came) and an earthquake arose.

And the seven angels, the ones having the seven trumpets, prepared them that they should blow.

And the first trumpeted! And hail and fire mixed with blood came and they were hurled unto the earth. And the third of the earth was burned, and the third of the trees was burned, and all the green grass was burned.

And the second angel trumpeted! And (what was) as a great mountain burning with fire was hurled into the sea. And the third of the sea became blood, and the third of the creatures, the ones in the sea, the ones alive, died; and the third of the ships were destroyed.

And the third angel trumpeted! And a great star, blazing like a torch, fell out of the sky upon the third of the streams and upon the springs of waters. And the name of the star is called, "The Wormwood." And the third of the waters became wormwood and many men died from the waters because they became poisoned.

And the fourth angel trumpeted! And the third of the sun was blasted and the third of the moon and the third of the stars so that the third of them was darkened; and the day, the third of it, did not shine; and the night likewise.

And I looked, and I heard a solitary eagle flying in mid-heaven sreeching in a loud voice, "Woe, woe, woe to the ones dwelling on the earth from the rest of the blasts of the trumpet of the three angels, the ones being yet about to trumpet."

### Chapter 9

And the fifth angel trumpeted! And I saw a star having fallen out of the sky unto the earth. And the key of the pit of the abyss was given to him. And he opened the pit of the abyss; and smoke went up out of the pit as smoke of a great furnace and the sun and the air were darkened. And locusts came out of the smoke upon the earth, and power, as scorpions of the earth have power, was given to them. And it was told to them that they shall not hurt the grass of the earth, neither any green (herb), neither any tree; except (they shall hurt) the men who do not have upon their foreheads the seal of God. And it was given to them that they shall not kill them but they shall be tormented five months. And their torment (was) as a scorpion's torment whenever it strikes a man.

## A TRANSLATION
### Revelation 8:1-9:21
### (continued)

And in those days men shall seek death and shall not find it; and they shall desire to die and death flees from them. And the images of the locusts (were) like horses having been prepared for battle and (crowns) upon their heads (were) as crowns like gold, and their faces (were) as faces of men and they were having hair like hair of women and their teeth were like (teeth) of lions and they were having breastplates like breastplates of iron and the sound of their wings (was) like noise of chariots of many horses rushing into battle. And they have tails like scorpions and stings and their power to harm humans five months (lies) in their tails. They have over them as king the angel of the abyss; in Hebrew his name (is) Abbadon and in Greek he has (the) name Apollyon.

The one woe (is) passed. Behold! After these (are) yet two woes.

And the sixth angel trumpeted. And I heard one voice from the four horns of the golden altar, the one before God, saying to the sixth angel, the one having the trumpet, "Loose the four angels, the ones having been bound at the great river Euphrates. And the four angels, the ones having been prepared for the hour and day and month and year, were loosed in order that they might kill the third of human beings. And the number of the soldiers of the cavalry (was) two hundred thousands of thousands; I heard the number of them. And in the vision I saw thus the horses and the ones sitting upon them, having breastplates of firey red, blue, and sulphur yellow; and the heads of the horses (were) as heads of lions, and fire and smoke and sulphur issues from their mouths. From these three plagues the third of human beings were killed, out of the fire and the smoke and the sulphur going out of their mouths. For the power of the horses is in their mouth and in their tails; for their tails (were) like serpents, having heads, and with these they hurt. And the rest of mankind who were not killed in these plagues, neither repented from the works of their hands that they should not worship the demons and the idols, the gold and the silver and the brass and the stone and the wooden which are not able either to see nor to hear nor to walk; and they did not repent from their murders neither from their sorceries nor from their fornication nor from their robberies.

## AN OUTLINE OF REVELATION 8:1-9:21

### The Goodness and Justice of God!

How does God exercise his essential nature of good in a moral universe that has gone evil? Is it possible for him to assert his sense of justice while retaining his own goodness? Can he condemn evil in judgment and at the same time redeem those who wish to rise to his level of life? How does the sovereign God rule and redeem in this world's moral environment? How can a God who is love exercise that love in an evil world?

Judgment is not the absence of love. Nor is it the contradiction of mercy. It is the only way love can exercise itself in immoral surroundings. He who will not judge evil does not love good! As light opposes darkness love opposes evil. And as light dissipates darkness so love drives out evil; it redeems from evil by judgment against it!

I. RESPONSE TO PRAYERS FOR MORAL INTEGRITY. 8:1-6
   1. Dramatic silence awaits awesome moral judgments. 1-2
   2. Prayers of "all the saints" presented to God. 3-4
   3. Divine judgments hurled upon the earth. 5-6

II. THE JUDGMENTS OF CREATION! 8:7-12
   1. The first trumpet sounded. 7
      A third of green herbs scorched.
   2. The second trumpet sounded. 8-9
      Third of sea creatures killed and shipping destroyed.
   3. The third trumpet sounded. 10-11
      Third of streams and springs poisoned.
   4. The fourth trumpet sounded. 12
      Third of light of heavenly bodies darkened.

III. JUDGMENTS AGAINST MANKIND. 8:13-9:19
   1. Three woes announced on those "dwelling on the earth." 13
   2. The fifth trumpet sounded.
      (a)The key to the "pit of the abyss."
      (b)Locusts like poisonous scorpions rise from the abyss for the judgmental purpose of hurting man.
      (c)Exception: Men with the "seal of God on foreheads."
      (d)The judgment against men limited to "five months." This the divine judgment of sin eating at man.
      (e)Apollyon their sovereign king.
   3. The sixth trumpet sounded.
      (a)Judgment of captivity from the "great river Euphrates."
      (b)Havoc and suffering from invading thousands kill a third part of humanity. This a typical captivity brought about by man's rebellion against God's rule.

IV. UNREPENTENT HUMANITY. 9:20-21
   1. "The rest of men" who survive the ravages of sin.
   2. The judgmental wrath of God did not produce:
      (a)Repentance from idolatry.
      (b)Or from the works of idolatry.

"I gave you cleanness of teeth in all your cities...yet you did not return to me." "Prepare to meet your God, O Israel."(Amos 4:6, 12) The "wrath of God" is for discipline and redemption.

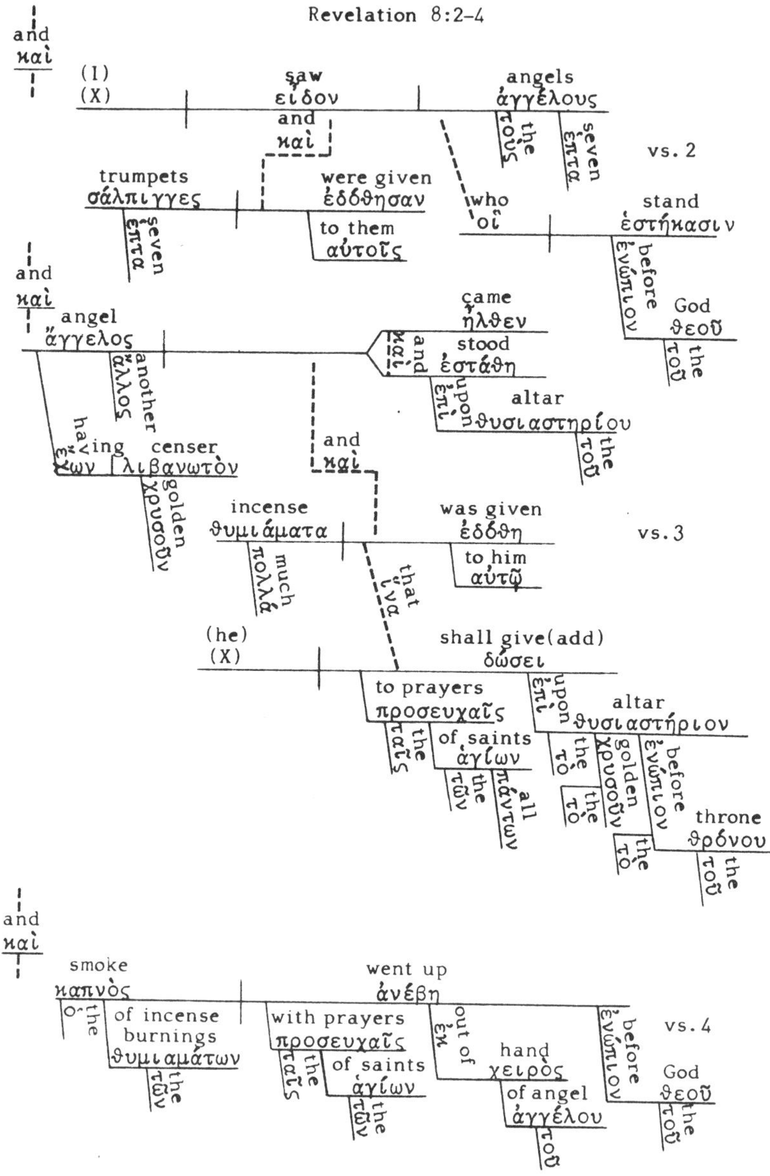

Revelation 8:2-4
and
καὶ
(I)
(X)
saw
εἶδον
angels
ἀγγέλους
the
τοὺς
seven
ἑπτὰ
vs. 2
and
καὶ
trumpets
σάλπιγγες
seven
ἑπτὰ
were given
ἐδόθησαν
to them
αὐτοῖς
who
οἳ
stand
ἑστήκασιν
before
ἐνώπιον
God
θεοῦ
the
τοῦ
and
καὶ
angel
ἄγγελος
another
ἄλλος
came
ἦλθεν
and
καὶ
stood
ἐστάθη
upon
ἐπὶ
altar
θυσιαστηρίου
the
τοῦ
having
ἔχων
censer
λιβανωτὸν
golden
χρυσοῦν
and
καὶ
incense
θυμιάματα
much
πολλὰ
was given
ἐδόθη
to him
αὐτῷ
vs. 3
that
ἵνα
(he)
(X)
shall give(add)
δώσει
to prayers
προσευχαῖς
the
ταῖς
of saints
ἁγίων
the
τῶν
all
πάντων
upon
ἐπὶ
altar
θυσιαστήριον
the
τὸ
golden
χρυσοῦν
the
τὸ
before
ἐνώπιον
throne
θρόνου
the
τοῦ
and
καὶ
smoke
καπνὸς
the
ὁ
of incense
burnings
θυμιαμάτων
the
τῶν
went up
ἀνέβη
with prayers
προσευχαῖς
the
ταῖς
of saints
ἁγίων
the
τῶν
out of
ἐκ
hand
χειρὸς
of angel
ἀγγέλου
the
τοῦ
before
ἐνώπιον
God
θεοῦ
the
τοῦ
vs. 4

## THE DIAGRAM OF 8:2-4

The sentence of verse two fits the pattern of compound-complex. It has two independent clauses to the first of which a dependent adjective clause is attached. The first clause affirms: "I saw the seven angels." By use of definite article τοὺς with ἀγγέλους the author calls attention to seven particular well-known angels. Jewish tradition gave names to angels. This group of seven was assigned a definite task of sounding judgments upon earth's inhabitants. The article points out "the" seven who were allotted this task. "Seven" signifies perfect judgment.

These seven angels are described by the dependent adjective clause announced by relative pronoun οἳ, "...who stand before God." ἑστήκασιν is perfect indicative active of ἵστημι to stand. It is intransitive here. These angels "took their stand and go on standing" in God's presence. Perfect suggests the permanency of their position "before God." The second of the independent clauses states, "...seven trumpets were given to them."

Verse three incorporates a compound-complex sentence. It has two independent and one dependent clause. The first clause declares "Another angel came and stood..." The compound predicate consists of two aorists which state the point-action fact that he "came and took his stand." ἐστάθη is ingressive aorist concentrating on the beginning of the act, he planted his feet and so "took his stand." The subject ἄγγελος is described by circumstantial participial phrase "having (a) golden censer."(ἔχων...)

The second independent affirms another fact about this "other" angel, "...much incense was given to him." ἐδόθη is an effective aorist looking to the finality of the act of giving.

The subordinate clause ushered in by ἵνα presents the purpose why "much incense was given to him." It was given "in order that he shall give to the prayers of the saints..." δώσει is future indicative meaning to "give" in the sense of "add." προσευχαῖς is probably best taken as dative although it conceivably might be associative-instrumental, "with." The angel was entrusted with the incense "that he shall add to the prayers of the saints..." The ἐπὶ phrase indicates the place where the incense shall be added, "upon the golden altar before the throne."

It should be observed that ἵνα normally introduces a purpose clause with a verb in the subjunctive. The text here has indicative although there are some manuscripts that have aorist subjunctive. If the indicative is the proper reading it would suggest a more positive affirmation of purpose; the difference between "might give" and "shall give."

Verse four depicts a simple sentence, "The smoke went up..." It has four prepositional phrases. "Of incense burnings" is genitive describing καπνὸς. "With prayers"(προσευχαῖς)is instrumental case, an adverbial idea describing the manner in which the prayers "went up." ἐκ with ablative "out of the angel's hand" is also an adverbial idea expressing source. "Before God" tells the place to which they "went up." Another adverbial phrase.

## Revelation 8:5-6

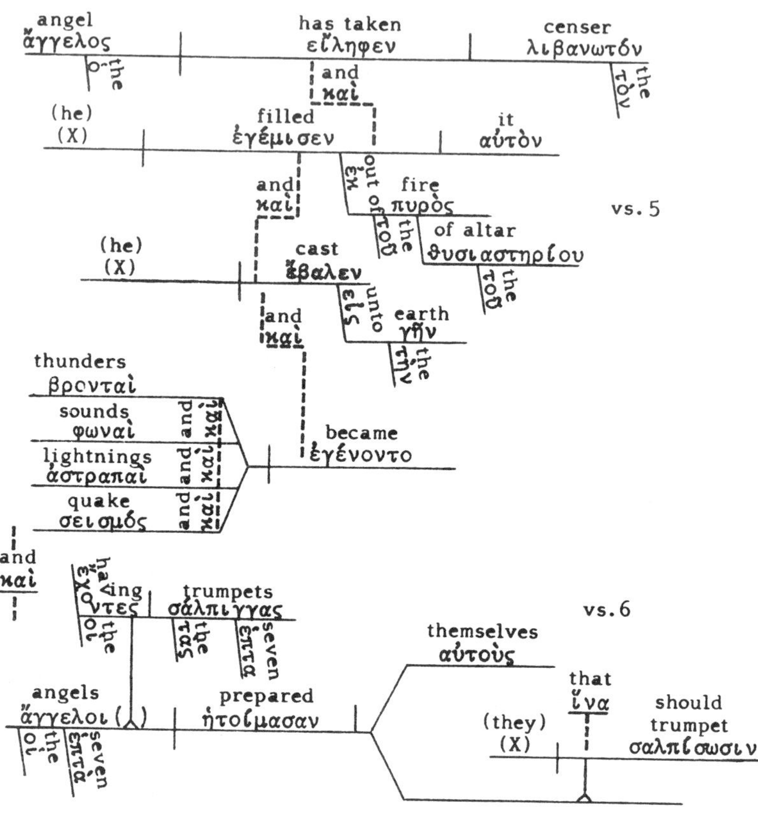

## THE DIAGRAM OF 8:5-6

Four independent clauses constitute a compound sentence. That's what verse five produces. The clause with which the sentence begins echoes the excited feelings of John, the author. It's as though he were reliving the very moment. "Look! the angel has taken the censer..." εἴληφεν is perfect indicative active. It's a dramatic perfect. That is, a perfect used by an author when he is narrating a story and his imagination becomes so lively that he envisions himself present and almost becoming a participant in the action. This dramatic perfect is made even more forceful by John's falling back immediately in the next three clauses to the more prosaic narrative aorists.

The second clause continues the episode by relating, "...he filled it out of the fire of the altar..." ἐγέμισεν is the normal narrative aorist used in telling a story. ἐκ with the ablative signifies the source from which the angel got that with which he filled the censer. Yet it is not only the source but is the thing itself with which he filled the altar. θυσιαστηρίου is probably genitive. It indicates the kind of fire, that is, "the fire which pertains to the altar." However, it might be viewed as ablative expressing the idea of separation. The fire was taken from the altar.

The third clause proceeds with the narrative about the angel and what he did in reference to the censer and the fire from the altar. "He cast it unto the earth..." ἔβαλεν is another narrative aorist. εἰς with accusative γῆν is a normal use of accusative case. The accusative limits an idea in "content, scope or direction." It limits an idea as to its time, its duration, its content. This εἰς phrase is adverbial in function here for it answers the question where.

The fourth clause completes the work of this "other angel." The entire work of this angel seems a portent signaling the judgments about to be sounded by the seven trumpet-angels. So this fourth clause adds, "...and thunders and sounds and lightnings and (an) earthquake became..." These violent disturbances of the forces of creation arose as a consequence of the fire from heaven's altar.

Verse six frames a simple sentence. It has but one clause though the subject "angels" is enlarged by an attributive participle in apposition. The verb "prepared" has a double object in the pronoun "themselves" and the noun clause (ἵνα) "that they should trumpet. The entire sentence reads, "And the seven angels, the ones holding the seven trumpets, prepared themselves that they should trumpet."

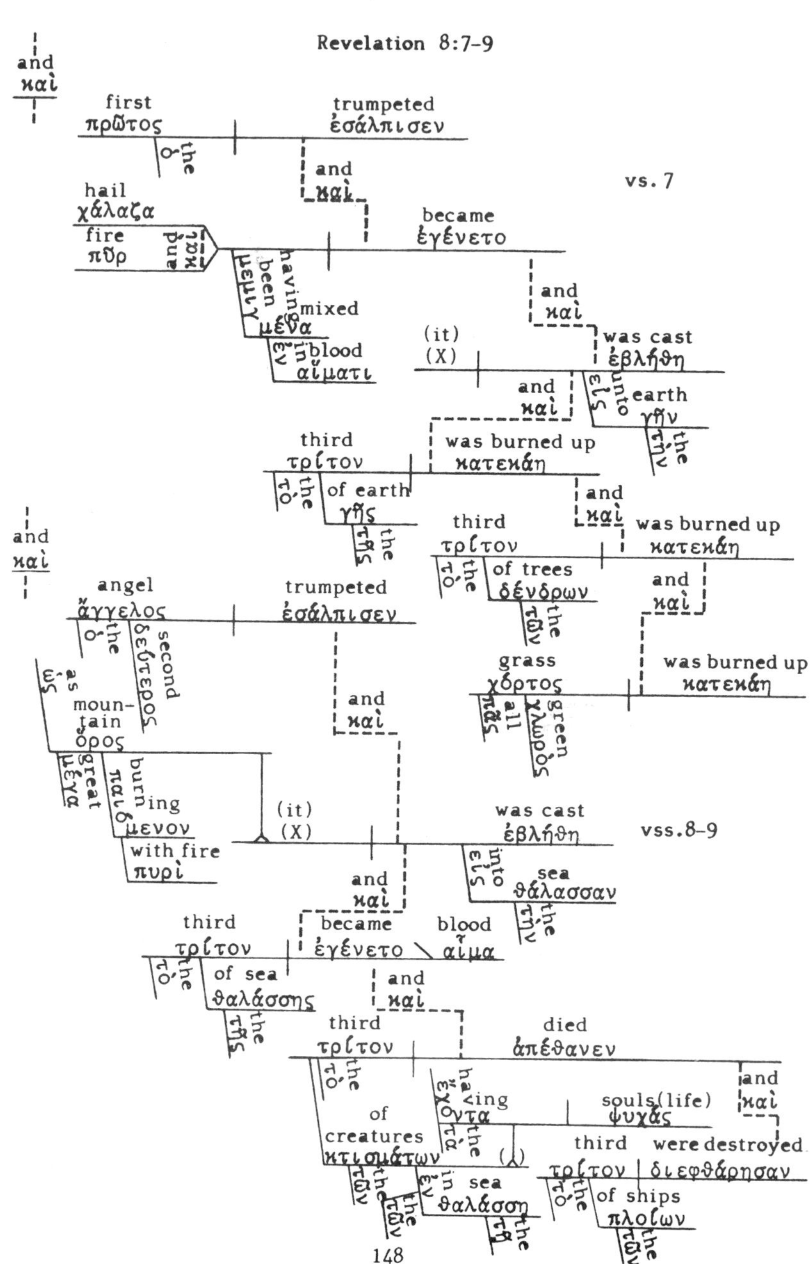
and
καὶ
first
πρῶτος
the
ὁ
trumpeted
ἐσάλπισεν
and
καὶ
vs. 7
hail
χάλαζα
fire
πῦρ
and
καὶ
became
ἐγένετο
having been mixed
μεμιγμένα
in
ἐν
blood
αἵματι
and
καὶ
(it)
(X)
was cast
ἐβλήθη
into
εἰς
earth
γῆν
the
τὴν
and
καὶ
third
τρίτον
the
τὸ
was burned up
κατεκάη
of earth
γῆς
the
τῆς
and
καὶ
third
τρίτον
the
τὸ
was burned up
κατεκάη
of trees
δένδρων
the
τῶν
and
καὶ
grass
χόρτος
all
πᾶς
green
χλωρὸς
was burned up
κατεκάη
and
καὶ
angel
ἄγγελος
the
ὁ
second
δεύτερος
trumpeted
ἐσάλπισεν
as
ὡς
moun-
tain
ὄρος
great
μέγα
burning
καιόμενον
with fire
πυρὶ
and
καὶ
(it)
(X)
was cast
ἐβλήθη
vss.8-9
into
εἰς
sea
θάλασσαν
the
τὴν
and
καὶ
third
τρίτον
the
τὸ
became
ἐγένετο
blood
αἷμα
of sea
θαλάσσης
the
τῆς
and
καὶ
third
τρίτον
the
τὸ
died
ἀπέθανεν
of
creatures
κτισμάτων
the
τῶν
having
ἔχοντα
the
τὰ
souls(life)
ψυχάς
in
ἐν
sea
θαλάσσῃ
the
τῇ
(X)
and
καὶ
third
τρίτον
the
τὸ
were destroyed
διεφθάρησαν
of ships
πλοίων
the
τῶν

## THE DIAGRAM OF 8:7-9

Revelation 8:7-9 embraces two sentences, both compound. The sentence of verse seven has six clauses "of equal rank." By definition a compound is a sentence in which all clauses involved are "of equal rank." That is, grammatically they match each other in importance. And that is true. There need be no question about that classification by grammarians. In this sentence of verse seven the first clause states what the first angel did. "The first (angel) trumpeted..."

The second clause reports that which arose ("became") when the first angel sounded his trumpet; "hail and fire mixed with blood became..." The perfect participle μεμιγμένα = "having been mixed" brings out the idea that this mixture was a "fixed" dose of judgment. God's judgment is not "cast down" arbitrarily. The consequence of sin is "fixed" in the nature of sin.

The third clause carries forward the account of what became of this mixture; "and it (the mixture of hail, fire and water) was hurled down unto the earth..." The verbs in all three of these first clauses are the usual narrative aorists used in reporting an historical account.

The next three clauses are also independent. But they relate the result of that which took place as a consequence of that which is reported in the first three clauses. These last three might have been made into adverb dependent result clauses. But they weren't! Why did the author make independent that which normally would be expressed in dependent? It reflects his own thinking as to the relative importance of what he's saying. He thinks of the result as on a par with that which occasioned the result. In this sentence he thought of the consequence of "equal rank" with cause of the consequence. The end equates with the beginning. Note too that the verb κατεκάη appears in the last three clauses. It is an effective aorist giving emphasis to the completion of the action. The earth, trees, grass were "thoroughly burned up."

Verses 8-9 contain five clauses of "equal rank." The initial clause tells that "the second angel trumpeted..." As in the previous sentence the second clause rehearses what happened: "(it) like a great mountain burning with fire, was hurled into the sea." The subject of this clause is an implied "it." The ὡς phrase is either in apposition to the "it" or it should be placed as an adjective phrase modifying the "it." The diagram presents it as appositional.

The next three clauses, though independent, suggest the idea of result just as the last three clauses in the previous sentence do. At the sounding of the second angel's trumpet a great burning mountain "was cast into the sea..." That resulted in three things: (1)"the third of the sea became blood." (2)"the third of the creatures of the sea died." (3)"the third of the ships were destroyed."

The present active participle ἔχοντα is an attributive. It with its object ψυχάς forms a phrase in apposition to κτισμάτων. It describes the "creatures in the sea" to be "the ones having life."

## Revelation 8:10–12

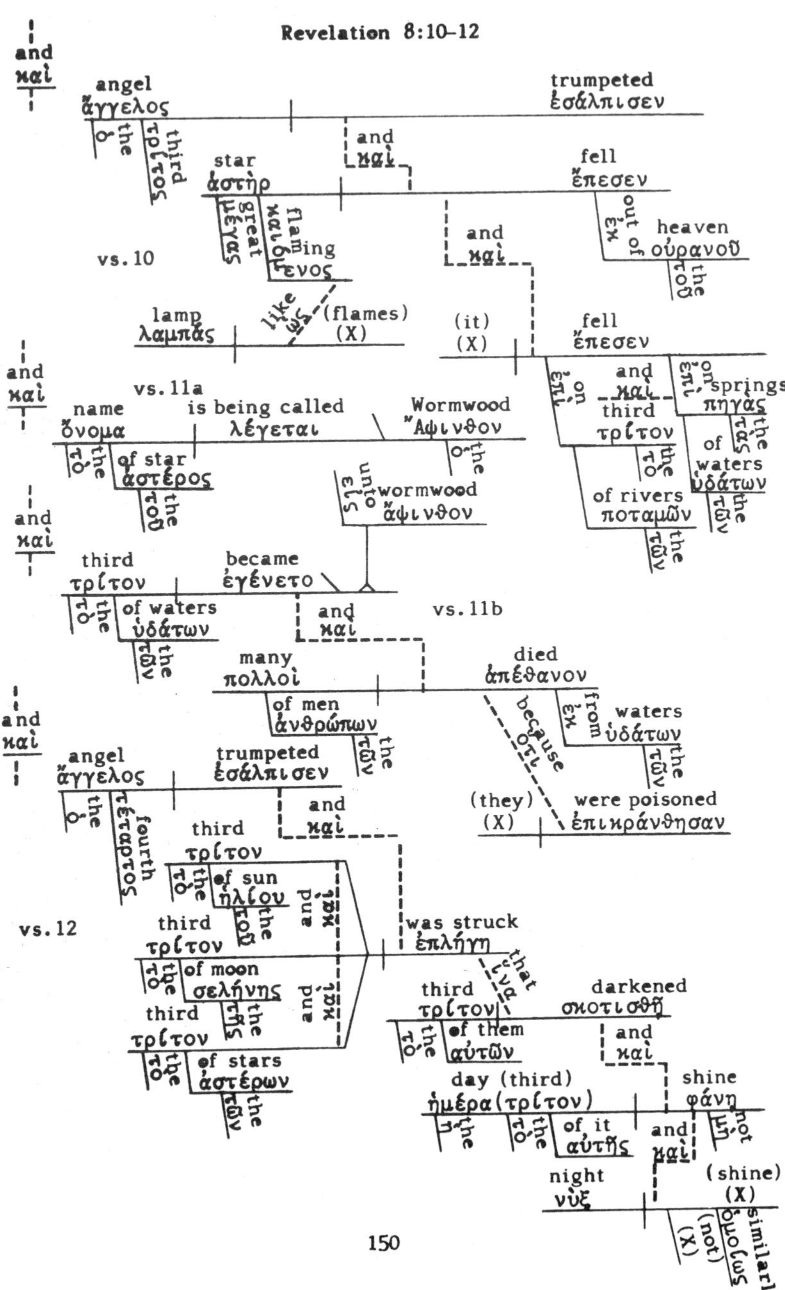

## THE DIAGRAM OF 8:10-12

Three independent clauses form the basic frame for the sentence of verse ten. However, one little adverbial dependent idea attaches itself to the second of these independents. So the sentence falls into the category of compound-complex.

The opening clause says: "The third angel trumpeted." The second clause advances the vision by designating what happened in the angel's exercising of his judgmental task: "a great star fell..." From whence it fell is incorporated in a prepositional adverb phrase, "out (ἐκ) of the heaven..." Modifying the subject, "star," is a circumstantial participle "flaming"(καιόμενος). It's to this participle that the dependent clause is joined. ὡς is the introductory conjunction. "The star, burning like a lamp (burns), fell..." It is a comparative adverbial idea.

The third main clause sets forth the specific judgments that came as a result of the fall of this flaming star, "...it fell upon the third of the rivers and upon the springs of waters."

In a simple sentence verse 11a gives a name to the star. "The name of the star is called Wormwood." Αψινθον is a feminie noun although here the masculine article appears with it. Apparently John was too excited to give attention to grammatical details. Or he may have been influenced by the masculine ἀστέρος. That would be aggreement "according to sense."

The third sentence (11b) of this page is a compound-complex. It has two independent clauses the second of which is supported by an adverbial dependent clause of cause. The first clause says, "The third of the waters became into wormwood." Preposition εἰς with accusative here constitutes an adjective phrase. It functions as a predicate adjective referring back to the subject τρίτον. This time "wormwood" is probably not a proper name as it was in the preceding sentence.

The next clause states what happened as a consequence of the waters having become bitter by means of poisoned wormwood: "...and many of the men died of the waters..." In the ὅτι causal clause the author gives a reason why the "many men died." "...because they (the waters) were poisoned."

Verse 12 embraces a sentence of five clauses, two independent followed by three dependent. After the pattern of the first three angels the initial clause declares, "...the fourth angel trumpeted." In telling what happened the second clause uses a compound subject, "the third of the sun and the third of the moon and a third of the stars..." The verb "was smitten"(ἐπλήγη)is aorist indicative passive of πλήσσω. It comes from the noun πληγή = blow, stroke "properly given by a sword or other weapon." Figuratively it came to mean a "stroke of calamity" such as a plague of divine punishment.

The ἵνα introduces three subordinate purpose clauses, "...that the third of them might be darkened," and that "the day, a third of it, might not shine," and that "the night similarly (might not shine)."

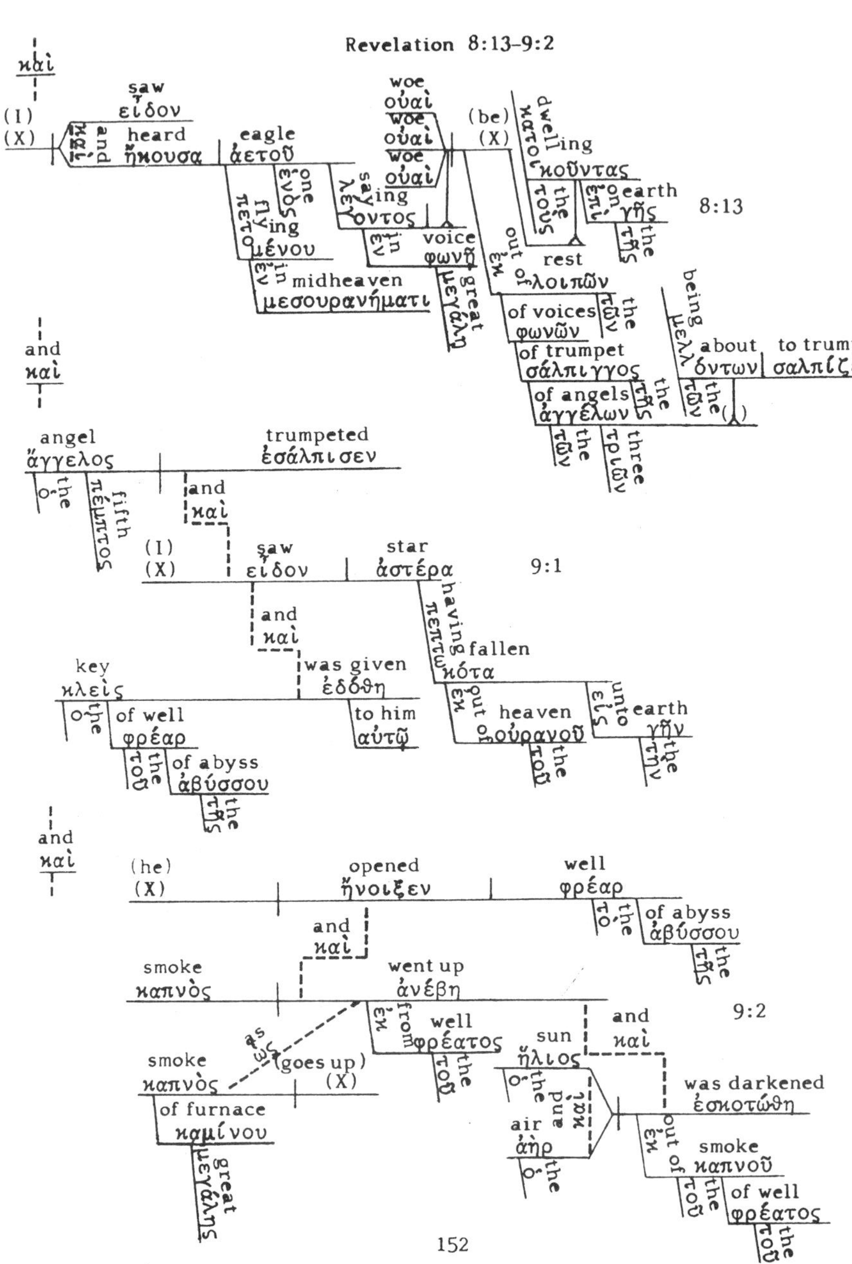
καὶ
(I)
(X)
saw
εἶδον
and
καὶ
heard
ἤκουσα
eagle
ἀετοῦ
one
ἑνὸς
fly
πετο
ing
μένου
in
ἐν
midheaven
μεσουρανήματι
say
λέγ
ing
οντος
in
ἐν
voice
φωνῇ
great
μεγάλῃ
woe
οὐαὶ
woe
οὐαὶ
woe
οὐαὶ
(be)
(X)
dwell
κατοι
ing
κοῦντας
the
τοὺς
on
ἐπὶ
earth
γῆς
the
τῆς
8:13
out of
ἐκ
rest
λοιπῶν
the
τῶν
of voices
φωνῶν
of trumpet
σάλπιγγος
the
τῆς
of angels
ἀγγέλων
the
τῶν
three
τριῶν
being
μελλ
about
όντων
the
τῶν
to trumpet
σαλπίζειν
and
καὶ
angel
ἄγγελος
the
ὁ
fifth
πέμπτος
trumpeted
ἐσάλπισεν
and
καὶ
(I)
(X)
saw
εἶδον
star
ἀστέρα
9:1
having
πεπτω
fallen
κότα
out of
ἐκ
heaven
οὐρανοῦ
the
τοῦ
unto
εἰς
earth
γῆν
the
τὴν
and
καὶ
was given
ἐδόθη
to him
αὐτῷ
key
κλεὶς
the
ὁ
of well
φρέαρ
the
τοῦ
of abyss
ἀβύσσου
the
τῆς
and
καὶ
(he)
(X)
opened
ἤνοιξεν
well
φρέαρ
the
τὸ
of abyss
ἀβύσσου
the
τῆς
and
καὶ
smoke
καπνὸς
went up
ἀνέβη
from
ἐκ
well
φρέατος
the
τοῦ
9:2
as
ὡς
smoke
καπνὸς
(goes up)
(X)
of furnace
καμίνου
great
μεγάλης
and
καὶ
sun
ἥλιος
the
ὁ
and
καὶ
air
ἀὴρ
the
ὁ
was darkened
ἐσκοτώθη
out of
ἐκ
smoke
καπνοῦ
the
τοῦ
of well
φρέατος
the
τοῦ

## THE DIAGRAM OF 8:13-9:2

Chapter 8 closes with a complex sentence. It has two clauses. The independent clause has a compound predicate, "I saw and heard..." ἀετοῦ is direct object in genitive after the verb of hearing. The cardinal number in genitive ἑνὸς has the force of an indefinite article. ἀετοῦ also has two circumstantial participles describing it. Present middle πετομένου in idea connects back to the verb "saw." "I saw an eagle flying..." The present active λέγοντος links up with the other main verb "heard." "I heard an eagle saying..." Each of these participles is modified by phrases introduced by ἐν and each of which are functioning as adverbs. The eagle was flying "in mid-heaven." And it was saying "in a loud voice."

The one dependent is a noun clause, direct object of the participle "saying." It has a triple-pronged compound subject, "woe, woe woe..." The ἐκ phrase modifies an understood verb. It expresses that the "woes" are to come as a result of ("out of") the sound of the next three angels' trumpets. A second modifier of the understood verb is the present attributive accusative participle κατοικοῦντας = "the ones dwelling..." Accusative case in this construction is somewhat unusual. Dative would be normal: "Woe be to the ones dwelling..." The personal interest dative reflects the idea of "for" or "against." Accusative limits an idea in "content, scope or direction." Either John again disregarded the refinements of grammar or else his choice of accusative expresses the limits of the "woes."

Chapter 9:1 accommodates a compound sentence of three clauses. "The fifth angel trumpeted..." is the first. It follows the pattern of the earlier four angel trumpets. The second clause affirms, "I saw a star..." An added fact about the star comes into view in circumstantial perfect participle πεπτωκότα = "having fallen." Both the ἐκ and εἰς phrases are adverbial modifying the participle and telling "from which" and "unto where" the star fell. The third clause reveals that "the key of the pit of the abyss was given to him." Antecedent to the pronoun αὐτῷ is "angel" back in the first of the three clauses. φρέαρ is "cistern" or "well." ἄβυσσος is an adjective formed from alpha privative with βυθός "depth." Resultant idea is "without depth" or "without boundary." In other words, "boundless." This expression has been translated "bottomless pit."

Verse two of chapter nine is compound-complex. It has three independent clauses and one dependent. Nothing distinctive about the opening clause: "And he opened the pit of the abyss." Here is a normal narrative aorist ἤνοιξεν with neuter accusative direct object φρέαρ. The second main clause divulges that "the smoke went up..." ἐκ with ablative φρέατος is adverbial telling from where the "smoke went up." That is, "from the pit." Attached to this second clause is the dependent adverbial comparative clause introduced by ὡς, "...as smoke of a great furnace (goes up)..." The final clause relates what happened as a result of this smoke going up. "...the sun and the air was darkened..."

## Revelation 9:3-5

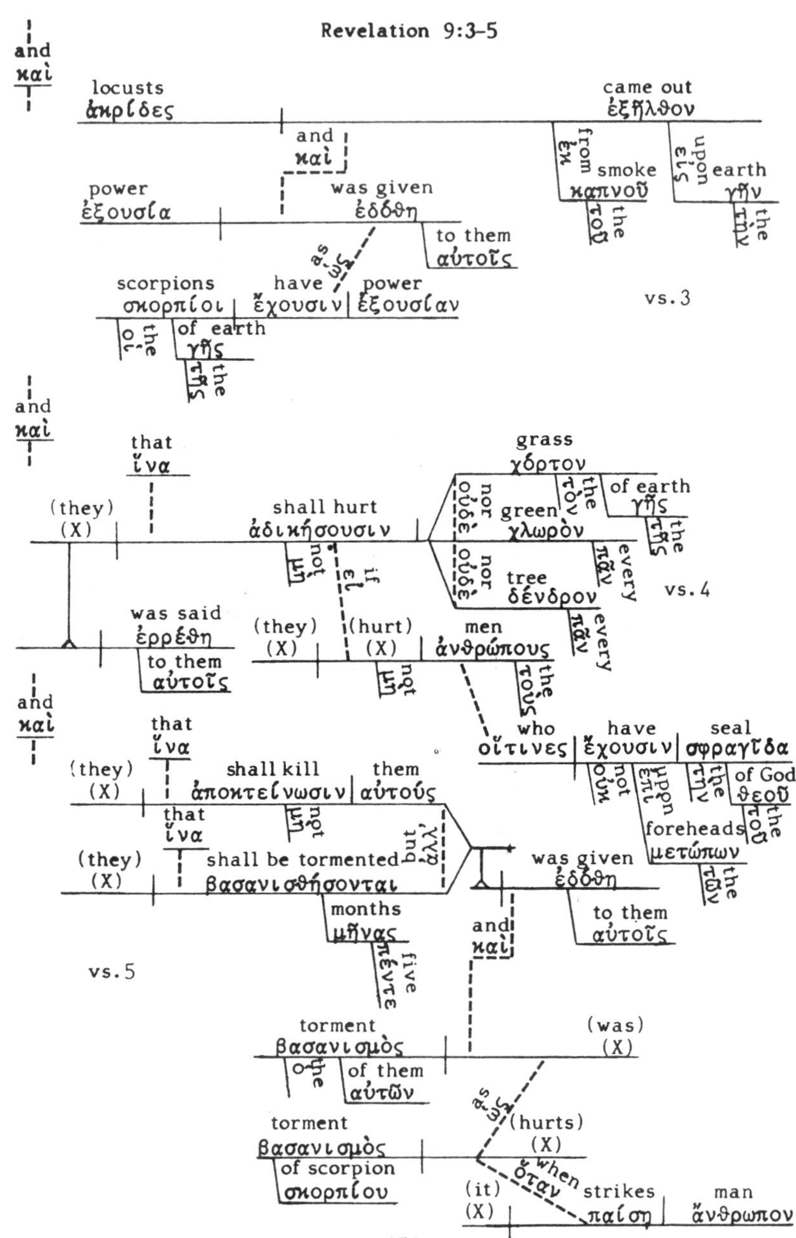

## THE DIAGRAM OF 9:3-5

Having set the stage in 9:1-2, verse three in a compound-complex sentence describes an infernal army of locusts that arose from the "pit of the abyss." The sentence possesses two independent clauses. First is the statement of that which the abyss disgorged. "And locusts came out..." Ablative with ἐκ tells from whence they came: "from the earth." εἰς with accusative indicates to where: "unto the earth."

The second main clause testifies, "power was given to them..." The noun ἐξουσία intimates that kind of power that lies inherent within rather than that which is imposed from an outside force. By its very nature evil has within it power to destroy. The rotting power of evil isn't imposed as punishment from outside the act itself. Native to the quality of sin is its own destruction. And to picture more concretely the power of these "locusts" to destroy, the author adds a subordinate adverb clause: "...as the scorpions of the earth have power..." It is a clause of comparison.

Verse four includes four clauses three of which are dependent. The one independent asserts, "It was said to them..." ἐρρέθη is aorist indicative passive of εἶπον. The content of what "was said" to these invading diabolical locusts finds expression in the dependent clauses. First is a noun clause serving as the subject of the verb "was said." It is introduced by ἵνα: "that they shall not hurt..." Precisely what they "shall not hurt" is found in the compound object: "grass of the earth," "nor any green," "nor any tree."

But this prohibition not to hurt natural creation is conditional. The condition is stated in the clause introduced by εἰ and an understood verb "shall hurt" borrowed from the preceding clause. This understood verb would be indicative as is ἀδικήσουσιν in spite of negative μὴ which is normally used with subjunctive. The particular "men"(ἀνθρώπους)under consideration are described in the adjective clause, "who do not have on their foreheads the seal of God." The logic involved in the three dependent clauses is determined by the conditional. It is a second class conditional determined as unfulfilled. "If they shall not hurt men, but they will..." The conclusion therefore is: "then they shall not hurt the grass etc..."

Verse five structures a five-clause compound-complex sentence. The verb of the first independent is ἐδόθη = "was given." Exactly what was given is stated in a compound subject. Each part of this two-pronged subject is made more prominent by use of ἵνα with each portion of the subject. "That they shall not kill them" was given. But "that they shall be tormented five months" was given. The second independent clause carries forward the idea of torment: "...their torment (was)..." Detailed description of this torment is set forth by two subordinate clauses. First is comparative ὡς clause: "...as a scorpion's torment (is)..." How much such a scorpion's torment hurts is further made plain by the ὅταν adverb clause: "...whenever it strikes (a) man."

## Revelation 9:6-9

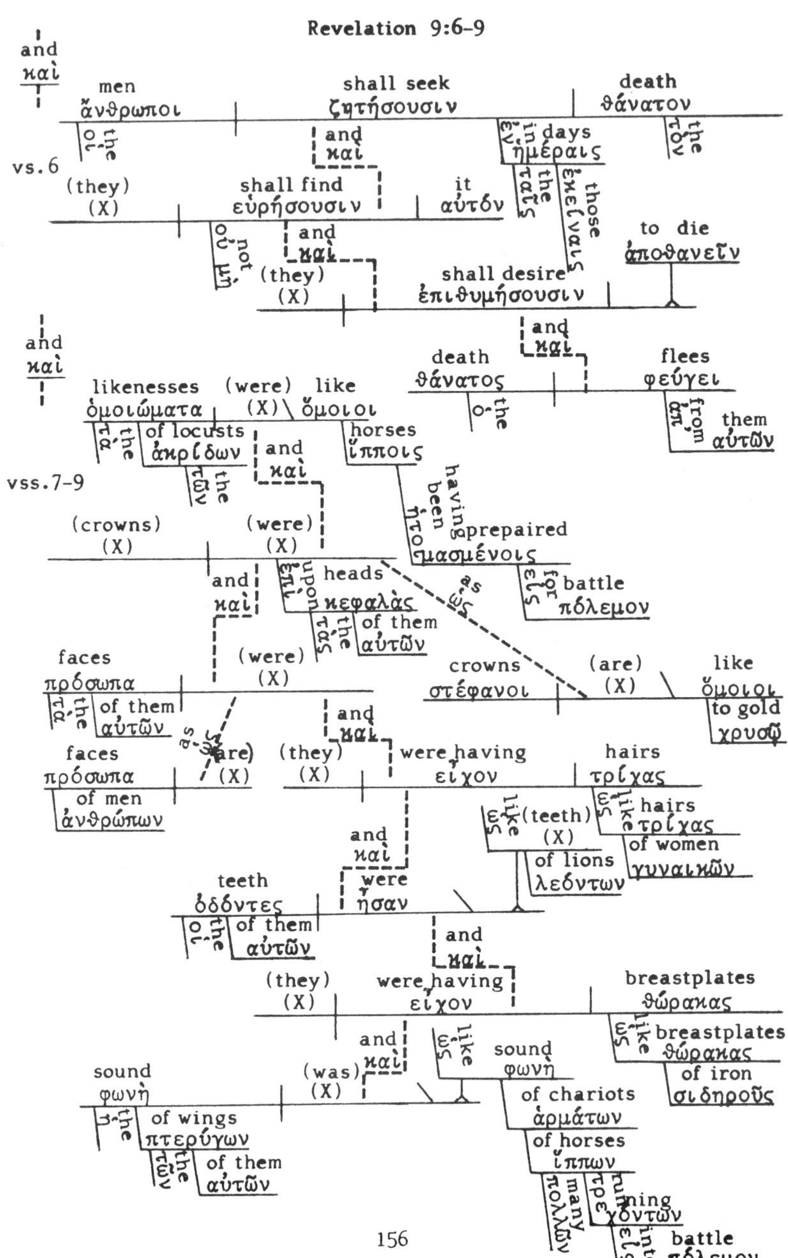

## THE DIAGRAM OF 9:6-9

The sentence of verse six has four clauses, all independent. That classifies this as compound. The sentence depicts the reaction of man to the onslaught of judgment inflicted by the locusts. The first clause states, "The men shall seek death." Prepositional ἐν phrase is adverbial suggesting when. The second clause contains emphatic double negative οὐ μὴ and declares, "they shall not find it." The third affirms their frustration: "they shall desire to die." Infinitive ἀποθανεῖν is accusative case object of the verb translated "shall desire." The final clause brings into view their hopelessness: "death flees from them." Of the verbs in these clauses the first three are future; the last is present though some manuscripts carry future.

As pictured in the diagram the sentence of verses 7-9 has nine clauses. Seven of them are independent with the remaining two dependent. Stripped of modifying elements the seven say, "likenesses were," "(crowns were)," "faces (were)," "they were having," "teeth were," "they were having," and "sound (was)."

The two dependent clauses use the adverb ὡς as introductory particles. The first ὡς clause is comparative adverbial modifying the second of the independent clauses: "...(crowns were) upon their heads as (ὡς) crowns (are) like gold..." Similarly the next ὡς clause modifies the next independent idea: "...their faces (were) as (ὡς) the faces of men (are)."

ὡς appears three more times in the sentence. But the diagram does not show them as introducing dependent clauses. One should remember "the mere adverb is a fixed case-form of a substantive, adjective, or participle, numeral, pronoun, or phrase used to modify verbs, adjectives, other adverbs or even substantives."(New Short Grammar of the Greek N.T., Robertson-Davis, pg.246). The next ὡς serves as a preposition (all prepositions are adverbs in a specialized use) with accusative τρίχας describing another τρίχας. "...they were having hairs like hairs of women..."

The last two times ὡς appears it is as introductory particle to a predicate nominative phrase which refers back to the subject in their respective clauses: (1)"like (teeth) of lions" and (2)"like sound of chariots etc..." In structure these expressions are no different than the first two ὡς clauses above. They might have been properly diagrammed as clauses thus making four dependent clauses in this sentence. However, the diagram sets them forth as predicate nominative phrases because this construction seems to tie them more closely to their respective subjects.

We note that a language has more than one way to express any given idea. Also we observe that a diagram, though an invaluable tool with which to analyze thought, may be more or less arbitrary as it sets up its devices to make relationships graphic to the eye. ὡς may be used in a variety of ways; it may convey various ideas. We've noted three of them in this sentence. One must apply himself to the context and then make a judgment as to what was in an author's mind when he wrote.

## Revelation 9:10–12

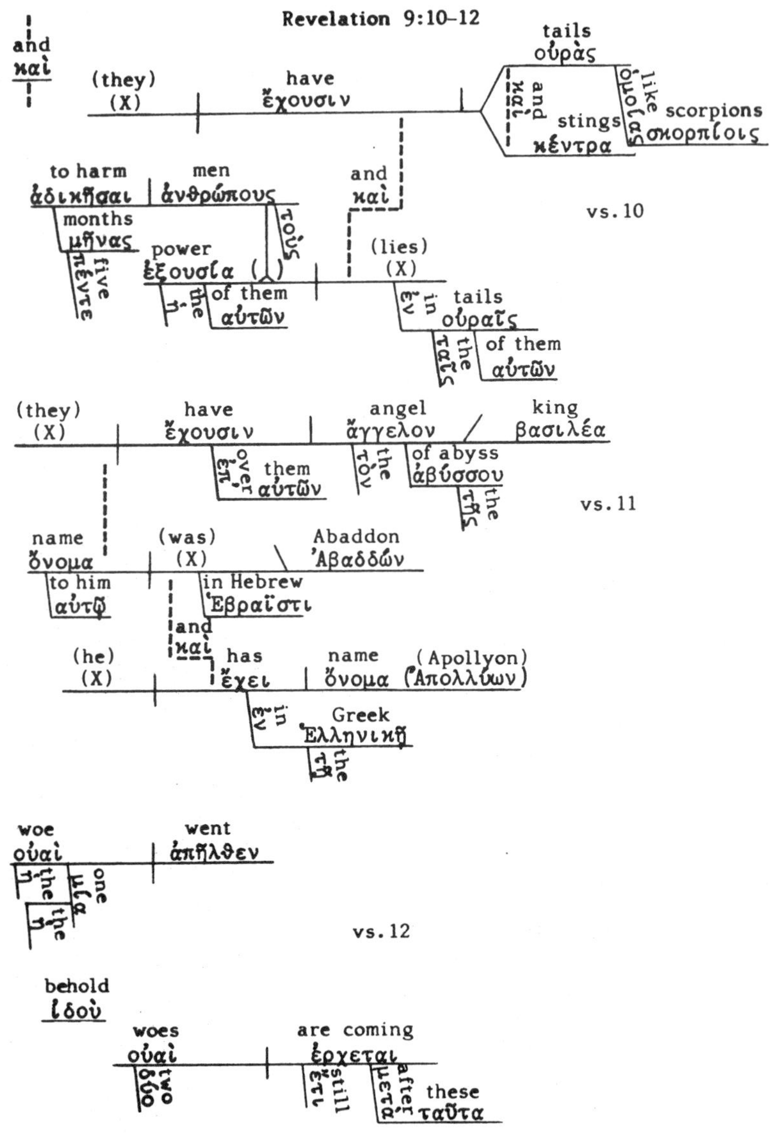

## THE DIAGRAM OF 9:10-12

Compound is the category into which the sentence of verse ten falls. It has two independent clauses. The first professes: "They have tails...and stings..." Their tails are described as being "like scorpions." ὁμοίας as a word of "likeness" has instrumental case after it, σκορπίοις = "scorpions." ὁμοίας is an adjective but in this construction it appears as though it were a preposition injecting an adjective phrase. Had the "scorpions" been nominative then "like" could have appeared as a subordinating conjunction introducing, "...like scorpions have tails..." Grammatical arrangements of one language don't always fit neatly into the patterns of another. And even within the same language identical words and forms may be used in different ways.

The second clause states: "...and their power...lies in their tails." To make a further identification of just how this power is to be applied the author adds an infinitive phrase in apposition to the subject. ἀδικῆσαι is aorist infinitive "to harm" which takes ἀνθρώπους "men" as its direct object. μῆνας is accusative extent of time.

Verse eleven admits of three clauses of equal rank, hence is compound. Asyndeton prevails between the first and second clauses. Such lack of formal connection often makes the two clauses so joined more sharply defined. The initial clause reads: "They have over them the angel of the abyss, (as) king." βασιλέα is objective complement. It indicates the particular function which the "angel of the abyss" has over "them."

The next clause identifies by name this "king." "...and name to him (was) in Hebrew, Abaddon." αὐτῷ is dative of possession. "In Hebrew" (Ἑβραϊστι) is an adverbial idea. The third clause restates the name but this time in Greek; "...and he has name, Apollyon, in the Greek." Ἑλληνικῇ for practical purposes functions as a noun though technically it is an adjective which would be modifying an understood "language."

Verse 12 consists of two simple sentences. The first one states: "The first woe went!" Note cardinal μία used as ordinal "first." ἀπῆλθεν is aorist indicative active. In this context it conveys the idea that the "first woe has happened!" οὐαὶ is an interjection though here with feminine article it takes on the force of a noun, subject of the sentence.

The second sentence of this verse gives a warning: "Behold! two woes are coming after these things!" In the first sentence "woe" is singular. Here it is used with "two" (δύο) and is treated as plural. Yet the verb ἔρχεται is singular. The μετὰ phrase is adverbial expressing <u>when</u> "these things" are coming.

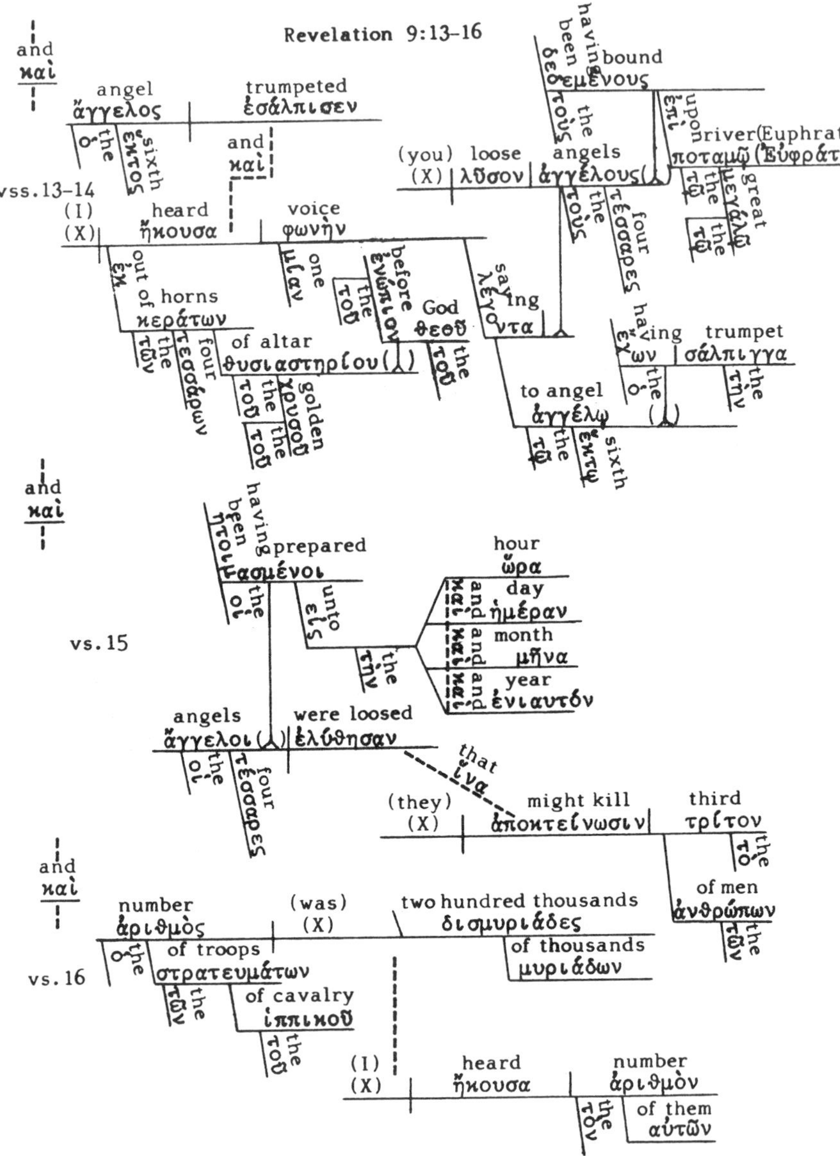
Revelation 9:13–16
and
καὶ
angel
ἄγγελος
the
ὁ
sixth
ἕκτος
trumpeted
ἐσάλπισεν
and
καὶ
vss.13–14
(I)
(X)
heard
ἤκουσα
voice
φωνὴν
one
μίαν
out of
ἐκ
horns
κεράτων
the
τῶν
four
τεσσάρων
of altar
θυσιαστηρίου
the
τοῦ
golden
χρυσοῦ
before
ἐνώπιον
God
θεοῦ
saying
λέγοντα
having been bound
δεδεμένους
the
τοὺς
upon
ἐπὶ
river
ποταμῷ
(Euphrates)
(Εὐφράτῃ)
great
μεγάλῳ
(you)
(X)
loose
λῦσον
angels
ἀγγέλους
four
τέσσαρες
having
ἔχων
trumpet
σάλπιγγα
the
τὴν
to angel
ἀγγέλῳ
sixth
ἕκτῳ
and
καὶ
having been prepared
ἡτοιμασμένοι
the
οἱ
unto
εἰς
the
τὴν
hour
ὥρα
day
ἡμέραν
month
μῆνα
year
ἐνιαυτόν
vs.15
angels
ἄγγελοι
four
τέσσαρες
were loosed
ἐλύθησαν
that
ἵνα
(they)
(X)
might kill
ἀποκτείνωσιν
third
τρίτον
the
τὸ
of men
ἀνθρώπων
and
καὶ
number
ἀριθμὸς
(was)
(X)
two hundred thousands
δισμυριάδες
of thousands
μυριάδων
vs.16
of troops
στρατευμάτων
of cavalry
ἱππικοῦ
(I)
(X)
heard
ἤκουσα
number
ἀριθμὸν
the
τὸν
of them
αὐτῶν

## THE DIAGRAM OF 9:13-16

Three clauses embellish verses 13-14. They are so disposed as to create a compound-complex arrangement. The two independent clauses affirm: "...the sixth angel trumpeted" and "I heard a voice..." Greek doesn't have an indefinite article but here the cardinal μίαν functions almost as if it were an "a." ἐκ with ablative is an adverbial phrase identifying the source from which the voice was sounded; "from the four horns..." θυσιαστηρίου is probably best classed as genitive of possession. It's the "horns of the golden altar..." Preposition ἐνώπιον with genitive is in apposition further identifying the "altar."

The dependent is a noun clause serving as direct object of the present circumstantial participle λέγοντα = "saying." It says, "loose the four angels..." Perfect passive participle with definite article labels these four angels as "the ones having been bound..." ἐπὶ with locative ποταμῷ is adverbial revealing where they had been bound. The one to whom the "voice" was "saying" the command is presented in the dative ἀγγέλῳ. And to this is added the appositional present attributive participle, "the one having the trumpet..."(ἔχων)

The next sentence (verse 15) is complex with just two clauses. Without its modifiers the one main clause declares, "...angels were loosed..." The definite article οἱ points back to the previously mentioned "four angels." And these four are further designated as "the ones having been prepared..." This perfect participle with article is attributive in apposition to the subject "angels." The preposition εἰς with accusatives expresses extent of time: "unto the hour and day and month and year..."

The ἵνα clause is the subordinate idea. It is adverbial in function expressing purpose. The reason for the loosing of the four angels was "in order that they mighty kill the third of men." The verb ἀποκτείνωσιν is present subjunctive, linear action. It flashes a moving picture of the death dealing jundgment, not just a still snapshot. τρίτον is an ordinal numeral used here as a noun, object of the verb "kill."

Verse 16 presents a two-part compound sentence. Its two clauses lack a formal conjunction to join them (asyndeton). The first clause creates the impression of the immensity of the multitudes of this army of judgment: "the number (was) two hundred thousands of thousands..." The subject "number" is characterized as being "of troops." Likewise the genitive translated "of thousands" adds a descriptive force to specify the kind of "two hundred thousands." The entire expression is designed to create the sense in the reader of a vast innumerable throng of the invading judgmental forces.

The final clause reinforces the impression left by the first. The author says, "I heard the number of them." In other words, I haven't overstated the numbers of the multitudes for "I heard the number..."

Revelation 9:17-19

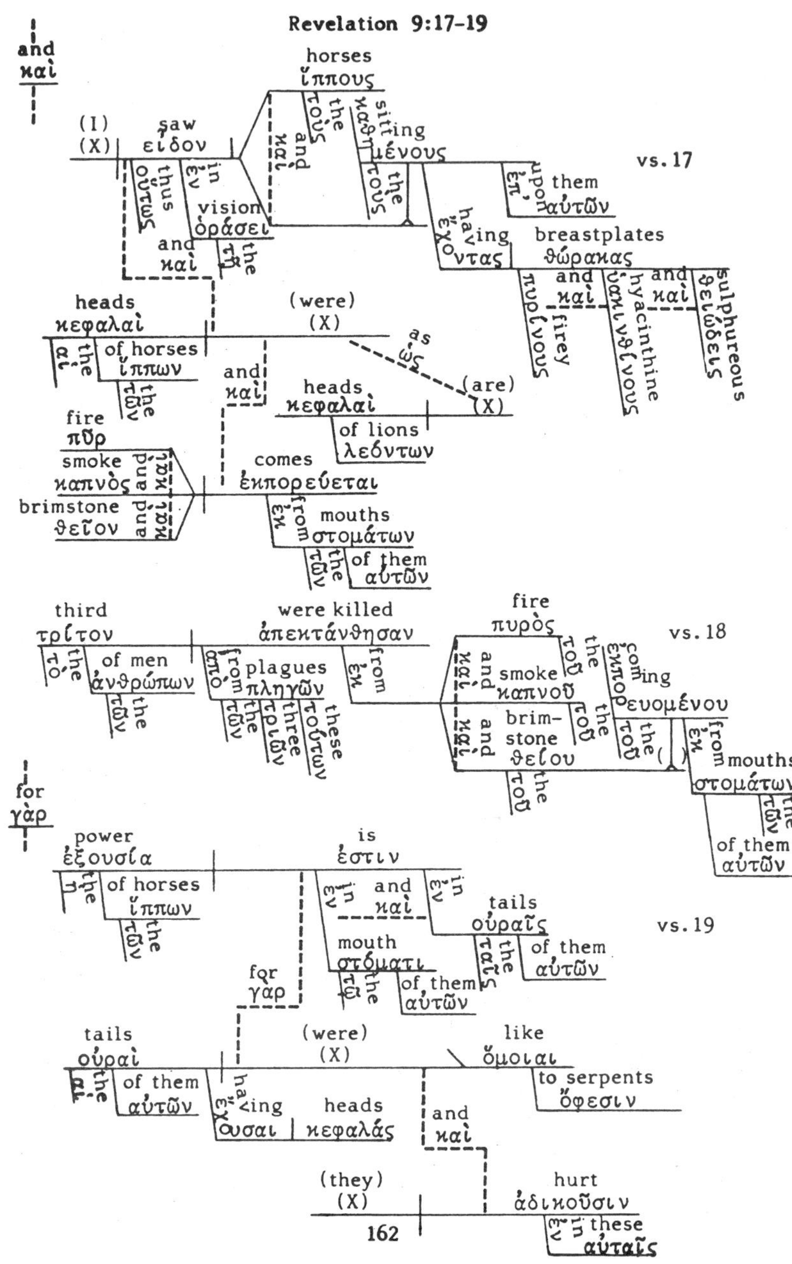

## THE DIAGRAM OF 9:17-19

The presence of a ὡς adverbial dependent clause turns verse 17 into a compound-complex sentence from what would otherwise have been a compound. The first clause announces the fact, "I saw..." Adverb "thus" (οὕτως) indicates the manner in which he saw. That is, the manner in which I here record. The ἐν phrase is adverbial; it points out where he saw; "in the vision." The content of that which he saw emerges in the double direct object, "horses" and "the ones sitting upon them." Present participle καθημένους is attributive = "the ones sitting." Added to this participle as a further description is a present circumstantial participle ἔχοντας = "having breastplates." The word translated "breastplates"(θώρακας) is made more horribly vivid by the adjectives "firey," hyacinthine" and "sulphureous."

The second main clause declares: "the heads of the horses (were)..." The description of the horses heads is carried forward by the ὡς dependent comparative clause: "as heads of lions (are)."

The third clause moves the description to its dramatic climax by disclosing that "fire and smoke and brimstone comes out of their mouths." These hellish horses, their riders and somber-red colors symbolize the terrors of evil and the judgments it inevitably brings on evil men.

Verse 18 has only one clause thus is categorized as simple. The bare clause states: "third were killed." To specify specifically who "the third" represents genitive ἀνθρώπων is thrust in: "the third of men." The verb ἀπεκτάνθησαν is aorist indicative passive plural. Though it has a masculine singular subject it is plural "according to sense." The expression "from these three plagues" (ἀπὸ with ablative) mirrors the source from which the killing derived. It's kin to a causal idea. They were killed because of the plagues. The cause is more specifically describe in the added ἐκ phrase, "from the fire and the smoke and the brimstone." θείου is more plainly pictured by appositional attributive participial phrase, "the one coming out of their mouths.(ἐκπορευομένου)

Verse 19 resorts to three independent clauses to portray its compound structure. The bare clauses without modifying elements say: "...power is...tails (were) like...they hurt..." The power is identified by genitive ἵππων = "of horses." The place where the power is located finds expression in the two ἐν phrases, adverb in function: "in their mouth" and "in their tails."

The subject of the second clause "tails" has a circumstantial participle describing it. ἔχουσαι is present active participle with κεφαλὰς as direct object: "having heads." ὄφεσιν is instrumental case after word of likeness.

The final clause points out that "...in these do they hurt..." ἐν with the locative "in these" is adverb idea locating where the power to hurt is. ἀδικοῦσιν is present tense linear action. The power to hurt is continuous and repetitious.

# Revelation 9:20–21

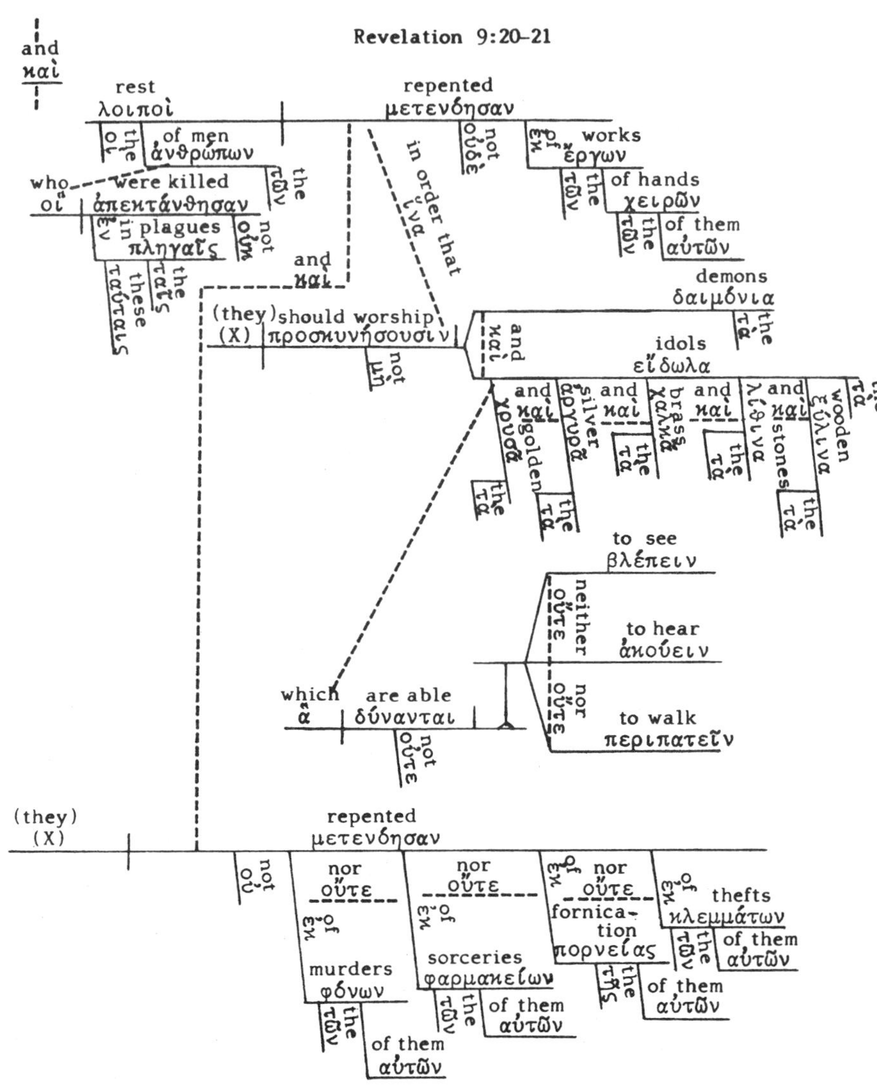

## THE DIAGRAM OF 9:20-21

Five clauses carry the flow of thought in 9:20-21. Two are independent and three are dependent. The burden of thought in both independent clauses is the failure to repent on the part of mankind who were not destroyed in the plagues that were let loose by the four angels of verses 14-15. Both the main clauses declare, "The rest of the men repented not" and "they repented not..." The very repetition insists on the importance of the idea. The fact that humanity doesn't respond in changing its mind (repentance) brings out the idea that the "plagues" were designed by God for redemptive purposes. In a world dominated by sin pain in punishment is as inevitable as fruit on a fruit tree. But pain is controlled by God to cure the sinner, not kill him. The fact that the patient doesn't respond redemptively to the surgery is a fact with which he has to live and die. The aorist tense in both these independent clauses is well-suited for underscoring fact as fact. Descriptive elaboration is not needed. The fact is: "they did not repent!!!"

The first of the three dependent clauses is adjectival describing ἀνθρώπων. It's introduced by the relative οἳ. It reads, "...who were not killed in these plagues..." ἐν with locative "plagues" conceives the killing as taking place "in" the plagues. It's the means by which the men were killed, sometimes referred to as the "instrumental use" of the locative.

The second of the dependent clauses is a negative adverbial inaugurated by ἵνα. The negative is μὴ. Such a negative purpose clause would normally have the subjunctive mode. But here the verb προσκυνήσουσιν is future indicative = "shall worship." This use of indicative rather than subjunctive might reflect John's excited ignoring of grammatical norms. On the other hand it could be deliberate. If so, since the indicative is the mode of positive affirmation, it would be a sharp emphasis on the purpose. No amount of punishment could persuade the "rest of the men" to repent. They weren't about to refuse to worship demons and the humanly made idols. Punishment drove them more firmly into their rebellious worship of their self-made gods.

The final of the dependent clauses is another adjective idea. It modifies the noun εἴδωλα. It describes the "idols." They are those "which (relative ἃ) are not able to see neither to hear nor to walk." The three infinitives that are objects of δύνανται are all present of linear action. Their inability to "be seeing," "be hearing," and "be walking" is continuous.

"The rest of mankind who were not killed in these plagues, neither repented from the works of their hands that they should not worship the demons and the idols,...and they did not repent from their murders..." These words offer a clue to the purpose of the "plagues" of the "seven trumpets." The judgments that came with the sounding of the trumpets hopefully would lead rebelling man to repentance. Punishment for sin is not wholly punitive. It's designed to be redemptive. Alas, those who escape the rapacious plundering of sin "repented not." Their sin persisted; their corruption compounded; their guilt multiplied.

We recall that the breaking of the seventh seal became the sounding of "seven trumpets." These trumpet judgments reveal God's method of maintaining a just governing in a world of wickedness. They uncover the secret of how the sovereign God rules and redeems in this degenerate immoral world. For judgment is not the absence of love. He who does not judge evil does not love good. In fact, judgment is the expression of love against the corrupting powers of evil. By its nature light to be light must destroy darkness. God is love, therefore he rules in judgments.

Prayers of the saints answered!

More awesome than ceaseless clamor of activity is total quiet. The sudden silence of heaven captured undivided attention. As the Lamb stretched forth to open "the seventh seal" the rapt consciousness of all heaven froze in anticipation. While thus gripped they beheld "another angel" moving silently until he stood "over the altar" from where "with the prayers of all the saints" he mixed the incense of heaven from his "golden censer." These "prayers went up before God out of the angel's hand." The moral conscience of the universe prays to the living God for justice to be done, divine vengeance be exercised on the moral injustices of history. In answer to this universal expectation of justice the angel takes the "fire of the altar, and cast it upon the earth..." The thunders and quakes that follow symbolize the answer to the "prayers of the saints." God rules in judgment. The seven trumpet angels depict God's judgments.

Judgments against creation!

The first four of the trumpets trigger judicial punishment upon various parts of creation. First, "hail and fire mingled with blood" burn the "third part of the earth...and of trees...and of green grass..." In quick succession a volcanic mountain "burning with fire was hurled into the sea" until a third part of fish in the sea and the ships on the sea perish. At the sounding of the third trumpet a great meteor-star like a "burning torch" fell upon a "third of the rivers" and "fountains of waters" This Wormwood star poisoned a "third part of the waters" and many men died because of the poisoned waters. The fourth trumpet angel darkened "a third part of the sun...moon...stars." Day and night were cut by a third. The fact that only "a third" was affected suggests that these judgments were mercifully limited. "God is not willing that any should perish." God wishes to stimulate man to repent. He designs punishment so that it may appeal to the conscience of man. He loves so much that any pain judgment inflicts will call men to turn toward Him. But if they refuse their very increased rebellion compounds their guilt and multiplies their pain.

Judgments against mankind!

Preceding the sounding of the fifth trumpet a flying eagle is envisioned spreading his wings in "midheaven." He screams forth three woes for "them that dwell on the earth." This forewarns that the coming three judgments are directed specifically to the people who inhabit the earth. This time it was more than creation which indirectly affects man's life on the planet. But painful punishment is to come straight onto rebellious human beings.

"The fifth angel sounded." This time when a "star fell from heaven" the "key to the abyss was given to him." Thus is indicated that this "star" was the fallen angel, Satan himself. So when he opened the pit and smoke arose "sun and air were darkened" signifying the darkening effect of sin let loose in the world. From this darkening smoke belched forth "locusts" that possessed the "power of scorpions." These powerful scorpion-like locusts were specifically instructed not to attack the natural creation but only the human. And even of men "only such men as have not the seal of God..." It's also important to note that the painful bite of the locusts was "not to kill" but only that men "should be tormented five months." This paints a portrait in symbolic colors of the power of sin to torment and harass. When Satan, king of the abyss, unlocked sin to do its destructive tormenting work on man he understood that by its very nature sin would carry its own painful punishment. The weight of guilt, the torment of conscience, the agony of remembered lies, the festering bleeding of adulterous betrayal, the restless unending pricking of one's inner spirit create a hell out of an otherwise heavenly life. If there were no hell for the devil and his angels these betrayals of sin would create a hell far more painful than fire that burns the body. Indeed, sin does not at first kill men. It torments them "five months." In the end it brings inevitable death. But in his mercy God allows sin only "to torment" for a limited period in the hopes that the torment would awaken man to repentance.

Yet in their folly men, instead of turning to God for mercy and forgiveness in repentance turn to suicide. "In those days men shall seek death, and shall not find it; they shall desire to die and death flees them." There's no way to escape the inexorable pain of punishment to him who will not repent. So the terrible armies of Satan's sin rush into battle and "the sound of their wings was as the sound of chariots, of many horses rushing to war." Appollyon rules in the realm of sin. But over one group of men he has no power; those on whose foreheads is the "seal of God." The evil locusts cannot penetrate the divine armor protecting God's people. Sin's power does not prevail over the sealing power of God's Spirit.

"And the sixth angel sounded." Another apocalyptic figure in symbolic terms paints a lurid picture of another judgment that ever has plagued the people of God. The great Babylonian captivity lay beyond the Euphrates. It was from that direction that Israel found herself swallowed up in her greatest humiliation. It came to the prophet as a shocking revelation that "the bitter and hasty nation" was "ordained for judgment" and that he was "established for correction."(Hab.1:12) Thus the sixth trumpet angel in Revelation was sent to "loose the four angels that are bound at the great river Euphrates." And those four who were destined for that "hour, month, day and year" were released that they might set loose "ten thousand times ten thousand horsemen." This innumerable horde of horsemen armed in fire and brimstone with "heads of lions" breathing "fire and smoke" broke into the ranks of humanity to kill "the third part of men" with the bite of mouth and tail. Short of total annihilation of humanity this was the ultimate punishment devised to incite repentance. But in spite of God's merciful design the "rest of mankind, who were not killed with these plagues, repented not of the works of their hands, that they should not worship demons, and the idols of gold, and of silver, and of brass, and of stone, and of wood; which are not able either to see nor to hear nor to walk; and they did not repent from their murders neither from their sorceries nor from their fornication nor from their robberies."

Man's maximum punishment for sin is that he must live and die with the gods of his own making. Sin is the punishment for sin. When a man leaves God out he will raise someone or something in God's place. That is an idol whether it be the stump of a tree of the primitive animist or the space technology of modern man. When he eliminates the God who created all things then man must live and die by his own creation. That's the pain under which man now lives. He is punished by daily terror of annihilation by his own scientific technology.

The living God of the Bible is "love." He does not act except in harmony with his own nature of love. The exercise of his righteous judgments against sin in people does not spring from personal hatred for the sinner. But he does love enough that he will not allow the sinner to wallow unnoticed or abandoned in his sin. God's nature of love prompts him to punish to correct; to tolerate man's pain that the cancerous sin may be removed from the sick soul. It is not the "will of God" that "<u>any</u> should perish but that <u>all</u> should come to repentance." Only <u>when</u> man refuses every <u>advance</u> of God's love in judgment does the great Captivity of eternity make its final and ultimate imprisonment of man. The great Babylonian Captivity became symbolic to the Revelator of the ultimate captivity of eternity. It has always been God's plan to give "cleanness of teeth" that men might "return to me." Only if and when "the rest of men...repent not..." is it that God leaves man to his final permanent captivity. God's wrath is for discipline and redemption. But God's love spurned leaves man a permanent captive.

"God so loved the world that he gave his only begotten son that whosoever believes on him might not perish, but might have eternal life."

## A TRANSLATION
### Revelation 10:1-11:19

And I saw another strong angel coming down out of the heaven, having been clothed with a cloud, and the rainbow was upon his head, and his face (was) as the sun, and his feet (were) as pillars of fire. And he was having in his hand a little book, having been opened.

And he placed his foot, the right one, upon the sea, but the left upon the land. And he cried in a loud voice as a lion roars. And when he cried the seven thunders sounded their voices. And when the seven thunders spoke, I was about to write; and I heard a voice out of heaven saying, "Seal which things the seven spoke and don't write them." And the angel whom I saw standing upon the sea and upon the land lifted his right hand unto the heaven. And he swore by the one living unto the ages of the ages, who created the heaven and the things in it, and the earth and the things in it and the sea and the things in it, that delay should be no more. But the secret of God is indeed completed in the days of the voice of the seventh angel whenever he's about to trumpet, as he announced unto his servants the prophets.

And the voice which I heard out of the heaven (was) again speaking with me and saying, "Go, take the scroll, the one having been opened in the hand of the angel standing upon the sea and upon the land." And I went off to the angel saying to him, "Give to me the little scroll." And he says to me, "You take and eat it, and it will embitter your stomach but in your mouth it shall be sweet as honey." And I took the little scroll out of the hand of the angel and devoured it, and it was in my mouth as honey (is) sweet; and when I ate it, my stomach was embittered.

And they say to me, "It's necessary that you again prophecy over peoples and nations and tongues and many kings."

### Chapter 11:1-19

And to me was given a reed like a measuring-rod, and (one spoke) saying, "Get up and measure the sanctuary of God and the altar and the ones worshipping in it." And the outer court of the temple leave out and don't measure it, because it's given to the Gentiles, and they shall trample the holy city forty two months.

And I will give to my two witnesses and they shall prophesy a thousand two hundred sixty days having been clothed in sack-cloth. These are the two olive trees and the two lampstands, the ones standing before the Lord of the earth. And if anyone wishes to harm them fire goes out of their mouth and it devours their enemies; and if anyone shall wish to harm them, it is necessary that he be killed in the same manner. These have the authority to shut the heaven that rain shall not shower for the days of their prophecy, and they have authority over the waters to turn them into blood and to smite the earth in every plague howevermuch

## A TRANSLATION
## Revelation 10:1-11:19
## (continued)

they shall wish. And whenever they shall complete their testimony, the wild beast, the one coming up out of the abyss, shall make war with them and shall conquer them and shall kill them. And their corpse (will lie) upon the street of the great city which is called spiritually Sodom and Egypt, where also their Lord was crucified. And they of the peoples and tribes and tongues and nations shall look on their corpse three days and a half and they don't permit their bodies to be placed in a tomb. And the ones dwelling upon the earth rejoice over them and make merry and shall send gifts to one another because the two prophets tormented (them), the ones dwelling on the earth. And after three days and a half the breath of life from God entered into them, and they stood upon their feet and great fear fell upon the ones beholding them.

And they heard a loud voice from heaven saying, "Come up here!" And they went up into heaven in the cloud and their enemies saw them. And in that hour a great earthquake happened and the tenth of the city fell - persons of men - seven thousands. And the rest became afraid and gave glory to the God of the heaven!

The second woe passed. Behold! The third woe comes quickly!

And the seventh angel trumpeted. And loud voices arose in heaven saying, "The sovereignty of the world became (that) of our Lord and his Christ, and he shall reign unto the ages of the ages."

And the twenty four elders, the ones sitting on their thrones before God, fell upon their faces and worshipped God, saying, "We thank you, Lord, the Almighty God, the being-one, the was-one, that you have taken your great power and reigned. And the nations got furious, and your wrath came. Also the time that the dead be judged, and the (time) to give reward to your servants, the prophets and the saints and the ones fearing your name, the little and the great, and (the time) to corrupt the ones corrupting the earth, (came)."

And the sanctuary of God opened, the one in the heaven, and the ark of his covenant was seen in his sanctuary and there arose lightnings and noises and thunders and earthquake and great hail.

## AN OUTLINE OF REVELATION 10:1-11:19

**The Sovereign Rule of God!**

Who really rules over and in this world? Man, the Devil, or God? Do human governments hold the ultimate power to govern? Or are there evil forces of mind and spirit controlling the real destiny of humanity? Or does God hold the reigns that drive human history toward a chosen goal? The seventh angel of the Revelation (11:15) trumpeted, "The sovereignty of the world became (the sovereignty) of our Lord and his Christ, and he shall reign forever and ever."

I. EATING THE LITTLE BOOK. 10:1-11
   1. Descent of the "strong angel."
      (a)His dress.
      (b)His burden - "a little book."
      (c)His roaring voice - "seven thunders."
   2. A Voice from Heaven-"seal what the seven thunders spoke."
   3. Message of the "strong angel."
      (a)Solemnity of his message.
      (b)"Delay shall be no more."
      (c)The "secret of God completed" - the seventh angel!
   4. Eating the "little book."
      (a)The command.
      (b)The prophet's willingness.
      (c)Effects: (1)sweet (2)bitterness.
      (d)The prophet experiences his message!
      (e)It's for universal consumption.

II. MEASURING THE TEMPLE OF God. 11:1-13
   1. The tools and limitations of measurement.
   2. The two witnesses.
      (a)Identity of the two witnesses.
      (b)Their work for a short, incomplete period.
   3. Treatment of the two witnesses.
      (a)By the wild beast from the abyss.
      (b)By the "ones dwelling on the earth."
      (c)By God.

III. DECLARATION OF SOVEREIGNTY OF GOD IN HIS CHRIST. 11:14-19
   1. The declaration: Sovereignty entrusted to the Lord's Christ.
   2. Its extent: forever!
   3. Song of approval by the "twenty four elders."
      (a)That "you have taken your great power and reigned..."
      (b)The world reaction: "got furious..."
      (c)But the time of God's judging has begun!

Christ is now the only supreme reigning king! His rule is open to all!

Revelation 10:1-3

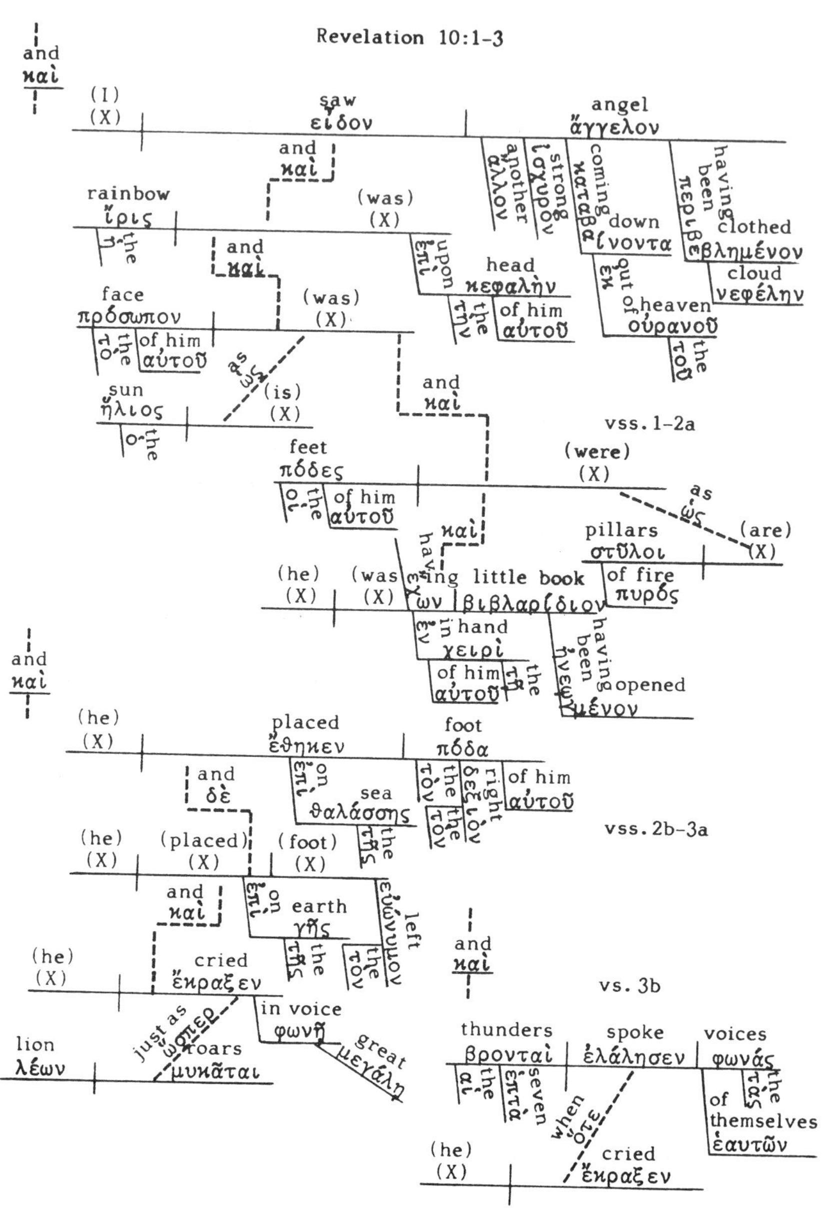

## THE DIAGRAM OF 10:1-3

Five out of the seven clauses in 10:1-3 are independent. The remaining two are adverbial dependent clauses of comparison, both ushered in by ὡς. Denuded of all modifying elements the five main clauses say: "I saw angel," "rainbow (was)," "face (was)," "feet (were)," and "he (was) having little-book." One can readily see the value of modifiers in filling out a more complete idea. The first full clause declares: "I saw another strong angel coming down out of heaven, having been clothed with a cloud." Present participle "coming down"(καταβαίνοντα) is circumstantial describing by its linear action the process of his descent. The ἐκ phrase is adverb indicating the source from whence he descended. Perfect passive participle περιβεβλημένον "having been clothed" is followed by accusative, normal with verbs of clothing or unclothing.

The full second clause states: "the rainbow (was) upon his head." The ἐπὶ phrase is adverbial denoting <u>where</u>.

If the third independent clause were left <u>bare</u> with no dependent clause to support it the meaning of the clause would alter greatly. The presence of the ὡς clause, though classed as "dependent," has an important function in making clear the author's point. He's not saying: "His face was..." He is saying: "His face was as the sun is..." or "as the sun shines..." The term "dependent" or "subordinate" does not indicate an idea of inferior importance. It merely means that the clause cannot stand alone as a complete sentence.

The same holds true of the fourth of the independent clauses. It too "depends" on a dependent ὡς clause to bring its idea to completion: "...his feet were as pillars of fire are..."

The final of the main clauses has a periphrastic verb form for its main verb, present participle ἔχων plus an understood "was." "He (was) having little-book in his hand having been opened." Adverb phrase "in his hand" expresses <u>where</u>. Perfect participle ἠνεῳγμένον "having been opened" is <u>circumstantial</u> describing "little book." The perfect tense suggests the fact that the book <u>stood</u> open.

Verses 2b-3 contain another compound-complex arrangement. It has three idependent and one dependent ideas. The second of the independent clauses is entirely elliptical except for its modifiers. It borrows its subject, verb, and object from the first clause. "He placed his right foot upon the sea and(he placed) his left (foot) upon the earth..."

The third main clause affirms: "he cried in a great voice." Once again the subordinate clause gives vital information that helps a reader to catch a more vivid picture of the explosive blast of the "great voice;" "...he cried in a great voice just like a lion roars."

Verse 3b is complex. ἑαυτῶν is reflexive pronoun: "The seven thunders spoke the voices of themselves" that is, "their own voices." ὅτε introduces a temporal adverb clause, "when he cried."

Revelation 10:4

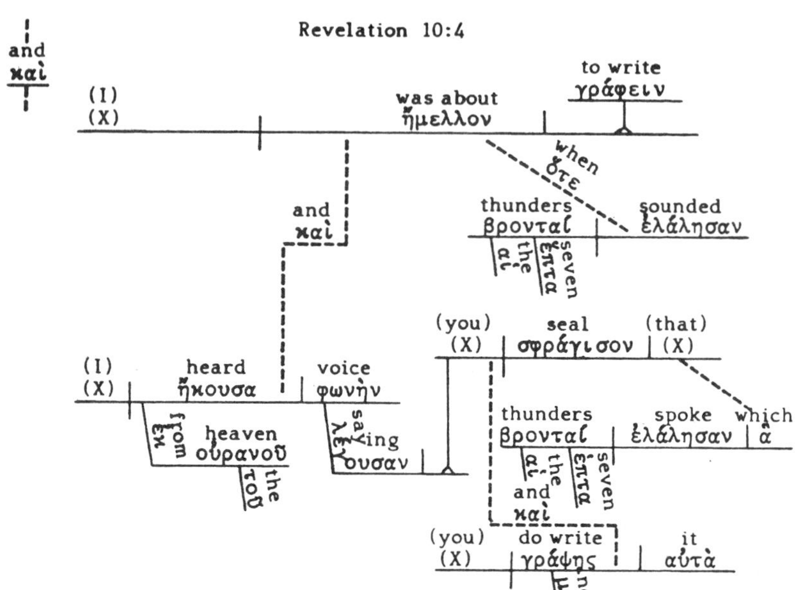

## THE DIAGRAM OF 10:4

The sentence of 10:4 includes two independent clauses with which are involved four dependents. The first independent publishes the action of the author: "I was about to write." The verb ἤμελλον is imperfect indicative active with a double augment. Syllabic augment ἐ also lengthens into temporal ἠ. The linear action of the imperfect has for its direct object the present active infinitive γράφειν "to write." The infinitive is inchoative = "beginning to write." The combination makes for a lively image of John's impulse to put into writing that which he saw. "I was about to begin to write..." The temporal adverbial dependent clause introduced by adverb ὅτε advises when he was "about to begin..." That is, "when the seven thunders spoke(sounded)."

The second independent clause brings in a restraining factor which interrupted his urge to write. It says, "I heard a voice..." The ἐκ expression reports the source from whence he heard. That is, "out of heaven." λέγουσαν is present participle describing "voice." This is an example of the participle used in indirect discourse, "I heard a voice saying..." A participle in indirect discourse, in contrast to an infinitive, presents an actual experience, not a hypothetical idea. John actually was hearing a voice.

Two noun clauses appear as objects of the verbal force in the participle. First, "Seal (that)..." Precisely that which he was urged to seal is set forth in an adjective clause describing an understood demonstrative pronoun "that." This adjective clause is ushered in by relative ἅ. "Seal (that) which the seven thunders spoke." σφράγισον is aorist imperative active. The tense stresses urgency. "Seal it! Clamp it tight! Don't even think of writing." This urgent idea is confirmed in the second noun-object clause in which aorist imperative active γράψῃς with negative μὴ appears. "Don't start to write it." Present imperative would have pressed, "Quit what your're doing." But aorist imperative demands, "Don't begin..."

**Revelation 10:5–7**

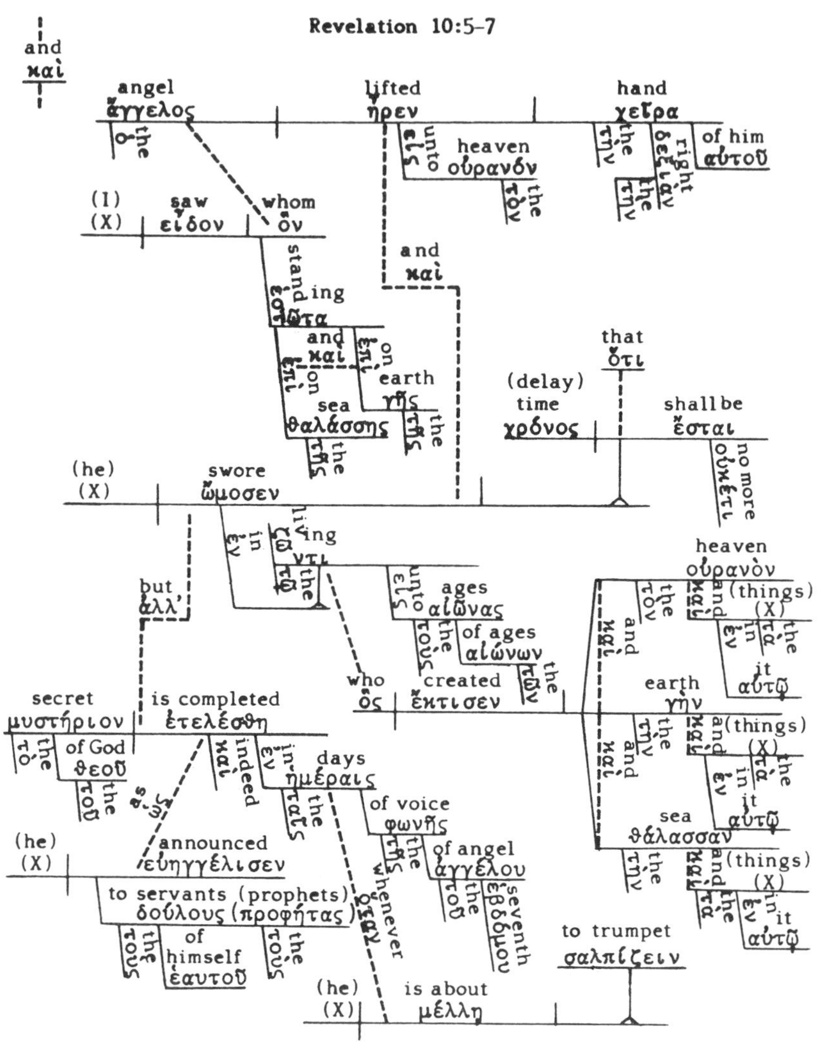

## THE DIAGRAM OF 10:5-7

The 83 words of 10:5-7 enfold one sentence. It has eight clauses three of which are independent and the others dependent. The first two independents tell what the "strong angel" did. He "lifted" and "he swore..." The final independent announces that "the secret(mystery)of God is completed."

This sentence takes up the action of the vision at the point at which John was hindered from writing. Article "the" with subject "angel"(ἄγγελος) points back to the "strong angel" who had (vs.2)placed his feet on earth and sea. In fact the subordinate relative ὃν clause gives a full description identifying the angel as the one "whom I saw standing upon the sea and upon the earth."

In telling his story John employs the narrative aorist indicative ἦρεν. The prepositional εἰς phrase serves as adverb indicating the direction toward which he "lifted his right hand."

In the second main clause John discloses that the angel "swore in the one living..." ἐν with articular attributive participle τῷ ζῶντι "the one living" is an adverbial idea. It expresses the basis or means of his oath. The use of the present participle "the living one" emphasizes God as the eternally existing One. The phrase "unto the ages of the ages" adds to this emphasis. Moreover, the addition of the adjectival relative ὃς clause makes more than clear that it is the eternal Creator-God "in" whom the angel swore. It's "the living One who created the heaven...etc..." The content of what he "swore" finds expression in the ὅτι noun clause, "delay shall no more be." The clause is object of the verb.

The third of the three independent clauses makes the triumphant announcement, "the secret of God is completed." ἐτελέσθη is aorist indicative passive of τελέω often translated "perfected," "completed" but containing in it the idea of "brought to an intended goal." It has to do with a purposed goal reached. A farmer plows and plants a field with a goal in mind. It includes of course a good crop. But his goal normally includes more than just a good crop. It encompasses food, shelter, clothing, and certain life-values for his family. In some cases more. But τελέω involves much more than just the passing of a season. It means to "arrive at a specific goal." The grand declaration of this third independent clause is the announcement of the fact: "the mystery of God indeed arrived at its purposed goal..."

Two subordinate clauses help support the idea of the main clause. ὡς brings in an adverb clause which reveals that the goal was not a late thought. On the contrary the "completed" mystery of God was "as he announced to his own servants, the prophets." εὐηγγέλισεν is aorist of a verb meaning to "announce good news." We would expect the term δούλους to be dative of indirect object. The accusative here might be treated as direct object of the verb "announce." "He gospelized his servants..." The diagram has chosen to place it as adverbial accusative under the verb. ὅταν introduces a temporal adverbial clause, "whenever he is about to trumpet."

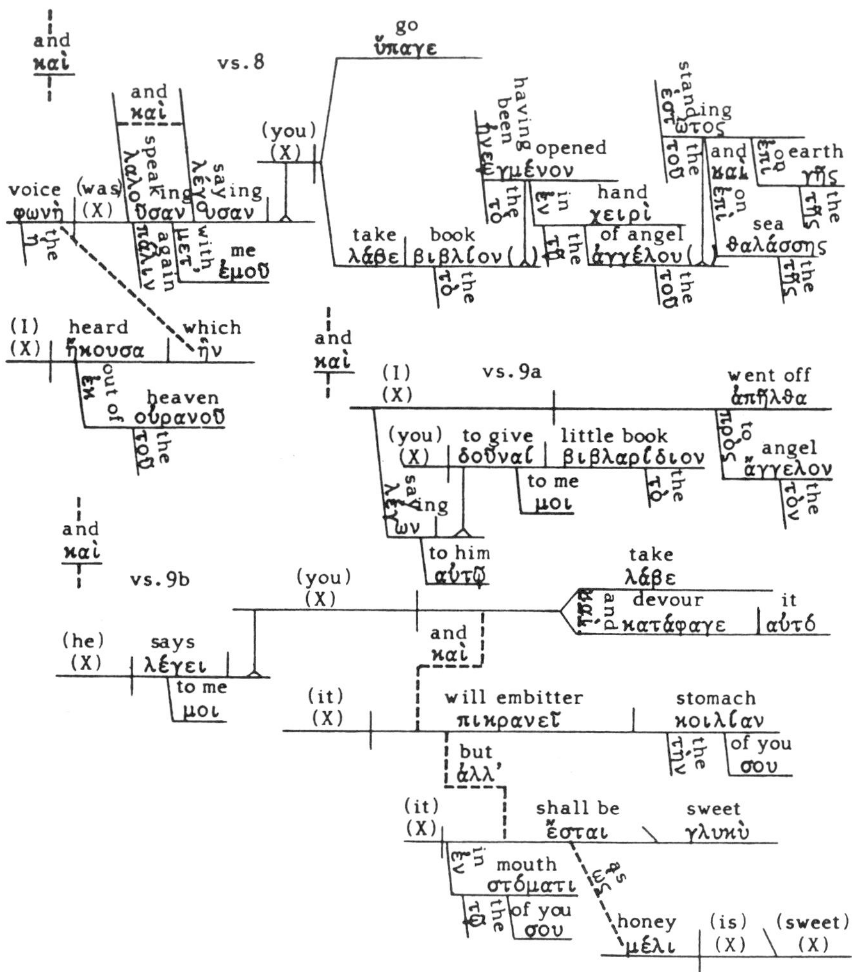
and καὶ
vs. 8
voice φωνὴ
the ἡ
(was) (X)
and καὶ
speaking λαλοῦσαν
again πάλιν
saying λέγουσαν
with μετ'
me ἐμοῦ
(I) (X) heard ἤκουσα
which ἣν
out of ἐκ
heaven οὐρανοῦ
the τοῦ
(you) (X)
go ὕπαγε
take λάβε
book βιβλίον
the τὸ
having been opened ἠνεῳγμένον
the τὸ
in ἐν
hand χειρὶ
the τῇ
of angel ἀγγέλου
the τοῦ
standing ἑστῶτος
the τοῦ
on ἐπὶ
sea θαλάσσης
the τῆς
and καὶ
on ἐπὶ
earth γῆς
the τῆς
and καὶ
vs. 9a
(I) (X)
went off ἀπῆλθα
to πρὸς
angel ἄγγελον
the τὸν
saying λέγων
to him αὐτῷ
(you) (X)
to give δοῦναί
little book βιβλαρίδιον
the τὸ
to me μοι
and καὶ
vs. 9b
(he) (X) says λέγει
to me μοι
(you) (X)
take λάβε
and καὶ
devour κατάφαγε
it αὐτό
and καὶ
(it) (X)
will embitter πικρανεῖ
stomach κοιλίαν
the τὴν
of you σου
but ἀλλ'
(it) (X)
shall be ἔσται
sweet γλυκὺ
in ἐν
mouth στόματι
the τῷ
of you σου
as ὡς
honey μέλι
(is) (X)
(sweet) (X)

## THE DIAGRAM OF 10:8–9

Verse eight entails a complex sentence of three clauses. The independent professes, "The voice (was) again speaking with me and (was) saying..." The verb is compound. Both elements of it are periphrastic consisting of present participles λαλοῦσαν and λέγουσαν coupled with understood "was." The subject φωνὴ is identified by an adjective relative clause ushered in by xx "which I heard from heaven." Direct object of "was saying" is a noun clause expressing an exhortation, "...go and take..." The two verbs ὕπαγε "go" and λάβε "take" combine linear action present with punctiliar aorist. "Be on your way and snatch..." The object of the verb "take," neuter noun βιβλίον, has a perfect passive attributive participle in apposition, "having been opened." The perfect tense calls attention to the fact that the book stood open. The phrase introduced by ἐν tells where the book was. It was "in the hand..." Genitive ἀγγέλου is possessive; the "angel's hand." To identify beyond doubt which angel, the attributive participle in apposition ἑστῶτος is inserted. It was "the angel, the one standing on the sea and on the earth."

The sentence of 9a has one independent clause which declares, "I went off." The aorist form ἀπῆλθα is substituted here for the usual ἀπῆλθον. There is no difference in meaning. A noun clause appears as direct object of circumstantial participle λέγων. This dependent clause might be classed as an infinitive phrase. Yet the infinitive δοῦναι with its implied accusative of general reference "you" turns into a practical clause in function. So we choose to classify this as a complex sentence of two clauses.

Verse 9b is clearly complex. But this time four dependent clauses sprout off the main idea, "he says to me." The initial noun clause performs as direct object of the main verb "says." "You take and devour it." The next two are also noun clauses, object of the same verb "says." "...it will embitter your stomach but it will be sweet..." To the third of the dependents two adverb expressions are attached. The ἐν phrase, "in your mouth" tells where the little book is to be sweet. ὡς inserts the last dependent clause, "as honey (is sweet)." This is an adverb clause of comparison.

Revelation 10:10–11

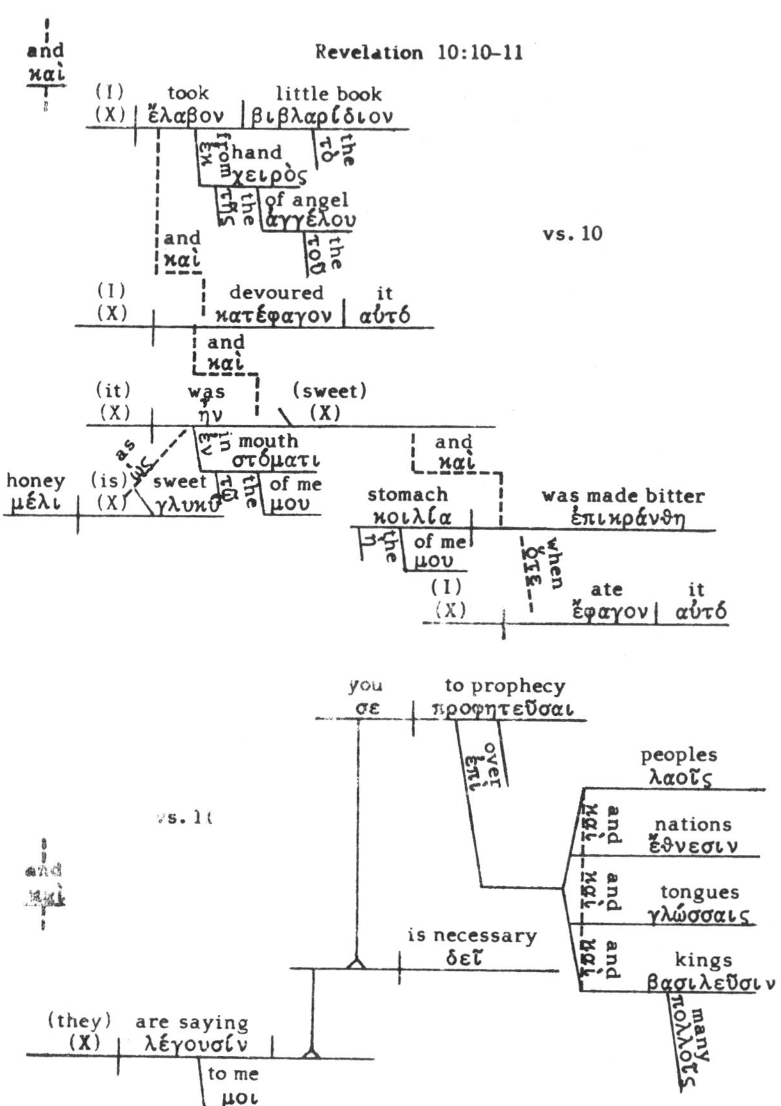

## THE DIAGRAM OF 10:10-11

With the gentle force of a skiff floating downstream verse ten drifts along carrying its thought to the reader. Of four independent clauses the first two relate what happened. "I took the little book...and I devoured it..." The one clarifying appendage to the first clause comes in the ἐκ phrase. In function it is adverbial telling the origin from whence the little book was taken: "from the hand of the angel."

Having announced in the first two clauses what happened, the second two independents state the effect of having eaten the little book. Were it not for two modifying ideas the third clause lacks clarity. One is a prepositional phrase indicating where "it" (the little book) "was." The other is a dependent adverb ὡς clause depicting a comparative standard of taste; "...it was (sweet) as honey (is) sweet."

The fourth independent clause propells the thought forward to another stage of development; "...my stomach was made bitter when I ate it." Thus comes to an end the flow of this compound-complex sentence.

In spite of the restraint placed on him in verse four to "seal up...don't write..." verse 11 reassures John of his prophetic responsibility. The sentence is complex with the independent clause stating: "they say to me..." A subordinate noun clause appears as direct object of λέγουσίν. "For you to prophecy over peoples...is necessary." The verb in the noun clause is impersonal δεῖ "it is necessary." Aorist active infinitive προφητεῦσαι is subject of δεῖ with pronoun σε performing as accusative of general reference with the infinitive. The prepositional phrase (ἐπὶ) has a compounding of four nouns translated "peoples and nations and tongues and many kings." The multiplying of synonyms relative to national groups underscores the idea that John's prophetic message is universal in its goal. Dative case of these nouns emphasizes the personal element in his message. It's not just abstract "truth." It is personally important and powerful.

## Revelation 11:1-3

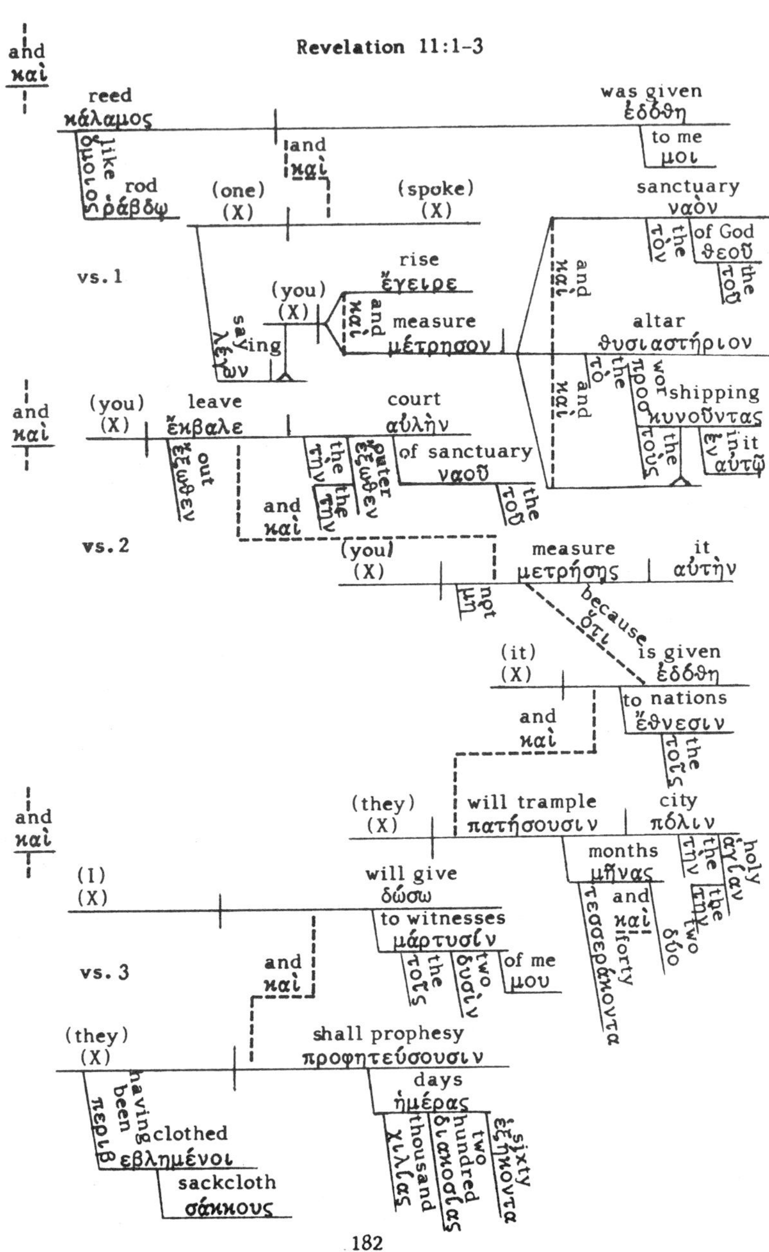

## THE DIAGRAM OF 11:1-3

Of the two independent clauses in verse one the second is implied by the context. The clauses declare, "a reed was given ..." and "(one spoke)..." To define clearly the "reed" the author inserts adjective phrase, "like a rod." ὅμοιος appears as a preposition. It is with the instrumental case.

The understood subject, "one," of the second independent clause expands by present circumstantial participle λέγων "saying." As object of this participle appears the noun clause, "rise and measure..." The presence of the noun clause transforms the sentence into a compound-complex. The aorist verb μέτρησον has a three-fold object: "sanctuary," "altar," and the attributive present participle προσκυνοῦντας, "the ones worshipping..."

Verse two is a unit of thought involving four clauses. Two are independent and two are dependent, so the sentence is compound-complex. The two independents are aorist imperatives. First is a positive and then the negative to reinforce the positive: "...do leave out...and don't measure..." literally means "cast out," "throw out." The context here intrudes the sense of "leave out." And the negative second clause confirms this sense of "leave out." In the task of measuring the temple "throw out the outer court..." By choice of word and tense the author conveys the compelling importance of leaving out the court of Gentiles. And as to the second independent, negative μὴ with aorist subjunctive indicates that John should not even begin to measure the "outer court."

To support these imperatives two adverbial clauses of cause are thrust in. ὅτι is the introductory subordinating conjunction. Reasons for leaving out and not measuring is "because it is given to the nations (gentiles) and they will trample the holy city..." ἐδόθη is narrative aorist depicting the fact that the outer court had been assigned to Gentiles. The future tense is naturally punctiliar unless strong factors in the context compel a linear idea. The presence of accusative extent of time in μῆνας etc. "forty two months" suggests that he may have the linear notion in mind. If it's linear he's describing the "trampling" of the city. If punctiliar he's merely setting forth the reality of the fact.

Verse three encloses two independent clauses. The sentence is compound. δώσω is future indicative active, "I will give..." To whom he will give is set forth in the dative indirect object, "to my two witnesses." But there is no direct object showing what he's going to give. That must be determined by context. That which he is going to give seems to refer to the responsibility of witnessing (testifying) the word of truth.

The second main clause confirms this by saying, "they shall prophesy." Once again the future προφητεύσουσιν is possibly point action yet more probably descriptive linear. The presence of accusative extent of time ἡμέρας suggests linear. Perfect passive participle "having been clothed" is circumstantial.

vs. 4

these οὗτοί | are εἰσιν \ olive trees ἐλαῖαι (αἱ the, δύο two) καὶ and lampstands λυχνίαι (αἱ the, δύο two) — ἑστῶτες standing (αἱ the) ἐνώπιον before κυρίου lord (τοῦ the) γῆς of earth (τῆς the)

καὶ and

vs. 5

fire πῦρ | goes out ἐκπορεύεται ἐκ of mouth στόματος (τοῦ the) αὐτῶν of them

καὶ and

(it) (X) | devours κατεσθίει | enemies ἐχθροὺς (τοὺς the) αὐτῶν of them

εἰ if — anyone τις | wishes θέλει | to harm ἀδικῆσαι | them αὐτοὺς

καὶ and

him αὐτὸν | to be killed ἀποκτανθῆναι (οὕτως thus) | is necessary δεῖ

εἰ if — anyone τις | shall wish θελήσῃ | to harm ἀδικῆσαι | them αὐτοὺς

these οὗτοι | have ἔχουσιν | power ἐξουσίαν (τὴν the) ( ) to shut κλεῖσαι | heaven οὐρανόν (τὸν the)

ἵνα so that — rain ὑετὸς | shower βρέχῃ (μὴ not) days ἡμέρας (τὰς the) προφητείας of prophecy (τῆς the) αὐτῶν of them

vs. 6

καὶ and

(they) (X) | have ἔχουσιν | power ἐξουσίαν ἐπὶ over waters ὑδάτων (τῶν the) — ( ) to turn στρέφειν | them αὐτὰ εἰς into blood αἷμα — καὶ and — ( ) to smite πατάξαι | earth γῆν (τὴν the) ἐν in plague πληγῇ (πάσῃ every)

ὁσάκις as often as — (they) (X) | shall wish θελήσωσιν (ἐὰν ever)

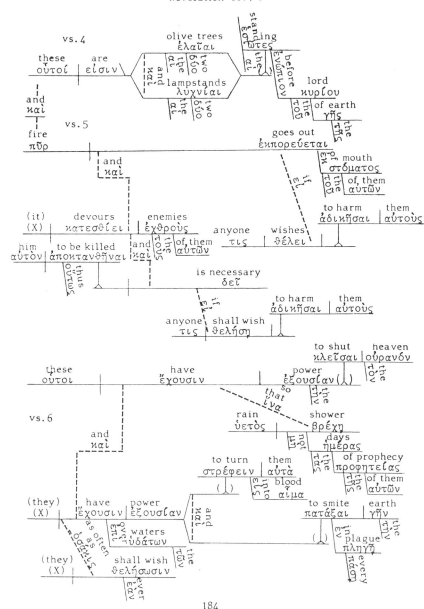

## THE DIAGRAM OF 11:4-6

In the sentence of verse four feminine plural article αἱ appears three times. The feminine nouns translated "olive trees" and "lampstands" refer back to masculine demonstrative pronoun subject οὗτοι. The articles apparently point to items well known. "These are the olive trees and the lampstands..." It's normal to use feminine articles with feminine nouns. But αἱ with masculine participle ἑστῶτες is unusual. The participle is obviously closely associated with the nouns with the feminine article. Hence the author just continued with the same feminine article in spite of its appearance with a masculine word. John might have used a feminine participial form. But though in apposition to predicate nominative nouns it points back ultimately to the masculine subject οὗτοι. The sentence, being of but one clause, is simple in structure.

As punctuated in Nestle's text verse five is compound-complex with three independent clauses. The complex element is found in two dependent adverbial "if" clauses. The first independent idea asserts, "And fire goes out..." The origin from whence it goes out is pictured in the ἐκ phrase, "...out of their mouth..." The second main clause continues, "...it devours their enemies..." κατεσθίει is an iterative present tense referring to repeated disposal of enemies. Preposition κατά in this compound verb is perfective. The fire "eats up(down)" with the finality of certain destruction. Both of these two independent ideas are conditioned by the εἰ "if" clause. This "if" plus present indicative θέλει makes a first class condition determined as fulfilled; "if anyone wishes to harm them..." The condition assumes that someone does wish to harm. Some manuscripts have aorist subjunctive; the diagram uses the indicative as in Nestle's text.

The third independent uses impersonal verb δεῖ "is necessary." As subject it has aorist passive infinitive "to be killed" with accusative of general reference αὐτὸν "him." It may be translated, "...that he be thus killed is necessary..." This necessity is determined by an "if" clause: "...if anyone shall wish to harm them." Use of subjunctive θελήσῃ makes this a third class condition undetermined but with prospect of fulfillment. This condition is less likely to happen than that of the earlier εἰ θέλει. The overhanging threat of their being killed made anyone less liable to "wish to harm them." Normally a third class condition would use ἐάν with subjunctive but here εἰ appears.

Verse six incorporates a compound-complex sentence. It has two independent clauses and two dependents. The two primary clauses testify, "these have power..." and "they have power..." In each instance the object "power" is expanded by infinitives in apposition: "power to shut..." and "power to turn them into blood and smite the earth..." ἵνα introduces a negative result idea. ὁσάκις presents an indefinite temporal clause, "...as often as they shall wish." ἐὰν here seems to be a "modal ἄν" emphasizing the indefinite idea.

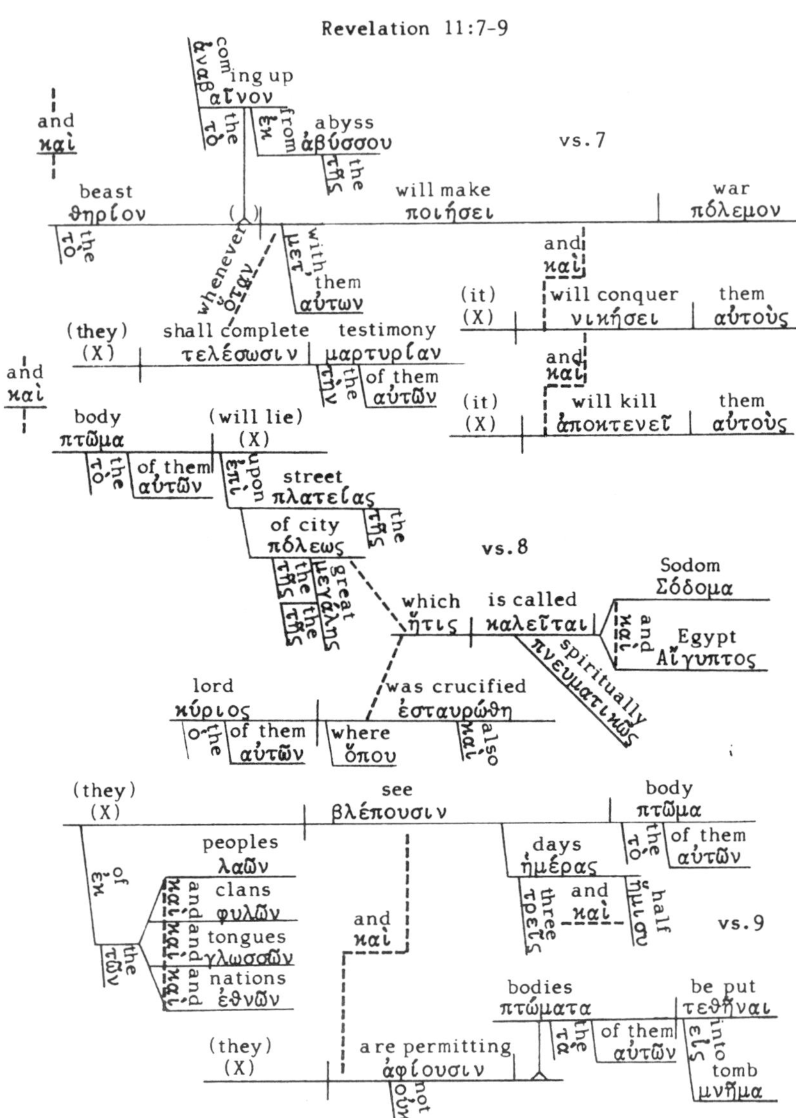
and
καὶ
coming up
ἀναβαῖνον
the
τὸ
from
ἐκ
abyss
ἀβύσσου
the
τῆς
vs. 7
beast
θηρίον
the
τὸ
will make
ποιήσει
war
πόλεμον
whenever
ὅταν
with
μετ'
them
αὐτων
and
καὶ
(it)
(X)
will conquer
νικήσει
them
αὐτοὺς
(they)
(X)
shall complete
τελέσωσιν
testimony
μαρτυρίαν
the
τὴν
of them
αὐτῶν
and
καὶ
(it)
(X)
will kill
ἀποκτενεῖ
them
αὐτοὺς
and
καὶ
body
πτῶμα
the
τὸ
of them
αὐτῶν
(will lie)
(X)
upon
ἐπὶ
street
πλατείας
the
τῆς
of city
πόλεως
the
τῆς
great
μεγάλης
the
τῆς
vs. 8
which
ἥτις
is called
καλεῖται
Sodom
Σόδομα
and
καὶ
Egypt
Αἴγυπτος
spiritually
πνευματικῶς
lord
κύριος
the
ὁ
of them
αὐτῶν
where
ὅπου
was crucified
ἐσταυρώθη
also
καὶ
(they)
(X)
see
βλέπουσιν
body
πτῶμα
the
τὸ
of them
αὐτῶν
of
ἐκ
the
τῶν
peoples
λαῶν
and
καὶ
clans
φυλῶν
and
καὶ
tongues
γλωσσῶν
and
καὶ
nations
ἐθνῶν
days
ἡμέρας
three
τρεῖς
and
καὶ
half
ἥμισυ
vs. 9
and
καὶ
bodies
πτώματα
the
τὰ
of them
αὐτῶν
be put
τεθῆναι
into
εἰς
tomb
μνῆμα
(they)
(X)
are permitting
ἀφίουσιν
not
οὐκ

## THE DIAGRAM OF 11:7-9

Three direct affirmations are made about "the beast" in the compound-complex sentence of verse seven. "The beast will make war and it will conquer them and it will kill them." In order to identify more clearly the beast present participle "coming up" is placed in apposition to the subject. Having the article the participle is attributive. The adverbial ἐκ phrase tells from whence the beast was "coming up." The linear tense of the participle may be classed as descriptive present. When the beast will accomplish all this conquest is depicted in the adverbial subordinate clause thrust in by the indefinite ὅταν; "...whenever they shall complete their testimony." The word translated "shall complete" is aorist active subjunctive of τελέω "bring to an end." The word carries the idea of arriving at a purposed goal. When the two "prophets," the "olive trees and lampstands," have fulfilled their work, that is, brought it to its intended goal then the "beast will make war...conquer...and kill."

Verse six entails a complex sentence of three clauses. The independent clause informs that "their body (will lie) on the street..." Which street is specified by genitive πόλεως, "of the great city." The author identifies the "great city" by two dependent clauses. The first is announced by the qualitative relative ἥτις "which by its very nature is called Sodom and Egypt spiritually." The other clause is heralded by ὅπου "where;" "...where their Lord also was crucified." This leaves no doubt that the city symbolized was Jerusalem. The tenses of the two verbs in the dependent clauses form a contrast. καλεῖται is present expressing linear action. ἐσταυρώθη is aorist passive expressing point action. The "great city" enjoyed an ongoing spiritual reputation; the Lord was crucified once and for all.

If we may take infinitive τεθῆναι with its accusative of general reference as a clause then verse four becomes compound-complex. Otherwise it's a simple sentence. Subject of the first main clause is "they" found in the verb endng. This "they" is explicitly defined by the four nouns of the ἐκ phrase. "They of the peoples and clans and tongues and nations..." The one definite article takes in all four nouns. This cluster of nouns strongly suggests the universality of those who "see their body." Linear present verb βλέπουσιν is "see" in the sense of "are looking" or "are staring..." "Three and a half days" is an adverbial accusative expressing extent of time.

In the second independent clause ἀφίουσιν is present active indicative of a later form of ἀφίημι. Here it means to "leave" or "permit." The negative is the strong οὐκ, used with indicatives. Object of the verb is the infinitive expression with accusative of general reference serving as if it were "subject." Infinitives by nature are "infinite" hence don't have "subjects." Here as a noun the infinitive is the real object of "permitting;" "..they are not permitting to be put..." The accusative sets forth the person or thing that performs the action of the infinitive.

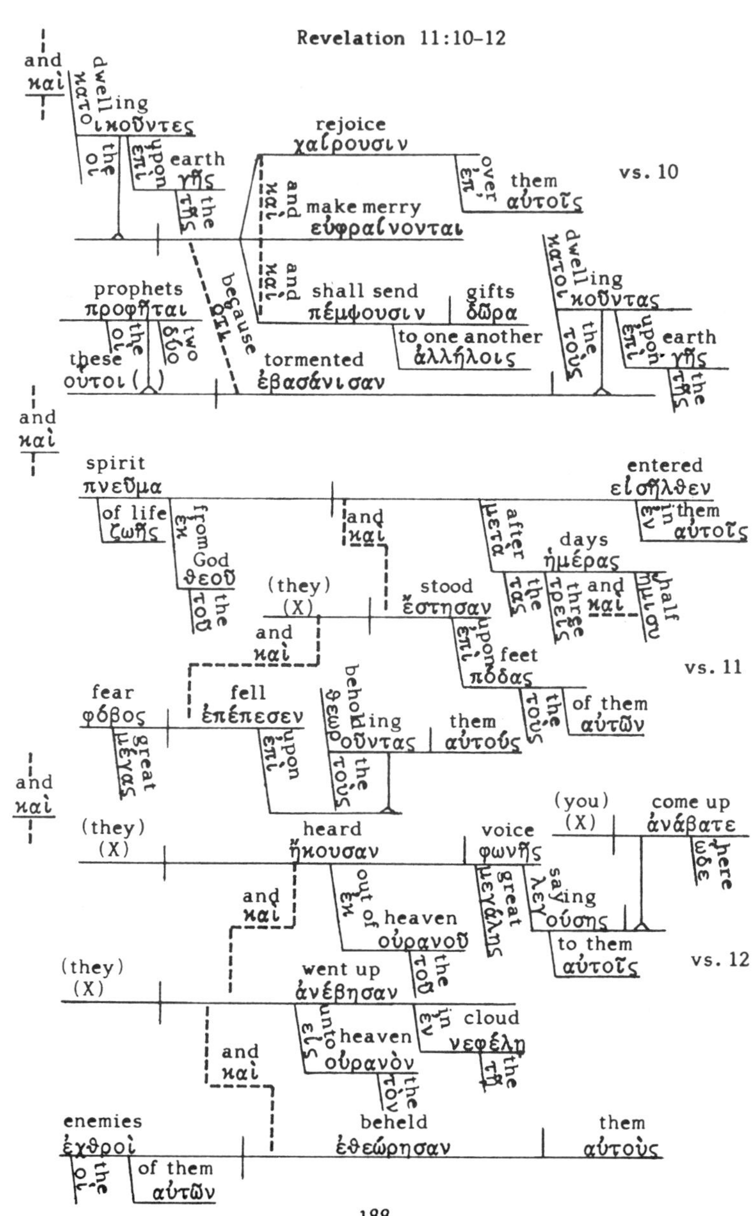
and
καὶ
dwelling
κατοικοῦντες
the
οἱ
upon
ἐπὶ
earth
γῆς
the
τῆς
rejoice
χαίρουσιν
and
καὶ
make merry
εὐφραίνονται
over
ἐπ'
them
αὐτοῖς
vs. 10
and
καὶ
shall send
πέμψουσιν
gifts
δῶρα
to one another
ἀλλήλοις
because
ὅτι
prophets
προφῆται
the
οἱ
two
δύο
these
οὗτοι
tormented
ἐβασάνισαν
dwelling
κατοικοῦντας
the
τοὺς
upon
ἐπὶ
earth
γῆς
the
τῆς
and
καὶ
spirit
πνεῦμα
of life
ζωῆς
from
ἐκ
God
θεοῦ
the
τοῦ
and
καὶ
entered
εἰσῆλθεν
in
ἐν
them
αὐτοῖς
after
μετὰ
days
ἡμέρας
the
τὰς
three
τρεῖς
and
καὶ
half
ἥμισυ
(they)
(X)
stood
ἔστησαν
upon
ἐπὶ
feet
πόδας
the
τοὺς
of them
αὐτῶν
vs. 11
and
καὶ
fear
φόβος
great
μέγας
fell
ἐπέπεσεν
upon
ἐπὶ
beholding
θεωροῦντας
the
τοὺς
them
αὐτούς
and
καὶ
(they)
(X)
heard
ἤκουσαν
voice
φωνῆς
great
μεγάλης
saying
λεγούσης
to them
αὐτοῖς
(you)
(X)
come up
ἀνάβατε
here
ὧδε
out of
ἐκ
heaven
οὐρανοῦ
the
τοῦ
vs. 12
and
καὶ
(they)
(X)
went up
ἀνέβησαν
unto
εἰς
heaven
οὐρανὸν
the
τὸν
in
ἐν
cloud
νεφέλῃ
the
τῇ
and
καὶ
enemies
ἐχθροὶ
the
οἱ
of them
αὐτῶν
beheld
ἐθεώρησαν
them
αὐτούς

## THE DIAGRAM OF 11:10–12

The sentence of verse 10 opens and closes with the identical expression. It's present active articular participle translated "the ones dwelling." It's an attributive particple. "Upon (ἐπὶ) the earth" is an adverbial phrase indicating where they "are dwelling."

The sentence is complex in structure having but two clauses. Subject of the independent clause is the above mentioned attributive participle in its first appearing. The predicate consists of three verbs declaring that "the ones dwelling...are rejoicing...are making merry and shall send gifts to one another..." Some manuscripts have present tense instead of future for "shall send." This would make "sends" parallel in kind of action to the first two verbs.

The rest of the sentence is a dependent adverb clause of cause introduced by ὅτι. It gives the reason why the earth dwellers "rejoice etc..." It was "because these, the two prophets, tormented the ones dwelling upon the earth." ἐβασάνισαν is aorist of punctiliar action to express the fact. The present linear tenses of the main clause are descriptive of the outburst of merry-making.

Verse eleven encloses a sentence with three independent clauses so it is classed as compound. The naked clauses declare: "spirit entered," "they stood" and "fear fell..." In the first clause the word "spirit" (πνεῦμα) may be, probably ought to be, translated "breath." The kind of breath is designated by genitive ζωῆς. The source of the breath by ἐκ with ablative, "from the God." When the breath entered is given by the μετὰ phrase, accusative extent of time, "after three and a half days."

The second clause states what happened when the breath of God entered them. "They stood upon their feet." Then the third clause declares the emotional response by "the ones beholding," "...great fear fell..." The verbs are narrative aorists presenting facts without descriptive elaboration. Yet the attributive participle θεωροῦντας is present tense. Its linear action suggests something of the wonder that gripped "the ones beholding" as they stood staring in fearful unbelief.

Verse 12 has three independent clauses. This time a dependent idea hangs off the first main clause. So the sentence is compound-complex. The first of the independents states, "They heard a great voice..." φωνῆς is direct object in genitive after verb of hearing. It specifies what they heard. That which the voice said is seen in a noun clause, object of the participle "saying." "Come up here." The source of this "great voice" is made known by the ἐκ phrase "out of heaven."

The second independent declares that "they went up..." The expression "unto heaven" tells where they "went up." The ἐν phrase informs how they "went up." That is, "in a cloud."

The final of the independent ideas asserts that "their enemies beheld them." The main verbs in this sentence are narrative aorists reporting facts as facts. The "two prophets" were treated differently by "the ones dwelling on the earth" from their treatment by heaven with its "breath of life from God."

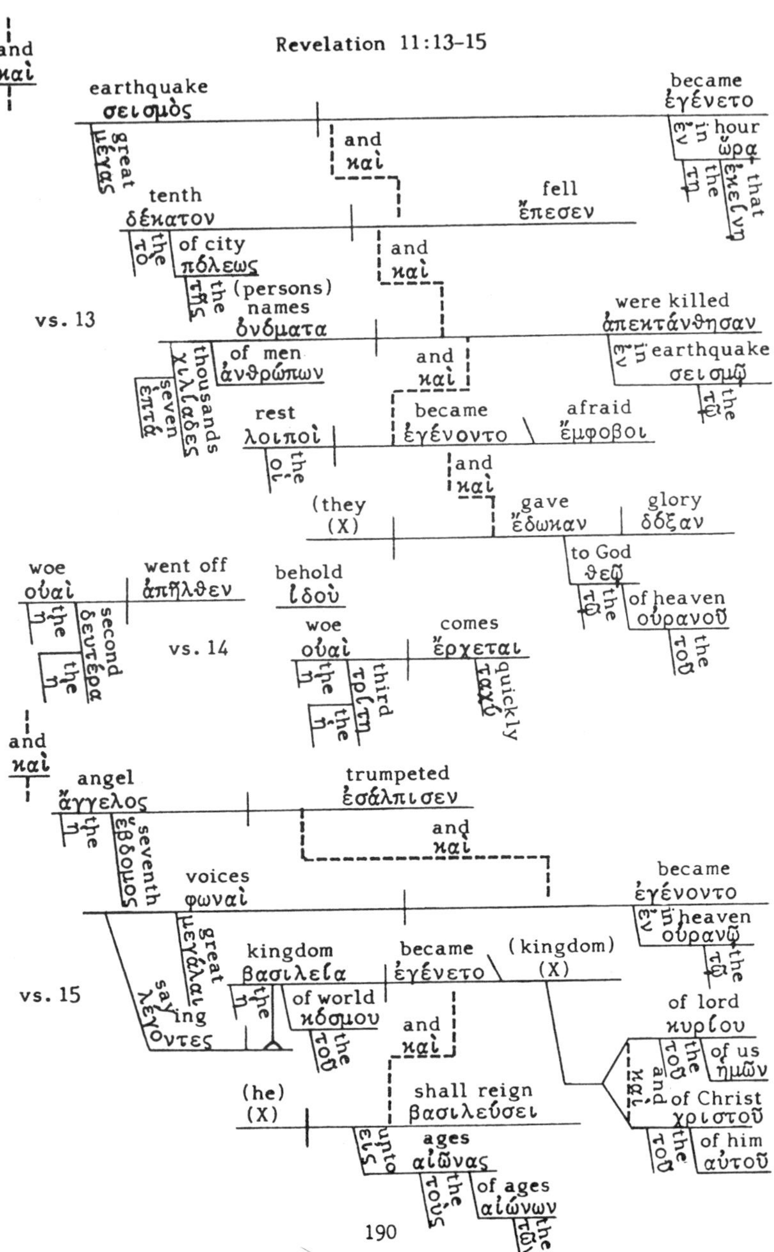
and
καὶ
earthquake
σεισμὸς
great
μέγας
became
ἐγένετο
in
ἐν
hour
ὥρᾳ
the
τῃ
that
ἐκείνῃ
and
καὶ
tenth
δέκατον
the
τὸ
of city
πόλεως
the
τῆς
fell
ἔπεσεν
and
καὶ
(persons)
names
ὀνόματα
of men
ἀνθρώπων
thousands
χιλιάδες
seven
ἑπτά
were killed
ἀπεκτάνθησαν
in
ἐν
earthquake
σεισμῷ
the
τῷ
vs. 13
and
καὶ
rest
λοιποὶ
the
οἱ
became
ἐγένοντο
afraid
ἔμφοβοι
and
καὶ
(they
(X)
gave
ἔδωκαν
glory
δόξαν
to God
θεῷ
the
τῷ
of heaven
οὐρανοῦ
the
τοῦ
woe
οὐαὶ
the
ἡ
second
δευτέρα
the
ἡ
went off
ἀπῆλθεν
vs. 14
behold
ἰδοὺ
woe
οὐαὶ
the
ἡ
third
τρίτη
the
ἡ
comes
ἔρχεται
quickly
ταχὺ
and
καὶ
angel
ἄγγελος
the
ὁ
seventh
ἕβδομος
trumpeted
ἐσάλπισεν
and
καὶ
voices
φωναὶ
great
μεγάλαι
saying
λέγοντες
became
ἐγένοντο
in
ἐν
heaven
οὐρανῷ
the
τῷ
vs. 15
kingdom
βασιλεία
the
ἡ
of world
κόσμου
the
τοῦ
became
ἐγένετο
(kingdom)
(X)
of lord
κυρίου
the
τοῦ
of us
ἡμῶν
and
καὶ
of Christ
χριστοῦ
the
τοῦ
of him
αὐτοῦ
and
καὶ
(he)
(X)
shall reign
βασιλεύσει
unto
εἰς
ages
αἰῶνας
the
τοὺς
of ages
αἰώνων
the
τῶν

THE DIAGRAM OF 11:13-15

Verse 13 presents five independent clauses, thus frames a compound sentence. The first clause announces, "...earthquake came..." Earthquake is described as "great." The verb is modified by an adverbial expression identifying when it came.

The second clause proclaims, "...the tenth fell." Genitive "of the city" specifies the particular kind of tenth, "the tenth of the city." Use of definite article "the" calls attention to a particular "tenth." It's "the tenth" of symbolic value not just any tenth.

The third clause has ὀνόματα "names" for its subject. But this term often translated "names" includes within it the idea of "person." In this context to speak of "seven thousand 'names'" is referring to that many "people." So the full clause may be translated, "...and seven thousand persons of men were killed in the earthquake..." The phrase "in the earthquake" is adverbial indicating the manner in which they were killed.

The remaining two clauses report how "the rest" responded to this devestating earthquake; "...the rest became afraid and they gave glory to the God of heaven." The verbs in all five clauses are narrative aorists. It's the tense used when one has no intent of vivifying with descriptive movement. Of the five verbs aorist of γίνομαι occurs twice, once singular and once plural. The root idea is more than just "be" or "was." Even "came" falls short of the basic idea. It means to "become" or "come into being," "spring out into life." In the first clause the author is saying more than that the earthquake existed. He's declaring that it "burst forth" as a living bud breaks forth because something within is pushing out into full display. Thus in the third clause "the rest" were more than filled with fear; "fear arose."

Verse 14 contains two simple sentences. First, "The second woe passed off." The second sentence says, "Behold! the third woe comes quickly! ἔρχεται is probably a futuristic present. "The third woe is going to come..."

In any interpretation of Revelation 11:15 is quite crucial. The sentence is compound-complex. It has two independent clauses which say, "And the seventh angel trumpeted" and "great voices became (arose) in heaven..." These voices were "saying" something as set forth in present circumstantial participle λέγοντες. Precisely what they were saying appears in two noun clauses, object of the participle. The first of these dependent clauses says, "the sovereignty of the world became (that) of our Lord and His Christ..." The final dependent promises, "and he shall reign unto the ages of the ages(forever)." The term βασιλεία is singular, not plural. Furthermore, it doesn't necessarily mean a territorial or politically structured "kingdom." It can mean, often does mean, and in this context certainly does signify "rule," "dominion," or "sovereignty." God, in his incarnation, projected himself into history and exercised his sovereign authority as king. This is what happened when the seventh angel trumpeted. The last clause says that his sovereign rule will not have any end.

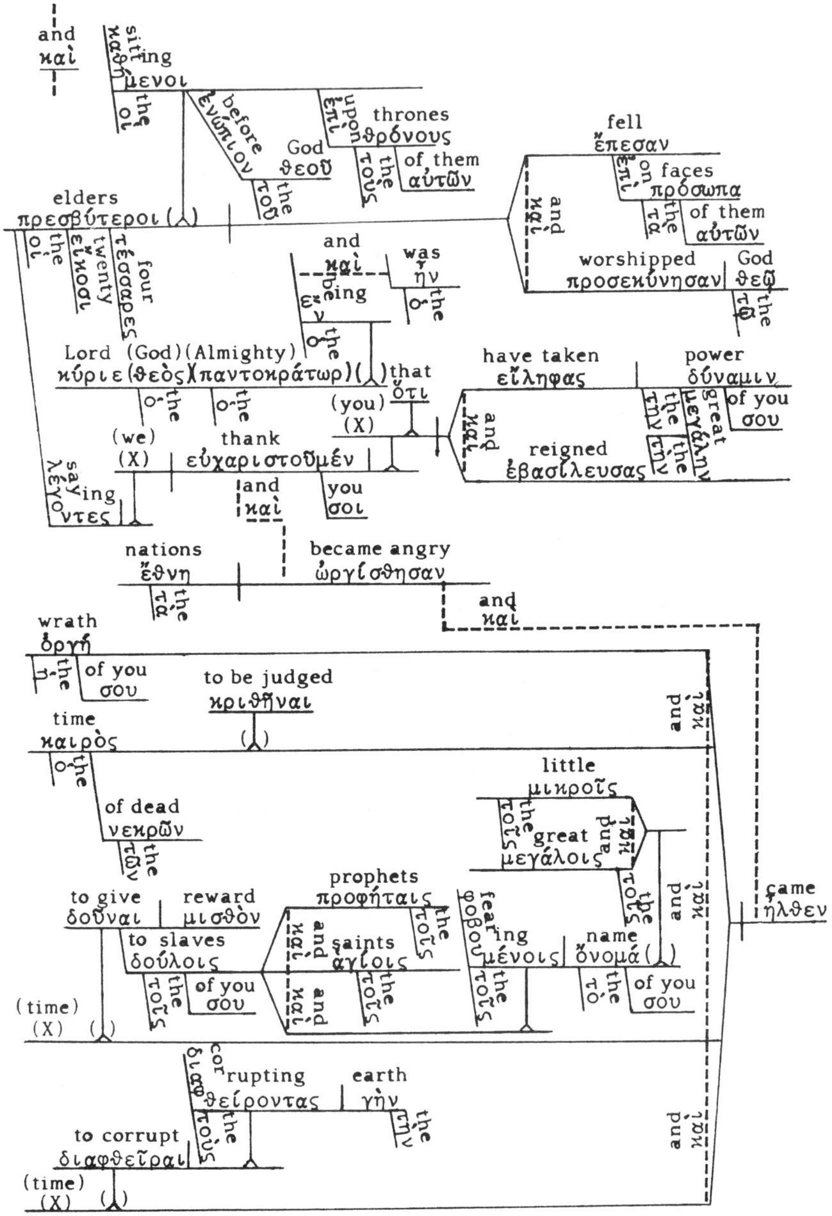

# Revelation 11:16-18

and
καὶ

sitting
καθήμενοι
the
οἱ

before
ἐνώπιον
God
θεοῦ
the
τοῦ

upon
ἐπὶ
thrones
θρόνους
the
τοὺς
of them
αὐτῶν

elders
πρεσβύτεροι ( )
the
οἱ
twenty
εἴκοσι
four
τέσσαρες

fell
ἔπεσαν
and
καὶ
on
ἐπὶ
faces
πρόσωπα
the
τὰ
of them
αὐτῶν

worshipped
προσεκύνησαν
God
θεῷ
the
τῷ

saying
λέγοντες

(we)
(X)
thank
εὐχαριστοῦμέν
you
σοι

Lord (God) (Almighty)
κύριε (θεὸς) (παντοκράτωρ) ( )
the
ὁ
the
ὁ

and
καὶ
being
ὢν
the
ὁ

was
ἦν
the
ὁ

(you)
(X)
that
ὅτι

have taken
εἴληφας
power
δύναμιν
the
τὴν
great
μεγάλην
of you
σου

and
καὶ
reigned
ἐβασίλευσας

and
καὶ

nations
ἔθνη
the
τὰ
became angry
ὠργίσθησαν

and
καὶ

wrath
ὀργή
the
ἡ
of you
σου

came
ἦλθεν

and
καὶ

time
καιρὸς
the
ὁ
to be judged
κριθῆναι
( )

of dead
νεκρῶν
the
τῶν

(time)
(X)
( )
to give
δοῦναι
reward
μισθὸν

to slaves
δούλοις
the
τοῖς
of you
σου

prophets
προφήταις
the
τοῖς
and
καὶ
saints
ἁγίοις
the
τοῖς
and
καὶ

fearing
φοβουμένοις
the
τοῖς
name
ὄνομά ( )
the
τὸ
of you
σου

little
μικροῖς
the
τοῖς
and
καὶ
great
μεγάλοις
the
τοῖς

and
καὶ

and
καὶ

(time)
(X)
( )
to corrupt
διαφθεῖραι

corrupting
διαφθείροντας
the
τοὺς
earth
γῆν
the
τὴν

## THE DIAGRAM OF 11:16-18

Verses 16 through 18 might well be divided into two sentences with a period coming at the close of verse 17. But Nestle's text treats this passage as one sentence. Hence the diagram presents it as one complex formulation. As complex it possesses but one independent clause. Shorn of all modifying elements the main clause declares: "...elders fell and worshipped..." The combination of adjectives translated "the twenty four" designates which elders. In addition an appositional attributive participle "the ones sitting before God upon their thrones" helps the reader to envision the elders more clearly. The expression "before God" signifies where they are sitting. "Upon their thrones" is another adverbial idea suggesting why they are sitting, that is, as reigning monarchs. In the predicate of this clause the noun θεῷ is dative (personal interest) after the verb "worshipped."

Present circumstantial participle λέγοντες introduces a series of subordinate clauses all but one of which are objects of the participle. First is, "we thank you..." A noun clause enclosing the content of that for which "we thank you" is seen in the ὅτι clause: "...that you have taken your great power and reigned..."

At this point a second sentence might begin. However, because it is part of what the twenty four elders were "saying" it seems well to include it as part of the one sentence. It is object of "saying." So the next dependent noun clause says, "...the nations became angry..."

Then comes the final dependent clause. It has one simple aorist verb "came"(ἦλθεν) but its subject is quite an extensive compound of four elements. And some of these elements are themselves somewhat complicated. The first subject is "your wrath," a very simple idea. To the second of the subjects, "the time of the dead," is added in apposition an aorist passive infinitive κριθῆναι "to be judged." The genitive νεκρῶν specifies the kind or quality of the "time" whereas the appositional infinitive insinuates the purpose of the "time."

Next comes the third of the subjects. It's a quite extensive apposition to a repeated understood "time." It is time "to give reward..." To whom the promised reward is given is set forth by dative δούλοις "to your slaves." Then in apposition to "slaves" is a three-pronged expression: "prophets," "saints," and "the ones fearing your name..." "Name"(ὄνομα)is object of the attributive participle "the ones fearing." And this "name" itself is expanded by a two-pronged appositional: "the little and the great." All these appositionals are datives calling attention to the quite personal relationship between the one giving and the ones receiving the promised "reward."

The fourth and final subject of the clause is another implied "time" accompanied by infinitive "to corrupt (διαφθεῖραι) with its direct object attributive participle "the ones corrupting..." The participle may be classed as a cognate accusative: "to corrupt the ones corrupting..."

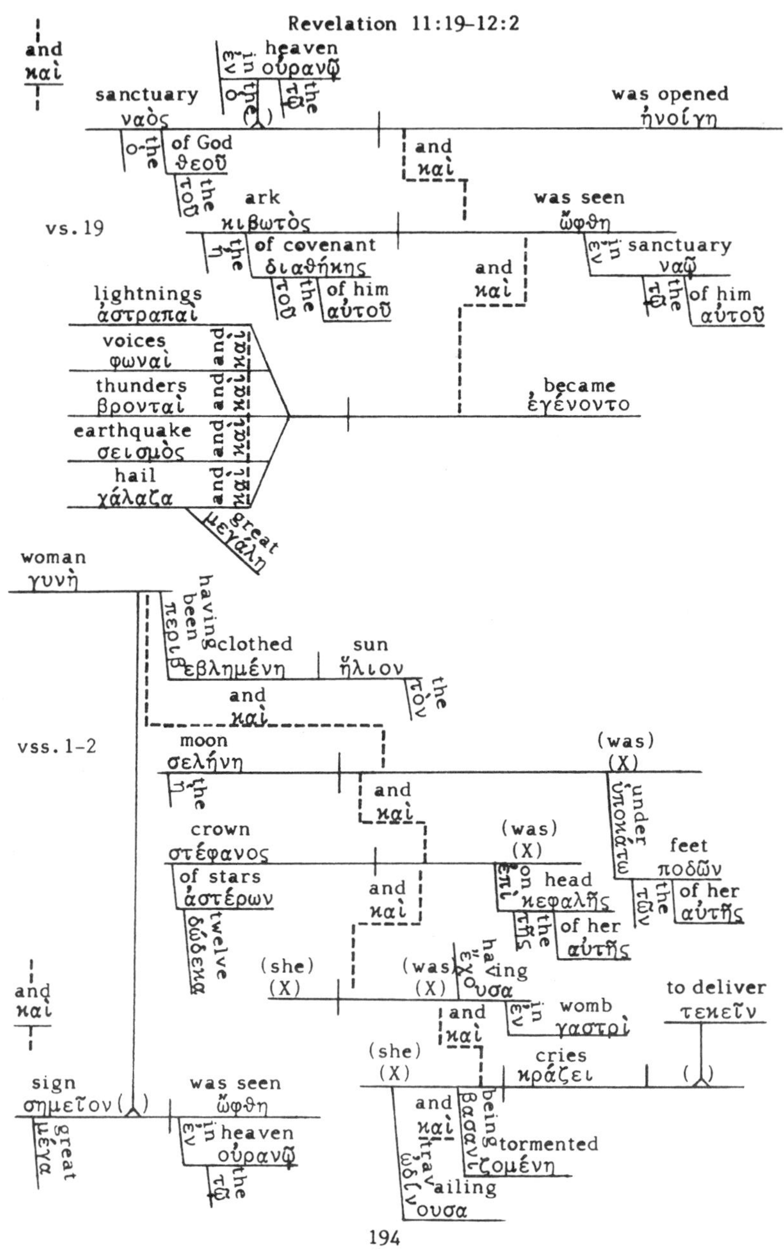
Revelation 11:19–12:2
and
καὶ
sanctuary
ναὸς
ὁ the
in ἐν
heaven
οὐρανῷ
the τῷ
was opened
ἠνοίγη
of God
θεοῦ
the τοῦ
and
καὶ
ark
κιβωτὸς
ἡ the
of covenant
διαθήκης
the τοῦ
of him
αὐτοῦ
was seen
ὤφθη
in ἐν
sanctuary
ναῷ
the τῷ
of him
αὐτοῦ
and
καὶ
vs. 19
lightnings
ἀστραπαὶ
voices
φωναὶ
thunders
βρονταὶ
earthquake
σεισμὸς
hail
χάλαζα
and καὶ
great
μεγάλη
became
ἐγένοντο
woman
γυνὴ
having been clothed
περιβεβλημένη
sun
ἥλιον
the τὸν
and
καὶ
vss. 1–2
moon
σελήνη
ἡ the
(was)
(X)
under
ὑποκάτω
feet
ποδῶν
the τῶν
of her
αὐτῆς
and
καὶ
crown
στέφανος
of stars
ἀστέρων
twelve
δώδεκα
(was)
(X)
on ἐπὶ
head
κεφαλῆς
the τῆς
of her
αὐτῆς
and
καὶ
(she)
(X)
(was)
(X)
having
ἔχουσα
in ἐν
womb
γαστρὶ
and
καὶ
to deliver
τεκεῖν
(she)
(X)
cries
κράζει
and
καὶ
being tormented
βασανιζομένη
travailing
ὠδίνουσα
sign
σημεῖον
great
μέγα
was seen
ὤφθη
in ἐν
heaven
οὐρανῷ
the τῷ

## THE DIAGRAM OF 11:19-12:2

11:19 holds within its embrace three independent clauses. It is therefore classed as compound. The first clause declares: "The temple(sanctuary)...was opened..." The word ναὸς is temple in the sense of the actual place or point of worship in contrast to the facilities such as buildings and grounds. It's the very holiest of holies. That it was God's sanctuary is indicated by genitive θεοῦ. It's location "in heaven" is detailed by the ἐν phrase in apposition to the subject. "The sanctuary of God, the one in the heaven..." The use of masculine definite article ὁ with the entire ἐν phrase not only makes the phrase definite but points to a particular well known sanctuary: "the one in heaven..." The one genuine sanctuary is "the one in heaven." All others are facsimiles.

The second clause adds an important fact as to that which "was seen" when God's heavenly sanctuary "was opened." It says: "...the ark of his covenant was seen in his sanctuary." The kind of "ark" is specified by genitive διαθήκης "of covenant." The place where it was seen is sketched by the adverbial ἐν phrase, "in his sanctuary."

The third clause depicts the violent reaction of the forces of creation, a symbolic view of divine judgment at God's taking his "great power and reigning." The clause has a compound subject of five nouns: "...lightnings and voices and thunders and earthquake and great hail became."

The first two verses of chapter 12 start out as a simple one-clause sentence with a single word in apposition to the subject "sign." But this one apposition γυνὴ is described by an added circumstantial participle, "having been clothed with the sun..." Then instead of continuing the description of this "woman" by use of additional participles the author tacks on four clauses. Each of the clauses furnishes a parallel idea to the initial participle. They say: "...the moon (was) under her feet," "crown of twelve stars (was) on her head," "she(was)having in womb..." and "(she), travailing and being tormented, cries to deliver." In view of these dependent clauses the sentence is complex.

The independent idea states that "A great sign was seen in heaven..." That "sign" was "a woman." Then follows the five descriptive expressions noted above beginning with perfect passive circumstantial participle περιβεβλημένη "having been clothed."

Present participle ἔχουσα "having" of the third dependent clause is predicate supplementary to an understood "was." Thus it helps form a periphrastic imperfect "was having." This verb along with ἐν γαστρὶ "in womb" is the usual way of declaring that "she was being pregnant."

The final clause pictures the "woman" in her birth pains. The two participles are circumstantial. Aorist infinitive τεκεῖν is object of the verb "cries" and vividly depicts the eagerness with which she desires her expected child. The symbolism is significant of the longing of the "people of God" for the deliverer.

## EXPOSITORY THOUGHTS ON 10:1-11:19

Before the sounding of the seventh trumpet announcing that God's "secret has been brought to its intended goal" a strong angel comes down out of heaven. A "little book" is in his hand. His coming from heaven indicates that he had a vision from God. The imagery of his dress and person speaks of the importance of his revelation. He's clothed with a protective cloud, a rainbow halo of hope about his head, his face glowing with the light of truth as bright as the sun's rays, walking with the firmness of feet purified with fire. The "little book" contained the ultimate truth of God's "secret" of the ages, the announcement of God's asserting his authority in His Christ about to be proclaimed in 11:15. The planting of his feet on land and sea symbolized the universality of the vision. It's for all! The rumbling of "seven thunders" notes God's judgments.

The seven thunders stimulate John to begin to write. But a "voice out of heaven" tells him to "seal up that which the seven thunders spoke and don't write." Warnings have done their work, God's rule in Christ has begun, God's reign is to be heralded. "Natural" judgments have exercised their discipline but without repentance. Hence "delay is to be no more," the time for proclaiming God's reign in Christ is at hand. The seventh trumpet is to sound God's long awaited "secret" that He rules in His Christ.

John becomes more than a spectator in this vision. He becomes involved as a participant. A voice from heaven exhorts him to "go take the little book" out of the hand of the angel. So John urged upon the angel that he "Give to me the little book." The angel surrendered the little book but with a word of command and prophetic warning. "Take and eat it; it will embitter your stomach though in your mouth it will be sweet as honey." In other words, John must master his message. He must be a part of his message, a participant in the prophecies and promises that he was commissioned to preach. He will become thrilled with the revelation of God's power, God's reign; excited over the hope of the victory in Christ over the Roman threat; overjoyed at the hope of heaven and final victory over death. How could honey be any sweeter?

But alas! In such a wicked world even the Christ's victory could not come without a Gethsemane and a cross. In announcing God's gospel of triumph John must include the judgments of God on rejection. Furthermore, he must point out clearly that for the Christian believer victory does not come without "taking up the cross and following" after the Christ. Without a cross there can be no crown, not in this kind of a world in which Satan is loose even for a little while. Thus that which is "sweet as honey" in the mouth is bitter as gall "in the stomach." But John accepts his prophetic task to herald this sweet-bitter message universally; to "peoples, nations, tongues and kings."

Part of John's responsibility as a participant is to evaluate the "temple of God." "To me was given a reed like a measuring rod..." And "someone" spoke to him, "Rise, and measure the sanctuary of God and the altar and those worshipping in it." But his instructions also dictated that he not measure "the outer court. ." Thus he symbolizes that his message includes a gauging of the Old Testament people of God, at least the Judaistic heritage as seen in the first century. That O.T. temple, altar, and "those worshipping" involved Elijah and Moses whose power "to shut the heaven" and "to turn the waters into blood" identifies them as the "two witnesses," the Law and the Prophets. The law and prophets were inviolable in their capacity to penetrate the society of God's people with the divine moral order. When anyone tried to tamper with God's truth they and their efforts fell flat. "If anyone wishes to harm them fire goes out of their mouth and it devours their enemies." One never "violates" God's law or the prophet's message. Disobedience only illustrates their inflexible truth. God's law always "devours its enemies."

But there came a time "whenever they (law and prophets) shall complete their testimony, the wild beast, coming up out of the abyss...shall conquer and kill them." That this symbolizes the destruction of Jerusalem is made plain in John's hint that the "great city" called "spiritually Sodom and Egypt" is where their "Lord was crucified." When the city of Jerusalem was destroyed in 70 A.D., its temple laid waste, its altar and worship crushed, its worshippers scattered, the world thought the restraints of God's law and prophets were dead. In fact, the nations "looked on their corpse three and a half days" and did not "permit their bodies" to be buried. So great was the victory of the beast over them that the peoples of earth burst into ecstatic rejoicing over the removal of such moral restraint to their "freedom" for license. Earth's peoples congratulated one another on their liberation from moral law. In their reverie they "sent gifts to one another." The "permissive age" arrives when God's law and prophetic judgments are overuled by the beast of the abyss.

But the triumph of the hordes of earth-dwellers is short lived. After the passing of three and a half days (a short indeterminate time) "the breath of life from God entered" the law and prophets. In other words, God's moral law and spiritual message can never be permanently destroyed. They can be twisted, thwarted, diverted, ignored, ridiculed, but they can not be eliminated from the fabric of human society. God's law and prophetic word are doing their surgical cutting to kill or cure no matter how much the followers of the beast of the abyss dismiss them. Thus the "breath (spirit) of life of God entered into them and they stood upon their feet..." In the gospel of the risen Christ the spiritual demands of the Old Testament law and prophets find new life. Law and prophet are reincarnated in the gospel of the New Testament. The spiritual quality and moral intent of the old message is raised and embodied in the gospel. "I did not come to destroy the law but to fulfill it." And it's because such renewed vitality of these moral principles that those who ignore them became terrified. When the divine law and prophet "stood upon their feet...great fear fell upon the ones beholding them."

Pain, suffering, destruction and death is as certain a harvest as any seed produces its inevitable crop. "The wages of sin is death!" Thus "in that hour" in which the "law and prophets" were whisked away into heaven "a great earthquake happened and the tenth of the city fell, persons of men seven thousands..." Like a destroying earthquake the "great city" of Jerusalem fell in 70 A.D. It was an earth-shattering event of judgment that was the complete, perfect ("seven thousands") vindication of God's moral judgment against a sinful society. "The rest became afraid and gave glory to the God of heaven."

## Declaration of God's Sovereignty in Christ!

At last comes the proclamation for which the world waited since the tragedy of Eden. "The seventh angel trumpeted." Immediately there arose from within heaven loud voices saying, "The sovereignty of the world became (that) of our Lord and his Christ, and he shall reign forever and ever." At long last there is a reigning monarch who has asserted his kingship and taken hold of sovereign power to wage victorious war against sin, Satan and death.

In this proclamation observe that "sovereignty" (kingdom) is singular, not plural as some versions carry it. Furthermore, the term does not, in this context, refer to a territorial or political unit. The English word "kingdom" does not represent the meaning of βασιλεία as used in the New Testament. "Sovereign," "rule," or "dominion" best reflect New Testament usage. "Kingdom of God" in our translations does not represent a political concept so much as the power of moral dominion over the spirits of people. Thus here in Revelation 11:15 the proclamation is that "the rule of the world became (the rule) of our Lord and his Christ..." At a point in time God entered into human history to take aggressive rule over the world in his Christ. That point was at the incarnation of God in the person of the virgin's son, Jesus the Christ. Said the angel to the virgin: "...he shall be called the son of the Most High...God shall give him the throne of his father David: and he shall reign...forever: and of his kingdom there shall be no end." Luke 1:32-33. This is confirmed in Rev.12:5 by the woman's "man-child" who is "to rule all the nations." And in Rev.12:10-12 by a "great voice in heaven" which says, "Now is come the salvation... and the sovereignty of our God, and the authority of his Christ..." God in Christ took his power and reigned beginning at Pentecost (Acts 2) and he still reigns. Furthermore, he shall go on reigning "forever and forever." "Of his kingdom there shall be no end."

The early Church saw in the risen ascended Christ fulfillment of messianic prophecy of Psalm 2:1. When the early church felt the heavy hand of the persecuting authorities the believers gathered together and reminded God of his present right of rule. In their prayer they quoted "Why did the Gentiles rage, and the peoples imagine vain things? The kings of the earth set themselves in array and the rulers take counsel against the Lord and against his anointed." Then they claimed the present threat of the Jerusalem authorities as an instance in which God must assert his active presence as sovereign king. It is clear that these early believers saw in the opposition of the Jerusalem powers a fulfillment of Psalm 2 in which the rule of God's Son-Messiah was foreshadowed. The reign of God in Christ as an existent ongoing reality was an example of their consciousness of the presence of the kingdom (sovereign rule) of God. At the incarnation God took "his great power and reigned." At that point in history "the sovereignty of the world became (that) of our Lord and his Christ." Furthermore, "he shall reign forever and forever." He has been ruling since the first century. He shall continue his rule through time and eternity.

The one who "was like a son of man" (Daniel 7:13) who was led into the presence of "the Ancient of Days" and to whom was given "authority, glory and sovereign power" and of whom it was said, "His dominion is everlasting...that will never be destroyed" (Daniel 7:14)---All these foregleams find their fulfillment in the birth, ministry, crucifixion, resurrection, ascension and exaltion of Jesus to the right hand of God. Thus it is a sound conclusion that in Revelation 11:15 John is asserting that the promised eternal reign of God in his Christ already was exercising itself then in the first Christian century. "Let all the house of Israel therefore know assuredly, that God has made him both Lord and Christ, this Jesus whom you crucified."(Acts 2:36)

It should not be forgotten that though evil seems predominant in our present society that does not nullify the fact that God is now in this world ruling in his Christ. When a Christian was brought before the Roman court in the first century he was given the option of owning Caesar or Christ as Lord. If he refused Caesar and affirmed faith in Christ he chose death. Who then was victor, Caesar or Christ? Certainly not Caesar! Christ was triumphant in that martyr's death. Caesar was defeated in his use of force to compel denial of truth. Christ reigned in that man. Christ ruled in that man in life and death! The early Christians were not defeated; they were only killed. In them Christ was victor both in time and eternity. Evil has no victors! Only defeat and death. God reigned "at the flood" and God, in his Christ, has taken "his great power" and reigns through all beastly governments who threaten and persecute God's people. Revelation 11:15 is the declaration of the fact of God's present sovereignty!

## A TRANSLATION
## Revelation 12:1-18

And a great sign appeard in the heaven, a woman having been clothed with the sun, and the moon (was) under her feet. And on her head was a crown of twelve stars. And she (was) pregnant and, travailing and being in birth pains, she cries to deliver.

And another sign appeared in the heaven. And behold, a huge firey red dragon, having seven heads and ten horns, and upon his heads seven diadems. And his tail drags the third of the stars of heaven and he hurled them unto the earth. And the dragon stood before the woman, the one being about to give birth, that whenever she shall bear, he might devour her child. And she bore a male child who is about to shepherd all the nations with an iron rod. And her child was snatched up to God and to his throne. And the woman fled into the desert where she has there a place having been prepared by God that there they might nourish her a thousand two hundred sixty days.

And war broke out in heaven. Michael and his angels waged war with the dragon. And the dragon and his angels battled but they did not conquer, neither was a place found for them in the heaven. And the great dragon was hurled out; the old serpent, the one being called "Devil" and the "Satan," the one deceiving the entire inhabited world, he was hurled down unto the earth, and his angels were hurled down with him.

And I heard a loud voice in the heaven saying, "Now became the salvation and the power and the sovereignty of our God and the authority of his Christ, because the accuser of our brothers was thrown out, the one accusing them day and night before our God. And they conquered him because of the blood of the lamb and because of the message of their testimony; and they did not love their soul (even) unto death. Because of this, rejoice, O heavens, and you, the ones tabernacling in them. Woe! the earth and the sea, because the Devil came down to you, having great rage, knowing that he has little time."

And when the dragon saw that he was hurled down unto the earth, he persecuted the woman who bore the male child. And to the woman was given the two wings of the great eagle in order that she might fly unto the desert unto the place where there she is being nourished a season and seasons and half a season from the face of the serpent. And out of his mouth the serpent spewed water like a river that he might make her as carried away by the flood. And the earth helped the woman and the earth opened its mouth and drank down the river which the dragon spewed out of its mouth. And the dragon became furious at the woman and went off to make war with the rest of her seed, the ones keeping the commandments of God and having the testimony of Jesus.

And he stood on the sand of the sea.

## AN OUTLINE OF REVELATION 12:1-18

### God Conquers Satan!

The conflict between God and Satan extends far beyond the limits of this world of sight and sense. It's a cosmic struggle that reaches farther in space and time, further in spirit and thought than the pygmy-size reach of the mind of mortal man in a material world. It is universal in the broadest sense. It's of the universe, not just of this Lilliputian earth.

The victory of God over Satan is past. It came in heavenly realms but on this earth at a time in history. Mopping up skirmishes still take place but the war is over. The battle of human redemption is past. That the good news of God's victory be heralded and confirmed to all who align themselves with God remains. Chapter 12 summarizes God's conquering Satan.

I. SIGNS OF THE COMING CONFLICT. 12:1-6
   1. Sign of the woman expecting to give birth. 1-2
      (a)Her exalted position.
      (b)Her pregnant situation.
   2. Sign of the firey red dragon. 3-4
      (a)His shrewdness and strength.
      (b)His earlier conquests.
      (c)His present purpose--devour the woman's child at birth.
   3. Birth and rescue of the woman's man child. 5
   4. Flight of the woman to safe nourishment. 6

II. GOD DEFEATS SATAN IN THE COSMIC CONFLICT. 12:7-12
   1. God's forces join battle with the dragon's. 7a
   2. Satan loses (a)the war (b)a "place" in heavenly realm. 7b-8
   3. The cosmic war injected into human history. 9
      (a)The dragon "hurled unto the earth."
      (b)His union with evil identified.
      (c)His angels hurled down into history with him.
   4. The Song of Victory by God's People.
      (a)The nature of the accomplished victory. 10a
      (b)The vanquished identified. 10b
      (c)The basis of the redemptive victory. 11a
      (d)Experiential evidence in the redeemed of the victory. 11b
      (e)Praise to heaven and its inhabitants. 12a
      (f)On earth the Devil has "little time" left. 12b

III. FINAL PHASE OF THE DEVIL'S DEFEAT. 12:13-18
   1. Mortally defeated the Devil rages against the woman. 13
   2. The woman provided a refuge of safety. 14
   3. In a second attack Satan seeks to drown her. 15
   4. The earth "helps" the woman to avoid drowning. 16
   5. Frustrated, Satan attacks the "rest of her seed." 17

Man's redemption is certain because of God's past victory on the plane of human history. Satan stands on the "sands of the sea" and surveys his defeat. John stands on the "sands of the sea" to survey God's triumph.

<u>Our</u> victory is assured by <u>his</u> victory. Redemption has been placed in our hands. It's up to us to "work it out."

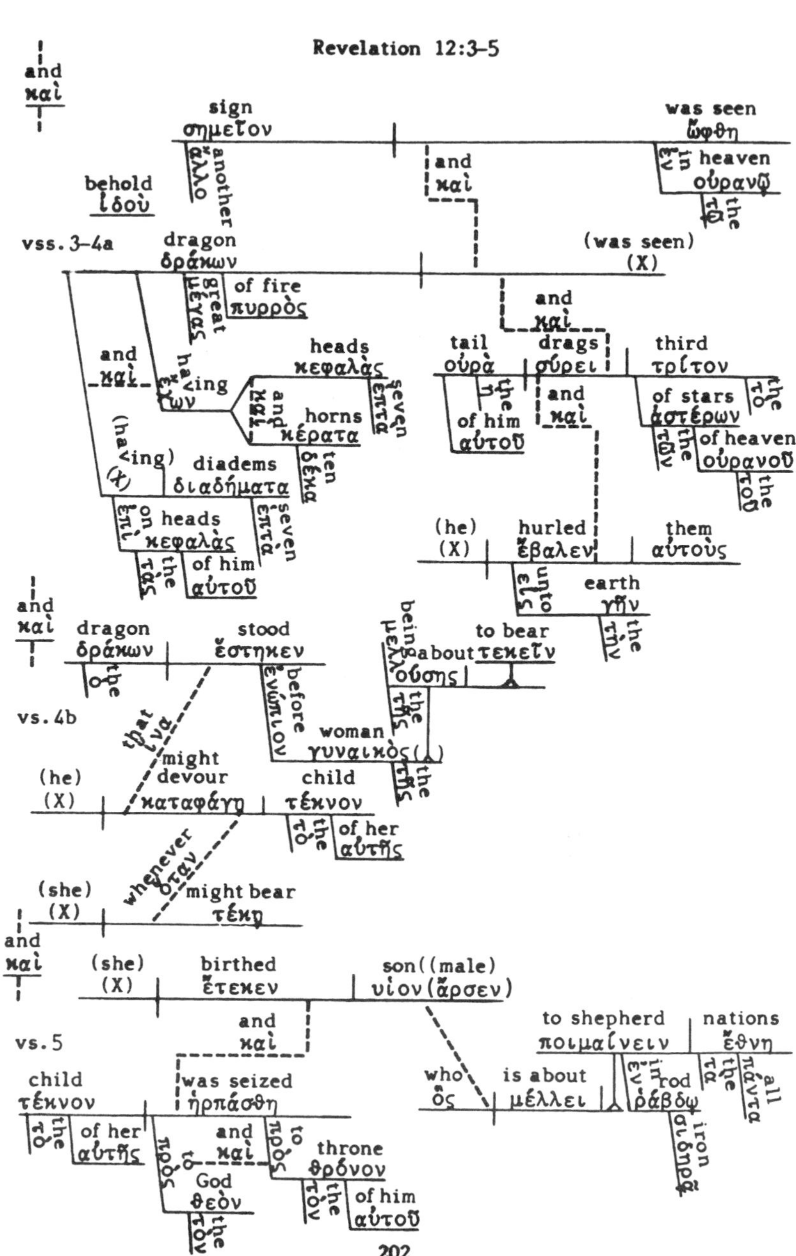
and καὶ
sign σημεῖον
another ἄλλο
was seen ὤφθη
in ἐν
heaven οὐρανῷ
the τῷ
and καὶ
behold ἰδοὺ
vss. 3-4a
dragon δράκων
great μέγας
of fire πυρρὸς
(was seen) (X)
and καὶ
having ἔχων
heads κεφαλὰς
seven ἑπτὰ
and καὶ
horns κέρατα
ten δέκα
(having) (X)
diadems διαδήματα
seven ἑπτὰ
on ἐπὶ
heads κεφαλὰς
the τὰς
of him αὐτοῦ
tail οὐρὰ
the ἡ
of him αὐτοῦ
drags σύρει
third τρίτον
the τὸ
of stars ἀστέρων
the τῶν
of heaven οὐρανοῦ
the τοῦ
and καὶ
(he) (X)
hurled ἔβαλεν
them αὐτοὺς
unto εἰς
earth γῆν
the τὴν
and καὶ
dragon δράκων
the ὁ
stood ἔστηκεν
before ἐνώπιον
woman γυναικὸς
the τῆς
being about μελλούσης
the τῆς
to bear τεκεῖν
vs. 4b
that ἵνα
(he) (X)
might devour καταφάγῃ
child τέκνον
the τὸ
of her αὐτῆς
whenever ὅταν
(she) (X)
might bear τέκῃ
and καὶ
(she) (X)
birthed ἔτεκεν
son ((male) υἱον (ἄρσεν)
vs. 5
who ὃς
is about μέλλει
to shepherd ποιμαίνειν
nations ἔθνη
the τὰ
all πάντα
in ἐν
rod ῥάβδῳ
iron σιδηρᾷ
and καὶ
child τέκνον
the τὸ
of her αὐτῆς
was seized ἡρπάσθη
to πρὸς
God θεὸν
the τὸν
and καὶ
to πρὸς
throne θρόνον
the τὸν
of him αὐτοῦ

## THE DIAGRAM OF 12:3-5

Four clauses of equal rank form the skeleton of the sentence of verses 3-4a. First is, "another sign was seen in heaven..." ὤφθη is aorist passive; it may be translated "appeared." However "was seen" gives stress on the passive idea. It stresses that those who did the "seeing" were actively involved. Their attention was captured by this "other sign." The phrase "in the heaven" is adverbial answering where the sign was seen.

The second clause identifies a "great dragon of fire" as being the central feature in the "other sign." Genitive πυρρὸς "of fire" is usually translated "red." Genitive specifies the kind of dragon. Two circumstantial participle phrases describe the dragon: "...having seven heads and ten horns" and "(having) on his heads seven diadems..." The participle is implied in one of these expressions. That implied "having" is modified by prepositional ἐπὶ phrase indicating where he was having the diadems.

The third clause says, "...his tail drags the third of the stars of heaven..." σύρει is descriptive present giving a moving picture of the action: "the tail is dragging..." τρίτον appears here as a noun direct object of the verb "is dragging." The "of stars" is a genitive idea specifying the kind of "third" involved.

The final of the four clauses states the fact: "He hurled them unto the earth." In the verb translated "hurled" the author returns to the narrative aorist rather than a linear descriptive tense. The sentence is compound.

Verse 4b represents a complex sentence. It has one independent and two dependent clauses. "The dragon stood" is the independent idea. Where he stood is presented in the ἐνώπιον phrase, "before the woman." The "woman" is distinguished by an attributive participle in apposition: "the one being about to bear."

The first of the subordinate clauses is incorporated by ἵνα portraying purpose: "...that he might devour her child..." ὅταν introduces an indefinite temporal idea, "...whenever she might give birth."

Verse five admits to being compound-complex. It has one dependent clause besides two independents. The first main clause states: "She birthed(bore)a son, a male." The direct object "son" is enhanced by appositional "male." Then is added an adjective clause further describing son as one "...who is about to shepherd in (with) a rod of iron all the nations." ἐν "in" is used only with locative case. Here the "shepherding"(ruling) is visualized as in the "rod" but may be translated "with." The idea of iron suggests the firmness by which the son rules. Ruling by "shepherding" suggests the gentleness of his ruling. He rules by leading, not by forcing.

The last independent clause reveals that "her son was seized (up) to God and to his throne." This "seize" is not that of capture but of rescue. πρός with accusative with persons announces a close personal relationship. He "was seized" to be "with God" in intimate personal association.

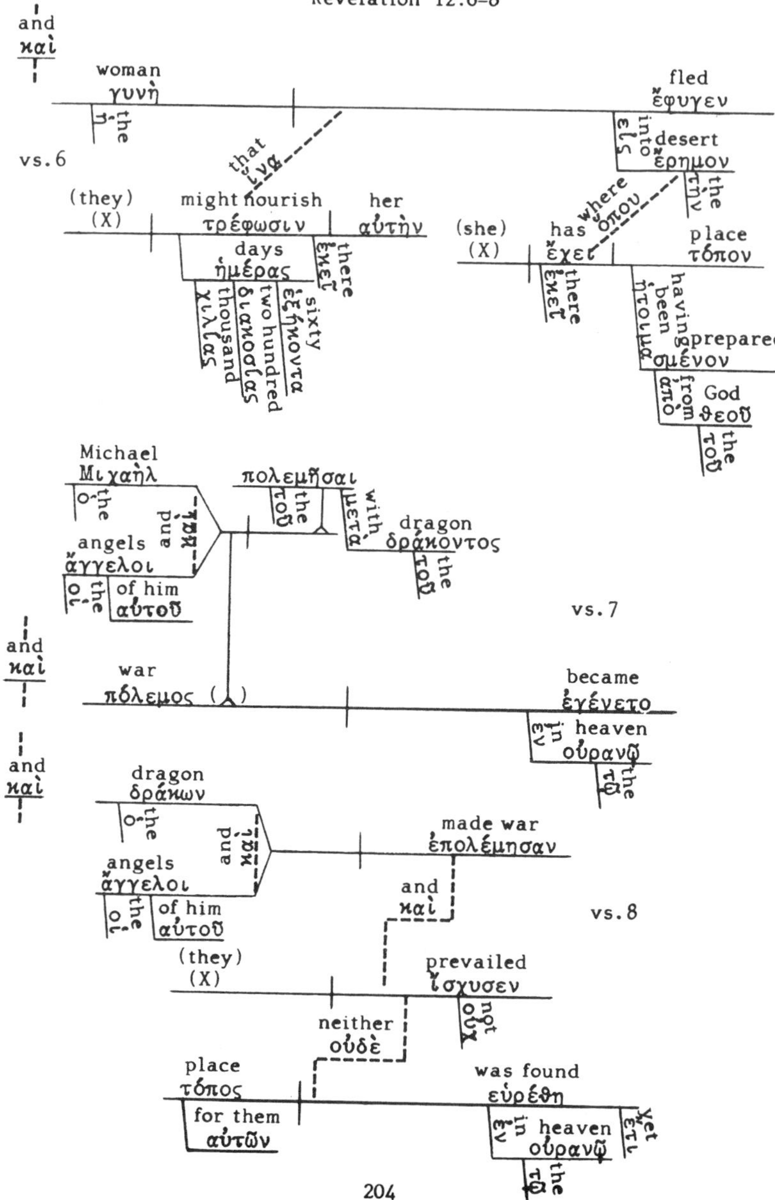
and
καὶ
woman
γυνὴ
the
ἡ
fled
ἔφυγεν
into
εἰς
desert
ἔρημον
the
τὴν
vs. 6
that
ἵνα
(they)
(X)
might nourish
τρέφωσιν
her
αὐτὴν
days
ἡμέρας
there
ἐκεῖ
thousand
χιλίας
two hundred
διακοσίας
sixty
ἑξήκοντα
where
ὅπου
(she)
(X)
has
ἔχει
place
τόπον
there
ἐκεῖ
having been
ἡτοιμα
prepared
σμένον
from
ἀπὸ
God
θεοῦ
the
τοῦ
Michael
Μιχαὴλ
the
ὁ
and
καὶ
angels
ἄγγελοι
the
οἱ
of him
αὐτοῦ
πολεμῆσαι
the
τοῦ
with
μετὰ
dragon
δράκοντος
the
τοῦ
vs. 7
and
καὶ
war
πόλεμος
became
ἐγένετο
in
ἐν
heaven
οὐρανῷ
the
τῷ
and
καὶ
dragon
δράκων
the
ὁ
and
καὶ
angels
ἄγγελοι
the
οἱ
of him
αὐτοῦ
made war
ἐπολέμησαν
and
καὶ
vs. 8
(they)
(X)
prevailed
ἴσχυσεν
not
οὐκ
neither
οὐδὲ
place
τόπος
for them
αὐτῶν
was found
εὑρέθη
in
ἐν
heaven
οὐρανῷ
the
τῷ
yet
ἔτι

## THE DIAGRAM OF 12:6-8

The three clauses of verse six arrange themselves so as to frame a complex sentence. The independent portion declares: "And the woman fled into the desert..." The prepositional εἰς phrase tells where she fled, hence is adverb in function. Describing the noun "desert" is a subordinate idea introduced by ὅπου "where." The clause is adjectival, "...where she has a place." This "place" is described by circumstantial perfect participle ἡτοιμασμένον "having been prepared." Perfect tense suggests that the "place" is stable, permanent, and fixed. Added to this participle is the ἀπὸ phrase "from God." Ablative case indicates that "God" is the source of the prepared place. The fact that the "from God" modifies the participle rather than "place" intimates that the preparation comes from God not to mention the "place." No wonder it's stable and permanent! The ἵνα clause proposes a purpose for the woman's fleeing. It was "in order that they might nourish her..." τρέφωσιν is present tense denoting durative continuing action.

That verse seven forms a simple sentence would seem guaranteed by the fact there is but one finite verb ἐγένετο "became." That clause says, "War in heaven arose(became)." The expression in apposition to the subject "war" has an infinitive to indicate the verbal action but it has no finite verb. Instead of the accusative of general reference with the infinitive the nominative case appears in both prongs of what serves as "subject," that is, the ones doing the action of the infinitive. Technically it isn't a clause yet practically it performs the function of a clause. Hence, with reason, we might classify it as complex. It is possible that an understood verb (ἐγένετο) might be supplied as verb following the two nominative subjects. In that case there's no doubt that the expression is a clause. The infinitive πολεμῆσαι would then be expressing purpose, a normal Greek idiom. That also would alter the classification to compound.

No question need arise as to how verse eight is to be classified. It is a compound of three independent clauses. Subject of the first clause is the compound expression: "The dragon and his angels..." The entire clause is a positive statement: "The dragon and his angels made war..." This is followed by a negative declaration: "...and they prevailed not..." Both verbs are aorists, statements of fact. The third clause is joined by the negative conjunction οὐδὲ "...neither was place found for them in heaven..." The genitive of pronoun αὐτῶν "of them"(their) seems best classed an objective genitive, "for them." The adverb ἔτι might seem to suggest that the "dragon and his angels" once had a place in heaven which they no longer occupy. But we recall that this is highly symbolic literature. Furthermore, the author does not speak of "heaven" so much as a locale but as a moral, spiritual condition in which any rebellious spirit had no "place." This war is that inaugurated at the incarnation, not at creation or before.

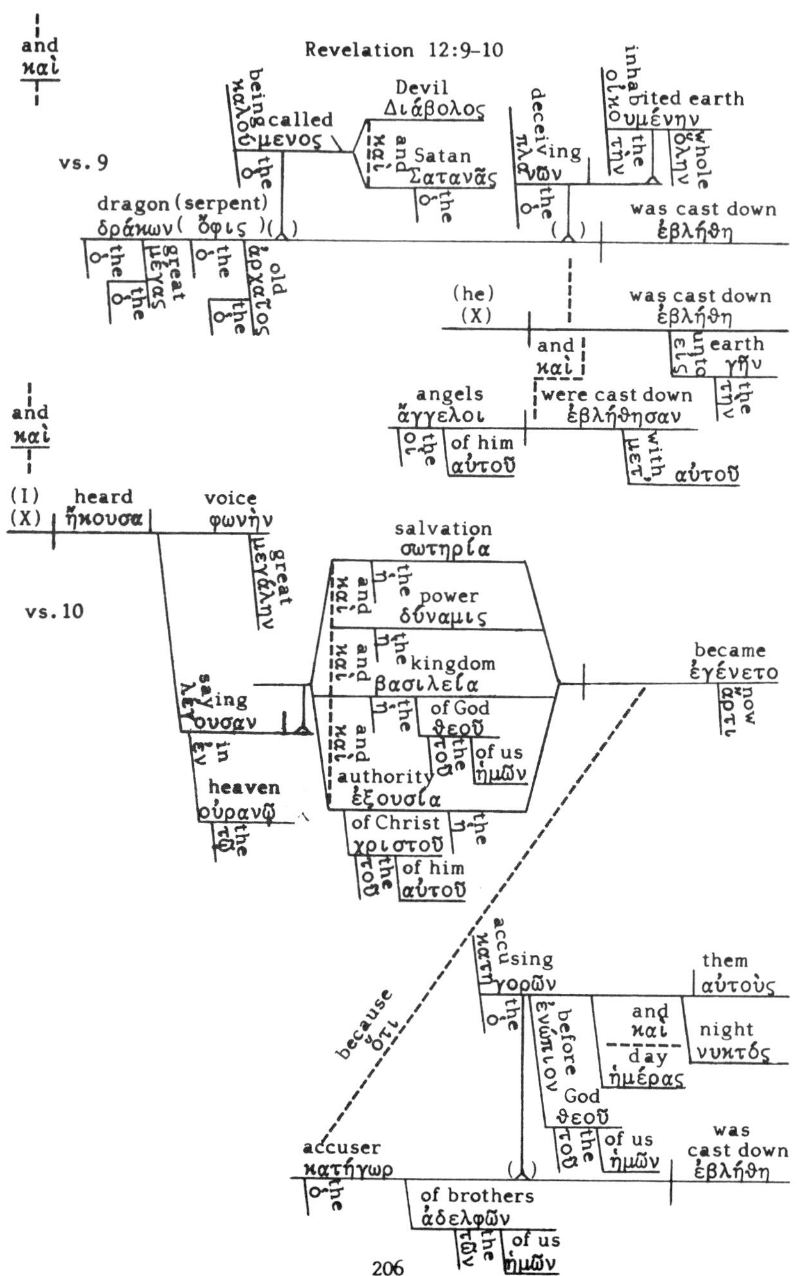
Revelation 12:9–10
vs. 9
and
καὶ
dragon (serpent)
δράκων ( ὄφις )
the
ὁ
great
μέγας
old
ἀρχαῖος
being called
καλούμενος
Devil
Διάβολος
and
καὶ
Satan
Σατανᾶς
deceiving
πλανῶν
inhabited earth
οἰκουμένην
the
τὴν
whole
ὅλην
was cast down
ἐβλήθη
(he)
(X)
unto
εἰς
earth
γῆν
angels
ἄγγελοι
of him
αὐτοῦ
were cast down
ἐβλήθησαν
with
μετ᾽
αὐτοῦ
vs. 10
(I)
(X)
heard
ἤκουσα
voice
φωνὴν
great
μεγάλην
saying
λέγουσαν
in
ἐν
heaven
οὐρανῷ
τῷ
salvation
σωτηρία
ἡ
power
δύναμις
kingdom
βασιλεία
of God
θεοῦ
τοῦ
of us
ἡμῶν
authority
ἐξουσία
of Christ
χριστοῦ
of him
αὐτοῦ
became
ἐγένετο
now
ἄρτι
because
ὅτι
accuser
κατήγωρ
accusing
κατηγορῶν
them
αὐτοὺς
before
ἐνώπιον
day
ἡμέρας
night
νυκτός
God
θεοῦ
of brothers
ἀδελφῶν
τῶν
was cast down
ἐβλήθη

## THE DIAGRAM OF 12:9-10

Verse nine accommodates three full clauses of equal rank. It is compound. The naked clause is: "...the dragon was cast down." Besides the adjective "great" the dragon is further identified by the noun in apposition, "serpent" which is named "the old serpent." Another appositional expansion is the attributive active participle καλούμενος "being called." That he is called "Devil" and "Satan" is indicated by predicate nominatives. There's another appositional describing the "dragon." It's another attributive present participle πλανῶν "deceiving." Object of this "deceiving" is yet another attributive perfect passive accusative participle οἰκουμένην "the inhabited earth." By expanding the simple subject "dragon" with such profusion of appositions the author fills full the image of the dragon for the reader. He leaves no doubt as to who the dragon is and his place in earth's affairs.

The second clause is reaffirming the thought in the first but without all the elaboration. It simply says: "...he was cast down unto the earth..." And the third is almost a post script affirming how thorough was the fall of the dragon for "his angels were cast down with him."

Verse ten also has three clauses but this time so arranged as to constitute a complex sentence. The single independent clause states: "I heard a great voice..." Sometimes the verb for "hear" takes a genitive as its direct object. But here it has accusative φωνὴν. However subtle there is a difference. Genitive calls attention to the fact a noise (voice) was heard. Accusative insists that the voice was not only "heard" but was heard with comprehension. John is saying that he heard more than a noise. He heard with understanding. That which he heard is set forth as direct object of the present circumstantial participle λέγουσαν "saying." This dependent noun-object clause has a compound subject of four parts:"...the salvation and the power and the kingdom of our God and the authority of his Christ..." Each separate part of this subject has its own definite article "the." This makes each member important in its own right while the combination of all four inflates the importance of the subject. The verb of the clause "became" (ἐγένετο) affirms what happened to this four-fold subject. Each of them "became," that is, each "arose," "blossomed out," "came into full force" by virtue of the inherent nature within them.

ἵνα introduces an adverb clause of cause setting forth the evidence lying back of the announcement of the "great voice." It's evident that salvation etc. came "...because the accuser of our brothers...was cast down." This "accuser" is plainly the same as the "dragon" since he's alluded to as "cast down." And this subject ("accuser") is also expanded by means of a present attributive participle "the one accusing them..." The prepositional phrase "before God" is adverbial in function because it tells <u>where</u> the accusing takes place. Genitives ἡμέρας and νυκτός are expressing the <u>kind</u> of time. That is, around the clock!

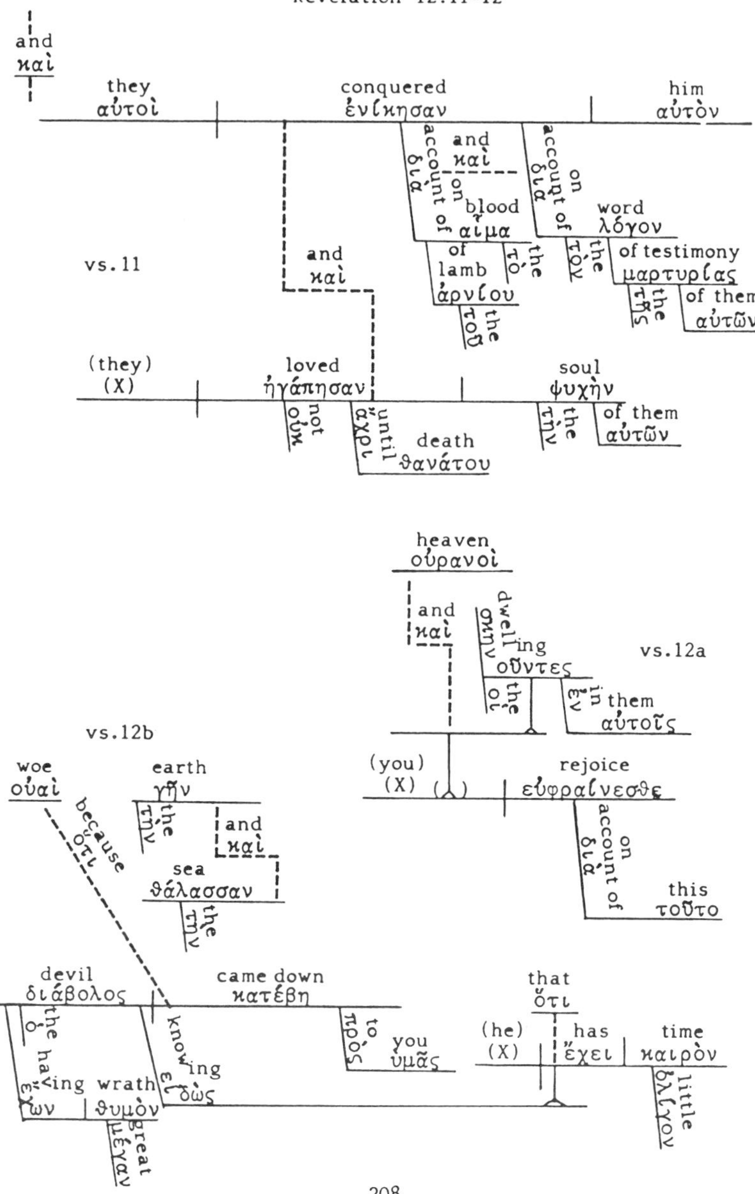
and
καὶ
they
αὐτοὶ
conquered
ἐνίκησαν
him
αὐτὸν
on account of
διὰ
and
καὶ
on
blood
αἷμα
the
τὸ
of lamb
ἀρνίου
the
τοῦ
on account of
διὰ
word
λόγον
the
τὸν
of testimony
μαρτυρίας
the
τῆς
of them
αὐτῶν
vs. 11
and
καὶ
(they)
(X)
loved
ἠγάπησαν
not
οὐκ
until
ἄχρι
death
θανάτου
soul
ψυχὴν
the
τὴν
of them
αὐτῶν
heaven
οὐρανοὶ
and
καὶ
dwell
σκην
ing
οῦντες
the
οἱ
in
ἐν
them
αὐτοῖς
vs. 12a
(you)
(X)
rejoice
εὐφραίνεσθε
on account of
διὰ
this
τοῦτο
vs. 12b
woe
οὐαὶ
because
ὅτι
earth
γῆν
the
τὴν
and
καὶ
sea
θάλασσαν
the
τὴν
devil
διάβολος
the
ὁ
came down
κατέβη
to
πρὸς
you
ὑμᾶς
know
ing
εἰδὼς
hav
ing
ἔχων
wrath
θυμὸν
great
μέγαν
that
ὅτι
(he)
(X)
has
ἔχει
time
καιρὸν
little
ὀλίγον

## THE DIAGRAM OF 12:11-12

Verse eleven deals with a compound sentence of two elements. The first clause states: "And they conquered him..." The opening conjunction "and" connects the thought to the preceeding sentence about the "brethren" who were being accused by the "accuser." The subject of the clause "they" has these "brethren" as its antecedent. That which "they" did is stated by the aorist verb translated "conquered." Direct object is the personal pronoun "him." Its antecedent is "the accuser" of the preceeding sentence. The underlying basis of the brethren's victory over the accuser is two-fold put forward by the two διὰ phrases: "...on account of the blood of the lamb" and "on account of the word of their testimony..." The second of the main clauses states an underlying philosophical and emotional reason lying back of their ability to conquer the accuser: "...they loved not their soul unto death..." The prepositional phrase inserted by ἄχρι functions as an adverb because it answers the questions <u>how</u> and <u>when</u>. That is, up to this degree and until death takes over.

In Nestle's text verse 12 is punctuated as a single sentence. The diagram divides it into two. Verse 12a has for its verb εὐφραίνεσθε "be rejoicing." It is present middle imperative exhorting to durative action: "go on rejoicing." The conquering of the "accuser" is cause for coninuous rejoicing. Middle voice places responsibility on the subjects to initiate as well as to continue the rejoicing. The subject "you" is amplified by two vocatives in apposition: "heavens" and "the ones dwelling in them." σκνοῦντες is present attributive participle. The expression, "on account of this" points back to the ideas of verses 10-11.

The arrangement of verse 12b involves some problems. The open exclamation "Woe" is left hanging with nothing but accusatives γῆν and θάλασσαν "earth and sea" standing apart. If copula verb "be" is inserted we could read "Woe (be) earth and sea..." But that would leave accusatives where nominatives should be. Some manuscripts reflect this problem by having an attributive participle τοῖς κατοικοῦσι "the ones dwelling" and the accusatives as object of the verbal force in the participle. In that case it might be translated: "Woe (be) to the ones dwelling in land and sea..." The diagram leaves it as Nestle's text has it. The accusative stands alone as a lossely attached adverbial accusative.

The remainder of the sentence contains two dependent clauses. ὅτι begins a causal adverb clause "because the devil came down." That's sufficient reason for a "woe." Two circumstantial participles are attached to the subject "devil." First, ἔχων "having great wrath..." And then εἰδὼς "knowing..." That which he knows is put in a noun clause (ὅτι) object of the participle "knowing." This object clause reports: "...that he has little time." Accusative καιρὸν expresses extent of time. The accuser's time for harming mankind is limited hence the greatness of his "wrath." θυμός in contrast to ὀργή is explosive, impetuous, irrational madness. Satan is incensed because he has but "little time."

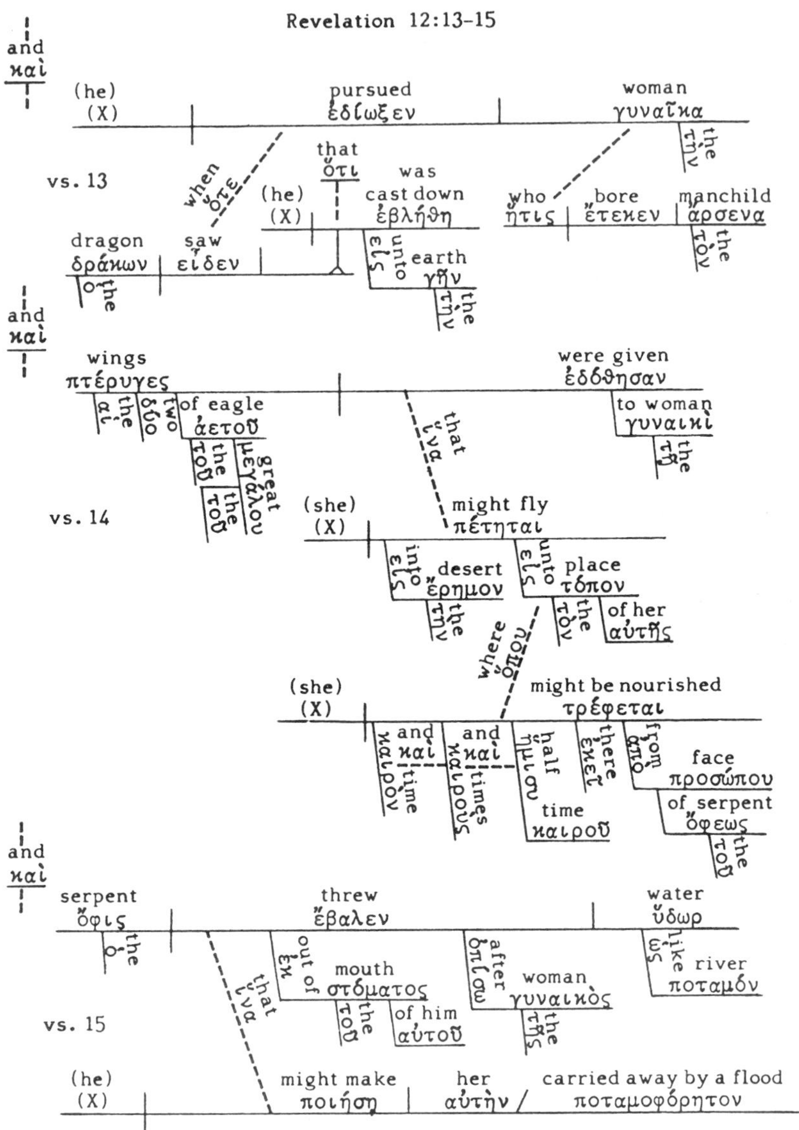
and
καὶ
(he)
(X)
pursued
ἐδίωξεν
woman
γυναῖκα
the
τὴν
vs. 13
when
ὅτε
that
ὅτι
(he)
(X)
was
cast down
ἐβλήθη
unto
εἰς
earth
γῆν
the
τὴν
who
ἥτις
bore
ἔτεκεν
manchild
ἄρσενα
the
τὸν
dragon
δράκων
the
ὁ
saw
εἶδεν
and
καὶ
wings
πτέρυγες
the
αἱ
two
δύο
of eagle
ἀετοῦ
the
τοῦ
great
μεγάλου
the
τοῦ
were given
ἐδόθησαν
to woman
γυναικὶ
the
τῇ
that
ἵνα
vs. 14
(she)
(X)
might fly
πέτηται
into
εἰς
desert
ἔρημον
the
τὴν
unto
εἰς
place
τόπον
the
τὸν
of her
αὐτῆς
where
ὅπου
(she)
(X)
might be nourished
τρέφεται
and
καὶ
time
καιρὸν
and
καὶ
times
καιροὺς
half
ἥμισυ
time
καιροῦ
there
ἐκεῖ
from
ἀπὸ
face
προσώπου
of serpent
ὄφεως
the
τοῦ
and
καὶ
serpent
ὄφις
the
ὁ
threw
ἔβαλεν
water
ὕδωρ
that
ἵνα
out of
ἐκ
mouth
στόματος
the
τοῦ
of him
αὐτοῦ
after
ὀπίσω
woman
γυναικὸς
the
τῆς
like
ὡς
river
ποταμόν
vs. 15
(he)
(X)
might make
ποιήσῃ
her
αὐτὴν
carried away by a flood
ποταμοφόρητον

## THE DIAGRAM OF 12:13-15

The sentence of verse 13 continues to narrate the dragon's implacable pursuit of the woman and her manchild. The sentence is complex. It's main clause states: "And he pursued the woman..." Who this woman was comes forth in the adjective clause modifying "woman." It's the woman "who bore the manchild." Subject in this dependent adjective clause is the qualitative relative ἥτις "who by her very nature." This child was no accident but the inevitable offspring of this particular "woman" by virture of who she was.

A second dependent clause is introduced by temporal conjunction ὅτε "when the dragon saw..." It's an adverbial clause indicating the time when the dragon pursued. Direct object of εἶδεν of this clause is a noun clause inserted by ὅτι "that was cast down unto the earth."

Verse 14 blossoms into a complex arrangement. It contains an independent clause supported by an adverbial ἵνα clause of purpose plus an adjective clause introduced by ὅπου "where." The independent clause carries the main idea: "The two wings of the eagle were given to the woman..." The purpose of such a gift was "in order that she might fly..." Where she was to fly is expressed in the εἰς phrase, "into the desert..." That phrase functions as an adverb. A second εἰς phrase indicates more specifically just <u>where</u> she was to fly, that is, "unto her place..." The adjectival <u>ὅπου</u> clause describes in more detail this "place." It is the "place" "where she might be nourished..." How long she is to be nourished is expressed by the accusatives extent of time translated "time and times and half of time." The adverb ἐκεῖ "there" is redundant. Ablative case with ἀπὸ "from the face of the serpent" suggestes that the woman is to be separated "from" and therefore protected from the destructive purposes of the serpent.

Verse 15 involves a two-clause complex sentence. The main clause describes what the old "serpent" did when he discovered that he couldn't destroy the woman. "The serpent hurled water..." The source from whence the water came is found in the ἐκ phrase "out of his mouth..." Another adverbial idea is seen in the ablative phrase (ὀπίσω) "after" or "behind the woman." It tells <u>where</u> he hurled the water. ὕδωρ is neuter accusative direct object of the verb "hurled." ὡς is treated here as a preposition. "He threw water like a river..."

The ἵνα brings in a dependent idea expressing purpose. The clause expresses purpose. He hurled the water "in order that he might make her as carried away by a flood." The serpent could not stop the flight of the woman so he tried to drown her. The word ποταμοφόρητον is a compound verbal used here in the predicate as objective complement. It is a word in current koine usage which literally means "carried away by a river."

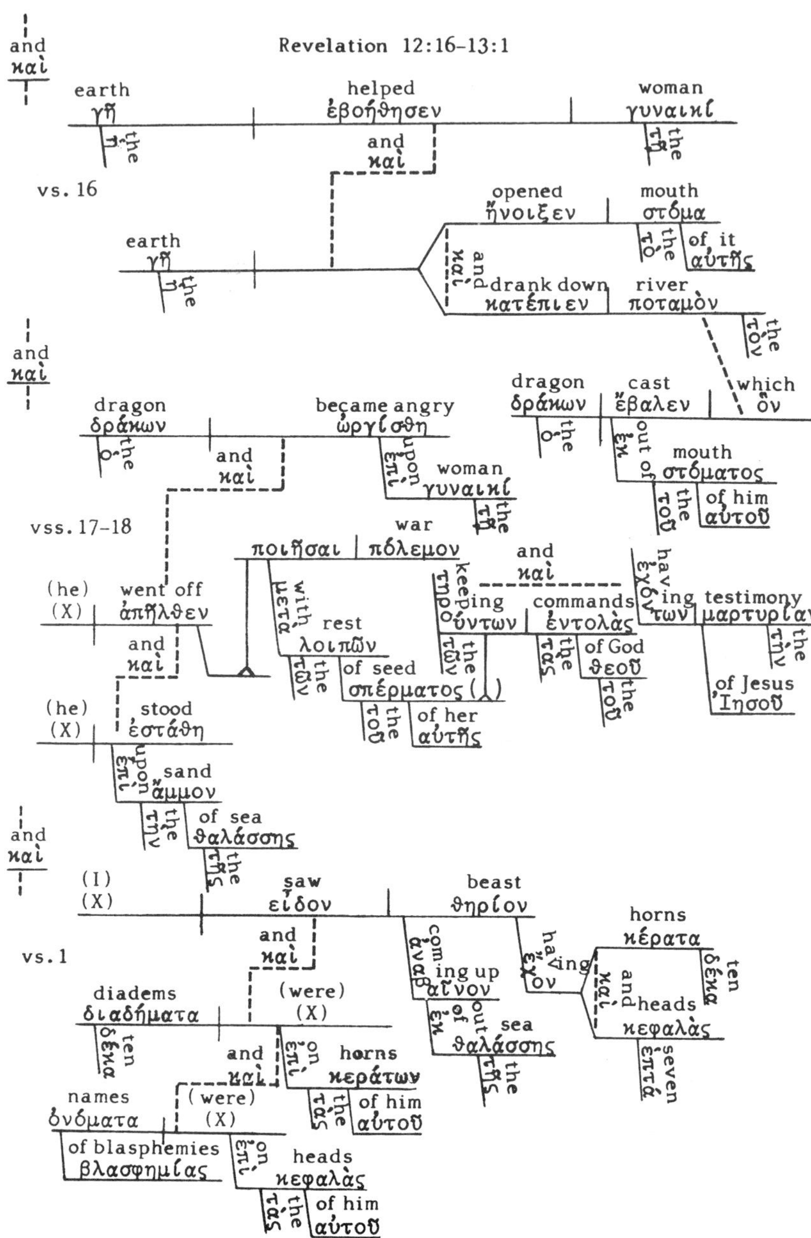
and
καὶ
earth
γῆ
the
ἡ
helped
ἐβοήθησεν
woman
γυναικί
the
τῇ
and
καὶ
vs. 16
opened
ἤνοιξεν
mouth
στόμα
the
τὸ
of it
αὐτῆς
earth
γῆ
the
ἡ
and
καὶ
drank down
κατέπιεν
river
ποταμὸν
the
τὸν
and
καὶ
dragon
δράκων
the
ὁ
cast
ἔβαλεν
which
ὃν
out of
ἐκ
mouth
στόματος
the
τοῦ
of him
αὐτοῦ
dragon
δράκων
the
ὁ
became angry
ὠργίσθη
upon
ἐπὶ
woman
γυναικί
the
τῇ
and
καὶ
vss. 17–18
war
ποιῆσαι
πόλεμον
with
μετὰ
rest
λοιπῶν
the
τῶν
of seed
σπέρματος
the
τοῦ
of her
αὐτῆς
keeping
τηρούντων
the
τῶν
and
καὶ
commands
ἐντολὰς
the
τὰς
of God
θεοῦ
the
τοῦ
having
ἐχόντων
testimony
μαρτυρίαν
the
τὴν
of Jesus
Ἰησοῦ
(he)
(X)
went off
ἀπῆλθεν
and
καὶ
(he)
(X)
stood
ἐστάθη
upon
ἐπὶ
sand
ἄμμον
the
τὴν
of sea
θαλάσσης
the
τῆς
and
καὶ
(I)
(X)
saw
εἶδον
beast
θηρίον
coming up
ἀναβαῖνον
out of
ἐκ
sea
θαλάσσης
the
τῆς
having
ἔχον
horns
κέρατα
ten
δέκα
and
καὶ
heads
κεφαλὰς
seven
ἑπτά
vs. 1
and
καὶ
diadems
διαδήματα
ten
δέκα
(were)
(X)
on
ἐπὶ
horns
κεράτων
the
τὰς
of him
αὐτοῦ
and
καὶ
names
ὀνόματα
(were)
(X)
of blasphemies
βλασφημίας
on
ἐπὶ
heads
κεφαλὰς
the
τὰς
of him
αὐτοῦ

## THE DIAGRAM OF 12:16-13:1

The compound-complex sentence of verse 16 has two independent clauses and one dependent. The opening clause states: "...the earth helped the woman..." The verb translated "helped" is a narrative aorist indicative. It has a dative (γυναικί) as direct object. The second of the main clauses has a compound predicate: "...the earth swallowed (literally "drank down") the river..." κατά "down" compounded with πίνω "drink" is the perfective use of the preposition. He thoroughly drank it; decisively gobbled it up(down). The noun-object "river" is described by a dependent adjective clause: "...which the dragon cast out of his mouth." The ἐκ phrase performs the work of an adverb telling "from whence" the dragon threw out the river.

A first glance at the sentence of 12:17-18 might lead one to suppose that a dependent clause is present somewhere. But not so! The sentence actually has but three clauses all of which are independent. Hence it is a compound sentence. The three clauses declare: "the dragon became angry..," "...he went off..," and "he stood..." Hanging from the first clause is an adverbial phrase, "at (ἐπί) the woman." This phrase answers the question as to <u>why</u> the dragon became angry. The tense of ὠργίσθη is an ingressive aorist signifying that he "became angry."

The second clause states:"...he went off..." Introducing the <u>purpose</u> for which he "went off" is the aorist infinitive ποιῆσαι "to make." That which he "makes" is the accusative noun "war." Those with whom he "makes war" are set forth in the μετά phrase "with the rest of her seed." σπέρματος "seed" is a collective noun. In spite of its singular number it has a plural combination in apposition to it: "the ones keeping commands..." and "the ones having the testimony of Jesus." Genitive Ἰησοῦ is objective genitive expressing the object of the testimony. On the other hand genitive θεοῦ is subjective; they are the commands which God gave.

The final of the three clauses states: "he stood." <u>Where</u> he stood finds embodiment in the ἐπί phrase, an adverbial idea: "...upon the sand of the sea."

The opening sentence of chapter 13 is also a triple-pronged compound formation. "I saw beast..." is the first clause. The object "beast" is described by two participles. One chronicles where and how the beast appears: "coming up out of the sea..." The second inserts a description as to what he's like: "having ten horns and seven heads..." The participles are predicate. But whether they are suppementary or circumstantial will be determined by their relation to the main finite verb εἶδον. In either case they are still adjectives describing "beast."

The last two of the clauses of this sentence add descriptions of the disposition of these "horns" and heads." The second clause states: "...ten diadems (were) upon his horns..." The third of the clauses relates: "names of blasphemies (were) upon his heads.." Both the ἐπί phrases represent adverbial ideas answering the question as to <u>where</u> the diadems and the names of blasphemies were.

## SOME EXPOSITORY THOUGHTS ON 12:1-18

Since the death and subsequent resurrection of the Christ it is not "truth forever on the scaffold." 'Tis sin, its moral allies and spiritual colleagues that hang from the scaffold's bar. The violent contortions of human society are but the evidence that it is choking in its death struggles. Revolutions, wars, murder and rape--these are the fruit of sin, the evidences of death. They are vivid tokens that the dying process has begun. Even the death of death is but a matter of time. Calvary and the empty tomb mark the point in time when the "sovereignty of the world became (that) of our Lord and his Christ." God is <u>now</u> reigning in his Christ. And that reign shall go on through time and eternity, history and heaven, now and "forever and forever." To the eye that is sensitive to ultimate reality divine doom has been pronounced. God's verdict of guilt and judgment of destruction is a matter of past history. The process of carrying out that judgment has been going on ever since Golgotha. And He, God in his Christ, has been reigning over His citizenry all through the centuries. He's still exercising that victorious reign in and over his kingdom.

Where, when, and how did God conquer Satan? If the victory in history belongs to God what does the present broil between God and Satan, right and wrong, signify? Why must the battle rage on?

### <u>Signs of the conflict!</u>

If any doubt remains that the Revelation is painted in symbolic colors the opening verses in chapter 12 should remove it. Verse one declares: "And a great sign(symbol)was seen..." and verse three joins in with: "And there was seen another sign(symbol)..." What is here described is history but in symbolic language.

First comes the "sign" of the expectant woman. The ornate clothing of the woman portrays her exalted dignity. She's adorned with the beauty of all creation; she wears creation like a crown. She's God's chosen; the one who produced the "manchild," God's son, man's saviour, the Christ child! Through the long anguished months of pregnancy the woman looked forward with great anticipation to the arrival of her manchild. It was the "people of God" who produced and awaited the child of God, the Christ.

But a second symbol signified that God's manchild would not appear on this earth without an ensuing struggle. The dragon of flaming red fire hovered with greedy avarice awaiting the birth of this saviour. His plan was to destroy the child before he could effect man's redemption. The dragon's seven heads symbolize his great wisdom. His ten horns image his mighty power. The seven diadems signify his perfect earthly authority. That his "tail draws the third part of the stars..." indicates his fiendish power over the rulers of earth. What can a lone pregnant woman do to protect her unborn child from such an array of force? How can her child ever reach his appointed destiny of ruling "all the nations with a rod of iron"(Ps.2 and vs.5) when the powers of evil are set to destroy her manchild before he draws his first breath?

These two "signs" are dramatic symbols which signified to the first readers the deadly, uncompromising nature of the warfare between God and the "old serpent." The great "accuser" is well aware that if he allows the manchild to live in human history his own power will be curbed and at last destroyed. If God "in flesh" is ever realized Satan has but "little time." Peace between good and evil is not negotiable. It's war to the end.

The woman "bore a male child." His appointed task was to "rule all the nations with an iron rod." With the incarnation the issue was clear, the battle lines drawn. Embodied in this-world rulers Satan attacked the manchild. From Herod's madcap murder of the Bethlehem infants through the perverse opposition of Jewish authorities, unto the combination of world-rulers that nailed the manchild to the cross Satan squandered his dirty-devices in his attempt to destroy the child. But it was to no avail for the "child was snatched up to God and his throne." The "best" Satan could do was to have the manchild crucified. But the resurrection turned that "defeat" into divine victory and the Christ ascended to the right hand of the sovereign God, there to share his ageless rule. And as for the woman who bore him! the "people of God" fled for refuge to a security prepared by God where she might be nourished a "thousand two hundred sixty days," symbol of a limited period of persecution. God's people, though living "in the world," are secure <u>from</u> the world.

## <u>The cosmic conflict</u>

The conflict is cosmic in proportions. The warfare rises beyond the mere "natural" order. It is more than meets the eye. It is an issue in which heaven itself is vitally involved. It is a war that "broke out <u>in heaven</u>." That's to say, it is a warfare which encompasses spiritual principles. Spiritual and moral realities are the things of "heaven" whether exercised in heaven, earth, or unknown galaxies! The birth of Jesus, the incarnation, the establishment of Messiah's rule on this earth is a cosmic, eternal event. It happened in history but it is above history in its issue. It is "in heaven." Satan met his sorest defeat in Jesus, particularly at the cross and the garden tomb. In this defeat Michael and his heavenly angels overcame the "Devil" and "hurled out the old serpent." "He was hurled down unto the earth and his angels with him." During his earthly life Jesus noted this fall: "I beheld Satan fall as lightning from heaven."(Luke 10:18)

Heaven rejoices over Satan's defeat at calvary. Heaven sings: "Now became the salvation and the power and the sovereignty of our God and the authority of his Christ..." But the earth?? "Woe the earth and the sea, because the Devil came down to you..." The defeat of Satan was not his destruction! This world is his in which to work for a "little time." In this world he will attack "the woman who bore the child," that is, God's people. So the deadly war goes on. Satan will embody himself in world rulers. His evil powers shall incarnate themselves within kings, governors, dictators, and all manner of world parliaments. The church must flee for a "season and seasons and half a season..." The period of persecution is limited in duration yet is very real. It will go on throughout human history.

Where do the people of God stand as this ruthless war rages on? They must live through this violent history. But they live as victors! "They conquered him (the dragon) because of the blood of the lamb and because of the message of their testimony; and they did not love their soul (even) unto death." These three factors sustain God's people amidst all the violence of the world's corrupt society.

First is "the blood of the lamb." The cross of Christ conquered for them the curse of sin and its issue in death. His victory assures their victory! Because he died and rose they live in, through, and beyond the corruptions of the world. His victory is a matter of record! And God's people share in that victory.

Another supporting factor is "the word of their testimony." Christ died and rose! Those are historic facts. But the significant meaning of the facts was proclaimed to God's people. The "good news" was testified to them. And they not only responded in faith but the "good news" became for them "the word of their testimony" to others. This "word" undergirded their life with meaning. It testified to a purpose for living. The word of witness about Jesus becomes a word for Jesus. And to the one who testifies it becomes an inner, subjective, tested word of experience. "We know that the son of God has come, and he has given to us understanding that we may go on knowing (experiencing) the true one; and we are in the true one in his son Jesus Christ."(I Jn 5:20)

A third supporting factor is the quality of their love for Christ; "they did not love their soul (even) unto death." God's people are not just "committed." They are committed to HIM. The incarnation, the establishment of God's rule in Christ revealed that life in this corrupted world is but a shadow of that which life really is. Jesus came to bring to light "life and immortality." The fact of life beyond life sustains life through all the turbulent times of Satan's warfare against "the rest of her (the woman's) seed." These children of the woman not only could but did say: "I hold not my life of...as dear to myself, so that I may accomplish my course and the ministry which I received..."(Acts 20:24) "...I am ready not to be bound only but also to die...for the name of the Lord Jesus."(Acts 21:13) Such love lives through the fires of persecution and the decay of death."

Furthermore, four realities are established because of the incarnation, the cross, and the resurrection. At calvary he wrought "salvation." God will not abandon man. He "so loved...that he gave his only begotten son" so that men might avoid the inevitable perishing of anyone who lives in this corrupt and corrupting world. Had he not come "in flesh" and established his Messianic rule there could have been no escape from the process of perishing. Did he not come that men "might not perish" as they certainly would have? Did he not come that men "might have eternal life" as indeed they would never have enjoyed had he not come? But now "salvation is come!"

"Now became the salvation and the power..." So too the power of God is established by the incarnation, cross, and resurrection. His is not a physical force that brushes aside anything or anyone that stands in his way. In fact it's more than just physical power that broke the bonds of death. It's moral force that brought the resurrection into the range of the possible. In its nature death is not able to keep down the morally chaste or the spiritually spotless. "The wages of sin is death." The fruit of moral perversion is the grave. Death is the inexorable consequence of sin. Death does not come because of purity or innocence. Hence there is no way for the grave to hold him who is morally pure or spiritually innocent. The resurrection of the Christ demonstrated God's power over the grave and revealed the cross to be his power over sin. By death God's power removed sin; by resurrection he surmounted death. "Now is come the salvation and the power..."

Now also is come "the kingdom of God." The prominate presence of Satan in this world doesn't mean that God does not reign. Evil battles against righteousness but it does not eliminate it. Satan wars against God's kingdom. That very fact testifies that God's kingdom is a reality. Otherwise the dragon would have no war to wage. In Jesus' earthly career God established his reign. And ever since God has been exercising his reign over all human hearts that yield to his rule. God is a real king over a real kingdom. His is not a make-believe! "Now is come...the kingdom of our God." In his Christ God invaded the affairs of men in behalf of their redemption. No way can he deny the fact of redemption. The past cannot be changed. Redemption is a matter of historical record. Victory has been permanently, unchangably provided for any man or all men who recognize in Christ their redemption. "Who is the one conquering the world if not the one believing that Jesus is the son of God? This is the one who came through water and blood..."(I Jn. 5:5-6) With the incarnation, death and resurrection the "last age" began. God's final deed of redemption has been completed. It is time now to announce it and let "every creature" claim it for himself.

Thwarted at every turn the "serpent spewed water like a river that he might make her as carried away by flood." All stops were pulled as Satan sought to drown the woman by every segment of society. Yet the very "earth helped the woman" and "drank down the river." The social institutions that turned on the woman for her destruction became the opportunities she exploited to aid the cause she advanced.

What's left for the dragon? Defeated at each point nothing remains but to rage in violent wrath. "The dragon became furious ...and went off to make war with the rest of her seed..." But he's doomed to failure! The Christ has already won the war by enabling his people to "keep the commands of God and hold tight to the testimony of Jesus." The people of God are well armed for the conflict. The war was won at Bethlehem, calvary and the garden tomb. Announcing the victory, enlisting recruits, and a mopping up campaign is that which remains.

## A TRANSLATION
### Revelation 13:1-18

And I saw rising out of the sea a beast having ten horns and seven heads and upon his horns ten diadems and upon his heads names of blasphemies. And the beast which I saw was like a leopard, and his feet were as of a bear, and his mouth (was) as a lion's mouth. And the dragon gave to him his power and his throne and great authority. And one of his heads (was) as though it were wounded unto death. But its deadly wound was healed. And the whole earth marvelled after the beast, and worshipped the dragon because he gave his authority to the beast; and they worshipped the beast saying, "Who is like the beast and who is able to war with him?"

And a mouth speaking great things and blasphemies was given to him; and authority was given to him to do (these things) forty two months. And he opened his mouth for blaphemies against God, to blaspheme his name and his tabernacle and the ones tabernacling in the heaven. And to do battle with his saints was given to him, and to him was given authority over every tribe and people and tongue and nation. And all the ones dwelling on the earth shall worship him, whose name has not been written in the book of the life of the lamb, the one having been slaughtered from the foundation of the world.

If anyone has ears, he is to hear! If anyone (is) for captivity he is to go unto captivity; if anyone shall kill with sword, it's necessary that he be killed with a sword. Here is the wisdom and the faith of the saints.

And I saw, coming up from the earth, another beast. And he was having two horns like a lamb, and he was speaking as a dragon. And he exercises all the authority of the first beast before him. And he makes the earth and the ones dwelling in it that they shall worship the first beast whose deadly wound was healed. And he does great signs that he even makes fire to come down out of heaven unto the earth in the presence of men. And he deceives the ones dwelling on the earth by the signs which were given to him to do before the beast, saying to the ones dwelling on the earth, that they should make an image to the beast who has the wound of the sword and lived. And to give breath to the image of the beast was given to him in order that the image of the beast might speak and he might make that howevermany if they shall not worship the image of the beast that they shall be killed. And he makes all, the slaves and the free, the poor and the rich, the great and the small, that they shall give to themselves a mark upon their right hand or upon their forehead and that anyone not be able to buy or to sell except the one having the mark (the name of the beast) or his number. Here is the wisdom! The one having understanding is to count the number of the beast for the number is of a human being. And his number is six hundred sixty six.

## AN OUTLINE OF REVELATION 13:1-18

### The Dragon and The Two Beasts

What are the agents through which Satan operates in human affairs? At what point does he invade human history to wreak his destructive ends? As a corrupting, morally subversive power how does he ply his practice? What is the relationship between his evil nature and the institutions and agencies of this world?

Under the apocalytic forms of a dragon and two beasts the author of Revelation deals with these questions. And that which Satan utilized in the late first century he has done repeatedly through the centuries unto this modern age.

I. THE DRAGON AND THE FIRST BEAST. 13:1-8
1. The beast rises "from the sea." - from below! 1a (cf.vs.11)
2. His power, position, and blasphemies. 1b
3. He's swift, strong and carnivorous. 2a
4. He holds the power, throne, and authority of the dragon. 2b
5. Though killed he lives. 3
6. The people worship the dragon because they idolized the beast. 4
7. Powers given to the beast include:
   (a)Blasphemy against God, his dwelling, his heavenly people. 6
   (b)War with and victory over God's saints. 7a
   (c)Exercise of universal power. 7b
   (d)Except for God's people, universally worshipped. 8

II. WISDOM AND FAITH OF THE SAINTS. 13:10
1. Possession brings responsibility to perform. 10a
2. The "wisdom and patience of the saints." 10b
   (a)In the matter of captivity.
   (b)In the matter of violent force.
   (c)In identifying the human enemy agent. 18

III. THE SECOND BEAST. 13:11-17
1. The second beast, rising "out of" earth, is deceptively contradictory in appearance and voice. 11
2. With the first beast's authority he enforces the worship of the first beast. 12
3. He possesses:
   (a)Marvelous miraculous "signs."
   (b)Power to give "breath" to image of the first beast.
4. He exercises power to regulate the economic details of the people by a "mark" of the beast.

Satan operates in human affairs through government and its provincial rulers, both political and religious. But having a human "number" (666) indicates that the government is human. The Christian recognizes that he is dealing with human powers. Only God in Christ is the ultimate authority!

## Revelation 13:2-3a

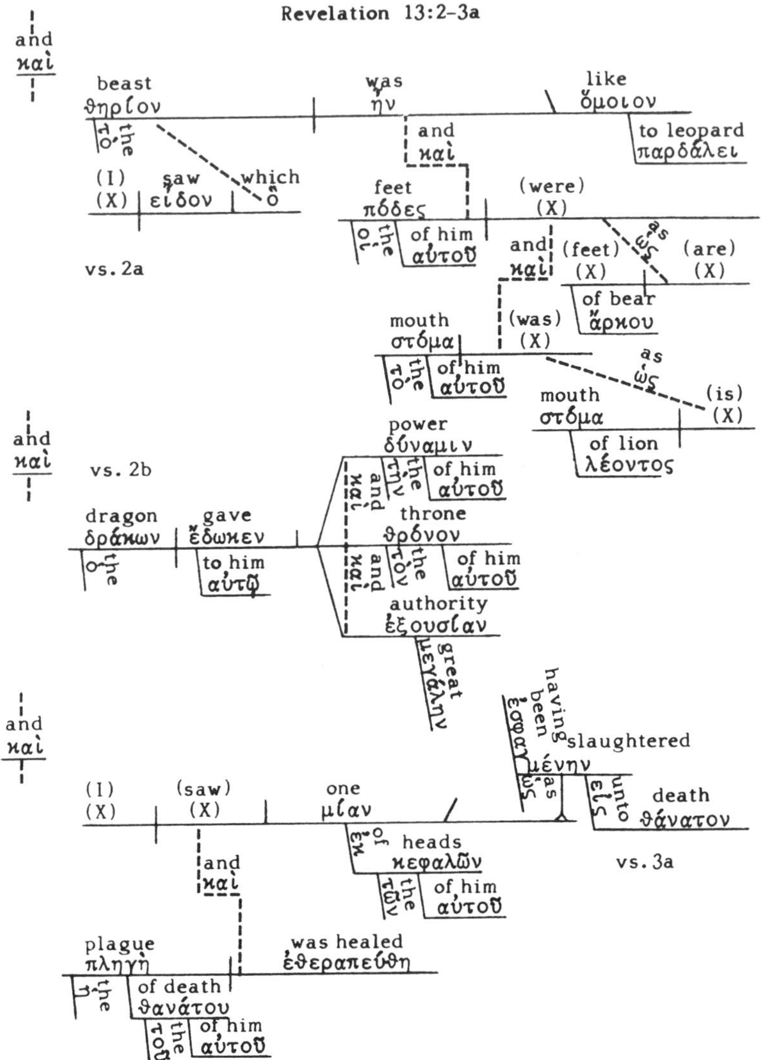

## THE DIAGRAM OF 13:2-3a

The six clauses of verse 2a form a compound-complex sentence. It contains three independent clauses and three dependent the combination of which give a graphic description of the beast. The first of the independents presents a general statement of what he is "like." "The beast was like to a leopard..." To the subject, beast, is added a dependent adjective clause identifying the "beast" as one "which I saw..." ὅμοιον "like" is predicate adjective pointing back to the subject. Words of likeness normally take instrumental case and hence παρδάλει is instrumental.

The next two independent clauses offer descriptions of particular feautures of "the beast." First his feet; then his mouth. To complete the descriptions each of these independents uses a dependent adverbial ὡς clause: "...his feet (were) as (the feet) of a bear (are)." Last comes "...his mouth (was) as lion's mouth (is)."

Verse 2b encases a simple sentence although it has a compound triple-pronged direct object. "The dragon gave to him his power and his throne and great authority." The appearance of the definite article with two of these objects, "power" and "throne," makes each object stand out as a distinct item. The addition of the adjective "great" with the third object gives to it a certain specific prominence. The personal pronoun "him" appears three times in this sentence. Its antecedent is "beast" in the preceding sentence. αὐτῷ is dative of indirect object. Dative is the case of "personal interest" and thus calls attention to the personal relationship between Satan and the "beast." Satan incorporates himself and his evil designs in the "beast." In this context the "beast" is a symbol for the Roman government.

Verse 3a constitutes a compound sentence of two clauses. The subject and verb of the first clause must be inferred from the context: "(I saw) one..." The ἐκ phrase is adjectival describing "one." But it is not genitive specifying which one. It is ablative separating "one" of the heads from the others of the seven heads which the beast had. The diagram presents the perfect participle "having been slaughtered" with its introductory "as" as objective complement.

The second of the independents reports that "...the plague of his death was healed." The noun πληγή comes from a verb meaning "to strike" or "smite." Hence the prime meaning of the noun is "a blow, stripe, wound." Here it seems to signify "blow." This is symbolic language to convey the idea that the evil embodied in one of the "heads" (one Roman emperor) reappeared in a successor.

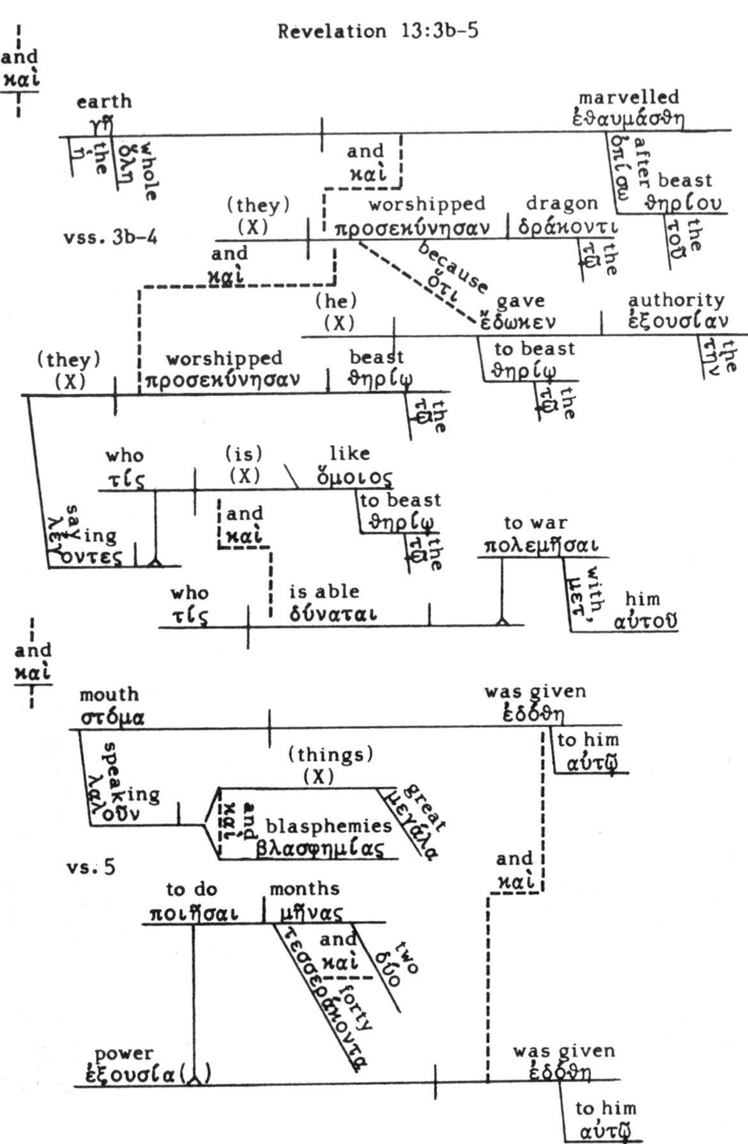
and
καὶ
earth
γῆ
the
ἡ
whole
ὅλη
marvelled
ἐθαυμάσθη
after
ὀπίσω
beast
θηρίου
the
τοῦ
and
καὶ
(they)
(X)
worshipped
προσεκύνησαν
dragon
δράκοντι
the
τῷ
vss. 3b-4
and
καὶ
because
ὅτι
(he)
(X)
gave
ἔδωκεν
authority
ἐξουσίαν
the
τὴν
to beast
θηρίῳ
the
τῷ
(they)
(X)
worshipped
προσεκύνησαν
beast
θηρίῳ
the
τῷ
who
τίς
(is)
(X)
like
ὅμοιος
to beast
θηρίῳ
the
τῷ
saying
λέγοντες
and
καὶ
to war
πολεμῆσαι
with
μετ'
him
αὐτοῦ
who
τίς
is able
δύναται
and
καὶ
mouth
στόμα
was given
ἐδόθη
to him
αὐτῷ
(things)
(X)
speaking
λαλοῦν
great
μεγάλα
and
καὶ
blasphemies
βλασφημίας
vs. 5
and
καὶ
to do
ποιῆσαι
months
μῆνας
τεσσεράκοντα
and
καὶ
two
δύο
forty
power
ἐξουσία
was given
ἐδόθη
to him
αὐτῷ

THE DIAGRAM OF 13:3b-5

The sentence of 3a-4 is compound-complex in structure. In the sentence the first of three independent clauses states, "The whole earth marvelled after the beast." ἐθαυμάσθη is aorist passive indicative of defective verb θαυμάζω "wonder at," "admire." A defective verb is one that is middle or passive in form but apparently active in meaning. Though the passive idea may still be vaguely present for all practical purposes the translation comes out as active. "The whole earth was marvelled" as though a "marvel" was being sent upon the whole earth. But the agent who did the sending of the marvel is left so far in the background that it is lost sight of entirely. So such verbs are translated to all appearances as though they were active. The end result is "the whole earth marvelled." In other words the earth did the marvelling. ὀπίσω is an "improper" preposition used with ablative. The phrase is adverbial: "after the beast." It suggests the direction toward which the marvelling was pointed. In other words, it deals with the question where.

The next two independent clauses give more specific details as to the form the marvelling took. "...they (the earth) worshipped the dragon" and "they worshipped the beast..." Stemming from the second independent is the ὅτι clause. It is an adverbial dependent explaining why "they worshipped the dragon," "...because he gave to the beast his authority..."

The third independent clause is amplified by circumstantial participle λέγοντες "saying." Two dependent noun clauses appear as direct objects of this participle "saying." They are interrogative clauses inquiring "...who (is) like to the beast" and "who is able to make war with him?"

The verb προσεκύνησαν "worshipped" which appears in the second and third independent clauses has datives as direct objects. That's the case of personal interest. By its nature worship tends to be personal. The idea in the verb and the case fit each other.

Verse five frames a compound sentence of two clauses. Both the clauses state that which was given "to him"(the beast). "A mouth was given to him..." and "...power was given to him." The verb in both clauses is aorist passive ἐδόθη "was given." The agent who gave the "mouth" and the "power" was apparently the dragon. The present participle λαλοῦν "speaking" describes the "mouth." A duet of direct objects of the participle is "great (things)" an "blasphemies."

Subject of the second clause is "power." It is expanded by the infinitive ποιῆσαι "to do" or "make." The diagram shows accusative μῆνας "months" as object of the infinitive. It could be thought of as an adverbial accusative extent of time and placed under the infinitive as though modifying it. In that case the infinitive would have an understood object ("these things").

Revelation 13:6–8

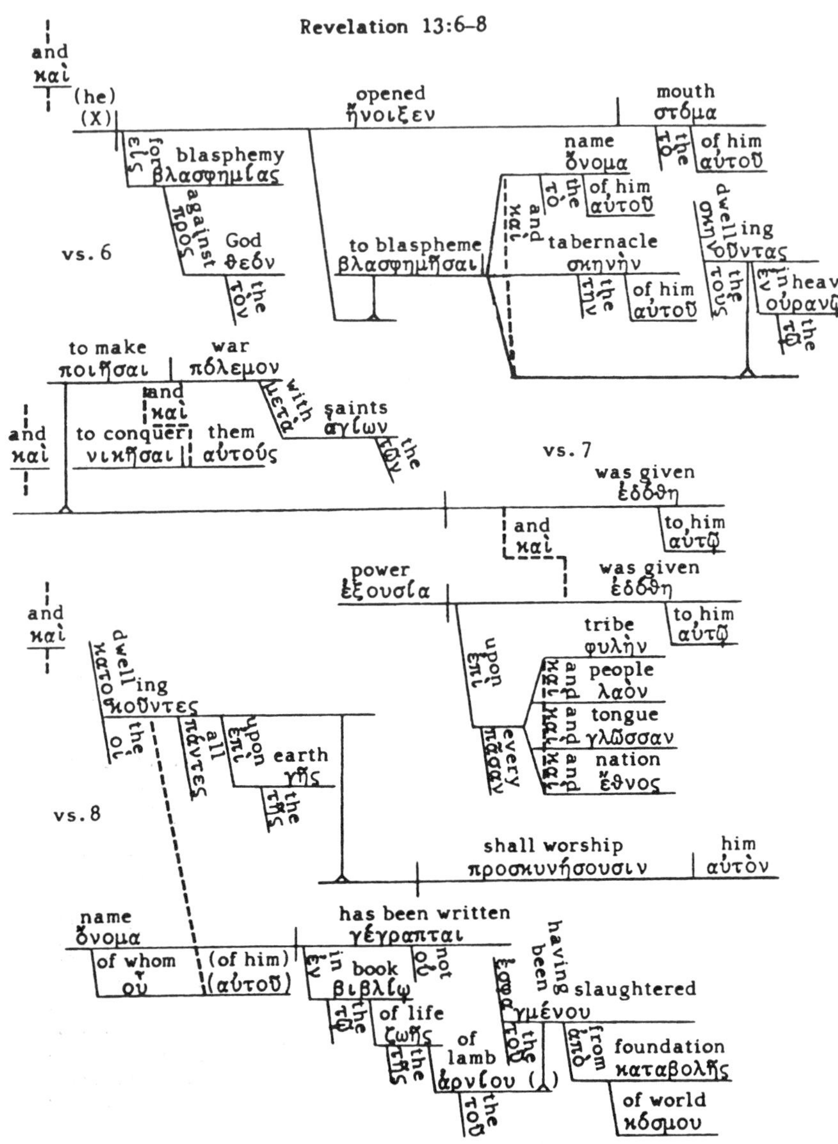

## THE DIAGRAM OF 13:6-8

Verse six admits of but one clause hence is a simple sentence. It declares; "...he opened mouth..." Antecedent of the subject "he" is the "beast" of the preceding sentences. The direct object "mouth" is identified by the article and genitive "of him." That which the beast did when he opened his mouth is set forth by two modifying expressions. First, the εἰς phrase "for blasphemies..." The εἰς in this expression definitely pronounces purpose. When πρός is used with a person it advances the idea of a "face to face" encounter. In this instance "against" God. Aorist infinitive βλασφημῆσαι "to blaspheme" also is an expression of purpose. It, with its triad of direct objects, presents in more detail the form the blasphemies took. The beast "opened his mouth to blaspheme the name (person) of him (God)..." He also purposed to blaspheme "the tabernacle of him..." That is, God's habitation where he welcomes worship. And he also purposed "to blaspheme "the ones dwelling in heaven..." That is, the people of God, angels of God and any others associated with heavenly habitation. The beast's angry animosity toward God and all he stands for is only outdone, if at all, by Satan who embodies himself in the beast.

Verse seven is compound in structure. It has two independent clauses. Both clauses join in declaring exactly what "was given" to the beast. The first clause enjoys a compound subject of two infinitives: "to make war...and to conquer..." The μετὰ phrase pictures with whom he makes war, "with the saints." The second of the clauses states that "power was given to him..." The vast extent of his "power" is seen in the prepositional phrase: "upon every tribe and people and tongue and nation." The ἐπὶ literally means "upon" though the context here allows a resultant idea of "over." His power is "over" in the sense that he presses with force "upon."

Verse eight states a negative idea in its independent clause "name has not been written..." The subject "name" is amplified by relative οὗ plus a redundant αὐτοῦ "of him." The antecedent to this singular relative is the plural "all the ones dwelling..." And this participial phrase serves as subject of the future indicative "shall worship." This dependent clause in conjunction with the independent makes of the sentence a complex arrangement.

Modifying the verb γέγραπται of the main clause is a prepositional phrase "in book," ἐν with locative tells where the name "has not been written." The "book" is specified by genitive ζωῆς. It's the book the quality of which is "life." And that "life" is further identified by a possessive genitive ἀρνίου "of lamb." In addition the "lamb" itself is further described by appositional perfect participle "having been slaughtered..." Slaughtering of the lamb was not an afterthought. It was "from" (ἀπό with ablative expresses source) the "foundation of the world." The source of the slaughtered lamb goes back into eternity past.

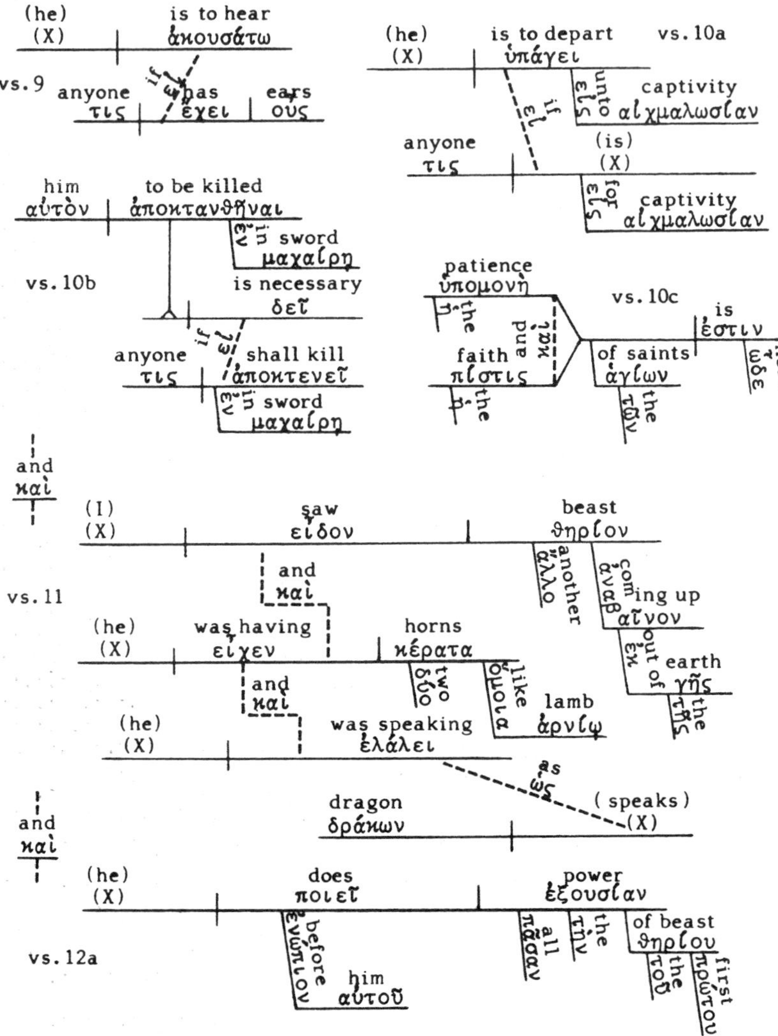
(he) (X) is to hear ἀκουσάτω
vs. 9
anyone τις
if εἰ
has ἔχει
ears οὖς
(he) (X) is to depart ὑπάγει
vs. 10a
if εἰ
unto εἰς captivity αἰχμαλωσίαν
anyone τις
(is) (X)
for εἰς captivity αἰχμαλωσίαν
him αὐτὸν
to be killed ἀποκτανθῆναι
in ἐν sword μαχαίρῃ
vs. 10b
is necessary δεῖ
if εἰ
anyone τις
shall kill ἀποκτενεῖ
in ἐν sword μαχαίρῃ
patience ὑπομονὴ
the ἡ
and καὶ
faith πίστις
the ἡ
vs. 10c
is ἐστιν
of saints ἁγίων
the τῶν
here ὧδε
and καὶ
(I) (X)
saw εἶδον
beast θηρίον
another ἄλλο
coming up ἀναβαῖνον
out of ἐκ earth γῆς
the τῆς
vs. 11
and καὶ
(he) (X)
was having εἶχεν
horns κέρατα
two δύο
like ὅμοια lamb ἀρνίῳ
and καὶ
(he) (X)
was speaking ἐλάλει
as ὡς
dragon δράκων
(speaks) (X)
and καὶ
(he) (X)
does ποιεῖ
power ἐξουσίαν
all πᾶσαν
the τὴν
of beast θηρίου
the τοῦ
first πρώτου
vs. 12a
before ἐνώπιον him αὐτοῦ

## THE DIAGRAM OF 13:9-12a

Three conditional sentences appear in verses 9-10b. All are first class conditions. That is, the "if" assumes the condition to be true. Since each of the three has but two clauses all are complex. The "if" clause prepares for and supports the conclusion. A conditional is a logical syllogism.

The first sentence says: "If anyone has ears, he is to hear." Being first class the protasis assumes that "any one" does have ears. In the light of that fact he has the responsibility to hear.

The next sentence declares: "If anyone (is) for captivity, he is to depart unto captivity." Again the "if" assumes the condition to be fact. It may or may not be but the logic of the sentence presumes that it is fact. Therefore the conclusion is inevitable. In other words, if one lives on the basis of forcing one's will on others until they become one's captive the inevitable result is that the captor will become a captive. He who forceably enslaves others will himself become a slave. That's the way God has made life.

The third conditional says the same thing but with even more compelling language. "If anyone shall kill in (the) sword..." That is, if one lives by the power of armed might..." the result is predictable. The killer will be killed! Subject of the main clause is infinitive ἀποκτανθῆναι "to be killed" with accusative of general reference αὐτὸν "him." The verb δεῖ implies logical necessity.

Verse 10c makes a positive statement on the basis of the logic of the preceding three conditional sentences. Verse 10c is a simple sentence having just the one clause, though it does have a double subject. "The patience and faith(trust)of the saints is here (in this principle)." The word translated patience is compounded out of two words, ὑπό "under" and μένω "remain." To remain under this principle of non-violence as a means of spiritual warfare takes a lot "remaining under" the load of persecution. And πίστις is more than a body of doctrine that one believes. It is an action noun suggesting "trusting" God's spiritual kingdom to be advanced or defended by spiritual instruments rather than force of the sword.

Verse 11 is compound-complex having three independent but only one dependent clause. The first clause states: "I saw a beast..." The adjective "another" indicates a difference from the earlier beast. ἀναβαινον "coming up" is present participle describing the beast as he rises into view. And the ἐκ phrase presents him as rising "out of the earth" whereas the first beast came from the sea. This second beast "was having"(linear imperfect)two horns" symbol of power though not seven, symbol of perfect power. Besides, his horns were "like a lamb." To the third main clause, "he was speaking," is attached the dependent adverb clause, "as a dragon (speaks)."

Verse 12a is a simple sentence: "he does(performs)power..." Where he performs this power is in the adverbial ἐνώπιον phrase "before him." The power of this second beast is specified by the genitive θηρίου "of the first beast."

## Revelation 13:12b-14

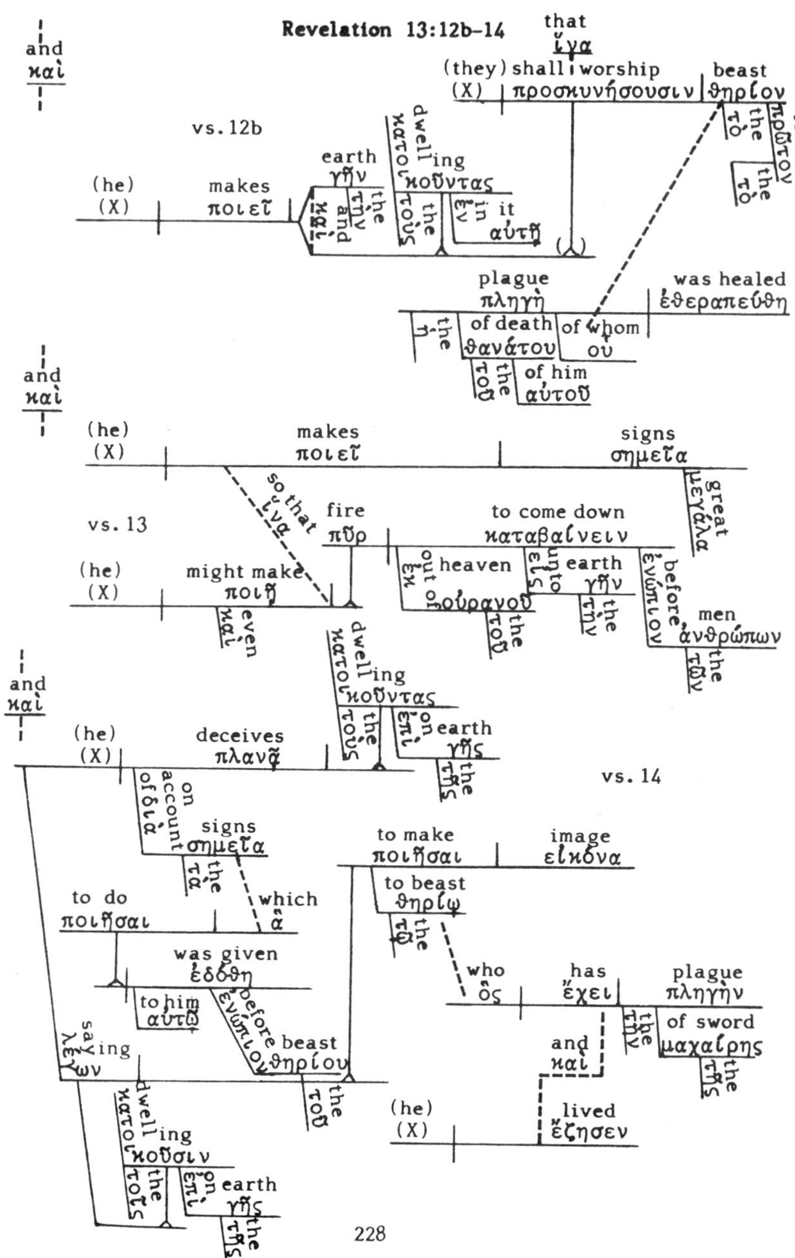

## THE DIAGRAM OF 13:12b-14

The sentence of verse 12b contains a brace of direct objects the second of which is the attributive participle κατοικοῦντας "the ones dwelling." The phrase "in it" which modifies the participle tells where they dwell. And the antecedent of the "it" is the first of the objects, "earth." If the sentence ended there and one should ignore the context a reader might suppose that "he made" in the sense of "created" the "earth" and its dwellers. But by the addition of a noun clause in apposition to the participial object the author conveys the idea that "he" made "the ones dwelling" do something they otherwise might not have done. And that is: "...that they shall worship the first beast..." The ἵνα launches the noun clause. It is a subfinal clause giving the content of that which the second beast "makes" them do. It should be noted that ἵνα usually uses the subjunctive but here appears with a future indicative. The indicative might suggest a more vivid expectation that "he" shall accomplish his intent. A further dependent clause is added to describe the object θηρίον "beast." It is adjective in function and is attached by the genitive relative pronoun οὗ "of whom." The full clause reads: "...whose stroke of his death was healed." The sentence, of course, is complex in structure.

The presence of a dependent adverbial ἵνα clause of purpose in verse 13 installs a complex element into the sentence. So, following only one independent clause the sentence is classed as complex. The main clause states: "He makes (produces) great signs..." Then the purpose clause points to the end in view: "...that he might even make..." The ascensive use of καὶ hints at the highest kind of sign. Precisely what that unusual sign might be comes out in a noun phrase, object of ποιῇ. The object phrase consists of present infinitive καταβαίνειν "to come down" with accusative of general reference πῦρ "fire." The three prepositional phrases modifying the infinitive are adverbial. They tell from whence(ἐκ), unto whence(εἰς) and where(ἐνώπιον).

That "he" succeeds with his deceptive signs is set forth in the main clause of the complex sentence of verse 14. "He deceives the ones dwelling on the earth..." The basis on which his successful deception is founded is expressed in the διὰ phrase, "on account of the signs." Then the "signs" are further described by an adjective relative clause (ἃ) "which (it) was given him to do." Infinitive ποιῆσαι is subject of the clause.

Present participle λέγων "saying" adds further circumstances which surround this deceptive work of the beast. Not only did he deceive by a show of signs but he accompanied that with persuasive deceptive "saying." Dative attributive participle κατοικοῦσιν "to the ones dwelling" indicates those to whom he speaks. The content of what he speaks is set forth by infinitive ποιῆσαι phrase "to make image of the beast." The particular "beast" to whom the image was to be made is described by two dependent adjective clauses: "...who has the stroke of the sword" and "he lived." ἔζησεν is ingressive aorist meaning "came alive."

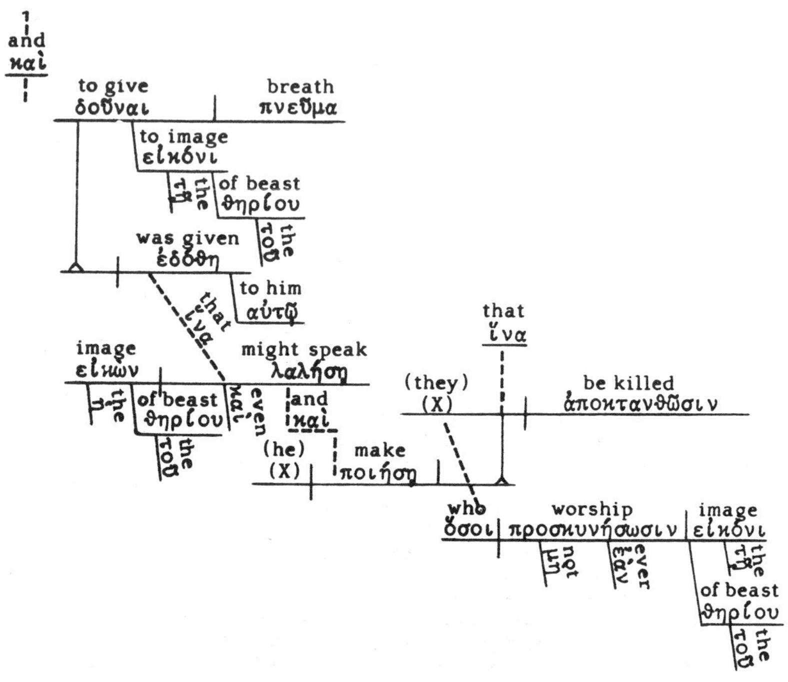
1
and
καὶ
to give
δοῦναι
breath
πνεῦμα
to image
εἰκόνι
τῇ
the
of beast
θηρίου
τοῦ
the
was given
ἐδόθη
to him
αὐτῷ
that
ἵνα
image
εἰκὼν
ἡ
the
of beast
θηρίου
τοῦ
the
might speak
λαλήσῃ
καὶ
even
and
καὶ
(he)
(X)
make
ποιήσῃ
that
ἵνα
(they)
(X)
be killed
ἀποκτανθῶσιν
who
ὅσοι
worship
προσκυνήσωσιν
μὴ
not
ἐὰν
ever
image
εἰκόνι
τῇ
the
of beast
θηρίου
τοῦ
the

## THE DIAGRAM OF 13:15

Of the five clauses making up the sentence of 13:15 four are dependents. So the sentence is complex. If all modifying elements are removed the bare independent clause says: "to give was given." δοῦναι is 2nd aorist infinitive of δίδωμι "to give." An infinitive is a verbal noun. It partakes of the nature of verb in that it has kind of action (tense) and voice and it may be used with cases as any other verb might. But it also shares in the nature of a noun. Though it is indeclinable and in a fixed form it is always in a case as are other nouns. It may be subject or object of verbs or serve in prepositional phrases as do other nouns. It's case must be determined solely by the context. In the present instance "to give" is in the nominative case, subject of the aorist passive ἐδόθη "was given," the main verb of the clause. As a verb the infinitive has a direct object, the accusative noun πνεῦμα "breath." This noun may be translated either "spirit" or "breath" according to the demands of the context. Here it is quite obviously "breath." The dative εἰκόνι "image" is indirect object. Genitive "of beast" specifies whose image to whom breath was given.

The first ἵνα inaugurates the first of the four dependent clauses. It expresses purpose, thus is adverb in function. The "breath" was given "...in order that the image...might speak..." This "speaking" of the image was apparently accomplished by ventriloquism so as to give the sense of life to the image.

And there is a second purpose clause: "...and that he make..." That which he was to "make" is expressed in a noun clause object of aorist subjunctive ποιήσῃ, "...that they be killed." This second ἵνα clause is subfinal, that is, it states the content or substance of that which "he make."

But who is the "they" who should be killed? "They" are identified and described in an adjective clause instigated by the relative ὅσοι "who." This is a quantitative relative which, when used with modal ἂν (ἐὰν), signifies "whoever-so-many." The verb for "worship" is aorist active subjunctive with negative μὴ. The clause may be translated: "...howsoever many shall not worship the image of the beast." These are "they" who shall "be killed." Refusal to worship the beast brought on capital punishment.

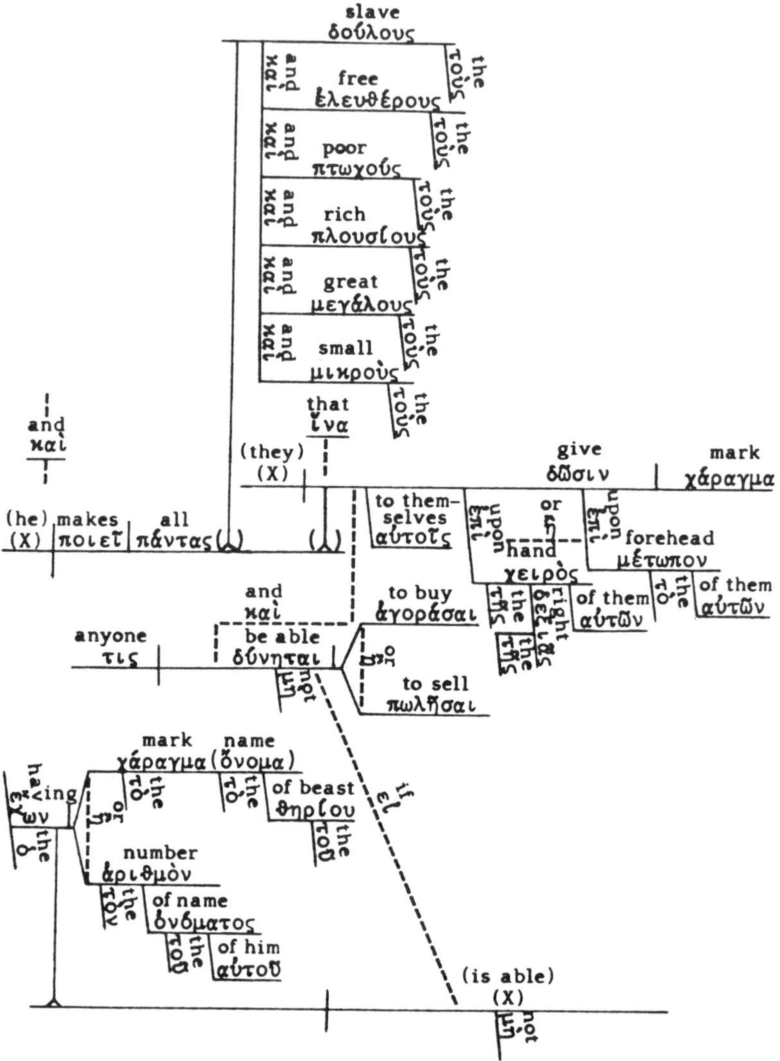
slave
δούλους
the
τοὺς
and
καὶ
free
ἐλευθέρους
the
τοὺς
and
καὶ
poor
πτωχούς
the
τοὺς
and
καὶ
rich
πλουσίους
the
τοὺς
and
καὶ
great
μεγάλους
the
τοὺς
and
καὶ
small
μικρούς
the
τοὺς
and
καὶ
(he) makes all
(X) ποιεῖ πάντας
that
ἵνα
(they)
(X)
give
δῶσιν
mark
χάραγμα
to themselves
αὐτοῖς
upon
ἐπὶ
hand
χειρὸς
the
τῆς
right
δεξιᾶς
the
τῆς
of them
αὐτῶν
or
ἢ
upon
ἐπὶ
forehead
μέτωπον
the
τὸ
of them
αὐτῶν
and
καὶ
anyone
τις
be able
δύνηται
not
μὴ
to buy
ἀγοράσαι
or
ἢ
to sell
πωλῆσαι
if
εἰ
having
ἔχων
the
ὁ
mark
χάραγμα
the
τὸ
or
ἢ
name
(ὄνομα)
the
τὸ
of beast
θηρίου
the
τοῦ
number
ἀριθμὸν
the
τὸν
of name
ὀνόματος
the
τοῦ
of him
αὐτοῦ
(is able)
(X)
not
μὴ

## THE DIAGRAM OF 13:16-17

These verses form a complex sentence of four clauses. The construction of the sentence follows the pattern of ποιεῖ in verses 12 and 15. "He makes all(πάντας)..." is essentially the independent clause. The object "all" is expanded by a series of accusatives in apposition,"..the small and the great, the rich and the poor, the free and the slaves..." The definite article appearing with each of the accusatives makes each separate class stand out with its own distinctness. Yet they are in pairs contrasting one class with its opposite. The first pair forms a chiasm, "the small and the great." The last two pairs place the more prestigious first. These are adverbial accusatives defining more sharply the "all."

Besides these appositional accusatives another apposition in the form of a ἵνα object clause follows πάντας "all." "He makes... that they give mark..." Even as the saints received God's seal so here the devotees of the beast get a "mark" identifying them as his. The two ἐπὶ phrases answer the question as to where the mark is placed: "...upon their right hand" or "upon their forehead." These would certainly be the most prominent and therefore most easily seen by the authorities or informers.

A second dependent noun clause parallel to the first ἵνα states the negative effect of not having the "mark" of the beast: "...and anyone is not able to buy or to sell..." This is an effective way to place social and economic pressure on the Christian believers. The infinitives ἀγοράσαι and πωλῆσαι are point action aorists, rather than linear ideas. They were not even able to enter the economic market, much less go on buying or selling.

The final subordinate clause is a negative first class condition. The condition is assumed as true. "...if the one having the mark is not able..." and he isn't. The attributive participle ἔχων is the subject of this dependent clause. Like infinitives, participles have a dual nature. Though not verbal nouns they are verbal adjectives. Here as a verb ἔχων takes as its direct objects both "mark" and "number." The "mark"(χάραγμα)was in fact the "name." Hence ὄνομα is placed in apposition to indicate that the "mark" was actually the "name" of the beast. And since in the ancient Greek the letters of the alphabet were used as the various numerals a person's "name" was often put into the corresponding numbers that went to make up his name. Thus ἀριθμὸν "number" is added as a second object of the participle. And "number" is explained by addition of genitive ὀνόματος "of his name." The number that went to make up his name was the "mark" of identity.

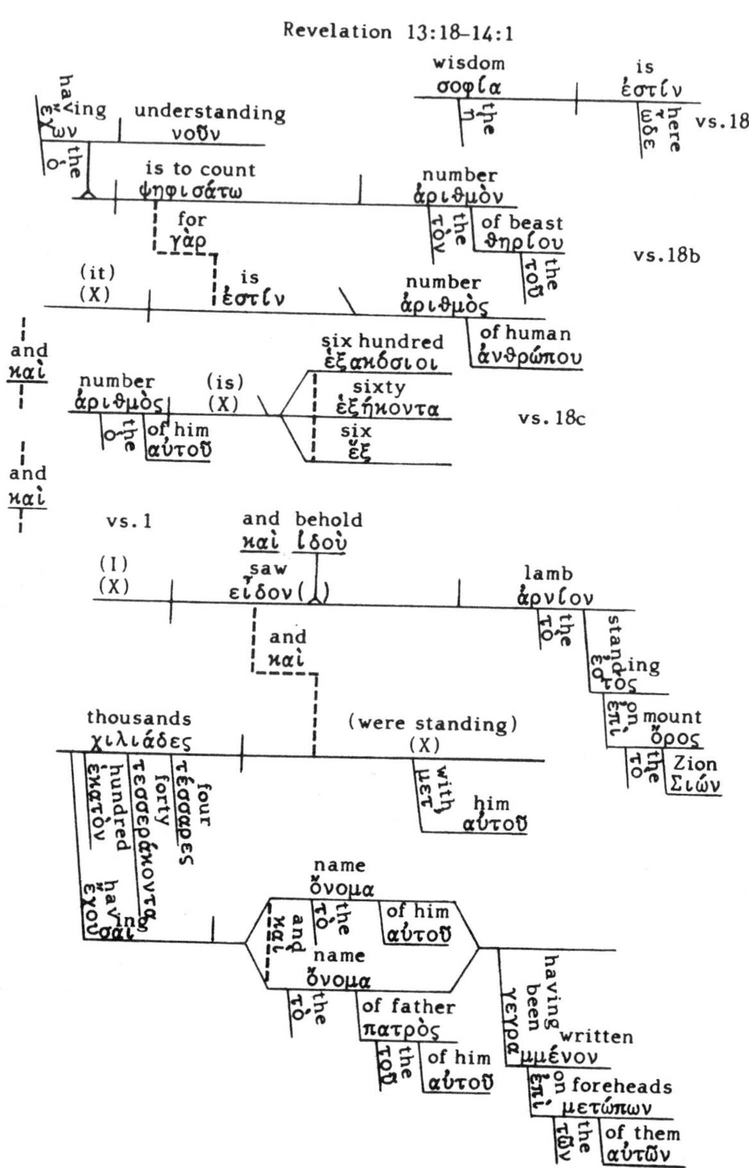
wisdom
σοφία
is
ἐστίν
the
ἡ
here
ὧδε
vs. 18a
having
ἔχων
understanding
νοῦν
the
ὁ
is to count
ψηφισάτω
number
ἀριθμὸν
the
τὸν
of beast
θηρίου
the
τοῦ
for
γὰρ
vs. 18b
(it)
(X)
is
ἐστὶν
number
ἀριθμὸς
of human
ἀνθρώπου
and
καὶ
number
ἀριθμὸς
the
ὁ
of him
αὐτοῦ
(is)
(X)
six hundred
ἑξακόσιοι
sixty
ἑξήκοντα
six
ἕξ
vs. 18c
and
καὶ
vs. 1
and
καὶ
behold
ἰδοὺ
(I)
(X)
saw
εἶδον
lamb
ἀρνίον
the
τὸ
standing
ἑστὸς
on
ἐπὶ
mount
ὄρος
the
τὸ
Zion
Σιών
and
καὶ
thousands
χιλιάδες
(were standing)
(X)
with
μετ
him
αὐτοῦ
hundred
ἑκατὸν
forty
τεσσεράκοντα
four
τέσσαρες
having
ἔχουσαι
name
ὄνομα
the
τὸ
of him
αὐτοῦ
and
καὶ
name
ὄνομα
the
τὸ
of father
πατρὸς
the
τοῦ
of him
αὐτοῦ
having been written
γεγραμμένον
on
ἐπὶ
foreheads
μετώπων
the
τῶν
of them
αὐτῶν

## THE DIAGRAM OF 13:18-14:1

Four words, one clause designate verse 18a as simple in form. It says: "Here is the wisdom." In the midst of all this symbolism "here is an occasion in which common sense(wisdom) needs to be used." Definite article with "wisdom" is to be noticed. It's "the" wisdom, well known, always desired but infrequently used!

Two clauses of equal rank elevate vs.18b into the compound category. Subject of the first clause is present articular attributive participle with its direct object: "The one having mind..." In other words, the one who has a mind should use it and apply wisdom in the matter of understanding the meaning of the "number of his name." This one having such a mind "is to count," aorist active. The object of such a count is "the number of the beast." The second clause supports the first by offering an underlying reason why one should count. "...for it is a human number." The genitive ἀνθρώπου "man" in this instance does not refer to an individual male but rather to humanity. The number involved is not supernatural, mystical, cabalistic. It's just like other numbers used by humans.

Verse 18c presents another simple sentence. "The number of him (the beast) is six hundred sixty six. The numerals involved in this number appear in the diagram as predicate nominative.

With 14:1 a turn in the developing thought occurs. Having presented the Forces of Evil (see outline) in the dragon and his two beasts the author now presents the Forces of Righteous Judgment in the person of the Christ. Verse one is a compound sentence of two clauses. The first clause states: "And I saw, and behold, the lamb..." The exclamation "and behold" seems best taken to be an appositional idea reaffirming the idea in the main verb εἶδον "I saw." That which he "saw" about the "lamb" finds expression in the perfect active participle ἑστὸς "standing." Where he was standing is made clear in the adverbial prepositional phrase sponsored by ἐπὶ "upon the Mount Zion.

The second clause adds a fact. Besides the lamb, "...thousands (were standing) with him..." The "with him" prepositional phrase tells where they "were standing." The numerals modifying the subject indicate how many "thousands." The present participle rendered "having" gives circumstances attending the "thousands." The "thousands", "having the name...the name..,(were standing) with him." ὄνομα appears twice as direct objects of the participle. Each time it appears there is a genitive to specify whose "name." It's "the name of him" (the lamb) and "the name of his father..." Then comes a circumstantial perfect participle giving an added description, "having been written..." The perfect tense registers the permanancy of the "name" which had "been written." Precisely where the names were written the ἐπὶ phrase exhibits. The name "has been written on their foreheads," The forehead symbolizes the area of intelligence in a human being.

## SOME EXPOSITORY THOUGHTS ON 13:1-18

Satan exercises his power over men through government and its bureaucracies not to mention other institutions of society. Jesus, by his death, resurrection and ascension, accomplished once and for all his eternal victory over sin and death. This is heaven's triumph over the dragon. There's nothing more Satan can do but explode in diabolical wrath. He wreaks his rage on this earth on any or all people who identify with the victorious Christ of God. For the "little while" yet remaining to him to wander up and down the earth he seeks "whom he may devour."

The little groups of Christians who were reeling under the press of government persecution needed encouragement. How explain the suffering of God's people? Why should believers persevere? Is there no end to government harrassment? Is Caesar or Christ winning spiritual allegiance? In view of present suffering of his people how interpret Christ's victory? An explanation of God's rule in the face of Rome's attitude would be encouraging. This John proceeds to give under the image of the two beasts of the dragon.

### The Dragon and the First Beast

From his island exile John looked west toward Rome. He beheld a beast "rising out of the sea." Ten horns protruding from the heads spoke of great power. Seven heads symbolized the succession of Roman emporers who exercised such vast power. The ten royal diadems on his heads were badges of authority. The "names of blasphemies" represented the practice of various emporers to insist on their own deity and to demand divine worship from their people. They demanded spiritual loyalty that belonged only to God. This beast was as swift as a leopard in its conquest of the human spirit, as irresistable as a bear in driving toward its goal, as frightening as a roaring lion in its display of its power. In the environment in which John wrote this beast was Imperial Rome. And John points out that Rome got is "power and great authority" from the dragon. That is, Rome exercised its power by evil principles. Rome was the embodiment of Satan's invitations to Jesus in his recorded temptations in the wilderness.(Matt.4:1-11)

That John refers to Rome is put beyond doubt when he writes, "One of its heads was...wounded unto death. But its deadly wound was healed." In this John mirrors the myth that Nero was to come back to life in the person of the reigning emperor, Domitian. This emperor reincarnated the vilest features of Nero. Christians may expect the same kind of treatment now as happened then. Indeed, the Christians would be the only ones who did not worship the beast. "The whole earth marvelled after the beast and worshipped the dragon because he gave his authority to the beast;...saying, 'Who is like the beast and who is able to war with him?'" Swayed by such a display of sensuous power Rome became the popular idol of the peoples of earth. Men are always overwhelmed by the rattle of the sword, the display of the senses and the excitment of the masses. Indeed, "Who is like the beast?"

## Powers of the Beast!

"And a mouth speaking great things and blasphemies was given to him..." How insecure! how inferior the beast feels! He assumes prerogatives that aren't his. Yet they "are given" to him. He's a big mouth! He boasts "great things." He flaunts blasphemies. He names himself "Saviour." He calls himself "Lord." He advertises himself as the "August One," beyond whom there is no God. Such were Rome's "blasphemies." Such are the presumptuous pretensions of all governments who take from men divine freedoms for which they were created.

But the beast's power is bridled. He could only do these blasphemies "forty two months," a limited time. In spite of claims the beast wasn't "Saviour," "Lord." Such presumptuous assertions were false in fact and doomed to defeat. But blind to his inevitable end he goes right on blaspheming "his name," (God's person), "his tabernacle," (God's spiritual house), and "they who dwell in heaven"(God's saints here and hereafter).

But we live in this world. John was an exile. He didn't live in a fantasy world. The Roman beast was even now putting God's people to death. Antipas of Sardis(2:13)was a prominent reminder. John knew that "to do battle with the saints was given to him," and incredible as it is, "to conquer them." If the Christian community was to survive faithfully it must deal with this. In view of Christ's victory at calvary and the tomb how does it happen that it "was given" to the beast "to conquer"? With no doubting hesitation John gives the answer. The beast's authority extended universally over "every tribe, people, tongue..." All "shall worship him..." But with a notable exception: "whose name has not been written in the book of the life of the lamb, the one having been slaughtered from the foundation of the world."

The beast's "conquering" of the saints is short lived. His so-called "conquering" stops at the cemetery. The name of a saint "written in the book of the life of the lamb" doesn't imply that God keeps a file system. Here too symbolism must play its rightful role in communication. When a "name"(a person) is "written"(incorporated) into the "life of the lamb" the life of the living Christ is in him. He is "in Christ" and Christ in him. "It is no longer I that live, but Christ living in me."(Gal.2:20) When the government demanded that Antipas of Sardis bow the knee to worship Caesar as God Antipas refused. Who conquered whom? The beast only conquered him in the sense that he killed God's saint. But the saint was victor! He refused to bow to Caesar. Antipas was not conquered; he was only killed! "This is the victory that gets the world conquered, our believing."(I Jn.5:4) "When Christ, our life, shall be manifested, then shall you also with him be manifested in glory."(Col.3:4)

Furthermore, this victory of Christ's life "in" his people is not an afterthought. It's God's grand forethought. It has been planned "from the foundation of the world." In the terms on which this world measures life the beast "is given" to conquer. But in terms of moral realities the victory belongs to the Christian.

## The Wisdom and Faith of the Saints

The faith of the saints leads to a wisdom far and beyond the wisdom of the world. Caesar says: Might makes right and the sword settles truth! But Christian faith relegates that to the world of illusion. The hard fact is that he who takes the sword to triumph shall by that same sword be conquered. Facts of history verify this. The law of logic not to say justice insists that he who kills by force shall by force be killed. To enslave men means that the slave-maker shall become enslaved. His own evil becomes his master. Armies of spear and sword, of shot and shell can "keep the peace" but they can't advance the cause of Christ. His is a warfare of the spirit, of truth, of right. It is not waged by police force. Armies of tanks and pistol packing police are necessary in this kind of a world to maintain "law and order." But do not be deceived into thinking that the kingdom of God can be defended or advanced by such methods. He who knows this spiritual fact is responsible to act accordingly. If we have ears we are responsible to hear. Captivity produces captivity; sword produces sword. But Christ's kingdom is advanced by the "sword of the spirit," the word of God. The "patience and faith" sights below the surface. Faith sees where sight is blind! Faith and patience penetrate truth even in areas of darkness where human wisdom fails. Anything that is merely human, faith sees.(vs.18) Beyond that God reveals. But he reveals it to faith.

## Rise of the Second Beast!

Once again John's vision was drawn toward the west. This time there loomed before him "coming up from the earth, another beast." Though they were but two in number his horns testified to his great power. But there was something different about these horns. They were "like a lamb." Power was present but concealed by a false front. The appearance of a gentle lamb was a veneer to cover the speech "as a dragon." Though buried by the fleece of a lamb he had "the authority of the first beast" for his voice was the roar of the dragon. His task would be accomplished by deceit and hypocrisy. Thus was the work of the emporer cult symbolized. To the priests of the Roman cult, the provincial authorities, was it given to enforce the worship of "divine" Caesar. "He makes the earth and its inhabitants that they shall worship the first beast whose deadly wound was healed." By whatever forms human society expresses itself the power of religion generates life. Even pagan religions stir imagination, develop ideas to feed the mind, and enlist the emotions to inflame action. Thus it is that this second beast came to the people with the deceptive show of "life." He did "great signs." He even made "fire to come down out of heaven." He gave "breath"(spirit of life)to the image of the beast. He made the "image of the beast speak" as though he had "life." By such magic means he duped the people to the extent that if they didn't worship "the image of the beast they should be killed." It was the task of the provincial authorities to force the cult of Rome on the populace. Capital punishment was the alternative.

Less overt but even more dangerous way of imposing the will of the state upon the adherents of the churches was social-economic pressure. Control thought and control work is more subtle than open, declared capital punishment. A "mark on the forehead" and a "mark on the right hand" would help "persuade" to devotion to the state. Manipulation of thought and labor opportunities is an instrument of coercion. And the second beast used this device. Not a single class of the populace escaped government manipulation. He made all, slave and free, poor and rich, noble and commoner "that they shall give to themselves a mark upon their right hand or upon their forehead" that he "not be able to buy or sell except the one having the mark of the beast or his number." The job market was controlled by the government. He who would not worship Caesar could not get a job or lost the one he had. The small business man found himself isolated from wholesale warehouses and boycotted by his customers. Whether it be polytheistic Rome in the first century or atheistic Russia in the 20th the method is the same. Social and economic opportunities are denied the servant of the Christ. Death by overt capital punishment or death by slow strangulation of the spirit--it embodies the evil will of the dragon by bestial government agencies. When religion, Christian or otherwise, becomes an arm of the state it stifles freedom of the spirit and the redemption of the soul. The issue was (and is) clear cut. Is it to be Caesar or Christ? God or government? Redemption or rebellion?

Common sense wisdom!

It doesn't take profound intellect to one who believes God is Creator to understand that rebellious humanity is doomed to ultimate defeat. Or that anything short of divine perfection is human imperfection. Satan has duped man into rebellion against God. He has engaged human institutions to beguile mankind. He appeals to patriotic fervor and peer pressure to embody and disguise his evil designs. "Here is wisdom. The one having a mind is to count the number of the beast." And it really isn't all that hard to count. For the number is the number that human beings use. The number is 666. The number 7 symbolizes perfection, completion, entireity! The number 6 is one short of 7, just short of perfection. It represents humanity in its sinful imperfection. The tripling of 6 into 666 merely marks the enormity of man's sinful imperfection. By force Rome unified a chaotic, divided, turbulent society. But the Roman pax still fell short of God's plan for a redeemed humanity. Roman law, Roman roads, Roman arms, Roman civilization kept the peace. But at the price of the freedom and redemption of the souls of men. Socialization is not salvation!

Whether the mystic 666 by gematria refers to Nero reincarnated in Domitian or not it still remains a symbol for human imperfection; a falling short of the divine plan of redemption. It is better to have the divine name than the human mark of the beast! "Here is wisdom." Here is common sense! "He that has ears to hear is to hear." If we have minds we are under obligation to use them.

## A TRANSLATION
### Revelation 14:1-20

And I saw, and behold, the lamb standing upon the Mount Zion, and with him 144,000 having his name and the name of his father written on their foreheads. And I heard out of the heaven as a sound of many waters and as a sound of loud thunder. And the sound which I heard (was) as harpists harping on their harps. And they sing a new song before the throne and before the four living creatures and the elders; and no one was able to learn the song except the 144,000, the ones having been purchased from the earth. These are those who were not defiled with women, for they are virgins. These are the ones following the lamb wherever he goes. These, first fruits to God and to the lamb, were purchased from men, and in their mouth a lie was not found; they are blameless!

And I saw another angel flying in midheaven, having eternal gospel to herald on the ones sitting on the earth and upon every nation and tribe and tongue and people, saying in a loud voice, "Fear God and give glory to him, because the hour of his judging came, and worship the one who made the heaven and the earth and the sea and springs of waters."

And another angel, a second, followed saying, "It fell! It fell! Babylon the Great, which made all the nations to drink of the wine of the wrath of her fornication."

And another angel, a third, followed them saying in a loud voice, "If anyone worships the beast and his image and receives a mark upon his forehead or upon his hand he also shall drink of the wine of God's wrath, unmixed in the cup of his wrath; and he shall be tormented in fire and brimstone before holy angels and before the lamb. And the smoke of their torment goes up unto ages of ages. And the ones worshipping the beast and his image don't have respite day and night, and if anyone receives the mark of his name. Here is the patience of the saints, ones keeping the commandments of God and faith in Jesus."

And I heard a voice from heaven saying, "Write! the dead are blessed, the ones from now dying in the Lord." Yea! the spirit says that they shall rest from their labors; for their works follow with them.

And I saw, and behold, a white cloud and upon the cloud one sitting like son of man having upon his head a golden crown and in his hand a sharp sickle. And another angel came out of the sanctuary crying in a loud voice to the one sitting on the cloud, "Send your sickle and reap because the hour came to reap for the harvest of the earth is ripened." And the one sitting upon the cloud threw his sickle upon the earth and the earth was harvested. And another angel came out of the sanctuary in heaven having also himself a sharp sickle. And another angel came out of the altar, the one having power over the fire and he called in a loud voice to the one having the sharp sickle, saying, "Send your sickle, your sharp one, and gather the clusters of the vine of the earth because the grapes of it got fully ripe." And the angel threw his sickle into the earth and gathered the vine of the earth and threw (it) into the great winepress of the wrath of God. And the winepress was trodden outside the city and blood came out of the winepress unto the bridles of the horses from a thousand six hundred stadia.

## AN OUTLINE OF REVELATION 14:1-20

Security of the Saints Amid Judgment on the Sinners!

If God be sovereign and if God be holy, it follows that judgment is inevitable on sin and sinners in this world of sin. If that be true, where do the righteous stand? Does the Christian have any assurance of security? Or will the wrath of God's judgment spill over and engulf the saints?

I. THE ETERNAL GOOD NEWS! 14:1-7, 12-13.
  1. The Lamb and his redeemed on Mount Zion. 1-5
    (a)The "name" written on their foreheads. The character of God written in the character of the redeemed.
    (b)The "new song" sung only by the redeemed. 2-3
    (c)The virgins, "unblemished" in character! 4-6
  2. The good news is:
    (a)Eternal.
    (b)Universal.
    (c)It prompts to worship of "the one who created..."
  3. Death for the saint becomes a "blessed" experience. 12-13
    (a)The "patience of the saints" is demonstrated by:
      (1)"Keeping the commands of God."
      (2)Keeping "the trust in Jesus."
    (b)Blessedness of death demonstrated by:
      (1)"Rest from their labors."
      (2)Their works follow with them."

II. THE CERTAINTY OF JUDGMENT. 14:8-11, 14-20
  1. The fall of the wicked city necessarily inevitable. 8.
  2. The citizens of the wicked city fall under judgment of the undiluted wrath of God. 9-11
  3. The sickle of judgment "thrown" into the world. 14-20
    (a)Son of man is Lord of the harvest. 14
      (1)He wears a "crown" and holds the "sickle." 14
      (2)The harvest comes when "the hour of harvesting" is ready. 15-16
    (b)Fulness of judgment on the "vintage" of the earth. 17-20

God provides adequate security for his saints in the midst of his judgmental wrath on the evil earth. The "name" of the Lamb and of the Father is the believer's promise of safe and fruitful living. And the assurance of blessedness in death. Their works follow "with" them.

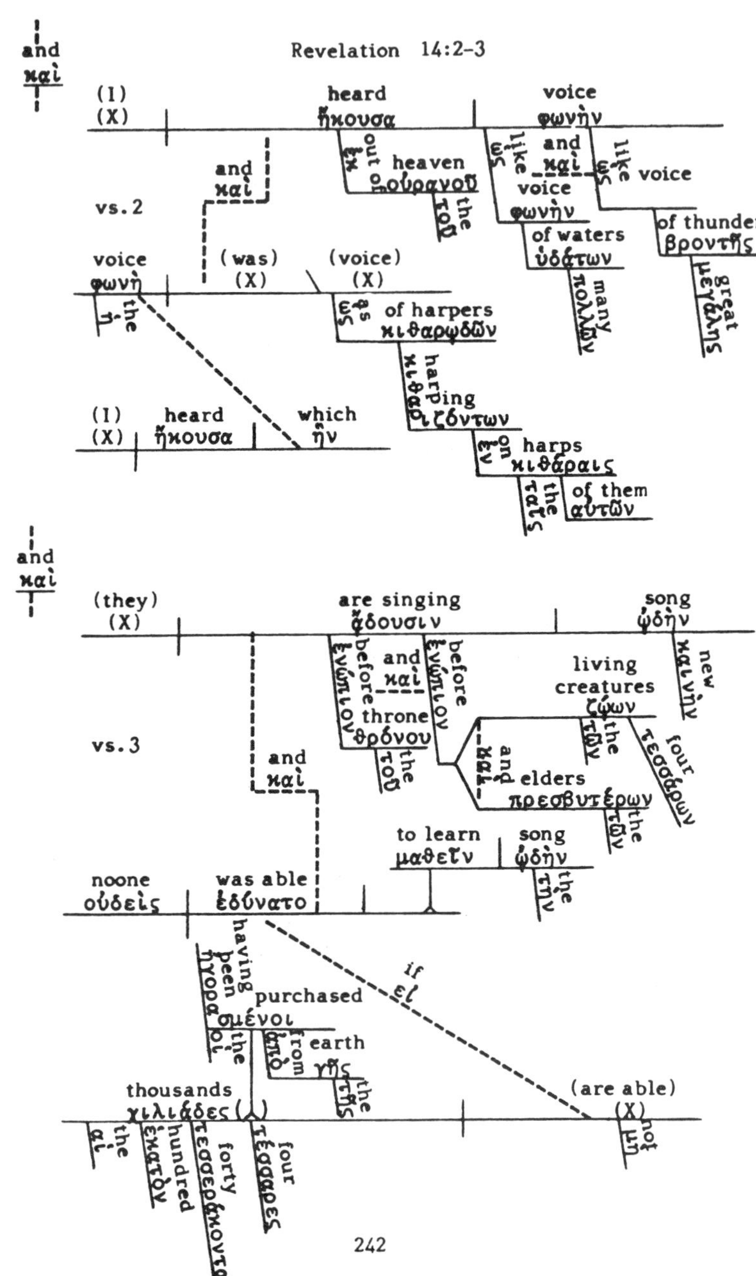
and
καὶ
(I)
(X)
heard
ἤκουσα
voice
φωνὴν
out of
ἐκ
heaven
οὐρανοῦ
the
τοῦ
like
ὡς
voice
φωνὴν
and
καὶ
like
ὡς
voice
of waters
ὑδάτων
many
πολλῶν
of thunder
βροντῆς
great
μεγάλης
vs. 2
and
καὶ
voice
φωνὴ
the
ἡ
(was)
(X)
(voice)
(X)
as
ὡς
of harpers
κιθαρῳδῶν
harping
κιθαριζόντων
on
ἐν
harps
κιθάραις
the
ταῖς
of them
αὐτῶν
(I)
(X)
heard
ἤκουσα
which
ἣν
and
καὶ
(they)
(X)
are singing
ᾄδουσιν
song
ᾠδὴν
new
καινὴν
before
ἐνώπιον
and
καὶ
before
ἐνώπιον
throne
θρόνου
the
τοῦ
before
ἐνώπιον
living creatures
ζῴων
the
τῶν
four
τεσσάρων
and
καὶ
elders
πρεσβυτέρων
the
τῶν
vs. 3
and
καὶ
to learn
μαθεῖν
song
ᾠδὴν
the
τὴν
noone
οὐδεὶς
was able
ἐδύνατο
having been purchased
ἠγορασμένοι
the
οἱ
from
ἀπὸ
earth
γῆς
the
τῆς
if
εἰ
thousands
χιλιάδες
the
αἱ
hundred
ἑκατὸν
forty
τεσσεράκοντα
four
τέσσαρες
(are able)
(X)
not
μὴ

## THE DIAGRAM OF 14:2-3

**Two independent clauses plus one dependent make verse two a compound-complex sentence.** The first clause proffers: "I heard a voice..." ἀκούω "hear" takes either genitive or accusative as object. When accusative is used emphasis falls on the comprehension of that which is heard. In other words, "I heard with understanding." John heard more "noise" than voice. He heard a noise "like waters" and "like thunder." The ὡς phrases might conceivably be diagrammed as two separate adverb dependent clauses. But in our diagram we have treated the ὡς as preposition and made them into adjective phrases modifying the object "voice." The ἐκ phrase is adverbial modifying the verb. It answers the question where.

In the second independent both verb and predicate nominative must be supplied from the context. "The voice (was noise)..." Describing this predicate nominative is another ὡς phrase this time used with genitive: "...as of harpers harping on their harps..." κιθαριζόντων is present participle the tense of which emphasizes their continuous playing. It is circumstantial participle, an added description of "harpers." Preposition ἐν indicates a "point within which" a thing rests or is conceived to take place. As used here the "harping" is conceived as taking place "in" the harps. English usage suggests "on" or "with" as acceptable translations.

Subject of this second main clause is φωνὴ "noise." Protruding from this subject is the adjective clause identifying the "noise" as the one "which I heard." Again the accusative case ἣν appears after the verb of hearing. He not only heard the noise but also understood its significance.

Another three-clause sentence arises in verse three, this one also complex in structure. The first clause announces that "they sing a song..." Subject "they" obviously refers to the "harpers" of the preceeding sentence. Present tense of the verb "are singing" declares that the singing is continuous (linear action). They "go on singing." The song is described by adjective καινὴν "new." This word for "new" denotes new in quality. It's a new kind of song, not merely new in time. The two ἐνώπιον phrases are adverbial telling where the singing is done: "...before the throne and before the four living creatures and the elders..."

The second independent idea declares that "no one was able to learn the song..." The linear action of imperfect ἐδύνατο indicates that the inability was a constant, continuous matter. The aorist of the infinitive μαθεῖν "to learn" calls attention to the fact rather than the process of learning.

The "if" announces a negative first class condition. "If the 144,000...are not able (and they aren't) then noone was able..." In apposition to the subject "thousands" is attributive perfect participle ἠγορασμένοι "having been purchased." It gives the reason why only these could learn the new song. The tense emphasizes the permanancy of their purchase "from the earth."

Revelation 14:4-5

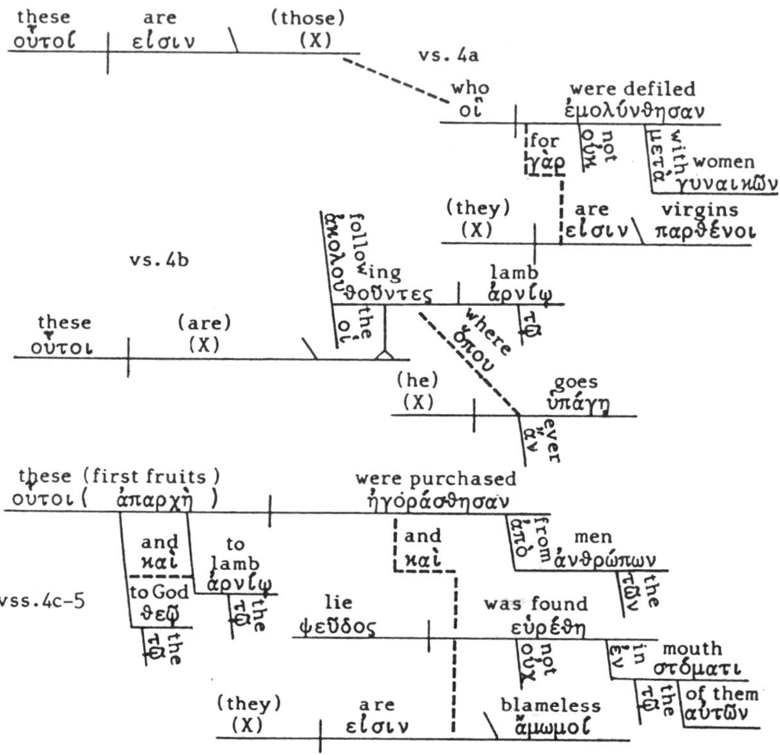

## THE DIAGRAM OF 14:4-5

The two dependent clauses which fill out the meaning of the sentence of verse 4a are adjectival. They are introduced by relative pronoun οἳ "who." They describe an understood predicate nominative "those" of the independent clause. The main clause affirms: "These are (those)..." The first dependent defines "those" as being ones, "who were not defiled..." The point at which they "weren't defiled" is depicted in an adverbial phrase "with women." The fact "women" are specifically designated is an incidental allusion to the fact this was written in a man's world. It could have been equally written: "who were not defiled with men..." The second dependent clause confirms this for it specifically says: "...they are virgins." The term "virgin" is as applicable to men as to women. This obviously refers to adultery or fornication whether commited by men or women. This second dependent is equal in rank to the οἳ clause and retains the force of the relative. The sentence is to be classed as complex.

Verse 4b has only two clauses, one independent and the other dependent. Thus it is complex in form. The sentence contributes a futher characterization of "these" referred to in the preceding sentence. "These are the ones following the lamb..." ἀκολουθοῦντες is a present active attributive participle "the ones following." The tense calls attention to the fact that they continually following. Whom they are following is set forward by object ἀρνίῳ "lamb." The dative as direct object is usual after the verb ἀκολουθέω. Presence of the definite article with "lamb" serves to point out both the lamb that has already been mentioned as well as the lamb that is "well known" to the readers of Revelation. The appearance of relative conjunction ὅπου signals an indefinite local clause with modal ἂν: "wherever he is going."

The sentence of verses 4c-5 is compound. It entertains three independent clauses. The first states: "These...were purchased..." ἀπαρχὴ "first fruits" is a singular collective noun in apposition to the subject. Conceivably it might be placed after the verb in the position of predicate nominative and referring back to the subject. However, the diagram has opted for apposition. In either instance it is closely identified with "these." Another choice to be made is where to place the two datives "to the God" and "to the lamb." Are they adverbial modifying the verb "were purchased" or adjectival modifying "first fruits" as the diagram has them? The ἀπὸ phrase is adverbial. It tells from where the purchase was made.

The second clause proposes that "lie was not found in their mouth..." The ἐν phrase is used as an adverb explaining where a lie was not found." That is, "in their mouth."

The final of the three clauses rises in thought to "...they are blameless." The fact that "they are blameless" and that a "lie was not found in their mouth" does not mean that these virtues formed the basis for their redeemed position. The first clause has already set forth that they "were purchased..." Thus these virtues are the authentic stamp of their purchase, not the cause for it.

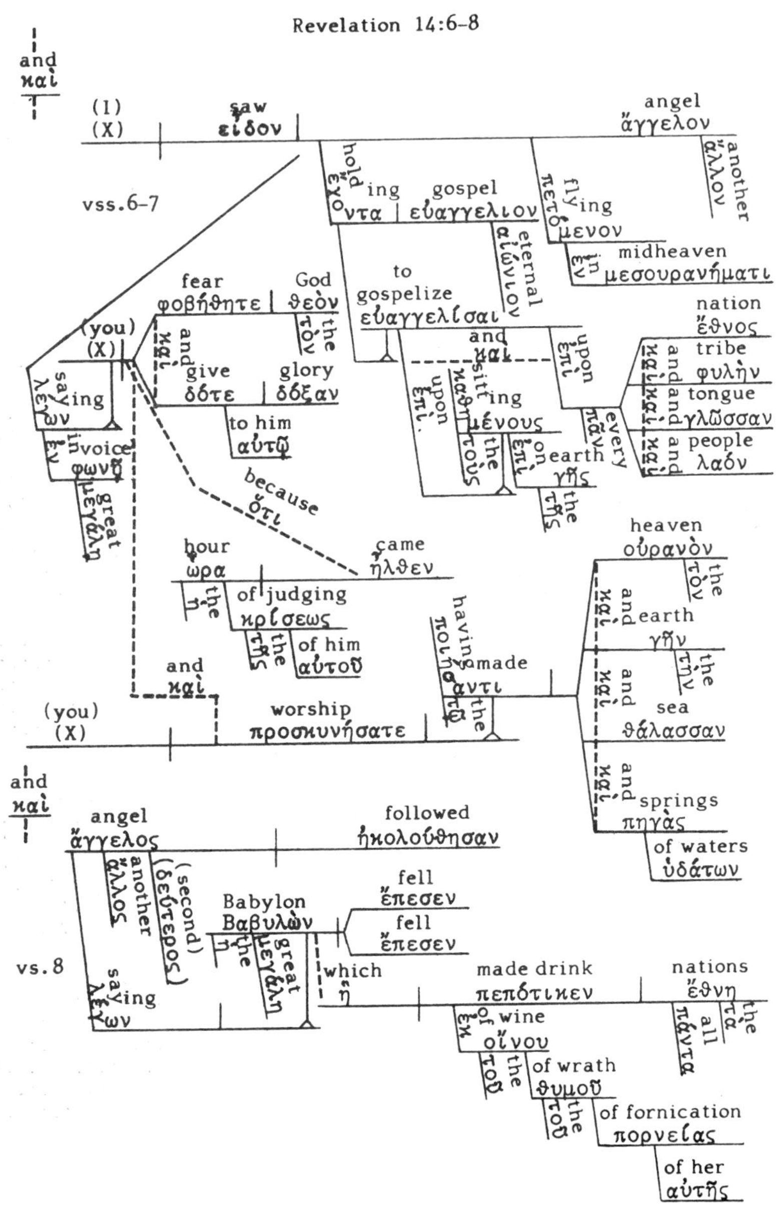
and
καὶ
(I)
(X)
saw
εἶδον
angel
ἄγγελον
another
ἄλλον
hold
ἔχο
ing
ντα
gospel
εὐαγγέλιον
eternal
αἰώνιον
fly
πετό
ing
μενον
in
ἐν
midheaven
μεσουρανήματι
vss.6-7
to
gospelize
εὐαγγελίσαι
and
καὶ
upon
ἐπὶ
sitt
καθη
ing
μένους
the
τοὺς
upon
ἐπὶ
on
ἐπὶ
earth
γῆς
the
τῆς
every
πᾶν
nation
ἔθνος
and
καὶ
tribe
φυλὴν
and
καὶ
tongue
γλῶσσαν
and
καὶ
people
λαόν
fear
φοβήθητε
God
θεὸν
the
τὸν
and
καὶ
give
δότε
glory
δόξαν
to him
αὐτῷ
(you)
(X)
say
λέγ
ing
ων
in
ἐν
voice
φωνῇ
great
μεγάλῃ
because
ὅτι
hour
ὥρα
the
ἡ
came
ἦλθεν
of judging
κρίσεως
the
τῆς
of him
αὐτοῦ
and
καὶ
(you)
(X)
worship
προσκυνήσατε
having
ποιή
made
σαντι
the
τῷ
heaven
οὐρανὸν
the
τὸν
and
καὶ
earth
γῆν
the
τὴν
and
καὶ
sea
θάλασσαν
and
καὶ
springs
πηγὰς
of waters
ὑδάτων
and
καὶ
angel
ἄγγελος
another
ἄλλος
(second)
(δεύτερος)
followed
ἠκολούθησαν
vs.8
say
λέγ
ing
ων
Babylon
Βαβυλὼν
the
ἡ
great
μεγάλη
fell
ἔπεσεν
fell
ἔπεσεν
which
ἣ
made drink
πεπότικεν
nations
ἔθνη
the
τὰ
all
πάντα
of
ἐκ
wine
οἴνου
the
τοῦ
of wrath
θυμοῦ
the
τοῦ
of fornication
πορνείας
of her
αὐτῆς

## THE DIAGRAM OF 14:6-8

Verses 6-7 constitute a sentence of 59 words in four clauses. Only one is independent; the sentence is complex. The main clause alleges, "I saw angel..." Besides adjective "another" two circumstantial participial phrases describe the object "angel." In the order they appear in the text (reversed on the diagram) the first is descriptive present πετόμενον "flying." "..in midheaven.." is adverial telling where he's flying. The next participle pictures the angel as "having the eternal gospel." The purpose for having it is expressed by aorist infinitive εὐαγγελίσαι "to gospelize." The reason the angel "has" the good news is to announce it. The two ἐπὶ phrases modifying the infinitive are adverbial revealing how widespread the good news is to be announced; "upon the ones dwelling on the earth" and "upon every nation, tribe etc."

The third circumstantial participle λέγων "saying" is nominative whereas the earlier two are accusative. Possibly John thinks of a beginning a new sentence. But rather than stating a fresh subject he follows the participial pattern already cruising through his mind. But regular or irregular it is nominative. It has for its object a dependent noun clause with a compound predicate. "You fear God and give glory to him..." The verbs "fear" and "give" are point action aorist imperatives. Aorist doesn't deny that one should go on continuously fearing God etc. it simply doesn't emphasize it. It rather insists that one do these things. The ὅτι adverb clause presents a strong reason: "...because the hour of his judging came."

A second noun clause, object of participle "saying" urges upon earth's inhabitants to "...worship the one having made the heaven and the earth etc..." Again the verb "worship" is aorist imperative insisting on the fact of worship though not at all denying the habit. Aorist participle ποιήσαντι is attributive "the one having made." As a verb it takes an object; here it has four.

Verse 8 has three clauses, two dependents, one independent. The main clause declares: "another angel, a second, followed..." Circumstantial participle λέγων modifies "angel," and introduces the dependent clauses. First is a noun clause, object of the participle. "The great Babylon fell, fell!" English versions often translate aorist indicative ἔπεσεν "fell" as if a past participle, "fallen." But this is indicative. It is a prophetic use indicating the certainty that the doom of the city will be consummated. A prophet sees the future as having happened.

A final dependent clause is an adjectival relative describing "Babylon," "...which has caused all the nations to drink..." Perfect πεπότικεν underscores the continued effects of Babylon's corrupting influence. The striking phrase of three genitives vividly depicts the contents of the drink that corrupted the nations. "...of the wine of the wrath of her fornication." The "wine" was really "the wrath." And the wrath was the issue of her "fornication." It's a chain of figures of speech using genitive.

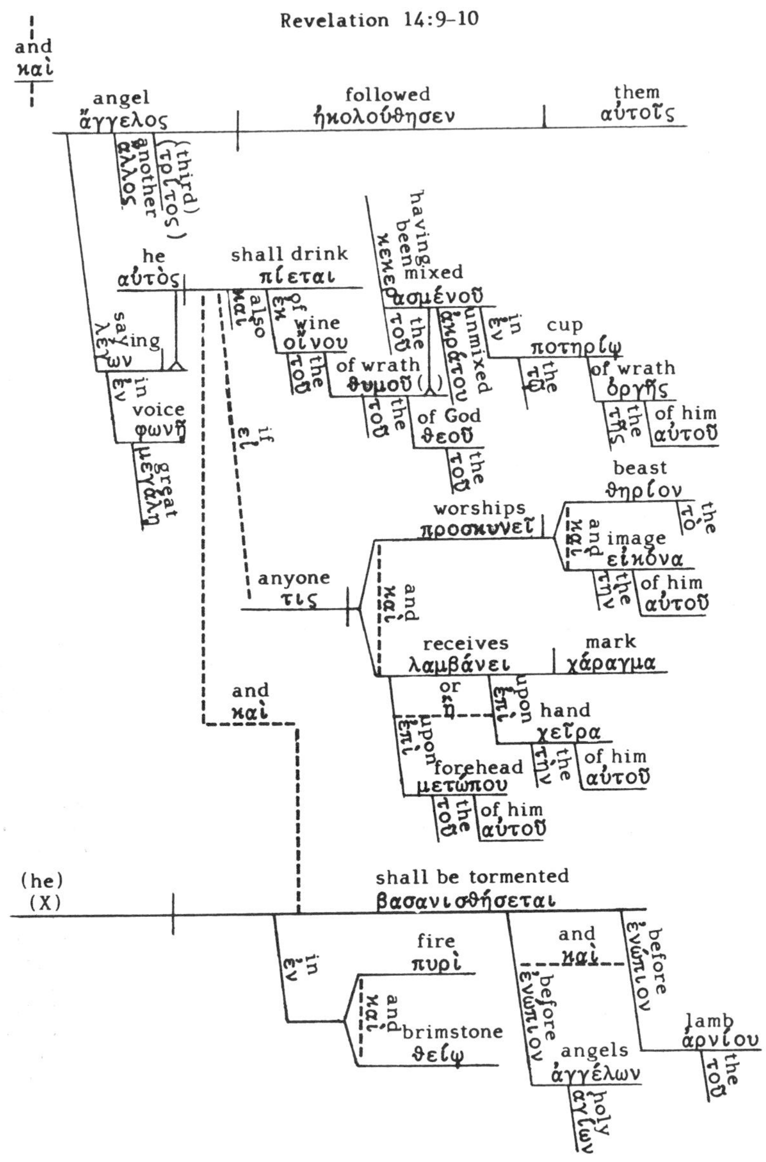
and
καὶ
angel
ἄγγελος
followed
ἠκολούθησεν
them
αὐτοῖς
another
ἄλλος
(third)
(τρίτος)
saying
λέγων
in
ἐν
voice
φωνῇ
great
μεγάλῃ
he
αὐτὸς
shall drink
πίεται
also
καὶ
of
ἐκ
wine
οἴνου
the
τοῦ
having been mixed
κεκερασμένου
the
τοῦ
unmixed
ἀκράτου
of wrath
θυμοῦ
the
τοῦ
of God
θεοῦ
the
τοῦ
in
ἐν
cup
ποτηρίῳ
the
τῷ
of wrath
ὀργῆς
the
τῆς
of him
αὐτοῦ
if
εἰ
anyone
τις
worships
προσκυνεῖ
beast
θηρίον
the
τὸ
and
καὶ
image
εἰκόνα
the
τὴν
of him
αὐτοῦ
and
καὶ
receives
λαμβάνει
mark
χάραγμα
or
ἢ
upon
ἐπὶ
hand
χεῖρα
the
τὴν
of him
αὐτοῦ
upon
ἐπὶ
forehead
μετώπου
the
τοῦ
of him
αὐτοῦ
and
καὶ
(he)
(X)
shall be tormented
βασανισθήσεται
in
ἐν
fire
πυρὶ
and
καὶ
brimstone
θείῳ
and
καὶ
before
ἐνώπιον
angels
ἀγγέλων
holy
ἁγίων
before
ἐνώπιον
lamb
ἀρνίου
the
τοῦ

## THE DIAGRAM OF 14:9-10

Only one sentence adorns page 248. Having but one independent and three dependent clauses it is complex in form. Sometimes an independent clause is referred to as the "main" clause. And that is true in the sense that it carries the basic idea (or ideas in a compound). However, often many of the significant facts that give color and import to the "main" clause appear in subordinate elements. That is true of this sentence.

The "main" clause states: "Another, a third, angel followed them..." The reason he followed was to speak a word of warning to the would-be Caesar-worshippers, those tempted to forsake Christ and bow to "the beast and his image."

The content of that which he spoke appears in the three subordinate ideas. The initial dependent is first class conditional, εἰ with indicatives:"...if anyone worships...and receives..." The conditions assume that some will. On the basis of that assumption two conclusions follow. They are set forth in two noun clauses both of which are direct objects of circumstantial participle λέγων "saying." "He shall drink..." and "he shall be tormented..." Exactly what he shall drink is depicted in the ablative phrase with ἐκ "out of." The source from which he shall drink is "wine." But the wine is characterized by the genitive θυμοῦ "of wrath." Another genitive identifies the wrath as being "of God," that is, divine wrath. This picture is made even more vivid by attributive perfect participle κεκερασμένου "having been mixed unmixed..." This kind of figure of speech, oxymoron, uses opposites to create an attention-grabbing idea. The adjective ἀκράτου "unmixed" derives from a verb meaning to "mix." The alpha privative on the adjective form transforms the meaning into <u>un</u>mixed. It was often used of wine unmixed with water. Here it presents a vivid picture of the fierce wrath of God that he who compromises his faith will have to swallow. The addition of an ἐν phrase intensifies the picture. The "unmixed mixture" was blended "in the cup of his anger."

We note that in this very intense portait of punishment coming the author uses both θυμός and ὀργή. The first is explosive, impetuous, sharp, vehement fury. The second represents a more settled principled anger. Such anger operates on the basis of regular moral and ethical criteria.

Another object of participle "saying" is the noun clause which promises: "...he shall be tormented..." Two adverb phrases modify the verb translated "tormented." The ἐν phrase tells how he will be tormented, "in fire and brimstone." the ἐνώπιον pair tell where he shall be tormented, "before holy angels and before the lamb." Is there any pain more punishing than the public shame and the ego-shattering humilation of evil in the presence of purity? It "burns" a wicked man up to have to endure the presence of pure people.

Revelation 14:11-13a

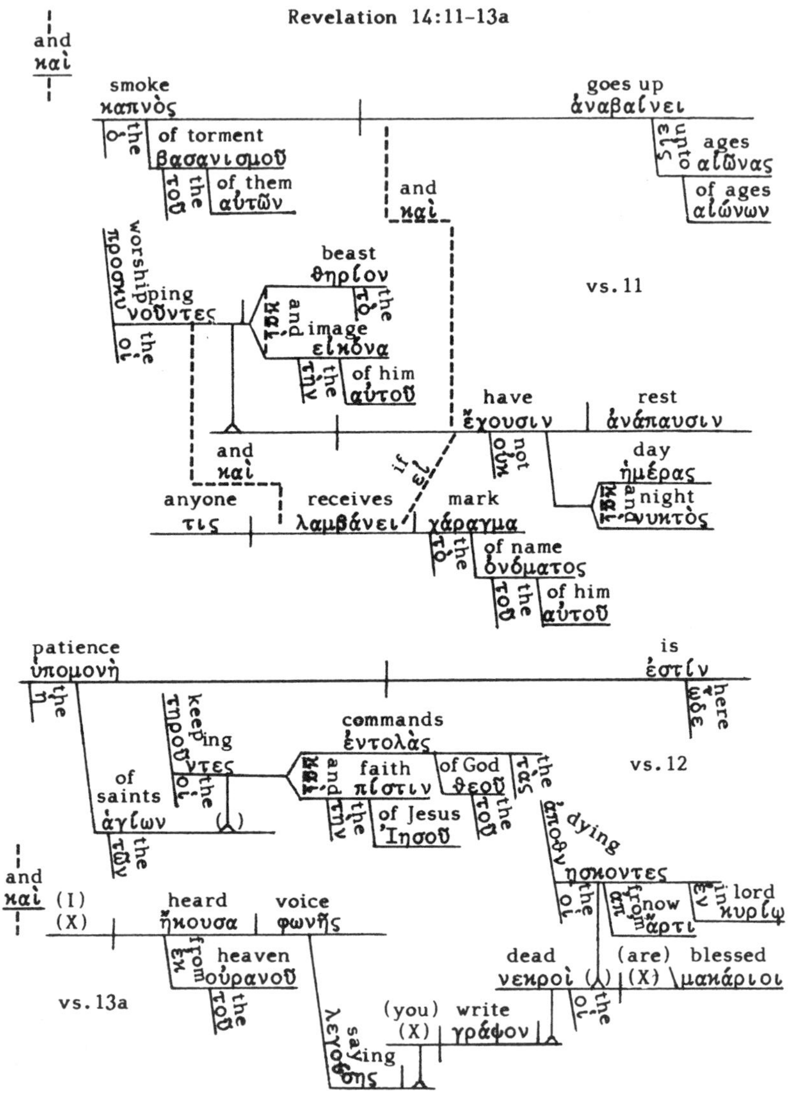

## THE DIAGRAM OF 14:11-13a

Something of a rarity occurs in verse 11. Three clauses appear one of which is an "if" clause. That, with the two independent clauses, classifies this as compound-complex. Yet the adverbial "if" clause is joined by coordinating conjunction καὶ to the attributive participial phrase "the ones worshipping," subject of the second independent. Such a connection would make of this a noun clause, part of a compound subject. Yet "if" is an adverb conditional. Can a clause be noun and adverb at the same time? Can it be subject of a verb and at the same time be a modifier of that verb? Logic says, "No." But people aren't always logical. Normally good grammar reflects good thinking. Grammar is logic spoken or written. But the mind wanders, repeats, makes false starts, inerrupts, makes new beginnings, and other involutions of illogical proceedure. Language may reflect the emotions of the moment. When that happens grammar becomes "irregular," "incorrect," "illogical." As John proceeded with the development of his sentence something like that happened. Logically he finished his thought with "...and his image(αὐτοῦ)." According to the second independent clause, "...the ones worshipping the beast and his image do not have rest day and night." Then he remembered another class who would "not have rest." So he added the "if" idea as an afterthought without adding another independent clause. It became another subject to the main verb already expressed. The construction may not be strictly logical but it was in keeping with the psychological mood of John's enlivened mind.

However one arranges it the sentence is compound-complex. The two main clauses say: "smoke went up...the ones worshipping etc...do not have rest..." ἡμέρας and νυκτὸς are genitives expressing kind of time; not accusative extent of time.

Verse 12 manifests a simple sentence: "The patience is here..." The kind of patience which is "here" is identified by the genitive ἁγίων "of saints." Of what that patience consists is found in present attributive participle in apposition to "saints." "The ones keeping the commands of God and the faith in Jesus." θεοῦ is subjective or possessive genitive. Ἰησοῦ is objective genitive; it's the faith of which Jesus is the object.

Verse 13a is a complex sentence: "I heard voice..." The ἐκ phrase is adverbial. It tells from where the voice came. Direct object is the noun φωνῆς in genitive after verb of hearing. Describing "voice" is present circumstantial participle (agreeing in case) λεγούσης "saying." Object of the participle is a noun clause: "You write..." Direct object of the verb γράψον is the dependent noun clause: "the dead are blessed." As a further identification of "the dead" is the appositional present attributive participle ἀποθνῄσκοντες "the ones dying." But it's more than just "the ones dying." It's "the ones dying in the Lord." More than that, when they are dying is produced by the "from now"(ἀπό) phrase. Both ἐν and ἀπό are adverbial ideas.

## Revelation 14:13b-15

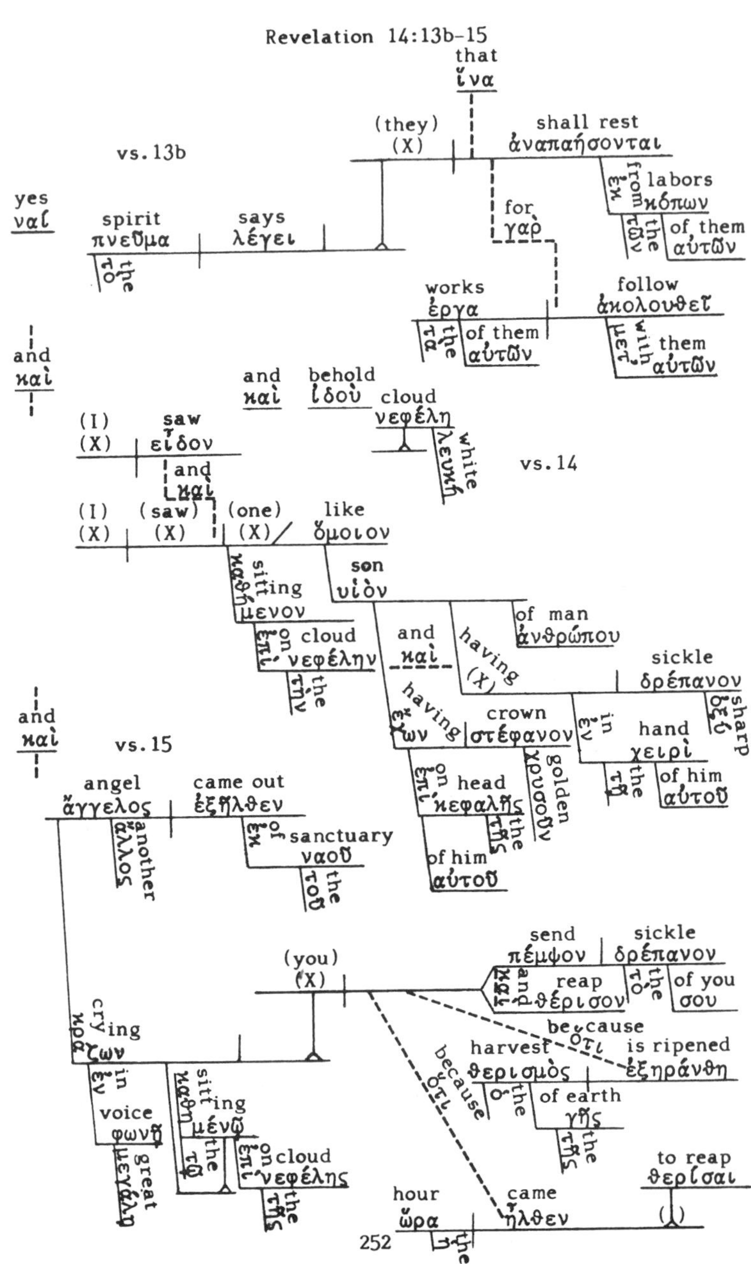

## THE DIAGRAM OF 14:13b-15

An interjection is the orphan of speech. It's an outburst of emotion, unattached grammatically to the sentence. But it is joined emotionally. It stands alone. The only way a diagram can picture an interjection is by placing it near but not joined to the sentence. So ναί "yes" is an interjection with the complex sentence of verse 13b.

"The spirit says..." is the burden of the independent element. What he says develops in the two dependent noun clauses, objects of the verb "says." ἵνα is a purport noun clause. It expresses the content of what the spirit says. It is direct object of the verb "says," "that they shall rest..." γὰρ is a coordinating conjunction that introduces another noun clause parallel to the ἵνα. Yet it does not give the content of what the spirit says. It gives a reason they will enjoy their rest. "...their works follow with them." μετά when used with genitive literally means "amidst," "mingling with." When it appears with accusative it indicates "after." When the righteous die their works follow along with them, not after. Their works are a part of them. Where they go their works go.

Verse 14 has only one true clause. Yet as diagrammed it is compound with two clauses showing. καὶ ἰδοὺ is a compound interjection accompanied by a nominative νεφέλη λευκή "white cloud." The entire expression stands apart as an emotional outburst. To force it into a clause would destroy the emotional effect. But the diagram does show two clauses. The first declares, "I saw..." and then is interrupted by the explosive "and behold..." The clause is restarted with a resumption (by implication) of the verb "I saw..." An understood "one" appears as direct object of "saw" much as an accusative followed the same verb in 14:1. The present participle καθήμενον describes this "one" as "sitting on the cloud." ὅμοιον is treated in the diagram as objective complement. Normally it would have instrumental case used with it but here accusative υἱὸν appears. This "son" is described by genitive ἀνθρώπου "of man" as well as two circumstantial participles (one implied) translated "having a golden crown" and "(having) a sharp sickle..."

Verse 15 embodies a complex collection of clauses. The one main clause states: "Another angel came out of the sanctuary..." Present participle κράζων "crying" describes "angel." That which he was crying is set forth in the noun clause object of the participle. This clause has a compound predicate. "You send your sickle and reap." There follows two ὅτι clauses. They perform the function of adverb giving supporting reasons why he should send forth and reap "...because the hour came to reap..." and "because the harvest of the earth is ripened." The aorist infinitive θερίσαι "to reap" is epexegetical. Epexegetical is to a verb what appositional is to a noun. In this instance the infinitive adds an explanatory idea to the verb with which it appears.

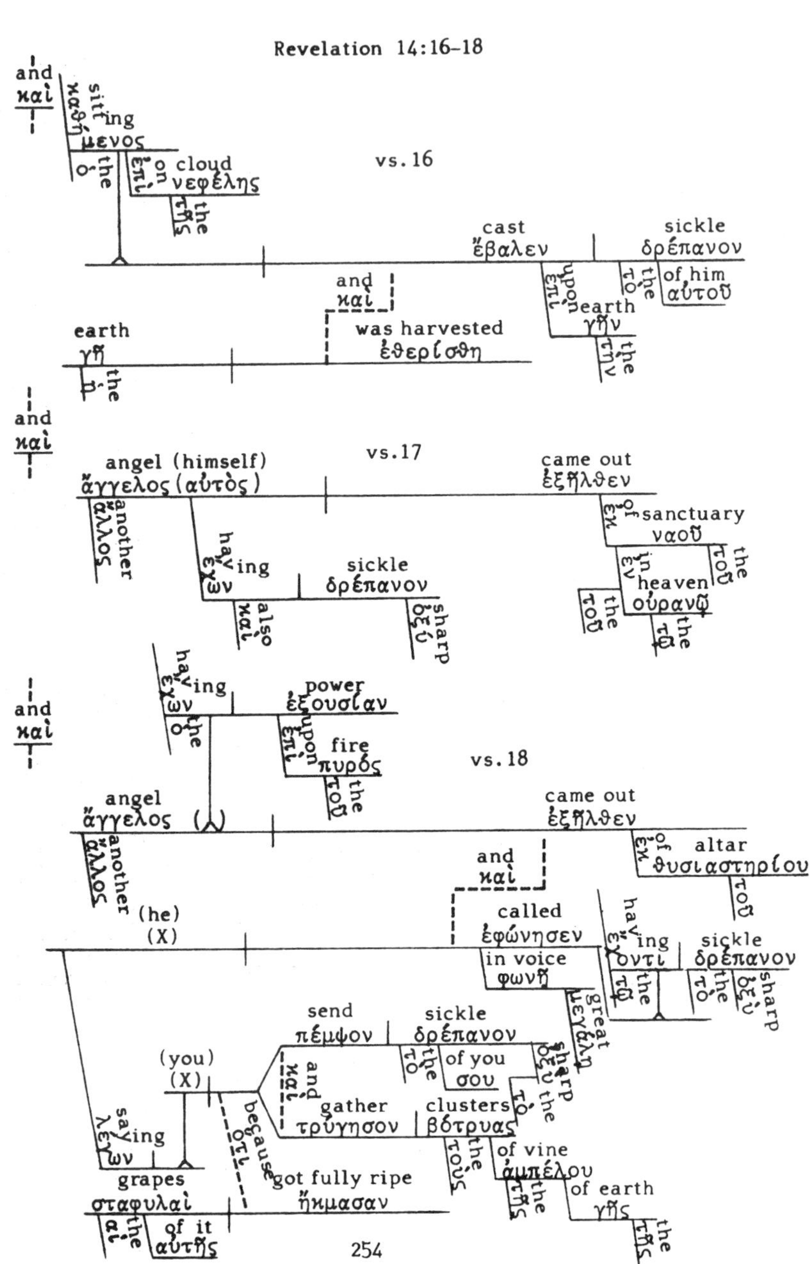
vs. 16
and καὶ
sitting καθήμενος
the ὁ
on ἐπὶ
cloud νεφέλης
the τῆς
cast ἔβαλεν
sickle δρέπανον
the τὸ
of him αὐτοῦ
upon ἐπὶ
earth γῆν
the τὴν
and καὶ
was harvested ἐθερίσθη
earth γῆ
the ἡ
vs. 17
and καὶ
angel (himself) ἄγγελος (αὐτὸς)
another ἄλλος
came out ἐξῆλθεν
of ἐκ
sanctuary ναοῦ
the τοῦ
in ἐν
heaven οὐρανῷ
the τῷ
having ἔχων
sickle δρέπανον
also καὶ
sharp ὀξύ
vs. 18
and καὶ
having ἔχων
the ὁ
power ἐξουσίαν
upon ἐπὶ
fire πυρός
the τοῦ
angel ἄγγελος
another ἄλλος
came out ἐξῆλθεν
of ἐκ
altar θυσιαστηρίου
the τοῦ
and καὶ
(he) (X)
called ἐφώνησεν
in voice φωνῇ
great μεγάλῃ
having ἔχοντι
the τῷ
sickle δρέπανον
the τὸ
sharp ὀξὺ
saying λέγων
(you) (X)
send πέμψον
sickle δρέπανον
the τὸ
of you σου
sharp ὀξὺ
and καὶ
gather τρύγησον
clusters βότρυας
the τοὺς
of vine ἀμπέλου
the τῆς
of earth γῆς
the τῆς
because ὅτι
grapes σταφυλαὶ
the αἱ
of it αὐτῆς
got fully ripe ἤκμασαν

THE DIAGRAM OF 14:16-18

There's nothing better than a diagram to dissolve a sentence into its component parts. It visually reveals relationships. But it is also true that a diagram destroys the effective style of a writer. This is amply illustrated in the sentence of verse 16. ἔβαλεν "he cast" is the verb of the initial clause. It's importance in the thought of the author is clear in that he placed the verb first in the sentence. But the diagram moves the subject into the first position. Articular attributive present participle καθήμενος is the subject: "the one sitting..." The ἐπὶ phrase tells where he is sitting: "upon the cloud." Another ἐπὶ phrase modifies the verb "cast" and tells where he cast his sickle: "upon the earth." The second of the two independent clauses proceeds to report that which happened when the sickle was cast on the earth: "...and the earth was harvested." The sentence is compound.

Verse 17 develops as a simple sentence. The bare clause states, "another angel came out..." The addition of pronoun αὐτὸς in apposition to the subject serves to make more prominent this angel: "the angel, he himself..." Further emphatic attention is given to the angel by the addition of present circumstantial participle ἔχων "having also a sharp sickle." Modifying the verb "came out" is the ἐκ phrase announcing from whence he came out: "...out from the sanctuary." Then, in order that the reader might know the particular "sanctuary" from which he came out the ἐν phrase is inserted with a repeated definite article τοῦ. It is not only the sanctuary "in heaven" but "the" one in "the heaven." It's "the in-the-heaven sanctuary."

Verse 18 produces a compound-complex array of clauses. The two independent ones say: "And another angel came out..." and "he called..." Once again an ἐκ phrase indicates from whence. "In a great voice" is adverbial in describing the manner in which he called. Present participle ἔχοντι "the one having" is attributive and conveys the indirect object. "...he called to the one having the sharp sickle..."

The dependent elements in this sentence of verse 18 are two. First, a noun clause object of circumstantial participle λέγων "saying." This clause has a compound object: "...send sickle..." and "gather clusters..." Second is the adverb clause of cause introduced by subordinating conjunction ὅτι "because its grapes became fully ripe." The aorist ἤκμασαν indicates the point at which the grapes "got fully ripe." Once the point of ripeness arrived no delay was permitted. The "sharp sickle (knife) was "sent" to cut the clusters.

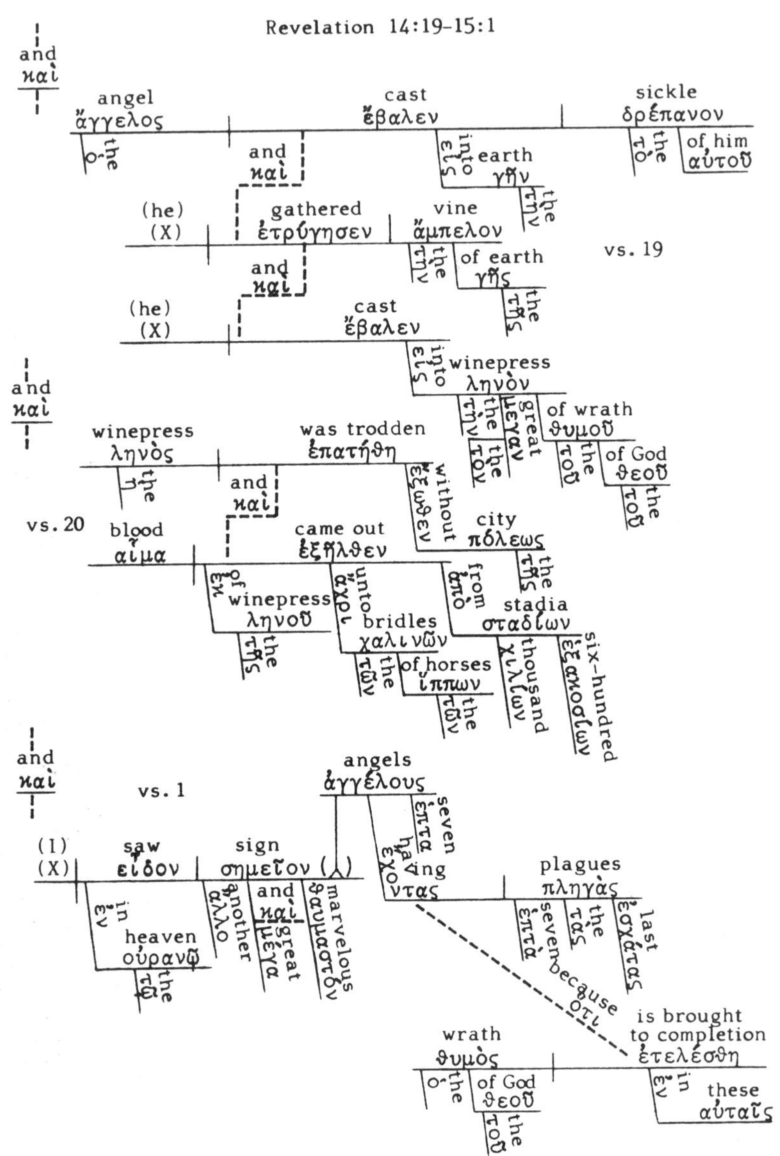
and
καὶ
angel
ἄγγελος
the
ὁ
cast
ἔβαλεν
sickle
δρέπανον
the
τὸ
of him
αὐτοῦ
into
εἰς
earth
γῆν
the
τὴν
and
καὶ
(he)
(X)
gathered
ἐτρύγησεν
vine
ἄμπελον
the
τὴν
of earth
γῆς
the
τῆς
vs. 19
and
καὶ
(he)
(X)
cast
ἔβαλεν
into
εἰς
winepress
ληνὸν
the
τὸν
great
μέγαν
of wrath
θυμοῦ
the
τοῦ
of God
θεοῦ
the
τοῦ
and
καὶ
winepress
ληνὸς
the
ἡ
was trodden
ἐπατήθη
without
ἔξωθεν
city
πόλεως
the
τῆς
vs. 20
and
καὶ
blood
αἷμα
came out
ἐξῆλθεν
of
ἐκ
winepress
ληνοῦ
the
τῆς
unto
ἄχρι
bridles
χαλινῶν
the
τῶν
of horses
ἵππων
the
τῶν
from
ἀπὸ
stadia
σταδίων
thousand
χιλίων
six-hundred
ἑξακοσίων
and
καὶ
vs. 1
angels
ἀγγέλους
seven
ἑπτὰ
having
ἔχοντας
plagues
πληγὰς
seven
ἑπτὰ
the
τὰς
last
ἐσχάτας
(I)
(X)
saw
εἶδον
sign
σημεῖον
in
ἐν
heaven
οὐρανῷ
the
τῷ
another
ἄλλο
and
καὶ
great
μέγα
marvelous
θαυμαστόν
because
ὅτι
wrath
θυμὸς
the
ὁ
of God
θεοῦ
the
τοῦ
is brought
to completion
ἐτελέσθη
in
ἐν
these
αὐταῖς

## THE DIAGRAM OF 14:19–15:1

The modifying ideas in verse 19 are words or phrases; no subordinate clauses. Three independent clauses classify this as compound. Disrobed of modifiers the clauses declare: "...angel cast sickle," "he gathered vine," "he cast."

The modifiers put meat on the bare bones. They add specific details and thus liven up the picture. Both subject ("angel") and object ("sickle") have definite article (ὁ) and (τὸ). These are samples of the anaphoric use of the article. They point back to a previous mention of nouns they modify. The εἰς phrase is adverbial in use answering the question where. He "cast into the earth..." αὐτοῦ is possessive genitive; it was "his" sickle.

The aorist ἐτρύγησεν "gathered" matches the aorists in the other clauses. They are narrative aorists reporting facts without any attempt at colorful description. The object ἄμπελον "vine" probably refers to the clusters of grapes, not the vine itself. In other words, the "vintage." The genitive "of the earth" specifies which vintage. It's the earth's, not any other than earth's.

In telling where he cast this vintage the third clause uses an adverbial εἰς phrase "into the winepress." The adjective "great" is made more forceful by repetition of the definite article τὸν. It's "the winepress, the great one." The repeated article is masculine τὸν whereas feminine τὴν appears with "winepress." ληνός is both masculine and feminine. We can't be sure why he changes gender of the article. Was it to shock the reader into realizing how "great" the winepress was?

The sentence of verse 20 is also compound. It has two clauses. "Winepress was trodden" is the denuded first clause. Again the article is anaphoric pointing to previously mentioned "winepress." The phrase "without the city" plays the role of adverb telling where. The third of the clauses has three prepositional phrases used adverbially. The use of ἀπὸ "from" is rather unusual to express "distance from." This is probably a symbol, exaggerated to suggest the entire earth.

The sentence of 15:1 represents a complex collection of clauses. "I saw sign" is the independent statement. Where the sign was located is in the ἐν phrase "in heaven." The attributes of the sign are identified by "another," "great" and "marvelous." Such adjectives express opinions. More specific concrete identification is found in the noun in apposition to "sign," ἀγγέλους "angels." Plural "angels" is viewed as one collective group describing the singular "sign." ἔχοντας is circumstantial participle describing "angels" as "having the seven last plagues." To sustain the claim of "having...plagues" a ὅτι causal clause appears, "...because the wrath of God is brought to completion in them." ἐτελέσθη is aorist passive of a word the basic meaning of which is "brought to its intended end," "brought to its purposed goal." God's use of "plagues" has design in mind from the outset. Nothing happens without purpose, not even plagues.

## SOME EXPOSITORY THOUGHTS ON 14:1-20

The vicious anger of the dragon toward the woman's child, the rise of two beasts to execute the dragon's purposes chilled the most dedicated saint. Where do the righteous stand in the face of these onrushing forces of evil? Are they abandoned to a dreadful fate? What may a moral man expect when he confronts a flooding tide of immoral power? Chapter 14 provides an answer.

Like sunshine breaking through storm clouds John sees a vision of "the lamb standing on mount Zion." With him "144,000 having his name and the name of his father written on their foreheads." Zion, solid, stable, secure amidst earth-shaking tumult of evil forces gives promise of solid footing for faithful saints yet in this world. He saw "the lamb," slaughtered but risen, directing his forces of righteousness from Zion's holy height. With the lamb was a complete crowd; not a single one missing, symbolized by the perfect number. They stand secure on Zion with the lamb. Christ reigns; Christ redeems; not one is forsaken or lost. We know because each of the 144,000 has "his name, and the name of his father written on their foreheads." The "name" identifies one as belonging to the lamb. It's the ID card for those who suffered and survived the forces of this world's beasts. The "name" signifies the kind of character stamped on each one standing with the lamb. It was stamped "on their foreheads," that is, in their mind, body and soul. What can evil do when one has absorbed the character of Christ, the "name" of the lamb, the redemption of God? This vision could not fail to lift the hearts of those yet facing martyrdom at the hands of the beast of Rome.

But there is yet more encouragement! A harmony sounded, music of "many waters," "harpers harping on their harps," strains of a "new song" which no one could learn except the 144,000" who were "purchased from the earth" and were "virgins," "not defiled with women." It was a new kind of song. That's the reason no one could learn it save those who "followed the lamb wherever he goes" and in whose mouth "a lie was not found." This rush of symbols multiplies the impression of the solid security of the saints. The purity of the saints on earth was their security to survive what Rome would do. The lie which "was not found" was their freedom from bowing to the false image of Rome's beast. The lack of "defilement with woman" was their triumph over the sexual vices of pagan permissiveness as well as the spiritual fornication of the cult of emperor worship. The "new kind of song" was the song of redemption. How can one learn to sing the song of redemption who hasn't been redeemed? And how can one not sing that song who has been redeemed? Character qualifies the singer to sing this song! These are "the first fruits to God and to the lamb..." To one who must choose between Rome's beast and God's Christ what greater inspiration could there be? An unfogged view of heaven's hereafter encourages to endure earth's here and now. Roots in heaven guarantees fruits on earth! The security of those there gives promise of security of those here!

Another encouraging sign appeared; "...another angel flying in mid heaven, having eternal good news to herald upon the ones sitting on the earth...upon every tribe..." This "messenger" of God is "flying." He's not passive, hidden in obscurity, not a side show on the fringe. No matter the storms on earth he's actively involved proclaiming heaven's "good news." Besides, it's "eternal good news." God's gospel is no afterthought, not a post script tacked on history's long epistle. It isn't an appendix as though God were caught off guard by Rome. His good news is "eternal," planned from "before the foundation of the world." God anticipated every deviation of sin, every diabolical move of the dragon. The gospel is "eternal." It confronts with triumph every painful persecution thrust onto the people of God.

Moreover, it's universal; to be proclaimed on the earth-dwellers of "every nation, tribe, tongue and people." No one is ever to be left out, neither in sunshine or shadow, peace or war, prosperity or poverty. Every man in every land at all times is to hear God's eternal good news. The proclamation contains simple appeals: "Fear God," "Judgment is here," "Worship the Creator not the creature."

To contrast the positive sign of the "eternal good news" a second angel proclaims the fall of Babylon(Rome). "It fell! It fell! Babylon the Great, which made all nations to drink of the wine of her fornication." There's no way for a government, civilization, culture, or city not to fall that is committed to sin. By its very nature opposition to God has within it the seed of its own downfall. If this world has a moral base, if God be good and omnipotent how can it be otherwise? The very fact that Rome, it's emperor, its sword, set itself up as divine guaranteed its ultimate disintegration. And that by the evil incorporated within its own system. The angel's use of past tense, "It fell! It fell!" before it happened indicates the certainty of the fall of the wicked city and all it stood for. Though the saints suffer it breeds hope to know that the persecutor is carving his own sepulchre.

In view of the certain destruction of the wicked city God's people need to be warned of the danger of compromise. Thus a third angel shouted aloud, "If anyone worships the beast...receives his mark on head or hand...he shall share in the same wrath which God pours on the doomed city." And remember this; God's wrath is undiluted. It's "unmixed" with anything that would make it more apetizing either as to intensity or as to extent. "The smoke of their torment goes up forever," not just for a moment of time. There's "no respite day or night." If one reject Caesar's image and clings to Christ he will die a painful death. Yet it's but for a moment of time. He who rejects Christ and cleaves to Caesar suffers torment eternally. If death for Christ seem an evil how much more is everlasting death apart from Christ? Is death in eternity to be preferred to death in time? Death in time is "for the moment." Death in eternity is permanent.

Patience! Patience! Patience! Such is saintly wisdom. To obey God is wise. To hold true to faith in Jesus is sound, sane and sensible.

**Blessed death!**

Again John heard a "voice from heaven" stating a paradox if ever there was one. "The dead are blessed!" And yet not all the dead are blessed. Beginning "now" it's the "ones dying in the Lord." Satan's most pernicious assault on God's highest creation, Man, is death. Man fears it, is enslaved by it, wards it off by superstition or science. He yields to it only out of necessity. Yet the voice from heaven declares "The dead are blessed, the ones dying in the Lord."

Among many reasons that might be given for such a shocking declaration two specific ones are named by the "voice." First, because they "rest from their labors." At the outset of history the word of God stated: "In the day you eat thereof you shall die." And from that tragic day man has ever been dying. Though he muffle it's ever ominous sound, hide from it by plush homes, massed money, and frenzied excitement man dies while he lives. We are walking corpses scurrying to find band-aids to cover the stench of the approaching grave. We're dead while we live! Our "life" consists of tiresome toil. We labor to find the "good life" and never are satisfied. Our thirst is never quenched; our hunger never appeased. We're always working, toiling, laboring, fighting, scrapping to "makes ends meet" and rise to a "higher" standard of living. And for what? A grave in the ground. But not so, those who "die in the Lord." They "rest from their heavy labors." By his own resurrection and life the Lord has removed the darkness of death, the futility of labor, the boredom of living a rat-race without hope. Death becomes a blessed relief.

A second reason why death "in the Lord" is "blessed" is because "their works follow with them." No cup of cold water given in the name of the Lord is lost. It journeys "with" the who gave it. That which I do "in the Lord" doesn't stay behind and some day catch up with me beyond the grave. It travels "with" me as and where I travel. It becomes a part of me. What I do I am! Hence, where I go my works go "with" me, here and hereafter! That which I believe motivates what I do. But what I do makes me what I am and what I become. I and my works are never separated. They, like I, survive the grave. That's the reason it is a blessing to die "in the Lord." Death is blessed because it is rest from the strain of toil in a sinful order; and because it honors my "works" done in such a sinful society.

And what are these toilsome labors? They are "keeping the commandments of God" in a society in which Caesar insists on being "God." To be right and to do right in a wrong world is to invite right to become a heavy load. But patiently keeping the righteous "commands of God" makes the saint wise and death a blessing. To "trust in Jesus" rather than to rely on Rome is to place a halo on death. Faith in Jesus is better than flowers on the grave. To obey God's commands and to trust Jesus are those "works" that follow through death into life eternal. They make the saint saintly and death a blessing. This indeed reveals "the patience of the saints."

## Certainty of Judgment

Do verses 14-20 speak of final judgment at the consummation of history? Or do they speak of the ongoing judgment in these "last days?" It may be, as some believe, that this is the "last" judgment. But of this we may be sure. The principle of judgment and he who judges are the same. In view of the fact that centuries have passed since Rome fell the judgment spoken of in verse eight obviously was not that which is called the "final" judgment. But he who judged Rome and who judges "the living and the dead" are one and the same. And the principles upon which all judgment rests are the same. If verses 14-20 are a vision of final judgment no specific time is fixed.

But in fact judgment is an ongoing process. Judgment proceeds on earth. There is no doubt of who does the judging. He sits on a "white cloud" and is "like unto a son of man." On his head is a "golden crown, and in his hand a sickle." Christ now reigns in judgment.

Coming forth "from the sanctuary" with God's instruction an angel appears crying to the Christ. "Send your sickle and reap." No need that he personally appear. He "hurled his sickle." Which is to say that he sent his instruments of judgment to execute his will. The inevitable result was that "the earth was harvested."

Yet another angel, this one "from out of the altar, the one having power over the fire" of the altar. Again he exhorts the "other angel" to "send your sickle, the sharp one and gather the clusters of the vine..." The sickle of divine judgment is "hurled to the earth" to perform its judicial work. Cutting through the speculation about when this judgment takes place the salient point is the fact of divine judgment. It is a process going on in history that reachs its culmination when Gods' goal in history is reached.

The immensity of the judgment is signified by the stream of blood which "came out of the winerpess unto the bridles of the horses from a thousand six hundred stadia." This is still symbolic language. 1600 stadia is approximately 165 miles in our terms. The chief point is the fact and enormity of God's judgment on human kind, here and herafter.

This whole chapter offers a vision of assurance of the safety of the saints who have gone on. And thus is an encouragement for those yet facing the ordeal of emperor worship. God provides security for his saints in the midst of his judgmental wrath on the earth. Even death becomes "blessed." And for sure there's no need to fear any final judgment beyond history. Saints are safe in the arms of Jesus!

## A TRANSLATION
Revelation 15:1-8

And I saw another sign in the heaven, great and marvellous, seven angels having seven plagues, the ultimate, because in them the wrath of God was brought to its ultimate end. And I saw as a sea, transparent, having been mixed with fire. And (I saw) the ones overcoming from the beast and from his image and from the number of his name, standing on the sea, the transparent one, having harps of God. And they are singing the song of Moses, the bond-servant of God and the song of the lamb, saying, "Great and marvellous are your works, Lord, the God, the Almighty! Righteous and true are your ways, O king of the nations! Who shall not fear, Lord, and glorify your name, because (you) only (are) holy, because all the nations will come and will worship before you, because your verdicts of judgment were manifested?"

And after these things I saw, and the sanctuary of the tent of the testimony in heaven was opened. And the seven angels, the ones having the seven plagues, came out, having been clothed with pure bright linen, having been girded about the breasts with golden girdles. And one of the four living creatures gave to the seven angels seven golden bowls being full of the wrath of God, the one living forever. And the sanctuary was filled with smoke of the glory of God and of his power, and no one was able to enter into the sanctuary until the seven plagues of the seven angels were brought to their ultimate goal.

## AN OUTLINE OF REVELATION 15:1-8
<u>Justifying God's Justice</u>!

The fierceness of divine wrath on Rome's world will bring indescribable suffering on humanity. Can such firey destiny for even wicked men be justified? Is God's nature of holiness opposed to inflicting such pain on human beings?

I. PREPARATION FOR SEVEN "LAST" PLAGUES. 15:1-2
   1. "Another sign" - seven angels with "last" plagues.
   2. Transparent sea, "mixed with fire." Judgmental providence.
   3. Conquerers standing "on the sea" with "harps of God."

II. THE SONG OF MOSES, SERVANT OF GOD! 15:3-4
   1. Moses' at Red Sea and Mt. Nebo, pattern of God's holiness.
   2. Conquerers' song of holiness for wrath upon the Beast.
      (a)"Just and true are your ways."
      (b)"You only are holy."
      (c)Fear, glory and worship come to you!

III. CONSUMMATION OF THE DIVINE WRATH. 15:5-8
   1. It's source: from sanctuary in heaven. 5
   2. It's agents: angels in "pure bright linen." 6-7a
   3. The topmost extent of the wrath. 7b-8

God's wrath expresses his holiness; his judgment expresses his love. Saints have nothing to fear from the wrath; the same holiness and love expresses itself in redemption.

## A TRANSLATION
## Revelation 16:1-21

And I heard a loud voice out of the sanctuary saying to the seven angels, "Go and pour out the seven bowls of the wrath of God into the earth." And the first went off and poured out his bowl into the earth. And a foul and malignant sore came upon the men, the ones having the mark of the beast and the ones worshipping his image. And the second poured out his bowl into the sea and it became blood as of a dead (man) and every living thing in the sea died. And the third poured out his bowl into the rivers and the springs of the waters, and they became blood.

And I heard the angel of the waters saying, "You, the one being and the one who was, the holy One, are just because you judged these. Because they poured out saints' and prophets' blood, and you gave blood to them to drink. You are worthy!" And I heard the altar saying, "Yea! Lord God, the Almighty, true and just are your judgings.

And the fourth poured out his bowl upon the sun; and it was given to him to burn men in fire. And the men were burned with a great scorch and they blasphemed the name of God, the one holding the power over these plagues; and they did not repent to give glory to him.

And the fifth poured out his bowl on the throne of the beast and his kingdom became darkened and from pain they gnawed their tongues and blasphemed the God of heaven because of their pains and because of their sores. And they repented not of their works.

And the sixth poured out his bowl upon the river, the great Euphrates; and its water dried up that the road of the kings from the sun-rising might be prepared. And I saw (emerging) out of the mouth of the dragon and out of the mouth of the beast and out of the mouth of the false prophet three unclean spirits, as frogs; for they are spirits of demons making signs which (spirits) go out upon the kings of the whole inhabited earth to gather them to the war of the great day of God the Almighty. Behold! I am coming as a thief! Blessed is the one watching and keeping his garments that he may not be living naked and that they should see his shame.

And they gathered them unto the place, the one being called in Hebrew, Harmageddon.

And the seventh poured out his bowl upon the air; and a loud voice came out of the sanctuary saying, "It has happened!" And lightnings and noises and thunders came; and a great earthquake came such as hadn't happened from when man became on the earth, so great was the earthquake. And the great city divided into three parts; and the cities of the nations fell! And the great Babylon was remembered before God to give to her the cup of the wine of his wrath. And every island fled and mountains were not found! And large hail as of a talent's weight, comes down out of heaven upon men; and the men blasphemed God because of the plague of hail, because that plague was terribly severe.

## AN OUTLINE OF REVELATION 16:1-21

Divine Wrath and the City of Man!

The seven "ultimate" plagues of God's wrath fall in swift succession on the city of Man. The city of earth is doomed. Its fall is as predictable as the harvest of any sowing of seed. Harvest is contained within the seed.

The holiness of the divine harvester assures also that his people and their persecution shall be justly avenged. The abuse of God's people does not go unnoticed.

I. THE WRATH OF GOD: FIRST SIX BOWLS. 16:1-12

1. "Foul and malignant sore" ate at men who have the stamp of the beast. This "sore" is "active evil" as it gnaws at the vitals of him who "worships the beast." 2
3. The second bowl fell on the sea; all living in it perished. Commerce from the sea destroyed. 3
3. Third bowl: Rivers and springs became "blood."
   (a)Fresh water polluted. 4
   (b)God's holiness demands this retributive justice. 5-6
   (c)Altar agrees:"true and righteous...your judgments." 7
4. Fourth bowl "fell on the sun..." 8-11
   (a)Failure of crops: drouth and famine. 8
   (b)Men "blasphemed" and "repented not." 9
5. Fifth bowl fell "on the throne of the beast." 10-11
   (a)Political discord: rebellion and revolt. 10
   (b)Men "repented not from their works." 11
6. Sixth bowl on the river Euphrates opens way for gathering of forces. 12

II. CONSUMMATION OF THE WRATH: SEVENTH BOWL. 16:13-21

1. Three evil agents gather the forces for battle. 13-14
2. Blessedness of those "keeping their garments clean." 15
3. The place of gathering: Harmageddon. 16
4. The seventh bowl poured out on the air." 17a
   (a)Prophetic voice from throne: "It has happened!" 17b
   (b)Signs of severity of judgment. 18
   (c)Man's city divided and "cities of nations fell." 19
   (d)Calamities of creation add to destructive forces. 20-21a
   (e)Men curse God because of severity of the destruction. 21b

God's holiness, judgment and the moral order. The holiness God means that judgment is inevitable in an immoral world society. The action of that holy character is continuously present in man's ongoing history.(Gal.6:7-8)(Rom.1:24,26,28) The wrath finds its ultimate expression in a final judgment. The final judgment is anticipated in every judgment within history.

Repentance is now available. This is the day of salvation!

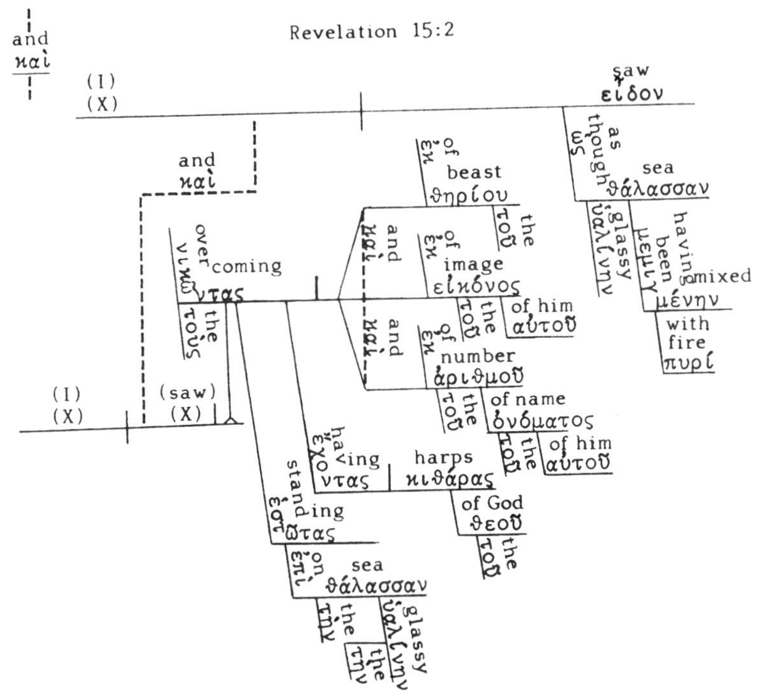


Were it not for coordinating conjunction καὶ 15:2 would have but one clause and hence would be simple. But the "and" indicates the author had a break in thought after his ὡς "as a glassy sea having been mixed with fire." So we have the second clause implied. This becomes a compound sentence.

The ὡς might have been treated as a dependent idea, "...as (I saw) a glassy sea..." This would have made the sentence compound-complex. But the diagram treats it as prepositional phrase. He did not see a sea. He saw something "like a sea."

Object of the implied verb "saw" of the second clause is the attributive participle νικῶντας "ones overcoming." Two participles modifying this express circumstances surrounding those overcoming; "standing on the glassy sea," and "having the harps of God." The three ἐκ phrases are placed in the diagram as though direct objects of νικῶντας. They very well could be placed under "ones overcoming" as adverbial ideas expressing "whence." However, the diagram elects to treat them as expressing noun ideas; "the ones overcoming (the things) out of the beast and out of his image and out of the number of his name." After all, a diagram is an attempt to picture relationships. Sometimes it can become somewhat arbitrary.

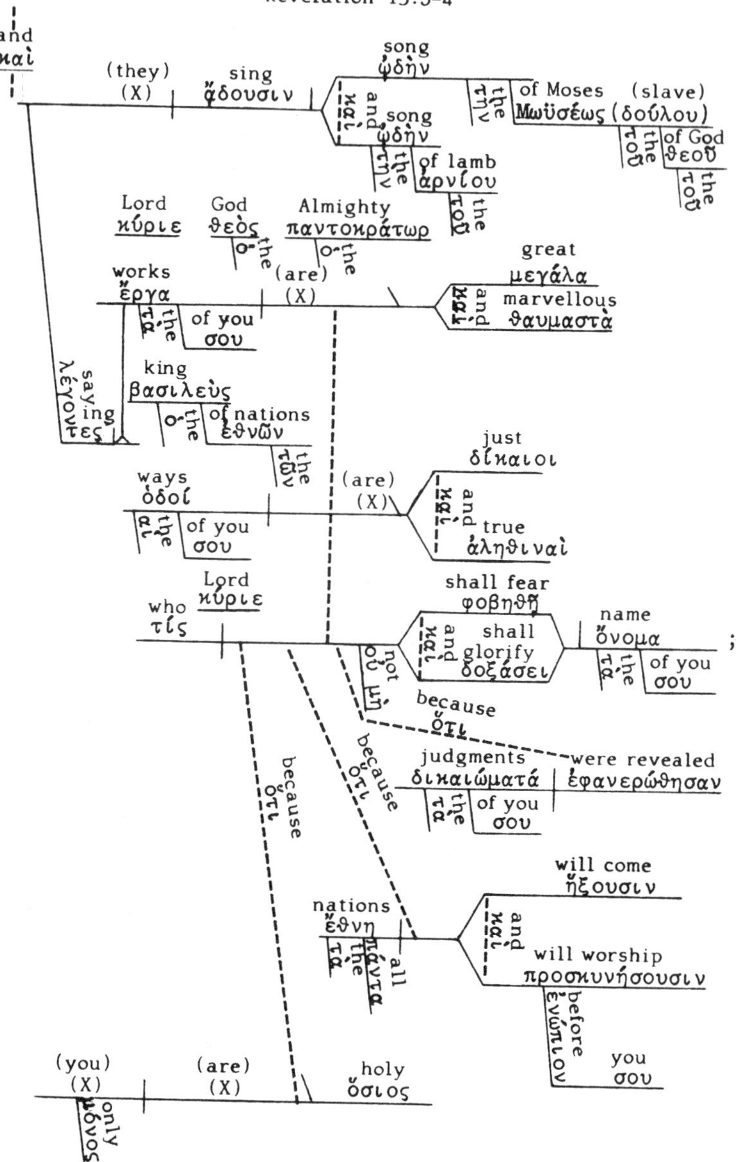
and καὶ
(they) (X)
sing ᾄδουσιν
song ᾠδὴν
the τὴν
of Moses Μωϋσέως
(slave) (δούλου)
the τοῦ
of God θεοῦ
the τοῦ
and καὶ
song ᾠδὴν
the τὴν
of lamb ἀρνίου
the τοῦ
saying λέγοντες
Lord κύριε
God θεὸς
the ὁ
Almighty παντοκράτωρ
the ὁ
works ἔργα
the τὰ
of you σου
(are) (X)
great μεγάλα
and καὶ
marvellous θαυμαστὰ
king βασιλεὺς
the ὁ
of nations ἐθνῶν
the τῶν
ways ὁδοί
the αἱ
of you σου
(are) (X)
just δίκαιοι
and καὶ
true ἀληθιναὶ
Lord κύριε
who τίς
not οὐ μὴ
shall fear φοβηθῇ
and καὶ
shall glorify δοξάσει
name ὄνομα
the τὸ
of you σου
;
because ὅτι
judgments δικαιώματά
the τὰ
of you σου
were revealed ἐφανερώθησαν
because ὅτι
because ὅτι
nations ἔθνη
the τὰ
all πάντα
will come ἥξουσιν
and καὶ
will worship προσκυνήσουσιν
before ἐνώπιον
you σου
(you) (X)
only μόνος
(are) (X)
holy ὅσιος

## THE DIAGRAM OF 15:3-4

There are seven distinct clauses in the sentence of 15:3-4. But only one is independent. Hence the sentence is complex. "They are singing the song...and the song..." Does the repetition of the definite article with repeated object ᾠδὴν indicate two songs? Yes and no! The author certainly thinks of them as distinct and wishes his readers so to think. They were possibly different in formal lyrics and thus two but the idea and feeling were the same and hence one. Both songs were one and the same in that they were songs of redemption. Moses' from Pharoah's pursuing army; the Lamb's from the dragon's pursuing evil.

λέγοντες is a present circumstantial participle modifying the subject "they." It introduces the content of the chorus. The rest of the sentence, directly or indirectly, hinges off this participle.

The first three of the dependent clauses are direct objects of the participle. They represent three stanzas giving the very words of the song. First, "Great and marvelous (are) your works." In the text the adjectives "great" and "marvelous" are placed first both for poetic effect as well as emphasis. The diagram ruins the poetic beauty but puts the subject first because it, in fact, is subject. The three-fold vocative with this clause, "Lord, God, Almighty" is adapted from the Psalms and prophetic parts of the Old Testament.

The second dependent noun clause affirms: "...your ways are just and true..." The reversal in order of subject and adjectives is the same in this clause as in the previous. Vocative, "King of the nations" (some mss. have "ages") is an adaptation of Jer.10:10.

The third noun-object clause provides a rhetorical negative question. "Who shall not fear and glorify your name?" The negative οὐ μὴ is very emphatic. φοβηθῇ is aorist passive subjunctive from defective verb φοβέομαι. A defective (depondent) verb is one that is passive in form but apparently active in meaning. The companion verb in this compound predicate is δοξάσει "shall glorify" and is future indicative. Aorist subjuctive and future indicative are very similar in meaning. Both are future as to time; both are punctiliar as to kind of action. The indicative might be a trifle more positive in its affirmation.

The final three dependent clauses conclude the song by giving reasons <u>why</u>! Certainly "anyone" would "fear" and "glorify" God's name "because (ὅτι) (you) only (are) holy." That's the first reason. Subordinating conjunction ὅτι "because" introduces each of these three adverbial dependent ideas. A second reason is "because all the nations will come and will worship before you." And third, "because your judgments were made known." God's sole and absolute holiness; his power to draw universal worship; his pronouncement of verdicts of judgment are potent reasons why "anyone" should "fear and glorify his name," his person.

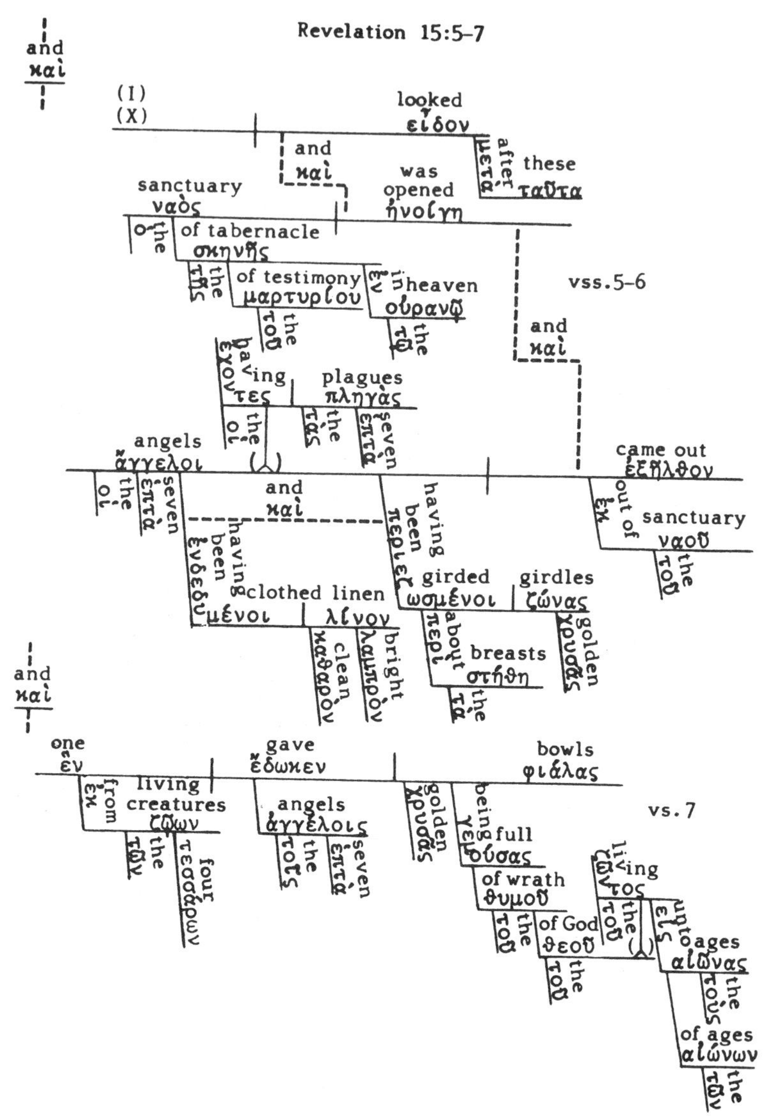
and
καὶ
(I)
(X)
looked
εἶδον
after
μετὰ
these
ταῦτα
and
καὶ
was
opened
ἠνοίγη
sanctuary
ναὸς
ὁ
the
of tabernacle
σκηνῆς
τῆς
the
of testimony
μαρτυρίου
τοῦ
the
ἐν
in
heaven
οὐρανῷ
τῷ
the
vss. 5–6
and
καὶ
having
ἔχοντες
plagues
πληγὰς
οἱ
the
τὰς
the
ἑπτὰ
seven
angels
ἄγγελοι
οἱ
the
ἑπτὰ
seven
and
καὶ
having
been
ἐνδεδυμένοι
clothed
linen
λίνον
καθαρὸν
clean
λαμπρὸν
bright
having
been
περιεζωσμένοι
girded
girdles
ζώνας
χρυσᾶς
golden
περὶ
about
breasts
στήθη
τὰ
the
came out
ἐξῆλθον
ἐκ
out of
sanctuary
ναοῦ
τοῦ
the
and
καὶ
one
ἓν
ἐκ
from
living
creatures
ζῴων
τῶν
the
τεσσάρων
four
gave
ἔδωκεν
angels
ἀγγέλοις
τοῖς
the
ἑπτὰ
seven
bowls
φιάλας
χρυσᾶς
golden
being
full
γεμούσας
of wrath
θυμοῦ
τοῦ
the
of God
θεοῦ
τοῦ
the
living
ζῶντος
τοῦ
the
εἰς
unto
ages
αἰῶνας
τοὺς
the
of ages
αἰώνων
τῶν
the
vs. 7

## THE DIAGRAM OF 15:5-7

The three clauses of verses 5-6 are all independent so we have here a compound sentence. Deprived of all modifiers they say: "I looked..." "sanctuary was opened..." and "angels came out." The initial clause has only one modifying element. It is an adverbial temporal phrase, "after these."

ναὸς "sanctuary" is subject of the second clause. The word is used when reference is made to the sacred place of worship in contrast to the more general ἱερόν which includes not only the sanctuary but the grounds and facilities attached thereto. Genitive σκηνῆς "of tabernacle" is probably best thought of as possessive. It is the "tabernacle's sanctuary" and is "the tabernacles's testimony" as well. So genitive μαρτυρίου specifies what kind of tabernacle it is. It's the tabernacle in which the "testimony" of God is present. The ἐν phrase is adjectival describing the tabernacle as being "the in-heaven" one.

Definite article οἱ, modifying ἄγγελοι "angels" subject of the third clause, is anaphoric. It points back to those seven angels who had the "seven ultimate plagues."(vs.1) Then in order to guarantee that no reader misundertand, he further defines these angels with a present articular participle, "the ones having the seven plagues. In this entire subject the article appears three times, all of them anaphoric. The author wants his readers to know for sure to which angels he is referring. Besides the attributive participle in apposition he brings in two additional circumstantial participles as added descriptions of "the seven angels." They are described as "having been clothed with clean linen" and "having been girded about the breasts with golden girdles." The accusatives λίνον "linen" and ζώνας "girdles" are accusative after verbs of clothing or unclothing. Prepositional phrase "about the breasts" is adverb in function telling where they were girdled. In similar fashion the ἐκ phrase modifying the main verb ἐξῆλθον "came out" is adverbial indicating from whence.

Verse seven involves a simple sentence. "One gave bowls" is the simple statement. Who this "one" was is identified by ἐκ with the ablative, "one of the four living creatures." Indirect object is "to the seven angels." Besides the adjective "golden" the direct object "bowls" is modified by circumstantial present participle and its modifiers "being full of the wrath of God." Genitive θεοῦ is further expanded by the present articular attributive participle ζῶντος "the one living unto the ages of the ages."

ζῴων is ablative with ἐκ. This noun ζῷον "living creature" appears a number of times in Revelation. By now it is a familar word; but a word about which some information may prove profitable. The word denotes the "vital element common to the whole animal creation."(Abbott-Smith Lex.pg.197) In contrast θηρίον the "brutal bestial element is emphasized."(ibid) ζῷον of course is the same root as ζάω "be alive." It is the life not the animal nature that is prominent.

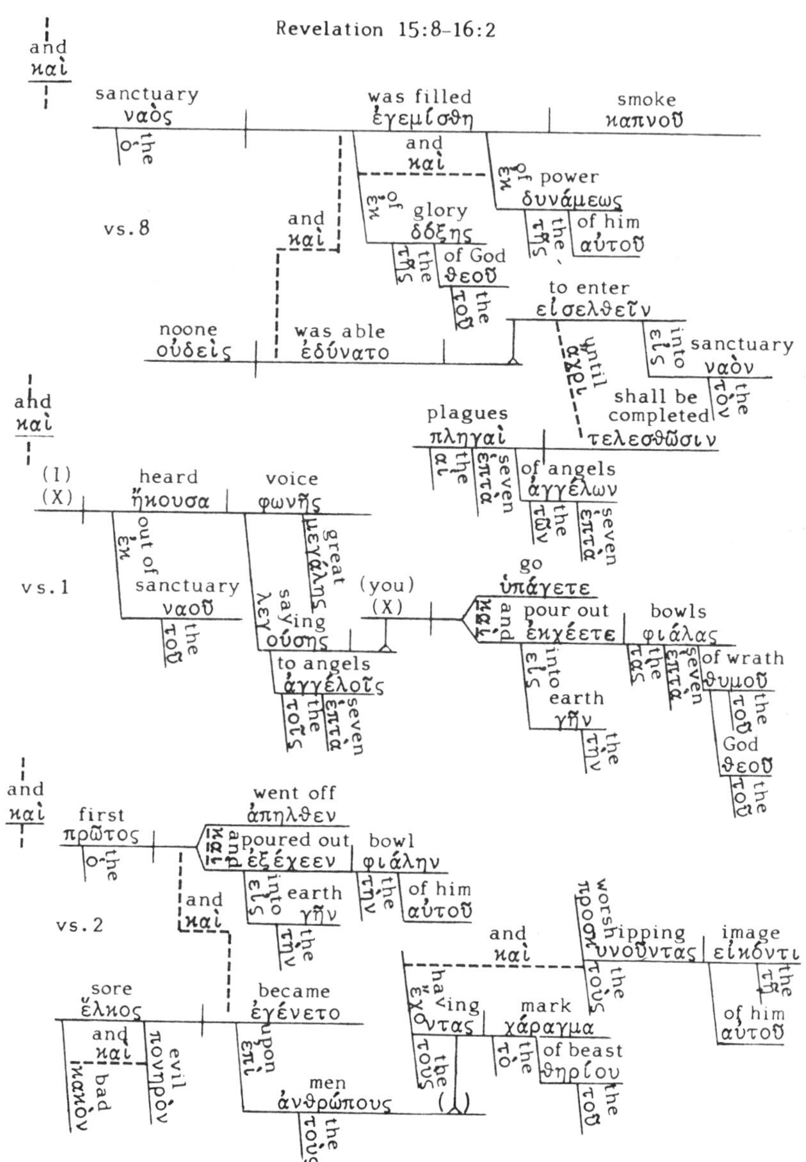
and
καὶ
sanctuary
ναὸς
the
ὁ
was filled
ἐγεμίσθη
smoke
καπνοῦ
and
καὶ
of
ἐκ
power
δυνάμεως
the
τῆς
of him
αὐτοῦ
of
ἐκ
glory
δόξης
the
τῆς
of God
θεοῦ
the
τοῦ
vs. 8
and
καὶ
noone
οὐδεὶς
was able
ἐδύνατο
to enter
εἰσελθεῖν
until
ἄχρι
into
εἰς
sanctuary
ναὸν
the
τὸν
shall be completed
τελεσθῶσιν
plagues
πληγαὶ
the
αἱ
seven
ἑπτὰ
of angels
ἀγγέλων
the
τῶν
seven
ἑπτὰ
and
καὶ
(I)
(X)
heard
ἤκουσα
voice
φωνῆς
great
μεγάλης
out of
ἐκ
sanctuary
ναοῦ
the
τοῦ
vs. 1
saying
λεγούσης
(you)
(X)
go
ὑπάγετε
and
καὶ
pour out
ἐκχέετε
bowls
φιάλας
the
τὰς
seven
ἑπτὰ
of wrath
θυμοῦ
the
τοῦ
God
θεοῦ
the
τοῦ
into
εἰς
earth
γῆν
the
τὴν
to angels
ἀγγέλοις
the
τοῖς
seven
ἑπτὰ
and
καὶ
first
πρῶτος
the
ὁ
went off
ἀπῆλθεν
and
καὶ
poured out
ἐξέχεεν
bowl
φιάλην
the
τὴν
of him
αὐτοῦ
into
εἰς
earth
γῆν
the
τὴν
vs. 2
and
καὶ
sore
ἕλκος
and
καὶ
bad
κακὸν
evil
πονηρὸν
became
ἐγένετο
upon
ἐπὶ
men
ἀνθρώπους
the
τοὺς
having
ἔχοντας
the
τοὺς
mark
χάραγμα
the
τὸ
of beast
θηρίου
the
τοῦ
and
καὶ
worshipping
προσκυνοῦντας
the
τοὺς
image
εἰκόνι
the
τῇ
of him
αὐτοῦ

## THE DIAGRAM OF 15:8-16:2

Two independent clauses and one dependent form the fabric of which the sentence of 15:2 consists. It is compound-complex. The sanctuary was filled with smoke" is the first thread of the fabric. Direct object of this first clause is genitive καπνοῦ "smoke," the usual case after verbs of filling. The verb translated "was filled" is normal narrative aorist expressing a fact as fact without any descriptive touch up a linear tense might supply. The two ἐκ phrases are adverbial for they report from where the smoke came that "filled" the sanctuary. It was from "out of the glory of God and out of his power."

The second independent clause declares: "...no one was able to enter..." Two adverb expressions, one an εἰς phrase and one a dependent ἄχρι clause, complete the sentence. Prepositional "into sanctuary" deals with the question <u>where</u>. The subordinate clause answers the question <u>when</u>, "...until the seven plagues of the seven angels shall be completed." Again the verb meaning "to bring to its intended goal" appears; τελεσθῶσιν "shall be completed" is aorist passive. The work of the seven bowl plagues is more than just a series of judgments. They are judgments that move toward a designed end. Thus comes to a close chapter 15.

### Chapter 16

Chapter 15 covered preparation in heaven for the pouring out of the seven bowls, God's ultimate punishments. Chapter 16 reports the pouring out of the bowls. Verse one is a complex arrangement that gets the action started. "I heard a voice..." Genitive direct object φωνῆς after verb of hearing. It came from (adverb) "out of the sanctuary." Circumstantial participle λεγούσης "saying" describes "voice." As direct object of the participle is a noun clause which states the content of what the "voice" was saying. "You go and pour out the vials..." Genitive θυμοῦ "wrath" is qualitative. The bowls consist of "wrath."

Verse two incorporates a compound construction. It contains two clauses. The first has a compound predicate and may be translated, "The first went off and poured out..." That which they poured out is seen in accusative φιάλας "bowls," direct object. Precisely where he poured it out is set forth by "into the earth," a prepositional phrase used as adverb.

The second clause says that a "sore became..." Two adjectives, synonyms, describe the sore. It was not only κακὸν "bad" but also πονηρὸν "evil." The first is "bad" and willing to be bad. But the second is actively evil, not only willing to be bad but agressively bad; not satisfied until it makes others bad. It is a festering sore, a putrid, cancerous growth. Second aorist verb ἐγένετο "became" indicates that the sore "arose" from forces inherent within. <u>Where</u> the sore appeared was "upon men," an adverbial idea. <u>Finally</u> the "men" are defined by a brace of participial phrases in apposition. They are "the ones having the mark of the beast" and "the ones worshipping his image."

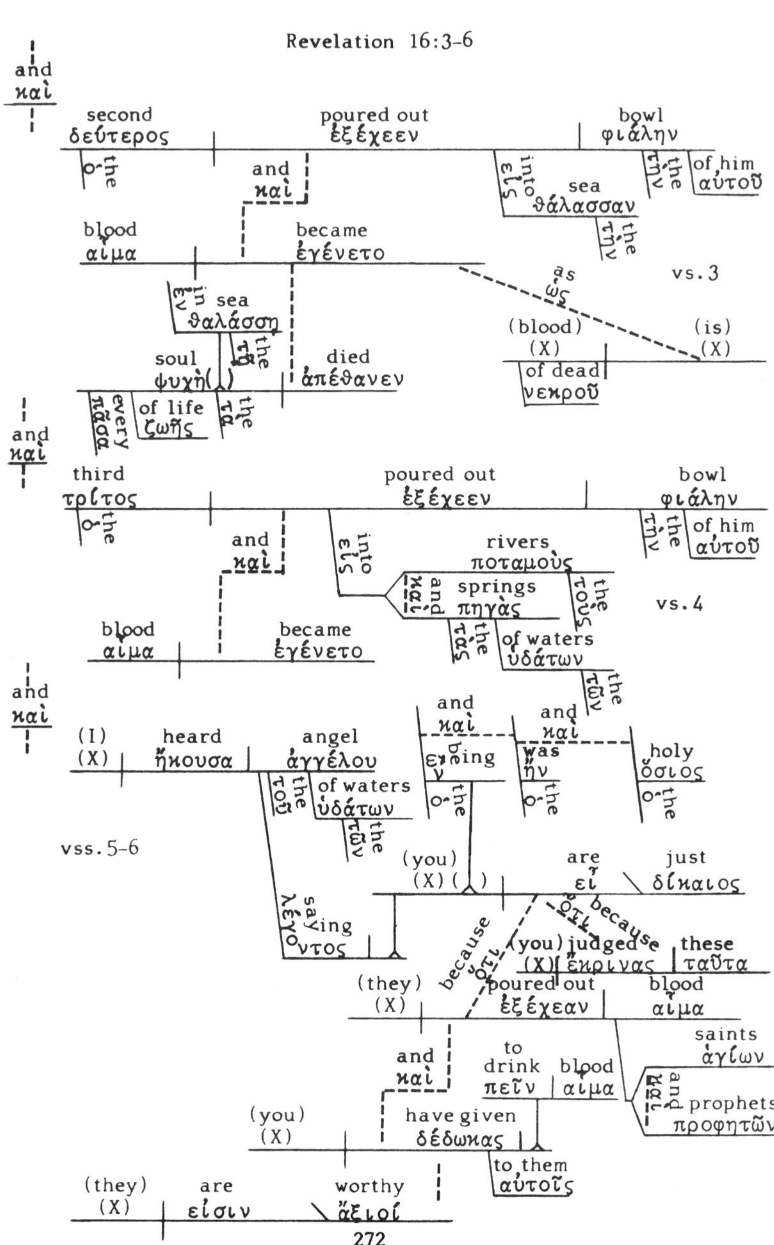
and
καὶ
second
δεύτερος
the
ὁ
poured out
ἐξέχεεν
bowl
φιάλην
the
τὴν
of him
αὐτοῦ
into
εἰς
sea
θάλασσαν
the
τὴν
and
καὶ
blood
αἷμα
became
ἐγένετο
as
ὡς
vs.3
(blood)
(X)
(is)
(X)
of dead
νεκροῦ
in
ἐν
sea
θαλάσσῃ
the
τῇ
soul
ψυχὴ
died
ἀπέθανεν
every
πᾶσα
of life
ζωῆς
the
τὰ
and
καὶ
third
τρίτος
the
ὁ
poured out
ἐξέχεεν
bowl
φιάλην
the
τὴν
of him
αὐτοῦ
and
καὶ
into
εἰς
rivers
ποταμοὺς
the
τοὺς
and
καὶ
springs
πηγὰς
the
τὰς
vs.4
blood
αἷμα
became
ἐγένετο
of waters
ὑδάτων
the
τῶν
and
καὶ
(I)
(X)
heard
ἤκουσα
angel
ἀγγέλου
the
τοῦ
of waters
ὑδάτων
the
τῶν
and
καὶ
being
ὢν
the
ὁ
and
καὶ
was
ἦν
the
ὁ
holy
ὅσιος
the
ὁ
vss.5-6
saying
λέγοντος
(you)
(X)
are
εἶ
just
δίκαιος
because
ὅτι
because
ὅτι
(you) judged
(X) ἔκρινας
these
ταῦτα
(they)
(X)
poured out
ἐξέχεαν
blood
αἷμα
saints
ἁγίων
and
καὶ
prophets
προφητῶν
and
καὶ
to
drink
πεῖν
blood
αἷμα
(you)
(X)
have given
δέδωκας
to them
αὐτοῖς
(they)
(X)
are
εἰσιν
worthy
ἄξιοί

## THE DIAGRAM OF 16:3-6

As diagrammed verse three is compound-complex. It seems best to take ὡς νεκροῦ as an abbreviated dependent clause, "as (the blood) of a dead (man is)." It is adverb in force; it speaks of the manner in which "blood became..."

The other three clauses of the sentence are independent and thus give the compound flavor to the construction. The first asserts the fact: "The second (angel) poured out his bowl into the sea." "Into the sea" is adverbial explaining where. The effect of the pouring of the second bowl is stated in the second of the independent clauses. "Blood became..." The result of that action is stated in the third main clause: "every soul of life...died." "Every soul of life" means "every living soul." Genitives are often adjectival in force. The plural neuter article treats the whole ἐν phrase as though it were a single noun: "the ones in the sea." The phrase is appositional to ψυχὴ "soul."

The sentence of verse four follows the compound pattern as that found in verse three. But this time no third clause reports the effect of the pouring of the bowl. And no dependent clause appears at all. The sentence says, "And the third (angel) poured out his bowl...and blood became." Again an εἰς adverbial phrase tells where the contents of the bowl were poured: "...into the rivers and the springs of the waters."

The sentence embodied in verses 5-6 is a bit more complicated. It has six clauses five of which are dependent. The sentence is to be classed as complex. The main clause asserts: "I heard the angel of the waters..." The verb for hearing has genitive ἀγγέλου for its direct object. The genitive ὑδάτων characterizes this angel as being the one "of the waters." Present participle λέγοντος "saying" is circumstantial. John did more than just hear an angel, he "heard an angel saying..." The content of that which the angel was saying is expressed in the five subordinate clauses which follow. First is the noun clause, direct object of the participle: "you are just..." In apposition to the subject "you" are the vocatives addressing God as "the being one and the was one and the holy one." ὅτι clauses set forth reasons why the angel could claim that God was "just." It was "because you judged these..." This is an adverb clause of cause. The ταῦτα "these" apparently refers to "these" who persecuted the believers to the death. The next ὅτι clause supports that; its an added explanatory (epexegetical) idea; "because they poured out blood of the saints and prophets." This second ὅτι carries forward to yet another suplementary reason: "...and you have given them to drink blood."

The last clause is added without any conjunction. It could be considered a separate sentence. In that case it would be a simple sentence. It declares: "They are worthy." This apparently refers to the fact that the "saints" and "prophets" are worthy. Hence God is just in pouring out his wrath on their persecutors.

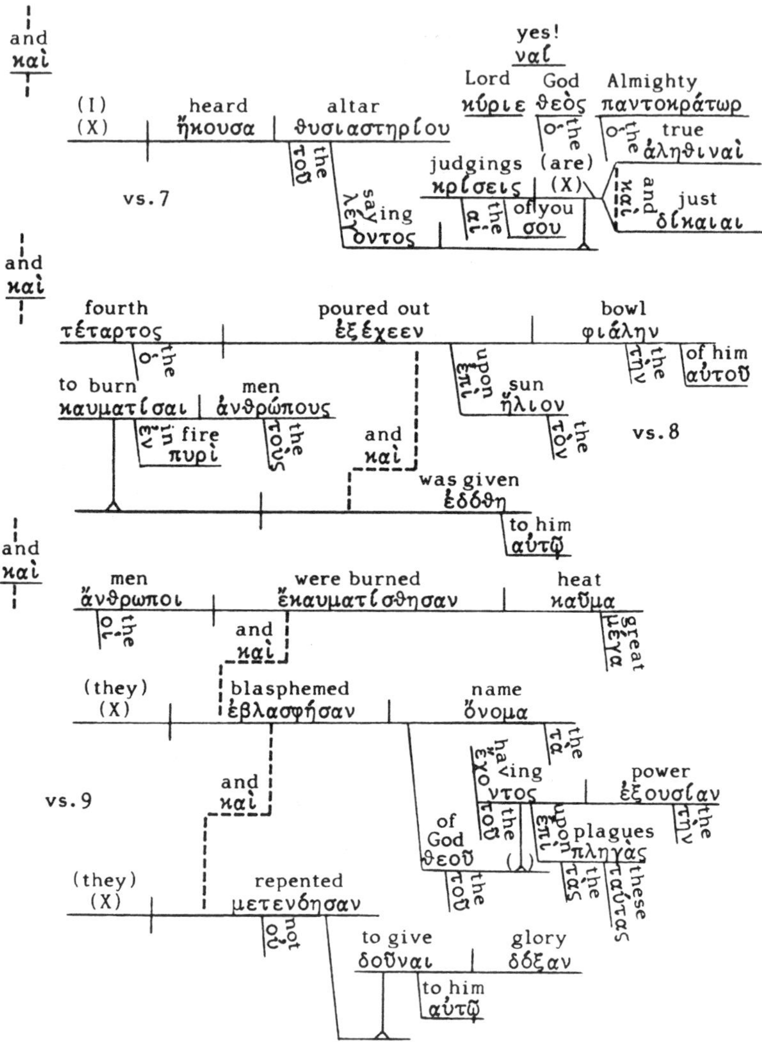
and
καὶ
(I)
(X)
heard
ἤκουσα
altar
θυσιαστηρίου
the
τοῦ
saying
λεγοντος
yes!
ναί
Lord
κύριε
God
θεὸς
the
ὁ
Almighty
παντοκράτωρ
the
ὁ
true
ἀληθιναὶ
judgings
κρίσεις
the
αἱ
of you
σου
(are)
(X)
and
καὶ
just
δίκαιαι
vs.7
and
καὶ
fourth
τέταρτος
the
ὁ
poured out
ἐξέχεεν
bowl
φιάλην
the
τὴν
of him
αὐτοῦ
upon
ἐπὶ
sun
ἥλιον
the
τὸν
vs.8
to burn
καυματίσαι
in
ἐν
fire
πυρί
men
ἀνθρώπους
the
τοὺς
and
καὶ
was given
ἐδόθη
to him
αὐτῷ
and
καὶ
men
ἄνθρωποι
the
οἱ
were burned
ἐκαυματίσθησαν
heat
καῦμα
great
μέγα
and
καὶ
(they)
(X)
blasphemed
ἐβλασφήσαν
name
ὄνομα
the
τὸ
having
ἔχοντος
the
τοῦ
power
ἐξουσίαν
the
τὴν
of God
θεοῦ
the
τοῦ
upon
ἐπὶ
plagues
πληγὰς
the
τὰς
these
ταύτας
vs.9
and
καὶ
(they)
(X)
repented
μετενόησαν
not
οὐ
to give
δοῦναι
glory
δόξαν
to him
αὐτῷ

## THE DIAGRAM OF 16:7-9

From verse seven springs a two-clause complex sentence. It declares: "I heard the altar..." This is either a personification of the altar or a reference to the "angel"(14:18)who "came out of the altar." The testimony which this "altar" gives supports that which the "angel of the waters" gave concerning the just judging of God. The participle λέγοντος "saying" is repeated. Object of the participle is the noun clause presenting the content of what he was saying. "Your judgments are genuine and just." God's judgments have no veneer to cover them; they are in keeping with the norm of that which is divinely right. The vocatives of address give added dignity and force to the praise of God's justice. "Yes, Lord! the God! the Almighty!" Verse eight narrates the pouring out of the bowl of the fourth angel. It does so in a compound sentence of two clauses. "The fourth poured out his bowl..." Nothing different here. But in the prepositional adverb phrase the preposition changes from εἰς to ἐπί, from "unto" to "upon." This fourth angel poured his bowl "upon the sun." The earlier three angels poured theirs "unto" whereas these last four pour theirs "upon."

The effect on the sun is expressed in the second clause, "and to burn men in fire was given to him." Back in 8:12 the fourth trumpet affected a third part of creation with darkness. Here the sun isn't blotted out; in fact, it's intensified to overheat creation. Aorist active infinitive καυματίσαι is subject of this clause. The "in fire" expression is adverbial; it intensifies the vision of the "scorching of men." The sun, the source of God's giving such universal blessing to humanity, becomes an instrument of his just judgment."

Another compound sentence occupies verse nine; this time with three clauses. The first clause presents the fact of what happened when this fourth bowl was emptied. "The men were burned with a great burn..." ἐκαυματίσθησαν "were burned" is aorist indicative passive. Accusative καῦμα "burn" is retained after the passive. καῦμα is cognate accusative: "they were scorched a scorch." Nouns ending in -μα are result nouns. Such nouns name the concrete result of the action in the verbs of the same root. καῦμα represents a "scorch," a "burn" a "char," a "singe" or such like.

The next two clauses of this sentence relate the positive and negative reaction on the part of humanity that got the scorch. First, "...they blasphemed the name of God..." The "name" as usual refers to the person. The attributive participle ἔχοντος "having" is in apposition to "God." This has the force of focusing attention on the God who is being blasphemed. The cursing is hurled against "the" God, "the one having power over the plagues."

The last clause is negative: "they repented not..." The form which the failure to repent took is pictured in the aorist active infinitive δοῦναι "to give" with its object δόξαν "glory." This infinitive partakes of the flavor of one expressing result.

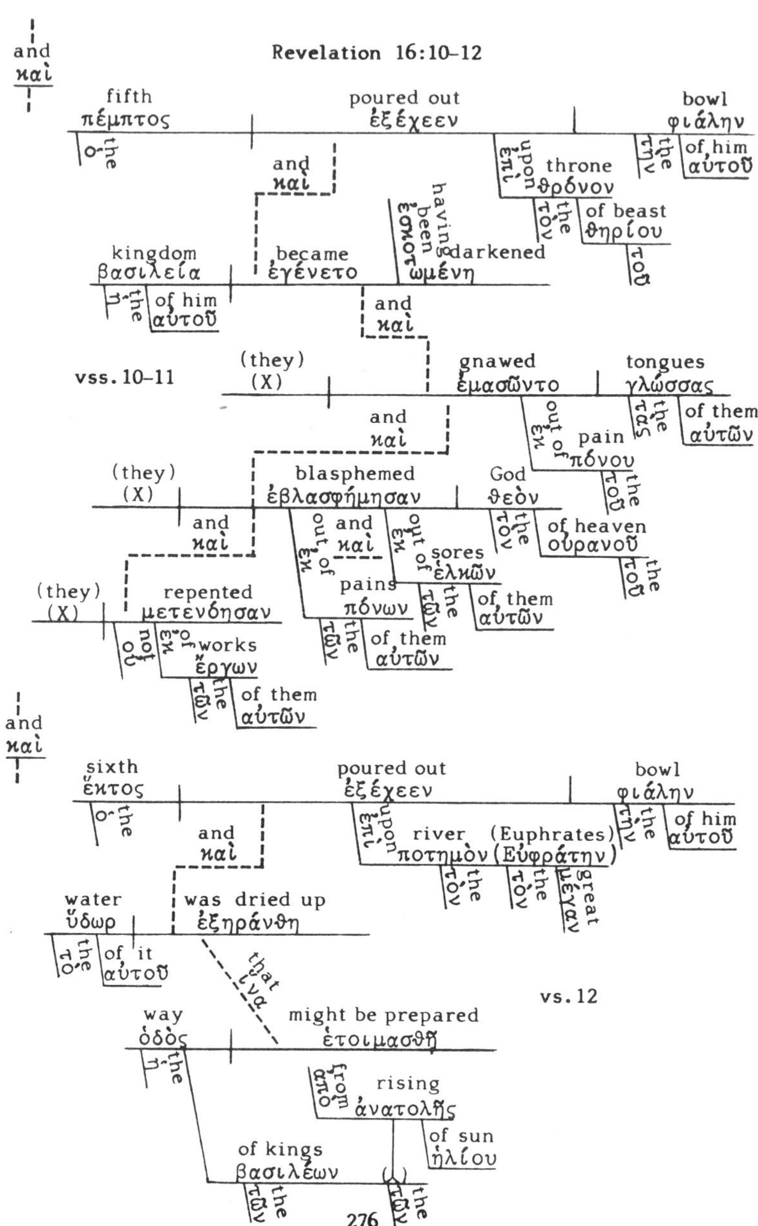

Revelation 16:10–12
and καὶ
fifth πέμπτος
the ὁ
poured out ἐξέχεεν
bowl φιάλην
the τὴν
of him αὐτοῦ
upon ἐπὶ
throne θρόνον
the τὸν
of beast θηρίου
τοῦ
and καὶ
kingdom βασιλεία
the ἡ
of him αὐτοῦ
became ἐγένετο
having been darkened ἐσκοτωμένη
and καὶ
vss. 10–11
(they) (X)
gnawed ἐμασῶντο
tongues γλώσσας
the τὰς
of them αὐτῶν
out of ἐκ
pain πόνου
the τοῦ
and καὶ
(they) (X)
blasphemed ἐβλασφήμησαν
God θεὸν
the τὸν
of heaven οὐρανοῦ
the τοῦ
and καὶ
out of ἐκ
and καὶ
out of ἐκ
sores ἑλκῶν
the τῶν
of them αὐτῶν
pains πόνων
the τῶν
of them αὐτῶν
(they) (X)
repented μετενόησαν
not οὐ
of ἐκ
works ἔργων
the τῶν
of them αὐτῶν
and καὶ
sixth ἕκτος
the ὁ
poured out ἐξέχεεν
bowl φιάλην
the τὴν
of him αὐτοῦ
upon ἐπὶ
river ποταμὸν
the τὸν
(Euphrates) (Εὐφράτην)
the τὸν
great μέγαν
and καὶ
water ὕδωρ
the τὸ
of it αὐτοῦ
was dried up ἐξηράνθη
that ἵνα
vs. 12
way ὁδὸς
the ἡ
might be prepared ἑτοιμασθῇ
from ἀπὸ
rising ἀνατολῆς
of sun ἡλίου
of kings βασιλέων
the τῶν
the τῶν

Verses 10-11 contain five clauses, all independent making the sentence compound. The first clause ratifies that "the fifth (angel) poured out his bowl..." Where he poured it out is exposed in the phrase "upon the throne of the beast."

The second clause advises as to what happened when this fifth bowl was emptied:"...his kingdom became darkened..." Antecedent of αὐτοῦ is "beast" of the preceding clause. The verb of the clause is periphrastic. It consists of aorist ἐγένετο "became" and perfect passive participle ἐσκοτωμένη "having been darkened." This combination of finite verb with participle forms a pluperfect passive. It may be paraphrased: "became as having been darkened." The action represents a point in the past at which the kingdom became darkened. But the perfect element insists that the darkness is a continuing effect extending right into the present. Mental, moral and spiritual darkness, with its intellectual confusion, its unsatisfied moral hungers and its spiritual famine is the form of God's judgment. The darkness comes at a point but continues unabated.

A striking feature of the third clause is the appearance of linear action imperfect ἐμασῶντο. It startles not only because of its more vividly descriptive action but also by contrast to the aorists which surround it. ἐμασῶντο sketches an animated picture of the intense, continuous "gnawing" as a result of the judgment of moral darkness. The intellectual confusion and moral webb entangling the beast's kingdom is an ongoing pain.

The last two clauses give positive and negative statements. Instead of turning to God in praise "they blasphemed God..." The source of their blasphemy is delineated in two ἐκ phrases" "...out of (because of) their pains" and "out of their sores..." These phrases are adverbial. The final clause states the negative result: "...they repented not of their works." ἐκ with ablative indicates either separation or origin. They didn't separate themselves from their works.

Verse 12 represents a compound-complex assortment. There are two independent clauses and one dependent. In the same pattern as the earlier five "the sixth (angel) poured out his bowl." Again an ἐπὶ phrase indicates where: "...upon the river..." But the author wants the reader to know which particular river. So he adds "Euphrates" in apposition. Old Testament association of God's use of Babylon beyond the Euphrates as his instrument of judgment was enough to warrant its symbolic use here.

The second independent clause relates the effect of this sixth judgmental bowl:"...the water was dried up..." Why? so that the Parthian armies might more easily advance. The adverb purpose ἵνα clause makes this clear: "...that the way of the kings...might be prepared." βασιλέων "of kings" is objective genitive: "the way for the kings." The ἀπὸ phrase is in apposition to "kings." From the "rising of the sun" means from the "east."

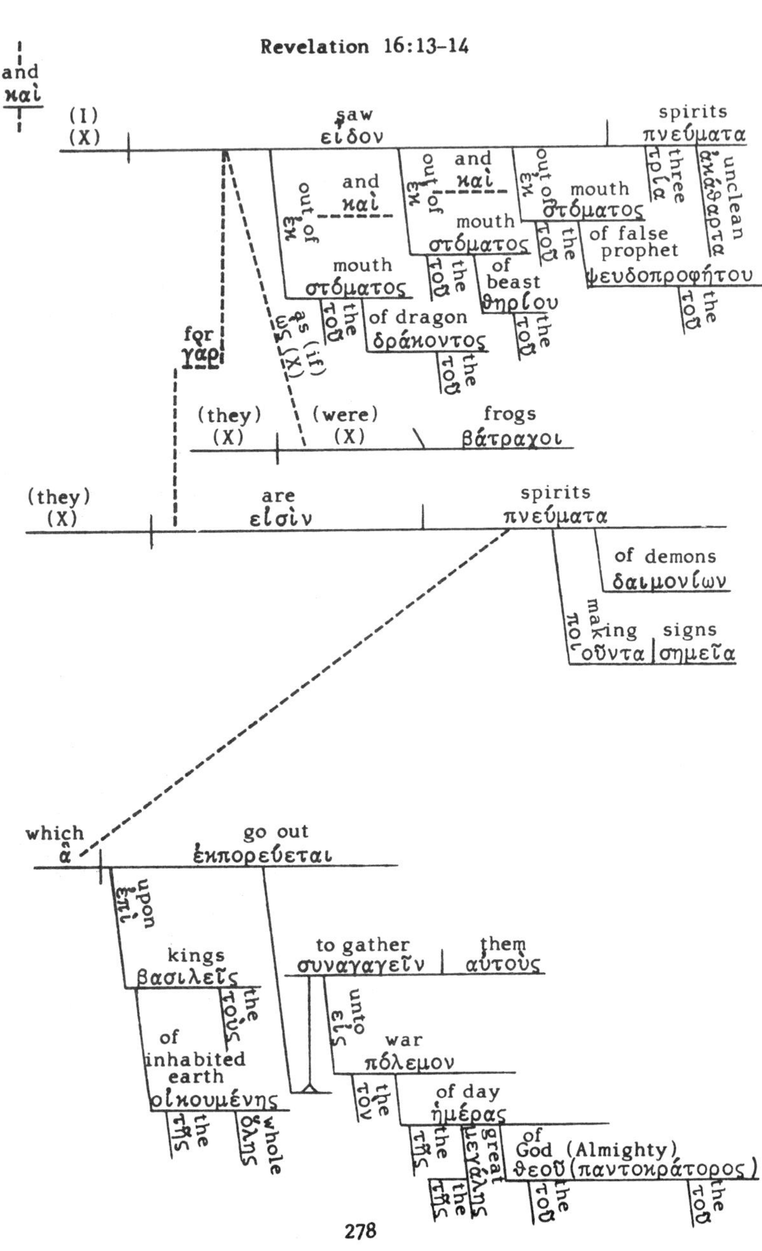
and
καὶ
(I)
(X)
saw
εἶδον
spirits
πνεύματα
three
τρία
unclean
ἀκάθαρτα
out of
ἐκ
and
καὶ
mouth
στόματος
the
τοῦ
of dragon
δράκοντος
the
τοῦ
mouth
στόματος
the
τοῦ
of beast
θηρίου
the
τοῦ
mouth
στόματος
the
τοῦ
of false prophet
ψευδοπροφήτου
the
τοῦ
for
γὰρ
as (if)
ὡς (X)
(they)
(X)
(were)
(X)
frogs
βάτραχοι
(they)
(X)
are
εἰσὶν
spirits
πνεύματα
of demons
δαιμονίων
making
ποιοῦντα
signs
σημεῖα
which
ἃ
go out
ἐκπορεύεται
upon
ἐπὶ
kings
βασιλεῖς
the
τοὺς
of inhabited earth
οἰκουμένης
the
τῆς
whole
ὅλης
to gather
συναγαγεῖν
them
αὐτοὺς
unto
εἰς
war
πόλεμον
the
τὸν
of day
ἡμέρας
the
τῆς
great
μεγάλης
the
τῆς
of God (Almighty)
θεοῦ (παντοκράτορος)
the
τοῦ
the
τοῦ

## THE DIAGRAM OF 16:13-14

Verses 13-14 encompass one sentence. Its four clauses represent two independent and two dependent. The ὡς expression might have been treated as adjectival modifying "spirits." But the diagram presents it as a subordinate clause, adverb in function. The first main idea is: "I saw spirits..." The words "three" and "unclean" are adjectives more clearly identifying "spirits." Three ἐκ phrases are adverb ideas which answer the question from where the sight of the spirits derived: "...out of the mouth of the dragon and out of the mouth of the beast and out of the mouth of the false prophet..." As mentioned above the ὡς in the diagram appears as an adverb clause. It is concessive in force: "as though (they were) frogs..." It presents the manner in which they were sighted by John. They weren't frogs but were seen "as though" they were.

Conjunction γὰρ joins the second independent idea to the first and declares: "...they are spirits..." The word translated "of demons" is genitive identifying the kind of spirits. Circumstantial participle ποιοῦντα brings in a description of the regular practice of these spirits. They are ones "making signs." Present tense of the participle graphically pictures the "making signs" as the habitual activity of such spirits.

These "spirits" are described by an adjective clause ushered in by relative pronoun ἃ "which." The pronoun is neuter plural and agrees in gender and number with its antecedent. The verb of the clause, however, is singular. It is normal Greek for neuter plural subjects to appear with singular verbs. ἐκπορεύεται is present tense, linear action. This "going out" is not a once-of-a-kind act. It is a habitual practice, regularly repeated. However, the immediate context focuses this habit onto a supreme instance in which the spirits "are (in the process of) going out." In other words in this context it is descriptive present. Where they are going is depicted by the ἐπὶ phrase: "upon the kings of the whole inhabited earth." Aorist infinitive συναγαγεῖν "to gather" expresses purpose and hence performs the work of an adverb: "to gather them unto war..." The "unto war" expression is an adverb idea telling where they are to gather them. The genitives "of day" and "of God..." specify the kind of war. It's not a war of swords and spears, shot and shell, but one "of the great day of the God the Almighty."

παντοκράτορος is a compound word constructed of πᾶς "all" and κρατέω "be strong, mighty." It is a name designating God from the standpoint of his great and strong power. It appears often in the Old and New Testaments. In the war here envisioned it is between the power of the dragon and his cohorts and the power of God. But he is the God who controls "all" the moral "might" to be victorious. It's a warfare of opposing spirits.

# Revelation 16:15-18

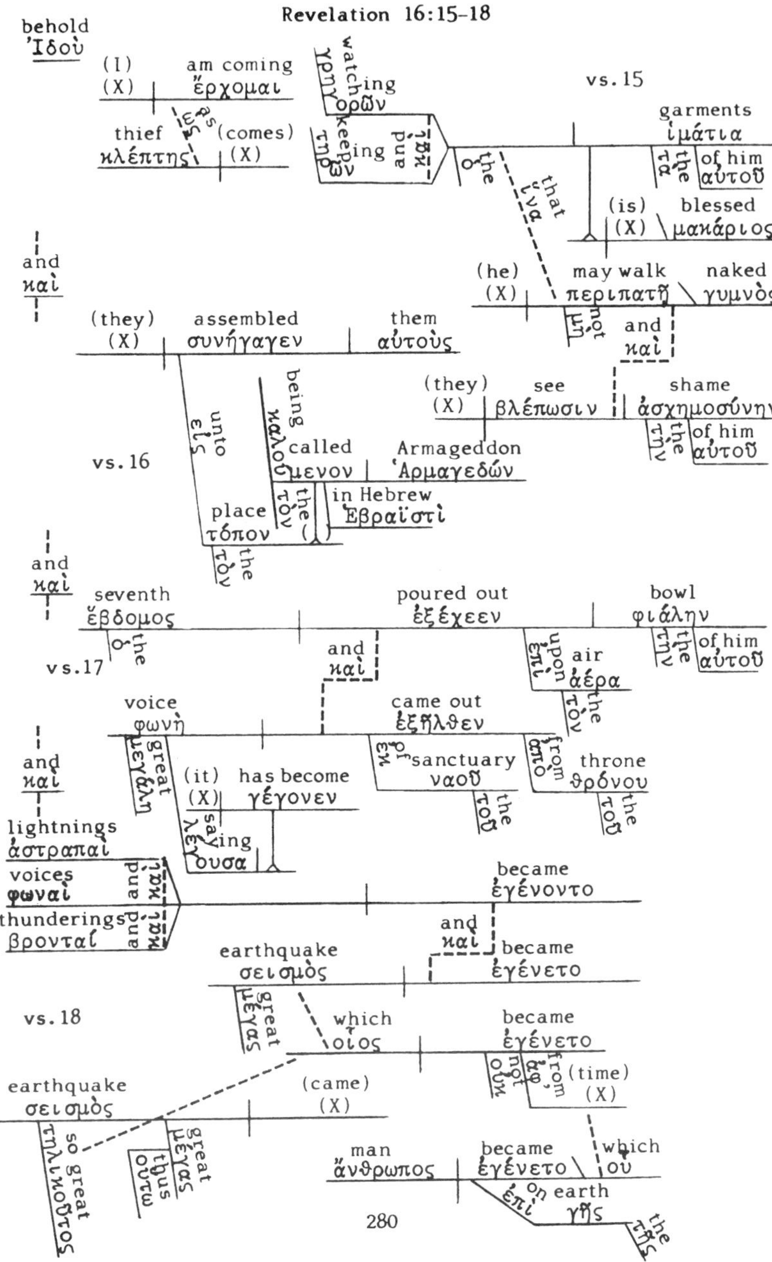

## THE DIAGRAM OF 16:15-18

In Nestle's text "Behold, I come as thief" isn't punctuated as a separate sentence. It forms an independent idea. If the entire verse is only one sentence it is a compound-complex. But it seems better to treat it as a separate complex sentence. That would leave the rest of the sentence a complex.

Ἰδοὺ is a form of εἶδον "see." It became an interjection whose role was to call attention! "lo!" or "behold!" It's not grammatically related to the sentence yet has no significance apart from one.

If the first four words are a separate sentence they form a two-clause complex. "I come" is the main assertion. The ὡς clause is a dependent clause of manner: "as a thief comes."

Taking the rest of verse 15 as a sentence it is a complex of three clauses. The essential assertion is: "The one watching and keeping his garments..." The single definite article with both participles suggests that the "watching" and "keeping" are closely related, two sides of one coin. The one watching keeps and the one keeping watches. ἵνα introduces two adverbial purpose clauses, a negative and a positive, "...that he may not walk naked" and "they see his shame." The contrast in action between aorist subjunctive περιπατῇ and present βλέπωσιν is to be noted. Tense is "kind of action." But it's the kind of action which the author wants the reader to visualize. It's not of neccesity the kind of action native (aktionsart) to the verb used. περιπατέω means "to walk around, to live," either of which is in its nature, without context, linear action. So when the author uses such a linear-root verb in the aorist he is expecting the reader to see the action as a point, not a process, a single act, not a repetition. Present βλέπωσιν is probably best taken as distributive. Each separate one of the "they" looks on his nakedness.

Verse 17 encases a compound-complex. The initial clause follows the pattern: "the seventh poured out his bowl." Again ἐπὶ designates where, an adverb idea. The second independent affirms: "...a great voice came out of the sanctuary from the throne." The one dependent idea appears as object of participle "saying." Perfect tense γέγονεν means "it has become and still is."

The five clauses of verse 18 are arranged as compound-complex. All verbs are aorists of γίνομαι "become." Subject in the first clause is a three-pronged compound, "Lightnings, voices, and thunderings..." These are three particulars of the created order. But so also is the subject of the second independent clause, "earthquake." Why does John present this phenomenon of creation apart and distinct from the other three? Note that the three dependents describe and expand the subject "earthquake." οἷος is qualitative relative, "which by its very nature." The adjectival οὗ clause describes an understood "time." τηλικοῦτος is adjectival describing "earthquake" indirectly through οἷος. The earthquake was so great that obviously it occupied the more prominent place in John's thought, much more than "lightnings, voices and thunderings."

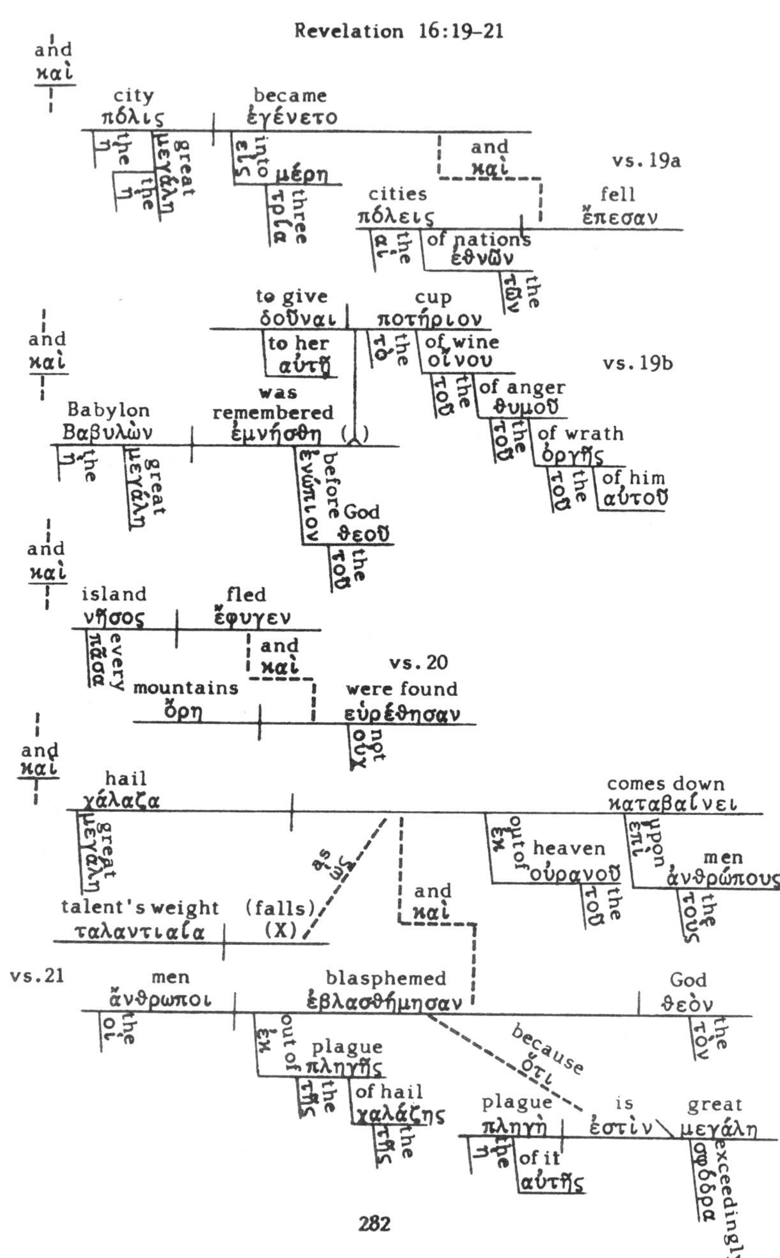
and
καὶ
city
πόλις
the
ἡ
great
μεγάλη
the
ἡ
became
ἐγένετο
into
εἰς
μέρη
three
τρία
and
καὶ
vs. 19a
cities
πόλεις
the
αἱ
of nations
ἐθνῶν
the
τῶν
fell
ἔπεσαν
to give
δοῦναι
to her
αὐτῇ
cup
ποτήριον
the
τὸ
of wine
οἴνου
the
τοῦ
of anger
θυμοῦ
the
τοῦ
of wrath
ὀργῆς
the
τοῦ
of him
αὐτοῦ
vs. 19b
and
καὶ
Babylon
Βαβυλὼν
the
ἡ
great
μεγάλη
was
remembered
ἐμνήσθη
before
ἐνώπιον
God
θεοῦ
the
τοῦ
and
καὶ
island
νῆσος
every
πᾶσα
fled
ἔφυγεν
and
καὶ
vs. 20
mountains
ὄρη
were found
εὑρέθησαν
not
οὐχ
and
καὶ
hail
χάλαζα
great
μεγάλη
as
ὡς
comes down
καταβαίνει
out of
ἐκ
heaven
οὐρανοῦ
the
τοῦ
upon
ἐπὶ
men
ἀνθρώπους
the
τοὺς
talent's weight
ταλαντιαία
(falls)
(X)
and
καὶ
vs. 21
men
ἄνθρωποι
the
οἱ
blasphemed
ἐβλασφήμησαν
God
θεὸν
the
τὸν
out of
ἐκ
plague
πληγῆς
the
τῆς
of hail
χαλάζης
the
τῆς
because
ὅτι
plague
πληγὴ
the
ἡ
of it
αὐτῆς
is
ἐστὶν
great
μεγάλη
exceedingly
σφόδρα

## THE DIAGRAM OF 16:19-21

Verse 19a constitutes a two-clause compound sentence. The first clause literally states: "The great city became into three parts..." We have noted before that the verb γίνομαι means "become" in the sense of developing from "within out," or "come to be." To say "the great city became into three parts" is to testify that something "within" the moral fiber of that city had to "come out." It "became" as surely as poison puss "becomes" from a boil that has come to a head. To translate this "divided into three parts" helps to make smooth English but fails to picture the putrid moral causes that lay behind the division of the city. The repetition of the definite article with adjective μεγάλη "great" increases the descriptive power of the adjective. It was not just "the city," it was "the city, the great one." The second of the clauses declares: "the city of the nations fell."

If the infinitive expression in verse 19b is not a clause then this is a simple sentence. The one clause attests: "The great Babylon was remembered..." Where he was remembered is made known by the ἐνώπιον prepositional phrase, "before the God." The aorist infinitive δοῦναι "to give" is epexegetic. That is, it adds an explanatory idea to define what is stated in the main verb to which it is added; in this instance "was remembered." In other words, the way Babylon (Rome) was "remembered" was "to give to her of the wine of the anger of the wrath of him." "Wine" is a metaphor. The multiplying of genitives intensifies the force of what the wine stands for. It is "anger;" "wrathful anger;" "his wrath." This chain of genitives is like a double underscoring.

Only eight words in verse 20 but they form a compound sentence. "Every island fled" is the first clause; "mountains were not found" is the second. Both verbs are aorists which portray the action as factual points rather than animated descriptions.

Verse 21 presents a compound-complex set of clauses. Each of two independent clauses has one dependent attached. The first idea is, "And great hail came down..." "Out of heaven" tells from where; "upon the earth" tells to where. Both expressions are adverbial. Subordinating conjunction ὡς ushers in an adverb clause of comparison; "as a talent's weight (falls)..."

The second independent clause reports what "the men" did after the great hail came down; "the men blasphemed God..." The prepositional ἐκ phrase is adverb in force. ἐκ with ablative, strictly speaking, expresses source or separation. The source of their blaspheming was "the plague of the hail." In this context the resultant idea is cause; "the men blasphemed because of the plague..."

Another adverbial clause follows introduced by ὅτι "because." It states: "because great is the plague of it exceedingly." An emphasis which the diagram is unable to show is that the adjective "great" is first in the clause and the adverb "exceedingly" is last. The first and last postions are always the most emphatic.

## SOME EXPOSITORY THOUGHTS ON 15:1-16:21

### Justice justified!

John saw another set of symbols. "I saw another sign, great and marvelous." No doubt as to what the sign was: "seven angels with seven plagues, the ultimate..." They're not the "last" in terms of time but in that no plagues are greater in pain, punishment or penalty. No anguish of end "time" can reach beyond the judgmental suffering of these "last plagues." John makes this clear: "because in them the wrath of God reached its ultimate." Any of God's judgments that may plague the consummation of history, the "end time," cannot in degree be more than these plagues on Rome in that time. These are the "ultimate."

This is symbol for John says, "I saw a transparent sea...mixed with fire..." If literal either the sea would quench the fire or the fire the sea. But this firey sea has "standing" on it a vast number "overcoming the beast...having the harps of God...singing the song of the lamb..." Thus, judgmental "wrath of God" which takes its source "in heaven" is approved by those who suffered under the beast of world power. They sing their sanction of the justice of God's wrath to be poured on Rome. "Great and marvellous are your works...righteous and true are your ways...you only are holy and righteous..." In view of the severity of these "ultimate plagues" how may men know that God's "great works" are "righteous" and that God is "holy"? The answer? "Because your verdicts of judgment were manifested." Not that your "verdicts of judgment" were pronounced, promised, prophesied or idealized. But that they were thrust into ongoing history; they were actually executed on the beast. God's wrath in judgment is more than hopeful theory, it is carried out in this world on a government that sets itself up as divine. He who opposes God experiences the ultimate wrath of God. Praise God, Hallelujah! Even as Moses, the servant of God, sang the song of victory over the ancient world power who enslaved God's people. It's the "song of the lamb."

John also saw a "sanctuary...in heaven," the "tent of the testimony," the point of worship where men meet God. The seven angels with the seven ultimate plagues "came out." Their "pure bright linen" clothing symbolized their holiness as having come from the immediate presence of God. To such pure agents was handed by "one of the four living creatures," God's creation, the seven bowls "full of the wrath of God." There's no inconsistency between the holiness of angelic agents and their tragic assignment. Purity and punishment are not opposites; they complement each other. Where sin is there's no purity without punishment. In the presence of evil, wrath expresses purity, judgment love.

"The sanctuary was filled with smoke." The smoke is as "the glory of God" and "his power." Yet "no one," man or angel, "was able to enter into the sanctuary" to share in God's glory and power "until the seven plagues...were brought to their end," their goal. Until judgment against evil is executed God's glory cannot be enjoyed.

The Pouring of the Seven Bowls!

Justice has been justified. The judgmental verdicts are to be executed. The bowls are poured on the city of Man. Divine vengeance is at hand. God's holiness is to be vindicated now in the historical processes involved in the disintegration of Rome.

The first angel "poured out his bowl unto the earth." In the language of symbolism John states what happened. "A foul and malignant sore came upon men." But it was limited to men "having the mark of the beast...and worshipping his image." This malignancy did not attack the ones refusing the mark of the beast. He who sets up any government, person, political party, system of thought, ideology as the supreme object of his worship and loyalty will have eating away at his soul guilt. When it grows and is compounded by feeding on itself it will utterly destroy him. Sin is moral cancer eating at the souls of men. It gnaws at his spiritual vitals ever increasing in mental, moral and spiritual pain.

"The second (angel) poured his bowl into the sea." What was the result in judgment? "It (the sea) became blood as of a dead (coagulated) and every living thing in the sea died." Trade and commerce, so dependent on the ocean lanes, dried up. Grains rotted on the docks, fruit and vegetables spoiled, commerce came to a standstill. The economic life stagnated; the resulting stench, both figurative and literal, became oppressive to men like the stench of putrid rotting blood. Sin in economic relations destroys economic prosperity. The odor of living becomes oppressive.

Judgment proceeds with accumulating effects. When the third angel poured out his bowl "into the (fresh) waters and springs of (drinking) waters," they turned into poison. When the spiritual sources of life become contaminated they seep out into all relations of men. When government, ignoring God, exploits its people, persecutes saints, ravages its reserves the result is acid rain, barren hills, gutted land, a depressed people. Its "fresh waters" dry up; its "natural" resources become exhausted. This is what eats from within to destroy a person, city, nation or empire that arrogantly assumes divine preogatives. The wrath of God increases in intensity as each bowl pours onto the earth-dwellers, that is, those who worship the image of the beast.

So severe is the wrath that John inserts a parenthetical relief. God entertains no personal hatred for sinful man. He "so loved that he gave his only son..." But he is eternally the Holy One. So the enormity of man's rebellion measures the enormity of the wrath. The "angel of the waters" said: "You...are just because you judged...they poured out saints' blood...you gave them blood to drink" Even the altar spoke: "Yea, Lord...true and just are your judgings." There's no way for a holy God to be just and not bring judgment on the rebellious sinner. The first readers must be reassured on this point. "An eye for an eye and a tooth for a tooth" is neither wrong, unjust or unfair. God himself honors this principle. But it's not personal vengeance. It's the holiness of God reacting in the presence of sin on the one who chooses sin as a life pattern.

The fourth bowl fell upon the sun, the source of energy, light, warmth and heat. Nothing in creation, man included, can live without the sun's energy. But too much of a good thing becomes harmful. The sun not only stimulates energy it mutes it. It not only warms, it muzzles men by overheating. Thus at the pouring of the fourth bowl "men were scorched with a great scorch." When the sun shines with no relief from shadow of a cloud or refreshing of rain crops wither in the fields, cisterns empty, springs become trickles, man and beast gasp for breath and many perish in death. Drouth, famine, hunger strike at the vitals of human existence. Economic depression, moral violence, lawlessness reflect the low spiritual valley in which man dwells. Unable to solve the attending problems men become irritated with each other, blame one another, and social unrest compounds the troubled society.

Would men recognize the hand of God in these judgments, repent of their rebellion, and turn to God in moral reform? "Many times I struck your gardens...with blight and mildew...yet you have not turned to me"(Amos 4:9) Judgment in punishment doesn't always lead men to repent. When the heart is far from God it does just the opposite. Rebellion increases. Thus when that Roman society was "scorched with a great scorch" they "blasphemed the name (person) of God, the one holding the power over these plagues and they did not repent to give glory to him." To the pervert any discipline from God confirms him in his perversion and determines him to greater depravity. And of course when this happens to enough people in and out of government it weakens the state, and leads to gradual disintegration until the government falls and society collapses of its own corruption.

The first four bowls hit man where it hurt by working through "natural" catastrophes and social disorders. The fifth bowl directly attacked man as represented by the "throne of the beast." As a result "the kingdom became darkened..." When government is controlled by second rate thinkers, immoral men with little souls, self-seeking senators, arbitrary bureaucrats insensitive to human needs, then man's "kingdom" is "darkened." And from pain men "gnaw their tongues and blaspheme God..." "Like priests like people" was never more true. Like leaders like people! Society is darknened. Men gnaw with pain, blaspheme God and "repent not of their works." Mental, moral and spiritual darkness never generates light. It merely compounds and confirms men in their sin. "They repented not of their works." "This is the judgment, that the light has come into the world, and men loved the darkness rather than the light; for their works were evil."(Jn.3:19)

"The sixth poured out his bowl upon the river, the great Euphrates." From Rome's viewpoint the Euphrates was the barrier from which the feared Parthians might invade. From the Jews'viewpoint the same river held memories of the great Babylonian captivity. It was from the East that invading hordes must swarm. The sixth bowl "dried up" the waters of the river "that the road of the kings from the sun-rising might be prepared." It signaled an open road for an invading army anticipating a great battle.

The approaching clash between God and the dragon propels an enlisting of the forces of evil. Under the symbol of three frogs which emerge "out of the mouth" of the dragon, beast and false prophet three unclean spirits "go out to the kings of the whole inhabited earth to gather them unto the war of the great day of God..." The propaganda machinery of the Roman government and its provincial "false prophet" is turned full force to the task of arousing the forces of evil against the power of God. The frogs are "unclean spirits" and "spirits of demons" under the control of propaganda facilities, the "mouth" of the dragon and his cohorts. They "show signs" and "magic" to persuade the "kings of the inhabited earth" to become Rome's allies in this "war of the great day of God the Almighty."

So far as God's hosts are concerned it's their task to be alert to what is coming. The battle belongs to God; the victory is assured. But God's soldier must be "watching and keeping" his garments that "he not be naked and they see his shame." The business of the believer is to keep clean and trust God for victory.

The place of gathering is Harmageddon, the hill of Meggido! The city of Meggido at the foot of Mt. Carmel guarded the pass into the plain of Esdraelon, bread basket of the ancient East. From Deborah to Josiah it was the scene of many strategic battles that affected the destiny of Israel. Thus it became a fitting symbol for the final war between sin and righteousness, God and evil. The forces at war are not material but moral and spiritual. Armaggedon pits the moral forces of God against the immoral forces of the dragon. What can be more fatal or final than good and evil, right and wrong, God and Satan? It's not a war of shot and shell but of soul and spirit. It's a battle for the souls of men.

"It has happened!" That's the final resolution between good and evil. That's God's verdict and history's decree on the war between God who is righeous and Satan who is evil. **γέγονεν** "it has happened" is perfect tense. That signifies the permanent result of the war. God's victory is not partial or temporary; it's for good! This ultimate display of the "wrath of God" was accompanied by tokens of divine displeasure, ligntnings, voices, thunders and earthquake! The city of Rome "divided into three parts" and allied "ciites of the nations fell." God does not "wink" at sin nor does he forget evil. His wrath is but stored up while he waits for repentance. The time comes when He "remembers." "The great Babylon was rememebred..." How? So as "to give to her the cup of the wine of his wrath." Islands fled! Mountains disappeared! Hail of a "talent's weight" descended. It's the final, ultimate, extreme, maximum expression of the wrath of God. The "plague was terribly severe" and "men blasphemed God because of the hail." For him who does not repent in time there is no repentance in eternity. Character formed here is not transformed hereafter. He who will not repent now cannot later. The only thing left for such men to do is to "blaspheme God." This is hell!

"It has happened!" Rome has fallen. This prophetic assurance is detailed in Chapters 17:1-20:10.

## A TRANSLATION
### Revelation 17:1-18

And one of the seven angels, the ones having the seven bowls, came, and he spoke with me saying, "Come! I will show you the verdict of judgment against the great harlot, the one sitting upon many waters, with whom the kings of the earth fornicated and (by whom) the kings of the earth were made drunk from the wine of her fornication."

And he carried me off in spirit. And I saw a woman sitting upon a scarlet beast being full of names of blasphemies having seven heads and ten horns. And the woman had been clothed with purple and scarlet and she had been adorned with gold and a precious stone and pearls. Upon her forehead she had a name having been written, a mystery, The Great Babylon, The Mother of Harlots and of the Abominations of the Earth. In her hand she had a golden cup full of abominations and the unclean (corruptions) of her fornication. And I saw the woman being drunk out of the blood of the saints and out of the blood of the martyrs of Jesus. And having seen her I marvelled a great marvel!

And the angel said to me, "Because of what did you marvel?; I will show you the mystery of the woman and of the beast, the one carrying her, the one having the seven heads and the ten horns. The beast which you saw, was, and is not, and is about to come up out of the abyss and goes unto destruction. And the ones living on the earth of whom their name has not been written on the book of life from the foundation of the world, (they) see the beast that was, and is not, and shall be (again).

"Here is the mind which is shrewd! The seven heads are seven mountains on which the woman sits. And the kings are seven! The five fell, one is, the other did not yet come, and whenever he shall come it's necessary that he remain a little. And the beast which was and is not, he himself is also eighth; and he is one of the seven and he is going unto destruction. The ten horns which you saw are ten kings who not yet received sovereignty but for one hour they receive power with the beast as kings (receive power). These have one opinion and they give to the beast their strength and power. These shall war with the lamb and the lamb will conquer them because he is lord of lords and king of kings and (because) those with him are called and chosen and faithful."

And he says, "The waters which you saw where the harlot sits are peoples and multitudes and nations and tongues. And the ten horns which you saw and the beast, these shall hate the harlot and they shall make her desolate and naked and they shall eat of her flesh and they shall burn her with fire. And God gave to their hearts to do his mind and to make (them) one mind and to give to the beast their sovereignty until the words of God shall be completed. And the woman which you saw is the great city, the one holding dominion over the kings of the earth."

## AN OUTLINE OF REVELATION 17:1-18

### The Scarlet Woman!

The city of man is a "harlot" riding a beast which comes "out of the abyss." The city of God comes "down out of heaven from God as a bride adorned for her husband." The city of man and the city of God have different origins; different destinies.

John is invited to "see" the verdict against the great harlot. He is to envision God's dealing with Rome, the wicked city of man.

I. THE SCARLET WOMAN, THE "GREAT HARLOT."
   1. Identity of the scarlet woman.
      (a)She sits "on many waters," many nations.
      (b)With whom "the kings of the earth fornicated."
         A "golden cup of abominations" in her hand.
      (c)Her gaudy dress and name stamp her character.
   2. The scarlet woman and the beast.
      (a)The woman rides the beast; mutually need one another.
      (b)Symbols identifying the beast.
         (1)Seven heads = mountains; seven hills of Rome.
         (2)Seven kings = seven emperors plus an "eighth" who is "one of the seven." Tiberius through Domitian.
         (3)He "was, is not, about to come out of the abyss and goes to destruction." Imperial power in the succession of emperors. Nero redivivus myth!
         (4)He's visible to the "ones living on earth."
   3. The provinces, the support of the wealth of Rome.
      "The woman is the great city, the one having rule over the kings of the earth."

II. THE SIN OF THE SCARLET WOMAN.
   1. Fornication of the spirit. Unfaithful as government. Truth compromised for the sake of power.
   2. Drunk with "blood of the saints."
   3. Mother of harlots; spawned a family of harlots.

III. THE WOMAN'S WAR WITH THE LAMB.
   1. Inevitable conflict based in the nature of the opposing persons and principles.
   2. Inevitable result: the lamb "overcomes." God through lamb is sovereign. Victory inexorable.!
   3. The reason: He "is king of king and lord of lords..."

IV DIVINE WRATH AND THE SCARLET WOMAN.
   1. The ten horns and the beast "hate the harlot...make her desolate...eat her flesh..." Internal revolt; disintegration.
   2. The power of the beast is limited to its contribution to the inescapable "completion" of "the words of God."

Rome's fall came through her disregard of the moral law which expresses God's holiness. God utilizes men, situations, circumstnaces and events in historical processes to release his wrath. By man's standard God works deliberately and slowly. Nevertheless, he is ever at work exacting justice on this earth.

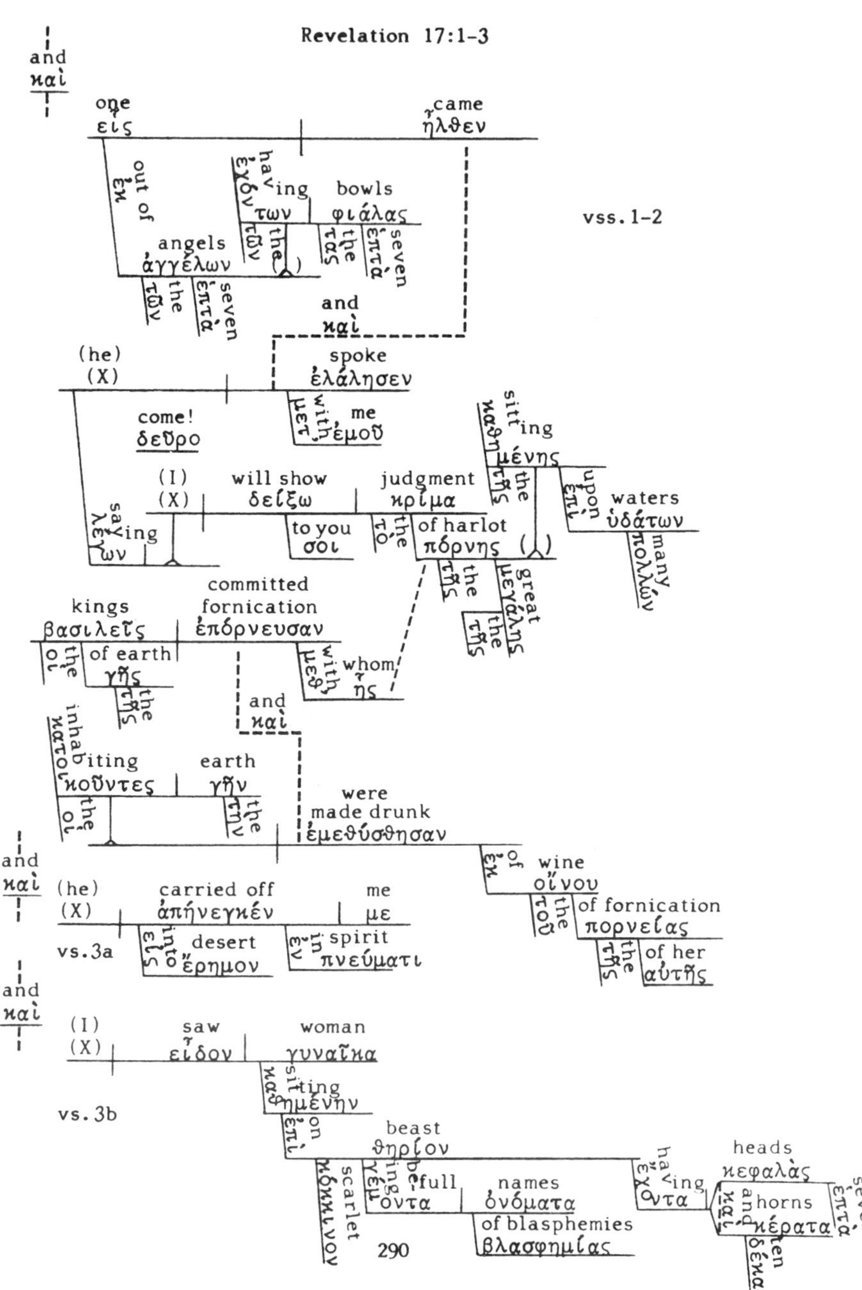
and
καὶ
one
εἷς
came
ἦλθεν
out of
ἐκ
having
ἐχόντων
the
τῶν
bowls
φιάλας
the
τὰς
seven
ἑπτὰ
angels
ἀγγέλων
the
τῶν
seven
ἑπτὰ
vss. 1-2
and
καὶ
(he)
(X)
spoke
ἐλάλησεν
with
μετ'
me
ἐμοῦ
come!
δεῦρο
sitting
καθημένης
the
τῆς
upon
ἐπὶ
waters
ὑδάτων
many
πολλῶν
(I)
(X)
will show
δείξω
judgment
κρίμα
the
τὸ
of harlot
πόρνης
the
τῆς
great
μεγάλης
the
τῆς
saying
λέγων
to you
σοι
committed
fornication
ἐπόρνευσαν
kings
βασιλεῖς
the
οἱ
of earth
γῆς
the
τῆς
with
μεθ'
whom
ἧς
and
καὶ
inhabiting
κατοικοῦντες
the
οἱ
earth
γῆν
the
τὴν
were
made drunk
ἐμεθύσθησαν
of
ἐκ
wine
οἴνου
the
τοῦ
of fornication
πορνείας
the
τῆς
of her
αὐτῆς
and
καὶ
(he)
(X)
carried off
ἀπήνεγκέν
me
με
into
εἰς
desert
ἔρημον
in
ἐν
spirit
πνεύματι
vs. 3a
and
καὶ
(I)
(X)
saw
εἶδον
woman
γυναῖκα
sitting
καθημένην
vs. 3b
on
ἐπὶ
beast
θηρίον
scarlet
κόκκινον
being full
γέμοντα
names
ὀνόματα
of blasphemies
βλασφημίας
having
ἔχοντα
heads
κεφαλὰς
seven
ἑπτὰ
and
καὶ
horns
κέρατα
ten
δέκα

## THE DIAGRAM OF 17:1-3

Verses 1-2 form one sentence. Whether it should be classed as complex or compound-complex must be determined by whether the subject εἱς "one" is subject of both ἦλθεν and ἐλάλησεν. Do these verbs form a compound predicate with the same subject? Or does each have its own distinct subject? The diagram treats them as two clauses, each with a separate subject. If that be correct then the sentence must be classed as compound-complex. When stripped of all modifying elements the two main clauses declare: "One came" and "he spoke." The subject "one" is limited by the adjective phrase ἐκ with ablative "of the seven angels." Then "angels" is further identified by attributive present participle in apposition ἐχόντων "ones having..." Object of the verbal force in the participle is accusative φιάλας "bowls."

The subordinate portion of verses 1-2 consists of three dependent clauses all of which stem from the circumstantial participle λέγων "saying." Direct object is the noun clause: "I will show to you the judgment of the great harlot..." κρίμα "judgment" is a result noun meaning "the verdict of judgment" not the process. The genitive πόρνης "harlot" is objective. It's the verdict pronounced of which the harlot is the object, in other words, on the harlot. This genitive is further described by the present attributive participle καθημένης in apposition; "the one sitting on the waters." Note the definite article appearing three times: "the harlot," "the great," "the one sitting." The article makes each word stand forth distinctly. The next two dependent clauses are adjectival further describing the harlot. She is "the one with whom (ἧς) the kings of the earth committed fornication." Also the one by whom "the ones inhabiting the earth were made drunk." ἐκ with ablative οἴνου reveals the source from where the drunkenness came. It was "out of the wine..." πορνείας "fornication" is qualitative genitive; it defines the kind of wine as being "of fornication." Back in 16:19 "wine" was described as being "of anger"(θυμοῦ). Genitives specify "this and not that," this <u>kind</u>.

The sentence of verse 3a has but one clause of seven words. It is classed as simple. "He carried me..." is the bare idea. A pair of prepositional modifiers put some meat on the bare bones. "...into desert" tells <u>where</u> he carried. "...in spirit" tells <u>how</u> or in what manner he carried.

Verse 3b furnishes another simple construction. Without its modifiers the clause reads, "I saw woman..." That the woman was "sitting" is expressed by the added predicate participle καθημένην. <u>Where</u> she was sitting is set forth by ἐπὶ and the accusative: "upon (the) scarlet beast..." Besides the adjective "scarlet" the "beast" is further described by the present circumstantial participle γέμοντα "being full." Verbs of fullness take the genitive but here plural accusative ὀνόματα "names." Another circumstantial "having" adds a further descriptive label on beast: "having seven heads and ten horns."

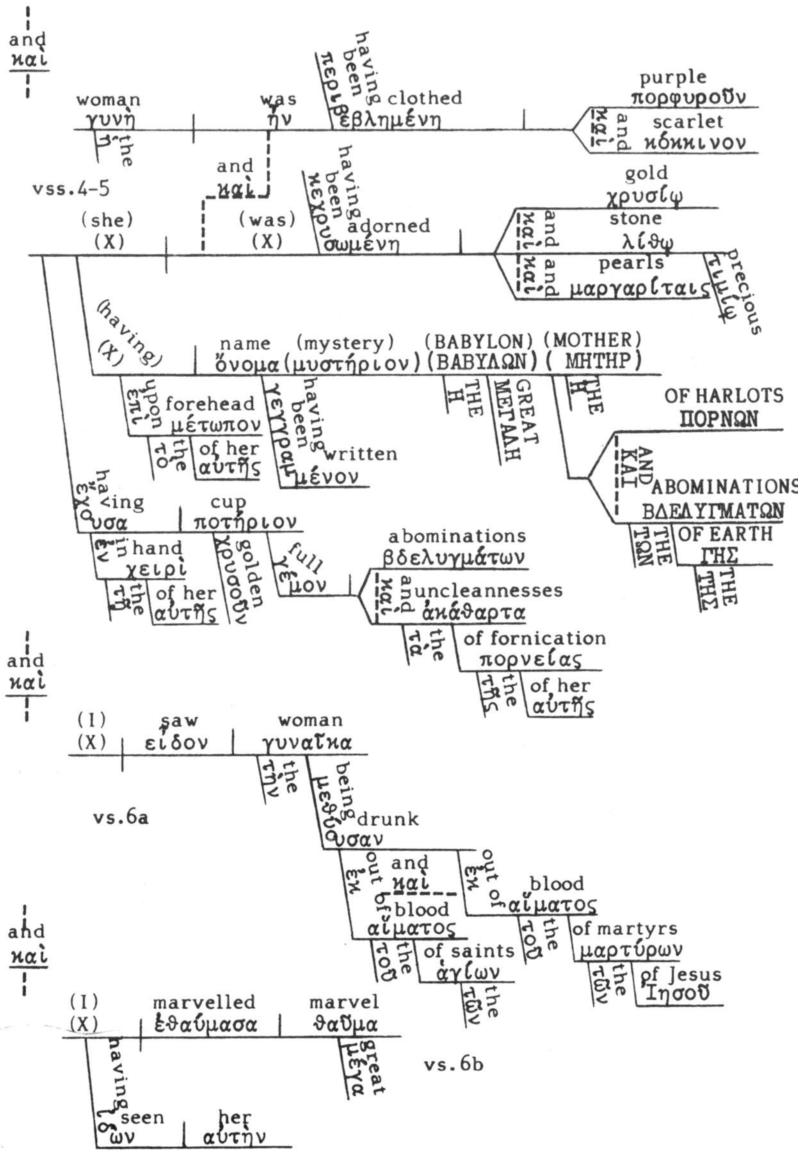
and
καὶ
woman
γυνὴ
the
ἡ
was
ἦν
having been clothed
περιβεβλημένη
purple
πορφυροῦν
and
καὶ
scarlet
κόκκινον
vss.4-5
and
καὶ
(she)
(X)
(was)
(X)
having been adorned
κεχρυσωμένη
gold
χρυσίῳ
and
καὶ
stone
λίθῳ
precious
τιμίῳ
and
καὶ
pearls
μαργαρίταις
(having)
(X)
name
ὄνομα
(mystery)
(μυστήριον)
(BABYLON)
(ΒΑΒΥΛΩΝ)
THE
Η
GREAT
ΜΕΓΑΛΗ
(MOTHER)
( ΜΗΤΗΡ)
THE
Η
OF HARLOTS
ΠΟΡΝΩΝ
AND
ΚΑΙ
ABOMINATIONS
ΒΔΕΛΥΓΜΑΤΩΝ
THE
ΤΩΝ
OF EARTH
ΓΗΣ
THE
ΤΗΣ
upon
ἐπὶ
forehead
μέτωπον
the
τὸ
of her
αὐτῆς
having been written
γεγραμμένον
having
ἔχουσα
cup
ποτήριον
golden
χρυσοῦν
in
ἐν
hand
χειρὶ
the
τῇ
of her
αὐτῆς
full
γέμον
abominations
βδελυγμάτων
and
καὶ
uncleannesses
ἀκάθαρτα
the
τὰ
of fornication
πορνείας
the
τῆς
of her
αὐτῆς
and
καὶ
(I)
(X)
saw
εἶδον
woman
γυναῖκα
the
τὴν
vs.6a
being drunk
μεθύουσαν
out of
ἐκ
blood
αἵματος
the
τοῦ
of saints
ἁγίων
the
τῶν
and
καὶ
out of
ἐκ
blood
αἵματος
the
τοῦ
of martyrs
μαρτύρων
the
τῶν
of Jesus
Ἰησοῦ
and
καὶ
(I)
(X)
marvelled
ἐθαύμασα
marvel
θαῦμα
great
μέγα
vs.6b
having seen
ἰδὼν
her
αὐτὴν

## THE DIAGRAM OF 17:4-6

A sentence with 51 words and as many visible modifiers as verses 4-6a have would surely have at least one dependent clause. But not so. Only two full clauses invade these verses and they both are independent. The sentence is compound. Other than one definite article the first clause has no modifiers. It declares: "The woman had been clothed..." The verb is periphrastic pluperfect constructed of imperfect ἦν and perfect passive participle περιβεβλημένη. A literal translation would be "...was having been clothed..." The perfective-completed action of perfect participle is thrown into the past by the imperfect ἦν. Verbs of clothing or unclothing normally take accusative case. So here both objects, "purple" and "scarlet," are accusative.

The second clause has another periphrastic pluperfect: "was having been adorned." Here too is another compound object, this time a three-fold one; "with gold and precious stone and pearls..." These objects are in the instrumental case, "...adorned with..." "Gold" χρυσίῳ is cognate with the participial part of the verb.

The rest of the sentence consists of two circumstantial participles and their modifiers. First is ἔχουσα "having a golden cup..." The ἐν phrase registers where, "in her hand." Direct object "cup" (ποτήριον) is pictured as "full of abominations and unclean things..." γέμον is neuter participle agreeing with the word it modifies. Verbs of fullnes usually take genitive. Here γέμον has genitive "abominations" as well as accusative "unclean things." This is either an instance of the author's excited carelessness as to grammar or he possibly could have been thinking accusative ἀκάθαρτα was to be another object after ἔχουσα. More likely this is a disregard of grammatical norms.

The second participle is another "having" but this time implied. The ἐπὶ phrase "upon her forehead" tells where. The name was "on her forehead." Agreeing with "name" and in apposition to it is "mystery." That the mystery-name was a fixed part of her character is emphasized by the perfect "having been written." This scarlet woman's person, her essential character, has been carved into her being; it was permanent. Then comes the name, "THE GREAT BABYLON." Such a name aroused memories of the despised city of captivity. In apposition is "THE MOTHER." The kind of mother is seen in the genitives "harlots and abominations..."

Verse 6a encloses a simple sentence. "I saw the woman..." But he saw more than the woman. He "saw the woman being drunken..." Present participle μεθύουσαν is circumstantial, an added predicate assertion about "woman." The source of her drunken condition is pictured in the ἐκ phrases: "out of blood..." The kind of blood is exhibited by the genitives translated "saints" and "martyrs."

Verse 6b embraces another simple sentence. ἰδὼν "seeing her" is 2nd aorist, a temporal circumstantial participle; "when I saw." The main idea is in the clause, "I marvelled a great marvel." θαῦμα is cognate accusative after ἐθαύμασα.

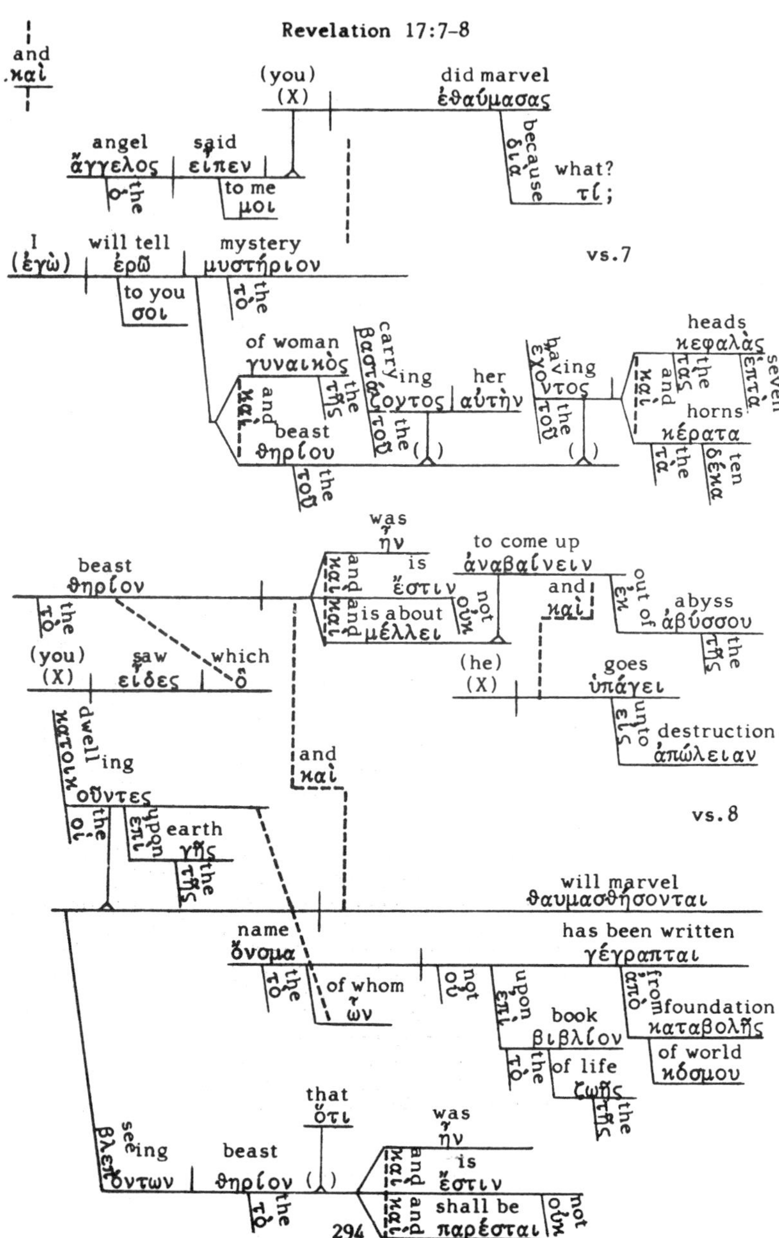
and
καὶ
(you)
(X)
did marvel
ἐθαύμασας
because
διὰ
what?
τί;
angel
ἄγγελος
the
ὁ
said
εἶπεν
to me
μοι
I
(ἐγὼ)
will tell
ἐρῶ
to you
σοι
mystery
μυστήριον
the
τὸ
vs.7
of woman
γυναικὸς
the
τῆς
and
καὶ
beast
θηρίου
the
τοῦ
carry
ing
βαστάζοντος
the
τοῦ
her
αὐτὴν
hav
ing
ἔχοντος
the
τοῦ
heads
κεφαλὰς
the
τὰς
seven
ἑπτὰ
and
καὶ
horns
κέρατα
the
τὰ
ten
δέκα
beast
θηρίον
the
τὸ
was
ἦν
and
καὶ
is
ἔστιν
not
οὐκ
and
καὶ
is about
μέλλει
to come up
ἀναβαίνειν
out of
ἐκ
abyss
ἀβύσσου
the
τῆς
and
καὶ
(he)
(X)
goes
ὑπάγει
unto
εἰς
destruction
ἀπώλειαν
(you)
(X)
saw
εἶδες
which
ὃ
dwell
ing
κατοικοῦντες
the
οἱ
upon
ἐπὶ
earth
γῆς
the
τῆς
and
καὶ
vs.8
will marvel
θαυμασθήσονται
name
ὄνομα
the
τὸ
of whom
ὧν
not
οὐ
has been written
γέγραπται
upon
ἐπὶ
book
βιβλίον
the
τὸ
of life
ζωῆς
the
τῆς
from
ἀπὸ
foundation
καταβολῆς
of world
κόσμου
see
ing
βλεπόντων
beast
θηρίον
the
τὸ
that
ὅτι
was
ἦν
and
καὶ
is
ἔστιν
and
καὶ
shall be
παρέσται
not
οὐκ

## THE DIAGRAM OF 17:7-8

If a sentence is determined by where a question mark or period is placed then two distinct sentences are enfolded in verse seven. The first is a two-clause complex. The independent clause records: "the angel said to me..." Direct object of the verb of the main clause, "said," is the noun clause, "On account of what did you marvel?" διὰ with accusative interrogative pronoun τί "what" may be rendered by the adverb "Why?"

The next sentence continues what the angel "said to me." In a sense it almost seems to be a part of the preceding sentence. It is in fact a continuation of the angel's speech. But after the question mark a new sentence begins. The diagram has a connecting broken line to indicate the close relationship. The new sentence (vs.7b) is simple in form since it has but one full clause. It states: "I will tell you the mystery..." ἐρῶ is future active of εἶπον. The brace of genitives translated "of the woman" and "of the beast" specifies the *kind* of mystery the angel proposes to tell. He purposes to reveal to John the secret about the woman and the beast. Then the "beast" is further identified by two present attributive participles in apposition. He is "the one carrying her" and "the one having seven heads and ten horns."

The scaffolding of verse eight is that of compound-complex. The subject of the first independent clause is θηρίον "beast." It is described by an adjective clause introduced by relative ὃ "which." "The beast which you saw..." The predicate of this first main clause is three-pronged; "was," "is," and "is about to ascend..." Present infinitive ἀναβαίνειν "to come up" "ascend" completes the verb μέλλει "is about..." It is epexegetic. The adverb idea *from where* is inserted by the ἐκ phrase, "out of the abyss." Parallel to the infinitive is the finite verb ὑπάγει "he goes." Preposition εἰς inserts an adverb idea indicating *where* he goes. ὑπάγει is a futuristic present: "he is going to go..."

The second main clause of verse eight has for its subject an articular attributive participle κατοικοῦντες "the ones dwelling..." These earth-dwellers are limited to those of whom the relative ὧν clause speaks. Those "whose name has not been written upon the book of life from the foundation of the world." Perfect tense γέγραπται "has been written" refers to an action which took place at a point in the past the effect of which still stands; "it stands written." The ἐπὶ and ἀπὸ phrases are both adverbial indicating *place where* and *time from whence*. Genitive ζωῆς "life" is appositional genitive; it is the "book" which is life.

Present circumstantial participle "seeing" is temporal "when they were seeing..." "Beast" is object of the participle; it is not subject of the following compound predicate. ὅτι is in apposition to "beast." It's the beast "that was and is not and shall be." Whenever these earth-dwellers see that beast "they will marvel." θαυμασθήσονται is future passive of a verb whose passive is defective. Passive in form; active in meaning, apparently.

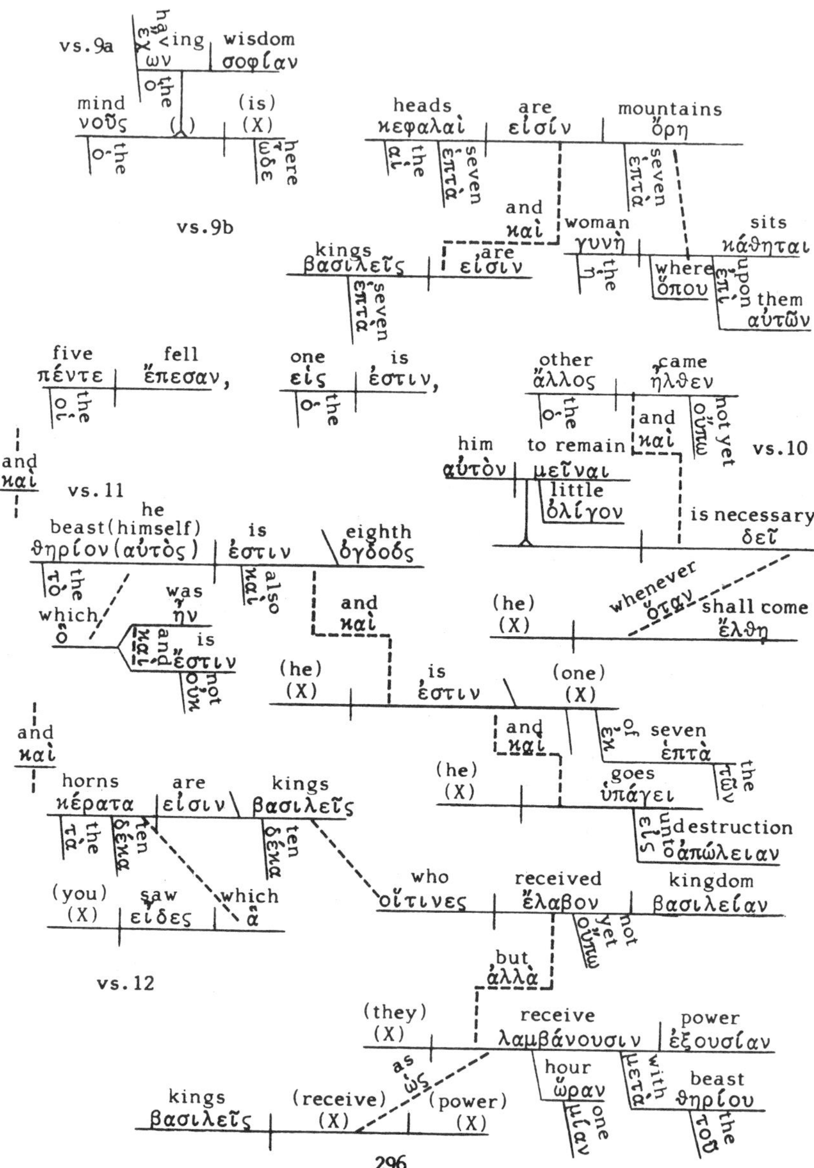
vs.9a
having
ἔχων
wisdom
σοφίαν
the
ὁ
mind
νοῦς
the
ὁ
(is)
(X)
here
ὧδε
vs.9b
heads
κεφαλαὶ
the
αἱ
seven
ἑπτὰ
are
εἰσίν
mountains
ὄρη
seven
ἑπτὰ
and
καὶ
kings
βασιλεῖς
seven
ἑπτά
are
εἰσιν
woman
γυνὴ
the
ἡ
sits
κάθηται
where
ὅπου
upon
ἐπ'
them
αὐτῶν
five
πέντε
the
οἱ
fell
ἔπεσαν,
one
εἷς
the
ὁ
is
ἔστιν,
other
ἄλλος
the
ὁ
came
ἦλθεν
not yet
οὔπω
and
καὶ
vs.10
him
αὐτὸν
to remain
μεῖναι
little
ὀλίγον
is necessary
δεῖ
and
καὶ
vs.11
he
beast (himself)
θηρίον (αὐτὸς)
the
τὸ
is
ἔστιν
eighth
ὄγδοός
also
καὶ
which
ὃ
was
ἦν
and
καὶ
is
ἔστιν
not
οὐκ
and
καὶ
(he)
(X)
whenever
ὅταν
shall come
ἔλθῃ
(he)
(X)
is
ἐστιν
(one)
(X)
of
ἐκ
seven
ἑπτὰ
the
τῶν
and
καὶ
(he)
(X)
goes
ὑπάγει
unto
εἰς
destruction
ἀπώλειαν
and
καὶ
horns
κέρατα
the
τὰ
ten
δέκα
are
εἰσιν
kings
βασιλεῖς
ten
δέκα
(you)
(X)
saw
εἶδες
which
ἃ
who
οἵτινες
received
ἔλαβον
kingdom
βασιλείαν
not yet
οὔπω
but
ἀλλὰ
vs.12
(they)
(X)
receive
λαμβάνουσιν
power
ἐξουσίαν
hour
ὥραν
one
μίαν
with
μετὰ
beast
θηρίου
the
τοῦ
as
ὡς
kings
βασιλεῖς
(receive)
(X)
(power)
(X)

## THE DIAGRAM OF 17:9-12

Verse nine divides into two sentences. The first is simple. It states: "The mind (is) here!" John adds to the subject a participle in apposition. The articular present participle ἔχων with its object defines the "mind" as "the one having wisdom." This is a variation of the same idea as that found in 14:18a.

Verse 9b forms a compound-complex sentence. Of two independent clauses the first avers "the seven heads are mountains..." An adjective clause describes "mountains." It is introduced by the adverb of place ὅπου "where" which here serves also as a conjunction; "...mountains where the woman sits..." The ἐπὶ phrase is redundant; it serves as an added adverb. The second dependent clause, as diagrammed, reads: "and seven kings are." In other words, "there are seven kings." Instead of appearing as attributive under "kings" the "seven" could be placed after the verb as predicate adjective and translated: "kings are seven." The seven mountains represent Rome. The seven kings are successive emperors.

Verse 10 has four independent clauses. No formal connective in the first three. "The five fell, the one is, the other did not yet come..." ἦλθεν is aorist with negative. Greek often uses aorist where English would use perfect, "has not yet come." Attached to this third independent is a fourth connected by καὶ; "and that he remain a little (time) is necessary..." Subject of this clause is aorist infinitive μεῖναι "to remain" with accusative of general reference as its "subject." αὐτὸν is adverbial accusative, extent of time. Supporting this fourth independent clause is the indefinite temporal adverb clause injected by ὅταν "whenever."

Verse 11 boasts of a compound-complex assortment of clauses. The only dependent begins by relative ὃ "which." It is adjectival describing subject "beast." The adjective ὄγδοός "eighth" can then be added as also describing the "beast." But the ὃ clause is attributive in force whereas ὄγδοός is predicate. Precidate adjectives assert something about a subject and can't be left out without bleeding the sentence to death. Attributive adjectives are incidental, which while important, may be left out without destroying the sense of the sentence. The three independent clauses all, with progressive force, help identify the "beast" as one of the seven Roman emperors who eventually is destined for "destruction." They say: "The beast himself is also eighth and he is one of the seven and he goes unto destruction."

The last sentence on this page is complex. The independent idea is: "The ten horns are ten kings..." Subject "horns" is described by adjective clause ushered in by relative ἃ. The horns are those "which you saw." βασιλεῖς is predicate nominate and is described by an adjective clause, the qualitative relative οἵτινες "who by their very nature." It reads: "...who did not yet receive (a) kingdom..." Connected to this by ἀλλὰ is another adjective idea describing "kings," "...but they do receive power..." Accusative ὥραν "hour" is extent of time. The last clause plays the role of adverb, "as (ὡς) kings (receive) (power)."

## Revelation 17:13-15

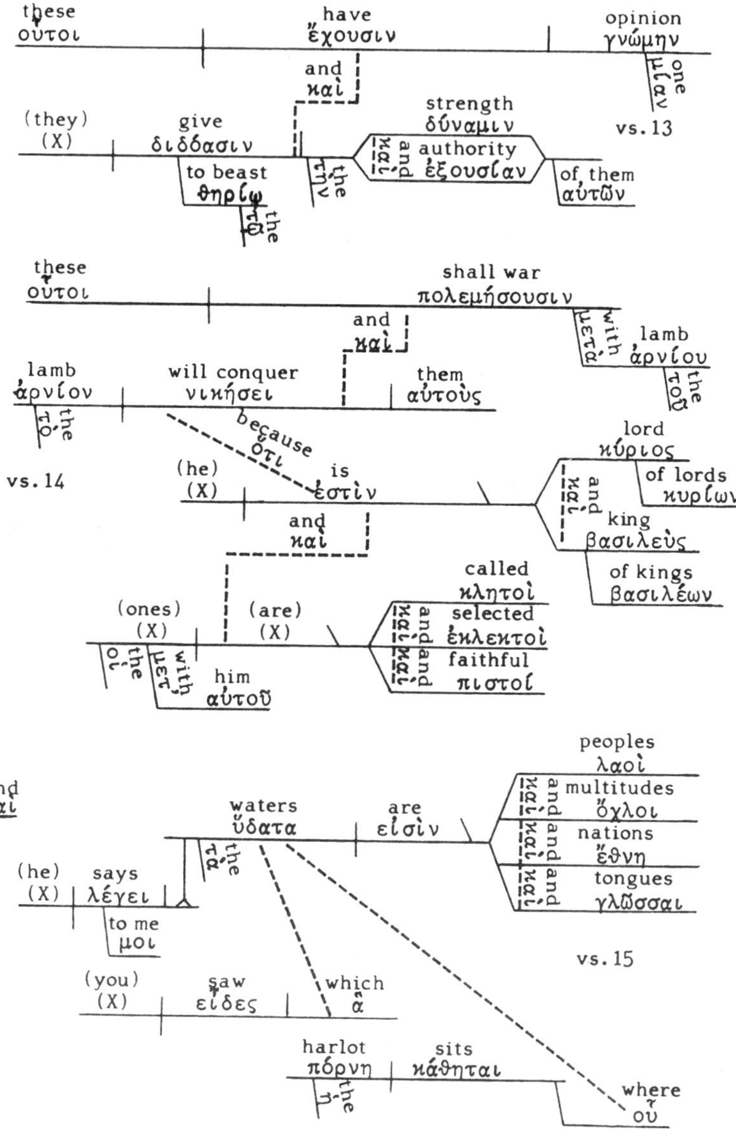

## THE DIAGRAM OF 17:13-15

Two clauses of equal rank constitute a compound sentence. Such is the sentence of verse 13. The first clause announces: "These have one opinion..." The object γνώμην "opinion" has its root in the verb γινώσκω "know." This noun came to mean "mind," "judgment," "opinion," "purpose." The subject οὗτοι "these" refers back to the succession of emperors. They are all of "one purpose," all have the same "mind," they respond to the situation in the same way. Just what way is stated in the next clause, "...and they give to the beast their strength and authority." διδόασιν "give" is present indicative active; the tense is probably best classed as distributive. That is, each in his own turn "gives" his "power and authority" that is in them as persons and as kings. δύναμιν gives attention to the explosive energy within each as a human. ἐξουσίαν refers to whatever power of authority rests in the office occupied. These "give to the beast." They, with "one mind" support the beast.

Verse 14 has four clauses, so arranged as to form a complex sentence. The first makes a statement: "These shall war with the lamb..." Preposition μετὰ with genitive is translated "with." It more frequently means "fellowship with" but on occasion, as here, conveys an idea of hostility. "These make war with (against) the lamb." The second independent clause pursues the outcome of the war by stating, "...the lamb will conquer them..." νικήσει is future indicative. As to action it's punctiliar. As indicative it affirms with positive conviction what is yet to come. He "shall conquer," no doubt about it. Lambs aren't exactly known for their bellicose, warlike traits. But by the indicative the angel left no doubt about the outcome of this war.

Two subordinate clauses support this conviction that "the lamb will conquer." They are inaugurated by ὅτι "because." The clauses function as adverbs of cause. The first contends: "...because he is lord of lords and king of kings..." This reflects what he is in himself. He's the "lords' kind of lord" as well as the "kings kind of king." He's not only "master," he's master of the masters, royalty among the royal. The next of the causal clauses furnishes a second reason why he'll conquer, "...because the ones with him (are) called and selected and faithful." Not only will he conquer because he is what he is in his own nature but also because of those alligned in fellowship with him in this all-out war. The Lord's army is made up of those specially "called," those carefully "selected," and those who are realiable, "trustworthy." Note that the article οἱ used with prepositional phrase μετ' αὐτοῦ "with him" treats that phrase as though it were a substantive, "the with-him ones."

Verse 15 is complex. "He says to me" is the independent element. A noun clause serves as object of the verb λέγει "says." The clause declares: "...the waters are peoples and multitudes and nations and tongues..." The subject "waters" is described by two adjective clauses, "which you saw" and "where the harlot sits."

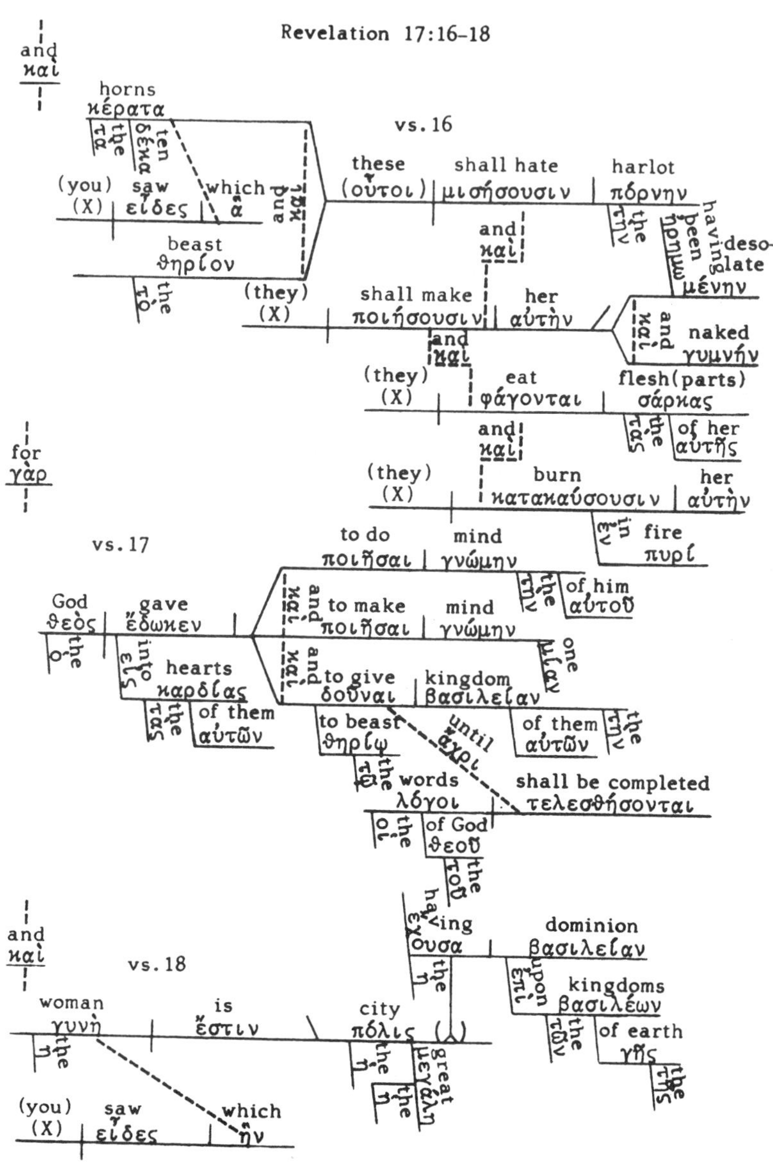
and
καὶ
horns
κέρατα
τὰ
the
δέκα
ten
vs. 16
(you)
(X)
saw
εἶδες
which
ἃ
and
καὶ
these
(οὗτοι)
shall hate
μισήσουσιν
harlot
πόρνην
τὴν
the
having been
ἠρημω
μένην
deso-
late
beast
θηρίον
τὸ
the
and
καὶ
(they)
(X)
shall make
ποιήσουσιν
her
αὐτὴν
and
καὶ
naked
γυμνήν
and
καὶ
(they)
(X)
eat
φάγονται
flesh (parts)
σάρκας
τὰς
the
of her
αὐτῆς
for
γὰρ
and
καὶ
(they)
(X)
burn
κατακαύσουσιν
her
αὐτὴν
ἐν
in
fire
πυρί
vs. 17
to do
ποιῆσαι
mind
γνώμην
τὴν
the
of him
αὐτοῦ
God
θεὸς
ὁ
the
gave
ἔδωκεν
and
καὶ
to make
ποιῆσαι
mind
γνώμην
one
μίαν
εἰς
into
hearts
καρδίας
τὰς
the
of them
αὐτῶν
and
καὶ
to give
δοῦναι
kingdom
βασιλείαν
of them
αὐτῶν
τὴν
the
to beast
θηρίῳ
τῷ
the
until
ἄχρι
words
λόγοι
οἱ
the
of God
θεοῦ
τοῦ
the
shall be completed
τελεσθήσονται
and
καὶ
vs. 18
having
ἔχουσα
ἡ
the
dominion
βασιλείαν
ἐπὶ
upon
kingdoms
βασιλέων
τῶν
the
of earth
γῆς
τῆς
the
woman
γυνὴ
ἡ
the
is
ἔστιν
city
πόλις
ἡ
the
μεγάλη
great
ἡ
the
(you)
(X)
saw
εἶδες
which
ἣν

## THE DIAGRAM OF 17:16-18

The sentence of verse 16 is compound-complex. It possesses four independent clauses. The only dependent modifies one element of the compound subject of the first independent clause. "The ten horns" and "the beast" form that subject. Describing "horns" is the relative (ἃ) adjective clause: "which you saw." The remainder of the sentence consists of the four main clauses. The demonstrative pronoun οὗτοι is in apposition to the compound subject, "horns and beast." The full clause, including all modifiers, reads: "And the ten horns which you saw and the beast, these shall hate the harlot..." μισήσουσιν "shall hate" is future indicative. Indeed, all the verbs of the four independent clauses are future indicatives. The rapid repetition of these indicatives multiplies the force of the positive affirmations. These are prophetic in power proclaiming as a certainty that which is to come.

The second of these clauses adds to its object αὐτὴν "her" a compound objective predicate complement. γυμνὴν "naked" is simple adjective. ἠρημωμένην "having been made desolate," being a participle, is an adjective but its verbal aspects of tense and voice give more impact to the idea. Perfect tense suggests that she has been "made permanently desolate." Passive voice intimates that agencies outside herself (not to mention those within) have worked to make her desolate.

The third clause proposes that "they shall eat her flesh..." The word translated "flesh" (σάρκας) is plural: "the parts of her flesh" they shall canabalize on her flesh, piece by piece. Quite a gruesome picture. The last of the clauses approves the declarations of the other three; "they shall burn her in fire." This sentence is a vivid picture of sin turning in on itself and bringing a just retribution for its own evil. Sin inevitably turns inward and consumes itself.

The sentence of verse 17 makes one statement but with three objects of the one main verb. "God gave..." is the statement. The εἰς phrase indicates where God put what he gave them, "into their hearts." The three objects appear as three aorist infinitives, each with its own direct object. He gave "to do (produce) his mind..." and "to make (have) one mind (the same opinion)" and "to give their kingdom (sovereignty) to the beast..." Infinitve δοῦναι is cognate to the verb. The subordinating conjunction ἄχρι announces a temporal adverb clause: "...until the words of God shall be completed (brought to their intended goal)."

In verse 18 we once again have a complex sentence. It has but two clauses. The independent clause testifies: "And the woman is the city..." Besides the adjective μεγάλη "great" modifying "city" an appositional attributive participle is added to identify more emphatically just who and what this city represents. She is "the one having dominion over (ἐπὶ) the kingdoms of the earth."

The dependent relative clause heralded by ἣν is adjectival descriptive of the subject "woman." "The woman which you saw."

## SOME EXPOSITORY THOUGHTS ON 17:1-18

Before the description of the catastrophic collapse of Rome is painted John is given a vision of the forces at work that lead to that inevitable debacle. Emptying six bowls of God's wrath has portrayed the increasing intensity of punishment on man. Now Rome, the city of Man, is itself to feel the fullness of the wrath. God's methods of bringing his wrath to bear are always the same. Forces within the social order, within historical processes, are his instruments of punishment.

One of the seven bowl-angels invited John: "Come! I will show you the verdict of judgment against the great harlot..." She is identified by three features. First, she is "sitting on many waters." These "many waters" symbolize "peoples and multitudes and nations and tongues."(vs.15) Rome drew her strength from the "many" national and cultural streams that flowed into her coffers. She became the repository of the wealth of her far-flung provinces.

A second feature of the woman was that she was a whore with whom "the kings of the earth fornicated." She wore the gawdy dress of a public prostitute. With brazen impudence she exhibited the jewels of her trade, "gold, precious stone, and pearls." In keeping with the practice of prostitutes she displayed on her forehead her professional name, The Great Babylon, Mother of Harlots." She carried her corruptions in her hand in a "golden cup." Fornication was a part of her every movement. She was not only the recipient of the wealth of the world but was also the source of all abominable corruptions flowing out into all the world.

We are dealing with symbols. Without doubt the "fornication" was literal. But more than that, it is symbolic of the prostitution of man's relationship to the living God by means of the Roman cult of emperor worship. She was the source of this kind of whoredom. She opposed with violence any who resisted her idolatrous whoredom which led her to get "drunk out of the blood of the saints and...martyrs of Jesus." Such a sight overwhelmed John: "I marvelled a great marvel!" How incredible it is to see the persistent enmity of the city of Man against the city of God! Not only in the day of Rome but in the day of Russia - or any other day in this world of rebellion against the divine moral order.

### The symbolism explained!

The angel marvelled that John marvelled. The meaning of the vision might puzzle, indeed, should puzzle, the uninitiated. But to a believer of John's maturity all should be plain. To an eye sensitive to eternal moral principles no amount of grotesque symbolism can hide the end of a corrupt government or an evil society. The consequences of sin is death; the inevitable result of evil is doom. It's as simple as that. But that no misunderstanding arise as to what society and what government was involved in the current judgment the angel explains the symbols. To identify the scarlet woman he draws on the physical setting and political history of Roman emperors, with which John was quite familiar.

"Here is the mind that is shrewd." The "mystery" isn't all that difficult. Be smart! The "seven mountains on which the woman sits" is Rome. Equally plain is reference to seven successive emperors: "the kings are seven;" beginning with Tiberias through Titus and now Domitian, "five fell." That is, five of these reigned, died and are gone. One "is," exists at the present. By leaving Nero out, who according to the redivivus myth, though he died would return alive, we arrive at "the other" who "did not yet come." That would be Nero returned in the person of Domitian who "himself is also eighth; and he is one of the seven." This creates a riddle for modern readers but to those who lived in the first century arena it was quite clear. It was a means of identifying the "beast" of Rome under Domitian's diabolical persecution complex. At the same time it encouraged the Christians to know that he wouldn't survive. It's logical that "he remain a little" time but it is also certain that "he is going unto destruction." No way can the beast win over God.

Besides the beast's "seven kings" another group of kings were enveloped in this war between the dragon and God's Christ. "The ten horns which you saw are ten kings." These weren't independent kings for they had "not yet gotten sovereignty." Yet "for one hour" (a brief time) they did get power with the beast." In other words, these "ten," the complete collection of dependent petty kingdoms and provincial rulers, ruled the Roman empire in conjunction with the beast. These "with one opinion," one united front, one cooperative judgment gave "to the beast their strength and power." Rome ruled because of the power of her provinces. All cooperated with the beast in his "war with the lamb." Rome's enmity to Christ was reflected in the administration of provincial power. But they could not conquer the lamb! Why? For two reasons. (1)Because of the nature of the lamb's authority. "He is lord of lords and king of kings." His is the ultimate, complete, final power. Right rules in the long run. (2)Because "those with him are called, chosen, faithful." He has a select army of trustworthy combatants. They follow faithfully where he leads!

The most startling fact is the revolt of the dragon's own allies. "The ten horns and the beast," the provinces and internal elements in Rome itself, shall turn on Rome and become its final executioner. "These shall hate the harlot." They will isolate her from her allies, "make her desolate." They shall strip her of her resources, "make her naked." They shall "eat of her flesh," ravage themselves on her material and spiritual assets. And "they shall burn her with fire" which literally came to pass. Rome was burned by her own citizens. Moreover, it was "God who gave to their hearts to do his mind...until the words of God be fulfilled." God never sleeps nor does he drouse through man's rebellions. He is ever at work through economic laws, social and psychological principles to right wrongs and bring justice to bear in behalf of his purpose and his people. As that ancient scarlet woman, "the great city" that "held dominion" but betrayed her trust so shall it be in succeeding scarlet governments who turn against God, his Christ and his people.

## A TRANSLATION
### Revelation 18:1-24

After these things I saw another angel coming down out of heaven having great power and the earth was illumined from his glory. And he cried in a loud voice saying, "Fallen, fallen (is) Babylon the Great and it became a habitation of demons, a hold of every unclean spirit and a hold of every unclean bird and hated thing, because all the nations have drunk of the wine of the wrath of her fornication, and the kings of the earth whored with her, and the merchants of the earth got rich out of the strength of her wantonness."

And out of heaven I heard another voice saying, "Come, my people, out of her that you may not share her sins and that you not receive of her plagues; because her sins are piled high unto heaven and God remembered her iniquities. Pay to her as she also paid and double the double according to her works; mix to her double in the cup with which she mixed. Howevermuch she glorified and wantonly indulged herself, by so much give to her torment and mourning. Because in her heart she says, 'I sit, queen and am not a widow and shall not see sorrow,' on account of this, in one day her plagues, death and sorrow and famine, will come; and she shall be burned in fire because strong(is)Lord, the God, the one judging her."

And the kings of the earth, shall weep and mourn over her, the ones having fornicated with her and having wantonly indulged (with her). Whenever they see the smoke of her burning; they will stand from afar because of fear of her torment, saying, "Woe! woe! the great city, Babylon, the mighty city! because in one hour your judging came!"

And the merchants of the earth weep and mourn over her for no one anymore purchases their produce, produce of gold and silver and precious stone and pearls and fine linen and purple and silk and scarlet and every thyine wood and every ivory vessel and every vessel of most precious wood and brass and iron and marble and cinnamon and amomum and incense and ointment and frankincense and wine and oil and fine flour and wheat and cattle and sheep and horses and chariots and bodies and souls of men. And the ripe fruit of the lust of your soul left you and all the dainty and gorgeous things perished from you and they shall not find them ever any more. And the merchants of these (wares), weeping and mourning, shall stand from afar because of the fear of her torment, saying, "The great city, the one having been clothed with fine linen and purple and scarlet and having been decked in gold and precious stone and with pearl, because such wealth was made desolate in one hour."

And every shipowner and every sea-faring passenger and sailors and howevermany trade by sea stood from afar and, seeing the smoke of her burning, were crying, saying, "What is like the great city?" And they threw dust on their heads and, weeping and mourning, they were crying, saying, "Woe! woe! the great city in which all those having ships at sea became rich from her wealth, because she was made desolate in one hour."

## A TRANSLATION
### Revelation 18:1-24
### (continued)

Be rejoicing, heaven and you saints and you apostles and you prophets, because God judged for you a verdict against her.

And a strong angel lifted a stone like a large millstone and he hurled (it) into the sea, saying, "Babylon, the great city, shall be hurled with violence and she shall not ever be found any more." And the sound of harpers and musicians and fluters and trumpeters shall not ever be heard in you any more; and craftsman of every craft shall not be found in you any more and a millstone's sound shall not be found in you any more and light of lamp shall not be found in you any more and bridegroom and bride's voice shall not be heard in you any more; because your merchants were the great ones of the earth; because with your sorcery all the nations were mislead and in her was found blood of prophets and saints and all the ones having been slaughtered on the earth.

## AN OUTLINE OF REVELATION 18:1-24
### Declarations of Doom!

In this vision are included declarations of the fall of the Roman Empire, of the provincial allies, and of the imperial city. The fall of the city of man is commensurate with the extent of its sin. It is paid back in kind and double degree. The millstone of God's justice may grind slowly but it grinds exceedingly fine.

I. DECLARATIONS FROM HEAVEN.
   1. An angel "having great authority." 2
      (a)"Fallen, fallen is Babylon the great!"
      (b)Habitation of "demons, unclean spirit,..hateful bird."
   2. "Voice from heaven." Warning to God's people to withdraw. 4
   3. Strong angel hurled stone into the sea. "The great city shall be hurled with violence; she shall never be found any more." 21
      (a)Arts cease. No more music. 22
      (b)Business & commerce cease. 22
      (c)Home life ceases. 23

II. DECLARATIONS FROM EARTH.
   1. "The kings of the earth who committed fornication with her." The suddenness of the destruction - "in one hour..!"
   2. "Merchants of the earth." Loss of markets for such variety of merchandise. "Such wealth desolated "in one hour."
   3. Sea-faring people. Wealth of the sea gone "in one hour."

The enormity of the judgment staggers the imagination, stupifies the mind of all who see and experience it. But such judgment brings joy to those who believe in the holy righteousness of God. "Be rejoicing, heaven and you saints and apostles and prophets, because God rendered a verdict against her."

God is good; "his righteousness endureth forever."

Revelation 18:1-3

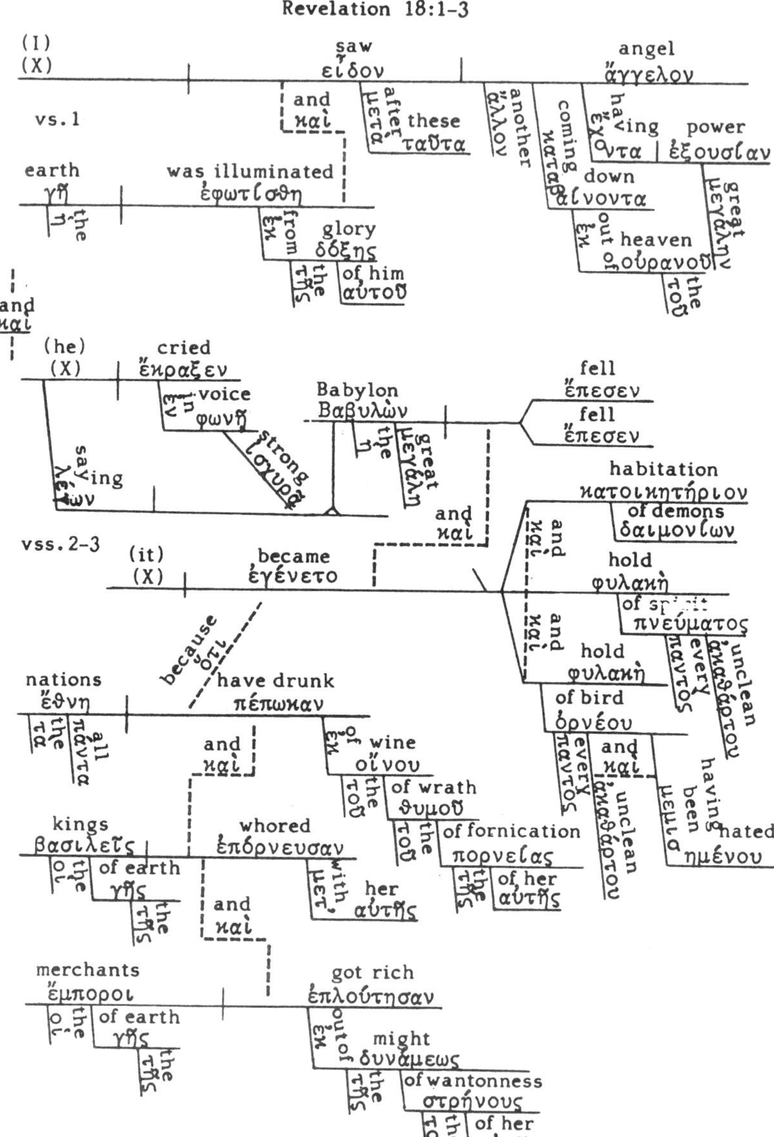

## THE DIAGRAM OF 18:1-3

The prepositional phrase "after these things" plays the role of temporal adverb in 18:1. It moves the narrative to a new stage. The sentence is compound with two clauses. The first states: "After these things I saw another angel..." Added descriptions of "angel" are two predicate participles both present tense, "coming down" and "having power." The ἐκ phrase, "out of heaven" indicates from where the angel was coming, an adverb idea. Another ἐκ phrase performs the same function in the other independent clause, "the earth was illuminated out of his glory."

Verses 2-3 project a complex sentence including five dependent ingredients. "He cried" is the bare announcement made by the sole independent clause. The manner in which he cried is presented in the ἐν phrase, "in a strong voice." The balance of the sentence, in one way or another, is attached to the circumstantial participle λέγων "saying." The first two dependent ideas are direct objects of the participle. "Fallen, fallen (is) Babylon, the great." This is a noun clause, the first object of "saying." It is worth noting that English has difficulty representing the Greek aorist indicative ἔπεσεν "fell." The finite verb, repeated in the predicate, literally reads: "Babylon the great fell, fell!" It ignores the circumstance that the city had not yet fallen and treats the fall as a fact already accomplished. So certain is the issue that the angel leaps into the future after the fact and looks back on it. It is a strong way of presenting prophecy. English seems less awkward with a past participle "fallen."

The next noun clause, also object of "saying," has for its verb ἐγένετο "became." Following it are three predicate nominatives pointing back to and describing the subject "it." Of course the antecedent of "it" is "Babylon" in the preceding clause. Each of these predicate nominatives presents a feature of Babylon that made it fit for falling. It was a "dwelling place," a "prison," and a "prison." Here is an excellent example of the value of the genitive as an important descriptive factor in language. Without genitives "of demons," "of every unclean spirit," and "of every unclean and hated bird" the clause wouldn't actually be saying much. These genitives plainly tell the <u>kind</u> of "habitation" etc.

The final dependent clauses display three reasons why the great Babylon fell and became such a haven for every foul thing. As often, ὅτι introduces an adverbial clause of cause: "...because all the nations have drunk of the wine of the wrath of her fornication." Instead of presenting οἴνου as object of the verb "have drunk" the ἐκ presents the "source" <u>from where</u> she drank. "Wine" is clearly a figure of speech; the genitive θυμοῦ "wrath" defines the kind of wine which the author has in mind. It's the wine which <u>is</u> wrath. Another genitive indicates the kind of wrath, that associated with fornication.

The last two dependent ideas append other causes for Babylon's downfall. "...the kings of the earth whored with her" and "the merchants of the earth got rich from the might of her wantonness."

Revelation 18:4-7a

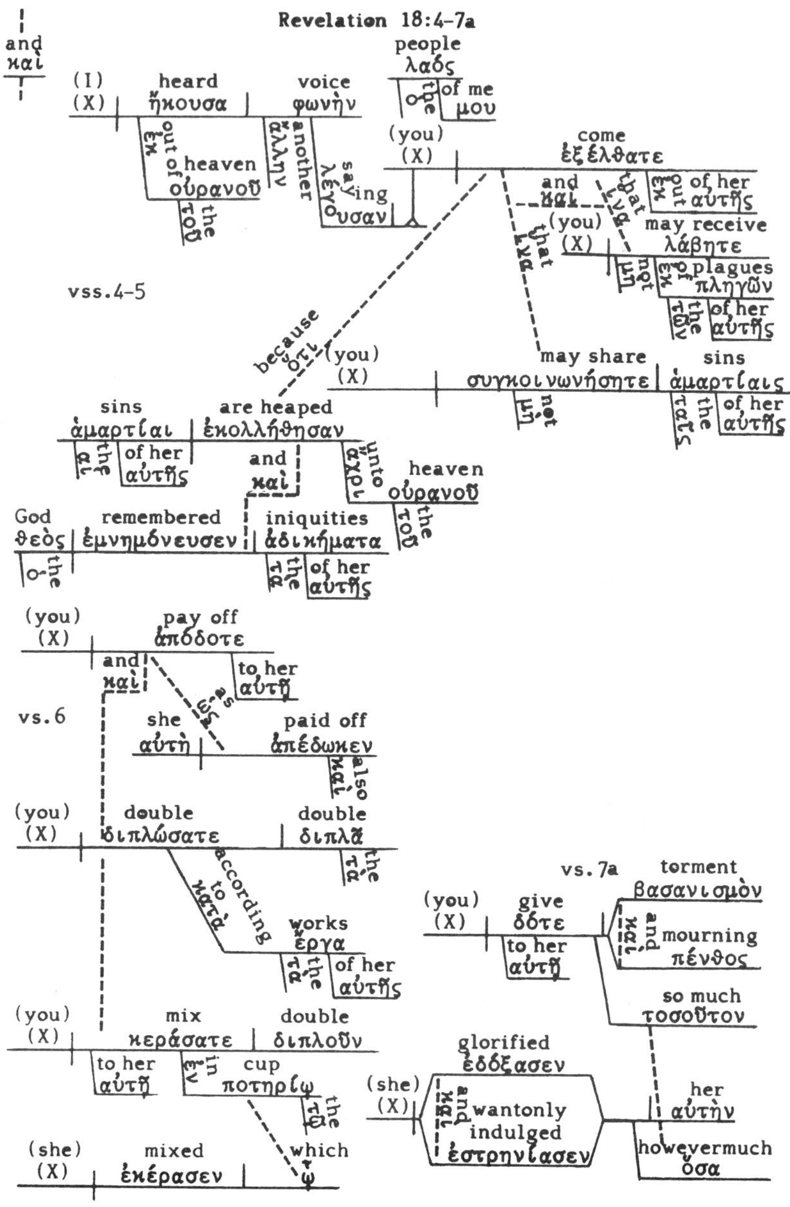

## THE DIAGRAM OF 18:4-7a

"I heard another voice out of heaven..." With this independent clause begins another complex sentence.(vss.4-5) It follows a similar structural pattern as the preceding sentence.(vss.2-3) It too has five dependent clauses. Circumstantial present participle λέγουσαν "saying" is accusative agreeing with the φωνὴν. "Voice" is accusative object of verb of hearing. Accusative, instead of genitive, may suggest that he not only "heard another voice" as a sound but that he heard it with understanding. The expression, ὁ λαός μου "My people" is nominative appearing as vocative. Imperative ἐξέλθατε "Come out," forms the first of the dependent clauses. It is object of the participle "saying."

Two ἵνα "that" clauses are adverbial of purpose: "that you may not share her sins" and "that you may not receive her plagues." συγκοινωνήσητε is a compound word made of preposition σύν "with" joined to κοινωνός "partner." It is aorist subjunctive with negative μὴ, "don't begin to share with." It takes as object associative-instrumental ἁμαρτίαις "sins," after a verb of sharing.

The two ὅτι clauses insert a couple of reasons why God's people should "come out." First, "because her sins are heaped unto heaven." A companion reason is: "because God remembered her iniquities" so as to bring judgment on her. The verb translated "are heaped" is aorist passive of a defective verb, passive in form but apparently active in meaning. "Unto heaven is an adverb idea indicating how much and how far her sins "were heaped." Object ἀδικήματα "iniquities" would normally be genitive after verb of remembering. Here accusative appears.

Verse six embraces a compound-complex arrangement. It has three independent elements and two subordinates. In the first clause aorist ἀπόδοτε "pay off" is imperative. The preposition ἀπό in composition with the simple verb is perfective in force. Not only "pay" but "pay off thoroughly, completely, in full." Perfective use of prepositions with verbs intensifies the meaning in the simple verb. It adds force. ὡς introduces an adverb clause of comparison: "...as she also paid off..."

The intensity with which just vengeance was urged is increased by the second independent idea: "you double the doubles..." The cognate accusative διπλᾶ adds its sharp sting. The prepositional κατὰ "according to" phrase sets up the standard upon which this doubling of repayment should be given: "according to her works."

The third of the independent clauses has no formal conjunction (asydeton) and for that reason is all the more keen, "...you mix double to her..." Where the mixing is done is "in her cup." Also where this doubled mix is to be mixed is set forth in an adjective phrase introduced by relative ᾧ "which."

Verse 7a is a complex with two clauses. The independent urges by aorist imperative δότε "Give to her torment and sorrow..." How much is to be given is pictured in adverb dependent clause ushered in by the indefinite relative ὅσα "howevermuch" and the correlative pronoun τοσοῦτον "by so much as..."

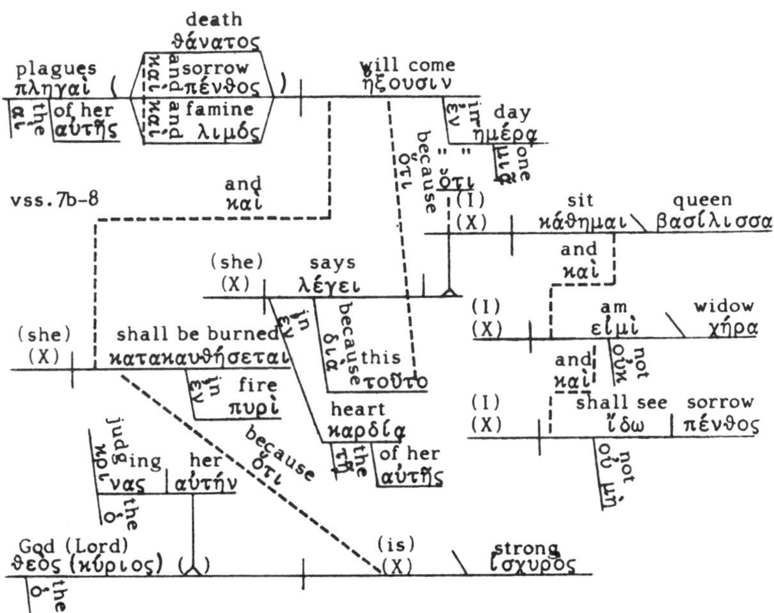
death
θάνατος
plagues
πληγαὶ
and
καὶ
sorrow
πένθος
will come
ἥξουσιν
αἱ
the
of her
αὐτῆς
and
καὶ
famine
λιμός
in
ἐν
day
ἡμέρᾳ
one
μιᾷ
because
ὅτι
" ὅτι "
and
καὶ
vss. 7b-8
(I)
(X)
sit
κάθημαι
queen
βασίλισσα
and
καὶ
(she)
(X)
says
λέγει
(I)
(X)
am
εἰμὶ
widow
χήρα
(she)
(X)
shall be burned
κατακαυθήσεται
in
ἐν
because
διὰ
this
τοῦτο
and
καὶ
not
οὐκ
in
ἐν
fire
πυρὶ
heart
καρδίᾳ
(I)
(X)
shall see
ἴδω
sorrow
πένθος
judging
κρίνας
her
αὐτήν
because
ὅτι
the
τῇ
of her
αὐτῆς
not
οὐ μὴ
the
ὁ
God (Lord)
θεὸς (κύριος)
(is)
(X)
strong
ἰσχυρὸς
the
ὁ

## THE DIAGRAM OF 18:7b-8

Two independent clauses of 18:7b-8 instill into the sentence the compound feature. They reveal the ghastly destiny which is coming on the wicked city of man. They say: "Her plagues...will come" and "she shall be burned in fire..." The general idea of "plagues" is spelled out in more specific detail by three nouns in apposition to the subject, plagues. They are: "death," "sorrow," and "famine." ἐν with locative forms an adverbial modifier expressing time, "in one hour." However, it's not extent of time as accusative would be but a point of time, a point within which "her plagues will come." And the point of time hints at the suddenness also with which the plagues will come. The second independent clause has but one modifier, an adverbial phrase, "in fire." That's the manner in which "she shall be burned." The preposition κατά "down" in composition with the verb "burn" is perfective in force. It brings in the idea of burning "thoroughly," "utterly," "completely." "She shall be utterly burned..."

Five subordinate clauses infuse the sentence with the complex quality. The sentence is thus compound-complex. The first of the dependents is formally announced by ὅτι "because." It is an adverb clause of cause detailing why the plagues will come: "because she says..." However, in the text the author gives his thought in a variation of Isaiah 47:8. And by the time he's made that allusion he has forgotten his ὅτι. So he starts his clause again, this time with διὰ τοῦτο "on account of this," another causal connecting phrase. The diagram places the ὅτι on the usual slanting line and the διὰ phrase below the verb of the clause, "he says."

The next three of the dependents are noun clauses direct objects of the verb "says." They represent three arrogant boasts of security: "I sit (as) queen and I am not a widow and I shall not see sorrow." The words translated "queen" and "widow" are predicate nominatives referring back to their respective subjects. But πένθος "sorrow" is neuter accusative direct object of ἴδω "shall see" with the strong double negative οὐ μὴ.

The final of the dependent clauses is another ὅτι adverb clause of cause: "...because the Lord God, the one judging her(is)strong." The predicate adjective ἰσχυρὸς "strong" is placed first in the text, the position of the strongest emphasis. Whether "Lord" or "God" is subject is a matter of judgment. Whichever is subject the other is in apposition to it. The diagram treats "God" as subject because of the presence of the definite article with it. Then there is added another apposition, the attributive aorist active participle κρίνας "the one judging." A diagram shows with vividness relationships but it doesn't always preserve the emphasis of the text.

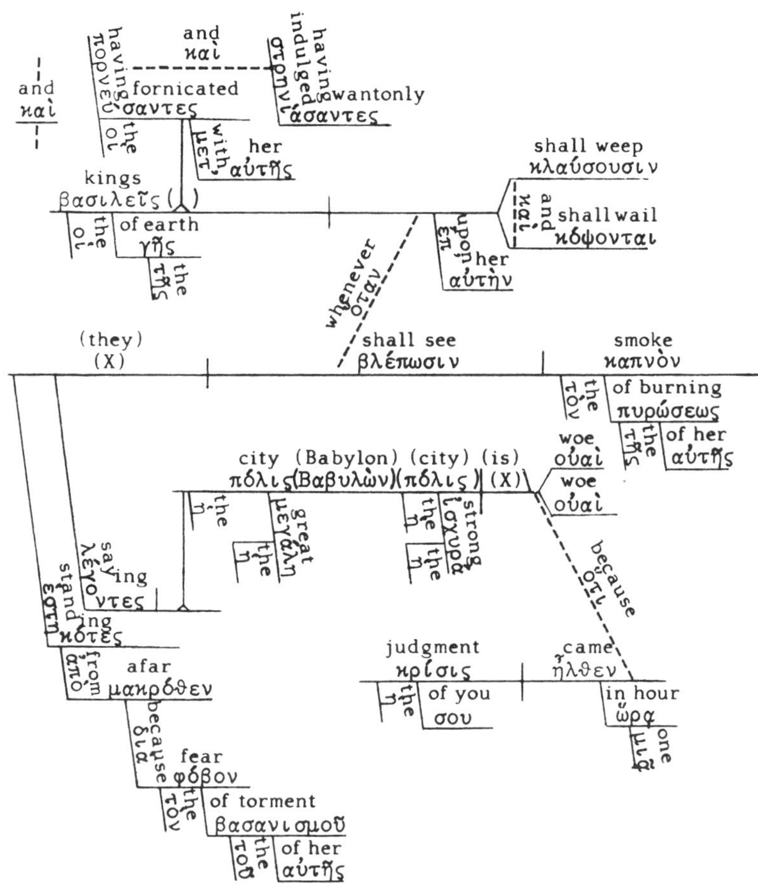
and
καὶ
having fornicated
πορνεύσαντες
the
οἱ
and
καὶ
having indulged wantonly
στρηνιάσαντες
with
μετ'
her
αὐτῆς
kings
βασιλεῖς
the
οἱ
of earth
γῆς
the
τῆς
shall weep
κλαύσουσιν
and
καὶ
shall wail
κόψονται
upon
ἐπ'
her
αὐτὴν
whenever
ὅταν
(they)
(X)
shall see
βλέπωσιν
smoke
καπνὸν
the
τὸν
of burning
πυρώσεως
the
τῆς
of her
αὐτῆς
city (Babylon) (city) (is)
πόλις (Βαβυλὼν) (πόλις) (X)
the
ἡ
great
μεγάλη
the
ἡ
the
ἡ
strong
ἰσχυρά
the
ἡ
woe
οὐαὶ
woe
οὐαὶ
because
ὅτι
saying
λέγοντες
standing
ἑστηκότες
from
ἀπὸ
afar
μακρόθεν
because
διὰ
fear
φόβον
the
τὸν
of torment
βασανισμοῦ
the
τοῦ
of her
αὐτῆς
judgment
κρίσις
the
ἡ
of you
σου
came
ἦλθεν
in hour
ὥρᾳ
one
μιᾷ

## THE DIAGRAM OF 18:9-10

"The kings shall weep and wail..." Such is the bedrock idea around which the sentence of verses 9-10 forms. This, therefore, is the sole independent clause of this complex sentence. Which kings shall do the weeping and mourning are specified by the genitive γῆς "of the earth." Where and why they shall wail find expression in επ' αὐτὴν "upon (over) her." Two aorist participles translated "the ones having fornicated with her and having indulged wantonly are in apposition with the subject "kings." Repetition of definite article οἱ with "kings" and the participles not only helps relate these epithets to each other but also makes each stand out distinctly, "the kings, the ones who fornicated...and indulged wantonly."

The rest of the sentence involves two circumstantial participles and three dependent clauses. The first of the dependents is ushered in by the indefinite ὅταν "whenever." Thus it is an adverb clause of time. It answers the question as to when the kings shall weep and wail: "...whenever they shall see the smoke of her burning." πυρώσεως "burning" is an action noun as are all nouns ending in -σις. αὐτῆς is objective genitive after an action noun.

The first of the two participles is ἑστηκότες "standing." It describes these "kings of the earth" as "standing from afar..." The "from afar" (ἀπό) expression is adverbial telling where they were standing. Why they were thus standing is seen in the διά phrase, "on account of the fear." What kind of fear? Genitive βασανισμοῦ "of her torment" answers this question. αὐτῆς is another objective genitive. It's the torment of which "she" (her) is the object.

The second circumstantial participle is λέγοντες "saying." As direct object of the participle a noun clause appears: "...the city, the great (one), Babylon, the strong (one) (is) woe, woe..." The clause does not say: "Woe (be) to the city..." It's not a prediction of woe. It's a factual statement of the condition of the city: "the city is woe!" The appositionals "Babylon, the strong city," not only help identify the city but they focus the spotlight even more intensely on the city.

The final clause of the sentence is an adverb clause of cause, another ὅτι clause: "because your judgment came in one hour." Once again an objective genitive appears after an action word, σου "of you" after κρίσις "judgment." The "you" is the object of the judging. The conflagration of such a large and impressive city of the world as was Rome might easily have been a subject of detailed vivid description. But aorist ἦλθεν "came" (happened) sets forth the destruction as a point, a matter of fact. Description may come later but for the present it's the suddenness and the fact that is important. This point idea is further enforced by instrumental case ὥρᾳ, point of time, "in one hour" rather than an accusative, extent of time.

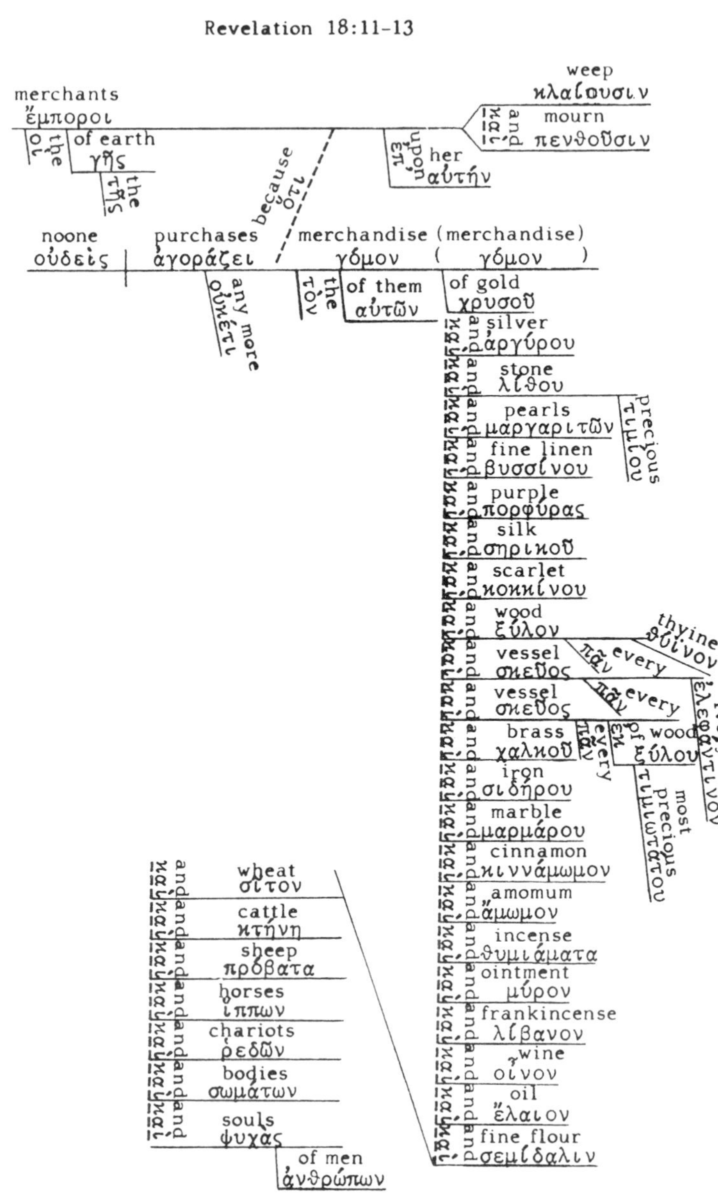
Revelation 18:11-13
and
καὶ
merchants
ἔμποροι
the
οἱ
of earth
γῆς
the
τῆς
weep
κλαίουσιν
and
καὶ
mourn
πενθοῦσιν
upon
ἐπ'
her
αὐτήν
because
ὅτι
noone
οὐδεὶς
purchases
ἀγοράζει
any more
οὐκέτι
merchandise (merchandise)
γόμον ( γόμον )
the
τὸν
of them
αὐτῶν
of gold
χρυσοῦ
silver
ἀργύρου
stone
λίθου
precious
τιμίου
pearls
μαργαριτῶν
fine linen
βυσσίνου
purple
πορφύρας
silk
σηρικοῦ
scarlet
κοκκίνου
wood
ξύλον
thyine
θύϊνον
vessel
σκεῦος
every
πᾶν
vessel
σκεῦος
every
πᾶν
ivory
ἐλεφάντινον
brass
χαλκοῦ
every
πᾶν
of
ἐκ
wood
ξύλου
most precious
τιμιωτάτου
iron
σιδήρου
marble
μαρμάρου
cinnamon
κιννάμωμον
amomum
ἄμωμον
incense
θυμιάματα
ointment
μύρον
frankincense
λίβανον
wine
οἶνον
oil
ἔλαιον
fine flour
σεμίδαλιν
wheat
σῖτον
cattle
κτήνη
sheep
πρόβατα
horses
ἵππων
chariots
ῥεδῶν
bodies
σωμάτων
souls
ψυχὰς
of men
ἀνθρώπων

## THE DIAGRAM OF 18:11-13

One independent clause and one dependent make verses 11-13 a complex sentence. After relating the reaction of "the kings" to the fall of Rome the author turns his attention to that of "the merchants." The independent idea is: "The merchants of the earth weep and mourn upon (over) her..." The verbs "weep" and "mourn" are present tense, probably dramatic presents so vivid was the scene as though it were even then before their eyes.

The underlying cause why the merchants weep and mourn is set forward in the adverbial ὅτι dependent:"...because no one any more purchases their merchandise." The noun γόμον "cargo" derives from the verb γέμω "be full." The verb referred particularly to a "full ship's cargo." The "cargo" listed in verses 12-13 was transported to Rome in ships. This was their "merchandise," that which made the merchants of Rome wealthy.

A second γόμον is in apposition to the first. Then begins a list of genitives that give specifics as to the kinds of merchandise the merchants of Rome traded. The pattern of genitives is interspersed with some accusatives. The list of identifying modifiers, for the most part, are single words. The list includes 29 commodities. Five of them are themselves modified by an added word or phrase; they include: "precious stone," "every thyine wood," "every ivory vessel," "every vessel of precious wood," and "souls of men."

This sentence is classed as complex. Its two clauses are quite simply and clearly arranged. The only thing unusual is the long list of modifiers detailing the γόμον "merchandise" in particular. These commodities reveal the widespread basis of Roman trade and commerce with the world community. They reflect the necessities and luxuries of a "this-world" society. These are the items with which the merchants of the world committed whoredom with the great harlot.

## Revelation 18:14-17a

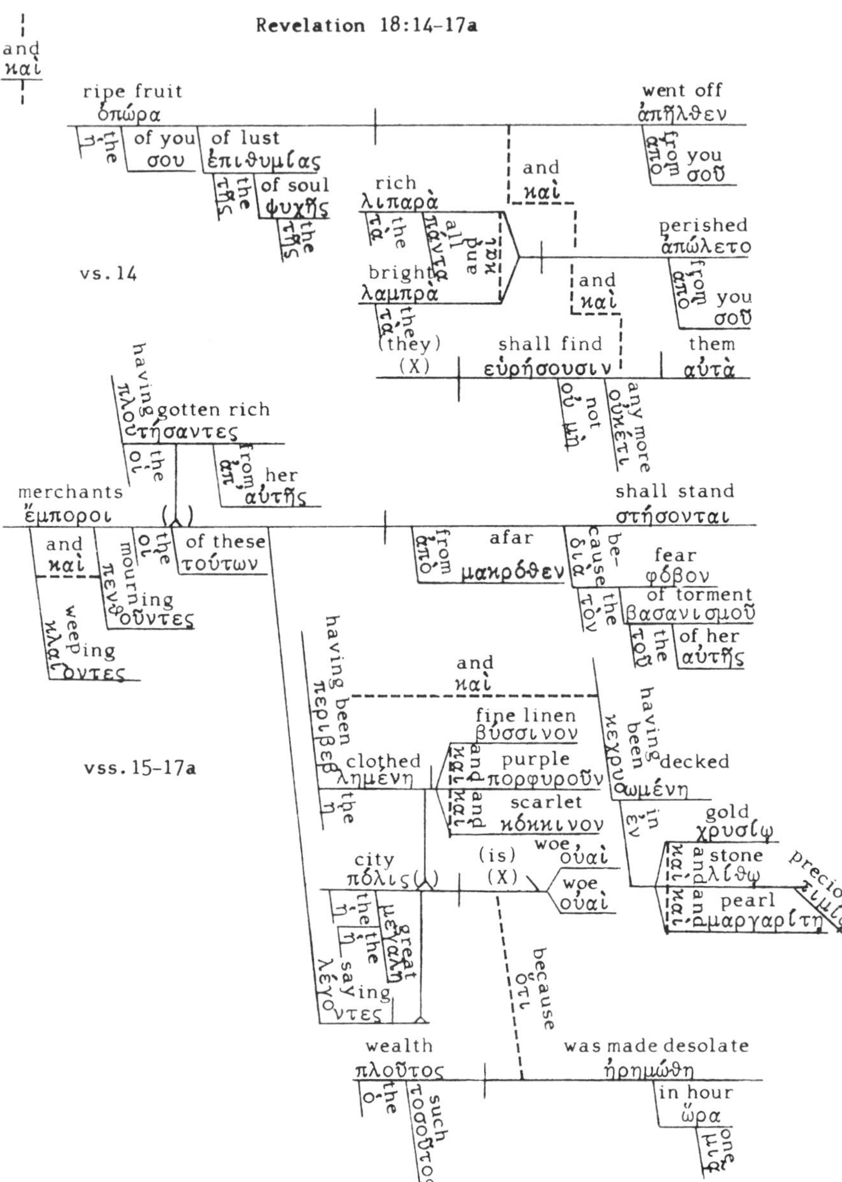

## THE DIAGRAM OF 18:14-17a

Three distinct clauses of equal rank form a compound sentence of verse 14. The first clause, shorn of its modifiers, attests: "ripe fruit...departed..." ὀπώρα "ripe fruit" appears only here in the New Testament. It refers to the "ripe fruit" that comes at the peak of a season; ripe autumn fruit; that stage when life is at its full strength, bursting with full energy. Both genitives σου "of you" and ἐπιθυμίας "of lust" specify details that help identify the particular fruit under consideration. It's the "glutted energy" that is the harlot's. It's also the desire (lust) of her soul at the peak of her energies for whoredom. The idea may be paraphrased: "the flush period of the lust of life," that time in the flush of life when energies are focused on sensual, material pleasures. This "went off from you..." ἀπὸ with ablative means that this period is once and for all (aorist) separated "from you."

The second clause has a compound subject, "rich and bright..." λιπαρὰ is neuter plural; the root of the noun contains the idea of "grease," "fat." Here it refers to "refined, rich, dainty foods." The root idea in λαμπρὰ is "bright," "shining," "brilliant." Here it alludes to the richly woven, gaudy, expensive clothing with which the harlot decorated herself. It too once-and-for-all "perished (another aorist) from you."

The most distinctive feature of the third clause is the repetition of strong negatives οὐ μὴ and οὐκέτι. English won't tolerate double negatives. But this "not never" is not only permissible but is the very strongest negative Greek produces.

Verses 15-17a frame a complex. Besides its independent there are two dependent clauses. The independent affirms: "The merchants shall stand..." What merchants? It's "these merchants, the ones having gotten rich from her..." This articular attributive participle is in apposition with subject "merchants." What's their bearing, their conduct, their manner and attitude while they stand? It's "weeping and mourning." These two present participles are circumstantial of manner and/or time. And where are they standing? "...afar off" answers that question. And why are they thus standing? "Because (διὰ) of the fear of her torment." Again we note αὐτῆς as objective genitive.

The two dependent clauses stem off the circumstantial participle λέγοντες "saying." First is the noun clause, direct object: "the city, the great (one) (is) woe..." In apposition to the subject "city" is a pair of attributive participial phrases: "the one having been clothed...and having been decked out." That in which she's "decked out" is expressed in an ἐν phrase: "in gold and precious stone and pearl." The singular of "stone" and "pearl" seems to be a collective idea. The earlier of these participles "having been clothed" has a triple-pronged compound direct object: "fine linen and purple and scarlet." These are accusatives after a verb of clothing.

The ὅτι clause brings in an adverb clause of cause: "because such wealth was made desolate in one hour." This is the reason for the "woe."

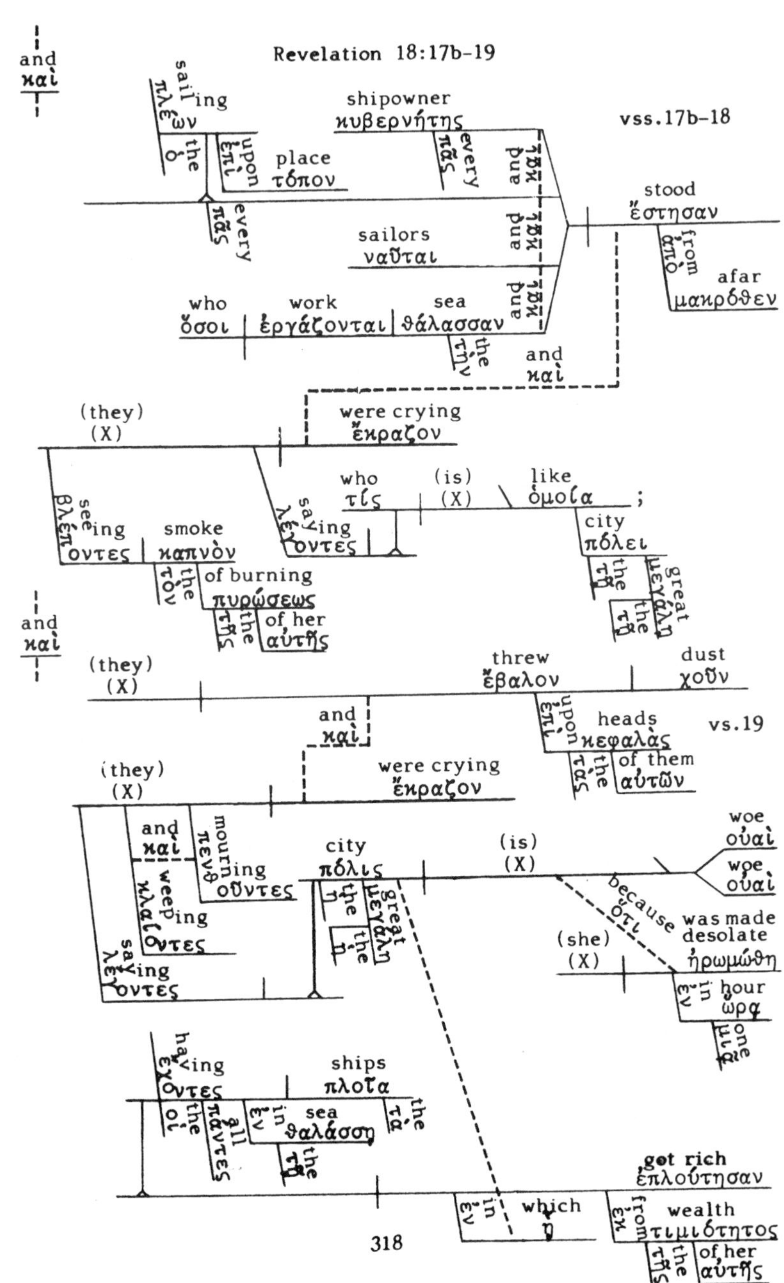
and
καὶ
sail
ing
πλέ ων
the
ὁ
upon
ἐπὶ
place
τόπον
every
πᾶς
shipowner
κυβερνήτης
every
πᾶς
and
καὶ
vss.17b-18
stood
ἔστησαν
from
ἀπὸ
afar
μακρόθεν
sailors
ναῦται
and
καὶ
who
ὅσοι
work
ἐργάζονται
sea
θάλασσαν
the
τὴν
and
καὶ
(they)
(X)
were crying
ἔκραζον
see
ing
βλέπ οντες
smoke
καπνὸν
the
τὸν
of burning
πυρώσεως
the
τῆς
of her
αὐτῆς
say
ing
λέγ οντες
who
τίς
(is)
(X)
like
ὁμοία
;
city
πόλει
the
τῇ
great
μεγάλῃ
the
τῇ
and
καὶ
(they)
(X)
threw
ἔβαλον
dust
χοῦν
upon
ἐπὶ
heads
κεφαλὰς
the
τὰς
of them
αὐτῶν
vs.19
and
καὶ
(they)
(X)
were crying
ἔκραζον
and
καὶ
mourn
ing
πενθ οῦντες
weep
ing
κλαί οντες
say
ing
λέγ οντες
city
πόλις
the
ἡ
great
μεγάλη
the
ἡ
(is)
(X)
woe
οὐαὶ
woe
οὐαὶ
because
ὅτι
(she)
(X)
was made desolate
ἠρημώθη
in
ἐν
hour
ὥρᾳ
one
μιᾷ
hav
ing
ἔχ οντες
the
οἱ
all
πάντες
in
ἐν
sea
θαλάσσῃ
the
τῇ
ships
πλοῖα
the
τὰ
got rich
ἐπλούτησαν
in
ἐν
which
ᾗ
from
ἐκ
wealth
τιμιότητος
the
τῆς
of her
αὐτῆς

## THE DIAGRAM OF 18:17b-19

Two independent units of thought shape the sentence of 18:17b-18 though two dependents appear in the course of the developing thought. Thus it is classed as compound-complex.

The subject of the first clause is compound made up of four members. All four relate to those who, in one way or another, derive their livelihood from the sea. κυβερνήτης is a "pilot" or "steersman." Nouns ending in -της are agent nouns. This word is of the same root as the verb κυβερνάω "to guide." So the agent who does the guiding on a ship is the "pilot." This may or may not be the owner. The second subject is attributive participle πλέων "the one sailing upon (to) a (particular) place." This is he who boards a ship to travel to a particular port on specific business. The general term of "sailors" is the third item of the subject. The final element of the subject is a relative clause: "however many are working the sea..." ὅσοι is quantitative relative "howevermany." This group would include fishermen, divers, ship-builders, etc. The clause states that all these "stood from afar..."

The second independent clause describes what they were doing as they "stood from afar." They "were crying..." The imperfect ἔκραζον draws an animated picture of their "crying." Besides, each of the four groups, in his own way and time(distributive idea), "was crying". Describing the subject "they" are two circumstantial participles. "Seeing the smoke of her burning" is probably best classed as temporal, "as they were seeing..." It may also include cause, "because they were seeing." Participle "saying" has a noun clause as its object: "who is like the city, the great (one)?" Words of likeness take the instrumental case. πόλει is instrumental.

The sentence of verse 19 also follows the compound-complex pattern. It has two independent and three dependent clauses. The independent elements state: "They threw dust..." and "they were crying..." "Upon their heads" tells <u>where</u> they were throwing the dust. That's an adverbial idea.

"Weeping" and "mourning" are two circumstantial participles that describe the "they," subject of the second independent clause. They suggest the manner in which the "crying" was conducted. A third such participle is "saying" which has for its direct object a noun clause: "the city, the great (one) (is) woe, woe!" Once again a reason for the "woe" is instigated by causal ὅτι "because she was made desolate in one hour." That, of course, is a subordinate adverb clause. Yet another dependent clause, this time adjectival, is proposed by ἐν ῇ "in which." It describes the noun "city." As subject of this clause is the articular attributive participle "the ones having"(ἔχοντες). The phrase "in the sea" is used as an adverb since it tells <u>where</u> they were having the ships. The verb of the clause "got <u>rich</u>" is aorist, point action. It's the fact of their getting rich that is the point, not a description of the process, hence the aorist. ἐκ with ablative "from her wealth" indicates the source of the seafarers' wealth.

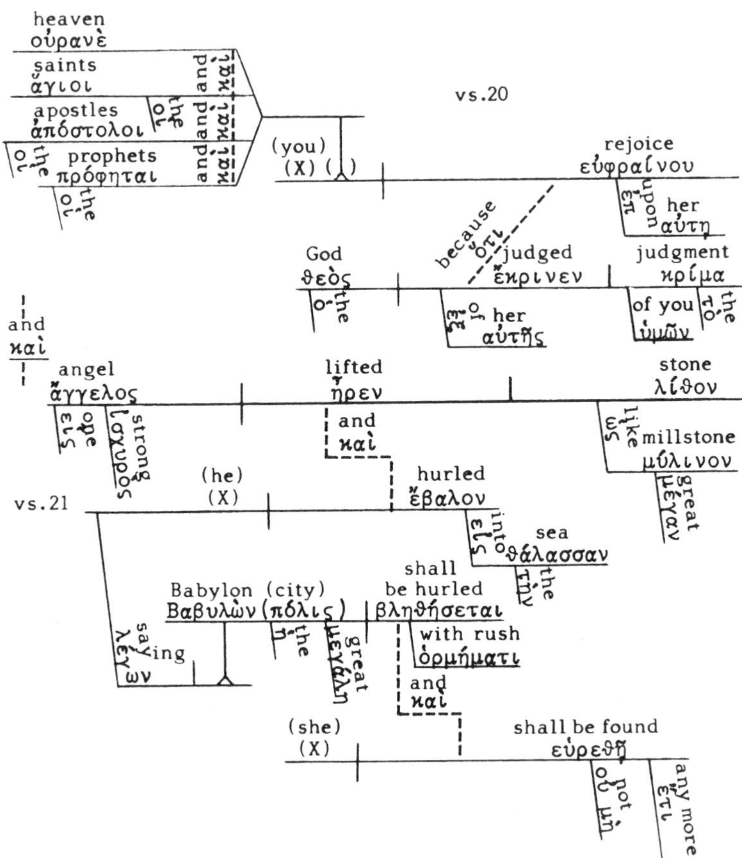
heaven
οὐρανὲ
saints
ἅγιοι
apostles
ἀπόστολοι
prophets
προφῆται
and καὶ
the οἱ
vs.20
(you)
(X)
rejoice
εὐφραίνου
upon ἐπ
her
αὐτῇ
because ὅτι
God
θεὸς
the ὁ
judged
ἔκρινεν
of ἐξ
her
αὐτῆς
judgment
κρίμα
of you
ὑμῶν
the τὸ
and
καὶ
angel
ἄγγελος
one εἷς
strong
ἰσχυρὸς
lifted
ἦρεν
stone
λίθον
like ὡς
millstone
μύλινον
great
μέγαν
and
καὶ
(he)
(X)
hurled
ἔβαλον
into εἰς
sea
θάλασσαν
the τὴν
vs.21
saying
λέγων
Babylon (city)
Βαβυλὼν (πόλις)
the ἡ
great
μεγάλη
shall
be hurled
βληθήσεται
with rush
ὁρμήματι
and
καὶ
(she)
(X)
shall be found
εὑρεθῇ
not
οὐ μὴ
any more
ἔτι

## THE DIAGRAM OF 18:20-21

Verse 20 enfolds two clauses, an independent and a dependent. Thus the sentence is complex. The verb of the main clause is present active imperative, "rejoice." Linear action signifies to "go on rejoicing." It is singular with "you" as subject. But the "you" is in apposition to a compound construction of four parts. First is vocative οὐρανὲ "heaven" with no article. The speaker addresses "heaven" for what it is, its nature. Then he divides those heavenly citizens into three particulars each with its distinct article: "the saints," the apostles," "the prophets." Apparently "heaven" (singular) encompasses these three groups as the ones called upon to "be rejoicing..." Heaven may have other inhabitants, angels, powers, principalities, etc. but this appeal is to those with whom the judgment pronounced has to do, those persecuted by the anti-christian harlot of this world.

The reason why heaven's citizens are exhorted to "rejoice" is set forth in the adverb ὅτι clause, "...because God judged the verdict of judgment (pertaining to) you (exacted) from her." The genitive ὑμῶν "of you" characterizes the verdict of judgment as relating "to you." Just what that relationship is must be determined by the context. ἐξ with ablative αὐτῆς is "from her" in the sense that the resulting judgment of God is demanded "from her," the harlot city. κρίμα is a result noun. It isn't the proceedure of judgment but the resulting verdict pronounced by the the judge.

Verse 21 unveils a compound-complex sentence. It accommodates two independent clauses and two dependents. Greek does not have an indefinite article. Sometimes the cardinal εις in its use almost has the force of "a" but is never quite the same. However, here εις appears to have its full force as a numeral. "One strong angel lifted stone like a great millstone." The fact that the stone was "great" is matched by the fact that, not just any angel, but "one particular strong angel" lifted it up. The second of the independent ideas relates what he did with the stone. "He hurled (it) into the sea."

That the action portrayed in the independent elements of the sentence is symbolic is confirmed by what the "strong angel" said. The circumstantial participle λέγων "saying" ushers in the dependent ideas. They consist of two noun clauses, direct objects of the participle: "Babylon, the great city, shall be hurled with a violent rush and she shall not ever be found any more." ὁρμήματι "rush" is instrumental of a -μα word. It is built off of verb ὁρμάω to "set in motion, urge on, rush." The result of the action in the verb is the creation of a "big splash," a "violent swish." In view of the fact the angel hurls this huge stone into a sea "big splash" conveys the idea quite well. The city will sink from view forever like a mountainous rock flung into an ocean. History confirms this. Any world power that violates its divine trust to govern righteously perishes from the earthly scene whether it be Aztec, Rome or Russia.

# Revelation 18:22-24

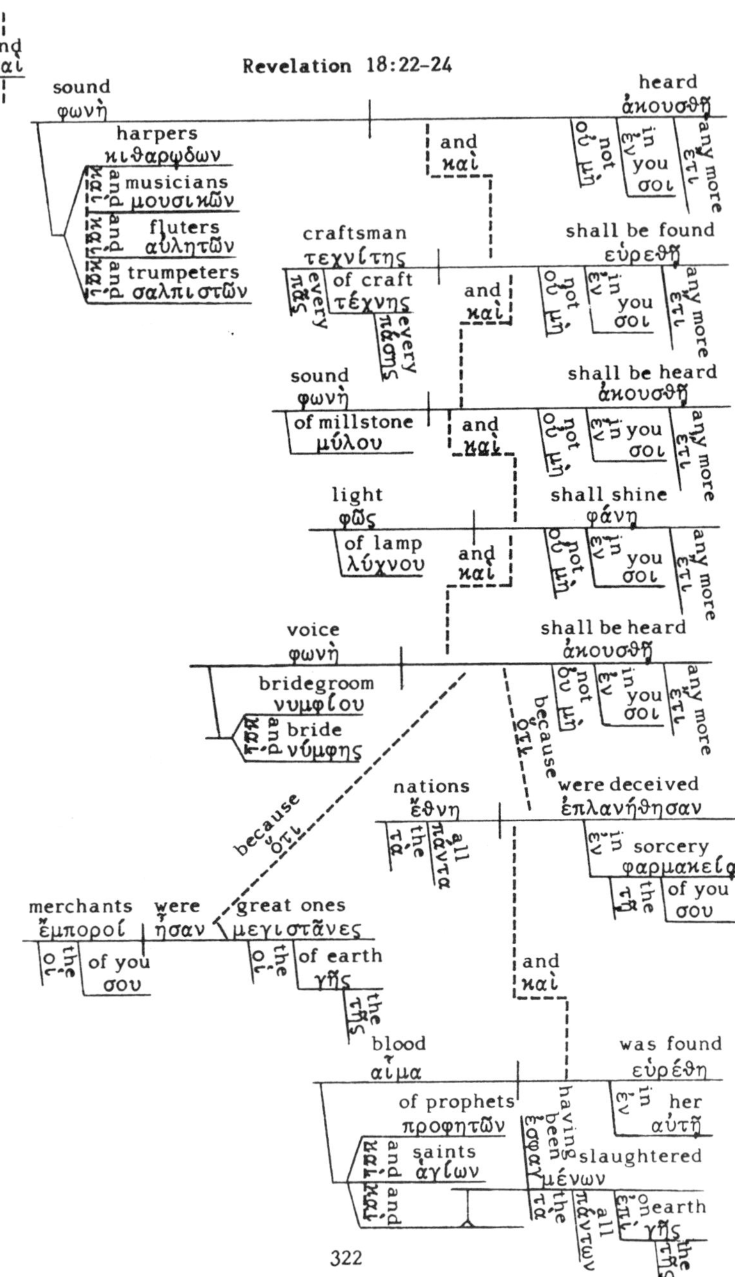

## THE DIAGRAM OF 18:22-24

The sentence of 18:22-24 consists of 88 words organized around eight clauses. The first five are independent; the last three are dependent. Thus, as to form, it is compound-complex.

In the five independent clauses the author sketches the falling apart of a whole civilization. Typical ingredients disappear from view. They include the arts, crafts, food, light and marriage. They are representative of man's culture. First, the arts! "The voice of harpers and musicians and fluters and trumpeters shall not be heard in you any more..." ἀκουσθῇ is aorist passive subjunctive with strong double negative plus adverb ἔτι "still" or "any more." With one exception (φάνῃ) this form of subjunctive appears in all five clauses along with both double negative and ἔτι. In this first of the independents the subject φωνὴ "sound" is defined by the four genitives representative of the arts. The genitive specifies the kind of sound; it's this kind, not that.

Subjects of the next four clauses follow the same pattern; a noun defined by genitive. τεχνίτης "craftsman" with -της ending expresses agent; one who does the crafting. He is defined by genitive τέχνης; "craftsman of every kind of craft." That includes the entire building trade. "Sound of millstone (μύλου) represents the food industry. "Light of lamp(λύχνου)typifies the lighting industry, both essential and frothy. Every night remains dark. "Voice of bridegroom and bride" suggests family life. An immoral society eventually falls of its own weight.

Three ὅτι clauses submit reasons why such a catastrophe befalls a great civilization. The first reason given is: "because merchants were the great ones of the earth..." Those of earth considered noble, the "beautiful people," were the money makers who profited from the commodities that ministered to the sensual seductive needs of the harlot.

A second reason is: "because all the gentiles were deceived (seduced) in your sorcery..." φαρμακείᾳ refers to "drugs," those which stupified the senses, dulled the intellect, and destroyed the human personality.

A third and final reason offered is: "because blood was found in her..." What kind of blood? Three genitives deal with that question. It's the "blood of the prophets," and "of the saints," and "of all the ones having been slaughtered (unjustly) on the earth." Perfect tense of attributive participle ἐσφαγμένων "having been slaughtered" gives emphasis to the permanent results of such slaughter. Murder of innocent blood cannot be recalled. Once done it's done!

## SOME EXPOSITORY THOUGHTS ON 18:1-24

The fall of Babylon is now portrayed in detail. The extent of her abominations is the measure of her fall. The "vision" may be divided into declarations originating "in heaven" and those from earth. From heaven come three pronouncements. First, from an "authoritative angel." Second, from a divine "voice from heaven." And third, a mighty "strong angel."

While John gazed with rapt attention he "saw another angel coming down out of heaven having great power(authority)..." His authority guarantees that his pronouncement is authentic. If you would avoid heaven's judgment, heed heaven's authority. The "whole earth was lighted from his glory." No longer can earth hide the destiny of destruction due the great harlot. In the light of heaven's authority Rome's doom is sure. Even before it happened the angel shouted aloud in prophetic certainty, "She fell! she fell! Babylon the great!" So complete is her fall she becomes the "prison" of "every vile spirit,..every hated scavenging bird..." Earth doesn't endure a vacuum. Every grisly, gruesome, fiendish, depraved evil rushes into the void of the shattered city to practice and compound its unholy shame. Evil feeds on itself; its ultimate end is to have to live in and with its own putrid self. With Rome it happened "because all the nations have drunk of the wine of the wrath of her fornication." She who fosters fornication will fall in her fornications. Besides, this judgment falls on her "because the kings of the earth whored with her and the merchants of the earth got rich out of her wantonness." One doesn't lead others into whoredom and ill-gotten gain without reaping the inevitable harvest of retribution. It's God's moral law.

John reports that he "heard another voice from heaven..." That this voice represented God is assured by its word addressed to "my people." He urged "my people" to "Come out of her that you have no fellowship with her sins and" thus "receive not of her plagues." God's people living in a sin-filled earth must endure the environment of sin. But they don't need to partake of the filth. Hence the urgent call to "come out." Get yourself disentangled from the meshes of its grasp. Free yourself from her whoredoms. Don't share her life style.

There are valid reasons why the Christian should carefully disentangle himself from suffocating clutches of the evil city. "Her iniquities are stuck in a stack as high as heaven." They've reached the point at which heaven must delay judgment no more. She is now to be repaid with exact precision that which she doled out to her innocent victims. Justice will meet justice in meticulous detail. "Mix to her double in the cup with which she mixed." Divine judgment is not sadistic. God doesn't double the punishment. But he does bring upon the evil city the same doubling of pain which she doubled onto his innocent people. Justice will not be unjust but it will exact justice in equal measure as evil dished out. Such is God's grace! Grace forgives wrong but it doesn't overlook it. God is gracious; therefore retribution is inexorable!

In verse 22 John tells of a highly symbolic act performed by an enormously strong angel. He lifted a "large millstone" and slung it with a "violent splash" into the sea. With the swish of the stone he voiced meaning to the symbol. "Babylon, the great city, shall be hurled with violence and she shall never be found any more." He announced that arts, commerce, and family life would disappear forever from the city. "Harpers, musicians,..shall never be heard..; craftsmen of every craft shall not be found." Millstones won't furnish flour for bakers nor lights provide for parties and pleasure. The joyous cry of bride and groom shall cease and family life disintegrate. All this because of the sorcery of the harlot and her slaughtering of "saints and prophets." Business, family, culture are matters of the past. The debasing of culture, extended economic depression, and disintegration of the family result from your merchants, your sorceries, your persecution of the "saints and prophets."

Declarations of the Earth.

"The kings of the earth...stand from afar because of fear of her torment..." They bewail the smoke of her burning "because in one hour, such a brief time, your judging came." These "kings" are the petty dependent governors of Rome's far-flung provinces. They held their power of governing by participation in the harlot's whoredoms, sorceries, and political ploys. When local magistrates betray their trust in order to stay in power both they and their central government shall fall "in one hour." Collapse will be sudden, complete, final!

Besides kings the "merchants of the earth weep and mourn over her..." The reason isn't hard to discover. Because "no one anymore purchases their produce..." When one's riches come as a consequence of the prostitution of moral fiber of peoples, when one's wealth is built up through manipulation of markets at the expense of human lives, when one's economic power comes as a result of multiplying markets through exploiting the weaknesses of humanity for luxuries that minister to the arrogant egotism of the flesh, then that wealth, that civilization, and that system "will be made desolate in one brief hour." Why is a merchant in business? To make money. That is not questioned. The issue is not a profit but why a profit? What is the motive for making money? To serve selfish sensual demands of the flesh? or to answer as a good steward toward God? That city of man that makes its money at the cost of God's moral and spiritual principles of stewardship is doomed to destruction "in one hour."

Rome's power rested not just in its provinces, not only in its merchants but in its entire sea-faring trade. In Rome's world lines of communication, transportation, trade, travel and education lay in the shipping lanes, weather, ports and products of the Mediterranean sea. Those who "worked the sea" became rich through involvement with Rome's prostitutions. So they too "threw dust on their heads" because "she was made desolate in one hour." When the means of communication, transportation, education and vacation become the servants of an immoral, persecuting government, such a system will inevitably fall "in one hour." That's God's moral law.

A TRANSLATION
Revelation 19:1-21

After these things I heard like a great shout of a large crowd in heaven saying, "Hallelujah! Salvation, and glory, and power (be) to our God because his judgings are true and just; because he judged the great harlot who corrupted the earth and avenged on her the blood of his servants." And they said a second (time), "Hallelujah! and her smoke goes up unto the ages of the ages."

And the twenty four elders and the four living creatures fell and worshipped God, the one sitting on the throne, saying, "Amen! Hallelujah!"

And a voice came out from the throne saying, "All his bond-servants, the ones fearing him, the little and the great, be praising our God."

And I heard like a noise of a large crowd and like a sound of many waters and like a sound of loud thunders saying, "Hallelujah! for (the) Lord our God, the Almighty, reigned! Let's rejoice and be glad; and we will give glory to him, because the marriage of the lamb came and his bride prepared herself. And that she should be clothed in fine clean, bright linen was given to her, for the fine linen is the righteous deeds of the saints."

And he says to me, "Write! The ones having been invited unto the marriage dinner of the lamb (are) blessed." And he says to me, "These are the true words of God." And I fell before his feet to worship him. And he says to me, "See that you don't do (that); I am a fellow bond-servant of yours and of your brothers, the ones having the testimony of Jesus." For the testimony of Jesus is the spirit of prophecy.

And I saw the heaven opened, and behold, a white horse; and the one sitting on him was called, "Faithful and True." And he judges and makes war in righteousness. And his eyes, a flame of fire; and on his head, many diadems; and having a name written which no one knows except he; and he had been clothed with a garment immersed in blood; and his name was called, "The Word of God." And the armies, the ones in heaven, were following him on white horses, clothed with fine clean white linen. And out of his mouth goes a sharp sword with which he might smite the nations and he will shepherd them with a rod of iron; and he treads the winepress of the wine of the anger of the wrath of God, the Almighty. And he has on his cloak and on his thigh a name written: King of kings and Lord of lords.

And I saw an angel standing in the sun and in a loud voice he shouted, saying to all the birds, the ones flying in midheaven, "Come! Gather together for the great feast that you may eat flesh of kings and flesh of captains and flesh of (the) strong and flesh of horses and those sitting on them and flesh all, of both freemen and slaves and of (the) little and (the) great." And I saw the beast and the kings of the earth and their armies having been assembled to make war with the one sitting on the horse and with his army. And the beast was captured and the false prophet with him, the one who, before him, made signs in which he misled the

## A TRANSLATION
Revelation 19:1-21
(continued)

ones who received the mark of the beast and the ones worshipping his image. The two were hurled alive into the lake of fire, the one burning in sulphurous fire. And the rest were killed with the sword coming out of the mouth of the one sitting on the horse. And all the birds were gorged out of their flesh.

## AN OUTLINE OF REVELATION 19:1-21
The Victorious Christ!

With increasing intensity, the war between God's sovereignty and the dragon has been pictured. In prophetic prospect God's wrath is exercised against Rome. The city falls! The decisive defeat of the three enemies moves to its inevitable climax. In this passage Christ and his army destroy the two beasts. They're cast unto their eternal destiny, the "lake of fire and brimstone."

I. THE HALLELUJAH CHORUS. 19:1-10
   1. Heaven's chorus sings the hallelujah. 2-3
      (a)"Salvation, glory, and power to God."
      (b)Because he judged the harlot.
      (c)Because he avenged the blood of his servants.
   2. A second "Hallelujah!" because "her smoke goes up forever."
   3. The 24 elders and four living creatures add "Hallelujah."
   4. A "voice from the throne" exhorts: "Praise God!"
   5. "Sound of a crowd...many waters...loud thunders..." add another "Hallelujah" and exhortation to "rejoice!"
      (a)Because of the "marriage of the lamb and his bride..."
      (b)The bride's clothing: "the righteous deeds of the saints."
   6. "The testimony of Jesus is the spirit of prophecy."
      (a)It's "true" that the wedding guests "are blessed."
      (b)Worship only him who is the subject of all prophecy.

II. THE VICTORIOUS CONFLICT. 19:11-21
   1. The name of him "sitting" on a "white horse."
      (a)"Faithful and True."
      (b)"King of kings and Lord of lords."
      (c)He "makes war in righteousness."
      (d)His "name" - "The Word of God."
   2. His equipment for warfare.
      (a)His eyes: "a flame of fire." Knowledge and insight.
      (b)Royal authority: "many diadems."
      (c)Deity: "Name...which no one knows."
      (d)His life's blood. Priestly sacrifice!
      (e)Offensive armament: "out of his mouth...a sharp sword."
      (f)Disciplinary government: "rod of iron" and "winepress of the wine of the anger of the wrath of God."
   3. Defeat and capture of the "beast and false prophet."
   4. Sentence executed: "Cast into lake of fire and brimstone."
   5."The rest" killed with sword of the conqering Christ.

Any government that patterns after Rome may expect the same end. With steady pace Christ moves through history.

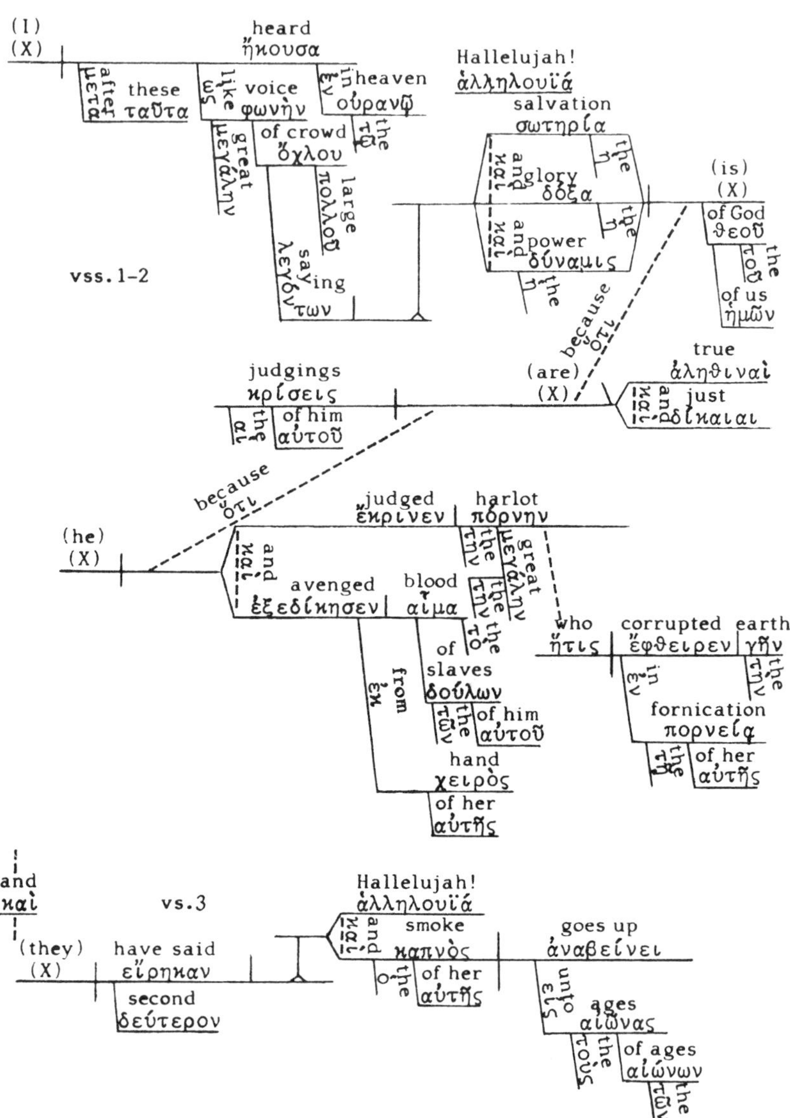

(I)
(X)
heard
ἤκουσα
after
μετὰ
these
ταῦτα
like
ὡς
voice
φωνὴν
great
μεγάλην
of crowd
ὄχλου
large
πολλοῦ
saying
λεγόντων
in
ἐν
heaven
οὐρανῷ
the
τῷ
Hallelujah!
ἀλληλουϊά
salvation
σωτηρία
the
ἡ
and
καὶ
glory
δόξα
the
ἡ
and
καὶ
power
δύναμις
the
ἡ
(is)
(X)
of God
θεοῦ
the
τοῦ
of us
ἡμῶν
vss. 1-2
because
ὅτι
judgings
κρίσεις
the
αἱ
of him
αὐτοῦ
(are)
(X)
true
ἀληθιναὶ
and
καὶ
just
δίκαιαι
because
ὅτι
(he)
(X)
judged
ἔκρινεν
harlot
πόρνην
the
τὴν
great
μεγάλην
the
τὴν
and
καὶ
avenged
ἐξεδίκησεν
blood
αἷμα
the
τὸ
of
slaves
δούλων
the
τῶν
of him
αὐτοῦ
from
ἐκ
hand
χειρὸς
of her
αὐτῆς
who
ἥτις
corrupted
ἔφθειρεν
earth
γῆν
the
τὴν
in
ἐν
fornication
πορνείᾳ
the
τῇ
of her
αὐτῆς
and
καὶ
vs. 3
(they)
(X)
have said
εἴρηκαν
second
δεύτερον
Hallelujah!
ἀλληλουϊά
and
καὶ
smoke
καπνὸς
the
ὁ
of her
αὐτῆς
goes up
ἀναβείνει
unto
εἰς
ages
αἰῶνας
the
τοὺς
of ages
αἰώνων
the
τῶν

## THE DIAGRAM OF 19:1-3

A complex sentence has but one independent clause. Ignoring modifying elements the independent idea of 19:1-2 is "I heard." Such a statement doesn't tell when, where, how or what was heard. Though an independent clause is a "group of words with subject and predicate that can stand alone" without modifiers it doesn't always say too much. Like flesh on a skeleton are modifiers to a clause. Meat, not bone, makes a tasty meal.

Verses 2-3 constitute a complex sentence. The μετὰ expression tells when "I heard," ""after these things." The ἐν phrase relates where "in heaven." ὡς as prepositional phrase points out how: "like a large crowd." All three expressions are adverbs in function.

After reporting when, where, and how the sentence uses present circumstantial participle λεγόντων "saying" in order to tell the reader what "I heard." Direct object of this participle is the noun clause, "...salvation and glory and power (is) of our God..." The ἀλληλουϊα "Hallelujah" is really Hebrew for "Praise Yahweh!" and serves as an exclamation. Genitive θεοῦ "of God" rather than dative "to God" is noticeable. The "salvation etc." is that which God gives; it is subjective genitive.

The remainder of the sentence consists of a pair of adverbial clauses of cause and an adjective clause. The general reason for the Hallelujah of praise is "because (ὅτι) his judgings (are) true and just..." God is "true and just" in all of his "judgings." But the next ὅτι clause gets down to the specific reasons for present praise: "...because he judged the great harlot and avenged the blood..." An ἐκ phrase modifies "avenged" to express the adverbial idea of from whence the vengeance was taken. It was "from her hand." Genitive δοῦλων "of slaves" identifies whose blood, it's "his slaves' blood," not anyone else's.

Worth noting is the aorist of the compound verb ἐξεδίκησεν "avenged." This demonstrates the perfective use of a preposition in composition. It adds intensity and finality to the simple verb idea. The root δικ has in it the idea of "straight," "upright." The verb δικέω is a causative or action word signifying "to make right." The prefixing of ἐκ intensifies the root idea. To "make right" completely, thoroughly, with finality means that he who judges (makes right) will see to it that a verdict is enforced, that wrong is punished to the exact measure.

The sentence concludes with the adjective clause describing "harlot." ἥτις "who" is a qualitative relative indicating "who by her very nature..." The harlot, being a harlot, by her nature "corrupted the earth..." The means was "in (ἐν) her fornication."

Verse three embodies a complex sentence of two clauses. "They have said..." is the independent idea. δεύτερον is an adverbial accusative "as a second thing" or "secondly." The "Hallelujah" appears in the diagram as if it were a clause. It really is an exclamation though the full idea may be thought of as a clause: "Praise (be) to God!" "Smoke goes up..." is a noun clause object of "have said."

# Revelation 19:4-5

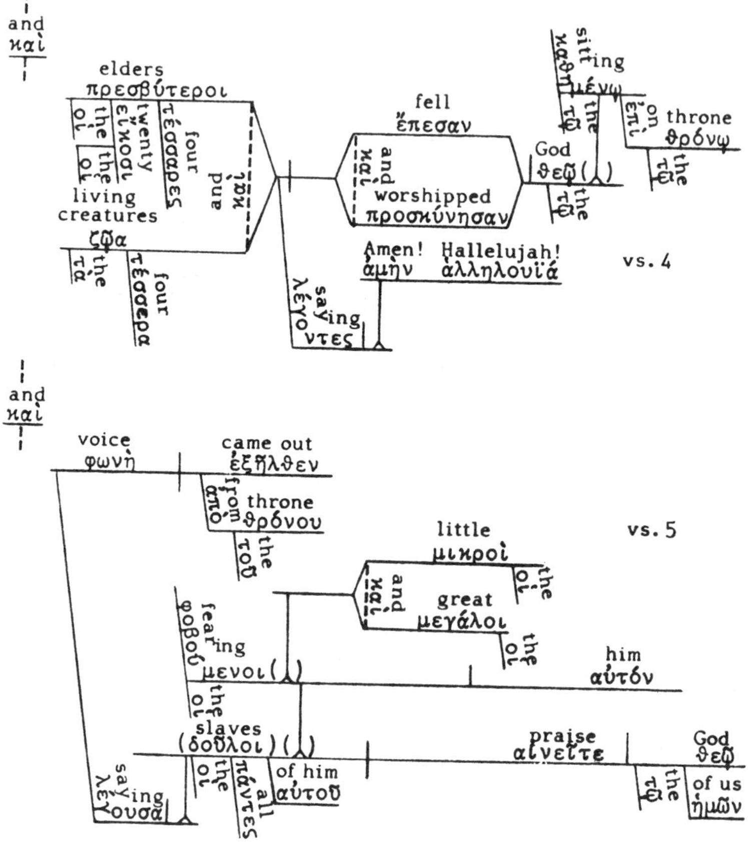

and
καί

elders
πρεσβύτεροι
the
οἱ
twenty
εἴκοσι
four
τέσσαρες
and
καὶ
the
οἱ
living creatures
ζῷα
the
τὰ
four
τέσσερα

fell
ἔπεσαν
and
καὶ
worshipped
προσεκύνησαν

God
θεῷ
the
τῷ
sitting
καθημένῳ
the
τῷ
on
ἐπὶ
throne
θρόνῳ
the
τῷ

saying
λέγοντες
Amen! Hallelujah!
ἀμὴν ἀλληλουϊά

vs. 4

and
καί

voice
φωνὴ
came out
ἐξῆλθεν
from
ἀπὸ
throne
θρόνου
the
τοῦ

saying
λέγουσα

praise
αἰνεῖτε
God
θεῷ
the
τῷ
of us
ἡμῶν

slaves
(δοῦλοι)
the
οἱ
all
πάντες
of him
αὐτοῦ

fearing
φοβού μενοι
the
οἱ
him
αὐτόν

little
μικροὶ
the
οἱ
and
καὶ
great
μεγάλοι
the
οἱ

vs. 5

## THE DIAGRAM OF 19:4-5

As diagrammed the sentence of verse four shows a compound predicate. In the text the verbs "fell" and "worshipped" are separated by more than a full line from each other. Furthermore, the two subjects are close to ἔπεσαν "fell." The sentence might be conceived as having two separate independent clauses. If so it would be a compound sentence. However, the ideas involved in the verbs are so closely related in their action that it seems best to bind them together as two parts of one compound predicate. Thus, as diagrammed, the sentence is to be viewed as simple. It possesses but one clause.

The subject is also compound. Each of the two subjects stands out as distinct. The definite articles with each insure that. These articles are anaphoric pointing back to chapter four where these two groups of worshippers were first mentioned: "The elders, the twenty four" and "the four living creatures." The verb for "worship" frequently takes the accusative as its direct object. But here the dative θεῷ appears. The dative gives somewhat more stress to the personal element that is obviously important if one is to worship the "living" God. In apposition to this dative object is the present attributive participle καθημένῳ "the one sitting." Precisely where he is sitting is seen in the ἐπὶ phrase, "upon the throne." The present circumstantial participle λέγοντες "saying" describes the subjects by telling what they were saying as they worshipped: "Amen! Halleluyah!" These two exclamatory words declare: "May it be so! Praise God!"

Verse five falls into the category of complex. Its independent clause affirms that a "voice came out." ἐξῆλθεν is a normal point action narrative aorist. It states a fact without description. The prepositional ἀπὸ phrase "from the throne" answers the question from where.

The sole dependent clause is a noun clause direct object of the present circumstantial participle λέγουσα "saying." "All his slaves are to be praising our God." αἰνεῖτε is present active imperative. It is an exhortation to "keep on praising..." Praise of God is not to be a one-time exercise; it is to be a continuing practice. Once again we note personal interest dative θεῷ as direct object underscoring the personal relationship of a worshipper to God who is living. The subject of this clause δοῦλοι "slaves" is expanded by the present attributive participle φοβούμενοι "the ones fearing." This participle is in apposition to "slaves" while it itself is enlarged by a brace of adjectives in apposition: "the great and the little." A definite article with each of the adjectives sets each forth as a distinct group. All humanity is classed as among either "the great" people or "the little" people, "the noble" or "the common."

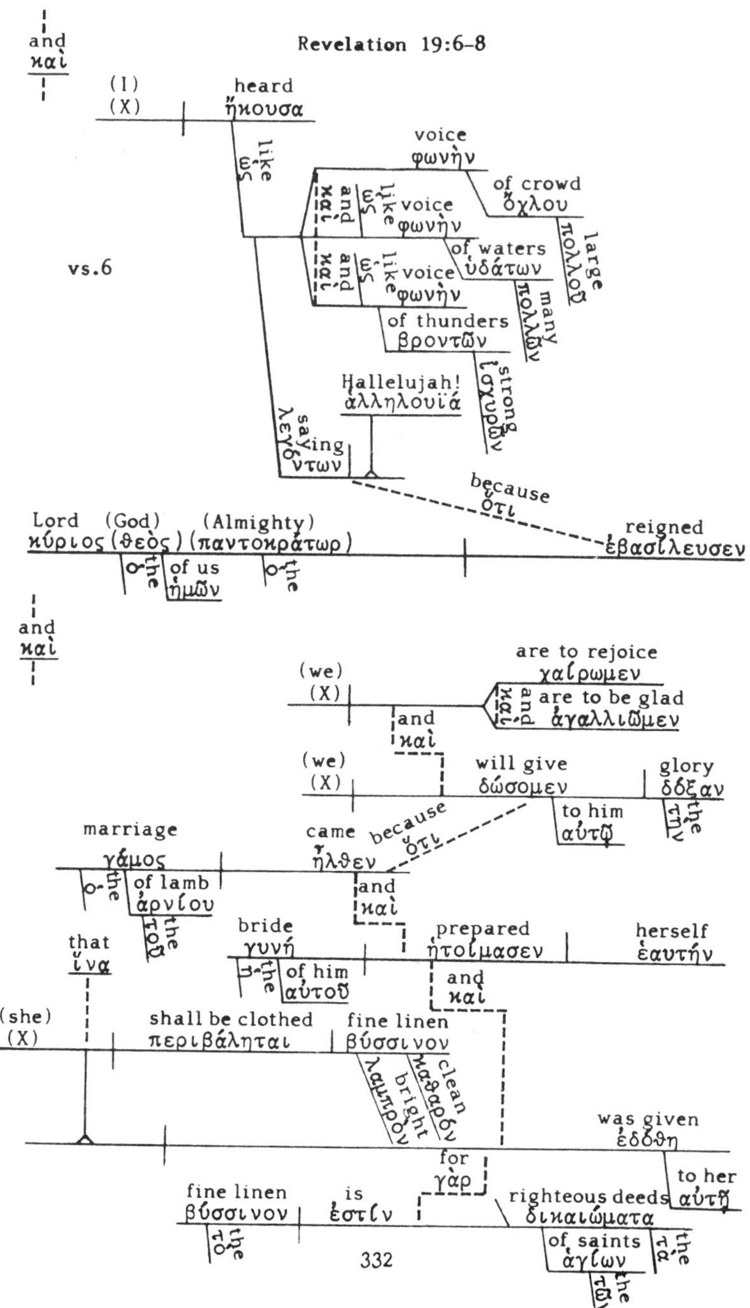
and
καὶ
(I)
(X)
heard
ἤκουσα
like
ὡς
voice
φωνὴν
of crowd
ὄχλου
large
πολλοῦ
and
καὶ
like
ὡς
voice
φωνὴν
of waters
ὑδάτων
many
πολλῶν
and
καὶ
like
ὡς
voice
φωνὴν
of thunders
βροντῶν
strong
ἰσχυρῶν
vs.6
Hallelujah!
ἀλληλουϊά
saying
λεγόντων
because
ὅτι
Lord
κύριος
(God)
(θεὸς)
(Almighty)
(παντοκράτωρ)
reigned
ἐβασίλευσεν
the
ὁ
of us
ἡμῶν
the
ὁ
and
καὶ
(we)
(X)
are to rejoice
χαίρωμεν
and
καὶ
are to be glad
ἀγαλλιῶμεν
and
καὶ
(we)
(X)
will give
δώσομεν
glory
δόξαν
the
τὴν
to him
αὐτῷ
because
ὅτι
marriage
γάμος
the
ὁ
of lamb
ἀρνίου
the
τοῦ
came
ἦλθεν
and
καὶ
bride
γυνὴ
the
ἡ
of him
αὐτοῦ
prepared
ἡτοίμασεν
herself
ἑαυτήν
and
καὶ
that
ἵνα
(she)
(X)
shall be clothed
περιβάληται
fine linen
βύσσινον
bright
λαμπρὸν
clean
καθαρὸν
was given
ἐδόθη
to her
αὐτῇ
for
γὰρ
fine linen
βύσσινον
the
τὸ
is
ἐστίν
righteous deeds
δικαιώματα
the
τὰ
of saints
ἁγίων
the
τῶν

## THE DIAGRAM OF 19:6-8

In the sentence of verse six ὡς appears three times introducing comparative phrases: "like a voice." They might have been shown as three distinct phrases hanging from the verb ἤκουσα "heard." But the diagram presents them as elements of a three-part compound. The independent clause states: "I heard..." It wasn't a "voice" that he heard but something "like a voice." Yet there were three distinct kinds of voices. It's at this point the genitives modifying "voice" demonstrate their value: "of a large crowd," "of many waters," "of strong(loud)thunders." The distinguishing feature is in the genitive rather than the case of the word they modify.

The present circumstantial participle λεγόντων "saying" lays the ground work for instilling a dependent ὅτι clause: "because Lord, the God, the Almighty reigned." The clause functions as an adverb. The subject, "Lord" is amplified by two appositional ideas each of which sets forth a particular aspect of the Lord. He is "our God," emphatic of a personal relationship between the "Lord" and the "voices." He is "Almighty" intimating the power of him who "reigned." The verb ἐβασίλευσεν "reigned" is aorist, an ingressive aorist calling attention to the fact that this "Lord" "took his reign." He "began to exert his power by beginning to execute his reign."

The song of the "voice of..." continues in another sentence. The seven clauses of verses 7-8 frame a compound-complex scheme. Two independent clauses and five dependents constitute the skeletal framework for the sentence. It is compound-complex.

The first of the independent clauses is an exhortation with a compound predicate. χαίρωμεν "be rejoicing" and ἀγαλλιῶμεν "be glad" are both present active subjunctives. They are volitive subjunctives appealing to the will: "let us be rejoicing..." of "may we be rejoicing etc..." In the second clause the future indicative δώσομεν "will give" changes the tone from exhortation to declaration of fact. Although it should be noted that some manuscripts have aorist subjunctive here which would continue this as an exhortation.

Following the main clauses three dependent causal ὅτι clauses present reasons why we should "rejoice etc..." They are: "because the marriage of the lamb came" and because "his bride prepared herself" and because "that she shall be clothed with shining, clean linen was given to her..." The verbs are all aorists "came," "prepared," and "was given." Subjects of the first two are single nouns. But subject of the third is a dependent noun clause, "she shall be clothed..." βύσσινον is object of the verb translated "shall be clothed." It is accusative after verb of clothing.

The final clause of the sentence changes the conjunction to γὰρ "for." It is closely associated with the 3rd of the ὅτι clauses. It really furnishes an explanation of the symbol "fine linen" mentioned in the subject-noun clause "she shall be clothed..." It states: "the fine linen is the righeous deeds of the saints."

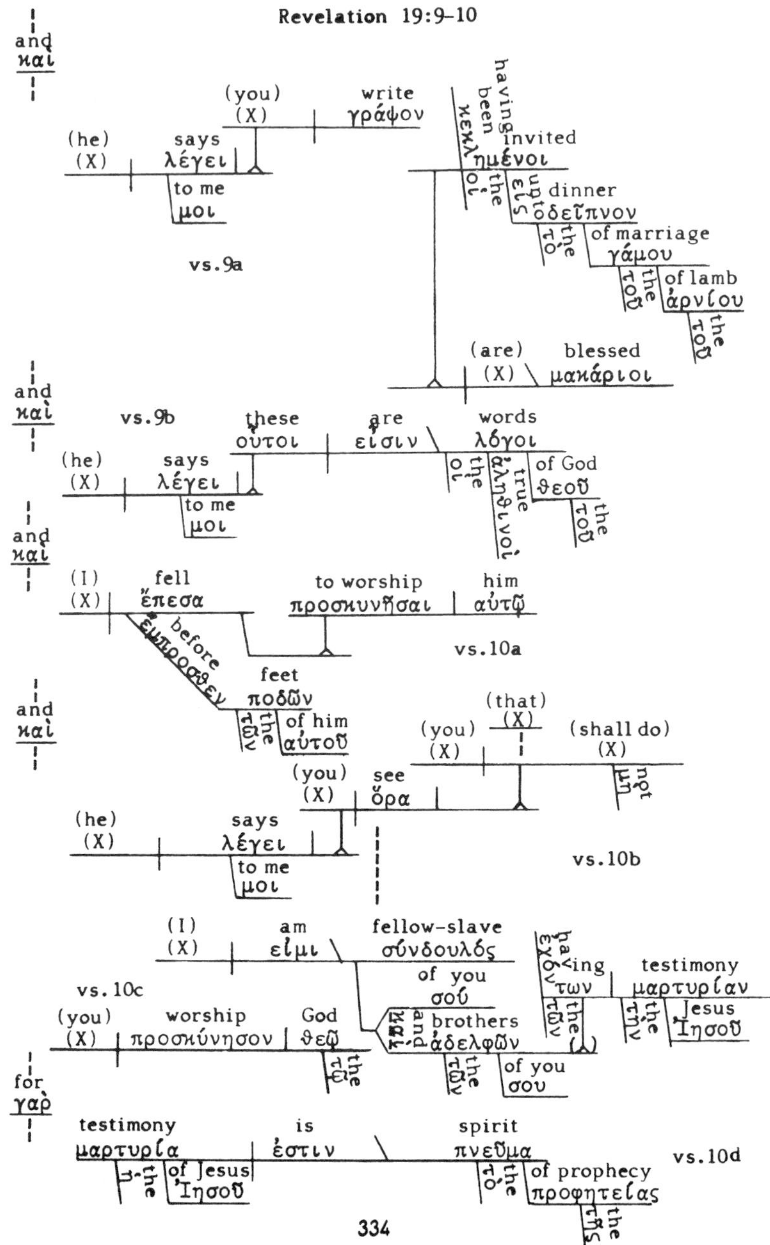
and
καὶ
(he)
(X)
says
λέγει
to me
μοι
(you)
(X)
write
γράψον
having been invited
κεκλημένοι
the
οἱ
unto
εἰς
dinner
δεῖπνον
the
τὸ
of marriage
γάμου
the
τοῦ
of lamb
ἀρνίου
the
τοῦ
vs.9a
(are)
(X)
blessed
μακάριοι
and
καὶ
vs.9b
(he)
(X)
says
λέγει
to me
μοι
these
οὗτοι
are
εἰσιν
words
λόγοι
the
οἱ
true
ἀληθινοὶ
of God
θεοῦ
the
τοῦ
and
καὶ
(I)
(X)
fell
ἔπεσα
before
ἔμπροσθεν
feet
ποδῶν
the
τῶν
of him
αὐτοῦ
to worship
προσκυνῆσαι
him
αὐτῷ
vs.10a
and
καὶ
(he)
(X)
says
λέγει
to me
μοι
(you)
(X)
see
ὅρα
(you)
(X)
(that)
(X)
(shall do)
(X)
not
μὴ
vs.10b
vs.10c
(you)
(X)
worship
προσκύνησον
God
θεῷ
the
τῷ
(I)
(X)
am
εἰμι
fellow-slave
σύνδουλός
of you
σοῦ
and
καὶ
brothers
ἀδελφῶν
the
τῶν
of you
σου
having
ἐχόντων
the
τῶν
testimony
μαρτυρίαν
the
τὴν
Jesus
Ἰησοῦ
for
γὰρ
testimony
μαρτυρία
the
ἡ
of Jesus
Ἰησοῦ
is
ἐστιν
spirit
πνεῦμα
the
τὸ
of prophecy
προφητείας
the
τῆς
vs.10d

## THE DIAGRAM OF 19:9-10

Verse 9a may be looked at as two sentences or as one. If one, then it is a complex with two dependent clauses. If two, as the diagram presents it, then the first is complex; the second simple. As a two-clause complex the first sentence says: "He says to me, 'Write.'" The independent element says: "He says to me." μοι is indirect object. That which he says appears as noun clause, object of "says." γράφον "write" is aorist imperative; the tense gives urgency to that which is commanded.

The second sentence of 9a is simple. Its subject is a participial phrase οἱ κεκλημένοι "the ones having been invited..." Where they have been invited is depicted in the εἰς phrase, "unto the dinner." The kind of dinner is specified in genitive γάμου "of marriage." Whose marriage is identified by genitive ἀρνίου "of the lamb." μακάριοι is a predicate adjective indicating what is said about "the ones having been invited..." That is, they "are blessed."

Verse 9b is a two-clause complex design. The same independent clause arises as in 9a: "He says to me..." Direct object of "says" is the dependent noun clause: "these are the true words of God." The adjective ἀληθινοὶ "true" has -ινος ending signifying material or substance of which a given thing consists. These "words of God" are more than about truth they are truth.

In verse 10a we are dealing with a simple sentence. The bare clause states, "I fell..." The prepositional expression ἔμπροσθεν "before his feet" indicates where. Aorist infinitive προσκυνῆσαι indicates the purpose or reason why "I fell." That is, "to worship him." Dative αὐτῷ "him" as direct object is used after the verb "worship" calling attention to the personal nature of such action.

The sentence of 10b is complex, this time with three dependent clauses. Again we have the same independent idea: "he says to me..." The next two clauses combine to form the direct object of the verb "says." ὅρα "see" is present active imperative. For an object of ὅρα a clause that is almost entirely elliptical must be used: "...(that) (you) (shall) not (do) (this)." A third noun clause which is also object of "says" follows: "I am a fellow-slave..." σύνδουλος is a compound word; preposition σύν joined to "slave" binds the angel who speaks to John the human as a co-servant, not an object of worship. This "fellow-slave" is further identified by genitives "of you" and "of your brothers." Present attributive participle ἐχόντων "ones having testimony" is in apposition to "brothers." Ἰησοῦ is objective genitive; it's the testimony given "to" or "about" Jesus, not that which Jesus gave.

Verse 10c may be taken as another object of "says" in 10b. Or as a separarte simple sentence as the diagram treats it; "Worship God."

10d is a simple sentence. "The testimony to Jesus (objective genitive) is the spirit of prophecy." (qualitative genitive) When the article appears with both subject and predicate nominative they are equal and interchangeable. The testimony...is the spirit. And the spirit is the testimony. They're one and the same.

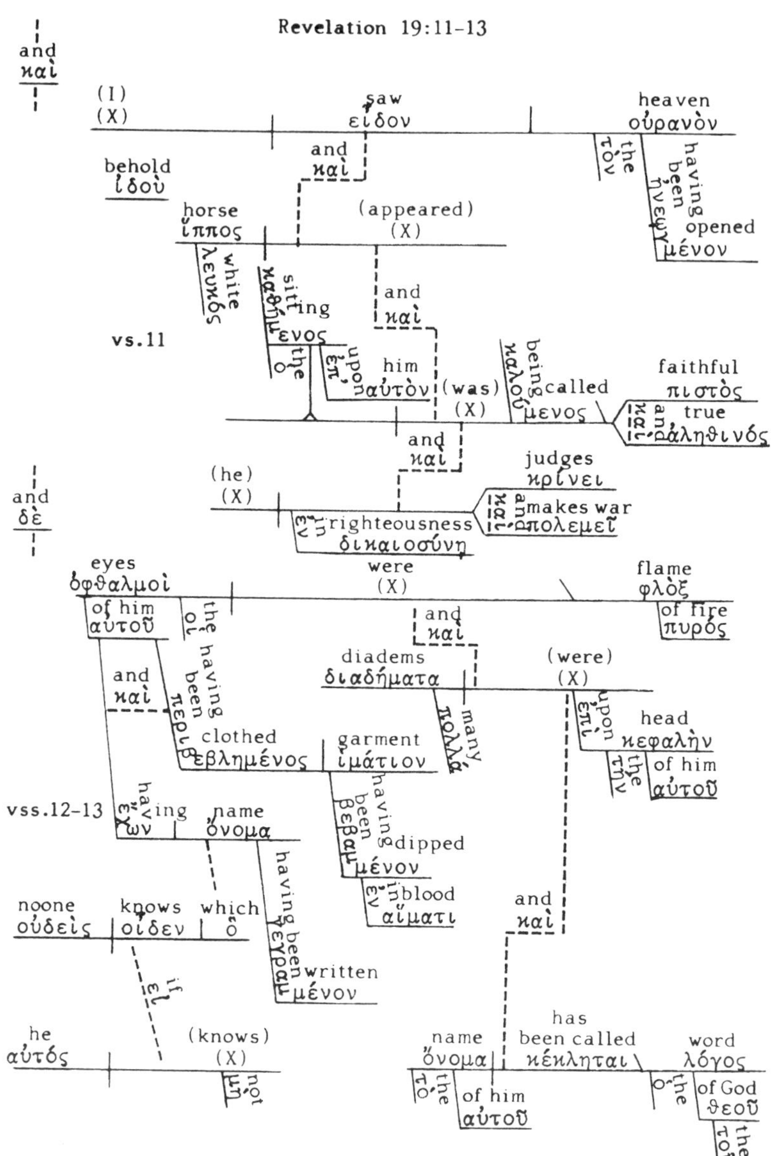
and
καὶ
(I)
(X)
saw
εἶδον
heaven
οὐρανὸν
the
τὸν
having been opened
ἠνεῳγμένον
and
καὶ
behold
ἰδοὺ
horse
ἵππος
white
λευκός
(appeared)
(X)
sitting
καθήμενος
the
ὁ
upon
ἐπ'
him
αὐτὸν
and
καὶ
vs.11
being called
καλούμενος
(was)
(X)
faithful
πιστὸς
and
καὶ
true
ἀληθινός
and
καὶ
judges
κρίνει
and
δὲ
(he)
(X)
in
ἐν
righteousness
δικαιοσύνῃ
and
καὶ
makes war
πολεμεῖ
eyes
ὀφθαλμοὶ
were
(X)
flame
φλὸξ
of him
αὐτοῦ
the
οἱ
of fire
πυρός
and
καὶ
having been clothed
περιβεβλημένος
diadems
διαδήματα
many
πολλά
(were)
(X)
upon
ἐπὶ
head
κεφαλὴν
the
τὴν
of him
αὐτοῦ
garment
ἱμάτιον
having been dipped
βεβαμμένον
in
ἐν
blood
αἵματι
vss.12-13
having
ἔχων
name
ὄνομα
having been written
γεγραμμένον
noone
οὐδεὶς
knows
οἶδεν
which
ὃ
if
εἰ
he
αὐτός
(knows)
(X)
not
μὴ
and
καὶ
name
ὄνομα
the
τὸ
of him
αὐτοῦ
has been called
κέκληται
word
λόγος
the
ὁ
of God
θεοῦ
the
τοῦ

## THE DIAGRAM OF 19:11-13

Four independent clauses form the framework of verse 11. The sentence is compound. The first clause announces another vision; at least another scene. "I saw the heaven having been opened..." Perfect participle ἠνεῳγμένον "having been opened" adds a description to object "heaven." He saw more than "heaven." He saw "heaven having been opened." Perfect tense says that heaven was not only "open" but that it continued to "stand open."

The verb of the second clause must be supplied from the context: "...white horse (appeared)..." A sentence must have a predicate; it must "say something" about its subject. Sometimes the emotional and psychological impact is greater without an expressed verb. So it is here: "Behold! a white horse!" But for a sentence to be a sentence it needs a verb, stated or implied. Here the diagram supplies "appeared."

The third clause has for its subject attributive participle καθήμενος "the one sitting." The verb of the clause is periphrastic imperfect "was being called." It is formed by an understood "was"(ἦν) plus supplementary participle καλούμενος "being called." Imperfect tense is linear action in past time. A periphrastic imperfect adds prominence to the linear action. "Faithful" and "true" are predicate adjectives pointing back to the subject. They assert something about the subject.

The final of the four clauses affirms: "and in righteousness he judges and does battle." The ἐν phrase is adverbial indicating the realm <u>within which</u> he performs his judging and war-making. Such is the sphere of the activity.

The sentence involved in verses 12-13 is compound-complex. It has three independent clauses and two dependent. The independents make three positive affirmations about the warrior on the "white horse: "His eyes (were) a flame of fire," "many diadems (were) upon his head," "his name has been called 'the word of God.'" Both φλὸξ "flame" in the first clause and λόγος "word" in the third are predicate nominatives referring back to their respective subjects. The term ὄνομα "name" goes beyond the idea of "name" as merely a distinguishing epithet. It contains the idea of the essential person. His "name" as "the word of God" means that he <u>is in his nature</u> "the word of God." Perfect tense κέκληται "has <u>been called</u>" suggests the fixed, permanent quality. He not only "has been" but "still is called..."

Participles ἔχων "having" and περιβεβλημένος "having been clothed" are nominatives without formal agreement with anything. In thought they are circumstantial describing αὐτοῦ "him." Object of "name" is described by adjective clause "which"(ὃ) noone knows." And that in turn is supported by the negative 2nd class condition determined as unfulfilled. Perfect participle γεγραμμένον also describes "name," the tense emphasizing that it "stands permanently written." Perfect participle βεβαμμένον "having been dipped" also indicates that the dipping is a fixed situation. The "garment" with which he "had been clothed" represents a permanent condition.

Revelation 19:14-16

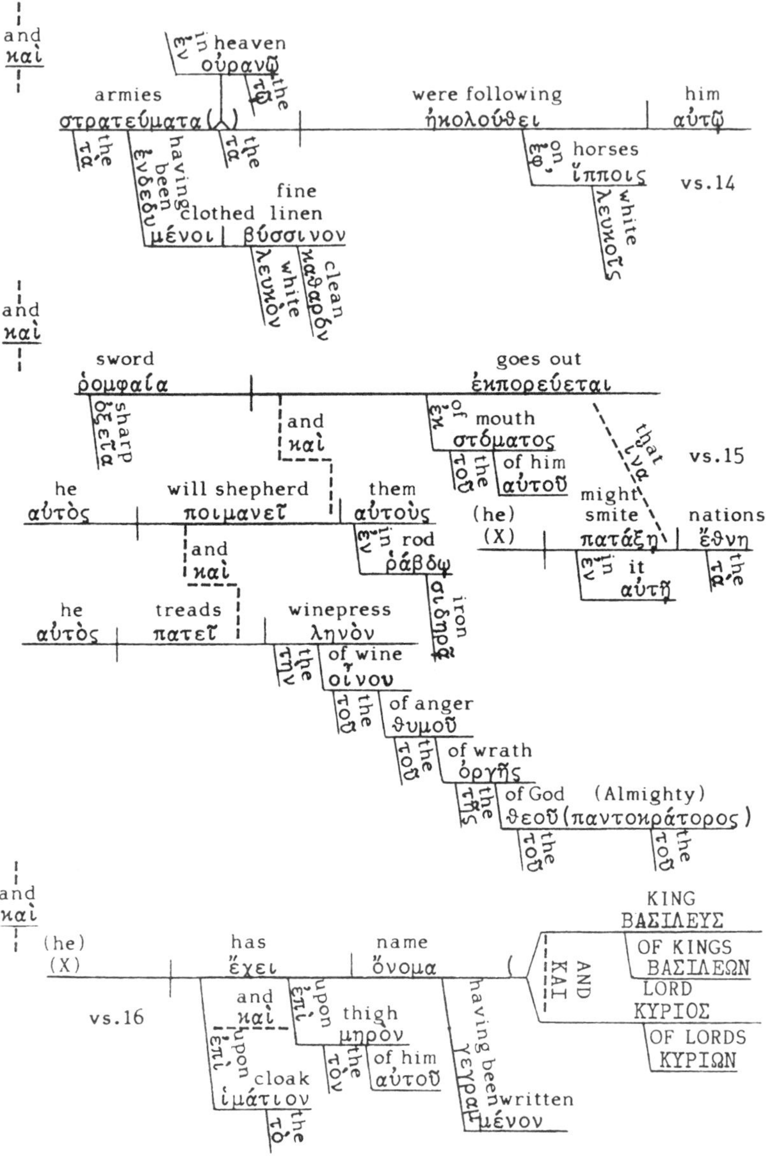

## THE DIAGRAM OF 19:14-16

Without any modifiers the bare clause of verse 14 sketches a moving picture:"...armies were following him..." Subject "armies" (στρατεύματα) is neuter plural of -μα result noun. Definite article τὰ points out specific armies. In view of the context it is almost the equivolent of personal pronoun "his." The repetition of this article signals a prepositional phrase in apposition to "armies," "the (ones) in heaven." Such a phrase identifies yet puts a limit on the nature of his armies; they are his reserve of spiritual forces "in heaven." That which enlivens this simple sentence with animation is the linear action descriptive imperfect ἠκολούθει "were following." It is normal for neuter plural to be used with singular verb. Perfect participle ἐνδεδυμένοι "having been clothed" is circumstantial with "armies." The tense suggests that armies not only had been but still are clothed. Verbs of clothing and unclothing take accusative hence βύσσινον "fine linen." The ἐφ' phrase "on white horses" is adverbial indicating manner.

Compound-complex characterizes the frame on which the sentence of verse 15 is built. "A sharp sword goes out..." is the affirmation of the first independent clause. The verb ἐκπορεύεται "goes out" is descriptive present. The ἐκ phrase, "out of his mouth," is adverb in function portraying "from whence." The only subordinate clause is an adverbial of purpose inaugurated by ἵνα, "that he might smite in it the nations."

The second independent clause asserts:"...and he will shepherd them..." Presence of the personal pronoun αὐτὸς as subject provides special prominence to subject "he." Verb ποιμάνει "will shepherd" is liquid future. Normally future is point action. But here the context seems to suggest linear: "...go on shepherding." This verb is sometimes transalated "ruling." To "shepherd" is the biblical concept of sovereign rule. The prepositional phrase (ἐν) "in iron rod..." is adverb in function indicating the <u>means</u> by which he would rule. Antecedent of the pronominal object αὐτοὺς "them" is "nations" in the preceding ἵνα clause.

The last of the independent clauses declares: "...and he treads the winepress..." The <u>kind</u> of "winepress" is specified by genitive οἴνου "of wine." This "wine" is followed by a chain of genitives, each specifying the <u>kind</u> of that which it modifies - the "anger" kind of wine, the "wrath" kind of anger, the "God" kind of wrath. Then θεοῦ "God" is itself defined by "Almighty" in apposition.

With only one clause verse 16 presents a simple sentence. Without its modifiers the clause states, "he has name..." Precisely what that name is finds expression in a two-pronged apposition, "King of kings Lord of lords. <u>Where</u> he "has" this name is pointed out by the two ἐπὶ phrases, "upon the (his) cloak and upon his thigh." They are both used adverbially.

Finally, there appears a perfect participle γεγραμμένον "having been written." As adjective it describes "name." As verb its perfect tense insists on the fact that the "name" "having been written" still stands permanently written.

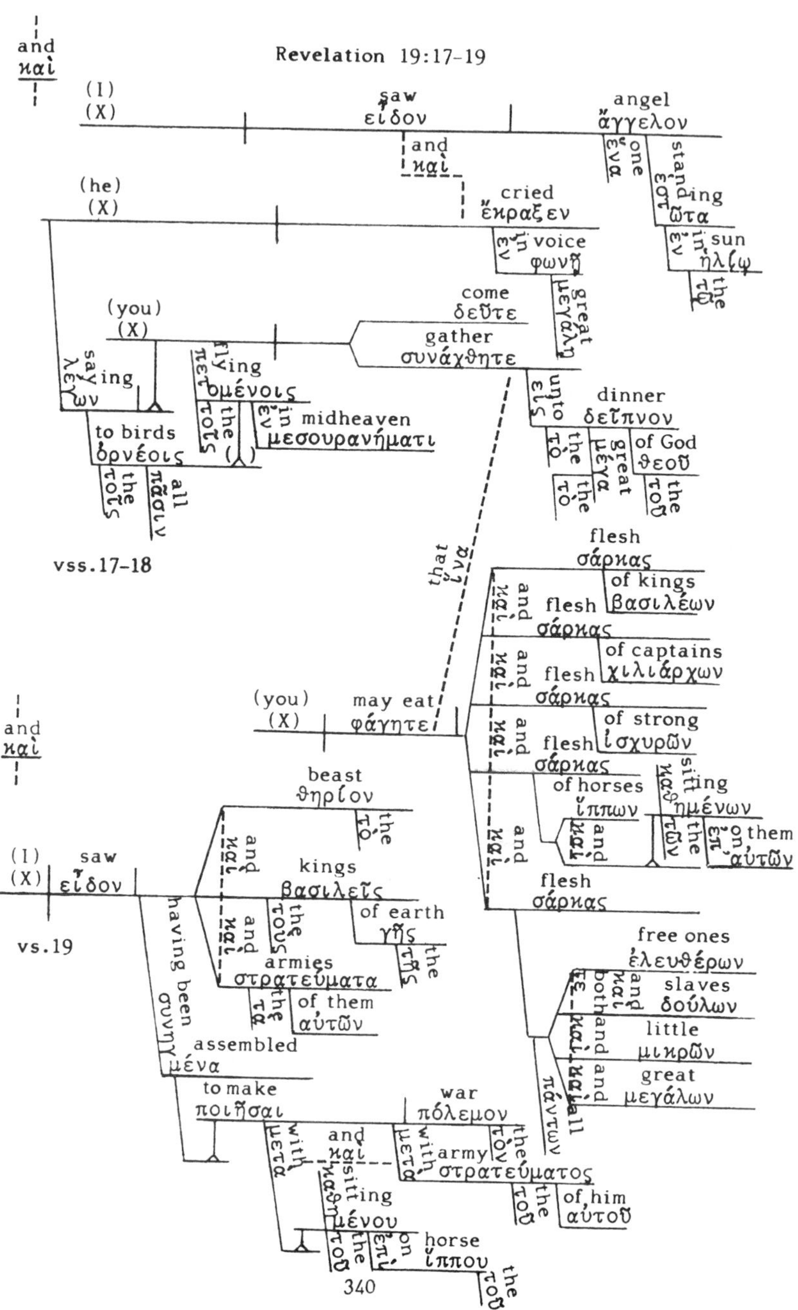
Revelation 19:17-19
and
καὶ
(I)
(X)
saw
εἶδον
angel
ἄγγελον
one
ἕνα
standing
ἑστῶτα
in
ἐν
sun
ἡλίῳ
the
τῷ
and
καὶ
(he)
(X)
cried
ἔκραξεν
in
ἐν
voice
φωνῇ
great
μεγάλῃ
saying
λέγων
to birds
ὀρνέοις
the
τοῖς
all
πᾶσιν
flying
πετομένοις
the
τοῖς
in
ἐν
midheaven
μεσουρανήματι
(you)
(X)
come
δεῦτε
gather
συνάχθητε
unto
εἰς
dinner
δεῖπνον
the
τὸ
great
μέγα
the
τὸ
of God
θεοῦ
the
τοῦ
vss.17-18
that
ἵνα
(you)
(X)
may eat
φάγητε
flesh
σάρκας
of kings
βασιλέων
and
καὶ
flesh
σάρκας
of captains
χιλιάρχων
and
καὶ
flesh
σάρκας
of strong
ἰσχυρῶν
and
καὶ
flesh
σάρκας
of horses
ἵππων
and
καὶ
sitting
καθημένων
the
τῶν
on
ἐπ'
them
αὐτῶν
and
καὶ
flesh
σάρκας
all
πάντων
free ones
ἐλευθέρων
both
τε
and
καὶ
slaves
δούλων
and
καὶ
little
μικρῶν
and
καὶ
great
μεγάλων
and
καὶ
(I)
(X)
saw
εἶδον
vs.19
beast
θηρίον
the
τὸ
and
καὶ
kings
βασιλεῖς
the
τοὺς
of earth
γῆς
the
τῆς
and
καὶ
armies
στρατεύματα
the
τὰ
of them
αὐτῶν
having been assembled
συνηγμένα
to make
ποιῆσαι
war
πόλεμον
the
τὸν
with
μετὰ
sitting
καθημένου
the
τοῦ
on
ἐπὶ
horse
ἵππου
the
τοῦ
and
καὶ
with
μετὰ
army
στρατεύματος
the
τοῦ
of him
αὐτοῦ

## THE DIAGRAM OF 19:17-19

Take four clauses; make two of them express independent ideas; deal with the other two as dependent and the result is a compound-complex sentence. Such is the sentence of 19:17-18. The first two are the independent clauses. They state the two basic ideas involved in John's next vision. "I saw one angel" and "he cried..." By means of perfect participle ἑστῶτα "standing in the sun" he relates what he saw this angel doing. The phrase "in the sun" is adverbial telling where the angel was standing.

The second of the independent clauses states an additional fact about that which the angel did. He cried "in a great (loud) voice." The phrase "in a great voice" performs as an adverb idea expressing the manner in which he cried.

The content of that which "he cried" is set forth by the present participle λέγων "saying." Those to whom he "cried saying" are pictured in an indirect object, dative ὀρνέοις "to all the birds." The "birds" are further identified by the attributive participle πετομένοις "ones flying..."

The first of the two dependent elements is a noun clause, direct object of the circumstantial participle "saying." It supplies the content of what the angel "cried." "Come! Gather together unto the great dinner of God..." δεῦτε is an adverb used almost as an exclamation and usually followed, as here, with an imperative command or exhortation. συνάχθητε "gather together" is aorist passive imperative. Preposition εἰς "unto" presents a purpose idea; the birds are urged to assemble "for (the purpose of eating) the dinner of God."

The ἵνα introduces a subordinate adverbial clause of purpose, "in order that you may eat..." The prepositional phrase in the preceding clause expressed purpose in general. This dependent ἵνα clause gives the purpose in detail; "...that you may eat kings' flesh...." The angel itemizes nine specific kinds of "fleshes" that go to make up the "great dinner of God." They are: "fleshes of kings," "of captains," "of strong(mighty)," "of horses," "of the ones sitting on them," "of all free," "of slaves," "little (common people)," and "of great(nobility)." It should be noted that σάρκας is plural = "pieces of flesh."

The sentence of verse 19 contains only one full clause. Strictly speaking it is a simple sentence. The clause includes a three-fold compound object. "I saw the beast and the kings of the earth and their armies..." This is the bare sentence. However the real burden of the sentence is set forward in the perfect participle συνηγμένα "having been assembled." Perfect tense indicates that it was a permanent assembling of these forces. The purpose for which they were assembled is presented in the aorist active infinitive ποιῆσαι "to make war..." Those "with" whom the beast and his allies are to make war are pictured in the two μετὰ expressions: "with the one sitting on the horse and with his army."

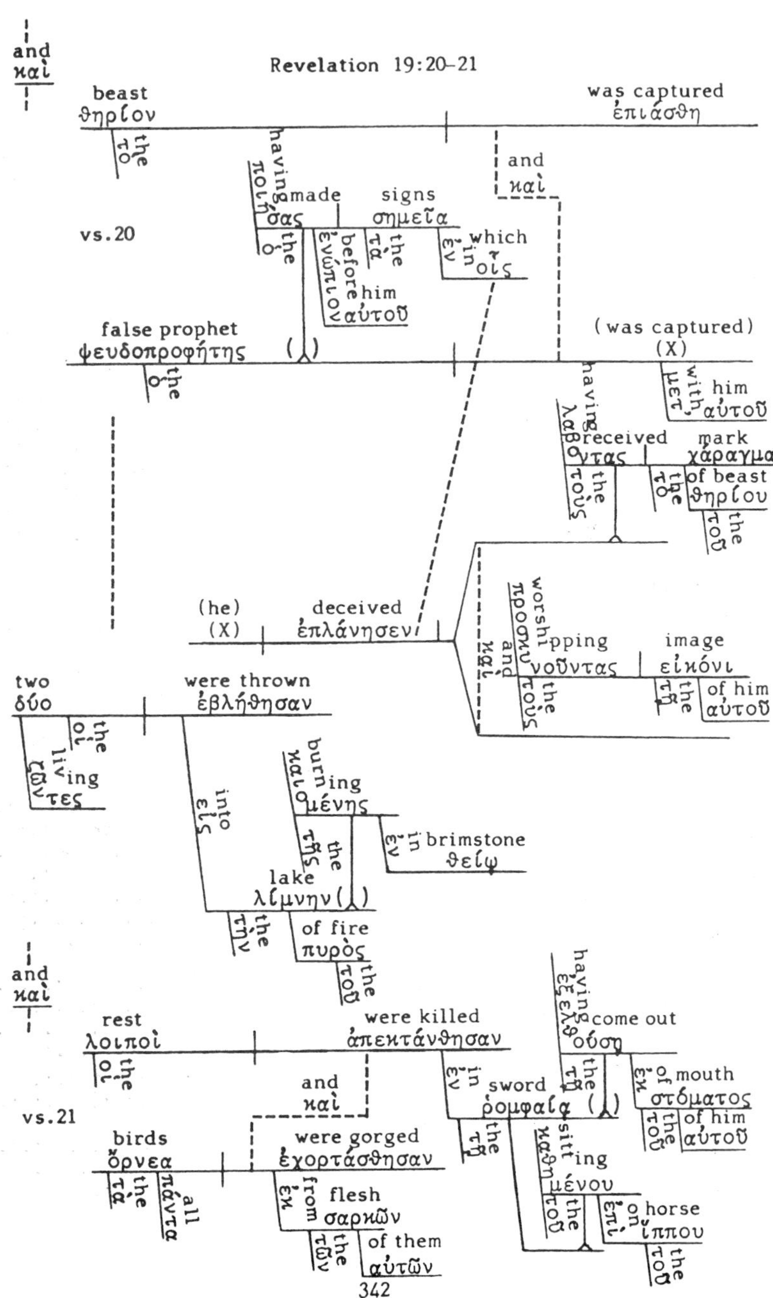
Revelation 19:20–21
and
καὶ
beast
θηρίον
the
τὸ
was captured
ἐπιάσθη
and
καὶ
vs.20
having made
ποιή σας
the
ὁ
signs
σημεῖα
the
τὰ
before
ἐνώπιον
him
αὐτοῦ
which
in
ἐν
οἷς
false prophet
ψευδοπροφήτης
the
ὁ
(was captured)
(X)
with
μετ'
him
αὐτοῦ
having received
λαβόντας
the
τοὺς
mark
χάραγμα
the
τὸ
of beast
θηρίου
the
τοῦ
(he)
(X)
deceived
ἐπλάνησεν
and
καὶ
worshipping
προσκυνοῦντας
the
τοὺς
image
εἰκόνι
the
τῇ
of him
αὐτοῦ
two
δύο
the
οἱ
living
ζῶντες
were thrown
ἐβλήθησαν
into
εἰς
burning
καιομένης
the
τῆς
in
ἐν
brimstone
θείῳ
lake
λίμνην
the
τὴν
of fire
πυρὸς
the
τοῦ
and
καὶ
rest
λοιποὶ
the
οἱ
were killed
ἀπεκτάνθησαν
and
καὶ
vs.21
in
ἐν
sword
ῥομφαίᾳ
the
τῇ
having come out
ἐξελθούσῃ
the
τῇ
of mouth
ἐκ
στόματος
the
τοῦ
of him
αὐτοῦ
sitting
καθημένου
the
τοῦ
on
ἐπὶ
horse
ἵππου
the
τοῦ
birds
ὄρνεα
the
τὰ
all
πάντα
were gorged
ἐχορτάσθησαν
from
ἐκ
flesh
σαρκῶν
the
τῶν
of them
αὐτῶν

THE DIAGRAM OF 19:20-21

Whether verse 20 contains one or two sentences must be determined by whether the last clause is viewed as a separate distinct sentence or just a third independent clause. This diagram treats that final clause as a distinct separate sentence. Yet its close connection in thought to the earlier part of the verse is indicated by the broken line that falls short of full attachment.

Thus verse 20a forms a compound complex sentence. It has two independent clauses and one dependent. The first clause announces: "The beast was captured..." ἐπιάσθη "was captured" is first aorist passive, indicative of πιάζω "take" "capture." This is a prophetic aorist; it treats the action as already having happened though in fact it is yet in the future. The fact and certainty of the fact is so inevitable the author feels that the aorist is appropriate.

The second of the independent ideas adds, "the false prophet (was captured)..." The verb is implied from the previous clause. The subject, false prophet, is more specifically identified by an attributive participial phrase, "the one having made the signs before him..." This false-prophet was captured "with him." μετά with genitive often suggests "fellowship with." Here it would seem to say, "the false-prophet was captured in conjunction with him." That is "in conjunction with the beast."

The subordinate clause is adjective in force because it describes "signs" through the ἐν οἷς phrase. "...signs in which he deceived the ones having received the mark of the beast and those worshipping his image." Aorist ἐπλάνησεν means "to lead astray." The tense gathers into one view all the many who were deceived, and that over a period of years and lumps them all together as a single fact: "he deceived..." The direct object is two-fold, both set forth in attributive participial phrases. (1)"the ones having received the mark of the beast..." Aorist tense. (2)"the ones worshipping his image..."Present tense; probably distributive present.

Verse 20b is a simple sentence stating, "The two were thrown..." ζῶντες is definitely a circumstantial participle; it describes the subject, "two," while at the same time enlivens the main verb "were thrown." "The two were thrown while being alive..." The εἰς phrase is adverbial telling where they were thrown alive; "into the lake of fire." Accusative λίμνην "lake" is further amplified by use of the attributive participle καιομένης "the one burning." Note genitive participle in apposition to accusative λίμνην.

Verse 21 is a compound sentence of two clauses. First, "The rest were killed..." The manner in which they were killed is set forth in the ἐν phrase: "...in the sword..." Attributive participle καθημένου "one sitting on the horse" specifies (genitive) whose sword. Another attributive participle ἐξελθούσῃ one having come out of his mouth" agrees in case with "sword" (locative) and is in apposition to it.

"All the birds were gorged" is the second independent clause. The ἐκ expression is adverbial. It pictures from whence "all the birds were gorged," that is, "from the pieces of their flesh."

## SOME EXPOSITORY THOUGHTS ON 19:1-21

### A Hallelujah Chorus! - 19:1-11

In his vision of the fall of the great harlot, the Seer of Patmos heard high praise to God from a "large crowd" in heaven. This lofty praise arose from the heavenly host for two reasons. First, "because his judgments are true and just." In the vortex that swirled Rome to oblivion as a world power God demonstrated that His "judgings" were at work through all the weary years of unjust sufferings. God had never neglected justice. The wheels of divine justice often appear to be non-existent. But such is not so. "Salvation, glory, and power" are ever present in the midst of this world's arrogant usurping of righteousness. God's judgment of evil powers in this demonic world is a process going on all the time. Wrong appears to be on the throne. But as a matter of reality (truth) the heavy wheels of divine justice are slowly, inevitably, bit by bit rolling with crushing power over every evil beast that the dragon rears in rebellion against God.

A second reason for such heavenly praise is because "he judged the great harlot who corrupted the earth and avenged on her the blood of his servants." Though God's judgings are a process going on that doesn't deny that his judgment comes to a climax; it reaches an apex; it comes full bloom in some cataclysmic political, economic, milatary debacle. As the center from which evil poured out to every sector of ancient society, as the center into which all the diabolic devices conceived in the depraved mind of man Rome collapsed "in one hour." It happened by no accident; it was the culmination of the heavy hand of the wrath of God. The "large crowd" of heavenly singers sang a second time, "Praise be to God! her (Rome's) smoke goes up forever and ever."

In symbolic language the prophet reported that such praise to the Lord God was universal in scope. "The twenty four elders and the four living creatures fell and worshipped God..." The people of God, the religious heritage of all ages "fell and worshipped" God because of his just judgment against the harlot. All aspects of the creation, "the four living creatures," they too "fell and worshipped" God because his true and righteous judgment pulverized Rome so completely. They too sang, "Amen! Praise ye the Lord!"

To this growing cry of victory a "voice came from the throne" exhorting "all his servants...the little and the great" to "Praise our God!" Rising to an incredible crescendo there responded a great crowd "like a sound of many waters...of loud thunders" uniting their voices to the hallelujahs. They added another specific reason for their victorious shout. "Hallelujah! for (the) Lord our God, the Almighty, reigned." Lying buried behind the visible faces of the dragon's beasts is not only the justice of God but also the active sovereign power of God. The power of Satan, though present, is on a leash. His power may hurt but only within limits. God is King; his will prevails; his righteousness rules. Any crowd whose voice rises from in heaven will of necessity proclaim the real sovereignty of God in history. "Let's rejoice and be glad" for God exercised his kingship. Rome's fall demonstrates God's sovereignty.

God "reigned!" So an appeal to "give glory to him" comes "because the marriage of the lamb came and his bride prepared herself." That this bride is the church is clear when John describes her bridal dress as "clean, bright linen" which linen "is the righteous deeds of the saints." So God's people of all time, here and hereafter, share in the victorious reign of God.

This fact so thrilled John that when the angel instructed him to "Write" about the people of God sharing in the "marriage dinner" he fell before the angel in adoration. But no! Whatever differences between angels and men, in one respect they are the same - servants, creatures of the Creator, bound to him in joyful servitude. And so far as this present human history is concerned their service centers in the "testimony of Jesus." The expression "of Jesus" is objective genitive signifying that the service they give is testimony about (to) Jesus. Preaching, whether of the Old Testament prophets or that of the preachers of the New finds its substance and essence in Jesus. The very breath of prophecy is Jesus. Without Jesus as its object, goal and end preaching would be but a vain display of human pride.

Jesus himself while on this earth was the "faithful witness" who said "He who has seen me has seen the Father." He testified to God and God's Kingdom and sealed his witness with his blood. This is the "testimony of Jesus." Men and angels continue testifying this testimony "of Jesus" each time they declare the gospel. Prophesying (preaching) the gospel is "testimony of Jesus."

## The Victorious Conflict - 19:11-21

Once again the Seer saw "the heaven opened." Coming forth was a warrior called "Faithful and True" sitting on a white horse. He came to "make war in righteousness." White symbolizes purity, eternity, victory. "In righteousness" plainly points to the spiritual nature of the war. It was not one of horses and chariots, of bow and arrow. As his instrument of war out of his mouth protruded "a sharp sword with which he might smite the nations..." In keeping with his name this sword was "the Word of God." And with such a spirit-filled sword "he will shepherd them(the nations)with a rod of iron."

In such apocalyptic imagery the author of Revelation struggles to portray the kind and method of spiritual combat by which God's pure, victorious forces overcome the dragon and his beasts in this world. "Put up your sword" said Jesus to his over-zealous disciple. The kingdom of God is not advanced by legions of soldiers bearing shot and shell. The Christ who rides the white horse conquers by the power of the Word of God. Who but Christ knows the nature and power of truth? His name "no one knows except he himself." His "name," that is, his person, his nature, its significance for man's redemption no one knows. Only he! Men trust him, believe him, obey him, though they do not really know him in the depths of his nature, his person! HE is the living Word of God who, with his victorious army of followers, conquers the Caesars and any other of the dragon's beasts. His is a spiritual conquest that conquers men with the gospel.

This "Word of God" warrior has other characteristics. His eyes were "a flame of fire." With penetrating power his insight into truth is absolute. Not just into abstract truth of the gospel but the particular truth about each man, friend or foe, believer or unbeliever. "There is no creature that is not manifest in his sight: but all are naked and laid open before the eyes of him with whom for us is the accounting."(Heb.4:13) I may hide myself from myself, and others, behind a bulwark of excuses, but there's no way to hide from him whose eyes are a "flame of fire."

Furthermore, "many diadems" were on his head. His head bore the symbol of royal authority. In fact, "many diadems" suggests absolute authority. In symbol it says the same as Jesus plainly claimed, "All authority has been given unto me in heaven and on earth."(Matt.28:18) As such and with his "sharp sword" he is well able to tread "the winepress of the wine of the anger of the wrath of God." By the power of his sword, the Word of God, he executes the divine wrath on the beasts of the dragon.

How could this warfare be other than the clash of spiritual forces when we note the clothing which the rider wears? "He had been clothed with a garment immersed in blood." The blood on his clothing symbolizes his sacrificial death for man's sin, the propitiatory sacrifice for man's redemption. Christ on the cross is the heart and core of every apostolic sermon recorded in the book of Acts. Without the cross there is no gospel; without the cross there can be no crown. "The word of the cross is to them that perish foolishness; but unto us who are saved it is the power of God."(I Cor.1:18) And this gospel is "the power of God unto salvation to everyone who believes."(Rom.1:16)

When we consider his insight into truth, his royal authority, his propitiatory blood sacrifice little wonder that he has on his cloak and thigh a name written; "King of kings and Lord of lords." This is not a name given to him at the end of or as a consequence of his victory. It's his name by virtue of who he is as a man. As incarnate deity, the living God come in human nature, fully man, he is "King of kings and Lord of lords." Already in this Revelation the author has referred to him as "the ruler of the kings of the earth."(1:5) And the author has made clear that Christ is king over kings when he declared, "The sovereignty of the world became (that) of our Lord and his Christ."(11:15) This all in keeping with what the angel Gabriel announced to the humble virgin in the quiet privacy of a Nazareth home, "...he shall be called the Son of the Most High: and the Lord God shall give him the throne of his father David: and he shall reign over the house of Jacob forever; and of his kingdom there shall be no end." He assumed his royal reign at the incarnation, ministry, death, resurrection, ascension and coronation as depicted in the New Testament scriptures. He came forth to conquer "in righteousness." And since that time his "armies, the ones in heaven were following him on white horses, clothed with fine clean white linen," the "righteous deeds of the saints."

The complete victory of the Warrior-Christ over the two beasts and their allies is sketched in the final scene of chapter 19. The harsh realism of the picture must not blind us to the fact that the author is consistently writing in symbols. An honest reader must, with self-discipline, follow the author's symbolism with equal consistency. The place a serious reader must start is always the age and circumstances of the author. This is true of any literature. The reader must never impose his state of affairs on an author's writing. So far as possible he must seek to place himself in the total environment that prompted the author to write. Having done that then he is in a position to see any parallells between the original situation and his own.

The battle, often called Armageddon, is not to be thought of as fought with physical armor. Amageddon (hill of Megiddo), though it gets its structure from a particuplar location, is symbolic of a deadly spiritual warfare between the forces of God's Christ versus the old serpent, the dragon, his beasts and their allies. Specifically it refers to the cosmic conflict going on "in righteousness" between Christ and Caesar, the kingdom of God and the kingdom of this world as embodied in Rome and empire. It's design is to symbolize for the first readers the total defeat of Rome by the Christ, the defeat of the empire by the kingdom of God.

John "saw an angel standing in the sun." In a "loud voice" he called all vultures "flying in midheaven" to "Come! Gather for the great feast that you may eat the flesh of" every kind and class of humanity; "kings, captains, strong, cavalry, free, slave, little and great." The beast, the kings, and their armies made war "with the one sitting on the horse and his army." The battle is not described. Only its issue is presented. "The beast (Imperial Rome) was captured and the false prophet (provincial priestly Emporer cult)" was also taken prisoner. And they both were "hurled alive into the lake of fire." In this highly symbolic language John encourages the "seven churches" (the whole church) that Rome and its persecuting Emporer cult are destined for final defeat under the attack of the Warrior-king, the Word of God. As a world power Rome fell to the advancing power of the gospel. Domitian died, the Emporer cult yielded, the church survived long after the Empire fell.

The vision is not complete until John tells, "...the rest were killed with the sword coming out of the mouth of the one sitting on the horse. And all the birds were gorged out of their flesh." The preaching of the gospel, the sword of truth either converted to Christ the "rest" of mankind, or was the sword of judgment that brought them to their "lake of fire." The word of God is a two-edged sword. It cuts to convert while at the same time it severs in judgment. To him who believes it's the means of salvation. To him who rejects it's the sword of damnation.

## A TRANSLATION
### Revelation 20:1-6

And I saw an angel coming down out of heaven having the key of the abyss and a great chain upon his hand. And he seized the dragon, which is the devil, even Satan, and bound him a thousand years. And he threw him into the abyss and shut and sealed over him that he might not any more deceive the nations until the thousand years shall be brought to their goal. After these things it is necessary that he be loosed for a brief time.

And I saw thrones and they to whom (right of judgment was given) sat upon them and judgment was given (to them). And I saw the souls of the ones having been beheaded because of the testimony of Jesus and because of the word of God, and who didn't worship the beast nor his image and who didn't accept his mark upon their forehead or on their hand. And they lived and reigned with the Christ a thousand years. The rest of the dead did not live until the thousand years was brought to its goal. This is the first resurrection. Blessed and holy is the one having part in the first resurrection; over these the second death does not have power, but they shall be priests of God and his Christ and they shall reign with him a thousand years.

## AN OUTLINE OF REVELATION 20:1-6
### Satan Bound and the Reign of the Martyrs!

Revelation is written in a code language of symbols. There's no reason for dropping the symbols at this point. The thousand years signify a limited period of history of spiritual warfare.

Satan is not destroyed, he is "bound." He's restrained, not annihilated. He's limited, not liquidated. 20:10 relates his eternal extinction. During the millennium period of history he's active but "bound" as to what he can accomplish.

I. THE BINDING OF THE DRAGON. 20:1-3
   1. An angel from heaven seizes the dragon, identified as Satan, and binds him a "thousand years." 1-2
   2. Confined to the abyss; sealed off from "deceit of nations" "until the 1000 years" accomplish God's purpose. 3a
   3. Logic demands his release for a "little time." No longer is he to be restrained; he's to be utterly destroyed! 3b

II. THE REIGN OF THE MARTYRS. 20:4-6
   1. Thrones from which ruled:
      (a)Martyrs: they reign in heaven! 4a
      (b)Those who didn't "worship the beast, his image, or receive his mark."
   2. These martyrs and faithful Christians.
      (a)Live & reign with Christ 1000 years."
      (b)Experience the "first resurrection" & avoid "2nd death."
      (c)Are "priests of God and his Christ."

Christians are priest-kings. Christ makes us rulers over self, sin, and death! The "thousand years" symbolizes Christ and his people's triumph over the forces of evil embodied in Rome and its allies. He still reigns! The millennium shall end when Satan is "unbound" for a "little time" in order that he be eternally destroyed.

## A TRANSLATION
### Revelation 20:7-10

And whenever the thousand-year period shall reach its goal, the Satan shall be loosed from his imprisonment and he will go out to deceive the nations, those in the four corners of the earth, God and Magog, (so as) to gather them unto war, the number of whom (is) as the sands of the sea. And they went up on the breadth of the earth and they encircled the camp of the saints and the beloved city; and fire came down from heaven and devoured them. And the devil, the one deceiving them was thrown into the lake of fire and brimstone where the beast and the false prophet also (had been cast) and they shall be tormented day and night unto the ages of the ages.

## AN OUTLINE OF REVELATION 20:7-10

Final defeat of Satan!

God could not be God and allow such evil as Satan not to be finally, fully and completely defeated. The very presence of evil raises a question of the moral and spiritual power of God. Inherent in the very idea of a good God is the impossibility of evil having a permanent place in the ethical, moral, spiritual universe. Even to tolerate Satan for a "little while" must have its constructive result if God's goodness be valid. So this brief passage is basic to the biblical story of sin and redemption. Satan's period of restraint, revealed under the symbolic form of a millennium, is followed by Satan's final permanent imprisonment.

I. SATAN'S FINAL WAR WITH GOD. 20:7-9a
   1. The end of Satan's thousand-year restraint. 7
   2. He mobilizes the nations for warfare against God. 8
   3. His strategy:
      (a) Mobilizes for world war of universal proportions: "over the breadth of the earth..." 9a
      (b) "Encircled the camp of the saints."
      (c) "And the beloved city." Seige war of attrition.

II. DEFEAT AND DESTINY OF SATAN. 20:9b-10
   1. "Fire came down from heaven and consumed them."
   2. Punishment prescribed:
      (a) "The lake of fire and brimstone."
      (b) The nature of the penalty: "tormented day ana night."

Human history as we have known it in this world is now over. The original purpose of God expressed in Genesis has been now accomplished by God's redemptive movement through history. The "image of God" has now been attained in man, God's creation. The primary force of evil has been overcome. Man has been redeemed. Satan has been thwarted and defeated. Eternity lies ahead with the city of God in prospect for redeemed humanity.

Revelation 20:1-3

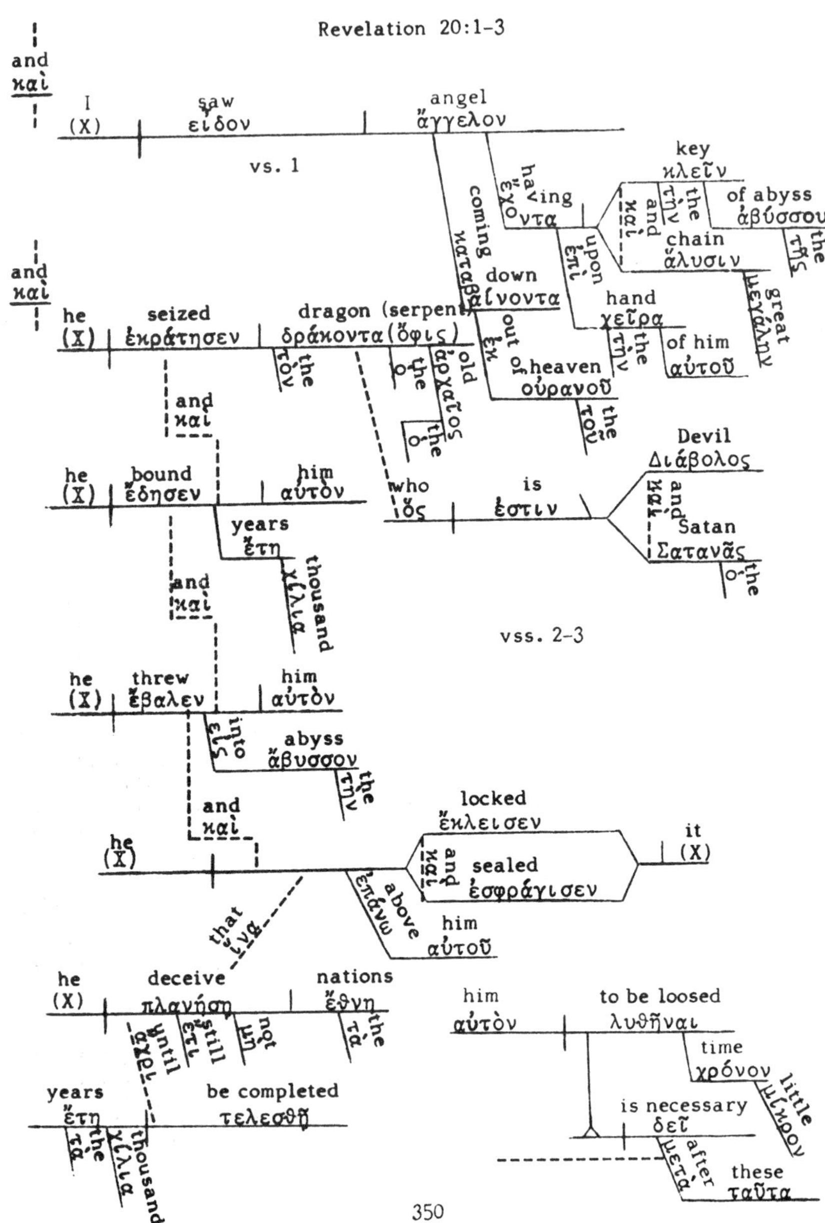

## THE DIAGRAM OF 20:1-3

Verse one is a simple sentence for it has but one clause. "I saw an angel..." Two participles are added to describe the direct object "angel." They are both descriptive presents: καταβαίνοντα "coming down," and ἔχοντα "having." Modifying "coming down" is the prepositional phrase "out of the heaven." It is adverbial expressing from where. "Having" has a brace of direct objects, "key" and "chain." The specific kind of "key" is defined by genitive ἀβύσσου "abyss." The ἐπὶ phrase modifying "having" conveys the idea of manner or circumstance.

Verses 2-3 contain eight distinct clauses. The final clause of verse three may be viewed as an independent sentence though Nestles text tacks it onto the others as an additional dependent clause. If taken as an independent sentence it is simple in form. It has the aorist passive infinitive λυθῆναι "to be loosed as subject of present indicative δεῖ "is necessary." Personal pronoun αὐτὸν "him" is accusative of general reference used as though it were a subject. "...after these things" is an adverbial expression presenting the idea of when. The diagram displays a broken line extending back toward the previous clause "until the thousand years be completed." The reader will make his own judgment as to whether this is to be treated as an independent sentence or to be more closely related to the sentence of verses 2-3a.

Treating 2-3a as a distinct sentence it is compound-complex in structure. It possesses four independent clauses and three dependent. The first idea is: "He seized the dragon..." Direct object δράκοντα "dragon" is expanded in two ways. ὄφις "serpent" is in apposition. Thus it would read, "...he seized the dragon, the old serpent." The author seems anxious that the dragon be thoroughly identified for he inserts an adjectival relative clause (ὅς) to identify him further, "who is (the) Devil and the Satan..."

The second independent clause declares, "...and he bound him a thousand years..." ἔτη is plural, accusative extent of time.

The third independent idea states that "he threw him..." Just precisely where he "threw him" is set forth in the prepositional εἰς adverbial phrase, "into the abyss."

The last of the independents states: "...and he locked and sealed(it)above him." The verbs ἔκλεισεν "locked" and ἐσφράγισεν "sealed" are both narrative aorists, as indeed are all the verbs of the independent clauses. The author is merely stating the facts as matters of fact with no attempt to describe. ἐπάνω "above" is one of the so-called improper prepositions. But it is just as much a preposition as any other. Here it is used with genitive αὐτοῦ "him" as adverb expressing where.

ἵνα "in order that" with subjunctive introduces an adverbial negative clause of purpose: "that he might not still deceive the nations." The ἄχρι "until" sets forth a temporal dependent clause "until the thousand years be completed." τελεσθῇ "be completed" is aorist passive subjunctive of τελέω "bring to an end," "bring to a goal," "complete," "fulfill."

## Revelation 20:4-5a

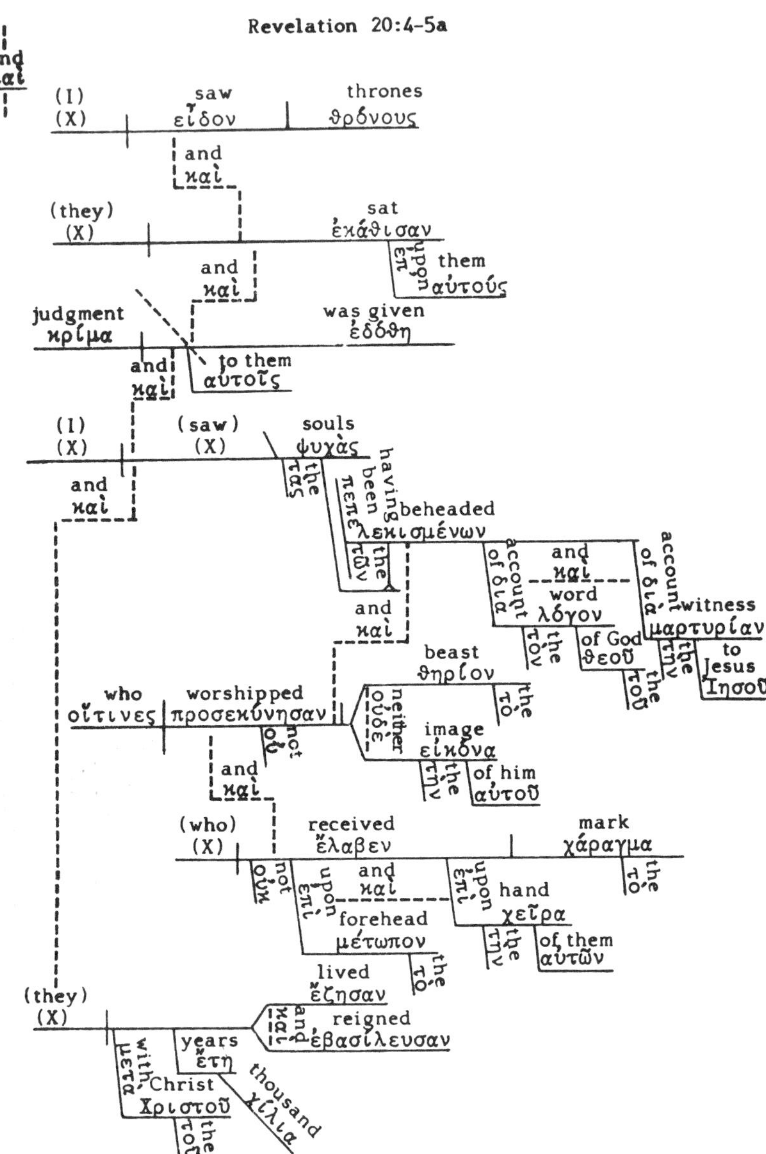

## THE DIAGRAM OF 20:4

Verses 4-5a involve one sentence. It is compound-complex as to classification. The sentence has five independent clauses; it also possesses two fully dependent clauses. However, the articular attributive participle which they parallel gives an idea that is essentially almost the equivalent of a dependent clause.

The initial independent clause states: "I saw thrones..." It has no modifying elements. The second has for its subject a "they" as reflected in the verb ending. But who this "they" is must be judged from the context. Possibly the Lord Jesus and the twelve. (Mt.19:28) The clause reads: "...and they sat upon them..." The phrase "upon them" serves as adverb since it tells where they sat.

The next clause says: "judgment was given to them..." The antecedent of αὐτοῖς "to them" is subject "they" of the preceding clause. The diagram shows a broken line pointing back in that direction. αὐτοῖς is indirect object. The -μα ending on κρίμα "judgment" indicates a verdict of judgment, not the process.

"I saw the souls" constitutes the fourth independent clause. To the object ψυχὰς "souls" is attached the attributive perfect participle mentioned above, πεπελεκισμένων "having been beheaded." The two διὰ phrases, "on account of the word of God" and "on account of the witness to Jesus" express reasons why, hence are adverbial. Placed in parallel to this participle yet being full clauses are two dependent ideas. First, "...who worshipped not the beast, neither his image..." Second: "...and who received not the(his) mark upon the forehead and upon the hand..."

The instrument most frequently used for execution in republican Rome was the πέλεκυς "battle-ax." From this comes the verb πελεκίζω "to cut off with an ax." The perfect participle of this verb in genitive with article appears, as already noted, in this sentence. Its perfect tense gives emphasis to the fixed permanency of the action; "the ones having been axed and who still are."

The fifth of the independent ideas affirms, "...and they lived and reigned with the Christ a thousand years." Both the verbs ἔζησαν "lived" and ἐβασίλευσαν "reigned are constative aorists. The subject "they," taken from the verb endings, has for its antecedent "souls" of the preceding clause. ἔτη "years" indicates extent of time as an accusative. The "with Christ" is also adverb in function indicating how they reigned, the circumstances under which they lived and reigned.

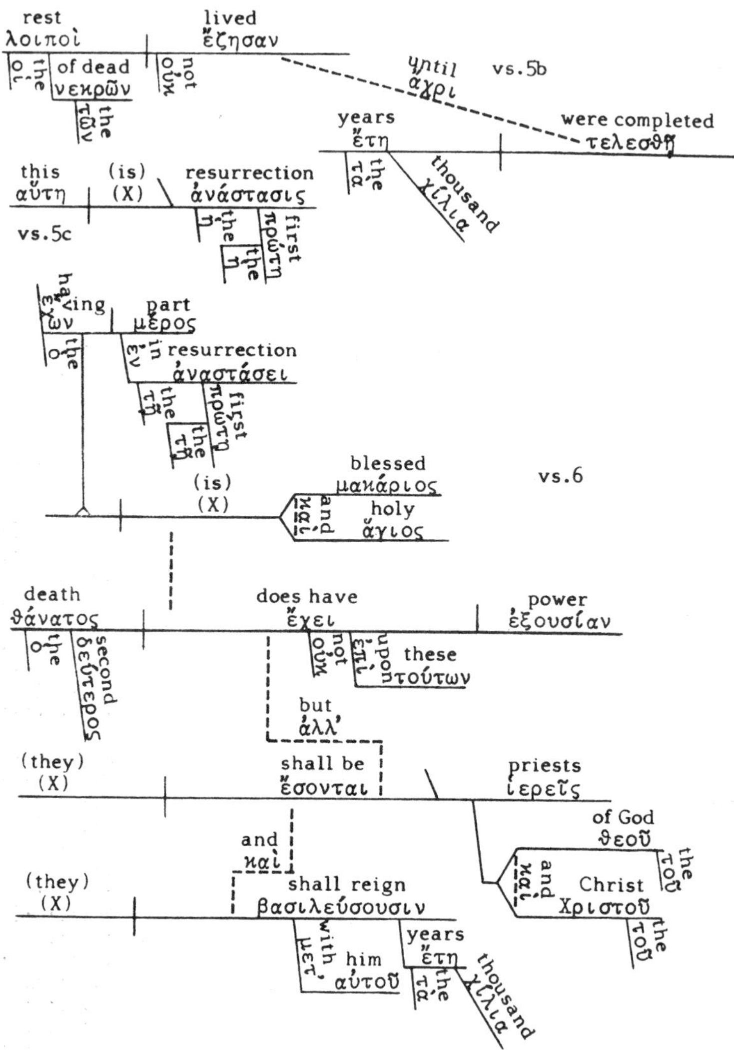
rest
λοιποὶ
οἱ
the
of dead
νεκρῶν
τῶν
the
lived
ἔζησαν
not
οὐκ
until
ἄχρι
vs.5b
years
ἔτη
τὰ
the
thousand
χίλια
were completed
τελεσθῇ
this
αὕτη
(is)
(X)
resurrection
ἀνάστασις
ἡ
the
first
πρώτη
ἡ
the
vs.5c
having
ἔχων
ὁ
the
part
μέρος
in
ἐν
resurrection
ἀναστάσει
τῇ
the
first
πρώτῃ
τῇ
the
(is)
(X)
blessed
μακάριος
and
καὶ
holy
ἅγιος
vs.6
death
θάνατος
ὁ
the
second
δεύτερος
does have
ἔχει
not
οὐκ
upon
ἐπὶ
these
τούτων
power
ἐξουσίαν
but
ἀλλ'
(they)
(X)
shall be
ἔσονται
priests
ἱερεῖς
of God
θεοῦ
τοῦ
the
and
καὶ
Christ
Χριστοῦ
τοῦ
the
and
καὶ
(they)
(X)
shall reign
βασιλεύσουσιν
with
μετ'
him
αὐτοῦ
years
ἔτη
τὰ
the
thousand
χίλια

## THE DIAGRAM OF 20:5-6

Verse 5 divides into two sentences. 5a is compound-complex. It has one independent and one dependent clause. It says, "The rest of the dead did not live until the thousand years were completed." ἄχρι is the harbinger of the dependent clause which presents a temporal idea. τελεσθῇ is aorist passive subjunctive of τελέω "complete," "finish." The word contains the idea of "bringing to an intended goal," a "consumation." Just what the goal is must be determined from the context, not the word. This aorist subjunctive might better be translated, "should be completed."

In the independent clause the subject λοιποὶ "rest" is defined by the genitive νεκρῶν as being "of the dead." But whose these "dead" are is not specified by any added word. Context alone must determine. The aorist verb ἔζησαν is ingressive and may be translated, "came alive."

The sentence of verse 5b is simple in form being of but one clause. "This is the first resurrection." ἀνάστασις "resurrection" whose ending is -σις is an action word. It might be rendered "This is the first rising." The repetition of the definite article with the adjective "first" sharpens more precisely the force of the adjective, "...the rising the first (one)."

Verse 6 incorporates four independent clauses; it contains no subordinate clauses. Subject of the first clause is the attributive present participial phrase ἔχων "the one having part in the first resurrection..." μέρος "part" is neuter accusative (gen.sg. μέρους) serving here as direct object of the participle. The ἐν expression, "in the first resurrection," is adverb in function indicating where he is "having." In this first clause the predicate (that which is said about the subject) is compound, "blessed and holy."

The second of the independent clauses lacks a formal connection (asyndeton) to the first. It states, "the second death does not have power over these..." In translating linear present ἔχει the diagram uses the English emphatic present "does have" rather than progressive "is having."

The strong adversative conjunction ἀλλά "but" joins the third independent clause to the second, "...but they shall be priests..." Instead of being subject to the "second death" "they" (the one having part in the first resurrection) "shall be priests." The kind of priest they shall be is announced in the genitives "of the God" and "of the Christ." Genitive is the case of specification.

The final of the four clauses declares, "...and they shall reign with him the thousand years." The definite article τὰ with ἔτη is anaphoric. It points back to earlier references of the thousand years. The verb βασιλεύσουσιν "shall reign" is future indicative active. Future tense on most occasions would be punctiliar action but here it appears linear. The servants of God not only "shall be" priests but they also shall "reign with him." The fact that it is to be a rule of a "thousand year" suggests linear action.

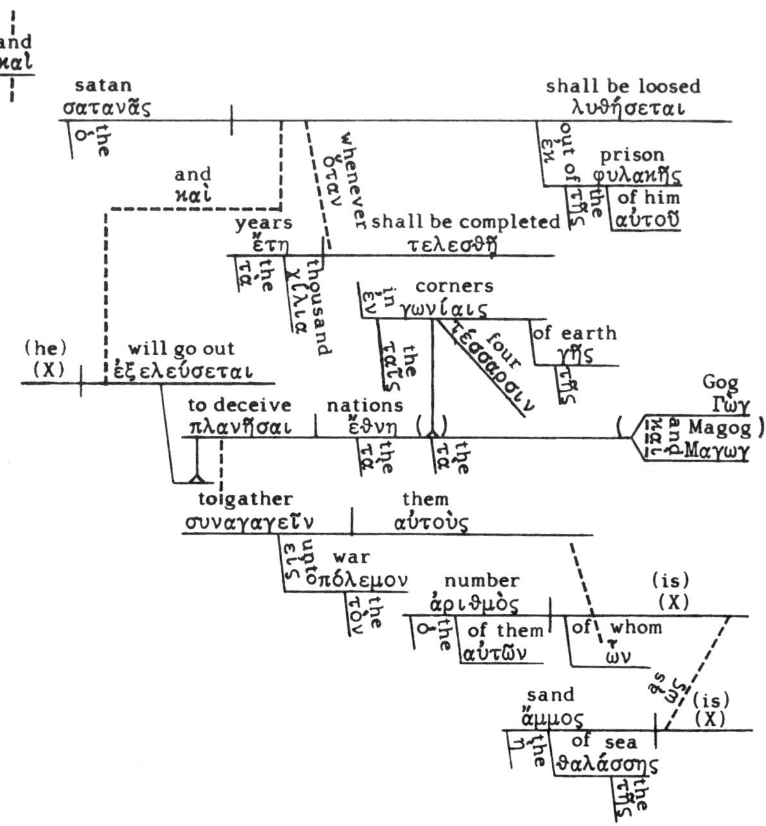
and
καὶ
satan
σατανᾶς
the
ὁ
shall be loosed
λυθήσεται
out of
ἐκ
prison
φυλακῆς
the
τῆς
of him
αὐτοῦ
and
καὶ
whenever
ὅταν
years
ἔτη
the
τὰ
thousand
χίλια
shall be completed
τελεσθῇ
in
ἐν
corners
γωνίαις
the
ταῖς
four
τέσσαρσιν
of earth
γῆς
τῆς
(he)
(X)
will go out
ἐξελεύσεται
to deceive
πλανῆσαι
nations
ἔθνη
the
τὰ
the
τὰ
Gog
Γὼγ
and
καὶ
Magog
Μαγωγ
to gather
συναγαγεῖν
them
αὐτοὺς
up to
εἰς
war
πόλεμον
the
τὸν
number
ἀριθμὸς
the
ὁ
of them
αὐτῶν
(is)
(X)
of whom
ὧν
as
ὡς
sand
ἄμμος
(is)
(X)
the
ἡ
of sea
θαλάσσης
the
τῆς

## THE DIAGRAM OF 20:7-8

The sentence of verses 7-8 encompasses a compound-complex arrangement. It employs two independent elements; it has three dependent clauses besides two infinitive phrases expressing purpose.

The first of the independent elements affirms that "The Satan shall be loosed out of his prison..." The definite article with "Satan" is anaphoric referring back to earlier uses of it, though it may also be demonstrative pointing out the Satan as well known. The ἐκ expression is adverbial because it indicates from where, that is, "out from his prison."

Attached to the first independent and introducing the initial dependent clause is the ὅταν "whenever." It heralds an indefinite temporal adverbial clause: "whenever the thousand years shall be completed..."

The second of the independent clauses affirms that "he will go out..." ἐξελεύσεται is future indicative middle. Attached to this independent are two infinitve expressions both of which declare the purpose of his going out. That is, "to deceive the nations" and "to gather them..." Both infinitives are aorist expressing point action. Being in the future they are announcing the action, not describing it. The direct object of "to deceive" is neuter plural ἔθνη "nations" to which is attached two appositional ideas. One, the ἐν "in the four corners of the earth" phrase. And two, the "Gog and Magog" idea. The ἐν phrase could conceivably modify the infinitive πλανῆσαι "to deceive" as an adverbial idea. The diagram has treated it as substantive in apposition to "nations." This is due to the presence of the definite article τὰ "the" making the whole phrase substantival.

The final two subordinate clauses stem off the second of the infinitive phrases, "to gather them..." The clause introduced by the relative ὧν is adjectival describing the pronoun αὐτοὺς "them" object of infinitive συναγαγεῖν "to gather together." The entire clause reads, "...whose number (is)..." In order to complete the idea initiated by this clause ὡς "as" appears. It might be treated as a predicate nominative expression after the understood "is" and referring back to the subject "number." However, the diagram presents is as an additional adverbial clause of comparison, "...as the sand of the sea (is)."

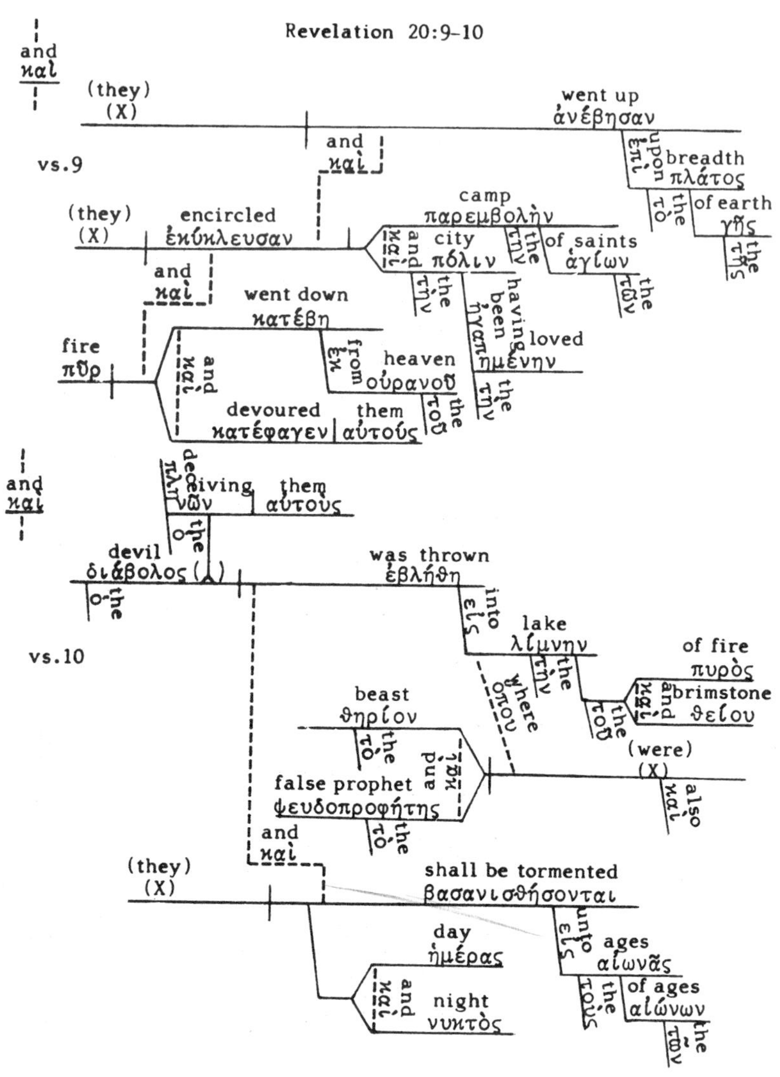
and
καὶ
(they)
(X)
went up
ἀνέβησαν
vs.9
and
καὶ
upon
ἐπὶ
breadth
πλάτος
the
τὸ
of earth
γῆς
the
τῆς
(they)
(X)
encircled
ἐκύκλευσαν
camp
παρεμβολὴν
the
τὴν
and
καὶ
city
πόλιν
the
τὴν
of saints
ἁγίων
the
τῶν
having been loved
ἠγαπημένην
the
τὴν
and
καὶ
went down
κατέβη
from
ἐκ
heaven
οὐρανοῦ
the
τοῦ
fire
πῦρ
and
καὶ
devoured
κατέφαγεν
them
αὐτούς
and
καὶ
deceiving
πλανῶν
the
ὁ
them
αὐτούς
devil
διάβολος
the
ὁ
was thrown
ἐβλήθη
into
εἰς
lake
λίμνην
the
τὴν
of fire
πυρὸς
and
καὶ
brimstone
θείου
the
τοῦ
where
ὅπου
vs.10
beast
θηρίον
the
τὸ
and
καὶ
false prophet
ψευδοπροφήτης
the
ὁ
(were)
(X)
also
καὶ
and
καὶ
(they)
(X)
shall be tormented
βασανισθήσονται
unto
εἰς
ages
αἰῶνας
the
τοὺς
of ages
αἰώνων
the
τῶν
day
ἡμέρας
and
καὶ
night
νυκτὸς

## THE DIAGRAM OF 20:9-10

Verse nine embraces three independent clauses. There are no subordinates so the sentence may be classed as compound. "They went up..." is the simple statement of the first clause. The verb ἀνέβησαν is 2nd aorist indicative active, certainly the appropriate tense and mode for declaring a fact as fact without polishing up the action by descriptive tools. An adverb device appears in the ἐπὶ phrase, "upon the breadth of the earth." It answers the question where.

The second clause confidently declares, "...they encircled the camp of the saints and the beloved city..." ἐκύκλευσαν "encircled" is aorist active indicative of κυκλεύω a late developing verb built on κύκλος "circle." The author uses aorists in announcing this vividly prophetic vision. The verb has two direct objects "camp" and "city." παρεμβολὴν "camp" may be used either of a camp or army. It is used in the Septuagint for the camp of the Israelites in the desert. The particular kind of camp is specified by genitive "of the saints (ἁγίων). The object πόλιν "city" is identified by means of an added attributive perfect participle ἠγαπημένην "having been loved." Its perfect tense is to be noted; the city not only has been loved but still is.

The third clause has a compound predicate; "...fire came down from heaven and devoured them." The preposition κατά prefixed to both verbs is perfective; it intensifies the action of the simple verb.

Compound-complex is the classification for the sentence contained in verse ten. It enjoys two independent clauses and one dependent. The ultimate destiny of the devil is the idea asserted in the first clause. "The devil, the one deceiving them, was thrown..." Where he was thrown is portrayed in vivid language in the adverbial εἰς phrase, "into the lake, the (one) of fire and brimstone..." Stemming off of λίμνην "lake" and describing it is the adjective dependent clause introduced by ὅπου "where." It reads, "...where the beast and the false prophet also (were)..."

The other independent clause relates the eternal consequences of the evil activity of the "beast and false prophet," "they shall be tormented day and night unto the ages of the ages." The terms "day" and "night" are in the genitive. This is not extent of time which would demand accusative. This is kind of time, normal to the genitive. The εἰς with accusative αἰῶνας expresses extent of time. βασανισθήσονται is future (prophetic) indicative passive of βασανίζω to "torture." The verb finds its origin in a noun which originally meant "touchstone," a dark stone employed in assaying metals. The noun developed the meaning of "examination by torture." The verb originally meant "to rub on the touchstone," "to put to the test." It developed into the meaning, "to examine by torture." Then the general meaning, "to torture," "torment."

## SOME EXPOSITORY THOUGHTS ON 20:1-6

John stated in 1:1 that God "signed" (gave in symbols) this Revelation. The symbols are consistently used through the whole of the book. Numerals are not symbolic in one place and literal in another. The reference to a "thousand years" in this passage is as symbolic as "ten days" is in 2:10 or "seven" is in 1:20. A thousand is merely 10x10x10. One thousand is symbolic of a long, yet indeterminate, limit of time. It was not meant to be a literal thousand years of exactly 365¼ days, no more, no less. It is rather the communication of an idea by means of cryptic code language. We look for the truth for which 1000 years is symbolic.

John saw in vision "an angel coming down from heaven," who, with a "key" and a "great chain" collared "Satan,..bound him a thousand years,..threw him into the abyss,..locked it over him that he not deceive the nations any more, until the thousand years be completed..." It is imperative to note that "to bind" does not mean to annihilate, obliterate or blot out. The ultimate destruction of Satan is not reported until 20:10. But here in verse two he is only "bound," and that for a limited though long time. Furthermore, to bind restricts activity, it doesn't eliminate it. Though bound and imprisoned Satan is able to carry on his nefarious opposition to God and his people. He's a gangster running his mob activity from prison's limitations. In fact this is confirmed by the last clause of verse three; "...after this it's necessary that he be loosed for a little while." He won't be bound forever but when he's "loosed" it will be but for a "little while" until his final and permanent destruction.(cf.20:10)

What John means by Satan's being "bound" is made more clear when we observe that Jesus conquered "demons" during his ministry. In Luke 9:31 the demons possessing the Garasenes begged Jesus "not to command them to depart into the abyss." They did not want their activity to be hampered, limited or imprisoned. That is, they did not want to be "bound." In Matthew 12:29 Jesus asks, "How can one enter a strong man's house and plunder his goods, unless he first binds the strong man?" Satan was the "strong man" whose house Jesus as the "stronger" man entered to "bind" him and "plunder his goods" by casting out (binding) demons from possessed people. When God became incarnate in the Christ Satan failed to destroy him; he "fell from heaven." But Satan pursued his enmity through the beasts of Rome and its provincial cult priests. In 16:12-15 "demonic spirits" gathered forces of the "whole world" to do battle at Armageddon. As Satan was "bound" during the earthly ministry of Jesus, so he's "bound" in his battle of his beasts against Christ's churches. He could not destroy the reign of God in his Christ through the beast of Imperial Rome.

This victory of Armageddon by Christ through the "binding" of Satan is confirmed in verses 4 and 6 of this same paragraph. John says he saw "thrones." Those who sat on these thrones were "those who had been beheaded on account of their testimony to Jesus...who had not worshipped the beast,...and did not receive the mark on their foreheads or hands. And they became alive and reigned with the Christ a thousand years." This "becoming alive and reigning" is described as "the first resurrection." Nothing is said about the "thrones" as being on earth. It's reasonable to view them as being in heaven. In earlier visions the thrones John saw were in heaven.(4:4) Some of those who sat on the thrones were martyrs; also others, not martyrs, but who successfully resisted government coercion. These too "lived and reigned." They were the faithful who endured under the persecution of Nero and Domitian. These were not Christians who reign with Christ on earth at some future date. They were those who were beheaded and refused the beast's mark under Domitian. They weren't raised from the dead on this earth; they "became alive" when beheaded, and they mounted their thrones and "reigned with Christ." "This is the first resurrection." The "rest of the dead," the non-believer or compromising, faithless Christian, didn't enjoy "becoming alive and reigning" with Christ and the saints during the thousand years. The millennium of verses 4-6 is the moral, spiritual reign of the Christ with his saints. It began with his crucifixion, resurrection, ascension and coronation. It continued through the triumphant conflict with Rome; it continues until the consummation of history at Christ's return.

"I have overcome the world;" "my peace I leave with you;" "the one believing on me, even if he die, shall go on living..." Can there be any Armageddon of shot or shell whose victory be greater than this? Is there any sovereign rule more triumphant than this conquering of moral weakness, spiritual corruption, or mortal frailty? Can the force of the sword make me more free, more kingly, more alive than the royal priesthood Christ gives me? I live in the millennium of God's timeless plan for man's redemption from sin and its consequence, death. 'Tis the reign of God in Christ; foreshadowed by prophet, announced by angels, established by Christ, proclaimed by apostles, embodied in his believing church.

## SOME EXPOSITORY THOUGHTS ON 20:7-10

During the reign of Messiah in history Satan has been "bound" but not destroyed. The reign of Christ with his saints has limited the dragon but not liquidated him. That must come at the end of history. In this paragraph John reports (it certainly isn't a long colorful, dramatic description) what occurs at the consummation.

For a "little time" Satan is "released" from the restraint of his millennium imprisonment. He goes out to scour the "four corners of the earth" to "deceive the nations." He'll embody himself in nations, institutions, governments, their foreign and domestic policies. He shall become in the end what "Gog and Magog" were in Old Testament times, ruthless enemy of God's people. By these agencies he will make an all-out attack against the kingdom of Christ. "As the sand of the sea in number" so will his forces be. He will "go over the breadth of the earth" with his evil forces and "will encircle the camp of the saints and the beloved city." In this vivid symbolic language does John picture the final onslaught of Satan for a "little time" against the present active rule of God's Christ with his saints. God's kingdom is now in history in the person and work of Jesus Christ. But there comes a final encounter between Christ and Satan on the plane of history. The compassing of the "camp of the saints" and of the "beloved city" symbolizes the final contest.

John does not dwell on details. In one unadorned statement he divulges the end. "Fire came down out of heaven and devoured them..." The destruction of the devil does not arise from the earth. It comes down "out of heaven" from God. Whatever "fire" symbolizes it utterly "ate them up," that is, they are finally, completely, utterly consumed. They aren't imprisoned or "bound" for an indeterminate period; they are thoroughly exterminated. The only other detail that John reports is the ultimate and permanent disposition of Satan. "The devil, the one deceiving them, was cast into the lake of the fire and brimstone, where also the beast and the false prophet (were cast), and they shall be tormented day and night unto the ages of the ages." Such is the rather prosaic way in which the biblical author relates the end of the Satan whose image casts its dark shadow over the long tragic valley of human history. How the end is to come he does not state. Only that God initiates it. When the end comes he does not tell, except to say that it is at the close of the "thousand years." It is enough to know that there will be an end when he who is the source of all evil will be thoroughly defeated and permanently destroyed.

Innate to the idea of God is the companion idea that good must triumph over evil. God must defeat, and that decisively, him who is the spring of all moral depravity and spiritual corruption. The nature of sin guarantees its defeat for it has within it the seed that has to end in self-disintegration. The "lake of fire and brimstone" is but the fruit of immoral activity; it's the predictable destiny of spiritual perversion. God could not remain God and permit the One source of all Evil not to be totally obliterated from the spiritual experience of such a divinely-imaged creature as man. Thus the vision of this paragraph is a logical necessity, a predictable fact of the future. Given the major premise of a good God, the minor premise that moral evil cannot forever survive in the presence of God, the inevitable logic demands a total end to evil. That which logic demands this vision revealed to John as a fact of the future. And through John to all generations.

What more is to be said? As we have experienced it, history is past. God has not only made man "in his own image" but, through redemption, has remade man in "his image." Evil in its source has been reduced to zero. That which lies ahead is resurrection, judgment, and the death of death, after which an incomprehensible vista of eternity stretches.

## A TRANSLATION
## Revelation 20:11-15

And I saw a great white throne and the one sitting upon it from the face of whom the earth and sky fled; and a place for them was not found. And I saw the dead, the great and the small, standing before the throne. And books were opened. And another book was opened which is the book of life. And the dead were judged out of the things having been written in the books according to their works. And the sea gave up the dead, that which was in it; and death and hades gave up the dead, that which was in them, and each was judged according to their works. And death and hades were thrown into the lake of fire. This is the second death, the lake of fire. And if anyone shall not be found written in the book of life, he shall be thrown into the lake of fire.

## AN OUTLINE OF REVELATION 20:11-15

### The Death of Death!

The curtain has been lowered on human history. As far as the drama of man's tragedy in history is concerned it is a thing of the past. But one event, anchored in history, but bridging into eternity must yet be portrayed. More than an encore it is the critic's encore.

What is the judgment on history? What is the judgment on man? What is the judgment on God? It's imperative that the entire universe have clear answers to these questions.

I. THE BASIS OF JUDGMENT. 20:11-12
1. The "great white throne." Purity of judgment!
2. The "earth and sky fled." Earth cannot distort judgment.
3. Universality of judgment. The "great and the small," "the sea...death and hades gave up the dead..."
4. The books of recorded deeds.
5. Another book: the "book of life."

II. THE VERDICT. 20:13-15
1. Death and hades were "cast into lake of fire." 13-14
   (a)Death - the horror of the experience eliminated.
   (b)Hades - the permanancy of death eliminated.
   (c)This is the "second death." - the death of death!
2. They who reject life "in Christ" choose death with death! 15

Death holds no concern for those written in the book of life. By its nature life excludes death. The death of death means that life prevails; death is no more. At worst it's but a shadowed memory of the past. At best a foil against which God's grace and love show up all the brighter.

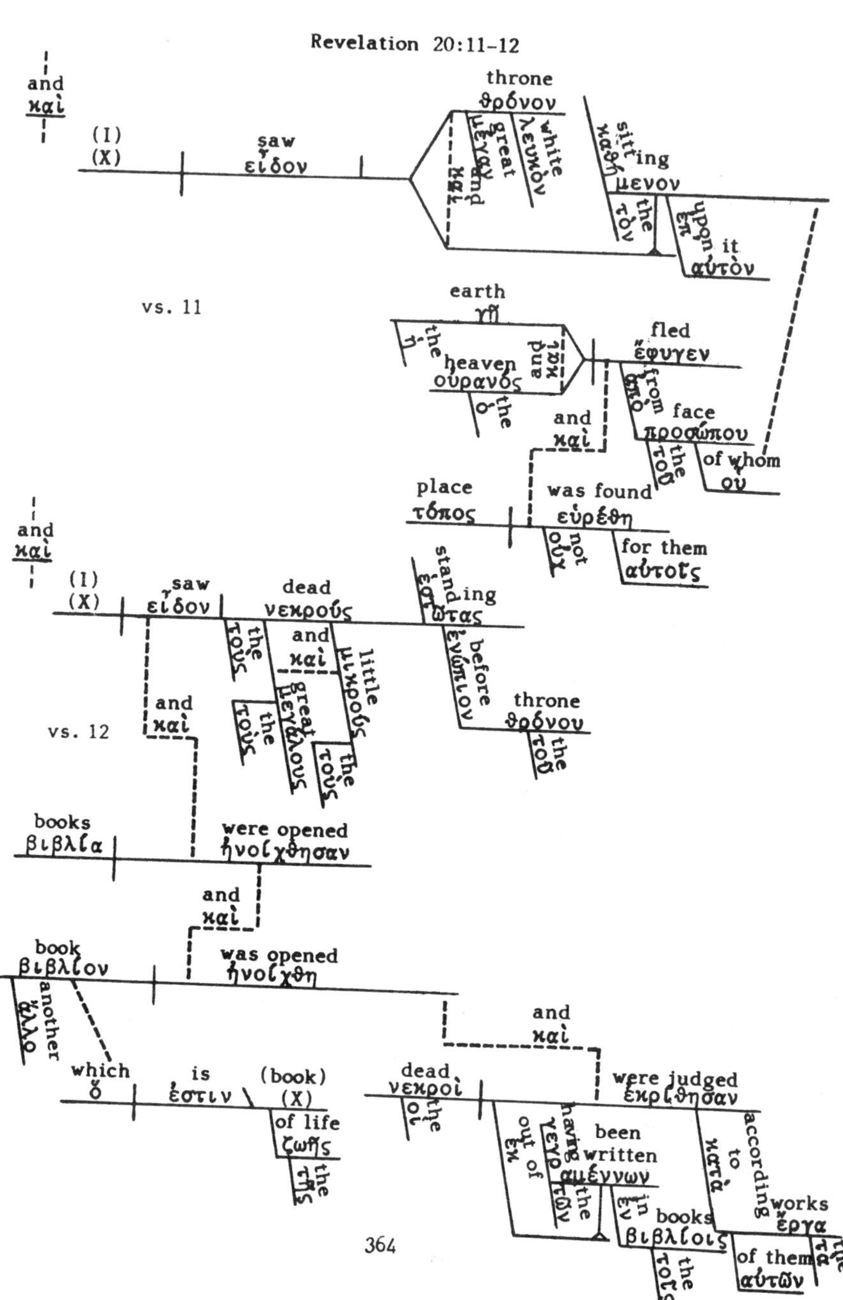
and
καὶ
(I)
(X)
saw
εἶδον
throne
θρόνον
great
μέγαν
and
καὶ
white
λευκὸν
sitting
καθήμενον
the
τὸν
upon
ἐπ
it
αὐτὸν
vs. 11
earth
γῆ
the
ἡ
and
καὶ
heaven
οὐρανὸς
the
ὁ
fled
ἔφυγεν
from
ἀπὸ
face
προσώπου
the
τοῦ
of whom
οὗ
and
καὶ
place
τόπος
was found
εὑρέθη
not
οὐχ
for them
αὐτοῖς
and
καὶ
(I)
(X)
saw
εἶδον
dead
νεκρούς
the
τοὺς
and
καὶ
little
μικροὺς
great
μεγάλους
the
τοὺς
standing
ἑστῶτας
before
ἐνώπιον
throne
θρόνου
the
τοῦ
and
καὶ
vs. 12
books
βιβλία
were opened
ἠνοίχθησαν
and
καὶ
book
βιβλίον
another
ἄλλο
was opened
ἠνοίχθη
which
ὅ
is
ἐστιν
(book)
(X)
of life
ζωῆς
the
τῆς
and
καὶ
dead
νεκροί
the
οἱ
were judged
ἐκρίθησαν
out of
ἐκ
having been written
γεγραμμένων
the
τῶν
in
ἐν
books
βιβλίοις
the
τοῖς
according to
κατὰ
works
ἔργα
the
τὰ
of them
αὐτῶν

THE DIAGRAM OF 20:11-12

One independent clause from which two dependents hang makes of verse 11 a complex sentence. The affirmation of the independent clause is: "I saw..." Precisely what he saw is depicted in a double object. First, "great white throne." And second, "the one sitting upon it." καθήμενον is attributive present participle with definite article.

The genitive relative pronoun οὗ "whose" is the bridge that links the dependent clauses to the participle in the main clause. The first of the dependents declares, "...from whose face the earth and the heaven fled..." Preposition ἀπὸ with ablative indicates whence, "from whose face..." hence is adverbial in function. The ablative is the case which best expresses separation. The second of the dependent elements avers: "...place was not found for them." Both the subordinate clauses use aorist tense.

One dependent clause added to four independents makes for a compound-complex classification. Such is the sentence of verse 12. The first independent states what the Seer "saw." "I saw the dead, the little and the great, standing before the throne..." The preposition ἐνώπιον "before" is one of the so-called "improper" prepositions. It is used with the genitive and means "in the sight of," hence "before." Here it introduces an adverbial idea of where. Whether perfect participle is circumstantial or supplementary may be debatable. The diagram has it as supplementary to εἶδον. John didn't see "the dead." He saw "the dead standing..." The participle carries the main idea in the predicate.

The second independent is the unmodified "books were opened-..." the verb ἠνοίχθησαν "were opened" is aorist passive of ἀνοίγω "to open."

The third independent idea speaks of one particular book, "...another book was opened..." This book is specially identified by the relative clause introduced by ὅ "which is (the book) of the life..." This dependent clause is adjectival in function. The understood "book" is described by genitive ζωῆς "of life." The genitive specifies the particular kind of book. It's the "life" kind, not any other kind.

The last of the independent clauses reports the destiny of "the dead." "The dead were judged..." How they were judged is set forth by two prepositional expressions; "out of (ἐκ) (the things) having been written in the books." The participle γεγραμέννων is attributive, "ones having been written." Its perfect tense suggests that the things "having been written" still stand as written; they are permanently fixed. The κατὰ phrase also indicates the how or basis on which they "were judged." It's "according to their works."

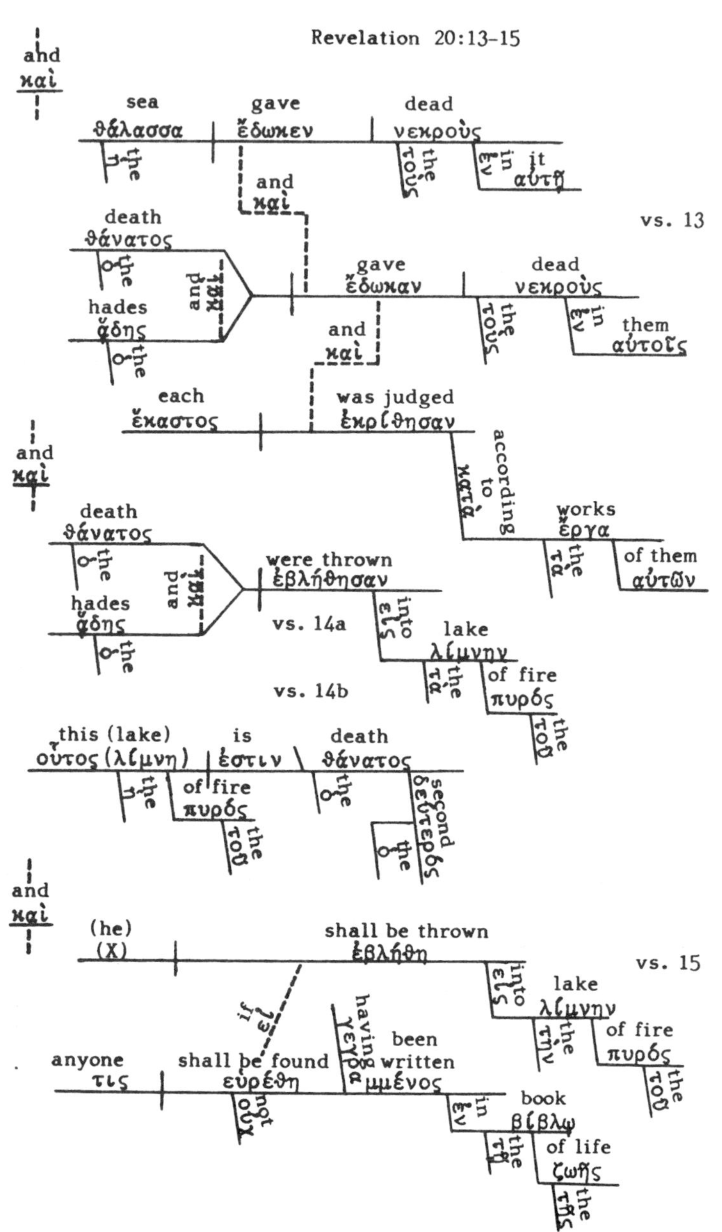
and
καὶ
sea
θάλασσα
the
ἡ
gave
ἔδωκεν
dead
νεκροὺς
the
τοὺς
in
ἐν
it
αὐτῇ
and
καὶ
vs. 13
death
θάνατος
the
ὁ
and
καὶ
hades
ᾅδης
the
ὁ
gave
ἔδωκαν
dead
νεκροὺς
the
τοὺς
in
ἐν
them
αὐτοῖς
and
καὶ
each
ἕκαστος
was judged
ἐκρίθησαν
according to
κατὰ
works
ἔργα
the
τὰ
of them
αὐτῶν
and
καὶ
death
θάνατος
the
ὁ
and
καὶ
hades
ᾅδης
the
ὁ
were thrown
ἐβλήθησαν
vs. 14a
into
εἰς
lake
λίμνην
the
τὰ
of fire
πυρός
the
τοῦ
vs. 14b
this (lake)
οὗτος (λίμνη)
the
ἡ
of fire
πυρός
the
τοῦ
is
ἐστιν
death
θάνατος
the
ὁ
second
δεύτερός
the
ὁ
and
καὶ
(he)
(X)
shall be thrown
ἐβλήθη
vs. 15
into
εἰς
lake
λίμνην
the
τὴν
of fire
πυρός
the
τοῦ
if
εἰ
anyone
τις
shall be found
εὑρέθη
not
οὐχ
having been written
γεγραμμένος
in
ἐν
book
βίβλῳ
the
τῷ
of life
ζωῆς
the
τῆς

## THE DIAGRAM OF 20:13-15

Three independent clauses determine 20:13 to be a compound sentence in structure. "The sea gave the dead in it," is the thought expressed in the first clause. The "in it" phrase is adjectival in effect since it limits or describes the object νεκροὺς "dead." The definite article τοὺς helps to substantize what would otherwise be an adjective νεκροὺς "dead." νεκρὸς is basically an adjective and therefore implies some substantive such as "bodies."

The second clause uses a compound subject to include all the dead, "...the death and the hades gave the dead in them..." Note a distinction between the noun "death" in the subject and adjective "dead" as direct object. The Greek word ᾅδης "hades" is worthy of diligent research to the student of the scriptures. Limitations of space forbid any lengthy discussion here. But in general it is to be observed that in the New Testament "hades" is treated as the abode of the departed, both the good and the bad. There are moral distinctions but it is a period of retention until the final judgment, the consummation of human history. ᾅδης is personified as holding the "dead" which it must disgorge before final judgment.

The last of the independent clauses asserts that "...each was judged according to his works." κατὰ with accusative is the normal construction by which to express the standard of measurement. Each will be judged measured by this standard.

Verse 14a embodies a simple sentence. Its one clause repeats the compound subject from the final clause of the preceding sentence "death and hades..." ἐβλήθησαν is aorist indicative passive. This tense is appropriate for reporting this final destiny of man's "last enemy." Aorist tense has a finality, an urgency, a decisiveness that fits it for this expression. Of course the εἰς phrase is adverb in usage since it indicates where.

Verse 14b also reflects a simple sentence. Demonstrative pronoun οὗτος is the subject. In apposition to it is the noun λίμνη "lake." The definite article with "lake" is anaphoric referring back to the earlier mentioning of the lake. The "of fire" phrase is adjectival specifying the kind of lake; it's the "lake of fire," not any other kind. The ordinal numeral δεύτερός "second" is used here as an adjective to limit θάνατος "death." "Death" is predicate adjective pointing back to the "this, the lake of fire." Thus the "the second death" is identified with "the lake of fire."

Verse 15 frames a complex sentence of two clauses. The first declares, "And he shall be thrown into the lake of fire..." The dependent clause is a first class conditional, the condition assumed to be true, "...if he shall not be found having been written in the book of life." γεγραμμένος is perfect passive participle. It supplements aorist passive εὑρέθη "shall be found." Together they form a perfect periphrastic verb which, with the negative, may be translated, "shall not have been written." Note the full force of the perfect tense, a permanent, fixed finality about the negative action. He hasn't been written and it's going to stay unwritten.

## SOME EXPOSITORY THOUGHTS ON 20:11-15

John has reported history behind; he now turns to eternity ahead! Spanning between history and eternity is resurrection, judgment and the death of death.

First in his vision is "a great white throne." The throne is that of the Almighty. This is clear from the fact that "earth and sky fled" from his face. Nothing of this earthy, temporal, physical, corrupted creation would be able to tamper with this king-judge. Besides, the throne was "white" symbol of purity, that which alone is eternal. The basis of judgment is purity!

A general resurrection, though not specifically mentioned, is implied. John asserts that he "saw the dead...standing. "Furthermore, "the sea gave up its dead...and death and hades gave up their dead..." The "dead" were no longer "dead" if they were "standing," nor if they had been disgorged from the "sea," "death," and "hades." This is that which follows the general resurrection.(Jn.5:28-29)

Moreover, the judgment is all-inclusive, absolutely universal. It includes "the great and the small," the noble and ignoble, kings and commoners, all that sea, land, death and hades gobbled up in their insatiate greed for victims. Obscurity does not allow escape; nor does nobility soften judgment.

"Books were opened." These are plainly those that contain the "deeds done in the body." We recall that the author is still writing in symbolic language. God doesn't need a literal filing system to find out what deeds we've done. Nevertheless, no deed or its consequences is lost in its effect on character.

"And another book was opened," this time identified as "the book of life." Judgment proceeds on the basis of what the books, including the "book of life," reveal. God's judgment is not based on any difficulty of his uncovering knowledge of our "deeds." But our deeds are the consequence of receiving or rejecting of God's grace in Christ.

Destiny for the redeemed is reserved for a later report of the coming New Jerusalem. The present passage records the verdict and execution of the "lost." "Death and hades are thrown into the lake of fire," which lake is defined as "the second death." "Death and hades are personified and dealt with as other victims. Here is the promise that these ravaging enemies will be eliminated. Death can no longer oppress! Dying shall be no more; nor shall there be any shadowy prison for the souls of men. The "second death" is the complete death of death! Eternity will harbor no such enemy. Death belongs only to time and history!

Furthermore, that which happens unto death and hades is the destiny of "anyone not found written in the book of life." He too "shall be thrown into the lake of fire." Life in its very nature debars death. Thus, he whose "name"(person)possesses "life" shall not be so consumed. Contrarily, he who shall not be found possessing "life" "shall be thrown into the lake of fire." History is over; life prevails; eternity is!

## A TRANSLATION
### Revelation 21:1-8

And I saw a new heaven and a new earth, for the first heaven and the first earth passed away, and the sea is not any more. And I saw the holy city, new Jerusalem, coming down out of heaven from God, having been prepared as a bride adorned for her man. And I heard a loud voice from the throne saying, "Behold the tabernacle of God (is) with men, and he will pitch his tent with them and they shall be his people and God himself shall be with them. And he shall wipe away every tear out of their eyes, and death shall not be any more; neither mourning nor cry nor pain shall be any more, because the first things passed away."

And the one sitting upon the throne said, "Behold! I make new all things." And he says, "Write! For these words are faithful and true." And he said to me, "They have happened! I (am) the alpha and the omega, the beginning and the end. To the one thirsting, I will give of the fountain of the water of life freely. The one being victorious will inherit these things and I will be to him God and he shall be to me, son. But to the cowards, and faithless, and polluted, and murderers, and fornicators, and sorcerers, and idolators, and all the liars, their portion (shall be) the lake burning with fire and brimstone, the second death.

## AN OUTLINE OF REVELATION 21:1-8
### Fellowship with God in the City of God!

What of God's people beyond history? What is their role in the New Jerusalem? What will life be when we "see him just as he is" and move into eternity? Can we be realistic about what lies beyond human experience? What does it mean to be in "heaven" with God and the people of God?

John paints the unpaintable, 21:1-22:5. He develops three ideas: (1)fellowship,21:1-8, (2)protection, 21:9-26, (3)provision,22:1-5. Here 21:1-8 he considers the aspect of fellowship.

I. THE NEW ORDER DESCRIBED. 21:1-5a
   1. A new kind of heaven and earth; the first "is no more." 1a
   2. No more separation. "The sea is no more." 1b
   3. Its origin: "...down from heaven" not up from beneath. 2a
   4. Its nature: "as a bride adorned for her man." 2b
   5. Presence of the eternal God living with his people. 3
   6. Final victory over earth's defeats; pain, sorrow, etc. 4-5

II. THE GUARANTOR OF THE NEW ORDER. 21:5b-6
   1. The word pledged. 5b-6a
   2. The promise. 6c
   3. The guarantor's capacity to fulfill his pledged word. 6b

III. THE HEIRS OF THE NEW ORDER. 21:7-8
   1. The "one overcoming shall inherit these things." Heaven is God's gift but it involves moral, ethical manifestations of redemptive grace. 7.
   2. Non-heirs offer sharp contrast to heirs. 8

Redemption is of God's grace; its effect is moral character made worthy for eternity of divine fellowship.

Revelation 21:1-2


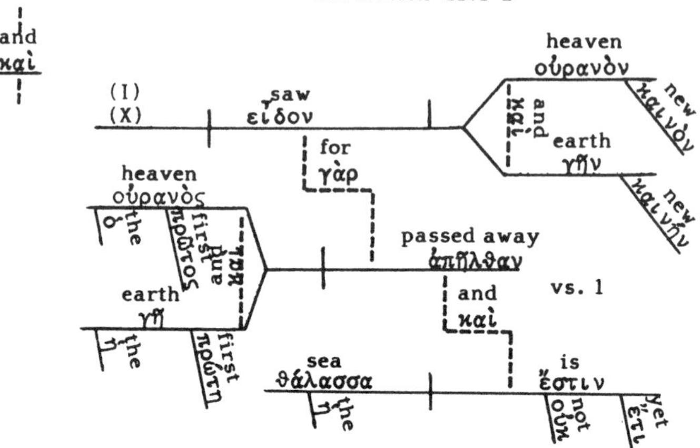

and
καὶ
(I)
(X)
saw
εἶδον
heaven
οὐρανὸν
new
καινὸν
and
καὶ
earth
γῆν
new
καινήν
for
γὰρ
heaven
οὐρανὸς
the
ὁ
first
πρῶτος
and
καὶ
earth
γῆ
the
ἡ
first
πρώτη
passed away
ἀπῆλθαν
and
καὶ
vs. 1
sea
θάλασσα
the
ἡ
is
ἔστιν
not
οὐκ
yet
ἔτι


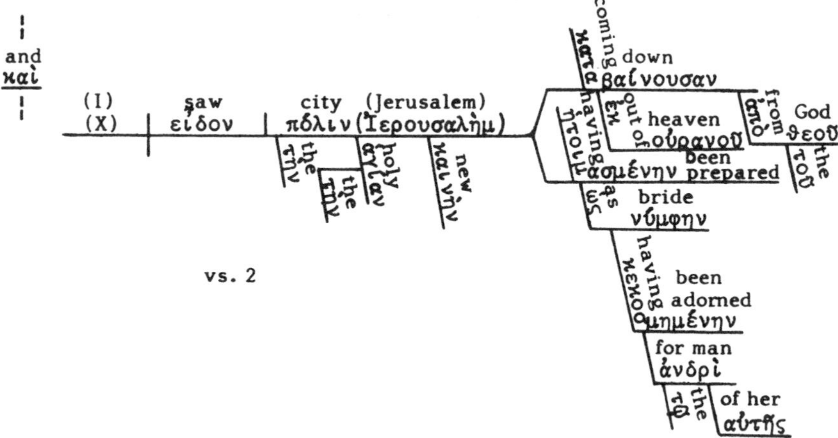

and
καὶ
(I)
(X)
saw
εἶδον
city
πόλιν
(Jerusalem)
Ἰερουσαλὴμ
the
τὴν
the
τὴν
holy
ἁγίαν
new
καινὴν
coming down
καταβαίνουσαν
out of
ἐκ
heaven
οὐρανοῦ
from
ἀπὸ
God
θεοῦ
the
τοῦ
having been prepared
ἡτοιμασμένην
as
ὡς
bride
νύμφην
having been adorned
κεκοσμημένην
for man
ἀνδρὶ
the
τῷ
of her
αὐτῆς
vs. 2

## THE DIAGRAM OF 21:1-2

In striking contrast to the preceding scene of the "lake of fire" is the next vision of a "new heaven and a new earth."(21:1-8)

Verse one thrusts forward a compound sentence of three clauses. First, John states: "I saw a new heaven and a new earth..." It is to be noted that the word for "new" is καινός. This signifies "new" in respect to kind or quality; that which is unused or to which one is unaccustomed; "brand new" so to speak. It contrasts to νέος "new" in the respect to time. So the "new heaven and new earth" are new in the sense of quality, character, condition. The idea is not that of this world renovated but an entirely new kind!

The second clause proclaims: "...the first heaven and the first earth passed away..." ἀπῆλθαν is aorist indicative passive of the defective verb ἀπέρχομαι to go away, depart. The verb literally means "to go off." It's possible that the preposition ἀπό prefixed to the simple verb could be the perfective use. If so that suggests the "arrival at a destination." The first heaven and first earth have served their purpose, arrived at their appointed destiny and have "gone away."

The third clause of verse one is a negative statement,"...the sea is not any more." οὐκ is a strong negative and here goes with the verb. ἔτι is an adverb which emphasizes the negation.

Verse two embraces a simple sentence. Denuded of any modifiers the bare sentence says: "I saw city..." Adjective ἁγίαν along with its repeated article defines the city as being "the holy city." This adjective means "holy" in the sense of "set apart," "dedicated." In apposition to "city" is Ἰερουσαλὴμ "Jerusalem" itself defined as "new" in the sense described above. This city, "New Jerusalem," is further described by two participles. καταβαίνουσαν "coming down" is present active describing the city as in the process of "coming down." The city descends "out of heaven" and it is "from God" not from man. The ἐκ and ἀπό phrases make this clear. The next participle is perfect passive ἡτοιμασμένην "having been prepared." The tense intimates that "preparing" resulted in a permanent condition. The city was "prepared" in the sense that it had been made suitable as a place for people redeemed into the nature and image of God. The ὡς expression is placed in the diagram as a prepositional phrase. If the νύμφην were a nominative case instead of accusative it would be diagrammed as a dependent adverbial clause, "as a bride is adorned..." But being accusative the ὡς appears as a preposition. "Bride" itself is described by circumstantial participle κεκοσμημένην "having been adorned." Perfect tense has its usual force, permanently adorned.

The participles, "coming down" and "having been prepared," appear on the horizontal line with εἶδον "saw." It seems best to take them as supplementary rather than circumstantial. They are more than incidental circumstances; they are essential to the sense of what John is saying. He isn't saying, "I saw the holy city,..." Rather he is saying, "I saw (that) the holy city, New Jerusalem, was coming down and had been prepared."..

Revelation 21:3–4

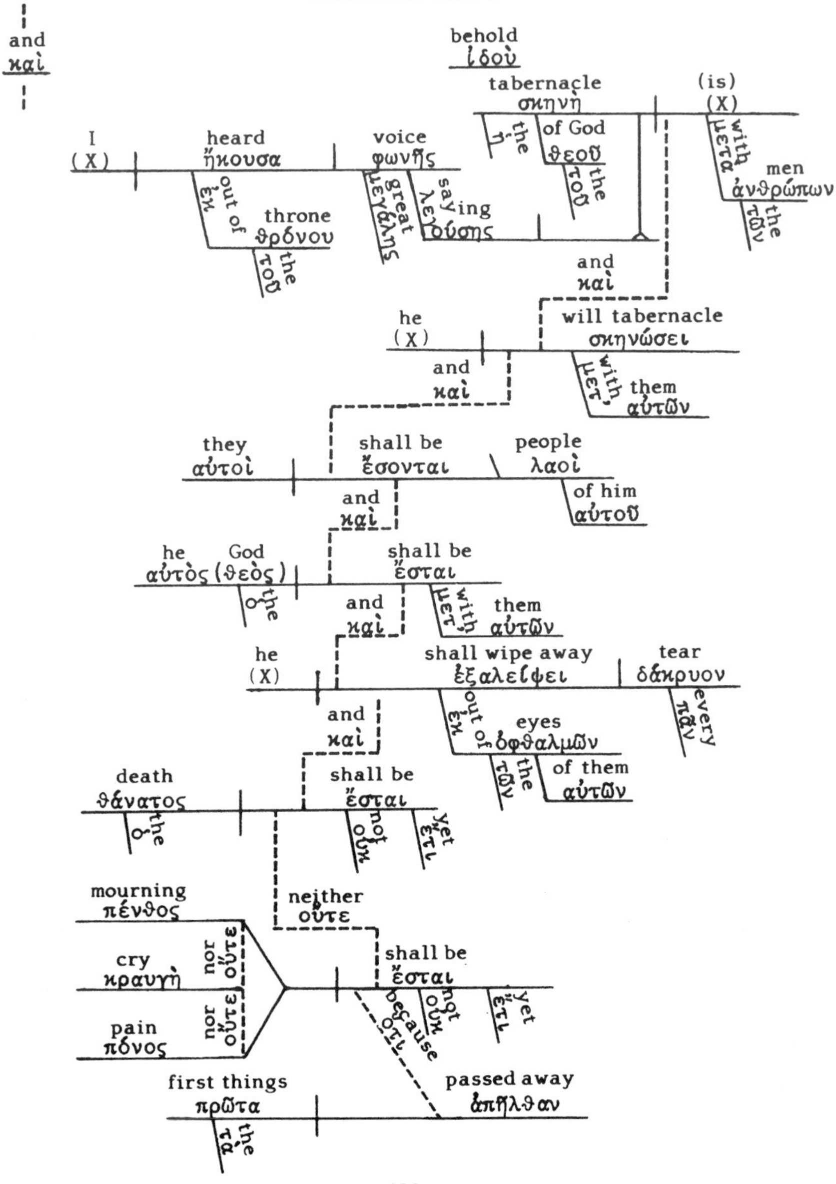

and
καὶ

behold
ἰδοὺ

tabernacle
σκηνὴ
the
ἡ
of God
θεοῦ
the
τοῦ

(is)
(X)
with
μετὰ
men
ἀνθρώπων
the
τῶν

I
(X)
heard
ἤκουσα
out of
ἐκ
throne
θρόνου
the
τοῦ

voice
φωνῆς
great
μεγάλης
saying
λεγούσης

and
καὶ

he
(X)
will tabernacle
σκηνώσει
with
μετ'
them
αὐτῶν

and
καὶ

they
αὐτοὶ
shall be
ἔσονται
people
λαοὶ
of him
αὐτοῦ

and
καὶ

he God
αὐτὸς (θεὸς)
the
ὁ
shall be
ἔσται
with
μετ'
them
αὐτῶν

and
καὶ

he
(X)
shall wipe away
ἐξαλείψει
tear
δάκρυον
every
πᾶν
out of
ἐκ
eyes
ὀφθαλμῶν
the
τῶν
of them
αὐτῶν

and
καὶ

death
θάνατος
the
ὁ
shall be
ἔσται
not
οὐκ
yet
ἔτι

neither
οὔτε

mourning
πένθος
nor
οὔτε
cry
κραυγὴ
nor
οὔτε
pain
πόνος
shall be
ἔσται
not
οὐκ
yet
ἔτι
because
ὅτι

first things
πρῶτα
the
τὰ
passed away
ἀπῆλθαν

## THE DIAGRAM OF 21:3-4

The sentence of 21:3-4 consists of nine clauses, eight of which are subordinate. Hence this sentence is to be classed as complex. The naked independent clause states: "I heard voice." The phrase "out of the throne" makes known the source from which the voice came; thus it's adverbial. The adjective "great" fixes the voice in the mind as "loud." The use of genitive as direct object φωνῆς "voice" suggests that the author wants emphasis to be on the fact of hearing. No question but that the content of what was said is clearly understood. The eight dependent clauses spell that out. But genitive object after the verb of hearing does emphasize the reality that all that follows was truly heard.

The initial dependent idea is: "Behold! the tabernacle of God (is) with men..." σκηνή literally means "tent." To the dweller in the ancient mid-east "tent" was quite normal as a dwelling place. It's reference here calls to mind the "tent of meeting" in the midst of the wandering Israelites in the wilderness. It represented God's presence in their midst. Here John draws on this Old Testament background for his imagery of God's real presence with his redeemed. Genitive θεοῦ "of God" specifies whose tent. "With men" indicates where.

The second dependent asserts: "...he will pitch his tent with them..." σκηνώσει is future indicative. It is a verb built from the noun. The idea is that God will make his dwelling "with men" who have for so many centuries longed for the personal presence and more intimate relationship with God.

The next two clauses form a couplet of ideas which reassure the intimate closeness of the relationsip between God and man. They read: "...they shall be his people and he their God shall be with them..." λαοὶ "people" is predicate adjective after copula verb ἔσονται "shall be." In the next clause of the two θεὸς "God" could be placed as predicate adjective and thus balance off with λαοί. But the diagram places it in apposition to the subject αὐτὸς "he" because of the presence of definite article ὁ with θεὸς.

The fifth of the dependents declares: "...he shall wipe away every tear from their eyes..." ἐξαλείψει "shall wipe out" is future indicative. The ἐκ prefixed to the verb form followed by ἐκ with the phrase "out of their eyes" alerts the reader to the emphatic fact that God is going to separate (ablative) tears of sorrow from the future of the redeemed. Tears of joy are not in view; only tears of sorrow. That's plain from what is said in the clauses which follow: "...the death shall not be any more, neither shall not be any more mourning nor cry nor pain..."

The last of the dependent clauses is an adverbial clause of cause introduced by ὅτι "because." It supplies the underlying reason for the doing away with the items of sorrow mentioned in the previous two clauses, "death" etc. The verb ἀπῆλθαν "passed away" is aorist. The tense is most appropriate for the statement of fact. Any more descriptive tense would be inappropriate here. It's enough to know that "death, mourning, crying, pain" are gone.

Revelation 21:5-6

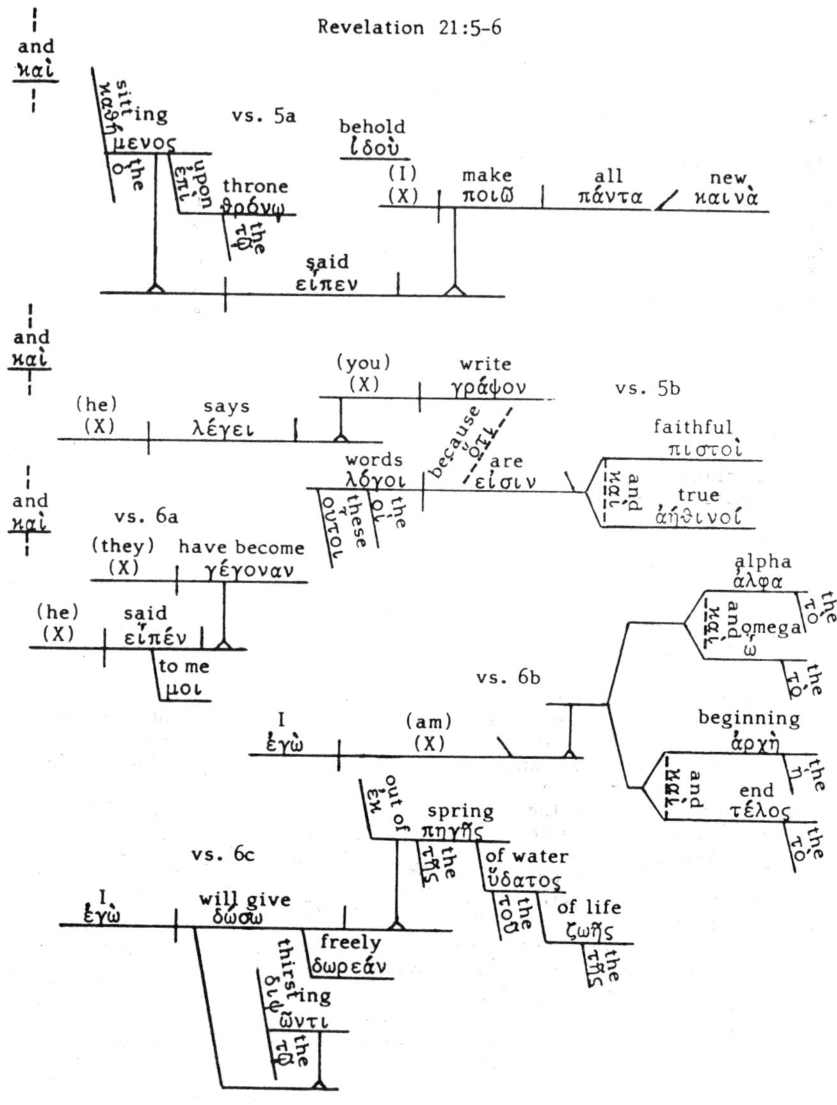

## THE DIAGRAM OF 21:5-6

By classification the sentence of 5a is complex. It contains two clauses. Subject of the independent clause is attributive participial phrase translated, "The one sitting upon the throne..." Participle καθήμενος "sitting" is present of defective verb κάθημαι "sit." A defective verb is one that is middle or passive in form but active in meaning apparently. The ἐπὶ "upon" expression plays the role of an adverb inasmuch as it indicates where. The dependent clause is the direct object of the aorist εἶπεν "said." After the exclamation "Behold" it reads, "I make all things new." καινὰ "new" is new in the sense of kind or quality. In this clause it is used as objective complement; it completes the idea in the object "all."

Verse 5b presents another complex sentence, this time with three clauses. The independent merely reports: "He says..." That which he says is presented in the noun clause, object of "says." It is an exhortation (or command), "...you write..." Then follows the other dependent clause introduced by ὅτι "because." It is an adverb clause of cause, giving the reason why he should write, "...because these words are faithful and true." "Faithful" and "true" are predicate adjectives pointing back to and affirming something about the subject λόγοι "words."

Still a third complex sentence appears in verse 6a. "He said to me..." is the main clause. Dative of the third personal pronoun μοι "me" is indirect object. The direct object consists of the other clause in this two-clause sentence: "...they have become." Perfect tense γέγοναν "have become" in this context appears to mean "they have come to pass," "they have happened." "It's over, done with permanently. The results are fixed."

Verse 6b is a simple sentence in structure. Use of the first personal pronoun ἐγὼ "I" gives to it a special prominence. It's as though the writer was underscoring "I" for special emphasis. The four nouns appearing as predicate nominatives each has its own definite article. Thus the speaker intends that each idea shall be distinct. Each has its own full force.

The final sentence on this page, verse 6c, is also simple in form. Again the first personal pronoun makes prominent the subject "I" as emphatic. "I will give..." is the bare clause. The prepositional ἐκ phrase might be properly placed under the main verb δώσω "will give." If we should place it there it would serve as adverb expressing source from whence. The diagram puts it as a direct object because the sense of the sentence suggests "water" as that which is "given." It would thus be construction according to sense rather than strictly a grammatical relationship. "Freely" is an adverb expressing manner. The present participle διψῶντι is attributive with article meaning "the one thirsting." It is used as indirect object.

Revelation 21:7-8

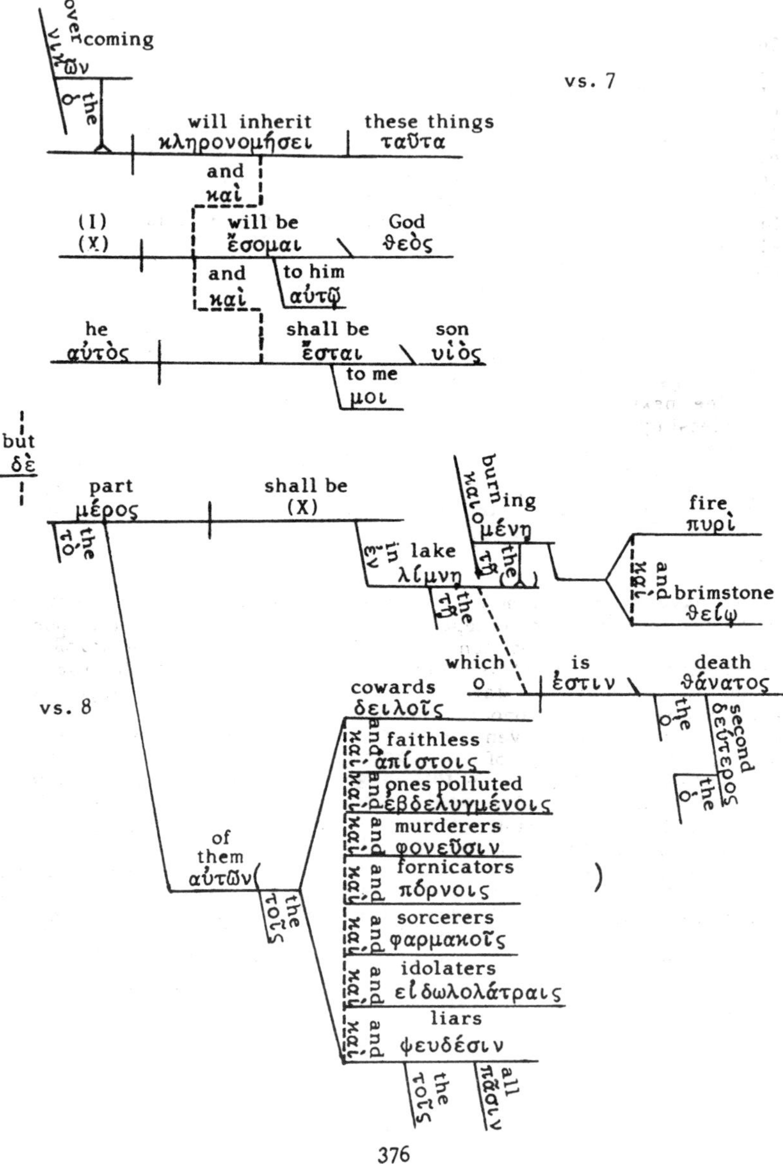

## THE DIAGRAM OF 21:7-8

Verse seven embodies a compound sentence of three clauses. Subject of the first clause is the articular attributive present participle ὁ νικῶν "the one overcoming." The linear action of the present tense is descriptive of a process going on. It reminds that the conquering on the part of the believer is an ongoing growth. The change involved in being remade into the "image of God" is not accomplished by an instantaneous act but by a gradual step-by-step transformation. However, this "one overcoming" "will inherit these things..." κληρονομήσει "will inherit" is point action future. The inheriting is not a process; it is a decisive, once-for-all act. The verb κληρονομέω means "to inherit." It is derived from the noun κληρονόμος "heir." To inherit is that action or experience involved in coming into one's heritage. All biblical ideas about "children, sons, heirs, inheritance, inherit" come to focus in this promise of 21:7. The object ταῦτα "these" refers to all the "new" things in the "new heavens and earth." These are the "things" the "one overcoming will inherit."

The next two clauses of verse seven spell out in detail two of the blessings that form part of the heritage. Or better, two phases of one great spiritual blessing to be inherited. "I shall be to him, God and he shall be to me, son." Both θεὸς "God" and υἱὸς "son" are predicate nominatives. The absence of the definite article with them calls attention to the quality or nature of "God" as deity and "son" as one who is son, that is of the same nature as deity.

Verse eight is formed after the pattern of a complex sentence. Without modifiers the independent clause states: "But the portion shall be..." Whose portion is designated by genitive αὐτῶν "of them." But this "them" is more particularly identified by use of a series of nouns in the dative case but which retain an appositional relationship to the pronoun "them." The definite article τοῖς lumps together the first seven of these nouns. These seven seem to appear as a variety of human corruption. By use of a second article with ψευδέσιν the speaker sets this particular form of corruption off to itself as especially evil, "all liars" regardless of what variety of corruption the lie happens to take. Liars are specially heinous sinners, utterly unreliable.

The ἐν expression is adverbial telling <u>where</u> their portion will be, "...in the lake..." Which lake is designated by use of an attributive participle in apposition, "...the one burning with fire and brimstone..."

The one dependent clause of this complex sentence is adjectival introduced by relative ὅ "which." It describes the "lake" as one "which is the second death."

## SOME EXPOSITORY THOUGHTS ON 21:1-8

What are the blessings of the future for the redeemed? What makes heaven heavenly? Can John picture in human language that which lies beyond our best experiences here?

That which lies beyond history is new. As useful and beautiful as the present dome of the sky with its myriads of twinkling stars is and as fruitful as this earth has been they can't compare with the "new heaven and earth" which shall be. It is not to be a transformation of this present heaven and earth. It will be new in quality, new in kind, new in essence. For one thing, there'll be no more anxious, heart-breaking separations for "the sea is not to be any more." And even as cities have drawn people together into social communities there will be a new city, a "new kind of Jerusalem" in which the redeemed may live in relaxed security. It comes "down" from God; it doesn't rise from fallen man. The new Jerusalem is not an evolution from below upward; it's a creation and revelation of God downward. It's bright and light with joy and gaiety "like a bride adorned for her husband."

That which makes such jubilance, such blithesome joy lies in the literal presence and real fellowship with the living God. During the dark days of this earth's experience it's been the lot of even the best of humanity "to seek God, if haply we might find him." But beyond history the search will be a thing of the past. God, in Christ, sought man here that man, in Christ, might be God's companion there. God himself speaks "from the throne." He declares: "Behold! the tabernacle (dwelling) of God (is) (in fellowship) with men, and he will make his dwelling with them, and they shall be his people and he, their God, shall be with them..;" In the wilderness wandering of ancient Israel the "tent of meeting" stood in the midst of the encamped people. It symbolized the presence of God with his people. But in this vision of John God's real presence is experienced apart from figurative symbols. "God shall dwell (in fellowship) (μετά) with them," God's personal presence eliminates all earth's defeats. "He shall wipe away every tear (of sorrow) from their eyes." And "death shall not be any more" nor any of its companion pains for there shall be "neither mourning, nor crying, nor anguish any more..." So accustomed are we to bitter sorrow and smarting pain, so ingrained is the experience of death, John finds it difficult to describe the experience of heaven's life with God. He must resort to negatives of our present ordeal in order to create imaginations of what life with God will be. There's more to be experienced than just the opposite of "mourning, cry, or pain." And eternal life is more than the absence of death. There's a quality of life to be tasted that thrills the spirit more than pain depresses. There are positive virtues that await our encounter. How can they be described when there is nothing in this world's life by which to compare them? We must be content to know that "the first things passed away." We abide in the promise of God, "Behold! I make all things new." And "I shall be your God!"

When "the one sitting on the throne" said "I make all things new," he immediately exhorted John to "write!" that which he had envisioned as told in verses 1-5a. Futhermore, a reason why he should write these things down with pen and ink is because "these words are trustworthy and true." They tell of things on which those reading may rely implicitly. These words are genuine!

After thus emphasizing the importance of the vision of 21:1-5a he ("the one sitting on the throne") adds an additional remarkable prophetic statement. "And he said to me (that is, to John), 'They have happened.'" What has happened? The making of all things new, the new Jerusalem, the presence of God with his people, the removal of pain and death and all that attends the old heaven and earth, along with the future blessedness promised -- these things, resting as they do on the word of him who is the Alpha and Omega, are treated as if they already have happened. "They have come to pass."(γέγοναν) The perfect tense indicates that they have come to pass and are matter of permanent record. They are as sure to happen as anything God has ever said; and it is permanent! It's God's pledged word. And he is well able to fulfill his pledged word. "I am the alpha and the omega, the first and the last" (the ultimate end toward which I have been working since the beginning).

The true "end," the real "last" is a matter of the spirit. The "goal" of history as indeed the goal of each human in history is at bottom a spiritual thirst. Humanity's restless rushing is at bottom a witness to its unconscious longing for spiritual satisfaction of deep thirst for life, that is for God! The image of thirst is often used in scripture to speak of an earnest sense of spiritual need, particularly a need for communion with God.(Is.44:3, Jn.4:14) Thus the promise is given with assurance: "To the one thirsting, I will give of the fountain of the water of life..." As water quenches a throat parched by desert heat thus every longing for life, for God, is to be quenched in this new order by "life." Moreover, it is to be a gratuitous gift; it's freely given because of redemption in Christ.

This "free" gift is given to the morally responsible. "The one conquering will inherit these things, and I will be his God, and he shall be my son." Home in the new Jerusalem is not "cheap grace." Accompanying the "gift" is responsible obedience. Orthodox doctrine demands orthodox deeds. God gives grace that life may be lived graciously, not corruptly. And as if to underscore this fact the readers of Revelation are shocked by a description of the destiny of those who fail their moral responsibility. "For the cowards, and faithless, and polluted, and murderers, and fornicators, and sorcerers, and idolators, and all the liars, their portion is the lake burning with fire and brimstone, the second death." Grace does not eliminate our moral responsibility; it makes it even more imperative. Grace grants help to live the ethical imperatives of the gospel of grace. We live in this world in a spiritual, moral relationship to the life which is to come. To him who is to live forever with God there is an obligation to live here worthy of being a son of God.

## A TRANSLATION OF REVELATION 21:9-27

And one of the seven angels of the ones having the seven bowls full of the seven ultimate plagues came and spoke with me saying, "Come, I will show you the bride, the wife of the lamb." And he carried me in spirit up to a mountain great and high. And he showed me the holy city, Jerusalem, coming down out of heaven from God, having the glory of God, (its light like a very precious stone, like a jasper, clear as crystal) having a wall great and high, having twelve gates, and at the gates twelves angels and names having been written which are the twelve tribes of the sons of Israel; from the east three gates, and from the north three gates and from the south three gates and from the west three gates. And the wall of the city (was) having twelve foundations and upon them twelve names of the twelve apostles of the lamb.

And the one speaking with me was having a golden measuring rod that he might measure the city and its gates and its wall. And the city lies foursquare, its length even as much as its breadth. And he measured the city with the rod, about 1500 miles; and the length and the breadth and the heighth of it are equal. And he measured its wall, a 144 cubits (by) human measure, which is(the)angel's. And the wall was inlaid jasper; and the city was pure gold like pure glass. The foundations of the wall of the city had been adorned with every precious stone; the first (was) jasper, the second sapphire, the third chalcedony, the fourth emerald, the fifth sardonyx, the sixth sardius, the seventh chrysolite, the eighth beryl,the ninth topaz, the tenth chrysoprase, the eleventh hyacinth, the twelfth amethyst. And the gates (were) twelve pearls; each single one of the gates was of one pearl. And the street of the city (was) pure gold like transparent glass.

And in it a temple I did not see; for the Lord God Almighty is its temple, and the lamb! And the city does not have need of the sun nor of the moon that they should shine in it, for the glory of God lighted it and the lamb is its lamp. And the nations shall walk by its light and the kings of the earth shall bring their glory into it, and its gates shall not be shut by day--for there'll be no night there. And they shall bring into it the glory and the honor of the nations. And every unclean (thing) and the one making filth and falsehood shall not enter into it -- only the ones having been written in the lamb's book of life!

## AN OUTLINE OF REVELATION 21:9-27

### Security in the City of God!

"Be not anxious" reflects man's insecurity! At every level safety drains our energy. God's city provides perpetual protection.

I. THE CITY OF GOD: ITS SECURITY. 21:9-14

1. In personal relationships: "the bride, the wife of the lamb."
2. It's from God "having the glory of God."
3. Its wall and gates promise security and free access.
4. Twelve foundation stones insure its eternal durability.

II. THE CITY OF GOD: ITS SIZE AND WORSHIP. 21:15-27

1. Infinite space! "The city lies foursquare."
2. No temple: God is personally present; sin entirely absent.
3. No light! God is its light; and the lamb its lamp.
4. No "filth and falsehood" insures its purity and peace.

The heavenly life is a state of spiritual dimensions.

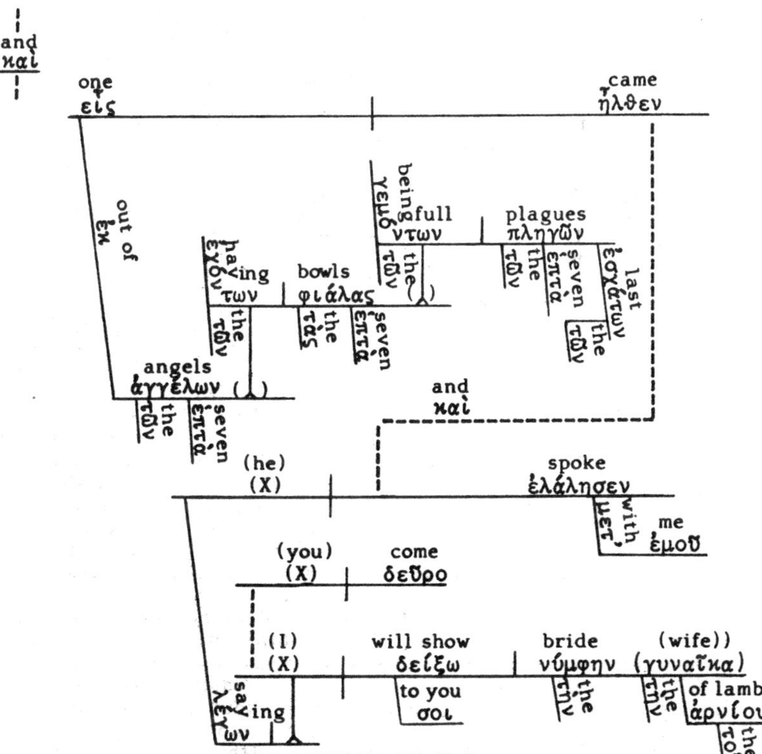


THE DIAGRAM OF 21:9

Verse nine is a compound-complex sentence of two independent and two dependent clauses. The independents say: "One came" and "he spoke." **ἐκ** with ablative "of the angels" is adjectival. It tells source from which. In apposition to "angels" is present attributive participle **ἐχόντων** "having," the object of which is **φιάλας** "bowls." That in turn has in apposition the attributive participle **γεμόντων** "being full." Verbs of fulness use genitive as object hence **πληγῶν** "plagues."

Modifying the subject "he" of the second independent is present circumstantial participle **λέγων** "saying." It has for its object two noun clauses: "you come" and "I will show you the bride, the wife of the lamb." **δεῦρο** is an adverb but on occasion, as here, may be used as an imperative. The diagram has it as a distinct clause.

In the second dependent **γυναῖκα** "wife" is in apposition to the object **νύμφην** "bride." Genitive **ἀρνίου** "lamb" specifies whose wife.

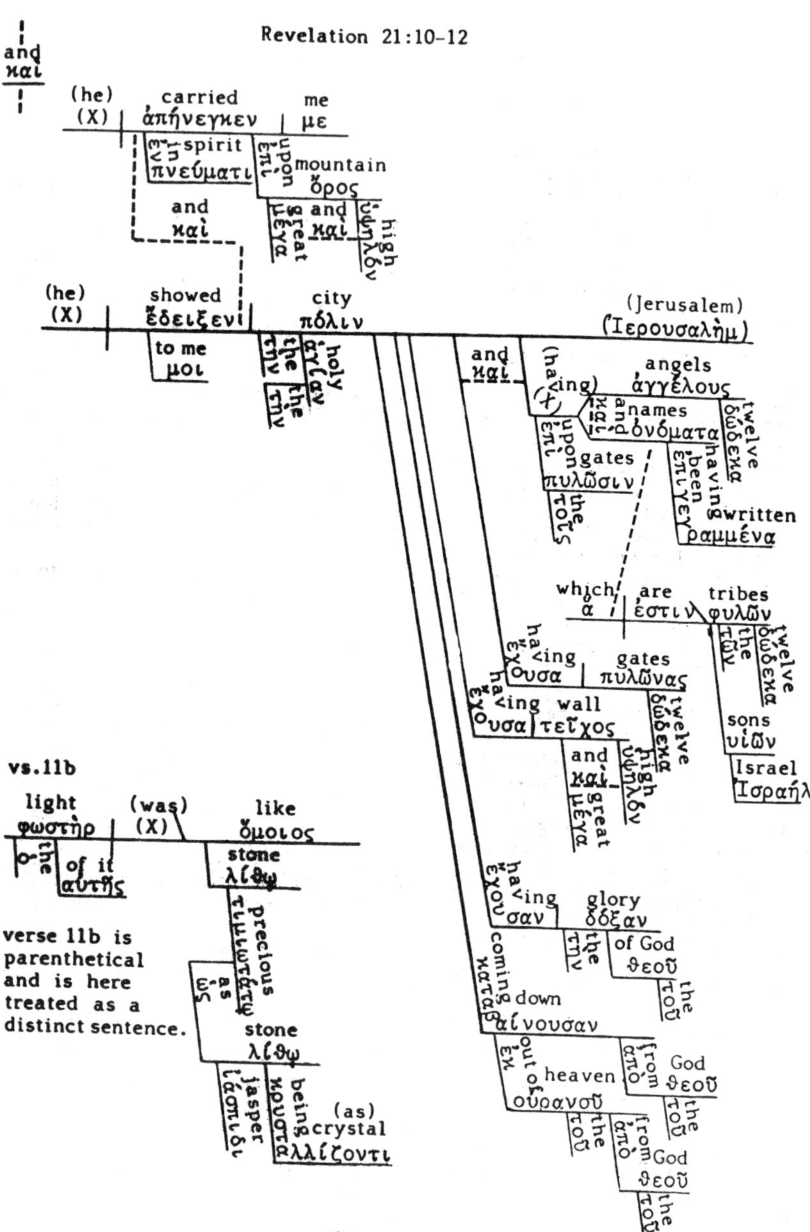
and
καὶ
(he)
(X)
carried
ἀπήνεγκεν
me
με
in
ἐν
spirit
πνεύματι
upon
ἐπὶ
mountain
ὄρος
great
μέγα
and
καὶ
high
ὑψηλόν
and
καὶ
(he)
(X)
showed
ἔδειξεν
to me
μοι
city
πόλιν
the
τὴν
holy
ἁγίαν
the
τὴν
(Jerusalem)
(Ἱερουσαλήμ)
and
καὶ
(having)
(X)
angels
ἀγγέλους
twelve
δώδεκα
and
καὶ
names
ὀνόματα
upon
ἐπὶ
gates
πυλῶσιν
the
τοῖς
having been written
ἐπιγεγραμμένα
which
ἅ
are
ἐστιν
tribes
φυλῶν
the
τῶν
twelve
δώδεκα
sons
υἱῶν
Israel
Ἰσραήλ
having
ἔχουσα
gates
πυλῶνας
twelve
δώδεκα
having
ἔχουσα
wall
τεῖχος
and
καὶ
great
μέγα
high
ὑψηλόν
having
ἔχουσαν
glory
δόξαν
the
τὴν
of God
θεοῦ
the
τοῦ
coming down
καταβαίνουσαν
out of
ἐκ
heaven
οὐρανοῦ
the
τοῦ
from
ἀπὸ
God
θεοῦ
the
τοῦ
vs.11b
light
φωστὴρ
the
ὁ
of it
αὐτῆς
(was)
(X)
like
ὅμοιος
stone
λίθῳ
precious
τιμιωτάτῳ
as
ὡς
stone
λίθῳ
jasper
ἰάσπιδι
being (as) crystal
κρυσταλλίζοντι
verse 11b is
parenthetical
and is here
treated as a
distinct sentence.

## THE DIAGRAM OF 21:10-12

Nestle's text has verses 10-12 punctuated as one sentence. The diagram presents verse 11b as a parenthetical interruption, a complete sentence itself. As organized it has but one full clause and hence would be classed as simple in structure. The clause states: "Its light (was) like a very precious stone..." But the rest of the sentence condenses into a adverb-prepositional ὡς expression what otherwise might be translated as an adverbial subordinate clause. Had it been expressed as a clause it would read, "...as a jasper stone is shining crystal clear." But the form in which it appears in the text reads: "...as a jasper stone being crystal clear." The present participle κρυσταλλίζοντι "being crystal clear" is circumstantial modifying λίθῳ "stone."

Eliminating verse 11, verses 10, 12 form a compound-complex arrangement. It has two independent clauses. And though it has but one dependent clause it does display five circumstantial participles all of which describe direct obect πόλιν "city" of the second independent clause.

The first independent idea affirms: "And he carried me in spirit upon(to)a great and high mountain..." The ἐν expression is adverbial inasmuch as it indicates the manner in which he was carried. The ἐπὶ phrase is also adverbial; it tells <u>where</u>.

The second independent clause alleges that "he showed to me the holy city, Jerusalem..." As indicated above, five circumstantial participles give added descriptions to πόλιν "city." First is the descriptive present καταβαίνουσαν "coming down." It has two prepositional phrases modifying it, both of which are adverbial; ἐκ express <u>from where</u>; ἀπὸ <u>from whom</u>. The next participle is also descriptive present with an object ἔχουσαν δόξαν "having glory." The term translated "glory" has a genitive modifying it identifying <u>whose</u> glory, that is, "God's." The next participle is a repeat of ἔχουσαν "having," this time with τεῖχος "wall" for its direct object. "Wall" is modified by two adjectives which describe it as "great and high." The fourth participle is a third repeat of "having." For its object this time πυλῶνας "gates" appears modified by the cardinal numeral δώδεκα "twelve." The final of the participles is understood, implied from the context. It too is "having" with two direct objects: "twelve angels" and "names." The "names" has a circumstantial perfect participle modifying it ἐπιγεγραμμένα "having been written." The perfect tense reveals that the names have been permanently fixed "upon the gates." This ἐπὶ phrase is adverbial modifying the implied participle "having." It tells <u>where</u> the names have been fixed.

The only dependent clause is adjective introduced by relative ἅ "which." It identifies the "names." It states, "...which are the twelve tribes of (the) sons of Israel."

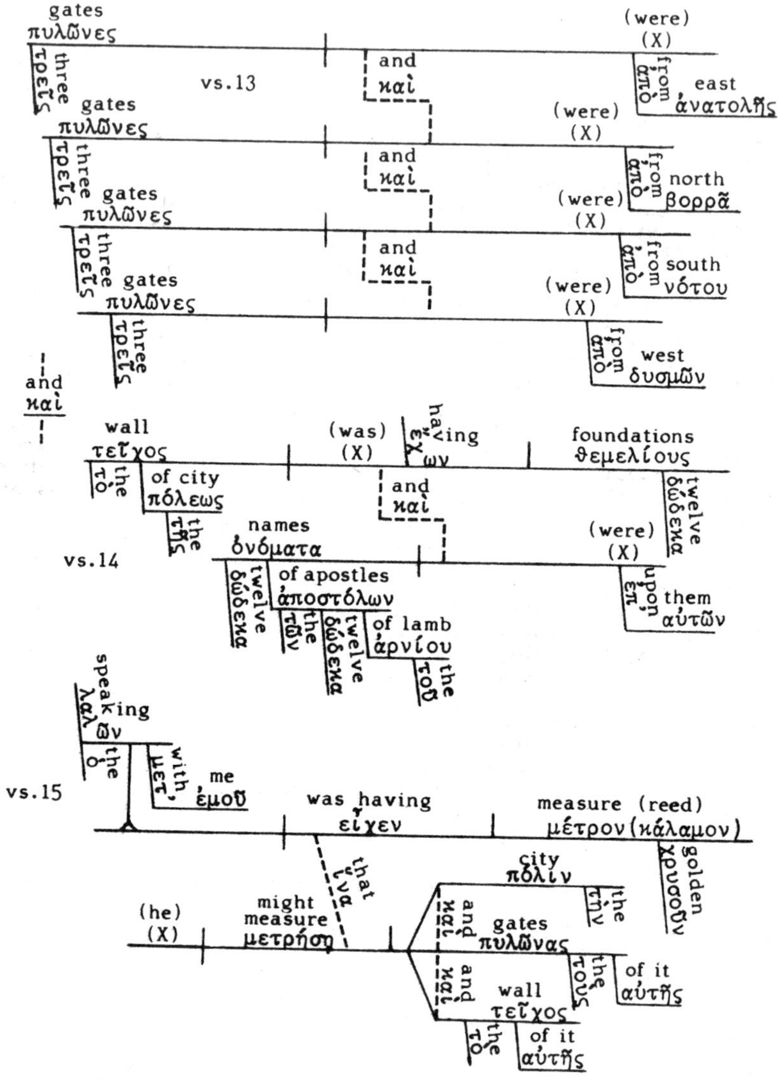
gates
πυλῶνες
three
τρεῖς
vs.13
and
καὶ
(were)
(X)
from
ἀπὸ
east
ἀνατολῆς
gates
πυλῶνες
three
τρεῖς
and
καὶ
(were)
(X)
from
ἀπὸ
north
βορρᾶ
gates
πυλῶνες
three
τρεῖς
and
καὶ
(were)
(X)
from
ἀπὸ
south
νότου
gates
πυλῶνες
three
τρεῖς
(were)
(X)
from
ἀπὸ
west
δυσμῶν
and
καὶ
wall
τεῖχος
the
τὸ
of city
πόλεως
the
τῆς
(was)
(X)
having
ἔχων
foundations
θεμελίους
twelve
δώδεκα
and
καὶ
vs.14
names
ὀνόματα
twelve
δώδεκα
of apostles
ἀποστόλων
the
τῶν
twelve
δώδεκα
of lamb
ἀρνίου
the
τοῦ
(were)
(X)
upon
ἐπ'
them
αὐτῶν
speaking
λαλῶν
the
ὁ
with
μετ'
me
ἐμοῦ
vs.15
was having
εἶχεν
measure (reed)
μέτρον (κάλαμον)
golden
χρυσοῦν
that
ἵνα
(he)
(X)
might measure
μετρήσῃ
city
πόλιν
the
τὴν
and
καὶ
gates
πυλῶνας
the
τοὺς
of it
αὐτῆς
and
καὶ
wall
τεῖχος
the
τὸ
of it
αὐτῆς

## THE DIAGRAM OF 21:13-15

Three sentences adorn this page. The first, verse 13, involves a compound structure of four clauses. Each of the four clauses follows the same pattern. In fact they are worded exactly the same except for the words representing the four points of the compass; "east," "north," "south," and "west." The sentence reads, "Three gates (were) from the east and three gates (were) from the north and three gates (were) from the south and three gates (were) from the west." The verb "were" must be supplied from the context. The cardinal numeral τρεῖς "three" appears as an adjective modifying the subjects. The ἀπὸ expressions are, of course, adverbial. They indicate from whence.

Verse 14 frames a compound sentence of two clauses. The first clause states: "The wall of the city (was) having twelve foundations..." The present participle ἔχων "having" is a predicate present participle supplementing an understood imperfect ἠν "was." Thus together they form a periphrastic imperfect. A periphrastic form of a verb gives added emphasis to whatever tense is involved in the periphrasis. In this instance, linear action.

The second clause of the sentence of verse 14 declares: "... twelve names of the twelve apostles of the lamb(were)upon them." Genitive ἀποστόλων "apostles" specifies whose names; genitive ἀρνίου "lamb" specifies whose apostle. The ἐπὶ expression is an adverb phrase indicating where.

The sentence of verse 15 manifests a complex category. It has two clauses. The independent has for its subject an attributive present participle λαλῶν "speaking." The main verb εἶχεν "was having" is imperfect of ἔχω. The root of this verb is σεχ, the Aktionsart of which is punctiliar, "get." When the augment is put on, εσεχ, the sigma dropped off and ε + ε = the diphthong ει. Direct object μέτρον "measure" has in apposition to it κάλαμον "reed."

The subordinate clause of this sentence of verse 15 is an adverbial clause of purpose ushered in by ἵνα "that." The verb μετρήσῃ "measure" is aorist subjunctive. It has for its direct object three nouns: "the city," "its gates," and "its wall."

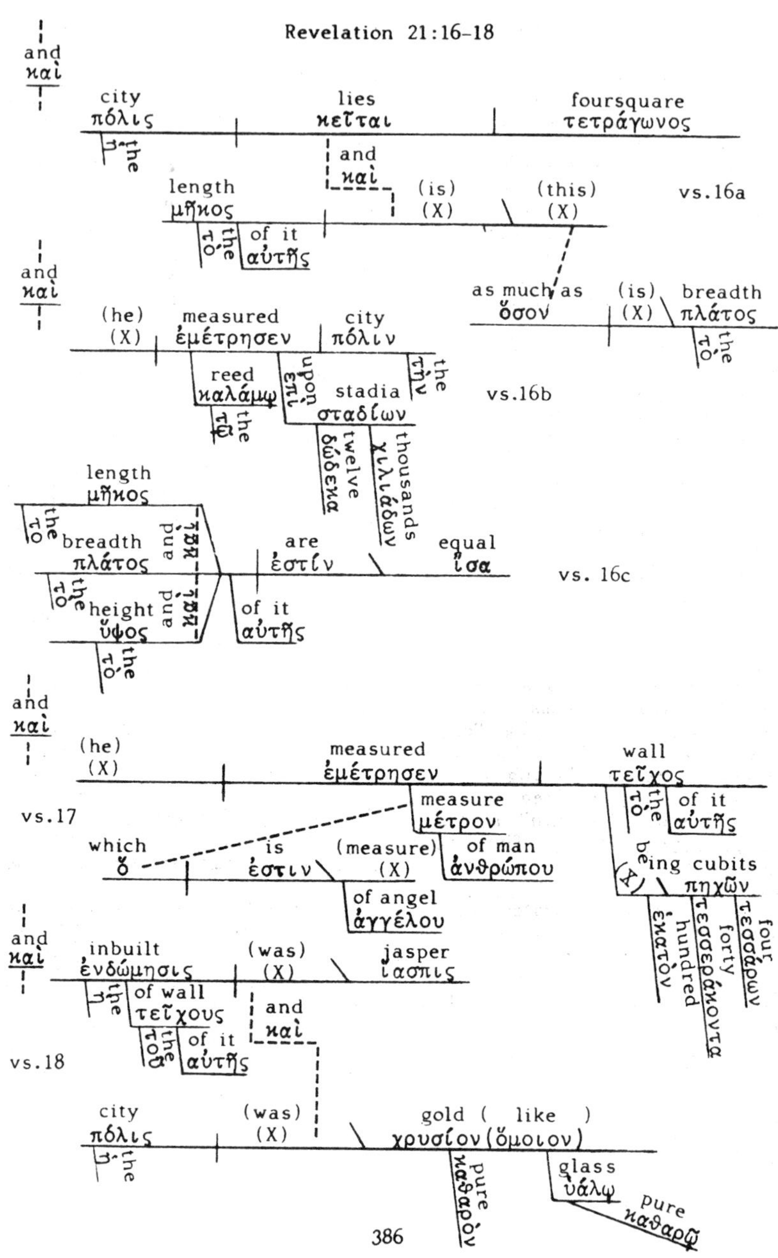
and
καὶ
city
πόλις
ἡ the
lies
κεῖται
foursquare
τετράγωνος
and
καὶ
length
μῆκος
τὸ the
of it
αὐτῆς
(is)
(X)
(this)
(X)
vs.16a
as much as
ὅσον
(is)
(X)
breadth
πλάτος
τὸ the
and
καὶ
(he)
(X)
measured
ἐμέτρησεν
city
πόλιν
τὴν the
reed
καλάμῳ
τῷ the
upon
ἐπὶ
stadia
σταδίων
twelve
δώδεκα
thousands
χιλιάδων
vs.16b
length
μῆκος
τὸ the
breadth
πλάτος
τὸ the
and
καὶ
height
ὕψος
τὸ the
and
καὶ
are
ἐστίν
equal
ἴσα
of it
αὐτῆς
vs. 16c
and
καὶ
(he)
(X)
measured
ἐμέτρησεν
wall
τεῖχος
τὸ the
of it
αὐτῆς
measure
μέτρον
of man
ἀνθρώπου
vs.17
which
ὅ
is
ἐστιν
(measure)
(X)
of angel
ἀγγέλου
(X) being
cubits
πηχῶν
hundred
ἑκατὸν
forty
τεσσεράκοντα
four
τεσσάρων
and
καὶ
inbuilt
ἐνδώμησις
ἡ the
of wall
τεῖχους
τοῦ the
of it
αὐτῆς
(was)
(X)
jasper
ἴασπις
and
καὶ
vs.18
city
πόλις
ἡ the
(was)
(X)
gold ( like )
χρυσίον (ὅμοιον)
pure
καθαρὸν
glass
ὑάλῳ
pure
καθαρῷ

## THE DIAGRAM OF 21:16-18

With two independent and one dependent clause the sentence of verse 16a is compound-complex. The only modifiers involved with any of the clauses are three definite articles and the genitive of the third personal pronoun αὐτῆς "of it." The pronoun is feminine because its antecedent πόλις "city" in the first clause is feminine. The two main clauses say: "And the city lies foursquare and the length of it (is) (this)..." "Demonstrative pronoun "this" (τοῦτο) must be supplied from the context. And describing it is the adjective dependent clause, "...as much as (is) the breadth (of it)." ὅσον is a neuter quantitative relative pronoun. πλάτος "breadth" is neuter predicate nominative pointing back to the pronominal subject.

The remainder of verse 16 may be treated as one compound sentence of two clauses. Or, as the diagram presents it, it may be treated as two distinct sentences, both simple in form.

Verse 16b asserts that "And he measured the city." καλάμῳ is instrumental case and may be translated "with a reed." It's adverb in function for it expresses manner. The ἐπὶ "upon" with genitive σταδίων "stadia" is used here rather than the usual accusative extent of space. Some manuscripts have the accusative. This idiom may be literally translated, "...on the basis of 12,000 stadia..."

Verse 16c reaffirms what has already been stated about the city in verse 15 but spells it out in different terms. "The length and the breadth and the height of it are equal." In other words, it is "foursquare," a perfect cube as was the Holy of Holies of the temple.

Verse 17 contains a complex sentence of two clauses. The independent clause affirms: "And he measured its wall..." Modifying "wall" is genitive πηχῶν "of cubits. "Cubits" might modify "wall" directly as a genitive but the diagram has inserted an understood present participle "being of one hundred forty four cubits." The accusative μέτρον "measure" expresses extent of space. The genitive ἀνθρώπου "of man" means "of a human." The measure is that of a human being. The dependent adjective clause adds the descriptive note that a human's measure is that "which is (the measure) of an angel."

Verse 18 incorporates a compound sentence of two clauses. The subject of the first clause is ἐνδώμησις "a building in." It is an action noun referring to that which is being built into the wall. The wall of this city had jasper built into it; inlaid with jasper. The use of the definite article with ἐνδώμησις "inbuilt" while ἴασπις "jasper" is without the article assures that the word with the article is subject; the word without it is predicate. The second clause continues the description by saying, "the city (was) pure gold..." The adjective ὅμοιον "like" is placed in apposition to "gold" to stir the imagination of a reader. It was pure gold "like pure glass." ὑάλῳ is associative-instrumental case after word of likeness.

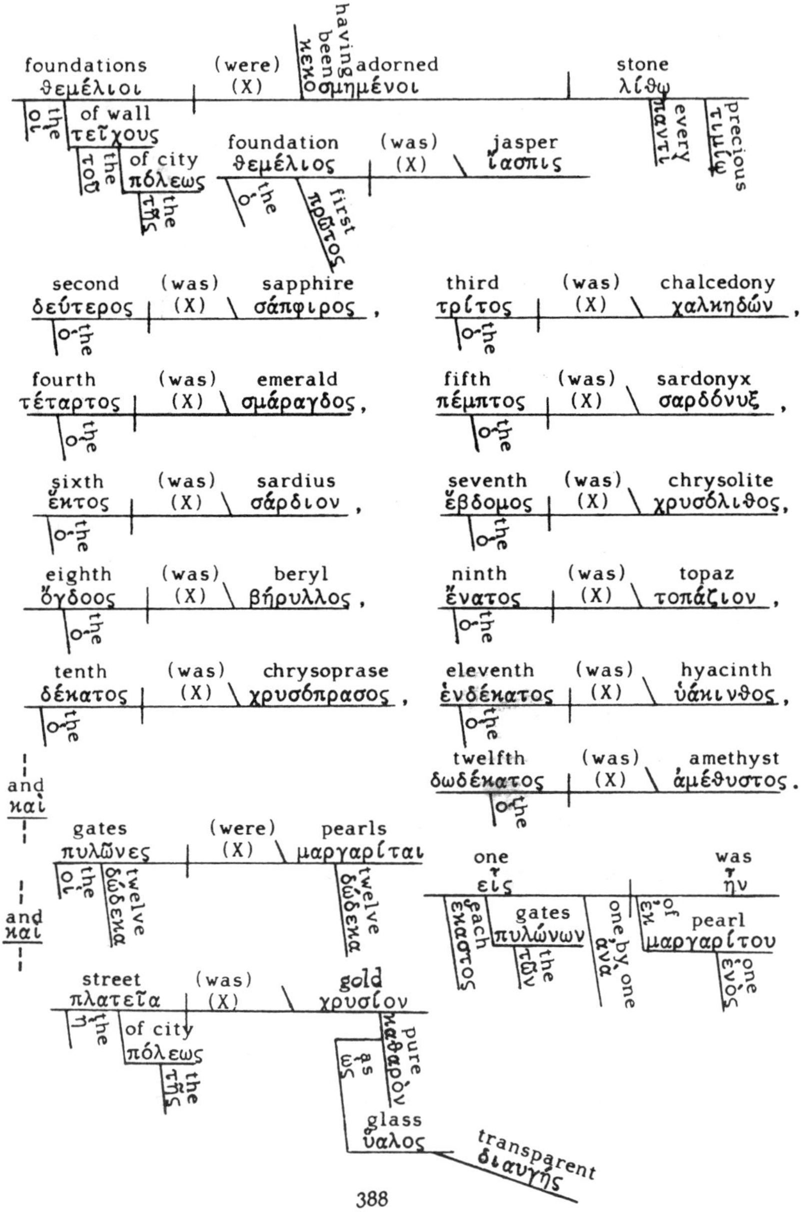

foundations θεμέλιοι | (were) (X) having been adorned κεκοσμημένοι | stone λίθῳ
οἱ the; of wall τείχους; τοῦ the; of city πόλεως; τῆς the; παντὶ every; τιμίῳ precious

foundation θεμέλιος | (was) (X) \ jasper ἴασπις
ὁ the; πρῶτος first

second δεύτερος | (was) (X) \ sapphire σάπφιρος, — ὁ the
third τρίτος | (was) (X) \ chalcedony χαλκηδών, — ὁ the
fourth τέταρτος | (was) (X) \ emerald σμάραγδος, — ὁ the
fifth πέμπτος | (was) (X) \ sardonyx σαρδόνυξ, — ὁ the
sixth ἕκτος | (was) (X) \ sardius σάρδιον, — ὁ the
seventh ἕβδομος | (was) (X) \ chrysolite χρυσόλιθος, — ὁ the
eighth ὄγδοος | (was) (X) \ beryl βήρυλλος, — ὁ the
ninth ἔνατος | (was) (X) \ topaz τοπάζιον, — ὁ the
tenth δέκατος | (was) (X) \ chrysoprase χρυσόπρασος, — ὁ the
eleventh ἑνδέκατος | (was) (X) \ hyacinth ὑάκινθος, — ὁ the
twelfth δωδέκατος | (was) (X) \ amethyst ἀμέθυστος. — ὁ the

and καὶ

gates πυλῶνες | (were) (X) \ pearls μαργαρῖται
οἱ the; δώδεκα twelve; δώδεκα twelve

one εἷς | was ἦν
ἕκαστος each; of gates πυλώνων; τῶν the; ἀνὰ one by one; ἐκ of pearl μαργαρίτου; ἑνός one

and καὶ

street πλατεῖα | (was) (X) \ gold χρυσίον
ἡ the; of city πόλεως; τῆς the; καθαρόν pure; ὡς as glass ὕαλος; διαυγής transparent

## THE DIAGRAM OF 21:19-21

According to the punctuation of Nestle's text 21:19-20 is one compound sentence. It contains 13 clauses. Asyndeton prevails throughout. The diagram doesn't even show any bare dotted lines to indicate connections between clauses. The final three clauses in this series are presented in the diagram as three distinct sentences even though Nestle joins the first two of them into one sentence.

The first clause in the series of verses 19-20 provides background color for the entire series. It declares: "The foundations of the wall of the city(were)having been adorned with every precious stone,.." λίθῳ "stone" is retained as object after passive verb. It is instrumental case. It might have been placed as adverbial under the verb. Had the sentence been active, not passive, it would have read, "Every precious stone adorned the foundations..." The diagram opted to retain λίθῳ as object. It still gives an adverbial idea much as an adverbial accusative. The verb is periphrastic pluperfect made by an understood imperfect "were" supplemented by perfect passive participle κεκοσμημένοι "having been adorned."

The second clause of this sentence is the first of a series of 12 that follow in an identical pattern. The pattern is first set by declaring:"the first foundation(was)jasper,.." The ordinal numeral πρῶτος "first" serves as an adjective modifying the subject θεμέλιος "foundation." The verb "was" must be supplied from the context. That is followed by a predicate nominative. This pattern follows in the next 11 clauses with the exception that the successive ordinal numbers appear in the diagram as subjects. It would be acceptable to deal with them as adjectives modifying implied subjects. But the presence of the article with each is sufficient grounds for treating them as substantives. At any rate the student will note that δεύτερος "second," τρίτος "third," etc. appear as subject in each clause.

The final three clauses appearing on this page are treated as three simple sentences. Verse 21a states: "And the twelve gates (were) twelve pearls." Verse 21b continues describing the gates by giving attention to each single gate. It reads: "Each one of the gates, one by one, was of one pearl." πυλώνων "of gates" is a normal use of the genitive to specify the kind of "one." The preposition ἀνὰ appears here in the distributive sense of "one by one." μαργαρίτου "pearl" is ablative with ἐκ expressing source from which. It's an adverbial idea.

The final sentence reaffirms, "The street of the city (was) pure gold..." Once again we note the ὡς used as adverbial preposition, "as pure glass." It might have been diagrammed as a dependent clause, "...as glass (is) pure." Had we used that form the sentence would be classed as complex. As diagrammed we treat the sentence as simple.

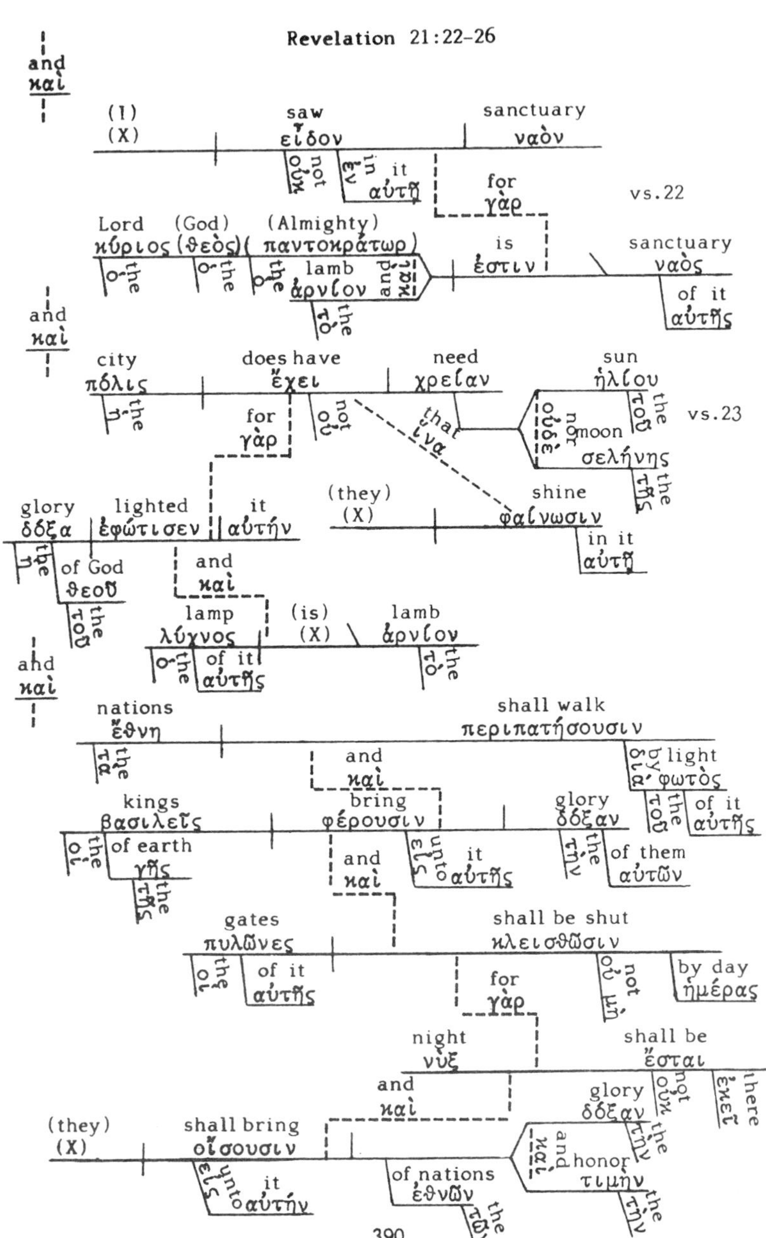
and
καὶ
(I)
(X)
saw
εἶδον
not
οὐκ
in
ἐν
it
αὐτῇ
sanctuary
ναὸν
for
γὰρ
vs.22
Lord
κύριος
the
ὁ
(God)
θεὸς
the
ὁ
(Almighty)
παντοκράτωρ
the
ὁ
lamb
ἀρνίον
the
τὸ
and
καὶ
is
ἐστιν
sanctuary
ναὸς
of it
αὐτῆς
and
καὶ
city
πόλις
the
ἡ
does have
ἔχει
not
οὐ
for
γὰρ
need
χρείαν
that
ἵνα
sun
ἡλίου
the
τοῦ
nor
οὐδὲ
moon
σελήνης
the
τῆς
vs.23
glory
δόξα
the
ἡ
of God
θεοῦ
the
τοῦ
lighted
ἐφώτισεν
it
αὐτήν
(they)
(X)
shine
φαίνωσιν
in it
αὐτῇ
and
καὶ
lamp
λύχνος
the
ὁ
of it
αὐτῆς
(is)
(X)
lamb
ἀρνίον
the
τὸ
and
καὶ
nations
ἔθνη
the
τὰ
shall walk
περιπατήσουσιν
by
διὰ
light
φωτὸς
the
τοῦ
of it
αὐτῆς
and
καὶ
kings
βασιλεῖς
the
οἱ
of earth
γῆς
the
τῆς
bring
φέρουσιν
unto
εἰς
it
αὐτῆς
glory
δόξαν
the
τὴν
of them
αὐτῶν
and
καὶ
gates
πυλῶνες
the
οἱ
of it
αὐτῆς
shall be shut
κλεισθῶσιν
not
οὐ μὴ
by day
ἡμέρας
for
γὰρ
night
νὺξ
shall be
ἔσται
not
οὐκ
there
ἐκεῖ
and
καὶ
(they)
(X)
shall bring
οἴσουσιν
unto
εἰς
it
αὐτήν
of nations
ἐθνῶν
the
τῶν
glory
δόξαν
the
τὴν
and
καὶ
honor
τιμὴν
the
τὴν

## THE DIAGRAM OF 21:22-26

Two clauses of equal rank joined in one sentence constitute a compound construction. Thus verse 22 is compound. The first clause is negative; the second positive. The first says: "I did not see a temple in it..." The word translated "temple" is ναὸς "sanctuary." It refers to the inmost holy room, the shrine in contrast to the whole temple area. It was the very place of worship. The second clause states the reason lying back of the absence of a sanctuary, "...for the Lord God the Almighty is its sanctuary, and the lamb." Since a sanctuary is the place where a worshipper meets God the presence of God in the new Jerusalem excludes the need for any special sanctuary. The subject in this second clause is a compound one. "Lord" has both "God" and "Almighty" in apposition. As the sentence begins that is the sole subject. It uses a singular verb. "The lamb" was added as an afterthought so as to identifiy the "Lamb" with deity. The author felt no need to change the number of the verb to conform to a plural subject.

Verse 23 incorporates a compound-complex. It has three independent clauses and but one dependent. The opening clause asserts, "And the city does not have need of the sun nor of the moon..." The negative οὐ goes with the verb, not the object. ἔχει is linear action present: the city goes on continuously not having need..." The dependent clause which stems off this independent is an adverb clause of purpose ushered in by conjunction ἵνα "in order that they should shine in it."

The two remaining independent clauses present reasons lying back of the city's lack of need for light from sun or moon. "...for the glory of God lighted it" and "the lamp of it (is) the lamb."

Verses 24-26 form one compound sentence of five clauses. The initial clause states one of the results of such illumination as the "glory of God" which radiates from the "its lamp," the Lamb. "And the nations shall walk through (διὰ "by means of") its light..."

The second clause makes the statement that "the kings of the earth bring unto it their glory..." In the first clause the future tense περιπατήσουσιν "shall walk" is punctiliar stating a fact. In this second clause φέρουσιν is present tense. Its linear action may be conceived as iterative; one after another "each king brings..."

In the third clause the double negative lends strength to the negation, "...the gates of it shall not ever be shut by day..." The ἡμέρας is genitive of time; the gates won't be closed at this kind of time, that is, daytime. Since the next clause states, "...night shall not be there..." that enforces the idea that the gates won't ever be closed. There is to be open access forever.

The final of the five clauses states: "...and they shall bring unto it the glory and the honor (wealth) of the nations." οἴσουσιν "shall bring" is future indicative active of φέρω "carry." Its punctiliar action is a statement of fact. The word translated "honor" is τιμή "that which is esteemed," "of value as to price." The precious valuables of the earth, "they shall bring."

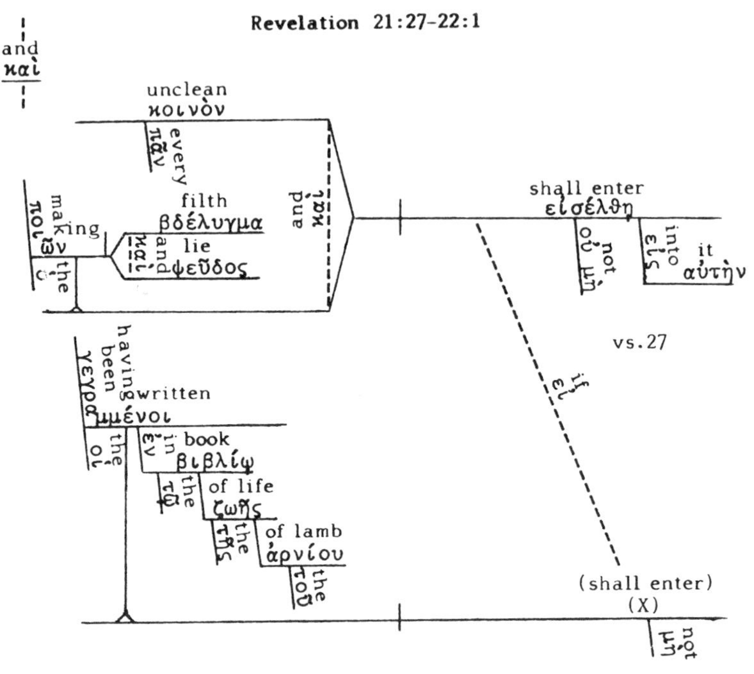
and
καὶ
unclean
κοινὸν
every
πᾶν
making
ποιῶν
the
ὁ
filth
βδέλυγμα
and
καὶ
lie
ψεῦδος
and
καὶ
shall enter
εἰσέλθῃ
not
οὐ μὴ
into
εἰς
it
αὐτὴν
vs.27
if
εἰ
having been written
γεγραμμένοι
the
οἱ
in
ἐν
book
βιβλίῳ
the
τῷ
of life
ζωῆς
the
τῆς
of lamb
ἀρνίου
the
τοῦ
(shall enter)
(X)
not
μὴ

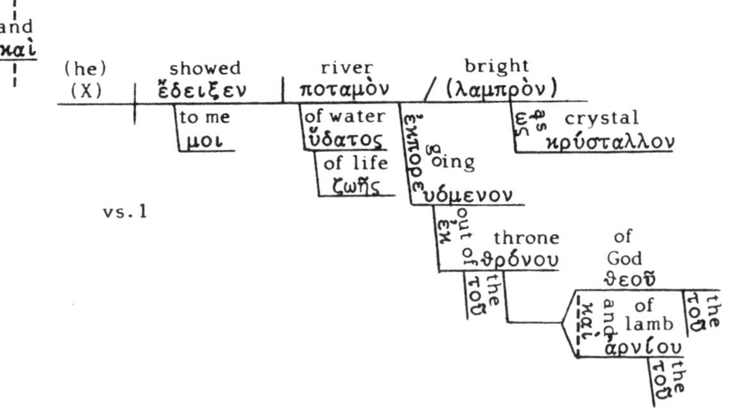
and
καὶ
(he)
(X)
showed
ἔδειξεν
to me
μοι
river
ποταμὸν
of water
ὕδατος
of life
ζωῆς
bright
(λαμπρὸν)
as
ὡς
crystal
κρύσταλλον
going
ἐκπορευόμενον
out of
ἐκ
throne
θρόνου
the
τοῦ
of God
θεοῦ
the
τοῦ
and
καὶ
of lamb
ἀρνίου
the
τοῦ
vs.1

## THE DIAGRAM OF 21:27-22:1

Besides one independent clause the sentence of 21:27 has one negative adverbial conditional clause. Hence it is to be classified as complex. The main clause makes a strong negative statement as to who shall not enter into this new Jerusalem. "Every unclean (person) and the one producing an abomination and falsehood shall not enter into it..." κοινὸν "common" in this context refers quite obviously to that which is "common" in the sense of "unhallowed." The opposite of hallowed or morally clean. βδέλυγμα "abomination" derives from the verb βδελύσσω "to make foul" which in turn comes from the verb βδέω "to stink." The -μα word is a result noun. Since it is derived from a verb meaning "to make foul" βδέλυγμα would be that which is made foul, a filthy, abominable thing. It is to be noted that the subject of this main clause is compound and that one item of the subject is portrayed by attributive present participle ὁ ποιῶν "the one making..." It's a person who actively produces a "filthy" thing and a "lie" who "shall not enter..." The negative οὐ μὴ is the strongest kind of negative. The preposition εἰς prefixed to the verb is reinforced by its repetition in the adverbial phrase εἰς αὐτὴν "into it."

The dependent "if" clause is a 1st class conditional determined as fulfilled. That is, "...if the ones having been written in the book of the life of the lamb (shall not enter) (and the "if" assumes for the sake of argument that they shall not) (then that surely means that) every common and the one making filth and lie shall (for certain) not enter into it." Such a translation seems somewhat heavy, awkward, involved, and obscure to the English reader. The sense is more easily apprehended by translating: "And every unclean (thing or person) and the one making filth and falsehood shall not enter into it, only (except) the ones having been written in the lamb's book of life (shall enter)." The negative μὴ in the "if" clause goes with the understood verb "shall enter."

The first verse of chapter 22 forms a simple sentence. The naked clause reads: "And he showed river..." μοι "to me" is indirect object. ποταμὸν "river" is direct object. λαμπρὸν "bright" is objective complement. The ὡς phrase, "as crystal," as it appears in the diagram, is an adverbial-prepositional expression. If κρύσταλλον were nominative instead of accusative it might have been treated as a subordinate clause of comparison, "...as crystal is bright." Genitive ὕδατος "of water" specifies the kind of river; but that "water" in turn is described by another genitive ζωῆς "life" which specifies the kind of "water" he's talking about. The participle ἐκπορευόμενον "going out" is linear present. It is circumstantial describing the continuous outflowing of the river of the water of "life." The ἐκ "out of" reveals the source out from which the flow of life is constantly pouring. It is "out from the throne of the God and from the lamb."

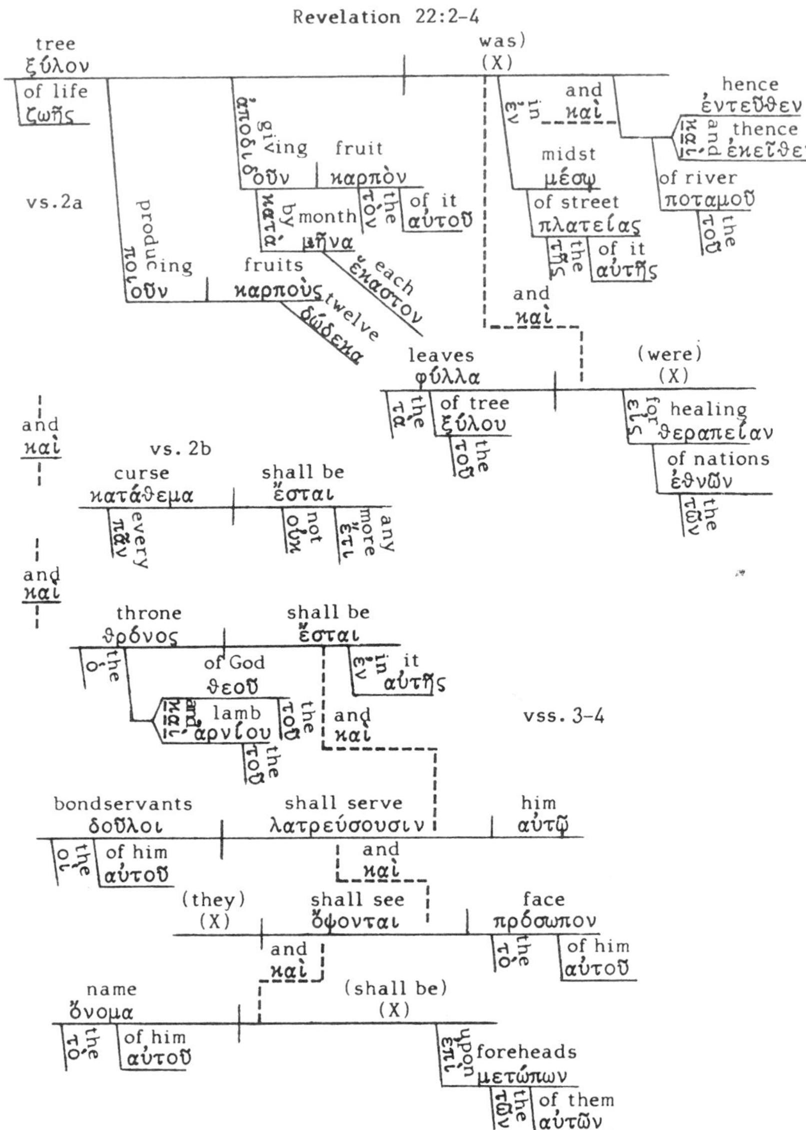
Revelation 22:2-4
tree
ξύλον
of life
ζωῆς
was)
(X)
in
ἐν
and
καὶ
midst
μέσῳ
of street
πλατείας
the
τῆς
of it
αὐτῆς
hence
ἐντεῦθεν
and
καὶ
thence
ἐκεῖθεν
of river
ποταμοῦ
the
τοῦ
giving
ἀποδιδοῦν
fruit
καρπὸν
the
τὸν
of it
αὐτοῦ
by
κατὰ
month
μῆνα
each
ἕκαστον
vs. 2a
producing
ποιοῦν
fruits
καρποὺς
twelve
δώδεκα
and
καὶ
leaves
φύλλα
the
τὰ
of tree
ξύλου
the
τοῦ
(were)
(X)
for
εἰς
healing
θεραπείαν
of nations
ἐθνῶν
the
τῶν
and
καὶ
vs. 2b
curse
κατάθεμα
every
πᾶν
shall be
ἔσται
not
οὐκ
any more
ἔτι
and
καὶ
throne
θρόνος
the
ὁ
of God
θεοῦ
the
τοῦ
and
καὶ
lamb
ἀρνίου
the
τοῦ
shall be
ἔσται
in
ἐν
it
αὐτῆς
and
καὶ
vss. 3-4
bondservants
δοῦλοι
the
οἱ
of him
αὐτοῦ
shall serve
λατρεύσουσιν
him
αὐτῷ
and
καὶ
(they)
(X)
shall see
ὄψονται
face
πρόσωπον
the
τὸ
of him
αὐτοῦ
and
καὶ
name
ὄνομα
the
τὸ
of him
αὐτοῦ
(shall be)
(X)
upon
ἐπὶ
foreheads
μετώπων
the
τῶν
of them
αὐτῶν

## THE DIAGRAM OF 22:2-4

Verse 2a admits of two complete clauses both of which are independent. Thus the sentence is compound. Ignoring all modifying elements they declare: "Tree of life (was) and the leaves of the tree (were)..." The verbs in both clauses must be supplied. The diagram uses "was" in the sense of "existed." Subject ξύλον "tree" of the first clause is defined by genitive ζωῆς "of life" to specify the kind of tree. In fact, it is an appositional genitive; it's the tree which is life. He's really talking about life, not a tree. "Tree" is also modified by two circumstantial participles: "producing twelve fruits," and "giving forth its fruit according to each month..." κατὰ with accusative indicates "according to this standard of measurement." That is, "month by month." Prepositional phrase introduced by ἐν tells where the tree was; it was "in the middle of its (the city's) street." The two adverbs also indicate where; "hence and thence," which is to say "on this side and on that side." The "tree" apparently was a full-fledged grove of trees lining the street of the city.

The second independent clause reports the purpose for which the tree existed: "...the leaves of the tree (were) for the healing of the nations." ξύλου "tree" is possessive genitive. Preposition εἰς "for" with accusative here expresses purpose.

Verse 2b is a brief clause constituting a simple sentence. It reads: "And every curse shall not be any more." The magnitude of its meaning should not be measured by the brevity of its length. This is a strong, important statement that there'll not be "any curse any more." Subject κατάθεμα "curse" in this strong form appears only here in the New Testament; ἀνάθεμα appears elsewhere. The word is compounded from preposition κατά "down" plus τίθημι "put" or "place." A "curse" is a "put-down." Since Eden man has been living under the "curse" from which all curses stem. In the new Jerusalem "every curse" shall not be any more. (ἔτι)

The sentence of 3-4, having four independent clauses and no dependents, is compound. The first clause announces the presence of the divine throne: "And the throne of the God and the lamb shall be in it..." Genitives "of God" and "of the lamb" indicate whose throne. The definite article with "God" as well as "lamb" gives **each** his own distinct individuality. They share as equals the throne. "In it" is an adverb expression indicating where.

The second and third clauses declare the class of inhabitants of the city, that is, "bondservants" and what they shall do and experience in the city. They "shall serve him" and "they shall see his face..." The future verb λατρεύσουσιν "shall serve" means to serve as worshippers. To "see his face" contemplates personal experience.

The final clause states: "...his name (shall be) upon their foreheads." ὄνομα "name" is associated with the essense of who or what a person is. His name "upon their foreheads" suggests not only do they "belong" to him but in so belonging they partake of his character.

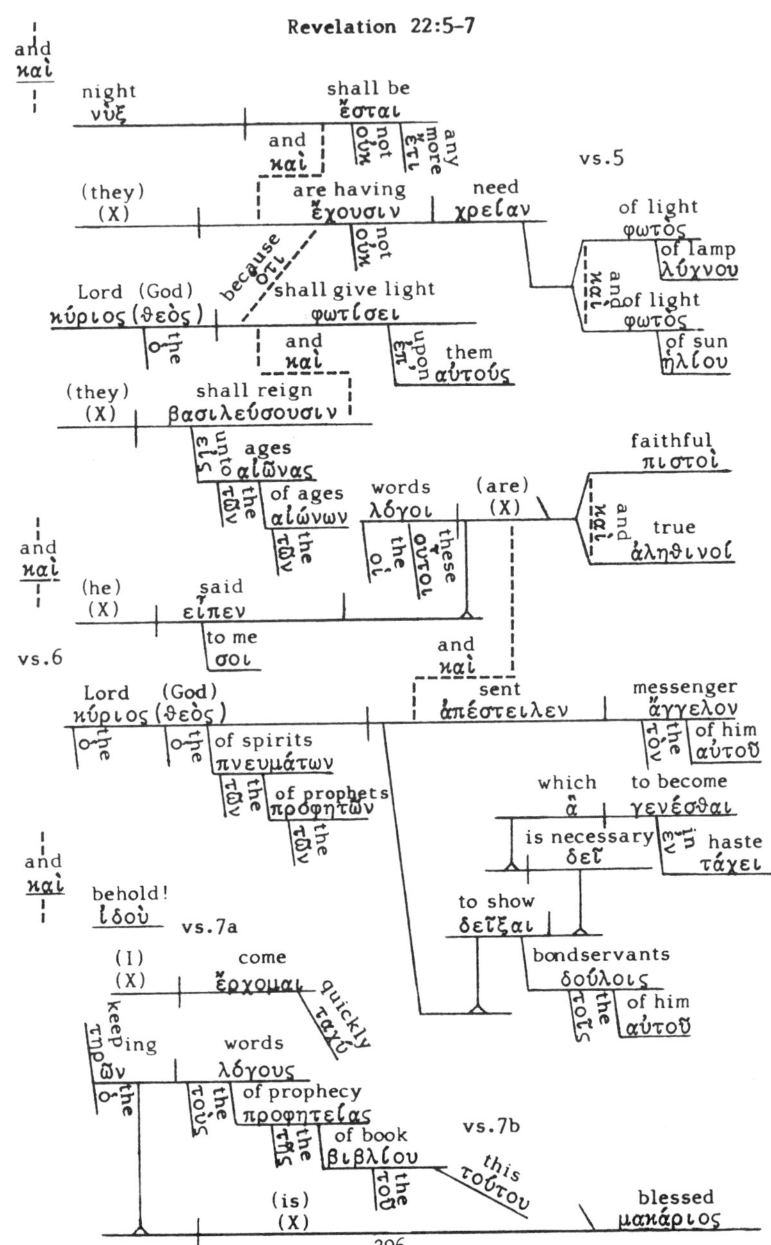
and
καὶ
night
νὺξ
shall be
ἔσται
not
οὐκ
any more
ἔτι
and
καὶ
vs.5
(they)
(X)
are having
ἔχουσιν
need
χρείαν
not
οὐκ
of light
φωτὸς
of lamp
λύχνου
and
καὶ
of light
φωτὸς
of sun
ἡλίου
because
ὅτι
Lord (God)
κύριος (θεὸς)
the
ὁ
shall give light
φωτίσει
upon
ἐπ'
them
αὐτούς
and
καὶ
(they)
(X)
shall reign
βασιλεύσουσιν
unto
εἰς
ages
αἰῶνας
the
τῶν
of ages
αἰώνων
the
τῶν
faithful
πιστοὶ
words
λόγοι
(are)
(X)
the
οἱ
these
οὗτοι
and
καὶ
true
ἀληθινοί
and
καὶ
(he)
(X)
said
εἶπεν
to me
μοι
vs.6
and
καὶ
Lord
κύριος
the
ὁ
(God)
(θεὸς)
the
ὁ
of spirits
πνευμάτων
the
τῶν
of prophets
προφητῶν
the
τῶν
sent
ἀπέστειλεν
messenger
ἄγγελον
the
τὸν
of him
αὐτοῦ
which
ἃ
to become
γενέσθαι
is necessary
δεῖ
in
ἐν
haste
τάχει
to show
δεῖξαι
bondservants
δούλοις
the
τοῖς
of him
αὐτοῦ
and
καὶ
behold!
ἰδοὺ
vs.7a
(I)
(X)
come
ἔρχομαι
quickly
ταχύ
keeping
τηρῶν
the
ὁ
words
λόγους
the
τοὺς
of prophecy
προφητείας
the
τῆς
of book
βιβλίου
the
τοῦ
this
τούτου
vs.7b
(is)
(X)
blessed
μακάριος

THE DIAGRAM OF 22:5-7

The description of the city "coming down from above" continues through 22:5. The sentence of verse five is compound-complex. The first two of its four clauses are independent. The first professes, "And night shall not be any more..." The second goes on to develop the theme of the absence of night by alleging, "...they are not having need of light of lamp and light of sun..." χρείαν "need" is accusative, direct object of the verb "are having." This "need" is limited by two genitives (φωτὸς) "of light" which specify the kind of "need." Then this "light" is itself described by two genitives, "of lamp" (λύχνου) and "of sun" (ἡλίου). In the city there's no need for either artifical or natural light.

There next follows a dependent clause stating the reason why there'll be no night, no light of lamp or of sun. It is an adverb clause introduced by ὅτι "because," "...because Lord, the God, shall give light on them..." The final of the four clauses is attached to the ὅτι clause by the coordinating conjunction καὶ "and." This would suggest that it is another subordinate clause. However, it's entirely possible that it be an independent clause parallel to the first two clauses. In that case the conjunction should be attached to the second clause, "they are having need." In either case it reads: "...and they shall reign unto the ages of the ages." This "reign" is not limited to a thousand years. It is "forever." Thus it's differentiated from the "millennium."

The description of the city is concluded. Verse six contains an added word to reinforce the truth of what the angel has shown in the preceeding vision. The sentence is complex. The one independent clause states: "And he said to me..." The content of what "he said" is presented in two noun clauses, objects of "said." First, "these words are faithful and true." Second, "the Lord, the God of the spirits of the prophets sent his angel..." To this last dependent clause is attached an aorist infinitive δεῖξαι "to show," expressing purpose direct object of this infinitive is the noun clause: "which (things) it's necessary to become in haste..." The verb δεῖ "is necessary" has for its subject the infinitive γενέσθαι "to become" with accusative of general reference ἅ "which." The ἐν "in haste" phrase is adverbial expressing how.

Verse 7a represents a simple sentence in structure. "Behold! I come quickly." ἔρχομαι "come" is quite possibly futuristic present, "I am going to come..." "Quickly" answers the question as to how he's going to come.

Verse 7b is also a simple sentence. The subject consists of a present attributive participial phrase: "The one keeping the words of the prophecy of this book..." The verb "is" is implied from the context. μακάριος "blessed" is predicate adjective pointing back to the subject. It makes an affirmation about the subject: "The one keeping...is blessed."

## A TRANSLATION
Revelation 22:1-7

And he showed me a river of water of life, bright as crystal, going out of the throne of God and the lamb. In the middle of its street and on each side of the river a tree of life producing twelve fruits, giving forth each month its fruit; and the leaves of the tree (were) for the healing of the nations. And every curse shall not be any more! And the throne of God and of the lamb shall be in it and his bondservants shall minister to him. And they shall see his face and his name (shall be) on their foreheads. And night shall not be any more; and they aren't having need of light of lamp and light of sun, because Lord, the God, shall shine on them and they shall reign unto the ages of the ages.

And he said to me, "These words are faithful and true; and the Lord, the God of the spirits of the prophets, sent his messenger to show to his bondservants which things it's necessary to come to pass quickly. And behold! I am coming quickly. Blessed (is) the one keeping the words of the prophecy of this book."

## AN OUTLINE OF REVELATION 22:1-7

Perfect Provision Restored!

In paradise lost (Gen.2:8-10) three essential elements were forfeited:(1)trees "good for food," (2)a pure river "to water the garden," (3)"the tree of life" offering an unfailing flow of health-giving energy. Food, water, and health are three requisites for human life; lost in Eden, restored in regained paradise.

I. PERFECT PROVISION FOR PERPETUAL LIFE! 22:1-2
   1. A "river of water of life, clear as crystal..."
      (a)Pure water.
      (b)Its source: "the throne of God and the lamb."
   2. Nutritious food: "tree of life" producing fruit year round.
      (a)Each month; symbol of plenty; no crop failures!
      (b)An orchard on "each side of river" accessible to all!
   3. Abiding health: "leaves of the tree for healing of nations."
      (a)Covering scars of the past.
      (b)Preventing any more diseases or wounds.

II. EMPLOYMENT IN PARADISE RESTORED! 22:3-5
   1. The nature of the government.
      (a)"The throne of God and the lamb" A monarchy!
      (b)We "shall see his face." Close personal relationship.
      (c)"His bondservants shall devotedly serve him."
      (d)His name "on their foreheads." Shall be "like him."
   2. The light of truth shines: "no night, no lamp, no sun..."
   3. Shall share sovereign power: "they shall reign forever."

III. CONFIRMATION OF THE VISION OF THE CITY. 22:6-7
   1. Reassurance: "These words are faithful and true."
   2. These things will come to pass "quickly."
   3. This prophecy is to be "kept," not just read!

Paradise lost made a hell; paradise regained makes a heaven! Eternity revealed gives meaning to life concealed. "Your life is hidden with Christ in God; when Christ, our life, shall be manifest, then you shall be manifested with him in glory."(Col. 3:4)

## SOME EXPOSITORY THOUGHTS ON 21:9-22:7

Life lies beyond life; beyond history! After sin has run its violent course and issued in its self-destruction along with all who identify with it, a society of redeemed humanity will appear. It is plainly prophesied; deliberately promised. It holds hope to all who groan, toil, and cry in this vale of tears. It's the promise of a new earth after this earth is no more.

John's word for new means a new kind of earth. He affirms that the "new Jerusalem," comes "down out of heaven from God." From the days of Enoch who first "built a city" to those who engineered the tower of Babel the cities of men have risen up from the earth; none have come down from God. Babylon, the Greek city-states, Rome, the United Nations have been begotten by the brain of man. They've been birthed from below, not from above. In vain have they sought peace, prosperity, health and long life for the peoples of this earth. The Roman peace was kept by the power of the Roman legions. Today we keep the peace, such as it is, by a precarious balance of nuclear arms. Man traces his human origin up from the mud of mammals, not down by creation of God. Humanism shapes its peace and prosperity by the collective folly of God-ignoring, God-denying world organizations. Thus men seek strength from beneath, not power from above.

What John asserts is that the "new earth" comes "down from God." The city of God is NOT going to arise; it's going to descend! The city in which men enjoy perfect partnership, perfect protection, perfect provision will not sprout from the institutions of men, educational, social, political, economic. It can't bloom from below.

The city promises perfect partnership; a face to face fellowship. We shall see him and "know him as he is." The joy of that city is not its geographical location, its unusual size, its bejewled appearance. It's the warm, intimate, personal fellowship between Creator and creature. The unutterable joy is like that of a wedding:"I saw the holy city...prepared as a bride adorned for her man."

Then John adds, "the tabernacle of God shall be with men, and he will live with them, and they shall be his people, and he shall be their God." I will move into the same house with God to live where he lives. He will be my father; I'll be his child. His other children will be my siblings. When he speaks to me he'll say, "Son!" And I'll answer, "Father!"

But there's more! He shall wipe away every tear (of sadness) from their eyes." Death, mourning, crying "shall be no more." I'll never stand by another open grave. I'll never carry the burden of a son going down the drain in drugs or drunkeness. Nor shall I see the heart-ache of divorce, the terrifying corruption of adultery, or the shattering trauma of a family fight. No unclean stain shall ever blot that fraternal companionship. "The cowards, the faithless, the polluted, and murderers, sorcerers, idolaters and all liars" will have been eliminated in the "second death." Sin shall not fracture the bond of citizenship in the city of God.

The "New Jerusalem" is the clear revelation that a country, nation, city, or family--any group commonwealth--does not consist in location, language, color, or economics. It's rather a matter of the heart, a unity in God, a community of character, a purity of moral and ethical behaviour centered in a common loyalty to the person and presence of the living God. Because God is the "first and the last" he is capable of giving "the water of life freely" to "him who thirsts." And throughout an ageless eternity I shall live fully conscious that I am fully accepted. Has he not promised, "I shall be to him God and he shall be to me son?"

The peace and security of the city of God comes from the kind of protection which God, not man, provides. John saw in that city "the glory of God." That is to say, it shined with the character of God, its maker. Its brilliance was like that of a priceless jewel, a "transparent crystal." In symbolic language the apostle impresses upon us the ultimate security when he says the walls were 1500 miles in length, breadth and height. No destruction can penetrate such colossal walls. No army can breach such secure ramparts. Man or devil cannot outflank this titanic haven of peace. No thief is inside; no enemy outside those solid embattlements.

Ancient cities normally had but one gate, open by day; barred at night. This reduced danger; increased protection. But the city of God has twelve gates, three on each of its sides. The gates never close. Which is to say that there is always free and open access into the divine city of refuge. And who is to enter the city? At each gate is an angel of God bearing a name of one of the twelve tribes of Israel. A symbol to say that all God's people enjoy unfettered liberty into and around the city. The foundation stones, twelve in number, consist of the richest, most sparkling, precious stones, symbolic of the beauty, permanent solid safety of the citizens. But the most striking stones are those which form the twelve gates. Each gate is a huge pearl. The pearl is the only precious stone that is formed by suffering. A grain of sand lodged in a clam irritates the living clam. To reduce the pain and protect itself the clam forms a hard substance around the grain which eventually turns into a beautiful pearl. I enter the city of God by a gate of pearl, the suffering of the son of God at Calvary. I cannot enter apart from his cross. But by that cross all have free access into God's holy city.

Speaking of security, what about a police force? Yet, who needs a police force where there are no criminals? "No defiled man, or one making a polluted thing, no lie or liar" lives in the city. Why police? Only "ones whose names are written in the book of life of the lamb" are living in the city anyway!

Should we inquire about government buildings? And what are the facilities for worship? Is temple or chapel to be found? The text says that there is no temple. God himself is present. He's available without hinderance or mystery. God is the sanctuary, the altar, the governor! Nor do I need street lights, or sewage system. God is the light. And as for sewage; there's no garbage! Who needs a Dempster-Dumpster?

**Man's dream of a golden age includes freedom from want; the want of wealth, health, and a meanful life.** This the city of God provides without measure. As for wealth, streaming "from the throne of God and the lamb" was a "river of water of life." It was as "bright as transparent crystal" flowing parallel to the main street! Between this main boulevard and the ever-flowing stream a grove of twelve trees was blooming. The trees lined both sides of the river producing twelve fruits, a food variety for an entire year. No one lacked drink; no one wanted for food. A perpetual uninterrupted supply! No poverty there! All are heirs of a billionaire father!

What signs of health are there? Besides the lack of a cemetery we note that there are no hospitals. This does not mean a paucity of health facilities; it means that there's no illness. No pneumonia to choke the breath, no cancer to devour the body, no broken bones or blind eyes or deaf ears. There are no healing drugs because there are no crippling diseases. The torment of disease and death has been cast into the lake of fire and brimstone.

On the positive side we've observed the "river of the water of life coming out of the throne of God..." Pure flowing, crystal clear water guarantees an uninterrupted flow of healthy life. In addition, on either side of the river are fruit trees producing fruit for each month of the year. Every tree bears life-giving, body-building, tasteful fruit awarding balanced nutrition for unending life. Besides fruit the tree of life produces healing herbs: "the leaves of the tree are for the healing of the nations." No plastic surgeon covers body blemishes like the therapeutic leaves of this tree covers the scars of sin cut by the cities of man. No dripping nose or pain of sinus, or migrain headache, or plaguing allergy, or any other affliction can penetrate the healing cover of the leaves of the tree of life. "There is NO curse any more!"

As God's freedmen, released from the slavery of sin, we "shall serve him" as priests; "we shall see his face and his name (shall be) on our foreheades." Which is to say that his character shall be our character. At last we shall attain the promise of Eden: to be "in the image" of God, fully divine in nature, pure in character with strength to resist the attack of any germ of sin. Nothing shall disrupt the health of the child of God. And with him we "shall reign forever and forever."

That this vision of the holy city is genuine, that it's accurate is given strong confirmation by the angel. He declares: "These words are faithful and true..." Even as God gave true messages through all his prophets of the past, so now "these words" are the genuine words of God. That which you've just seen are to come to pass "quickly."

Besides all this, the vision of the city brings a message that is to be "kept." The vision of the future is to give power to endure the present. Words of prophecy, this prophecy, are given to guide moral action, not just to satisfy idle curiosity about the future. "Blessed is the one keeping the words of the prophecy of this book."

## A TRANSLATION OF REVELATION 22:8-21

And I, John, (am) the one hearing and seeing these things. And when I heard and saw, I fell to worship before the feet of the angel, the one showing me these things. And he says to me, "Don't! I am your fellow servant and of your brothers, the prophets, and of those keeping the words of this book. Worship God!"

And he says to me, "Don't seal the words of the prophecy of this book for the time is near. The one being unjust is to be unjust still, and the filthy is to be filthy still, and the righteous is to do righteousness still, and the holy is to be holy still. Behold! I come quickly and my wage with me to give to each as is his work. I am the alpha and the omega, the first and the last, the beginning and the end. Blessed the ones washing their robes that their right shall be to the tree of life and that they shall enter by the gates into the city. Outside are the dogs and the sorcerers and the fornicators and the murderers and the idolaters and everyone loving and making a lie."

"I, Jesus, sent my messenger to testify these things to you for the churches. I am the root and offspring of David, the bright morning star."

The spirit and the bride say, "Come!" And the one hearing is to say, "Come!" And the one thirsting is to come; the one wishing is to take the water of life freely.

I testify to everyone hearing the words of the prophecy of this book: "If anyone shall add to them God shall add to him the plagues written in this book and if anyone shall take away from the book of this prophecy God shall take away his portion from the tree of life and from the holy city, from the things having been written in this book."

The one testifying these things says, "Verily, I am coming suddenly!"

Amen! Come, Lord Jesus! The grace of the Lord Jesus be with all.

## AN OUTLINE OF REVELATION 22:6-21

<u>The Credibility of the Revelation</u>!

When faith is threatened and life is marginal the credibility of him to whom man yields allegience is critical. We must rest on the trustworthy word of a trustworthy person. Evidence and promise must be clear and unclouded.

I. THE IMPORTANCE OF THE VISION.

1. The claim: "faithful and true." It's trustworthy. 6a
2. The divine source.
   (a)"God of the spirits of the prophets." 6b
      (1)John, the human agent. 8
      (2)An angelic agent. 9
   (b)The Lord Jesus. 13, 16
3. Its immediate relevance. 10-11
4. Sacred integrity of the book, the record of the Vision. 18-19

II. THE BEATITUDES OF THE VISION.

1. Blessed are the obedient. 7a
2. Blessed are the cleansed. 14-15
3. Those who respond to the three-fold invitation. 17

III. THE NEARNESS OF THE VISION.

1. Soon! Suddenly!
2. Believers' attitude: "Come, Lord Jesus!"

Paradise lost has now become paradise regained. We look forward to the consummation of history; the "beginning" of eternity!

## Revelation 22:8-9

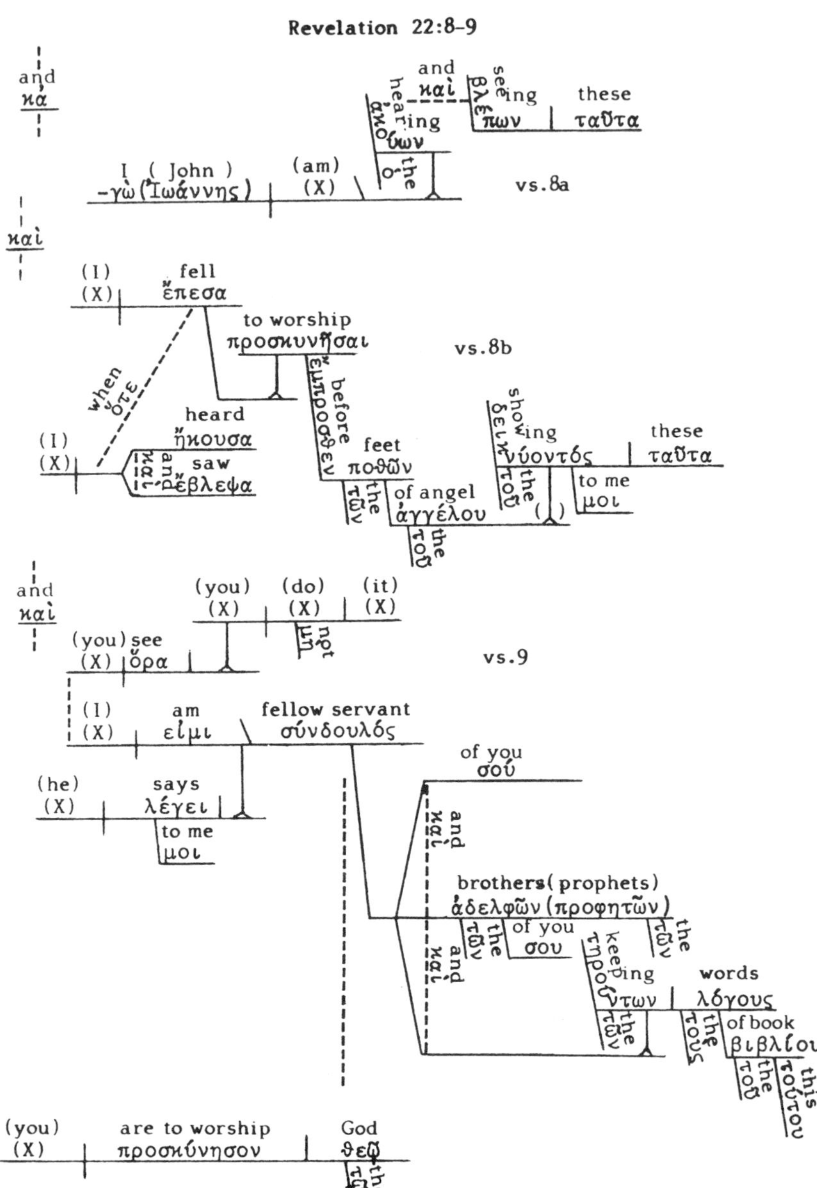

## THE DIAGRAM OF 22:8-9

22:8a is a simple sentence. Its subject is the emphatic use of first personal pronoun ἐγὼ "I" in an abbreviated form due to crasis with καὶ "and." Copula verb "am" is supplied from context. Predicate nominative consists of a brace of attributive present participles "hearing" and "seeing." The single article joining them brings "the one seeing and hearing" into a closer identity.

Verse 8b is a complex sentence of two clauses. The dependent is a temporal clause advanced by ὅτε "when." It marks the time when the action of the main clause took place. "When I heard and saw, I fell..." Infinitive προσκυνῆσαι "to worship" expresses the purpose: "I fell to worship..." The place where the worship was to take place is indicated by prepositional phrase ἔμπροσθεν "before the feet..." Whose feet is identified by the possessive genitive ἀγγέλου "of the angel..." The particular angel spoken of is set forth by attributive participle in apposition, δεικνύοντός "the one showing these things to me."

Of the five clauses in the sentence of verse nine four are subordinate. And one of them is almost entirely elliptical; it has to be filled in from the context. The main clause introduces the sentence: "He says to me..." The four dependents are noun clauses, three of them objects of λέγει "he says." "I am fellow-servant..." is the first. Modifying σύνδουλός "fellow-servant" and identifying whose servant are three possessive genitives, (1)"of you" (2)"of your brothers," (3)"of the ones keeping the words of this book." In apposition to one of the genitives, ἀδελφῶν "brothers," is προφητῶν "prophets."

The second dependent clause consists in the text of but one word, ὅρα "you see..." It is present imperative. The object of this imperative verb is the elliptical clause referred to above. The negative μὴ "not" is the only word not implied. "You see (that you do it) not."

The final clause could be a separate simple sentence. But because it's part of what "he says" it's probably best to treat it as an additional object clause: "...worship God!" προσκύνησον is aorist imperative, quite appropriate punctiliar action in a rather sharp exhortation. "Don't even let it enter your mind to worship anyone other than the One Living God!"

and
καὶ

vs. 10

(he) (X) | says λέγει | to me μοι

(you) (X) | seal σφραγίσῃς | words λόγους
μὴ not
τοὺς the
of prophecy προφητείας
τῆς the
of book βιβλίου
τοῦ the
τούτου this

for γὰρ

time καιρὸς | is ἐστιν \ near ἐγγύς
ὁ the

vs. 11

being unjust ἀδικῶν
ὁ the
be unjust ἀδικησάτω
ἔτι still

and καὶ

filthy ῥυπαρὸς | be filthy ῥυπανθήτω
ὁ the
ἔτι still

and καὶ

righteous δίκαιος | do ποιησάτω | righteousness δικαιοσύνην
ὁ the
ἔτι still

and καὶ

holy ἅγιος | be holy ἁγιασθήτω
ὁ the
ἔτι still

Behold
Ἰδοὺ

vs. 12

(I) (X) | am coming ἔρχομαι
ταχύ quickly

and καὶ

wage μισθός | (is) (X) \ to give ἀποδοῦναι
ὁ the
of me μου
μετ' with ἐμοῦ
to each ἑκάστῳ
ὡς as

work ἔργον | is ἐστὶν
τὸ the
of him αὐτοῦ

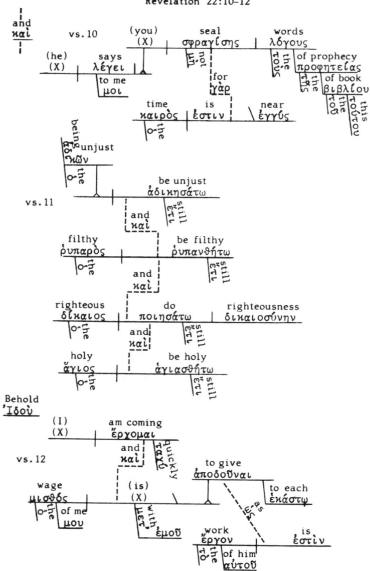

## THE DIAGRAM OF 22:10-12

Verse 10 comprises a complex sentence of three clauses. "He says to me" is the independent clause. The two dependents function as direct objects of λέγει "says." Both are noun clauses. The first exhorts: "...don't seal the words of the prophecy of this book..." σφραγίσης "seal" is an ingressive aorist subjunctive with negative. It urges: "...don't begin to seal or even think of sealing..." The second dependent offers a reason for the book's being left unsealed, its message left open: "...for the time is near." The word καιρός is "time" in the sense of fitness, a definite season. But χρόνος is "time" in the sense of duration.

Verse 11 entails a compound sentence of four clauses. They constitute a series of imperatives that are commands only in the sense that they represent judgments of God. The first says: "The one being unjust is to be unjust still..." The angel speaking isn't suggesting that God is urging the unjust to keep on being unjust. He is pronouncing God's judgment on the unjust. He punishes injustice with more of the same falling on him who is unjust. Sin is punished with more sin. So the second clause adds: "...the filthy is to be still filthy (with more filth)..."

The next two clauses pronounce the judgment on the opposites, the "righteous" and the "holy." They too will have more of the same. God rewards righteousness with more righteousness: "...the righteous is to still do (more) righteousness..." And "...the holy is to still be (more) holy." All verbs in verse 11 are aorists, "the tense of urgency."

The sentence of verse 12 involves a compound complex. The first independent idea reaffirms: "Behold! I am coming quickly..." The second independent clause in conjunction with the dependent ὡς "as" adverbial clause presents an accompanying consequence of the "coming." It says:"my wage (is) with me to give to each as is his work." "Wage is with me" is the independent clause. Infinitive ἀποδοῦναι "to give" is predicate nominative. The ὡς clause is adverb of manner.

Revelation 22:13–15

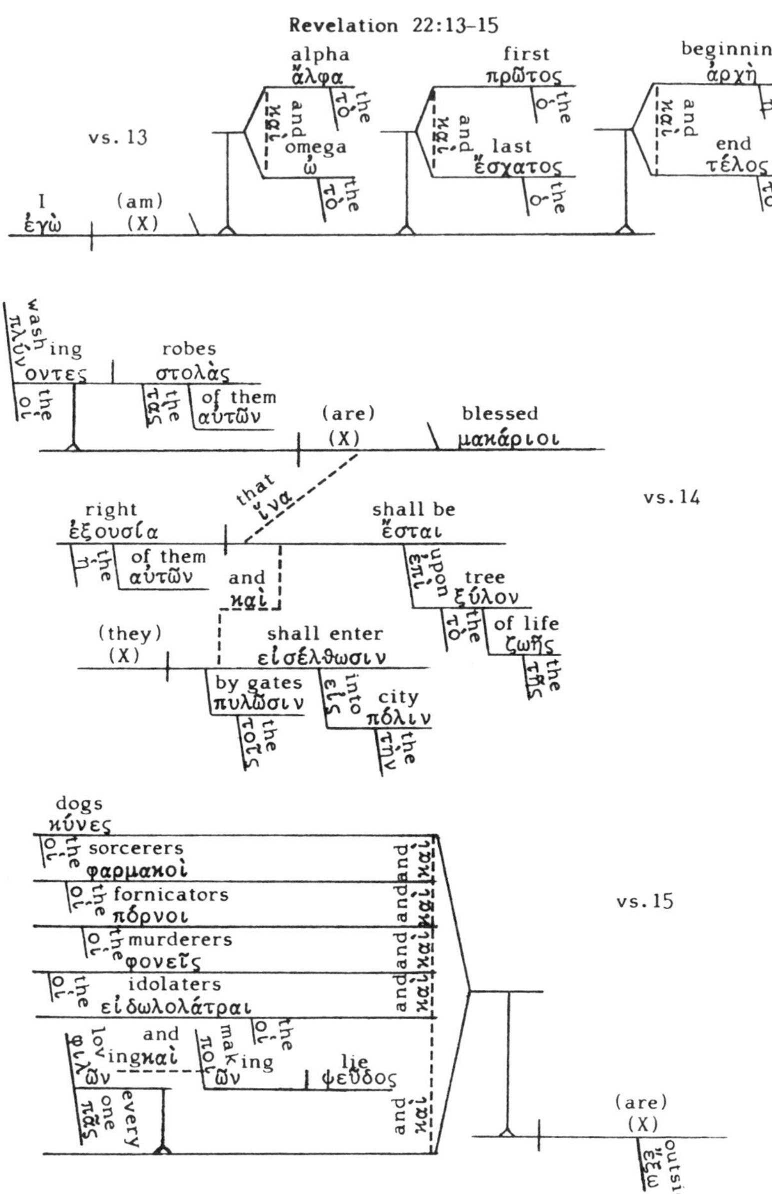

## THE DIAGRAM OF 22:13-15

Three predicate nominatives appear in the sentence of verse 13. Each of the three contains a pair of epithets which describe some feature of ἐγὼ "I" the subject. Since the sentence consists of but one clause it is simple in form. The presence of the first personal pronoun as subject magnifies its weight in the sentence. "I (am) the alpha and the omega, the first and the last, the beginning and the end." By repeating the predicate three times with words which mean essentially the same thing adds to the prominence of who and what the "I" really is. And the presence of a separate definite article with each of the epithets makes each stand out as a distinct feature.

The sentence of verse 14 encompasses a complex arrangement of three clauses. The independent clause contains a beatitude, "Blessed (are) the ones washing their robes..." Subject is the attributive participle πλύνοντες "washing." Its present tense probably should be classed as disributive, that is, each separate one who washes is "blessed." The adjective, "blessed," is predicate.

The ἵνα clause introduces two subordinate adverbial purpose clauses: "...that their right shall be upon (to) the tree of the life..." In expressing purpose ἵνα normally goes with subjunctive but here future middle indicative ἔσται "shall be" appears. The root meaning of preposition ἐπὶ is "upon." The context modifies its meaning; "to" is probably best here. The general idea is: "...when they come upon the tree of life their right is to have access to it..." Genitive ζωῆς "of life" defines the "tree" as being "life." They have access to "life." Definite article with "tree" points out a particular tree, one mentioned earlier in this vision and so well known as "the" tree.

The second dependent clause of verse 14, joined by καὶ "and," is also purpose; "...that they shall enter by the gates into the city." εἰσέλθωσιν "shall enter" is aorist subjunctive, normal mode in such purpose clauses. πυλῶσιν "by gates" is instrumental indicating means by which. The εἰς "into" expression is adverbial denoting <u>where</u>.

Verse 15 offers a simple sentence with a compound subject of six elements. "...(are) outside." is the predicate. Adverb ἔξω "outside" tells <u>where</u>. The subjects combine five nouns plus two present attributive participles joined in one noun phrase. Five elements of the subject have their own distinctive article. The participial phrase uses πᾶς "every one." This indicates that in the mind of the author each particular group stood out clearly as a well-defined class of sinners. They are: "The dogs, and the sorcerers, and the fornicators, and the murderers, and the idolaters, and everyone loving and making a lie."

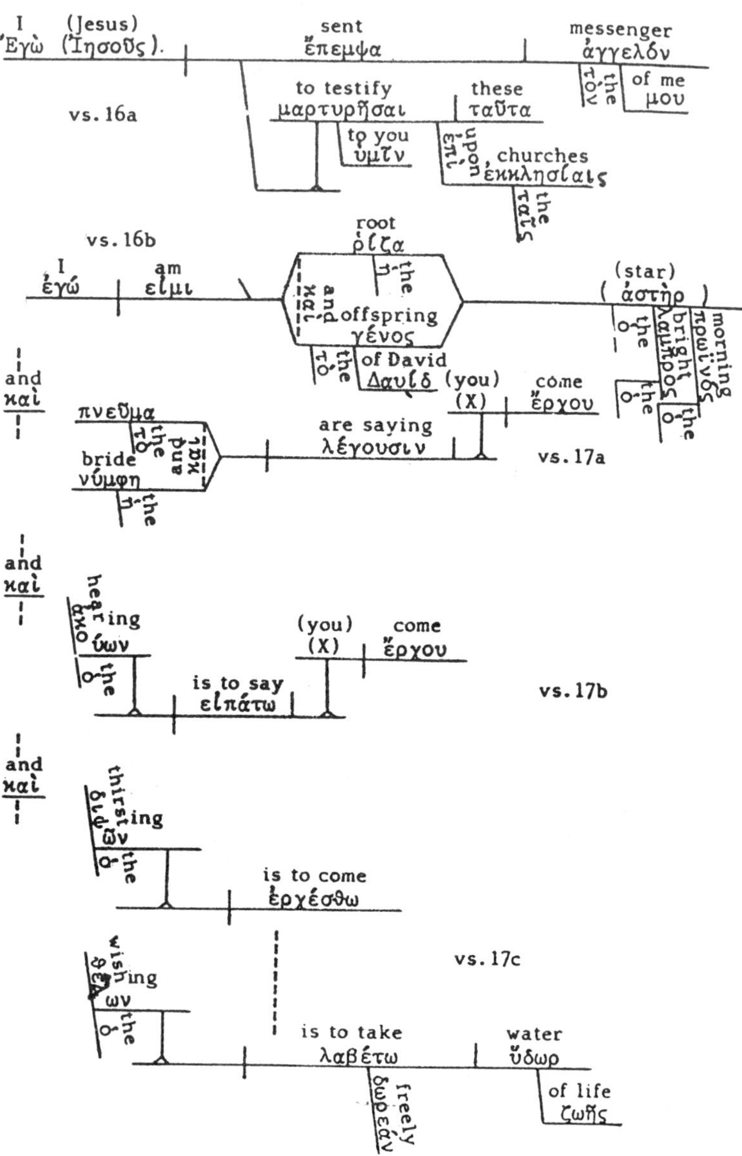
I (Jesus)
Ἐγὼ (Ἰησοῦς).
sent
ἔπεμψα
messenger
ἄγγελόν
the τὸν
of me μου
vs. 16a
to testify
μαρτυρῆσαι
these
ταῦτα
to you
ὑμῖν
upon ἐπὶ
churches
ἐκκλησίαις
the ταῖς
vs. 16b
root
ῥίζα
the ἡ
I
ἐγώ
am
εἰμι
and καὶ
offspring
γένος
the τὸ
of David
Δαυίδ
(star)
( ἀστὴρ )
the ὁ
bright λαμπρὸς
morning πρωϊνός
the ὁ
the ὁ
and
καὶ
πνεῦμα
the τὸ
and καὶ
bride
νύμφη
the ἡ
are saying
λέγουσιν
(you)
(X)
come
ἔρχου
vs. 17a
and
καὶ
hearing
ἀκούων
the ὁ
is to say
εἰπάτω
(you)
(X)
come
ἔρχου
vs. 17b
and
καὶ
thirsting
διψῶν
the ὁ
is to come
ἐρχέσθω
vs. 17c
wishing
θέλων
the ὁ
is to take
λαβέτω
water
ὕδωρ
freely
δωρεάν
of life
ζωῆς

## THE DIAGRAM OF 22:16-17

The sentence of 16a identifies the one who "sent" his "angel" and the purpose for which he sent him. Once again we meet the emphatic personal pronoun ἐγὼ "I" as subject. And this time the "I" is identified by an apposition Ἰησοῦς "Jesus." Jesus is the one who "sent my messenger..." The purpose for which he sent the angel is expressed by aorist infinitive "to testify" (μαρτυρῆσαι). Where or to whom the angel was "to testify" is seen in the ἐπὶ phrase "upon the churches." The context here suggests that the preposition might be translated "before" or "to." Whenever the messenger came "upon" a church he was to testify!

Verse 16b presents another simple sentence. First personal pronoun again appears as strong emphasis on the subject. εἰμι "am" is a normal connecting verb between subject and predicate nominatives. It's often implied but here expressed. Predicate consists of two nouns, "root" and "offspring" to which is attached another noun in apposition "star." All three of these predicate nouns have their own definite article. Thereby each is set off as clearly separate. Indeclinable Δαυίδ "David" is genitive identifying whose offspring. "Star" not only has its definite article but the two adjectives modifying it, "bright" and "morning" each has the article repeated. Thus the adjectives stand out more clearly.

Verse 17 contains three brief sentences, two complex, the third compound. The independent clause of 17a declares: "And the spirit and the bride are saying,.." Both "the spirit" and "the bride" as individual entities do the "saying" as evidenced by a definite article with each. λέγουσιν "are saying" is present tense, linear action, emphasizing the continuous and continuing invitation. The dependent is a noun clause object of "saying." It is present imperative ἔρχου "come." Subject "you" is in the verb ending.

Verse 17b is patterned after 17a except there is but one subject and it is a substantized present attributive participle, ἀκούων "the one hearing." Verb εἰπάτω "is to say" is aorist imperative, an urgent exhortation. The dependent clause of 17b is exactly the same as that of 17a, "You come!"

Verse 17c forms a compound sentence. Asyndeton obtains between the two clauses. The first exhorts: "And the one thirsting is to be coming..." Again the subject consists of a present attributive participle διψῶν "thirsting." The predicate is ἐρχέσθω "is to be coming." It is durative action present, he is to "keep on coming" as often as he needs his thirst quenched.

The second independent clause also has an attributive present participle as subject, θέλων "one wishing." λαβέτω "is to take" is aorist imperative. It focuses on the act of taking rather than the action of taking. It looks to the point, not the repetition, though aorist doesn't deny repetition. How is he to take? That is answered in the adverb δωρεάν "freely." What is he to take? The object ὕδωρ "water" supplies the answer. What kind of water is it? Genitive ζωῆς "life" specifies that.

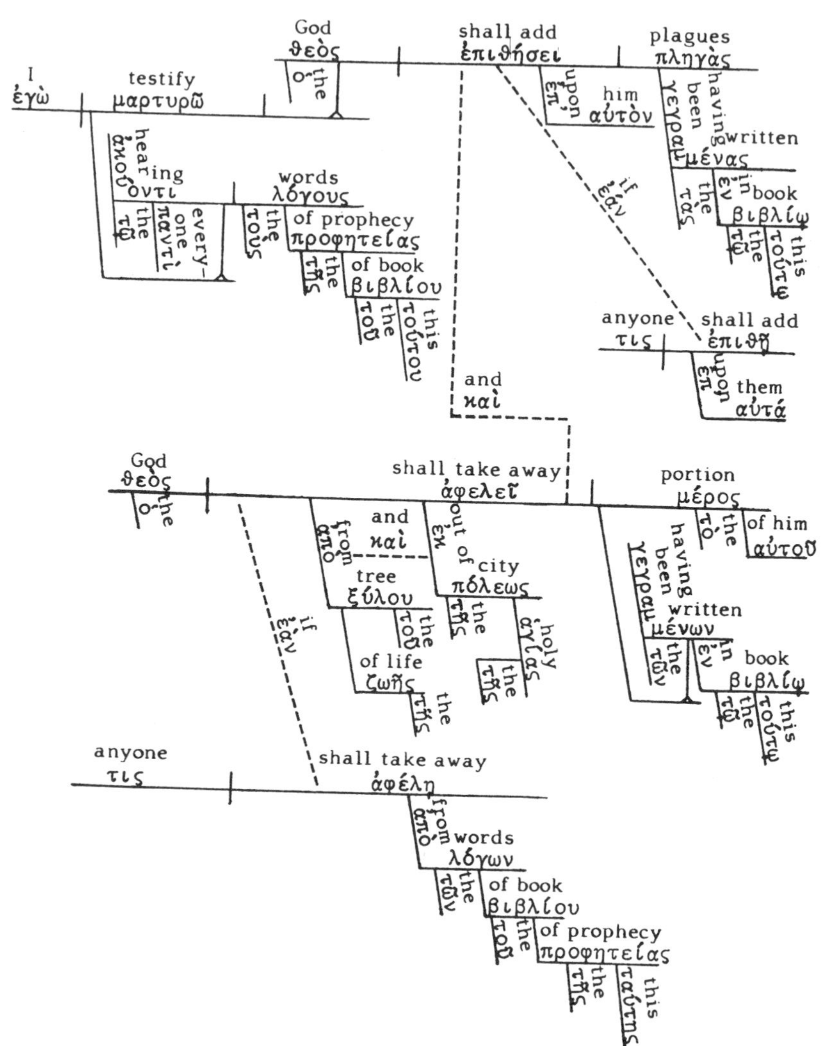
I
ἐγὼ
testify
μαρτυρῶ
God
θεὸς
ὁ the
shall add
ἐπιθήσει
plagues
πληγὰς
ἐπ' upon
him
αὐτὸν
having been written
γεγραμμένας
τὰς the
ἐν in
book
βιβλίῳ
τῷ the
τούτῳ this
hearing
ἀκούοντι
τῷ the
παντὶ every-one
words
λόγους
τοὺς the
of prophecy
προφητείας
τῆς the
of book
βιβλίου
τοῦ the
τούτου this
if
ἐάν
anyone
τις
shall add
ἐπιθῇ
ἐπ' upon
them
αὐτά
and
καὶ
God
θεὸς
ὁ the
shall take away
ἀφελεῖ
portion
μέρος
τὸ the
of him
αὐτοῦ
having been written
γεγραμμένων
τῶν the
ἐν in
book
βιβλίῳ
τῷ the
τούτῳ this
from
ἀπὸ
and
καὶ
out of
ἐκ
tree
ξύλου
τοῦ the
of life
ζωῆς
τῆς the
city
πόλεως
τῆς the
holy
ἁγίας
τῆς the
if
ἐὰν
anyone
τις
shall take away
ἀφέλῃ
ἀπὸ from
words
λόγων
τῶν the
of book
βιβλίου
τοῦ the
of prophecy
προφητείας
τῆς the
ταύτης this

## THE DIAGRAM OF 22:18-19

The entire of verses 18-19 embraces one sentence. In structure it is complex. It possesses one independent and four dependent clauses. The independent affirms: "I testify..." The one to whom he "testifies" is in dative attributive participle ἀκούοντι "everyone hearing." It is indirect object. λόγους "words" is direct object of the verbal action in the participle. This object is itself more specifically identified by the series of genitives translated "of the prophecy of this book."

The four dependent clauses are divided into a pair of noun clauses, objects of "testify." Each of these object clauses finds support from adverbial third class conditional clauses. The first noun-object clause with its conditional says: "If anyone shall add upon (to) them, God shall add upon him the plagues having been written in this book..." ἐάν "if" with subjunctive ἐπιθῇ "shall add" is the normal construction for third class conditionals, undetermined but with prospect of determination. "If anyone shall add" and they just may do that. The independent clause gives the conclusion (apodosis), "God shall add..." The perfect passive participle γεγραμμένων "having been written" is circumstantial giving an added description of πληγὰς "plagues" object of verb ἐπιθήσει "shall add."

The second of the independents is likewise supported by third class condition: "...if anyone shall take away from the words..." and it's possible someone might! ἀφέλῃ is aorist of ἀφαιρέω. Ablative is the case of separation or origin. Here λόγων is ablative with preposition ἀπὸ "from" to express separation.

The conclusion based on this third class condition states, "God shall take away his portion..." μέρος "portion" is neuter accusative object of verb "shall take away." The ἀπὸ "from" and ἐκ "out of" phrases are both adverbial. ἀπό is "from the side of" while ἐκ is "out from within." Both are ablative ideas of separation though each has its shade of meaning. He's going to be separated "from the tree," and he's going to be put "out of the holy city."

Revelation 22:20-21

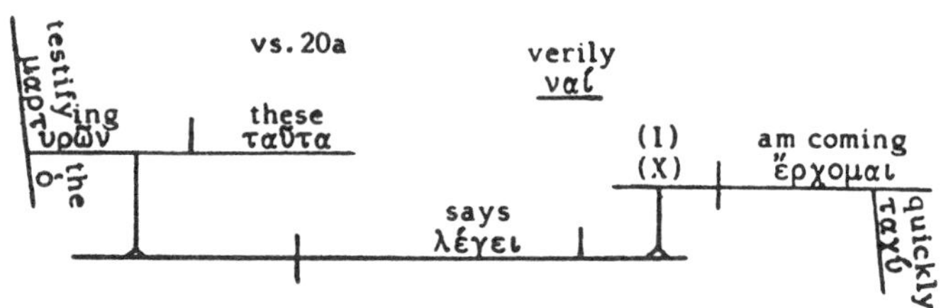


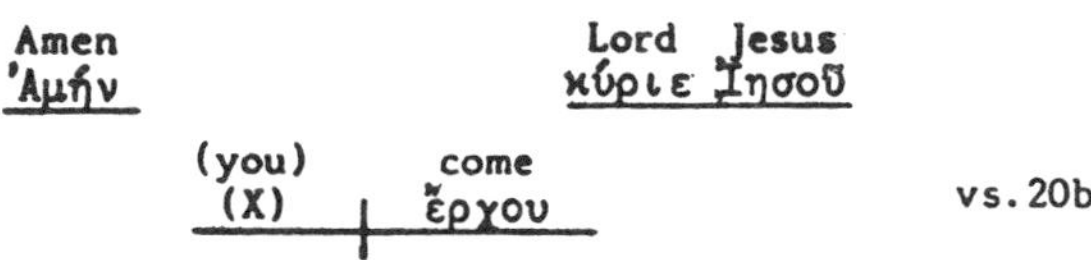


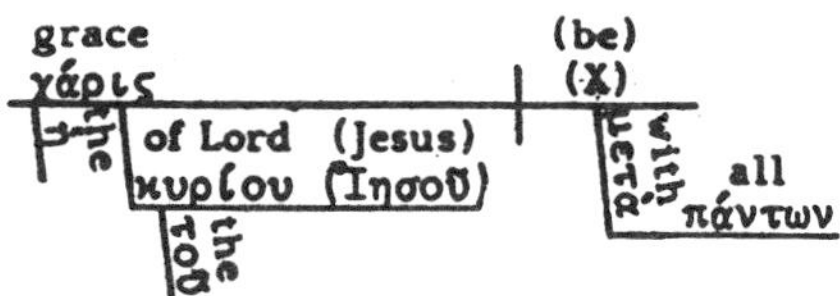


THE DIAGRAM OF 22:20-21

The words of 20a form a complex sentence. Subject of the main clause is present attributive participial phrase, "the one testifying these..." The one dependent is a noun clause object of verb "says." After an exclamation, "Yea verily" the clause states a promise: "I am coming quickly."

Verse 20b is John's response to the words of Jesus in 20a. "Amen! Lord Jesus! Come!" It is a simple sentence with subject "you" contained in the verb ending.

Verse 21 is John's benediction. In form the sentence is simple. The verb "be" is implied. Subject χάρις "grace has the definite article suggesting a particular grace. Genitive κυρίου "lord" with appositional Ἰησοῦ "Jesus" specifies the grace of which he speaks. "With all" is adverbial indicating <u>where</u> the grace is extended.

## SOME EXPOSITORY THOUGHTS ON 22:8-21

"And I, John, the one hearing and seeing these things." God's disclosures came through human beings in historical situations. If we would hear God and "not take away from" the words of his revelations we must understand those men and situations. The men through whom God spoke are not to be worshipped as deity. Even angelic messengers shrink from that.(vs.9) But when God speaks we are to accommodate ourselves to his method of speech.

"Don't seal the words of the prophecy of this book; for the time is near." The Revelation is relevant to the time in which it was given. Because of its relevance to that situation it speaks to any similar situation in later history. The book is a message of hope in persecution. Don't withhold such a message.

"He that is filthy is to be filthy still..." Man was not made for sin. But if he sins and persists in clinging to it he shall be turned over to sin. His punishment is within the nature of sin itself. Character formed here won't be transformed hereafter."Today is the day of salvation." "He that is righteous is to be righteous still." Righteousness carries its own reward. Heaven is a moral, spiritual state in which holy people socialize with God and each other on a holy plane, made possible by redemption through Christ. "Behold! I come quickly; and my reward is with me, to render to each man according to his work." The "washing" of redemption puts within reach for sinful human beings "the tree which is life!"

The "spirit and the bride say, 'Come.'" "The one hearing is to say, 'Come.'" "The one thirsting is to 'Come!'" In view of God's purpose in creation, a creature "in his image," in view of God's unfolding work in history, culminating in Calvary and the empty tomb, sin need be no barrier to the "tree of life." God's Holy Spirit invites all to "Come!" Christ's bride, his church pleads, "Come!" He who hears and responds to these invitations urges, "Come!" Man has been given an inborn thirst for God. Man cannot rest until he rests in God. All his restless thirst can be quenched by drinking at the fountain of the water of life. All who thirst can slake that thirst "freely." Let him who will, "Come!"

The integrity of "the words of the prophecy of this book" place a solemn demand of integrity on him who reads, handles, or teaches "the words...of this book." Before the printing press protected the published copies of a book the demand on the copyist or editor was doubly sacred. He who presumes to reproduce an author has no right to alter the text, message, or meaning. If this be true for books of secular design how much more for a book of sacred design! One who reads, teaches, or interprets "shall not add to" nor "take away" from the book of God's revelation. There's no place for dedicated ignorance however sincere, no place for personal prejudice, no place for careless laziness in handling God's word. And this is true whether on the level of the ancient copyist or a twentieth century interpreter.

"Come! Lord Jesus!"